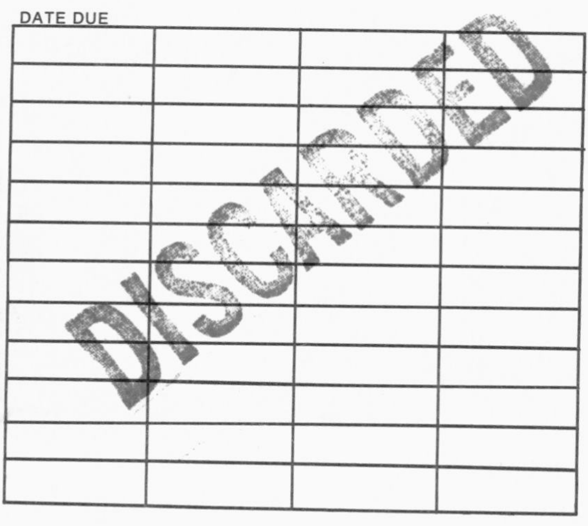

YORK COLLEGE
PENNSYLVANIA
Servire est vivere

Prehistory of the Nile Valley

STUDIES IN ARCHEOLOGY

Consulting Editor: Stuart Struever

Department of Anthropology
Northwestern University
Evanston, Illinois

Charles R. McGimsey III. **Public Archeology**

Lewis R. Binford. **An Archaeological Perspective**

Muriel Porter Weaver. **The Aztecs, Maya, and Their Predecessors: Archaeology of Mesoamerica**

Joseph W. Michels. **Dating Methods in Archaeology**

C. Garth Sampson. **The Stone Age Archaeology of Southern Africa**

Fred T. Plog. **The Study of Prehistoric Change**

Patty Jo Watson (Ed.). **Archeology of the Mammoth Cave Area**

George C. Frison (Ed.). **The Casper Site: A Hell Gap Bison Kill on the High Plains**

W. Raymond Wood and R. Bruce McMillan (Eds.). **Prehistoric Man and His Environments: A Case Study in the Ozark Highland**

Kent V. Flannery (Ed.). **The Early Mesoamerican Village**

Charles E. Cleland (Ed.). **Cultural Change and Continuity: Essays in Honor of James Bennett Griffin**

Michael B. Schiffer. **Behavioral Archeology**

Fred Wendorf and Romuald Schild. **Prehistory of the Nile Valley**

Michael A. Jochim. **Hunter-Gatherer Subsistence and Settlement: A Predictive Model**

in preparation

Stanley South. **Method and Theory in Historical Archeology**

Prehistory of the Nile Valley

Fred Wendorf

Department of Anthropology
Southern Methodist University
Dallas, Texas

Romuald Schild

The Institute for the History of Material Culture
Polish Academy of Science
Warsaw, Poland

with Sections by Bahay Issawi

Geological Survey of Egypt
Cairo, Egypt

ACADEMIC PRESS New York San Francisco London

A Subsidiary of Harcourt Brace Jovanovich, Publishers

ACADEMIC PRESS, INC.
111 Fifth Avenue, New York, New York 10003

United Kingdom Edition published by
ACADEMIC PRESS, INC. (LONDON) LTD.
24/28 Oval Road, London NW1

Library of Congress Cataloging in Publication Data

Main entry under title:

Prehistory of the Nile Valley.

(Studies in archeology series)
Bibliography: p.
Includes index.
1. Geology, Stratigraphic–Quarternary.
2. Geology–Nile Valley. 3. Man, Prehistoric–
Nile Valley. 4. Nile Valley–Antiquities.
I. Wendorf, Fred. II. Schild, Romuald.
QE696.P88 556.2 75-13097
ISBN:0–12–743950–1

PRINTED IN THE UNITED STATES OF AMERICA

To Rushdi Said

Our friend and colleague

Contents

Part II Synthesis

List of Contributors

Numbers in parentheses indicate the pages on which the authors' contributions begin.

Abdel-Kadder Attia (339), National Research Center, Dokki, Egypt

Roman Chlebowski (325), Polish Academy of Sciences, Warsaw, Poland

A. Gautier (349, 365, 369), Geologisch Instituut, University of Gent, Belgium

P. H. Greenwood (383), Zoology Department, British Museum of Natural History, London, England

Fekri A. Hassan (331, 339, 343), Wayne State University, Detroit, Michigan

Bahay Issawi (3, 23, 43, 93, 109, 151), Geological Survey of Egypt, Cairo, Egypt

Janina Kossakowska-Such (327), Polish Academy of Sciences, Warsaw, Poland

Wieslawa Przybylowska-Lange (321), Polish Academy of Sciences, Warsaw, Poland

Romuald Schild (27, 47, 95, 113, 121, 155, 229, 389), Polish Academy of Science, Warsaw, Poland

Elizabeth J. Todd (383), Zoology Department, Queen Elizabeth College, University of London

Fred Wendorf (27, 47, 95, 113, 121, 155, 229, 389), Department of Anthropology, Southern Methodist University, Dallas, Texas

Introduction

The study of Paleolithic materials from the Nile Valley began before World War I (Schweinfurth, 1903, 1904, 1905, 1909; Currelly, 1913; Sterns, 1917), but the first systematic surveys and excavations were undertaken during the late 1920s and 1930s. These resulted in the classic studies by Caton-Thompson and Gardner (1934, 1946, 1952); Sandford and Arkell (1929, 1933, 1934, 1939), and Vignard (1921a, b, 1923, 1928, 1934a, b, 1935a, b, 1947, 1955a, b, c, 1957). World War II and the subsequent political developments in Egypt terminated these initial systematic studies. Also, interest was slow in returning, in part because an erroneous impression had developed from the earlier work that Nilotic Paleolithic materials were both scarce and culturally retarded in comparison with adjacent areas of the Near East. Thus, with few exceptions (Myers, 1958, 1960; diCesnola, 1960), for nearly 20 years after World War II no large scale research was concluded on prehistoric materials in the Nile Valley.

The modern investigation of the prehistoric settlements along the Nile Valley began in 1961, stimulated by the international campaign to salvage the archaeological material which was to be inundated by the reservoir of the New High Dam at Aswan (Fig. 1). These initial efforts were concentrated in both Egyptian and Sudanese Nubia, extending as far south as the Third Cataract, and northward up to the Kom Ombo plain. They revealed a rich and complex sequence of prehistoric settlements and forever dispelled the earlier belief that few prehistoric remains existed along the Nile. In addition, the cultures along the Nile were shown to be fully as advanced as those in adjacent areas in the Near East. For example, evidence was found which suggested that the Nile Valley may have been one of the earliest scenes where ground grain was utilized as an important economic resource. It was felt that this initial use of grain might well have led to food production, one of the most important discoveries in human history. We now know that this is probably not correct, for true food production seemingly does not appear in Egypt until around 4000 B.C.

Several of the Nubian expeditions, although concerned primarily with Pharaonic and later materials, undertook limited excavations at Paleolithic sites (Chavaillon and Maley, 1966; Siirianen, 1965; Marks, 1970; and Vinogradov, 1964), but there were three major groups concerned primarily with prehistoric materials. One of these was the University of Colorado group working in a small area on the west bank near Wadi Halfa; Sudan (Irwin *et al.* 1968, Green *et al.*1967). A second group was the joint Yale University-Canadian National Museum party with a major effort at Kom Ombo, just north of Aswan, but also doing some work in Egyptian Nubia, mostly along the east bank of the river (Reed, 1966; Smith, 1966; Butzer and Hansen, 1968; Wendt, 1966; Kleindienst, 1967; Churcher, 1972).

One of the largest groups active in the Nubian campaign was the Combined Prehistoric Expedition, composed of scholars from several European and American institutions and universities. The major results of this work were published by Southern Methodist University (Wendorf, 1965, 1968), the organizing sponsor of the Combined Prehistoric Expedition. Another major report dealing with a survey of the adjacent desert was published by the University of Utah (Hester and Hoebler, 1970). When the Nubian salvage campaign was concluded in 1965 by the rise in the waters of the Aswan Reservoir, several of the participants in the Combined Prehistoric Expedition decided to continue their joint research along the Nile, and to concentrate their efforts downstream from Aswan. The major emphasis of this post-Aswan project was focused on the problem of Final Pleistocene prehistory, particularly those settlement just before, during, and after the first evidence for the use of ground grain. The primary sponsors of the work were Southern Methodist University, The Institute of the History of Material Culture, Polish Academy of Sciences, and the Geological Survey of Egypt. From time to time other institutions also contributed personnel or provided services to the project. These were: The British Museum of Natural History; Laboratory of Paleontology, University of Gent, Belgium; the Laboratory of Quaternary Studies, Polish Academy of Sciences; Isotopes, Inc.; Research Laboratory for Archaeology, Oxford University; and the University of Oklahoma.

The post-Nubia campaign along the Nile began in January, 1967 with a survey along the west bank of the Nile from just north of Aswan to Armant, near Luxor, Egypt. Two major areas were selected for more detailed studies: one, at El Kilh near Idfu; the other, just north of Isna. During the 1968 season the survey was extended from Luxor to Nag Hammadi on both the east and west banks, with major effort near Dishna, and more limited investigation at Makhadma village, both of these on the east bank, and several test sections were recorded on the west bank in a stretch extending from approximately opposite Luxor to Sohag. The 1969 season was spent on a partial survey of both banks between Tahta to Asyut and along the west bank to Mallawi; however, the major effort of that campaign was concentrated in the northern part of the Fayum depression. For subsequent seasons it was planned to extend the survey northward to the Mediterranean and then return to several key areas (El Kilh, Esna, Fayum, and one small area north of Aswan). Unfortunately, however, the increasingly tense international situation and local Egyptian security regulations forced us to terminate, hopefully only temporarily, our research along the Nile Valley.

Several preliminary accounts and notes dealing with post-Nubian work have been published (Wendorf and Said, 1967; Wendorf, Said, and Schild, 1970a, b; Said, Wendorf, and Schild, 1970; Said, Albritton *et al.*, 1972a, b; Schild, 1971; Phillips, 1970, 1972; Hassan, 1972). Three monographs dealing with sites in the Isna and Dishna areas have also been published (Phillips, 1973; Lubell, 1974; Hassan, 1974). The present study, however, offers considerable revision of many of the previous statements in these earlier publications. These revisions are the result of extensive reexamination of the entire body of data, including that obtained in Nubia, and some additional analyses not available when the preliminary accounts were written.

Preface

The purpose of this present study is to bring together all of the available data concerning the stratigraphy, chronology, and paleoenvironments which prevailed during the Final Pleistocene and Early Recent along the Nile from Nubia to the Mediterranean. Despite this goal, however, we recognize that the data are incomplete. In the first place, several of the analyses are not yet finished, especially the paleomagnetic, heavy mineral, and pollen studies. And then, only the initial phase of the planned research was accomplished. We had hoped to return to several key localities to conduct more extensive excavations. Despite these limitations, there still remains a large body of data including a large series of carefully recorded sections, numerous radiocarbon and thermoluminescent dates, the analyses of animal and fish remains, the diatom studies, the preliminary pollen counts, and a few heavy mineral and mechanical analyses. Together these form the framework for the synthesis presented here. It is felt that these data should be made available now, rather than delay further, particularly since a series of monographs dealing with the local prehistoric industries have already begun to appear (Phillips, 1973; Lubell, 1974;

Hassan, 1974), and these present only a restricted and, at most, a regional view. This volume is intended to reconcile the stratigraphic and environmental framework for the recognized archaeological entities, taking them together, and to provide a synthesis of the entire Nile Valley from below the Second Cataract in northern Sudan to the Delta.

The second half of this study presents brief descriptions and the characteristics of the major archaeological taxonomic entities defined in the post-Nubia work. It includes only very general typological and technological outlines of these groups so that the reader may have a reasonable impression of their contents. Since the emphasis of the post-Nubian work was on the Final Pleistocene and Early Recent, the earlier phases of the history of the Nile received very limited attention, and thus none of the archaeological materials from these earlier periods is included in the summary.

Early in the work it became apparent that the Final Pleistocene deposits along the Valley were preserved only in isolated local areas, usually where fossil embayments and large wadi mouths occurred. This geomorphic situation did not permit the continuous tracing of the units from one area to the next. Nevertheless, the repetitive lithostratigraphic pattern facilitated the recognition of the major units wherever they occurred. Furthermore, many of these units seemed to be clearly comparable to those seen in Nubia above the First Cataract. The comparison was also facilitated by some similarities in associated archaeological materials and, most convincingly, by the numerous parallels in radiocarbon dates. For this reason, in the preliminary accounts we employed the formal terminology established by de Heinzelin in Nubia. As our work progressed, and the additional data became available, several revisions in de Heinzelin's sequence seemed to be necessary. We now recognize a fundamental error was made by our utilization of the Nubian formal terminology in isolated areas several hundred kilometers below the First Cataract. This volume attempts to correct this error, but rather than offer a new formal terminology, thereby increasing the overflow of local formal names, and particularly in the absence of some of the critical required supporting data, we tried to establish local litho-stratigraphic sequences in each of the worked areas, and compared these one to another chronologically, using radiometric and archaeological data. The regional sequence thus developed was then compared with that established by Butzer and Hansen (1968) at Kom Ombo and by de Heinzelin and Albritton in Nubia (in Wendorf, 1968).

It is evident from these comparisons that along the entire stretch of the Nile simultaneous pulsations of the level of the Nile occurred, recorded by synchronous alluvial deposits and recessional downcuttings. To facilitate the understanding of this history we have utilized a combined terminology drawn from both de Heinzelin, and that of Butzer and Hansen. This terminology is considered to be informal and may not be entirely identical with the meaning originally attached to the formational names. These combined terms refer only to the events of aggradation or recession and not to the lithostratigraphic units. Table 15 compares the local lithological sequences, the informal names, and some of the formal names used by de Heinzelin, Butzer and Hansen.

Acknowledgments

It is entirely appropriate that this book is dedicated to our friend and colleague, Dr. Rushdi Said, General Director of the Egyptian General Organization for Mining and Mineral Research, whose support of the project from its inception was a vital factor in its success. Dr. Said also participated in the project as Senior Geologist whenever his busy schedule would permit, and his creative mind was a source of constant stimulation. Dr. Said's associate, Dr. Bahay Issawi, Senior Geologist in the Egyptian Geological Survey, is the author of several sections dealing with the pre-Quaternary geology. On the project, however, he had an even more responsible assignment. It was he who organized the camp, saw that we were properly fed, and took care of the multitude of problems which constantly arise during the operation of large expeditions. Dr. Issawi also served as surveyor and geological consultant. Most of the published maps were prepared by him.

All of the work was conducted under licenses issued by the Egyptian Department of Antiquities. The Department, through the personal interest of Dr. Gamal Mukhtar, Under Secretary of State for Culture and Antiquities, facilitated our research by assigning Mr. Achmed Said Hindi as Inspector of Antiquities on each of our field seasons. Mr. Hindi, although trained as an Egyptologist, developed a keen interest in prehistory, and thus participated as a full member of the expedition.

Several scholars took part in the project. They were, in alphabetical order: Claude C. Albritton, Southern Methodist University; Robert DuBois, University of Oklahoma; Achilles Gautier, University of Gent; C. Vance Haynes, Southern Methodist University; Thomas R. Hays, University of Texas at Arlington; Michal Kobusiewicz, IHKM, Polish Academy of Sciences; David Lubell, University of Calgary, Alberta; and James L. Phillips, University of Illinois at Chicago Circle.

Most of the artifact illustrations in this volume were prepared by Mrs. Lucy Addington, Southern Methodist University. The remaining artifacts (Figs. 191, 193-198, and 202) were drawn by Miss Iza Niewiadomska.

Generous financial support for the Nile prehistory project was provided by Grants No. 1386 and 1886, from the National Science Foundation, and by Grant 2423 from the Foreign Currency Program of the Smithsonian Institution. To these institutions and their staffs we wish to express our thanks not only for their confidence in us as scholars in providing support for our work, but also for their help throughout the project.

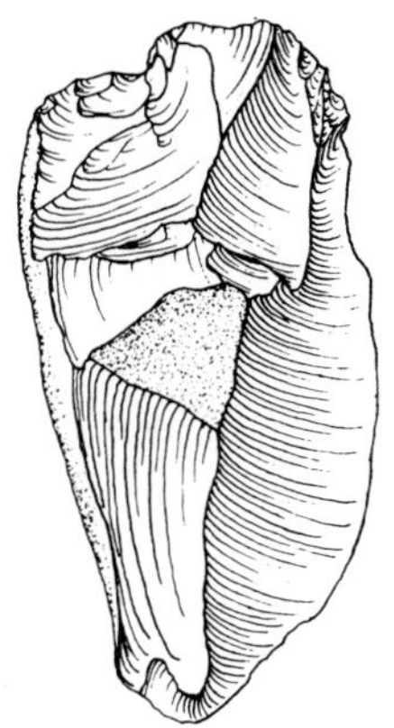

PART 1

Description

An Introduction to the Physiography of the Nile Valley

BAHAY ISSAWI

Egypt is located at the northeastern corner of Africa, overlooking the Mediterranean Sea, with a coastline that stretches approximately 1000 km in an east–west direction. The country lies midway on the old roads connecting Europe with the Far East, occupying a unique and central position in the Old World. Egypt also forms an integral part of the great African Sahara, lying to the west, which assigns a desert aspect to the country. Through the wilderness of the Sahara flows the great river, the Nile, giving fertility to the desert and attracting people to live beside its banks. The Nile flows 1520 km in Egypt, but it penetrates deeply into Africa, nearly to its center, creating relations with the African countries and giving both Nilotic and African perspectives to the country.

The Egyptian part of the Nile runs in a north–south direction for a distance of about 800 km between the Sudan frontier and Cairo (Figure 1). Slightly north of Cairo the river splits into two major branches, the Rosetta in the west (236 km) and the Damietta in the east (242 km), before reaching the sea. The two branches of the Nile embrace the fertile land of the Delta—22,000 km^2. The shape of the Nile valley is usually compared to that of a palm tree, the linear portion in Upper Egypt being the stem, while the branches of the palm are represented by the Delta with its intricate network of canals and drains.

During its Egyptian course the Nile seldom receives any water from the surrounding deserts. In very rare cases, during cloudbursts, some wadis, especially in the Eastern Desert, are flooded, and their water flows to the Nile.

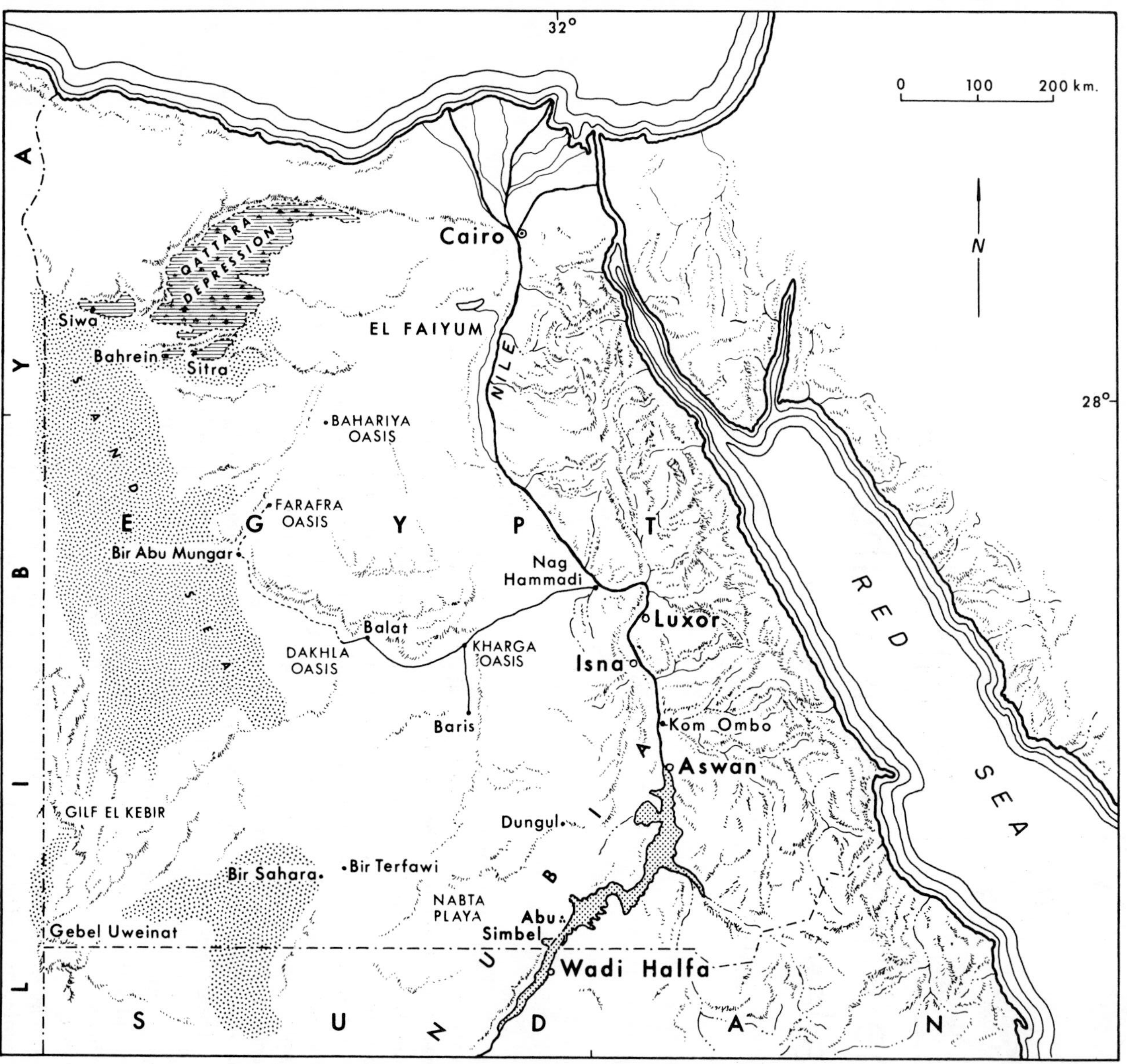

Figure 1. Map of Egypt showing position of major areas discussed in the text.

The Nile divides the area south of Cairo into two unequal geomorphic zones. Each has its own physical characteristics and differs considerably from the other. The area east of the river, the Eastern Desert, is famous for its rugged mountains, steep scarps, and conspicuous valleys, which have an external drainage system to either the Red Sea or the Nile. West of the Nile, the Western Desert is characterized by the flat, monotonous pediplains located between the Nile in the east and a relatively high scarp to the west. The pediplains are dissected by shallow wadis, which generally fan out before reaching the river, forming several mud pans and playas. The drainage is mainly internal.

Physiographic Divisions

Halfa–Aswan Province

The Nubian Nile flows between Halfa and Aswan, a distance of 350 km, in a very narrow valley during most of its course, bordered by abrupt cliffs. Between Adindan and Kalabsha the cliffs on both sides of the Nile are made of sandstone and quartzite beds of Upper Cretaceous–Lower Tertiary age. The beds are generally horizontal or slightly dipping (2°) northward. The sandstone is vari-colored—black, brown, brownish red, faint yellow to white. The dark colors are, however, more prominent, giving to the Nubian area a characteristic brown tint that contrasts greatly with the paler colors of the limestone plateaus farther west and with the bright colors of the crystalline rocks of the Eastern Desert.

On both sides of the Nile, the sandstone country is highly dissected by faults, which have an east–west trend south of Kurusku Highland. North of this highland, the faults generally trend north–south, with the east–west system of faults less developed—though some of them may be of considerable length, e.g., Kalabsha Fault (130 km). The effect of these structural lines on the relief of the Nubia area may be seen in the orientation of the ridges, the shape of the geomorphic features, and partly in the course of the river itself. The ridges, cliffs, and wadis in the south trend mainly east–west, whereas north of Kurusku these features assume a north–south direction. Between Kalabsha and Aswan granite and granitic gneiss (of the Aswan type, Late Precambrian) make their appearance below a thin cover of Nubia Sandstone, which may wear away in many places, and the river cuts its channel in the igneous rocks. The presence of sand dunes near the river is a very special feature that marks its Nubian course. Every cleft or hollow in the sandstone country is filled with yellow sand. The sand also partly covers the slopes of the sandstone ridges and sometimes forms twinkling patches near the summits of the cliffs that border the Nile. Said and Issawi (1966) classify this part of the valley into four distinct geomorphic zones, which they consider as structurally delineated. Further work on the area has shown that Aswan–Kushtanna Plateau is extended farther south to cover what has been named by these authors Alaqi–Abusku Depression. Thus the Nubia area can be subdivided into three units from south to north: (1) Halfa–Ballana Plateau, (2) Kurusku Highland, and (3) Alaqi–Aswan Plateau. The three units probably owe their existence to a group of faults that strikes more or less east–west, limiting the Kurusku Highland at both its north and south edges.

Halfa–Ballana Plateau

The Nile incises its valley in a horizontal or gently dipping (2° to the north) country of sandstone beds. The river flows in a northeast–southwest direction with minor bends in its course. On both sides of the river, a nearly flat pediplain surface, sloping gently toward the Nile, is observed. These surfaces overlook the Nile with steep scarps; each may rise 180 m above the river's edge. In a very few cases, where relatively major wadis open into the channel, the scarps retreat into the desert, giving rise to a longitudinal stretch of land very near to the river. These areas were the centers of farming in Nubia before the construction of the Aswan High Dam and the complete flooding of these plains, e.g., the Ballana–Abu Simbel area.

On both sides of the river, conical and table-like hills litter the undulating pediplain surface. These mesas and buttes attain different sizes and heights, varying from a few meters to 500 m in length and rising from 5 m to 100 m above the surface. When one approaches the Kuruska Highland, huge isolated masses of sandstone are observed, e.g., Gebel El-Sadd, occupying an area of about 10 km^2 and rising 180 m above the wadi level.

Kurusku Highland

This highland stands as a mass of rugged, mountainous land that attains a general elevation of 300 m above sea level, with higher peaks that may reach up to 500 m. In all its course through Egypt, the Nile never crosses an area with such marked and rugged physiography as the Kurusku stretch. The area is covered by Nubia Sandstone beds, which are generally dipping a few degrees toward the north. It is only near structural lines, mainly faults, that higher angles are observed. The southern part of the highland is wilder, rougher, more desolate and mountainous than the northern part. It is almost impassable even by light cars, while in the north access to the river is possible through wider gaps in the massive block. The uniqueness of the area is further heightened by the fact that for a distance of about 15 km the Nile flows in a northwest–southeast direction, against its normal trend. The acute bending in the river's course in this area may be due to a Quaternary uplift leading to the intricate topographic physiography of this highland. The wadis running along the surface of this mass drain it to the surrounding deserts, and by headward erosion and river capture two main streams join each other, giving rise to the present shape of the river (Said and Issawi 1965),

Alaqi–Aswan Plateau

The wild relief of Kurusku diminishes gradually northward, giving rise to widely spaced ridges and isolated Nubia Sandstone patches. The ridges are generally dissected by minor wadis, forming a trellis system of drainage that feeds low-lying areas—mud pans, known locally as *hatiya* or *naga*. The ridges may, in places, bear structural evidence of uparching movement, especially when encircling huge flat areas of up to 300 km^2.

The sandstone beds, exposed on these ridges, may dip away from the flat areas, giving rise to prominent hogbacks. Igneous outcrops are occasionally observed at the core of these structures, covering parts of the flat areas; otherwise they are the sites of silt and mud deposits with a thin veneer of drifted sand above. These mud pans, or playa surfaces, are well observed east of the Nile at Seiyala and west of it at Dakka.

From Alaqi to Aswan the Nile crosses a granite area that is covered by thin beds of sandstone. These beds may wear away in places because of structural reasons or intense erosion, as the river cuts its channel in the crystalline rocks. At Bab Kalabsha, where the river passes through very hard granites and granitic gneisses, its width is only 200 m, making this the narrowest part of the Egyptian Nile. In the Alaqi–Aswan stretch, the river has no floodplain on both sides, which is another unique feature in this area.

On both sides of the river between Kalabsha and Aswan, longitudinal parallel ridges of sandstone are common, rising several tens of meters above the surface. On the east side, the sandstone ridges may attain higher altitudes, up to 90 m above the river; sometimes they rise abruptly from the water's edge, forming precipitous cliffs. The ridges on the west bank extend to the west in a more or less monotonous rolled, undulating pediplain surface as far as the Sinn El-Kaddab scarp. This pediplain surface stretches between the scarp to the west and the Nile to the east, nearly to the latitude of Luxor farther north. The relief of this surface is low, attaining an average height of 200 m above sea level and an average width of 40 km. The pediplain is characterized by its internal drainage pattern, in contrast to the other side of the river where most of the ephemeral wadis drain their water to the Nile. Here, on the east side of the Nile, the cliffs bordering the river gain more height farther east, and the patchy thin sandstone cover over the crystalline rocks decreases gradually, giving place to the more complex and rugged peaks that mark the landscape of this part of the Eastern Desert.

Aswan–Cairo Province

At Aswan the Nile passes through an igneous channel, with several islands in the course of the river, and perfect conditions for a cataract are developed. Although the southern Nubia province manages to throw a shadow of its physiographic characteristics over the Aswan area, this area is generally acknowledged as the southern part of Upper Egypt.

North of Aswan the Nile loses its cataract characteristics, and the igneous obstacles in its course give place to sand and silt islands, probably resting over igneous knobs or covering sandstone beds in the river's channel. The cliffs bordering the Nile, on both sides at Nubia, continue farther north, but those on the left bank rapidly lose their height, and the precipitous scarp overhanging the Nile at Aswan is no longer observed. Instead, longitudinal parallel ridges of sandstone and clays covered by varying thicknesses of gravel characterize the west bank of the Nile. The scarp east of the Nile runs contiguous to the river, where the water almost washes the base of the cliff during most of its course, except for a few areas in the stretch between Aswan and Cairo, e.g., Kom Ombo Plain. This plain is a wide, featureless surface that is structurally delineated.

Farther north, at Luxor, the river suffers an acute bend, Qena Bend, which is the major loop of the Nile during its Egyptian course. This bend marks off a relatively narrow valley in the south from a wider section to the north.

The Fayum Depression, located 60 km southwest of Cairo, is an usurped oasis from the Western Desert, yet it belongs to the Nile Valley by virtue of its close proximity and connection with the river through the Bahr Youssef Canal.

For the 965 km stretch between Aswan and Cairo, the Nile has a general north–south trend, though it may flow to the northwest or the northeast during parts of its course. The level of the river is 83 m above sea level near Aswan and 12 m near Cairo; thus it acquires a gradient of 1:13.6 along this stretch.

From the general features of the different parts of the Nile Valley and the surrounding terrain in this province, the valley can be divided into several units: (1) the Aswan area, (2) the Aswan–Luxor stretch, (3) Kom Ombo Plain, (4) Qena Bend, (5) the Naga Hammadi–Cairo stretch, and (6) Fayum Depression. The main geomorphic characteristics of these six zones are briefly discussed in the following paragraphs.

Aswan Area (Figure 2)

The cataract area stretches for about 10 km along the course of the river north and south of Aswan City. Along this strech the river passes through several islands of igneous rocks, which divide the main river into several streams. The Nile water wanders among these islands, and the channel attains an exceptional width, ranging from 4.7 km south of Aswan Dam to 1.5 km north of the dam. Among these igneous islands the river forms rapid after rapid in the narrow streams, 150 m in width, between the small islets that partially bar the Nile.

As a result of the construction of Aswan High Dam, located 7 km south of the old dam, this scenery of small islands and rapids will completely disappear under water. The islands and rapids north of the old dam will be the only relic of the main Aswan cataract, mostly covered by Lake Nasser.

On both sides of the Nile in the Aswan area, steep scarps rise directly from the water's edge, and as in Nubia, the floodplain north and south of Aswan is more or less confined to the river course. The scarps are formed mainly of igneous rocks that are covered by different thicknesses of sandstone and clay beds. Sheets of deflated sands cover most of the face of the western scarp, while sand dunes fill all the hanging wadis in this scarp. The contrast in the color of the yellow sand, the green color of the vegetation on the islands, and the blackish-red color of these granitic islands gives Aswan its very special picturesque view.

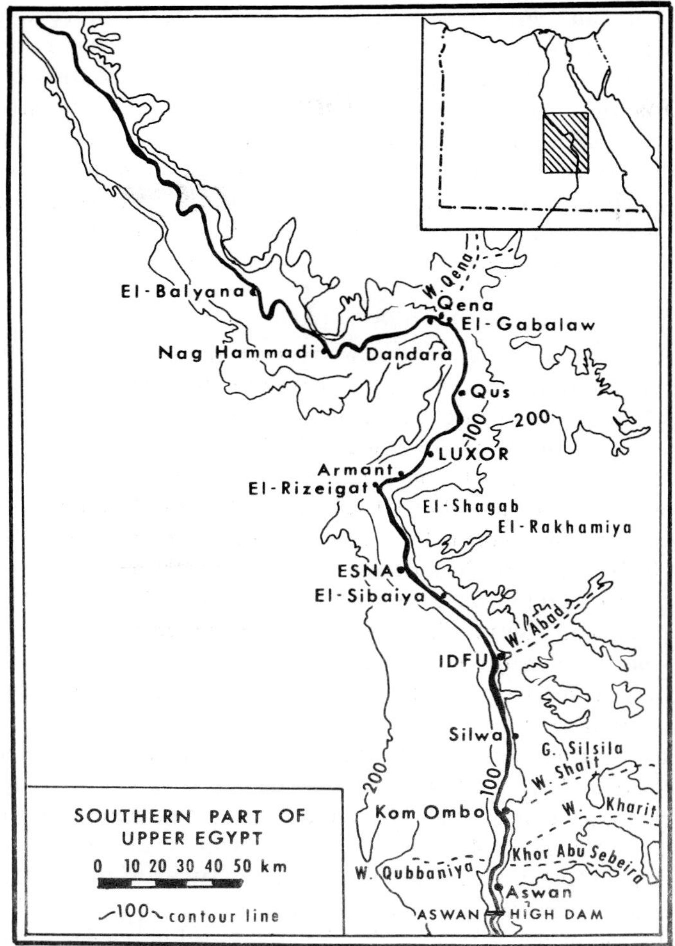

Figure 2. Map of Nile valley and southern part of Upper Egypt.

The effect of weathering on the granitic rocks on the watercourse gives a very peculiar crust and color. The crust, known as cataract crust, is usually found coating the igneous hummocks in the river's course and attains a thickness of up to 5 cm. Ball (1907) explains the origin of this crust as due to the penetration of the water inside the crystalline rocks, filling the pore spaces and dissolving some of the minerals to form a new, insoluble compound that is later deposited on the surface of the rocks.

The origin of Aswan cataract is considered by some authors as due to structural deformations affecting the Aswan area, while others believe there was undulating surface of the igneous rocks underlying a thin sandstone cover that was removed by the running water. Recent mapping of the High Dam area

(Za'tout and Gad 1961) shows a great number of faults cutting through the igneous rocks of the Aswan area, having both an east–west and a north–south direction. On the other hand, geological studies on the west bank of the Nile prove the irregular surface of the crystalline rocks. Thus the combined effect of both factors may result in the appearance of igneous islands in the river's channel and, hence, its division into several streams. The difficulty with which the river degrades a channel in this area, owing to the hardness of the igneous bedrock in comparison to the less hard sandstone in the south and the soft limestone in the north, may also lead to the fanning out of the Nile.

The Aswan–Luxor Stretch

North of Aswan the Nile flows in a general northerly direction for about 40 km before it turns abruptly to the west near Kom Ombo. Running for a distance of 5 km in an east–west direction, the Nile reassumes its northerly direction until north of Idfu, a stretch of 65 km. From north Idfu the river meanders to the northwest, where it flows 80 km in this direction as far as El-Rizeigat. The river then flows back to the east for 10 km and toward the northeast for another 15 km before reaching Luxor. The east bend at El-Rizeigat is the southern part of the Qena Bend.

The igneous rocks outcrop at the foot of the cliff bordering the Nile slightly northeast of Aswan, while the main part of the cliff is made of sandstone and clay beds. Ferruginous (hematitic) sandstones, interbedded with this sequence, are mined from different places in the wadis north of Aswan, while China clay, found on both sides of the river, is quarried for the porcelain industry and also for building the main body of the High Dam. The eastern cliff rises 100 m above the floodplain, whereas the western cliff is considerably lower. The latter extends further west to form a dissected pediplain surface, assuming a width of 25–45 km until it reaches the main Limestone Plateau.

This pediplain surface is a northern continuation of the southern Nubia pediplain and fringes the Nile to the latitude of Luxor. The surface of the pediplain is gently undulating, made of several broad benchlike terraces, interfingering and occasionally overhanging each other. The width of the terraces varies from a few hundred meters to 4 km, and the relief is on the order of from 5 m to 20 m. The slopes of these terraces near the wadi floor display a very irregular dendritic pattern marked with gravels derived from the terraces and sands of the adjacent wadis. The surface of these terraces is covered by gravels derived from the western Limestone Plateau. The gravels increase in size from cobbles to boulders as the plateau is approached.

The strip of this pediplain that bounds the valley is hummocky and highly dissected by wadis and gorges, and attains the highest altitude within this surface. This hummocky part is no longer observed near Isna, where the floodplain of the river opens into the pediplain surface. At Isna latitude, the western Limestone Plateau approaches the river because of a major promontory that protrudes toward the Nile, and the width of the pediplain surface is only 10 km. Farther north, the pediplain opens out again, coping with the recession of the Limestone Plateau to the west, and attains a width of 30 km. At El-Rizeigat, the western plateau bends toward the river and runs in a northeast direction until near Luxor, where it nearly touches the west bank of the Nile.

The main wadi running over the pediplain surface west of the Nile is El-Qubbaniya Wadi, which joins the Nile 15 km north of Aswan. The feeders of this wadi drain a considerable area, both in the Limestone Plateau and in the pediplain surface. The mouth of the wadi is blocked by deflated sand and silt derived from both sides of the wadi, indicating a phase of complete dryness during recent years. The banks of the wadi are made of sandstone and sandy clay beds covered by gravels at the top, while the slopes are highly covered with sand. Incision is in the range of 5 m near the Nile; it increases gradually westward, reaching up to 40 m in the central part of the wadi.

Other minor wadis run along the western scarp face, north of El-Qubbaniya Wadi, and continue eastward through the pediplain surface. Most of these wadis fail to reach the Nile; instead, they fan out, forming several mud pans. The hummocky edge overlooking the Nile acts as a divide between the river in the east and the pediplain surface in the west. Smaller wadis of insignificant length flow on either side of the divide. All these wadis are dry, and only during cloudbursts (probably one every 5 years) does an appreciable amount of water fill these dry channels.

The eastern side of the valley differs in its physiographic features. The sandstone cliff bordering the Nile at Aswan continues farther north, leaving, in places, only a few meters of shore between the cliff and the river. Northward, near Kom Ombo, the cliff bends abruptly to the east, overlooking a vast plain to the north–the Kom Ombo Plain. This plain is limited on the northwest by the sandstone cliffs of Gebel El-Silsila. Here, the river narrows, having a width of 350 m, but it soon opens out again north of Silwa, attaining its normal width of over 700 m. Near Idfu, the mouth of Abad Wadi opens into the floodplain of the Nile, increasing the potential of the cultivable land in this area.

North of Idfu the sandstone scarps on both sides of the river are covered with phosphatic and hard oyster limestone beds of Upper Cretaceous age, forming plateaus of considerable width, especially east of the Nile, e.g., El-Hagaria El-Moustaha, 20 km^2. Farther north, successive younger strata overlie the phosphatic beds and contribute to the buildup of the mountainous terrain at El-Sibaiya. Here the phosphatic beds are mined extensively.

At the latitude of Isna the phosphate beds no longer outcrop on the surface. The impressive mountainous mass of El-Rakhamiya El-Shagab, which rises some 550 m above the floodplain, is made of Lower Eocene limestone overlying shales and chalk beds. This range extends farther north, running contiguous to the river and leaving only a thin strip of land 0.7 km wide.

In contradistinction to the wadis on the western side, all the main wadis east of the Nile drain the eastern plateaus to the Nile. The silting of the wadis, a characteristic feature for the western wadis, is no longer observed here. Rainfall over the Eastern Desert is rare but more frequent than over the Western Desert, hence, the washing away of any accumulated sand and silt in the wadis' channels. The contrast between the eastern and western wadis is best noted at Khor Abu Sebeira on the east opposite El-Qubbaniya Wadi. In the former the sand and silt in the wadi channel are continually washed away by the flood of water running occasionally through the wadi, whereas El-Qubbaniya Wadi is more or less completely silted up.

The width of the Nile floodplain follows the bending of the surrounding scarps either away from or toward the river. Whenever the scarps run near the river, the valley narrows on the same side and opens on the other side. Between Aswan and Luxor the eastern cliffs are generally adjacent ot the Nile, except for the Kom Ombo Wadi area and several other small patches, with the valley wider on the west side. The average width of the valley in this stretch, excluding the Kom Ombo Plain, is 2.8 km; the maximum is 7.5 km at Idfu; and the minimum is 350 m, which is the width of the river itself at Silwa Gorge. These figures represent the state of the river before the High Dam was built. Now the picture is changing completely, and the floodplain of the Nile in the Idfu area, for instance, has penetrated 25 km farther east along Abad Wadi. At Isna, where an active reclamation program is taking place, the floodplain gains a few kilometers west of the Old Valley. The picture is not yet clear, since the reservoir behind the dam has not reached its full capacity and the process of land-gaining out of the surrounding desert is taking place.

Kom Ombo Plain

The sandstone cliff bordering the Nile east of Aswan stretches 30 km in a north–south direction before turning abruptly eastward, giving rise to a wide plain at its foot. This plain stretches about 35 km eastward and another 30 km to the north, where it is again limited by another sandstone scarp of Gebel El-Silsila. Both sandstone scarps are fault scarps with the Grabenal Wadi at Kom Ombo in between, where Upper Cretaceous–Lower Tertiary chalk, shale, and limestone beds are exposed. This section is covered by different thicknesses of Quaternary strata. The sedimentary sequence in the grabenal area assumes an earthy white color that contrasts with the dark yellowish-brown color of the surrounding sandstone cliffs.

The Kom Ombo Plain is a flat, undulated surface with inconspicuous ridges that fade out rapidly in the surrounding plain. The plain rises 20–25 m above the river, with several still-higher Quaternary terraces on both sides. The terraces are well developed on the east bank of the Nile, attracting the attention of several archaeologists and Pleistocene geologists (Vignard 1923, 1935, 1955; Sandford and Arkell 1939; Butzer and Hansen 1968; and others).

The northern cliff is higher and more consistent than the southern scarp. The first stands 100 m above the river, whereas the southern cliff rises 30–40 m above the Nile. The faults limiting the plain are transverse, east–west (approximately) in direction, crossing the Nile to be observed also on the western side.

The continuation of the Kom Ombo Plain to the west is relatively masked by the rising of the hummocky ridge that limits the western pediplain surface to the east. Passing this ridge, toward the west, a huge flat area covered with sand sheets extends nearly to the foot of the western Limestone Plateau. Several white outcrops of Upper Cretaceous–Lower Tertiary beds are observed on the west bank, forming 10–15 m ridges in this flat plain.

The widening of the Kom Ombo plain to the east is helped by the opening of two main wadis, namely, Shait Wadi in the north and Kharit Wadi in the south, in the eastern part of the plain. These two wadis drain a considerable area of the central Eastern Desert and fanning out form the eastern part of the Kom Ombo Plain before reaching the Nile.

The scarp in the north (Gebel El-Silsila) and the Kom Ombo Plain represent a perfect geomorphic setup of scarp, pediment, and bajada surface. The pediment, or zone of planation, is narrow—several hundred meters wide—in contrast to the vast zone of deposition represented by the Kom Ombo Plain. This indicates an old stage in the geomorphic cycle of the plains evolution.

Qena Bend

At El-Rizeigat, the Nile swings suddenly to an east–west direction, flowing for about 6 km before it heads toward the northeast. Past Luxor a major loop in the river's course is noticed, and at north Qus the Nile changes its course to attain a north–south direction. At El-Gabalaw, the river heads to the northwest as far as Dandara, where it changes its direction, assuming an east–west trend. Between Dandara and Nag Hammadi, the river flows in a west–southwest direction with several meanders, the largest of which is the oxbow curve east of Nag Hammadi. North of this curve the Nile flows back to the northeast. The distances between the different trends in the course of the river forming Qena Bend are indicated in the following table.

Trend of the Nile	*From*	*To*	*Distance in km*
West–East	El-Rizeigat	South Armant	6.0
Northeast–Southwest	South Armant	North Qus	65.0
North–South	North Qus	El-Gabalaw	15.0
Northwest–Southeast	El-Gabalaw	Dandara	15.0
East–West	Dandara	Nag Hammadi	50.0

The Qena Bend constitutes the waist of the Eastern Desert, as the river never approaches the Red Sea (150 km to Safaga on the Red Sea) except in this area. Probably that was one of the reasons that the area played an important role in old Egyptian history, since it is centrally located in the valley and near the Red Sea coast. For a long time during the Pharaohs' rule, Luxor (or Thebes) was the capital of Egypt, and in its western limestone cliffs the famous tombs of kings and queens were hewn, while the greatest temples of Old Egypt were built on both sides.

North of Armant, a major promontory of the western Limestone Plateau protrudes toward the Nile, filling the western side of the Qena Bend. The promontory rises about 430 m above the river, trending in a northeast direction and leaving a very thin strip of land on the left bank of the Nile. This strip thins out gradually north of Armant, but it soon gains the stretch of land that fills the major loop north of Luxor and again diminishes in width until west of Dandara. Here the desert edge overhangs the Nile for a distance of about 10 km, and the floodplain is restricted to the other side of the river. At Nag Hammadi the conditions are reversed; the eastern scarp approaches the Nile greatly, and the floodplain is confined to the west side, assuming a width of about 15 km.

On the eastern side of the river, the limestone scarp banking the valley south of Luxor, El-Rukhamia El-Shagab, retreats eastward in a huge arc that encircles the Nile bend and comes near the Nile opposite Nag Hammadi. All along this mountainous arc, which encompasses the concave side of the Qena Bend, deeply incised valleys run toward the river. The most important of these is Qena Wadi, which is also one of the major valleys in Egypt. The feeders of this valley drain the Southern Galala Plateau on the Gulf of Suez, 300 km further north.

The desert area east of the Nile is made up of three main steps overhanging each other before the main semicircular scarp to the east is reached. These are more or less parallel to the 100, 200, and 300 m contour lines and highly covered by gravel and boulder wash. The sedimentary section both east and west of the Nile is made of Lower Eocene limestone and shale at the top and Paleocene shales and chalk at the base. Quaternary silt and gravel terraces flank the Nile and stretch inside the surrounding deserts. In places east of Luxor, phosphatic beds of Upper Cretaceous age outcrop at the base of the scarp, overlaid by different thicknesses of shales and limestones.

The bend of the Nile at Qena is most probably structural in origin. Mapping on both sides of the bend reveals several deformational features, mainly fault lines. Some of them cross the Nile.

The Nag Hammadi–Cairo Stretch

North of Nag Hammadi the Nile swerves in the direction of the Red Sea and the valley broadens appreciably, giving rise to the main cultivable area in southern Egypt. For this long stretch (550 km) the river clings tenaciously to the right-hand side of the valley, sometimes hugging the foothills of the impressive steep cliffs that frequently rise abruptly from the water's edge.

Past Nag Hammadi, the Nile flows in a northwest direction to Manfalut, a distance of about 200 km. Between Manfalut and Samalut, 135 km, the river trends north–south, whereas from Samalut to El-Wasta, 140 km, the Nile has a northeast direction. North of El-Wasta, for a stretch of 85 km, the river heads northerly to Cairo. The general outlook of the channel in this stretch resembles a big arc; its concave side faces the Western Desert, whereas its convex side embraces the northern part of the Eastern Desert.

Between Nag Hammadi and Manfalut the eastern cliff runs in a very irregular pattern close to the river. Whenever the river meanders and the convex side of the loop faces the Eastern Desert, the whole U-shaped area is full of Nile silt and is highly inhabited. Generally the Nile in this stretch is undulated, running in a zigzag way, probably owing to the lithological characteristics of the river's bed. As may be anticipated from the surrounding scarps, which are made of alternating hard and soft Lower Eocene limestone beds, the Nile must have dug its channel in beds with different hardnesses. The river incises more rapidly in softer limestone beds, shifting its course gradually away from the hard, resisting beds. This may also explain the various depths of the river at one section, reflected in the difficulty of navigation through the Nile north of Qena. The difference in hardness of the river's bedrock probably is not the only reason for the zigzag way of the channel, but structural lines have undoubtedly contributed to shaping the channel.

The river is characterized in this stretch by a number of islands, some of which have considerable area, e.g., east and southeast of El-Balyana.

The eastern scarp bordering the Nile rises about 300 m above the floodplain, whereas the western cliff is progressively lower and more northward. Both scarps are highly undulated, forming many embayments and promontories. The embayments in the east are very narrow, occupied by deeply incised wadis that have conspicuous banks even near the river. Some of the wadis may fan out midway between the scarp and the river, contributing to the width of the floodplain, e.g., opposite El-Balyana, where the floodplain has its maximum width—19 km. The embayments on the west side are smooth in outline, and the wadis have no distinct channels. The incision is shallow near the scarp face, and most of the wadis fail to reach the Nile.

North of Manfalut the eastern scarp closely bounds the Nile, leaving tiny flat patches that are the only inhabited areas east of the river. The meandering of the river is less developed than south of Manfalut; the channel is marked by a number of islands, which are smaller in area toward the north. The floodplain of the Nile decreases in width north of El-Wasta, in spite of the fact that a more or less continuous strip of land banks the river on the east. The average width of the floodplain north of El-Wasta is 8.3 km, whereas to the south at Beni Suef it reaches 23.0 km owing to the widening of the valley to the west.

Nearly at the latitude of Beni Suef, the scarps on both sides of the Nile recess back, leaving a wide, open plain between the floodplain and the scarp. These plains are old Nile terraces that attain a higher altitude than the enclosed floodplain, a difference of 20 m, thus hindering any reclamation program. Recently since the completion of the High Dam, it seems possible to gain more land out of these plains.

The cliffs on both sides of the Nile are formed of Middle Eocene Limestone and have more or less the same physical characteristics as their southern continuation. The eastern scarp runs contiguous to the Nile until north of Samalut, where it bends eastward and then northward in a very irregular pattern, having many indentations alternating with projecting spurs, points, and promontories. It rises 200–250 m above the floodplain. Several deep wadis cut through this scarp; the major ones reach the Nile. The most important of these are the wadi at El-Assiyti in the south and Tarfa in the north. Both have an east–west direction, emerging from the southern Galala Plateau, and some feeders of El-Assiyti are entangled with those of Qena Wadi. The wadis' floors are highly covered with limestone boulders and blocks, which may stretch to cover the plains near the Nile.

The limestone beds dip gently northward, though in places opposite Maghagha major north–south faults disturb this inclination. The channel of the river in this area is partly delineated by faults.

The western scarp fades out gradually to the north, attaining an altitude from 50 m to 100 m above the floodplain. It has a very smooth outline, with minor wadis crossing the face of the scarp; none of these reach the river. Opposite El-Fashn the scarp abruptly changes its direction to the west, encircling the Fayum Depression. The bend is structurally controlled, and the scarp follows an east–west trending fault. The scarp makes a major detour around the depression before it emerges again from the west, overlooking the Nile at the latitude of El-Ayat. From here on it runs in a north–south direction, parallel to the Nile, as far as Cairo. The scarp has a low altitude along the El-Ayat–Cairo stretch, more or less 50 m above the floodplain. Sand dunes are very common, running north–northwest, south–southwest parallel to the prevailing wind. These are found filling cavities in the scarp face and shallow wadis, and sometimes stretch to cover parts of the plain between the Nile and the scarp. Thin parallel ridges and isolated patches, 15 m in height, are not uncommon near the floodplain.

North of Maghagha the eastern scarp runs at a regular distance from the Nile, about 15 km, in a north–south direction. The scarp keeps this trend until it passes Cairo, where it bends toward the east. Gebel El-Mokattam rises 200 m above Cairo, while the scarp attains higher altitudes southward and eastward—400 m above the floodplain. This portion of the scarp has an irregular outline with deep-cut wadis; most of them have an east–west trend, running toward the Nile.

Fayum Depression

The inland delta of the Fayum Depression is a semioasis located 60 km southwest of Cairo (Figure 3). The depression is sometimes known as "little Egypt"; the Bahr Youssef Canal, which feeds it with Nile water, is its "upper Egypt", whereas the intricate system of canals and terraces resembles the Delta and Lake Qarun is analogous to the coastal lakes of the Delta.

The depression is similar to other depressions in the Western Desert, yet it differs from them by its connection with the Nile and also by the fact that its floor is covered with Nile silt. Through its connection with the Nile, Fayum is always looked upon as a part of the Nile valley and not as an oasis in the Western Desert.

The depression covers an area of 12,000 km^2, with a general slope to the northwest where Lake Qarun is situated. The depression is carved in Middle–

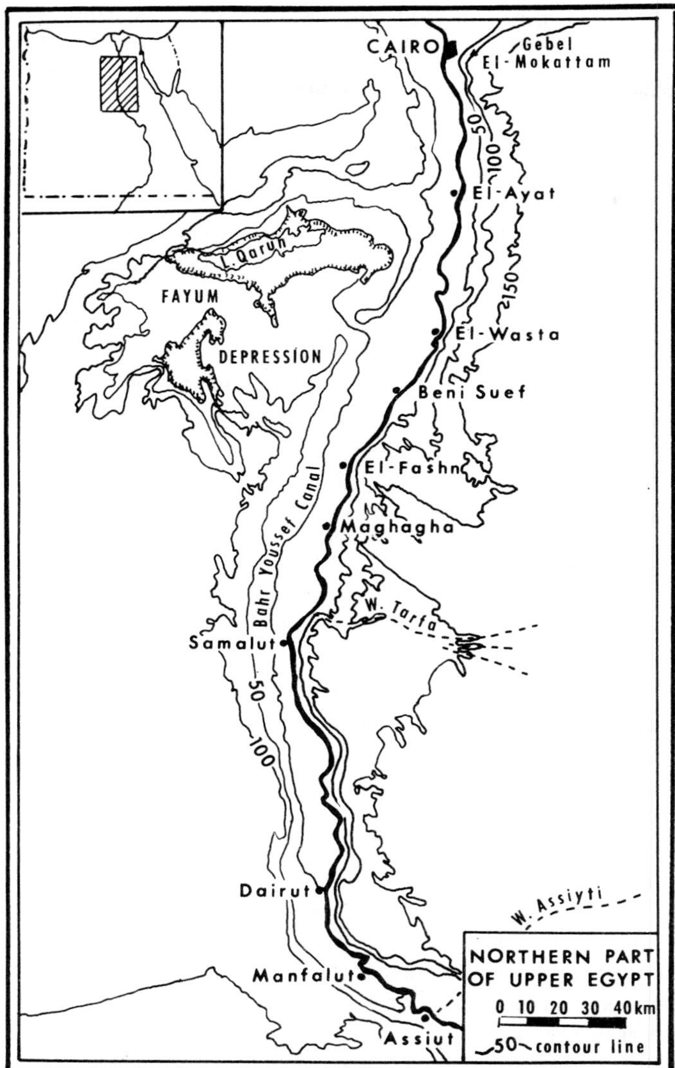

Figure 3. Map of Nile Valley near Fayum.

Upper Eocene and Oligocene beds. Basalt, probably of Oligocene age, caps the northern scarp, while Oligocene, Lower Miocene, and Pliocene gravel terraces are found on different scarps and partly in the depression. Quaternary deposits are present within the depression floor at different elevations, ranging from 40 m above sea level to 2 m below sea level (Caton-Thompson and Gardner 1929).

As in most of the Western Desert depressions, the north wall is a steep, nearly vertical cliff, while the southern and western escarpments are relatively low. The northern scarp rises 300 m above the floor of the depression, whereas the southern scarp rises only 80 m. The northern scarp is made of several benches overhanging each other, with several isolated mesas and buttes on the surface of each bench.

The eastern part of the depression, facing the Nile, is a flat area where the Fayum Depression opens into the floodplain of the river. Through this wide gap the Bahr Youssef Canal enters the depression. The canal joins the Nile at Dairut, 60 km north of Assiut, and flows for about 200 km in a very zigzag way parallel to the Nile. In the depression, Bahr Youssef feeds many canals, which are distributed in a triangular shape to cover the whole green area of Fayum province. All these canals have a blind end, and none of them reach Lake Qarun, north of the depression.

The cultivated area in the depression is bounded on the north by a low area below sea level that encircles Lake Qarun and stretches north and west to the foot slope of the northern scarp. Emerging from this low area, the floor of the depression rises gradually to make the undulating plains that encompass the Fayum Depression. These undulating plains are, in turn, surrounded by a semicircular scarp that is a part of the western scarp bounding the Nile valley. The low area surrounding the lake is covered by sand dunes and sand sheets. It has an altitude that ranges from -44 m at the southern side to -10 m on the northern shore of the lake. Several marshy ponds are seen in the southern part of this area.

The undulating plains are nearly flat, formed of several rock-cut benches stretching away from the lake to the surrounding scarps, and sometimes form considerable wide steps overhanging each other. These steps are covered by blown sand with hard knobs of rock coming out of the surface, giving the typical Karafish type of weathering. Over some of these benches, especially those to the north and northeast, extensive mud flats and Quaternary silt and diatomaceous earth deposits are well developed. The elevation of these plains varies from 0 to +25 m, with still higher mesas and buttes; some of them may rise 80 m from the surrounding plain, e.g., Qaret El-Gindi.

Lake Qarun is an oval-shaped depression. The long axis trends approximately east–west and has a length of 40 km whereas the maximum width is 9 km. Measured near its center, the maximum depth of the lake is 7.6 m, and the lowest point lies -45 m below sea level. The lake covers an area of 215 km. The average salinity of the lake is 3%, and it varies seasonally, reaching its maximum during August and its minimum in March. This depends on the temperature—hence the degree of evaporation—and also on the amount of saline drain water poured into the lake.

The Nile Delta (Figure 4)

Slightly to the north of Cairo, by 23 km, the Nile bifurcates into two main branches, flowing northeast and northwest toward the Mediterranean Sea.

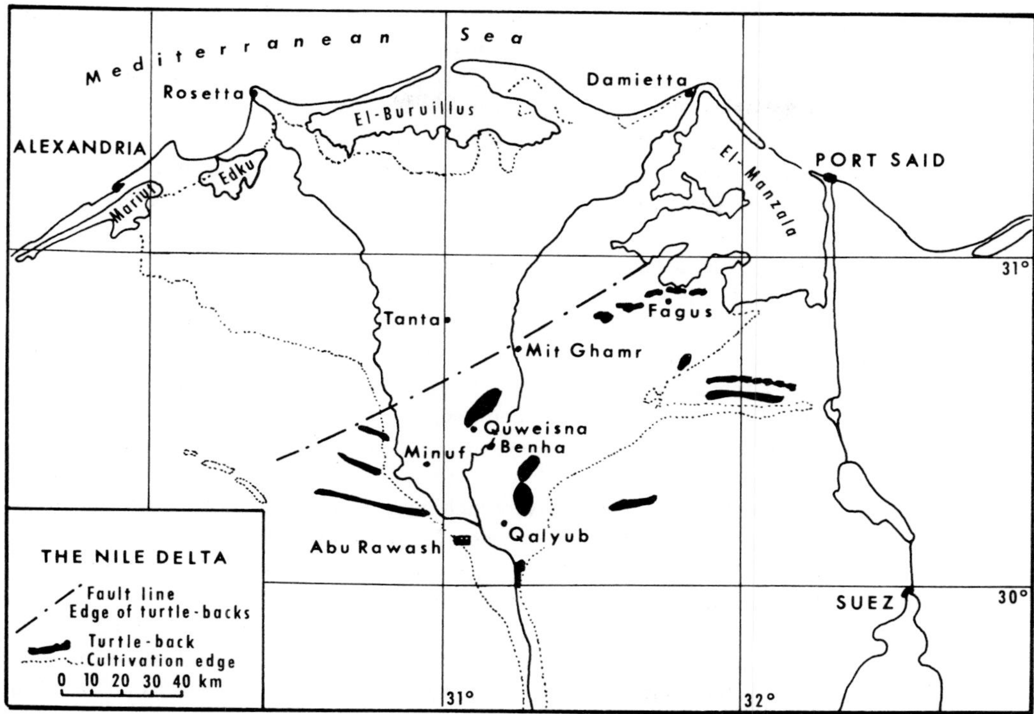

Figure 4. Map of Nile Delta.

The two branches embrace the Nile Delta, the most densely populated part of Egypt. Beyond the apex, the Delta stretches 170 km in a north–south trend, attaining a base of 220 km along the Mediterranean Sea and covering an area of 22,000 km^2, which represents 63% of the inhabited area of Egypt. The triangular-shaped plain is studded with an intricate network of canals and drains, the former along the higher tongues of the land, the latter in the hollows. The overall shape of the Delta is usually compared with the back of a leaf, on which the ribs mark the higher land with basins of lower land between them (Hamdan 1964).

Throughout history the canal mesh has evidently been highly variegated, and many fossil branches have been recognized. The whole loses itself in a coastal marshy area of waste land, the Bareri, pitted with a series of lagoons, some interior and some connected with the sea.

The physiographic setup of the area south of the Delta enhances the fanning out of the Nile in the area north of Cairo and the formation of such an extensive delta. To the east of Cairo the eastern scarp bends eastward, whereas the western scarp fades gradually into the flat Western Desert. This geomorphic pattern gives a flat surface in northern Egypt over which the Nile wanders, depositing its loads, gaining from the sea and forming its great Delta. On this deltaic surface the river splits into different branches. Only two of them are of importance now, while relics of the older ones are still observed in many parts of the Delta. Probably the Nile deserts some of these channels owing to a slight tilting of the Delta, which leads to damming and silting of these branches. Recent drilling for oil in the Delta has shown different structural features as well as thick basalt sheets below a section of Neogene strata that is overlaid by Nile sediments. Both geophysical and drilling works in the delta indicate a major fault that crosses the Nile at Mit Gamr and runs in a southwest direction, cutting the other branch of the Nile near Minouf. The parallelism of the two main branches of the Nile with the Aqaba and Suez gulfs of the Red Sea has long been considered as evidence for the structural setup of the Nile branches. Both the northeast and northwest trends of these branches represent a major system of deformation in the structural framework of the country.

The flat areas east and west of the Delta are covered mainly by Miocene and Pliocene sediments, and they are very gently inclined toward the northeast and northwest, respectively. Approaching the Delta, Quaternary silt and gravel terraces are very common. Only near Cairo do older rocks outcrop; Middle and Upper Eocene strata nearly encircle the city, while at the northwest an Upper Cretaceous exposure, the Abu Rawash Dome, is recorded.

The Delta area itself slopes to the north, with a gradient of 12 m in its entire 170 km stretch—approximately 1:14. Nearly the whole land of the Delta is highly fertile, made of alternating clay, clayey sand, medium to coarse sand, and a gravel bed at base. Basic elements are common in this sequence, carried by the Nile from the Ethiopian volcanic plateau. The northern part of the Delta is a bareri area with three main lakes connected with the Mediterranean through narrow straits.

Growth of the Delta

The estimated growth of the Delta was 12 feet per year before the construction of Aswan High Dam. This small rate of growth in comparison to other rivers (Mississippi, 250 feet/year; Volga, 1000 feet/year) is due to the fact that the river flows in a very arid zone for almost 2500 km before reaching the Mediterranean. In this arid stretch the river very rarely receives water from the surrounding deserts. On the contrary, the Nile loses some of its water through evaporation and lateral seepage, which diminishes the power of the river as a transporting agent and leads to a gradual deposition of its load along the course of the river before reaching the sea. With the complete damming of the river by Aswan High Dam, and continuous silting behind the dam, the rate of the Delta's growth will certainly decrease to a very low value. The effect on the northern coast of the Delta will be great and dangerous, since it will be continuously abraded by wave action. The drop of the Nile silt south of Aswan High Dam will also lead to a rejuvenation in the geomorphic cycle of the river, and the Nile will start degrading its channel, since the fortification of the banks will hinder any lateral effect. Continuous degradation of the river's channel will result in lowering the water level of the Nile and, hence, difficulty in irrigating the surrounding lands. Leaving these problems for several specialists to solve, the counterpart of them is the great amount of electricity generated from the dam as well as the extensive land to be reclaimed.

Turtle-backs

Turtle-backs are deposits of sand, sandy clay, and impure silt, yellow in color and forming higher longitudinal hummocks over the Delta surface. They appear as yellow islands in the green fields of the Delta, rising, generally, 10–12 m above the surface; some may rise only one meter above the surface. Four of these turtle-backs are found near Quweisna, two between Benha and Qalyub, one near Fagus, and five near Manzala, occupying an average area of 2 km^2 each.

With this distribution it is easy to draw a line dividing the Delta into two parts: Southeast of this line the turtle-backs are present, whereas northwest of it none are found. This line coincides approximately with the fault just mentioned, which crosses the Delta in a northeast–southwest direction. The Delta part northwest of this line is characterized by its fine, well-sorted, thick Upper Nile sediments, e.g., 43 m at Rosetta and 48 m at Damietta. Southeast of this line, the Upper Nile sediments are thin and ill-sorted, with gravel bands in the silt (Attia 1954), e.g., 8.5 m at Minuf. The turtle-backs may represent relics of the southern ill-sorted beds of the old buried branches of the Nile. Sandford and Arkell (1939) consider these turtle-backs as relics of Middle Paleolithic silts analogous to the deposits of the Delta sides, "Others have almost certainly increased in size at the expense of the fields by sand and dust accumulating around them." Ball (1939) regards these features as the more consolidated and more resistant portions of deltaic deposits "that were formed in the sea around the mouths of the river at a time when sea level was considerably higher relative to the land than it is at present day. As the relative level of the sea falls, the less compacted portions of the deposits were disintegrated by water-action and their material redistributed beneath the water. The more resistant portions remained in position and formed islands [p. 32]."

The Northern Lakes

The northern coast of the Delta is characterized by the presence of a chain of lakes, most of them connected with the Mediterranean Sea. The northern shores of these lakes are smooth, separated from the sea by a strip of sand. The southern coasts are very irregular, with many bays, giving rise to the marshy and swampy areas that characterize the northern part of the Delta. The lakes cover a 380 km stretch of the northern coast of Egypt between Port Said in the east and Alexandria in the west.

Lake El-Manzala, the largest of these lakes, is located at the northeastern corner of the Delta, east of the Damietta Branch, attaining a length of 47 km and a width of 30 km. The depth of the lake varies from 0.7 m to 1.5 m. Several hundreds of islands are found in the lake, formed mostly of silt and sand. They are almost flat, having an altitude of 20 cm to one meter above sea level. Wild, dense vegetation marks the shores of the islands, but they are barren inside.

Lake El-Buruillus, which is next in importance, is oval in shape, located in the northern central part of the Delta near Rosetta Branch. The long axis of this lake extends in an east–west direction for 56 km, whereas its shorter axis, measured near its center, is 17.5 km. The lake tapers on both ends and has a 400 m wide opening to the sea. On both sides of this opening, a narrow stretch of land separates the sea from the lake, but in places it may reach a width of 5 km. The islands in this lake are few in number (about 70), in contrast to those in Lake El-Manzala.

Lake Edku is located directly west of Rosetta Branch, occupying a comparable position to Lake El-Manzala. Edku is also oval in shape, having a smaller area (20 km) and average width (9 km) than the other lakes. The northern shore of the lake is covered by sand dunes, while the southern shores are swampy. The lake has a number of smaller islands and a 250 m wide gap in its northwest part connecting it with the sea.

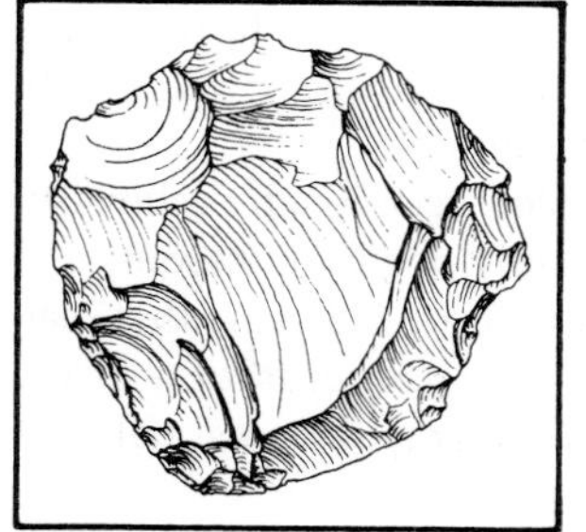

General Geology of the El-Kilh Area

BAHAY ISSAWI

The El-Kilh area lies on the west bank of the Nile about 15 km north of Idfu. The Nile Valley in this area is narrow—2 km wide—and limited to the west by a dissected flat pediplain surface that extends westward as far as the footslopes of the impressive limestone plateau. In places, especially near the valley, this surface is highly littered by conical and flat-topped hills and also by low ridges. These topographic features rise 10–40 m from the surrounding pediplain surface. On both sides of these ridges and hills run small, shallow, dry streamlets that very soon fade into the relatively flat area encircling these features. Practically none of these drainage lines reach the river; owing to the very rare precipitation, the channels of these streams are filled with drifted sand, sometimes rising to cover the slopes of the adjacent hummocks and ridges.

Variegated Shale

The oldest exposed rocks in the area belong to the Nubia Formation. The upper beds of this formation, known as the "Variegated Shale" member, make up the whole thickness of the isolated mesas and buttes as well as the lower part of the massive Gebel Ayat, 10 km north of Kilh. To the south of Kilh, the lower member of the Nubia Formation outcrops. Thus opposite Idfu, dark, ferrugineous sandstone beds are exposed, covering parts of the desert surface west of the cultivation and also forming many higher ridges and hummocks.

The variegated shales are mainly gray-green in color, occasionally yellowish-brown or attaining darker colors. The shales are sandy, highly gypseous, and saliferous. The gypsum occurs in the form of white clots or filaments that may lie parallel or oblique to the shale's bedding planes. The concentration of the white salts may be so high in places that it obscures the gray or green color of the shales.

Intercalated within the shale sequence are friable pale yellow to white sandstone beds that may pinch in the shale section when followed horizontally. The variegated shale has a thickness of 80 m in the Kilh area, best exposed at Gebel Ayat and the hummocks east of Kilh. The beds are poorly fossiliferous, yet Nakkady (1950) was able to collect some vertebrate remains from similar beds on the east bank of the Nile. The age assigned to these remains is Lower Maestrichtian.

The Duwi Formation

The Duwi Phosphate Formation overlies, with seeming conformity, the Variegated Shale member. The formation is best exposed at Sibaiya and the area north of El-Kilh. The Duwi is generally made of three phosphate beds (average thickness: 70 cm) interbedded with marl, shale, chert, and limestone. The section is usually capped by a hard oyster limestone bed, 2 m thick, while the average thickness of the whole unit is 10 m. The beds are fossiliferous with *Ostrea Villei*, *O. rili*, etc., and the fossil assembalge assigns a Lower Maestrichtian age to the formation.

The Dakhla Formation

The Dakhla Formation conformably overlies the Duwi Formation, and the shale beds of the Dakhla stretch to cover the pediplain surface between the Nile and the western Limestone Plateau. Along this stretch, 40 km, the beds of the Dakhla Shale are covered by variable thicknesses of Quaternary gravel and silt deposits.

The Dakhla is made of gray-to-green shales, soft, compact in places, highly gypseous, and saliferous. The gypsum and salts are found filling cracks and fissures either diagonal or parallel to the bedding planes, or may be present between the shale folios. The salts are variable, mainly sodium nitrites or nitrates; rarely chlorides and less commonly K-salts are found. The veinlets of salts and gypsum attain a few millimeters in thickness and sometimes are found as pockets and irregular concentrations among the shale beds. The natives usually dig in both the beds of Dakhla and Variegated Shale to extract these salts and use them as local fertilizer. The presence of salts in the beds of Variegated, Dakhla, and Esna (not represented in the Kilh area) Shale and their mode of occurrence, filling cracks and fissures, may indicate a secondary origin for such salts.

The Dakhla Formation assumes a residual thickness, in the Kilh area, of 60 m at Gebel Kom Meir. The beds are highly fossiliferous, including both macro- and microassemblages of micro- and macrofossils, which allocate a Lower Maestrichtian–Paleocene age to this formation (Said 1962; El-Nagger 1966).

Quaternary Deposits

These deposits cover the low-lying ground in the hummocky area near the Nile as well as the surface of the western pediplain. Thick Nile silt deposits fill what is supposed to be old Nile branches in the area north and south of Kom Meir. Drilling for phosphate in this area by the Geological Survey of Egypt has revealed a 70 m section of fluviatile sands and siltstone north of Sibaiya covering the Duwi Formation. The silt in the area of El-Kilh is highly saliferous, probably owing to the washing of salts from both the Dakhla and Variegated shales and their redeposition in the nearby area within the Nile silt. Gravel benches are common west of Kilh covering the surface of the pediplain. The gravels are mainly Lower Eocene limestone; they increase in size as the western scarp is approached.

Structures

Structurally the area is gently inclined to the northwest, with an average angle of 2°. Gentle warping of the beds by compression movements is clear in the area, since several flat, wide folds are observed in the area of Gebel Ayat and farther southeast of Kilh.

Faults are of minor importance, but probably are obscured by the thick Quaternary deposits.

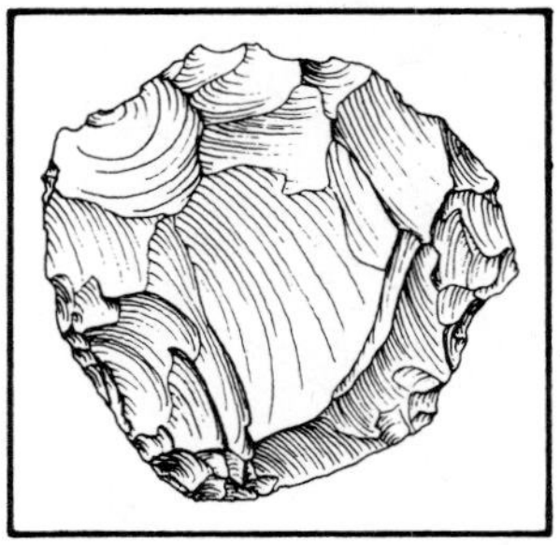

Quaternary Stratigraphy and Archaeology of the El-Kilh Area

Introduction

Six sites were recorded in this area (Figure 5). Four of them are situated on the slopes of rounded shaly hillocks that protrude out of the otherwise flat floor of the valley. These Dakhla Formation hillocks are covered by patches of gravels, and their footslopes are partially mantled by remnants of highly saliferous silts—much of which has been quarried by local farmers for salt. The areas between the hillocks as well as the slopes are packed with small pits that were dug during these quarrying activities. These pits give the landscape the appearance of a battlefield and, unfortunately, also destroyed most of the occupation areas at two sites and damaged two others. The two undisturbed sites in this area are both at somewhat lower elevations. One is on the surface of an eroded silt, while the other is partially *in situ* in the top of a recessional sand bar.

The El-Kilh Sites

Site E71P1

This site occupies a flattish surface 110 m long by 56 m wide on the southeast footslope of a small conical hill, the largest of a series of four such hills scattered along this section of the valley. The center of the site is 87.77 m above sea level and about 5 m above the modern Nile floodplain in this area (between

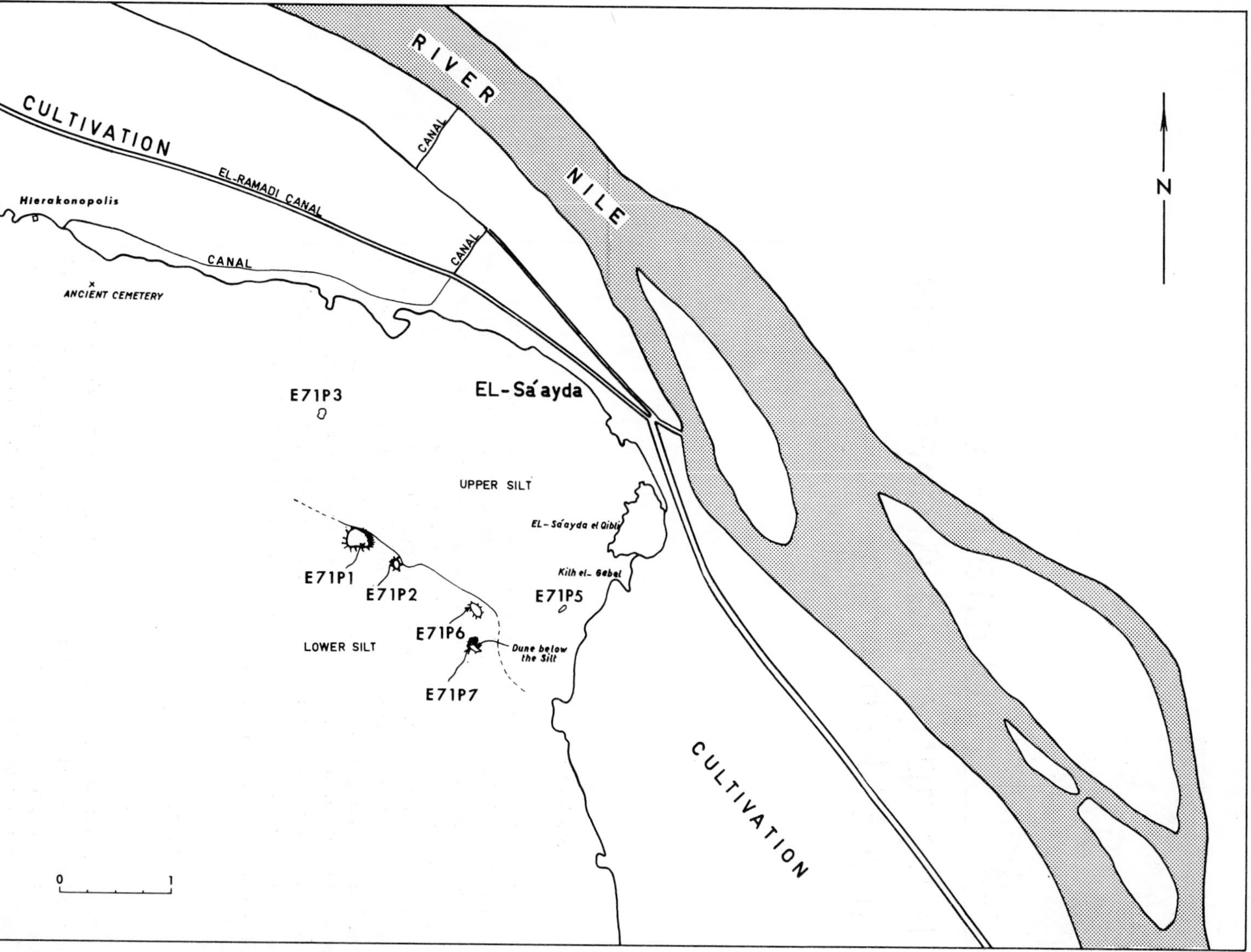

Figure 5. Map of El-Kilh area showing location of sites E71P1–E71P7.

Figure 6. View of Site E71P1, looking north. Note litter of artifacts in Area A behind figures.

82 m and 83 m above sea level). The surface of the entire site was evenly covered by numerous stone artifacts without evident clusters or concentrations (Figure 6). The fresh appearance of many of these artifacts indicated that they had recently been exposed by wind erosion.

The site was arbitrarily divided into four areas, three of which (A, B, and C) were squares 16 m on a side; the fourth (D) was an irregularly shaped disturbed section along the south margin of the site (Figure 7).

Several concentrations of *Unio* shells were noted within the site area, and the vicinity of four of these *Unio* clusters was selected for test excavation. Trench 1 was 14 m long; Trench 2, 12 m long; Trench 5, 6 m long; and Trench 6, 4 m long. All of them were 2 m wide. These trenches disclosed the presence of artifacts *in situ* within a very loose, friable, sandy silt unit and in an underlying soft, slightly consolidated silt (Figure 8). The distinction between these two layers of silt is regarded as a secondary phenomenon possibly due to leaching of the chlorides or weathering of the upper silt. The cultural horizon ranges from 30 cm to 50 cm in thickness, being thicker at the southern end of the footslope. The trenches did not disclose any traces of cultural stratification. Artifacts tended to be concentrated in a layer from 20 cm to 30 cm below the surface, and decreased rapidly at the bottom of the slightly consolidated silt.

Trenches 1 and 2 in Area A yielded the following fauna: *Bos primigenius*, *Alcelaphus buselaphus* (hartebeest), *Hippopotamus amphibius*, *Felis libyca*, *Gazella rufifrons* (red-fronted gazelle), *Nesokia indica* (rodent), *Unio abyssinicus*,

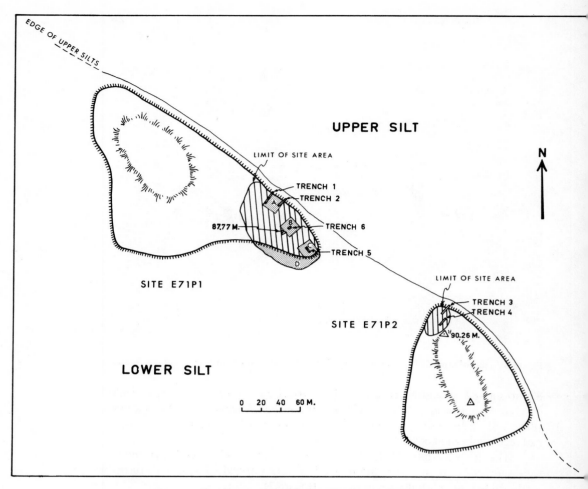

Figure 7. Sketch map of area at Sites E71P1 and E71P2.

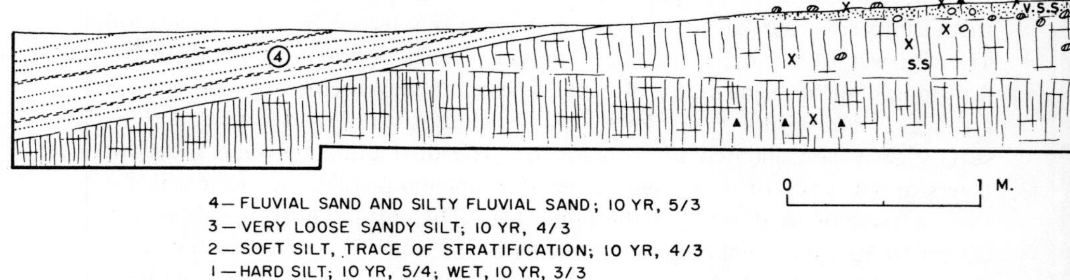

Figure 8. Profile of Trench 1, Site E71P1, Area A.

1. Yellowish-brown (10YR 5/4), slightly sandy silt; unstratified; consolidated; medium angular blocky structure. Rare cultural material found in a thin horizon 20–30 cm from the top. Base unexposed.

2. Dark brown (10YR 4/3), medium-sandy silt; weak traces of horizontal stratification; unconsolidated; passes into (1) and (3). Stone artifacts, fish and animal bones, *Unio* shells, burned and unburned stones found within top 20–30 cm. Basal part sterile.

3. Dark brown (10YR 4/3), medium-sandy powdered silt; unstratified; very loose,

Cleopatra bulimoides, and numerous remains of Nile catfish of the family *Clariidae*. Other than fish, the most common remains were hartebeest and *Bos.*

Trench 6 at Area B yielded few faunal remains other than fish, most of which were *Clarias* sp.; *Barbus* sp. and *Labeo* sp. were also found. Mammals were represented by *Bos* and hartebeest.

Trench 5 in Area C was the most productive in faunal remains. The most numerous mammal was hartebeest, followed by *Bos* and a few examples of *Gazella* and *Hippo*. Most of the fish were Nile catfish, *Clarias* sp., represented by at least 50 individuals estimated to range from 14 cm to 100 cm in length. Two examples of *Barbus* sp. were also noted. *Unio* were the only shellfish noted.

Below the two soft silts there was a third unit of very hard, consolidated silt of unknown thickness. In Trench 1 of Area A this consolidated silt yielded a thin (approximately 10 cm thick), very poor cultural layer some 60 cm below the upper cultural horizon and 30 cm below the contact between the hard silt and the overlying softer unit. This lower culture layer yielded only a few flakes and several *Unio* shells.

Along the eastern margin of the site, the artifact-bearing silts were truncated by a series of sediments consisting of very fine fluvial sand and silty fluvial sand with silt lenses. No artifacts were found in this unit.

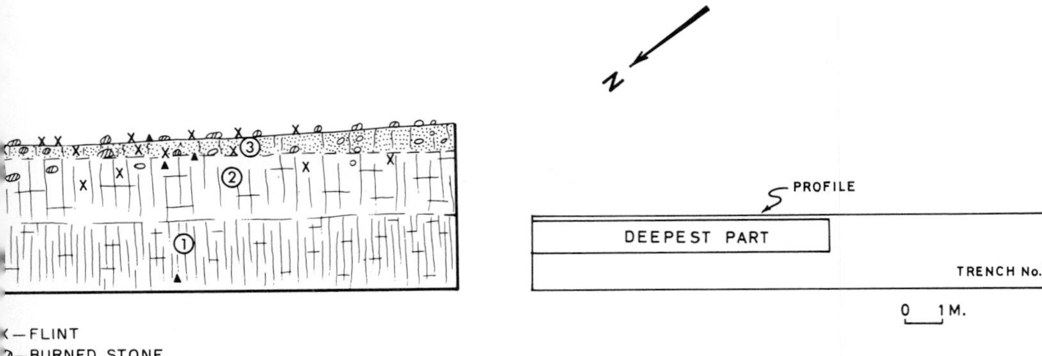

clear, single-grain structure. Stone artifacts, fish and animal bones, *Unio* shells, burned and unburned stones occur throughout this layer. Surface littered with cultural remains showing clear traces of eolian sheen. A sample of *Unio* shell gave a radiocarbon date of 15,650 BC ±300 (I-3419).

4. Brown (10YR 5/3), fine and medium-grained fluvial sand rich in mica and heavy minerals with thin (up to 1 cm) layers of sandy, unconsolidated silt; continuously stratified with bedding dipping 20% to 30% toward the river; loose, single-grain structure of sand. This unit clearly truncates underlying sandy silt units. Entirely sterile.

Five radiocarbon dates have been obtained from this site, all on *Unio* shell and all from the upper cultural horizon:

Trench 1, Area A	15,650 BC ±300 (I-3419)
Trench 2, Area A	15,000 BC ±300 (I-3248)
Trench 6, Area B	15,500 BC ±300 (I-3418)
Trench 6, Area B	15,300 BC ±300 (I-3249)
Trench 5, Area C	15,850 BC ±330 (I-3417)

Site E71P2

A second conical hillock, slightly smaller than the one at site E71P1, is located approximately 150 m to the southeast. The north side of this shaly knoll has a gently sloping surface mantled with silt. This silt had been extensively destroyed by the mining activities of the natives in search of salt, and the surface had also been recently deflated by wind action. A dense concentration of occupation debris, some 25 m by 30 m in area, occurred at the northern tip of this knoll, partly imbedded in the upper part of the silt (Figure 9).

Two trenches were excavated in the eastern portion of the concentration. Trench 3 was 10.5 m long and 2 m wide, while Trench 4 was 8 m long and 2 m wide. Two small test pits were also dug, and these as well as the native quarry trenches provided additional information on the stratigraphy of the site. The *in situ* cultural remains occurred in a firmly cemented, salt-encrusted silt 10–15 cm in thickness that overlay a soft silt with a maximum thickness of 25 cm. The soft silt, in turn, was underlaid by a silt that was firmly cemented by calcium carbonate (Figure 10). The stratigraphic context of the occupation debris at

Figure 9. View of Site E71P2, looking southeast. Note disturbance from excavation by local villagers quarrying for salt.

Site E71P2 is closely similar to that noted for the upper occupation level at Site E71P1, the only difference being the absence of a salt crust at Site E71P1.

The older units were also truncated by a series of fluvial sand and silty fluvial sediments similar to those at Site E71P1. The position and altitude of the truncated portion of the older units in the trenches at the two sites suggests the extent and direction of the contact between the lower silts and the overlying fluvial sands and silts. This contact could also be observed on the ground surface for a distance of approximately 1.5 km.

The trenches from this site yielded only a few faunal remains. These included *Bos* (most numerous), followed by hartebeest, gazelle, hippopotamus, and a few *Clarias* sp. Nile catfish. The relative paucity of catfish remains distinguishes this site from E71P1.

Site E71P6

A third small knoll is located some 750 m southeast from Site E71P2 (Figure 5). The northward tip of this knoll had a small, dense concentration of artifacts and burned stone covering an area 20 m by 10 m and eroding from a very loose sandy silt. The center of the concentration was 89.30 m above sea level, or about 6.3 m above the modern floodplain.

A single trench, 2 m by 2 m, was cut from the north edge of the concentration toward the center. This trench revealed artifacts and a few *Unio* shells *in situ* within the very loose, sandy silt, about 10 cm thick, under this a soft silt some 30 cm thick, deepening toward the Nile. The soft silt rested directly on bedrock shale of the Dakhla Formation.

Only five identifiable bones were recovered. These were *Bos primigenius* and *Alcelaphus buselaphus* (hartebeest).

Site E71P7

Some 250 m south of Site E71P6 is a fourth site located on another small hillock (Figure 11). Three distinct occupation areas were observed on the north edge of the hillock (Figure 12). Locality A is the westernmost. It is roughly circular in outline and 12 m in diameter. The southern edge (the highest point) is 87.95 m above sea level. Locality B is located about 14 m to the east and is oval in outline, 18 by 14 m. The third and smallest concentration, Locality C, is located immediately adjacent to the south, and is a rough oval 10 m by 6 m. Locality C may originally have been somewhat larger. The southern and eastern edge of this concentration was bounded by an extensively disturbed salt-quarrying area, and a number of artifacts were recovered from the quarry spoil dumps. Locality A had also been partially disturbed by quarrying. All of the surface concentrations, however, were accidental and do not reflect the original clustering of artifacts. All of the concentrations were within a slopewash and had been moved downslope an unknown distance.

Four trenches were cut into the site, two in Locality A and one each in the others (Figure 13). Trench 1 at Locality A (2 m by 2 m) was placed at the

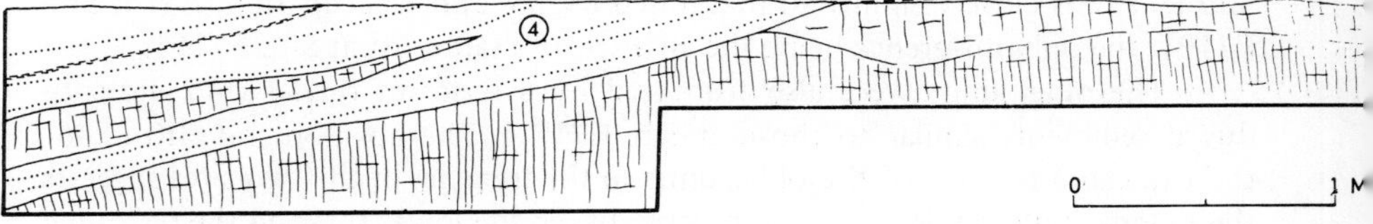

4—FLUVIAL SAND AND SILTY FLUVIAL SAND
3—VERY LOOSE SANDY SILT CONSOLIDATED BY SALT CRUST DESTROYED, CULTURAL LAYER

Figure 10. Profile of Trench 3, Site E71P2.

1. Yellowish-brown (10YR 5/4), slightly sandy silt; unstratified; consolidated; medium angular blocky structure. Sterile.

2. Dark brown (10YR 4/3), medium-sandy silt; unstratified; unconsolidated; passes into (1). Single, partially exposed stone artifact just at the top of this unit.

3. Removed by salt-quarrying activities but observed in patches beyond the trench, a unit of dark brown silt cemented by salt crust, containing cultural layer with stone artifacts, fish and animal bones, and rare *Unio* shell.

4. Brown (10YR 5/3), fine and medium-grained fluvial sand rich in mica and heavy minerals; continuously stratified with bedding, dipping almost evenly 20%–30% toward the river; loose, single-grain structure. Lenses and thin layers of sandy, unconsolidated silt occur throughout this sterile unit, clearly truncating the underlying older sediments.

southern edge of the surface concentration. Two units were revealed. The upper unit was a coarse sand slopewash with gravels and pebbles in a powdery matrix. Traces of stratification roughly following the slope were observed. Weathered artifacts were recovered from this unit. Below the slopewash was a brownish, weakly cemented, medium-grained sand, possibly of aeolean origin. In the top of it to a depth of 20 cm was a cultural layer containing artifacts and large angular stones.

Downslope, 7.2 m from the north corner of Trench 1, another trench was excavated in the area previously highly damaged by salt quarrying. This trench, 3 m by 1 m, is designated Trench 4. It was placed between quarry pits in one of the few undisturbed areas. The upper unit here was a thin veneer of soft silt. It overlay the brownish, presumably aeolian sand seen in Trench 2. Here the sand contained cultural material in the upper 30 cm and became lighter in color with depth. A few fish bones of the families *Clariidae* and *Bargidae* were recovered from the cultural layer in this trench.

In Locality B, Trench 2, which covered an area 2 m by 1.5 m, was dug in the center of the surface concentration. This trench revealed a similar stratigraphy to that noted in Trench 1. The only difference was a pseudo-cultural layer (concentration of weathered artifacts) within the more or less horizontally stratified slopewash. Fresh artifacts were recovered within the top 25 cm of the underlying

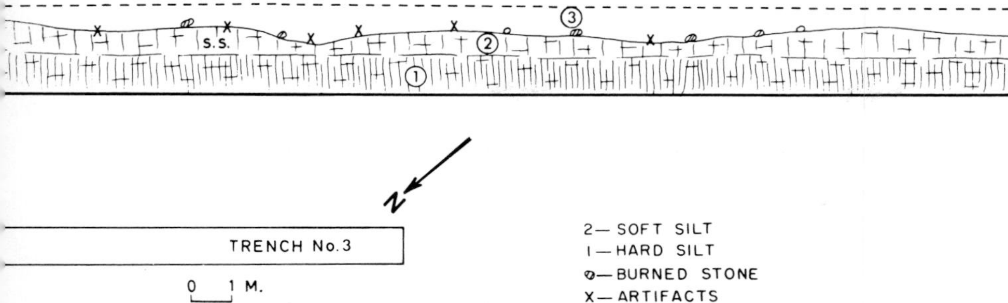

sand. Associated with these artifacts were a few bones from *Bos primigenius, Hippopotamus amphibius,* an unidentified bird, and a few fish of the family *Clariidae.*

Trench 3, a small pit 1 m by 1 m, was placed in the center of surface concentration C. It reveals the same stratigraphic sequence as that in Trenches 1 and 2; however, only a few artifacts were recovered from the occupation horizon at the top of the presumed dune sand unit.

The situation revealed in the trenches suggests an extensive occupation area extending a distance of approximately 60 m along the northern edge of the hillock. Much of the site, particularly on the upper slopes of the hill, has been destroyed by slopewash. The excavations were not sufficiently extensive to determine the possible limits of the site up- and downslope, nor the internal clustering of the occupational remains.

Site E71P3

Slightly west of north from Site E71P2, and approximately 1 km distant, is an eroded embankment of indurated silt standing about 1 m above an extensive area of fluvial sands stratified with silts. On the surface of this silt remnant occured scattered artifacts, burned mammal bones, and other cultural debris over an irregular oval area approximately 25 m by 50 m. A few patches of burned silt were observed within the site area. Most of the artifacts were weathered, but a few were fresh and appeared to have been exposed only recently.

The entire site area was collected. None of the burned bone fragments were identifiable.

Site E71P5

The youngest site studied in the El-Kilh area is located about 800 m northeast of Site E71P7. This chronologically most recent site, identifed as E71P5, is situated at the edge of an extensive area of silt and fluvial sand. The silts, recording an episode of Nile aggradation earlier than occupation of the site, were eroded during a period of lower Nile levels, and a channel was cut more than 3 m deep. The floor of the channel is filled with fluvial sand. There was a small

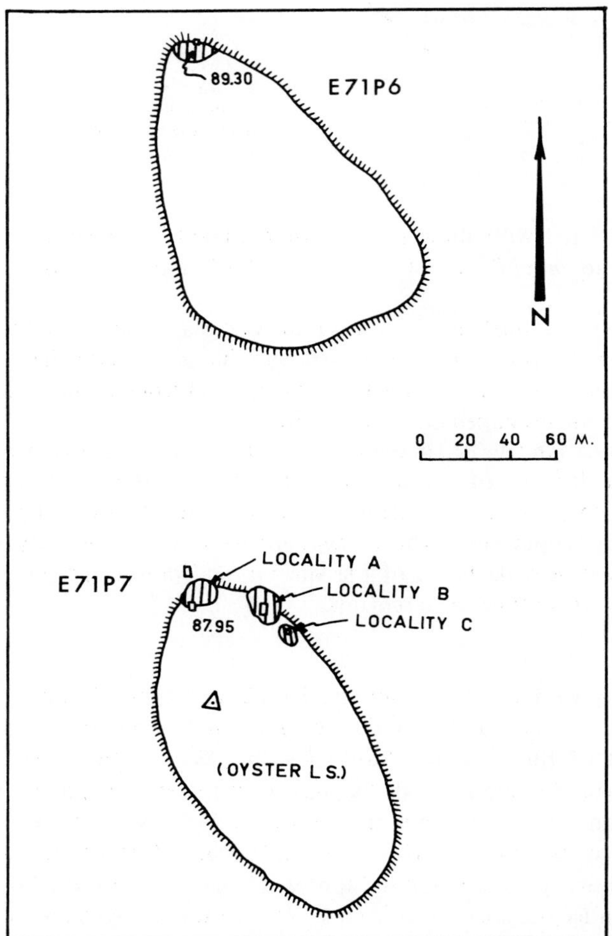

Figure 11. Schematic map showing location of Sites E71P6 and E71P7.

Figure 12. View of Site E71P7, looking southeast. Occupation concentration begins behind figures and to right.

occupation on the silt bank overlooking the edge of the channel and another, possibly contemporaneous, occupation below the bank on the fluvial sand floor of the eroded depression. Subsequent wind erosion removed about 1 m of the fluvial sand that had filled the channel, except in the area protected by the numerous cultural debris, leaving the occupied area standing as a low oval mound some 50 m long and 15 m wide (Figure 14).

The oval mound on the floor of the eroded depression is designated as Area A. The concentration on the adjacent silt bank is identified as Area B. Numerous *Unio* shells and artifacts were littering the surface of the mound at Area A. Some of these were fresh and had been exposed only recently. At Locality B the artifacts were thinly scattered and intensively weathered, and there was no evidence of *in situ* material. Surface collections were made at both localities, and three 10 m by 1.5 m trenches were excavated in the western part of the fluvial sand mound at Area A. The trenches yielded numerous fresh cultural remains, but they were limited to the upper few centimeters. The artifacts occurred in the top of the fluvial sand, and some were covered by small patches of silt. Besides the very numerous *Unio*, the associated fauna were limited to a few bones from *Bos primigenius*, a single bone from a hartebeest, and several bones of Nile catfish (*Clariidae*), the latter from individuals reconstructed to be from 40 cm to 65 cm in length.

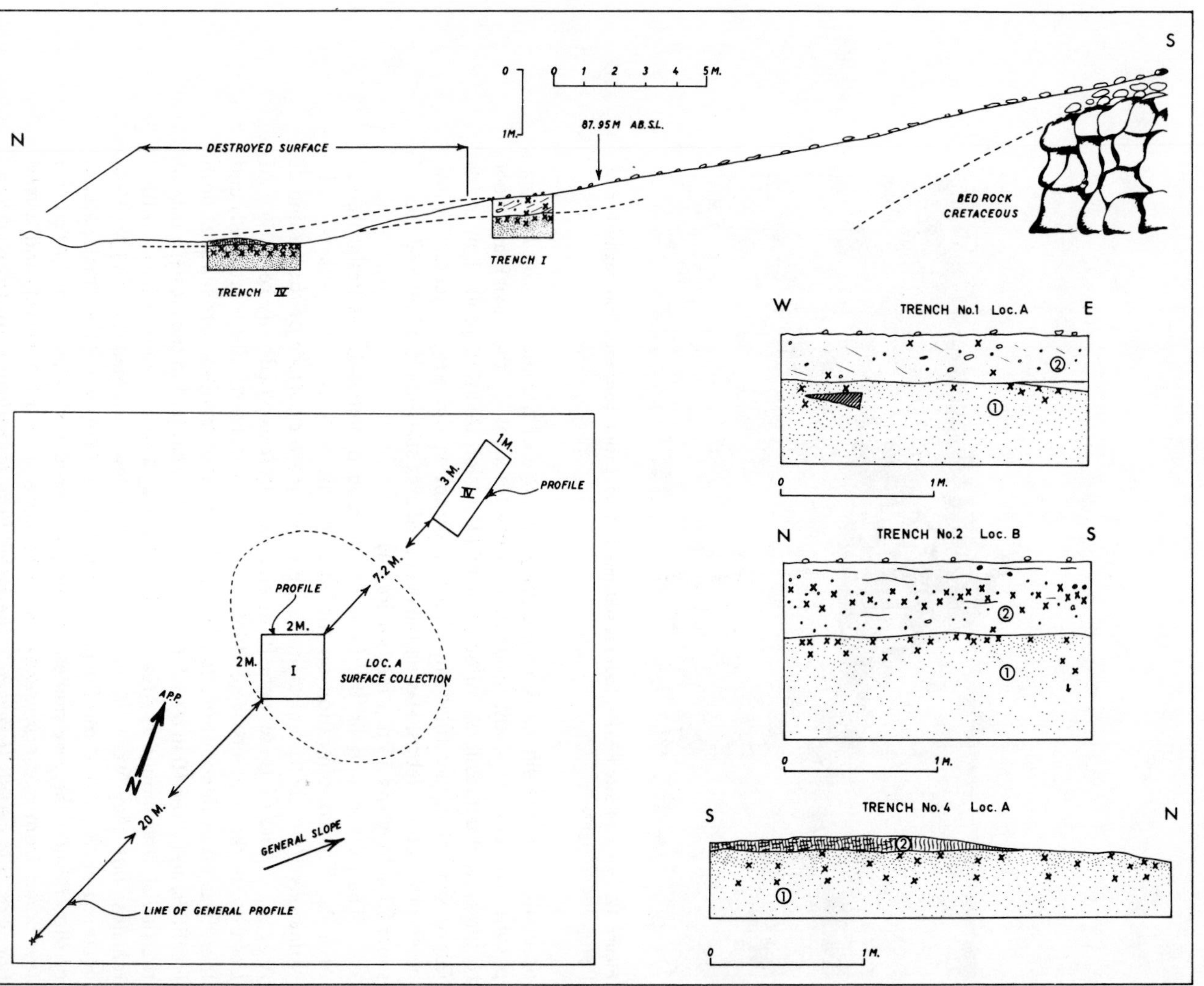

N
S
0
1M.
0 1 2 3 4 5M.
DESTROYED SURFACE
87.95M AB.S.L.
BED ROCK
CRETACEOUS
TRENCH I
TRENCH IV
W
TRENCH No.1 Loc. A
E
②
①
0
1M.
3M.
1M.
IV
PROFILE
7.2M.
PROFILE
2M.
2M.
I
LOC. A
SURFACE COLLECTION
APP.
N
20M.
GENERAL SLOPE
LINE OF GENERAL PROFILE
N
TRENCH No.2 Loc. B
S
②
①
0
1M.
S
TRENCH No. 4 Loc. A
N
②
①
0
1M.

Figure 13. Plan and profiles of trenches at Site E71P7.

Area A, Trench 1

1. Yellowish-gray, medium and coarse-grained, slightly consolidated sand; unstratified with chipped stone artifacts and unworked stones in upper 20 cm. Separated from overlying sediment by clear unconformity.

2. Pale brown, unsorted, fine to coarse-grained sand with numerous pebbles, cobbles, and slabs mostly of local derivation. Pebbles and gravels are usually subangular to angular with slightly rounded edges. Weak traces of foreset stratification with short, noncontinuous strata dipping *ca.* 30% down the slope. Loose to unconsolidated. Dispersed more or less rolled artifacts throughout the layer. Surface littered with subangular stones and rolled and eolised stone artifacts.

Area A, Trench 2

1. Yellowish-gray, medium to coarse-grained sand, unconsolidated to slightly consolidated near the top; unstratified; calcareous. Contains numerous stone artifacts in top 10–15 cm together with some animal and fish bones. Single artifacts occur down to 20 cm below the surface of this unit. Separated from overlying sediment by sharp unconformity.

2. Pale brown, unsorted, fine to coarse-grained sand with numerous pebbles subrounded to angular; loose to unconsolidated; weak traces of horizontal but essentially foreset stratification. Visibly worn artifacts concentrated in a 15–20 cm thick horizon in the middle of this unit. Less numerous but also worn artifacts dispersed below and above this horizon. Surface littered with worn artifacts and pebbles.

Trench 4

1. Yellowish-gray, medium to coarse-grained, and slightly consolidated to consolidated or almost cemented in top 20 cm; unstratified; contains numerous stone artifacts and rare fish bones in upper 20 cm.

2. Brown silt unconformably overlying Unit 1. Medium angular blocky structure; unstratified; consolidated to cemented by salt crust in places; sterile. Original surface destroyed by salt-quarrying activities.

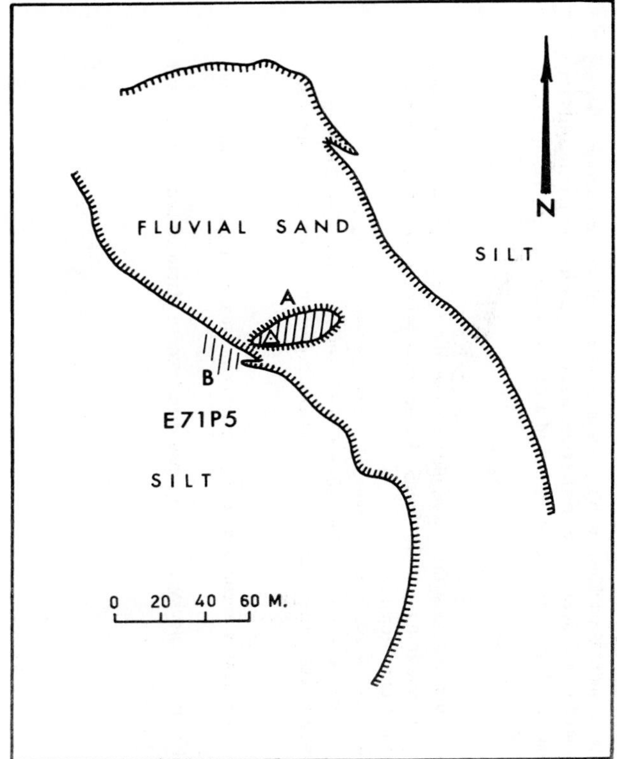

Figure 14. Schematic map of Site E71P5 and vicinity.

A sample of *Unio* shell from this site, associated with the occupation, dated 9610 BC ±80 years (I-3760).

Discussion of the Stratigraphy at El-Kilh

The excavations in this area disclose two distinct units of silt and fluviatile sand. The oldest silts are preserved at Sites E71P1, E71P2, E71P6, and E71P7, where they reach maximum elevations slightly below 90 m above sea level, or about 7 m above the modern floodplain. The similarities in lithology as well as elevation strongly indicate that all of these silts represent the same dynamic event. The end date for this episode of siltation is indicated by the series of radiocarbon dates between 15,000 and 15,850 BC at Site E71P1.

At Site E71P7 the older silt overlies a sand unit, regarded as aeolian, that may represent a period of dune formation that elsewhere (in the Isna area, to be discussed later) is clearly contemporary with the maximum of an aggradational phase of silt. Our trenches at the El-Kilh locality, however, were too restricted to determine if this aeolean unit also interfingered with the maximum of silt aggradation; however, this relationship is highly likely. Such an interpretation would correlate the aeolean sediment here with the dune member of the older silt at Isna. If this assumption is correct, then Sites E71P1, E71P2, E71P6, and E71P7 are all of the same general age.

Pronounced truncation of the older silts was observed in the trenches at Sites E71P1 and E71P2 and could also be seen on the surface for a distance of at least 1.5 km (Figures 6 and 7). This truncation is followed by the deposition of a broad, thick unit of channel sediments consisting mainly of fine-grained sand with lenses of silt. Toward the river these fluvial sands are replaced by more consolidated silts, presumably of the same age. This arrangement would suggest the presence of a channel adjacent to the older silt face and shallow water with less velocity to the east (toward the present river) of this deep channel.

The strongest points of evidence for the age of these younger Nile sediments are their stratigraphic position and the presence of a Sebilian site at their eroded top. These would indicate a correlation with the Late Sahaba Formation in Nubia (de Heinzelin, in Wendorf 1968), roughly dated between 10,000 and 12,000 BC (Wendorf *et al.*, 1970).

This correlation, in turn, would suggest that the following lowering of the Nile is represented by the fluvial sands at Site E71P5. If this assignment is correct, then the date of 9610 BC for the site suggests that the post-Sahaba recession began began slightly before 9600 BC.

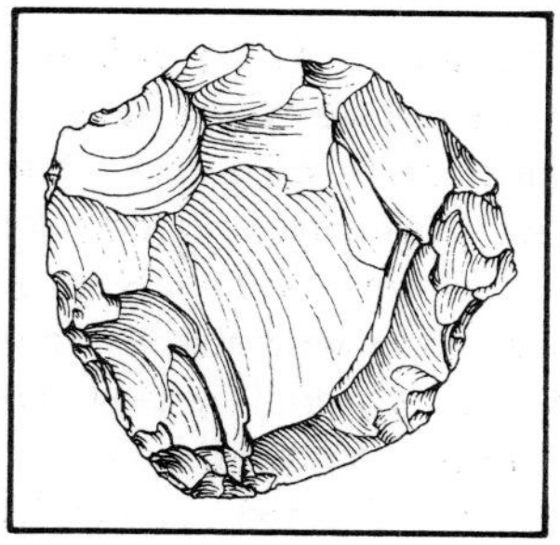

Geology of the Isna Area (West of the Nile)

BAHAY ISSAWI

The main part of Isna Town lies on the west side of the Nile 50 km south of Luxor. The floodplain of the river has its maximum stretch on the west side, while on the east an immense limestone plateau seems to cling to the river, leaving a thin strip of land.

The floodplain west of the Nile is limited by a pediplain surface that rises gradually westward toward a precipitous limestone plateau—El-Homra El-Shamkha. El-Homra is a promontory of the main Limestone Plateau, which overlooks the Nile from the west. The plateau surface of El-Homra attains the highest altitudes in the Egyptian Western Desert—606 m above sea level, excluding Gebel Uweinat and the Gilf el-Kebir Plateau in the extreme southwest corner of Egypt. The surface is dissected by a few deeply cut furrows marking north–south joints. Of interest is the steam rising from these fissures and, hence, the flourishing algae that cover the top of the jointed limestone.

The plateau surface is also marked by the several benches or steps that soon fade in the surrounding surface. Low conical hummocks formed of hard, persistent limestone weathered to a dark gray litter the surface of El-Homra.

The scarp face limiting El-Homra to the east runs in a very irregular manner, forming several embayments and promontories. The embayments are the sites of the wadis that drain the plateau surface. Because of the very rare precipitation, the wadis are nearly blocked by huge tabular or cubical limestone boulders. The gradients of the wadis are rather steep and irregular.

The pediplain surface stretches eastward for a distance of 12 km before it merges into the floodplain. The relief of the pediplain surface is low, ranging from 100 m near the floodplain to 300 m at the footslope of El-Homra. The pediplain surface is a monotonous rolled, undulating surface highly covered with limestone gravels. The gravel bed may assume a considerable thickness—8 m before the bedrock is reached. There are many parallel ridges separated by very shallow wadis, 2–3 m deep. The channels of the wadis are covered by sand and gravels, which may rise to cover the slopes of these ridges. Practically none of these wadis reach the Nile, and the pattern of drainage is ill-defined. The wadis may wander over the flat surface before fanning out in a low area of the pediplain surface.

Stratigraphy

The oldest exposed unit in the area is the Phosphate Formation noticed a few kilometers south of Isna near the cultivation edge. Phosphate beds, intercalated in a sequence of marl, shale, and oyster limestone strata, are the rock units of this formation. The sequence is partly exposed but mostly covered by either Nile silt or younger formations. The thickness of the phosphate in the south Isna area never exceeds 4 m, but farther south, at Sibaiya, it may reach 10 m.

The Dakhla Shale overlies the Phosphate Formation with seeming conformity. In contrast to the east bank of the Nile, where the Dakhla is well developed (120 m thick), only the residual thickness of the Dakhla is exposed on the western side. The Dakhla ranges in thickness from a few meters to 40 m in some of the isolated hills west of Sibaiya. Recent drilling for phosphate on the pediplain surface has revealed a much thicker (80 m) section of this formation. The Dakhla Shale is mainly grayish in color, varying to greenish and yellowish brown. Salt and gypsum pockets and filaments are common, while pyrite nodules are of minor importance.

The beds are highly fossiliferous, and El-Naggar (1966), after a detailed study on the macro- and microfossil assemblages collected from the east bank of the Nile, allocates both the phosphate and the lower Dakhla beds to the Maestrichtian age. The upper Dakhla beds belong to the Paleocene (Said and Sabry 1964; El-Naggar 1966).

The Tarwan Chalk that overlies the Dakhla Shale on the east bank of the Nile is lacking on the west. It is not exposed in El-Homra, since the base of this scarp is made of the overlying Esna Shale. Most probably it is covered by Quaternary deposits at the pediplain surface and disappears below the surface at El-Homra.

The lower part (60 m in thickness) of the impressive El-Homra Promontory is Esna Shale. The lower part of the Esna is still hidden below the surface at the southern end of El-Homra. Farther south along the western scarp, the overlying

Thebes Formation comes into contact with the Esna Shale, indicating a northwest–southeast fault that bounds the promontory to the west.

The Esna Shale is light gray, iron stained, with marl intercalations, generally thinly laminated, paper-like, and occasionally compact and massive. The age of this unit is Paleocene at the base, Lower Eocene at the top (Said and Sabry 1964; El-Naggar 1966).

The Thebes Formation comprises the upper part of El-Homra Promontory and the surface of the plateau. The thickness of this unit varies from 100 m to more than 250 m at El-Homra. The Thebes is formed of thick- to thin-bedded limestone, soft to hard, including flint bands, crystalline in places, occasionally siliceous and dolomitized. Marl bands are common, while thin shale intercalations increase at the base. The Thebes belongs to the Lower Eocene (Said 1960).

The Quaternary deposits are varied and complex. They comprise the tufa and travertine rocks that partly cover the slopes of El-Homra, the gravel sheets over the pediplain surface, the Nile silts, and the deflated sand near the cultivation edge.

Structures

The area is gently inclined (2–3°) to the northwest. This is well observed in the phosphate outcrops near the Nile and also at El-Homra. El-Naggar (1966) mapped some small, shallow folds near Sibaiya trending northwest–southeast. Recently El-Hinnawi and El-Deftar (1970) have recorded several folds running northeast–southwest at El-Homra and the adjacent areas. These authors also noticed a number of faults that dissect the scarp face of El-Homra and the western plateau. The faults trend generally in a north–southeast direction. A major fault having the same trend was also observed by Issawi west of El-Homra Promontory; this fault extends for a distance of 20 km. The throw of this fault is to the west *ca.* 70 m. The continuation of these faults on the eastern pediplain surface is not certain, since the thick Quaternary cover hinders the tracing of structural features.

Quaternary Geology and Archaeology of the Isna Area

Introduction

In 1967, about 9 km northwest of Isna, the Ministry of Agrarian Land Reform was in the process of developing an extensive land reclamation project under contract to Bonifica, an Italian company (Figure 15). Large areas were being leveled, canals were being dug, roads were being constructed, and several new villages were being completed. The new reclaimed area was occupied by Nubians displaced by rising waters behind the New High Dam at Aswan. Within the leveled and irrigated areas, several large sections were left more or less undisturbed. These were mostly fossil dune fields not suitable for cultivation. Although most of these areas were still intact when visited in 1967, a few had been partially destroyed by construction activities and others were threatened with destruction in the near future as the dunes were quarried for sand (Figure 16). These dune fields and sandy areas contained numerous prehistoric settlements, some of which were destroyed immediately after our investigations.

The newly reclaimed area lies parallel to the Nile along the west bank, from 3 km to 5 km from the river (Figure 17). The floodplain here is about 80 m above sea level, and the new reclaimed lands are from 5 m to 10 m higher. West of the reclamation project the landscape rises rapidly to the gravel-strewn foothills that front the Eocene limestone escarpment.

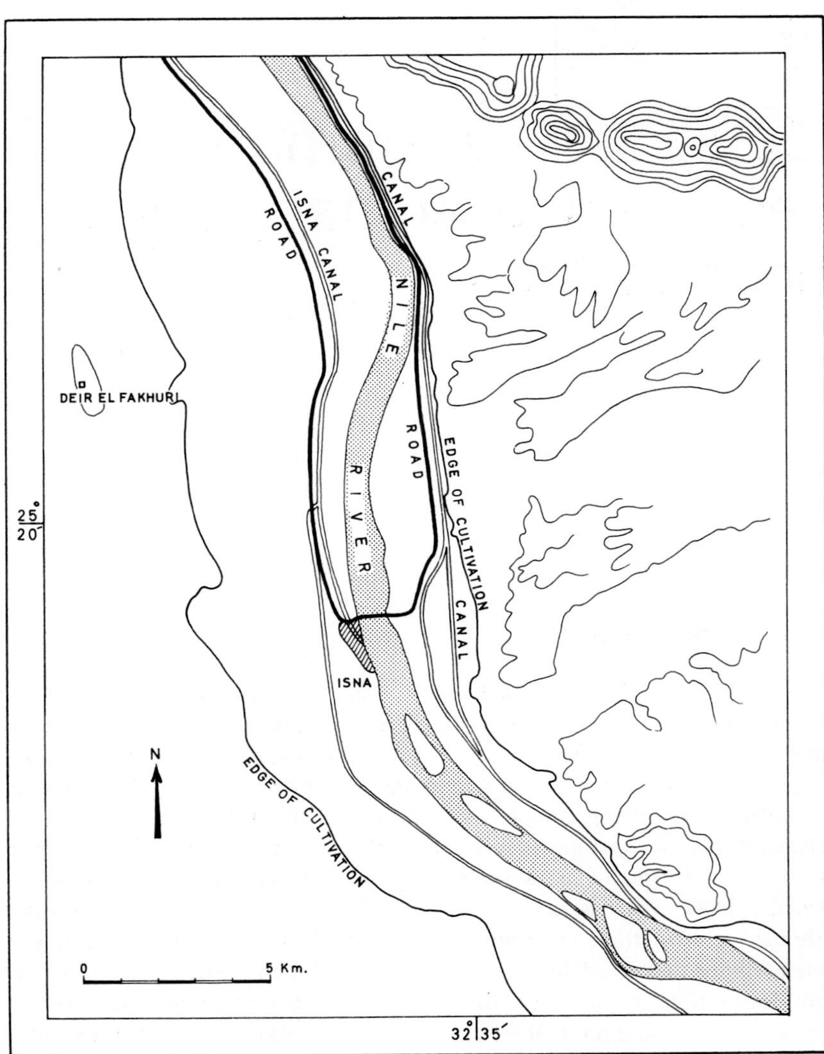

Figure 15. Map of Isna area showing location of Isna and Deir El-Fakhuri Monastery.

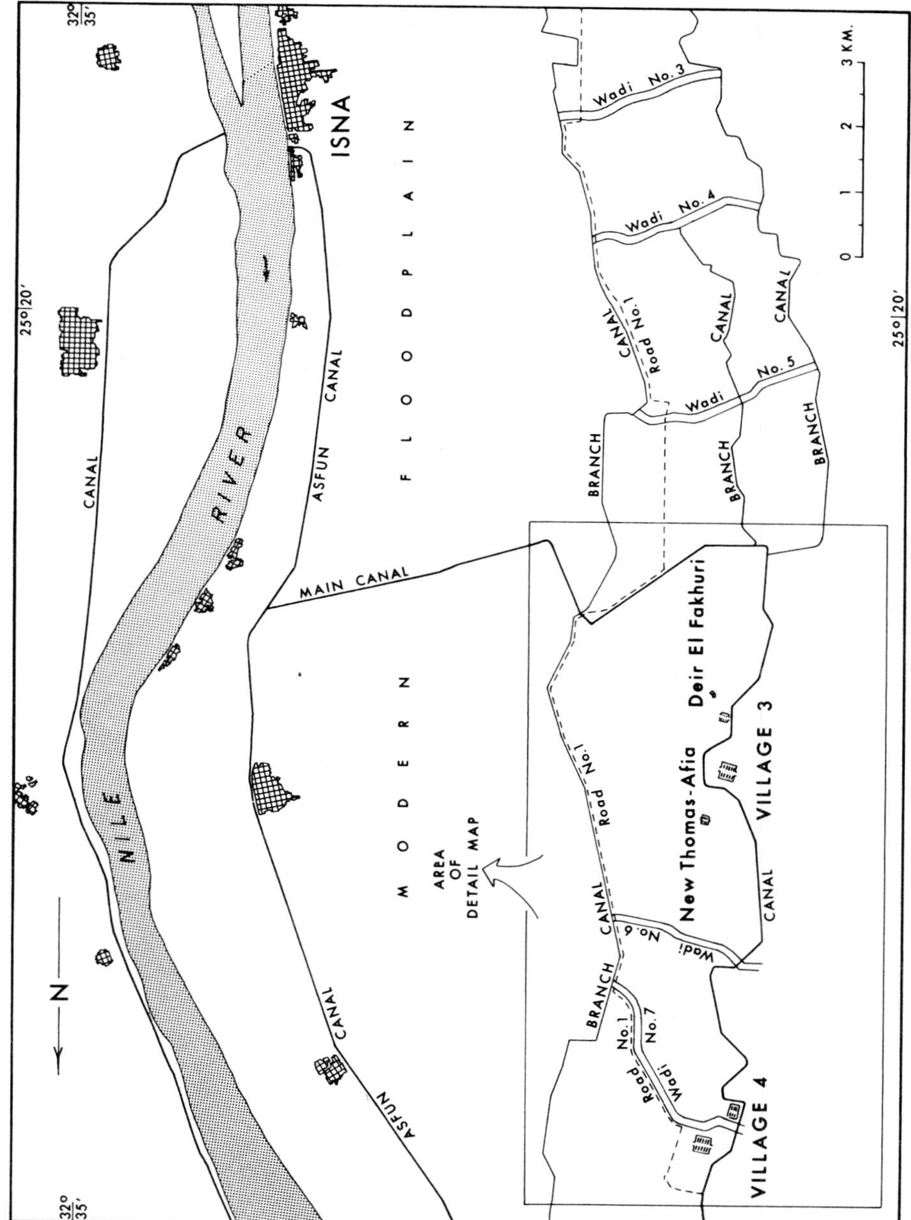

Figure 16. Map of recently developed irrigation area near Deir El-Fakhuri Monastery.

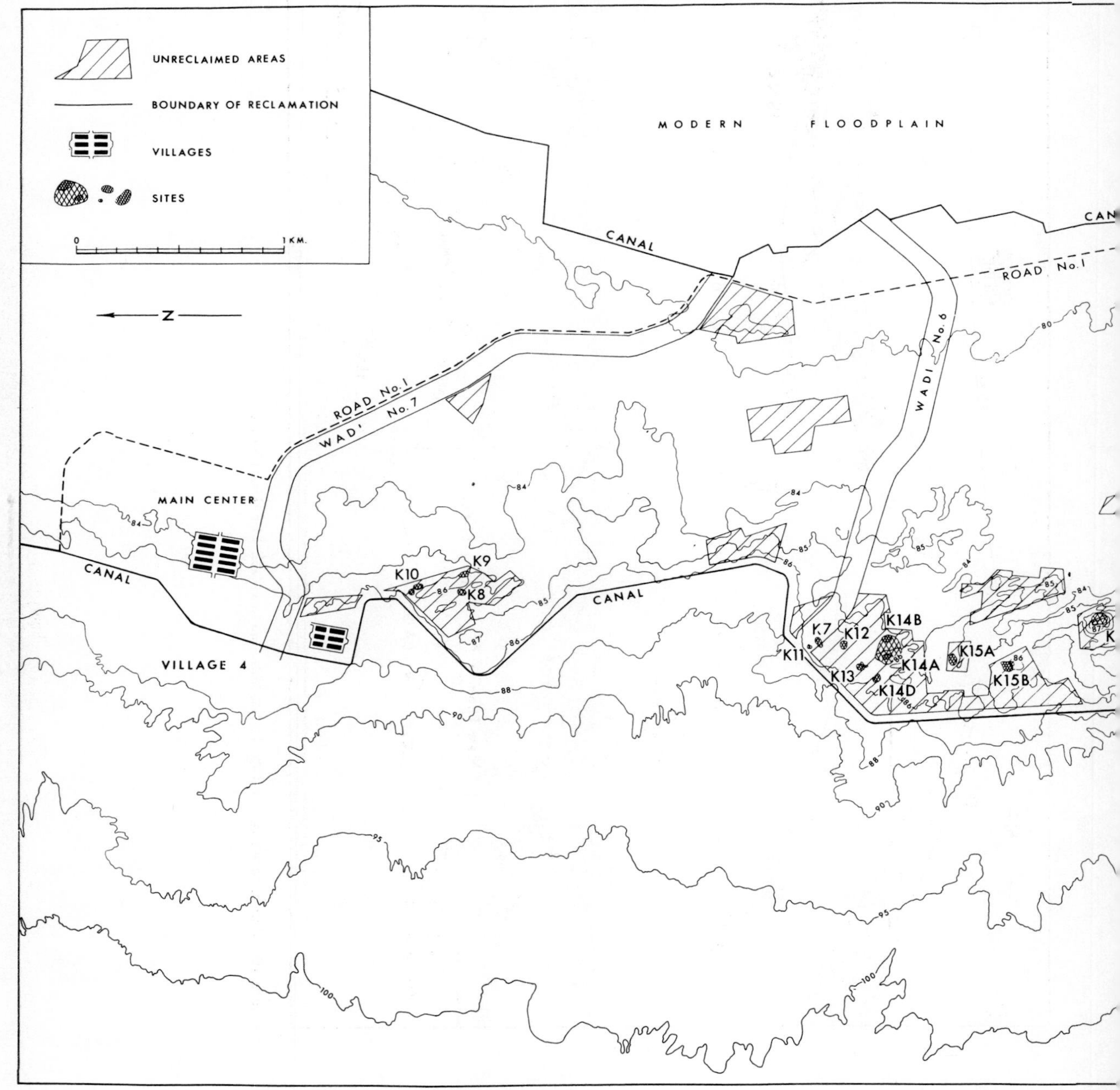

Figure 17. Detail map of recently developed irrigated area at Deir El-Fakhuri showing locations of sites investigated.

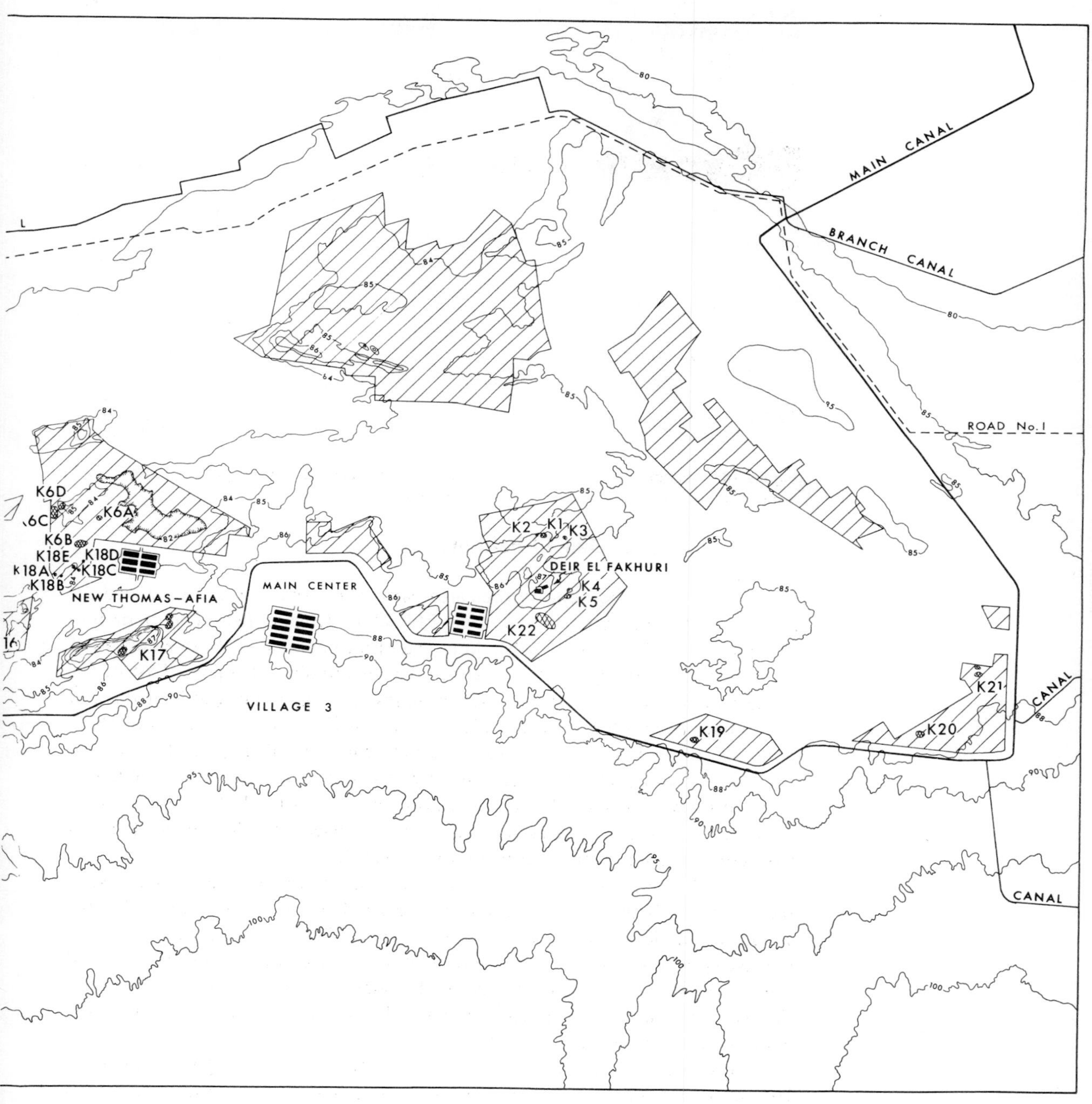
MAIN CANAL
BRANCH CANAL
ROAD No. 1
K6D
K6A
K6B
K18E
K18D
K18C
K18B
NEW THOMAS-AFIA
K17
MAIN CENTER
VILLAGE 3
K2
K1
K3
DEIR EL FAKHURI
K4
K5
K22
K19
K20
K21
CANAL
CANAL

Figure 18. Abandoned monastery at Deir El-Fakhuri near Isna, looking north. Site E71K5 is located in the deflated area of center foreground.

Sites at Deir El-Fakhuri

One of the largest undisturbed areas within the Isna project surrounded the abandoned Coptic monastery of Deir El-Fakhuri (Figure 18). The monastery occupies a prominent rise, a fossil dune, the surface of which is at an elevation of 87 m above sea level, about 2 m above the surrounding silt plain. East of the monastery is a series of small conical mounds, also fossil dunes, at least three of which have been intensively occupied in the past (E71K1, E71K2, and E71K3). South of the monastery is a large sand field with several flat, slightly elevated rises, one of which also was occupied (E71K4). Next to it, on a flat and highly deflated surface, was another concentration of artifacts (E71K5). About 100 m to the west of the monastery is a large, flat area covered by silts on which a very large concentration of artifacts was noted (E71K22).

Just beyond and about 2 m below the tops of the occupied dunes east of the monastery is an extensive flat area where a dark brown silt was exposed at the surface at an elevation of 85 m above sea level. The large silt area west of the monastery is of a different color, grayish, more calcareous, and between 1 m and 2 m higher than the brown silt east of the dunes. Large patches of the grayish silt also occur around the south and east sides of the monastery and mantle the underlying aeolean sands.

The sites in the sandy areas are all relatively small (ranging from about 200 m^2 to 1000 m^2 and roughly oval in outline, and belong to the same general cultural tradition. The surface materials at these five smaller sites were totally collected (Figure 19). The larger locality is on a deflated silt surface, covering

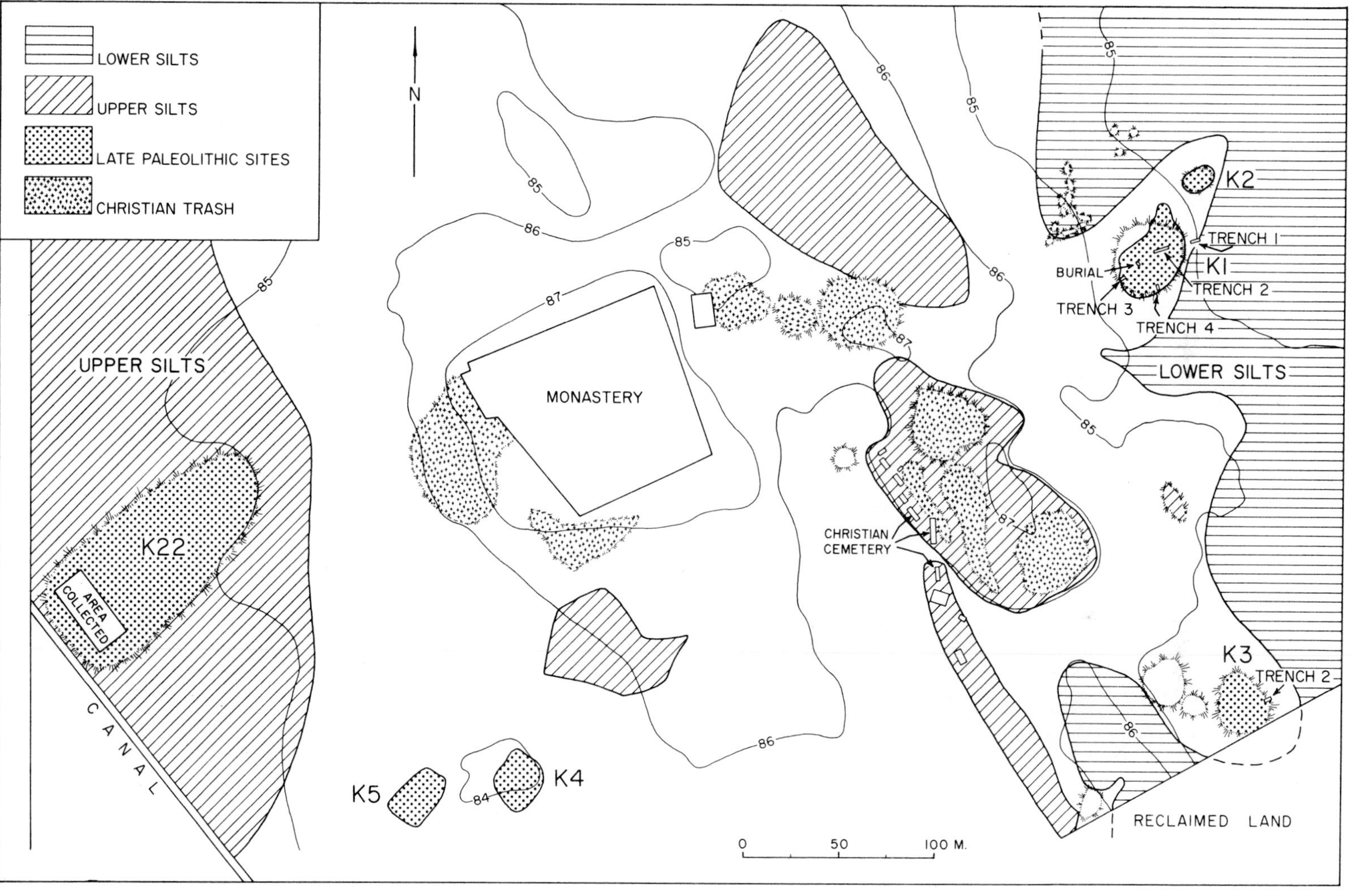

Figure 19. Map of immediate vicinity of Deir El-Fakhuri Monastery showing location of Sites E71K1, E71K2, E71K3, E71K4, E71K5, and E71K22. Hatched areas are remnants of upper silt. Shaded areas show limits of artifact concentration and indicate trash dumps of Christian age.

Figure 20. South face of Trench 1, Site E71K1 showing interfingering of dune and silt. Massive silt at base of trench. Compare with profile in Figure 21.

about 7000 m^2, and representing an entirely different industry. It was only partially collected by taking a complete sample from a rectangular area 18 m by 40 m, where the artifacts were most densely concentrated.

At Site E71K1, four trenches were excavated; two trenches were dug at E71K3, and two pits were dug at E71K22. These trenches, together with observations at several exposures in the vicinity, permit us to reconstruct the general stratigraphy of the Deir El-Fakhuri area.

The lower sediment is a firmly cemented, cracked, dark brown, calcareous silt that interfingers with the overlying dune sand (Figure 20). The interfingering silts on the backs of the dunes are represented by layers up to 20 cm thick, truncated at the top by deflation during subsequent movement of the dune. The fronts of the dunes show numerous thin (1–2 cm thick) strings of silt draped over the sand, representing maxima of Nile floods that covered the dune fronts while the dunes were slowly migrating eastward. Scarce vegetation grew on the dune shore during this period of deposition. Carbonate casts of the plant roots occur in the upper edge of the dune face where the face is preserved. In front of the dunes, after they became stabilized, the silt was built up and the dense border zone admixed with the still slightly agrading silt. These silts now occupy an extensive area immediately east of the dune remnants.

This dynamic sequence of events shows that the dune accumulation is clearly contemporaneous with the maximum accumulation of this lower silt and that the stabilization of the dunes coincides with a gradual reduction of the flood (Figure 21).

The cultural debris at Site E71K3 was partially worked down into the reworked sand–silt sediments at the dune border zone during the closing phase of this aggradation. The occupation horizon at Site E71K1 was also partially covered by a few thin patches of silt that lay over the top of the dune. The age of these silt patches is unknown. They may be remnants of a final phase of the older silt or of a later aggradational event. Two radiocarbon dates were obtained on *Unio* shell from these sites. The sample from E71K1 dated 16,070 BC ±300 years (I-3416), and that from E71K3 dated 15,640 BC ±300 years (I-3415).

The occupations at Sites E71K1–E71K3 appear to have been situated at the forward edge of a dune field that abutted the floodplain, while Sites E71K4 and E71K5 seem to have been located in the middle of this extensive dune field and back some distance from the edge of the floodplain (Figure 22). It seems unlikely that these last two sites were occupied when the edge of the dune field was at this position, for subsequent erosion as the dunes moved forward would have exposed them to pronounced wind scour, of which there is no evidence on the artifacts. A different site situation is suggested. Furthermore, there are some cultural differences evident between these two localities and those at the dune front.

To the west of the monastery, where the large, flat surface of grayish silt is exposed, two small test pits disclosed a diatomaceous pond sediment under the grayish silt and overlying a wedge of dune sand that pinches out to the west. Below the wedge of dune sand where this was present, and directly below the diatomite elsewhere, was a brownish lower silt unit. This situation suggests that the dune field was an island or peninsula partially surrounded by the floodplain during the final phase of the lower silt aggradation.

The upper grayish silt in this area contains a thin burned layer near the top. At Site E71K22 only a few artifacts were fresh, and none were found in the sediment. The cultural debris occurred on top of the eroded surface of the grayish silt and above the burned layer. The burned layer is therefore older than the occupation of this site.

Site E71K1 yielded numerous mammal remains, most of them found on the freshly deflated surface of the knoll. The most numerous was hartebeest (*Alcelaphus buselaphus*), represented by 100 bones. This was followed by *Bos primigenius. Gazella rufifrons, Nesokia indica,* and *Lepus capensis.* Six individuals of *Clarias* sp. ranging in length from 20 cm to 110 cm, one *Barbus* sp., and another specimen tentatively identified as of the family *Cichlidae* were found. A few *Unio* shells were also present.

Site E71K3 yielded fewer mammal remains, but hartebeest still predominated (45 bones), followed by *Lepus capensis, Bos primigenius, Gazella rufifrons, Nesokia indica,* hippopotamus, *Felis libyca* (?), and an unidentified

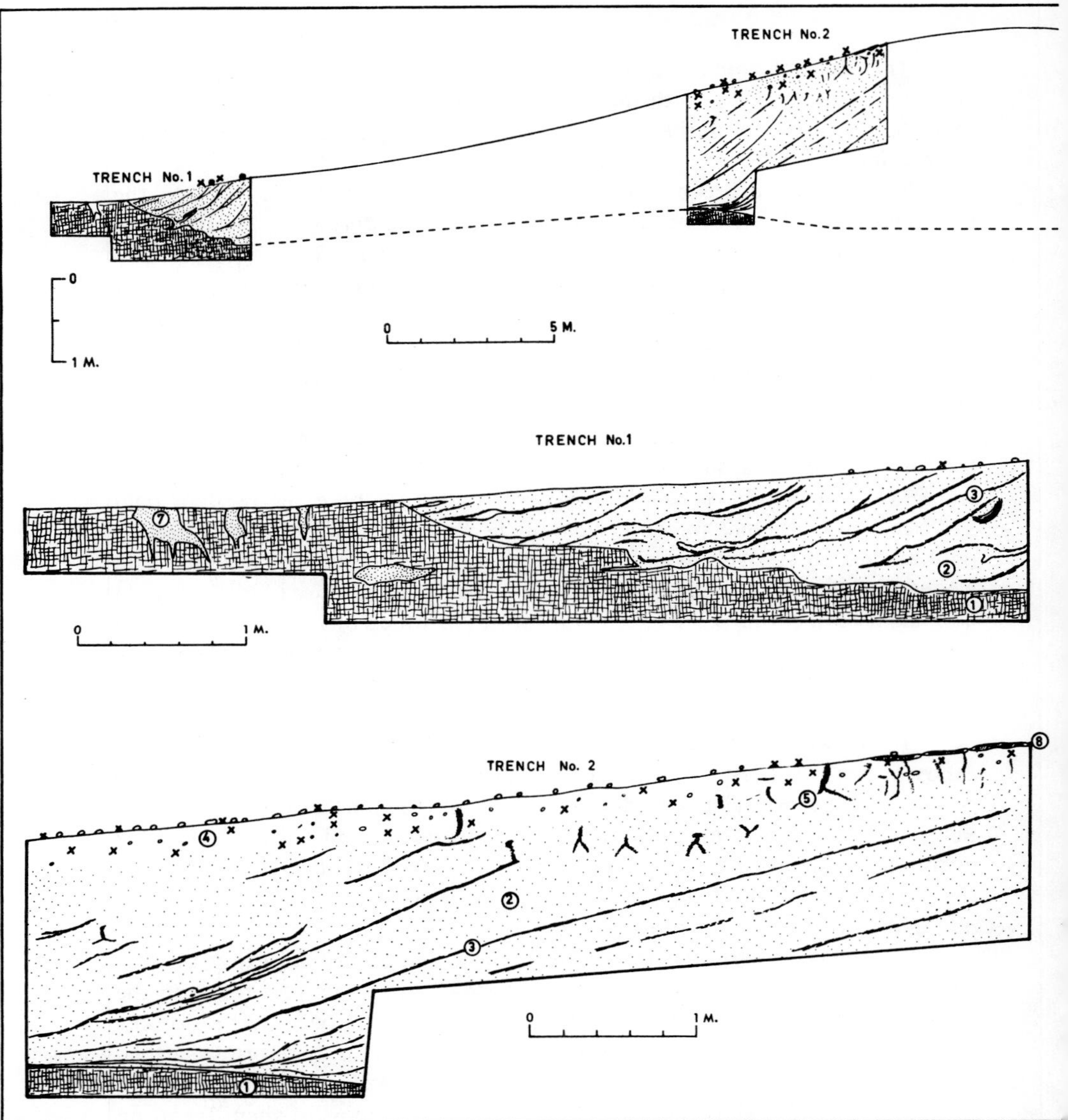

Figure 21. Plan and profiles of Trenches 1–4 at Site E71K1.

1. Brown (10YR 4/3), slightly sandy, clayey silt with medium angular blocky structure. Rare slickensides; unstratified, rare lenses of medium to coarse-grained dune sand; consolidated to cemented; highly calcareous; sterile.

2. Yellowish, medium and coarse-grained, loose calcareous dune sand. Clear stratification with foreset dipping of *ca.* 20%–40% to east. Rare oxidation stains concentrated mainly near the top. Very numerous, network-forming, root drip casts near the top down to *ca.* 50–60 cm from the dune surface. Human occupation remains in form of very numerous chipped stone artifacts; animal and fish bones litter the deflated dune surface and are also dispersed within the top 20 cm of this unit.

3. Brown (10YR 4/3), thin streaks and thicker layers of sandy silt within the dune; continuous and very thin (0.5–2.0 cm) in frontal part of the dune; generally much thicker

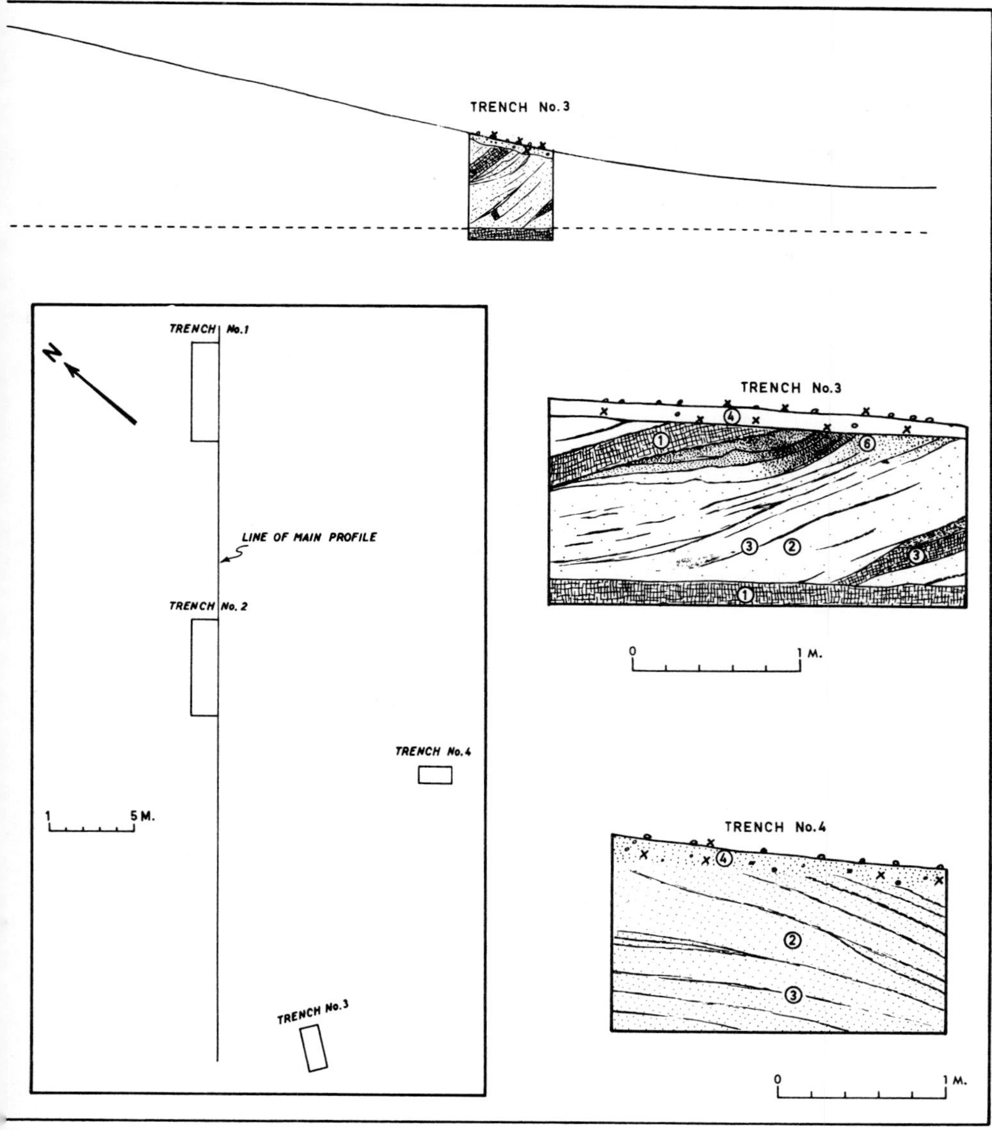

(to *ca.* 20 cm) and truncated in the back. No traces of stratification within the silt layers; unconsolidated to cemented in the back side of the dune; highly calcareous; archaeologically sterile, showing medium, angular blocky structure when thick.

4. Occupation horizon within the dune. A sample of *Unio* shell from this horizon gave a radiocarbon date of 16,070 BC ±330 (I-3416).

5. Root drip casts.

6. Brownish, coarse sand and silt with truncated silt streaks; cemented; calcareous; sterile.

7. Dehydration cracks filled with coarse sand.

8. Very thin patches of brownish-gray, sandy silt covering in places the surface of the dune and the occupation horizon.

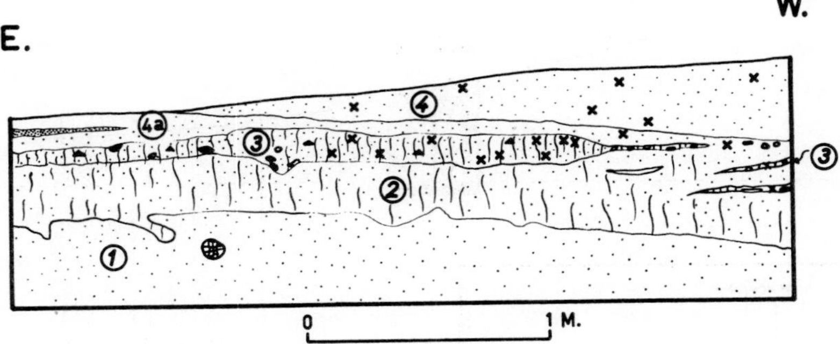

Figure 22. Profile of south face of Trench 2 at Site E71K3.

1. Yellowish, medium and coarse-grained dune sand; loose; calcareous with fossil rodent holes observed. Sterile.

2. Brown (10YR 5/3), silty sand with lenses of reworked cultural layer and dune sand; very weak traces of stratifaction with a foreset dip; consolidated to cemented; calcareous. Interfingers with underlying dune in places.

3. Brown (10YR 4/3), very sandy silt or silty sand; unstratified; consolidated to cemented; highly calcareous with fishbone breccia in places, stone artifacts and *Unio* shells. A sample of these gave a radiocarbon date of 15,640 BC ±300 (I-3415).

4. Light, yellowish-brown (10YR 6/4) dune sand with light silt admixture; loose to unconsolidated; calcareous, with slightly reworked cultural material.

4a. Same as (4) but slightly lighter in color with lenses of clear dune sand.

bird. Fish remains included 108 individuals of *Clarias* sp., two individuals of *Heterobranchus* sp., two individuals of *Barbus* sp., and one from the family *Cichlidae*, probably *Tilapia* sp. Burned *Unio* shells also occurred.

Site E71K4 yielded only a hartebeest and *Bos*, while E71K22 yielded only two examples of *Bos*.

There are obvious differences in the frequencies and distributions of the faunal remains at these sites. It would be extremely hazardous, however, to postulate different economic specialization at these localities on this basis. The apparent emphasis on mammal remains at E71K1 may be due to the differential preservation of surface and subsurface remains. Most of the fishbones and some of the mammal materials at E71K3 were recovered from the buried cultural layer in Trench 2, where fish clearly predominated. For this reason it seems safe to conclude only that these communities enjoyed a mixed economy based on both fishing and hunting.

A human burial was found near the top of the west slope of the dune knoll of Site E71K1 (Figure 23). The top of the skull, several teeth, and a few long bone fragments were eroding from the surface of the dune when first noted. Excavation confirmed that most of the burial had been exposed and removed by deflation. The remaining skeletal fragments, including a calvaria and a badly worn mandible, were cemented with calcium carbonate and had carbonate-replaced rootlets affixed to the bone.

Figure 23. Burials at Site E71K1.

A reconstruction of the sequence of events related to the burial suggests that when the pit for the burial was first excavated several large carbonate root casts were broken and the body was placed over these broken remnants. These root casts presumably date to an earlier period of vegetation when the dune was immediately adjacent to the river. The dune continued in its eastward migration and eventually covered the vegetation, which then was replaced by carbonates from the highly charged ground water. Such carbonate replacement presumably occurs rapidly under proper conditions. There are no indications to date the burial except with the occupation of the site, which the single radiocarbon date indicates occurred around 16,000 BC.

Sites in the Vicinity of Wadi No. 6

Northwest of Thomas Afia Village by about 1 kilometer is another large fossil sand dune area, irregular in outline, from 300 m to 500 m wide and 1200 m long. The dune area borders the western limit of the cultivated area and Branch Canal No. 2. A large wadi (No. 6) defines the northern limit of the dune area, while the eastern and southern edges abuts the leveled and cultivated area of silt (Figure 24). Several pronounced dune knolls stand about 2–3 m above the surrounding sandy plain and reach a maximum elevation of nearly 89 m above sea level. Each of these knolls has been occupied in the past, and in most areas the occupation debris was on the deflated dune surface. In a few places, however,

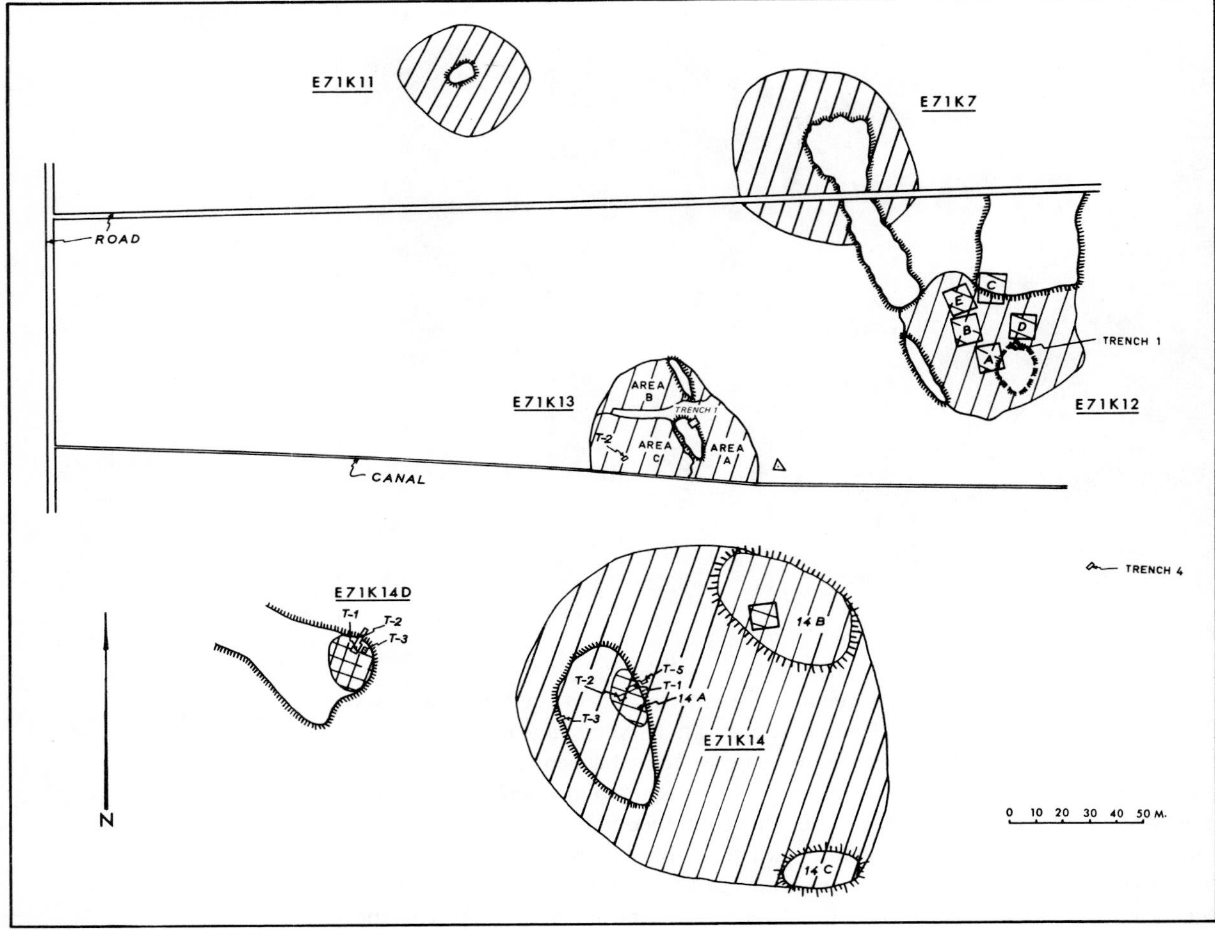

Figure 24. Map of sites in vicinity of Wadi No. 6. Hatched areas indicate extent of artifact concentrations.

patches of silt or other sediment preserved remnants of occupation floors, while two localities had extensive debris within an exposed fossil soil. Six sites were recorded from this area, and two of these had more than one locality. Collections were taken from four sites, all of which had some material *in situ*.

E71K12

The first of these sites is located near the north edge of the sand area, where there is a large, irregular oval (60 m by 65 m) and dense concentration. It is designated Site E71K12. The concentration was bounded on the north and

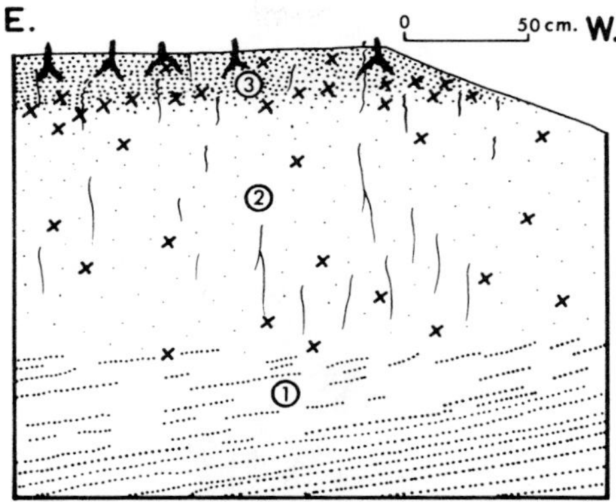

Figure 25. Profile of Trench 1, Site E71K12, Area D.

1. Yellowish, medium and coarse-grained dune sand; loose; calcareous; well stratified with foreset dipping of *ca.* 5–15°. Sand laminae continuous near the bottom of the trench, becoming broken and discontinuous at the contact with unstratified part of the dune and just below this contact. Single, chipped stone artifacts at the contact with unstratified, overlying part of the dune.

2. Yellowish, medium and coarse-grained dune sand; unstratified; consolidated to cemented by heavy concentration of calcium carbonate diminishing toward the stratified part of the dune. Numerous oxidation stains (limonite) in patches and elongated, irregularly vertical and/or semi-verticalstreaks seemingly repeating fossil root traces. Chipped stone artifacts and few animal bones almost evenly dispersed throughout this portion of the dune.

3. White, grayish, medium and coarse-grained dune sand; unstratified; cemented by heavy concentration of calcium carbonate. Near and on the surface a mat of root drip calcareous casts. Stone artifacts observed throughout the layer, with a line of a more dense occurrence at about 20 cm below the surface.

west sides by low remnants of cemented dune sand. A third remnant occupied the center of the concentration. The cemented aeolian sands in the remnants had a mat of calcareous root casts covering their surface and retarding deflation. A line of artifacts could be seen eroding from the edges of the remnants about 20 cm below the surface and below the calcareous root casts. Five collections were made from the deflated surface surrounding the remnants. Each collection was taken from an arbitrary area 10 m by 10 m, labeled A–E. A small pit, 2 m by 2 m, was excavated in the edge of the center remnant (Figure 25).

E71K13

Just 70 m west of Site E71K12 was another large, oval, very dense concentration about 60 m in diameter (Figure 26). The south side of this concentration, designated as Site E71K13, was bordered by a canal, and construction and leveling had entirely destroyed the site beyond the canal. The surface of the western third of the remaining site area had also been disturbed by bulldozer leveling. Two flat, slightly higher remnants stood in the center and at the edge of

Figure 26. View of sediments in Trench 1, Site E71K13. Note yellowish dune sand at top with vertical streaks and stains, presumably from vegetation. Artifacts occur in this unit and on surface.

the site, and as at E71K12, the top of the remnants was a firmly cemented dense sand with calcareous root casts. The entire site was divided into three arbitrary areas (A, B, and C), and two small trenches were dug. Trench 1 was placed in the center of the site and measured 1.5 m by 2 m (Figure 27); Trench 2 was 1 m by 3 m (Figure 28).

E71K14

Across the canal bordering Site E71K13 on the south, some 30 m distant, there was a larger scattered concentration, roughly circular and 140 m in diameter (E71K14). The site occupies a large, flat mound of sand standing from 1 m to 2 m above the surrounding plain. There were three denser subconcentrations within the site limits, labeled A, B, and C. Each subconcentration was on a low knoll that stood slightly above the rest of the dune mound. These knolls, however, do not reflect the original topography, but have persisted because the concentration of artifacts at two of them retarded wind deflation and a silt patch protected the third. The hillock covered by the silt patch was near the western edge of the site limits, and the subconcentration was near the eastern edge of the silt remnant.

A fourth concentration, Area D, assigned to this site was located approximately 50 m to the west on another, lower knoll marked with patches of silt and cemented pond sediments.

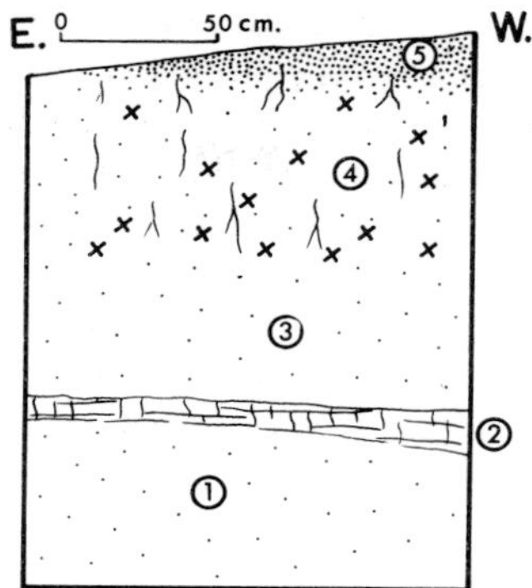

Figure 27. Profile of Trench 1, Site E71K13, Area A.

1. Yellowish, medium and coarse-grained dune sand; loose with single-grain structure; stratification not observed; sterile.

2. Brownish, silty sand; unconsolidated with limonite discoloration stains along the top and within the layer; weak, angular blocky structure; sterile.

3. As in (1).

4. Yellowish, medium and coarse-grained dune sand; unstratified; consolidated to cemented by heavy concentration of calcium carbonate diminishing toward (3); limonite discoloration stains observed throughout this unit in the form of small patches and/or elongated vertical and semivertical streaks. Extremely numerous chipped stone artifacts and less numerous animal remains dispersed with this layer down to unit (3).

5. Grayish, medium and coarse dune sand; unstratified; cemented by very heavy concentration of calcium carbonate. Abundant root drip casts and extremely numerous stone artifacts throughout the unit. Surface littered with lag artifacts, clearly deflated.

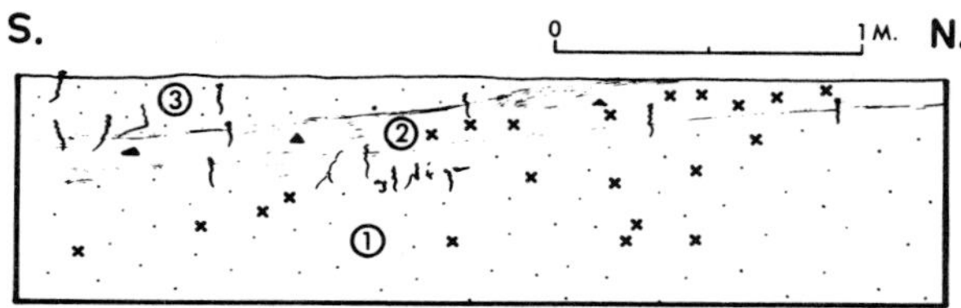

Figure 28. Profile of Trench 2, Site E71K13, Area C.

1. Yellowish, medium to coarse-grained dune sand; calcareous; loose, single-grain structure; a few limonitic discoloration stains, as observed before, dispersed within this unit. Stone artifacts within upper 40 cm evenly dispersed.

2. Dark gray, medium and coarse sand with powdered burned bone; loose, single-grain structure; unstratified; upper and lower limit not sharp. Numerous stone artifacts and burned bone fragments; a few root drip casts.

3. Light, yellowish, medium and coarse-grained dune sand; unstratified; loose, single-grain structure; possibly culturally sterile, seems to contain a few root casts. Surface exposed by bulldozer. It is possible that this unit was formed during the bulldozer leveling of the dune.

The surface concentration at Localities A and D were totally collected, while only a 10 m by 10 m square was collected at Locality B. No collection was taken at Locality C. A series of trenches were dug at Localities A and D, and beyond the site at the foot of the sand mound to the east (Figures 29–35).

E71K15

Some 300 m south of Site E71K14 is another circular sand mound about 40 m in diameter, 1.5 m higher than the adjacent area and completely surrounded by cultivated fields. The surface of this mound was littered with stone artifacts

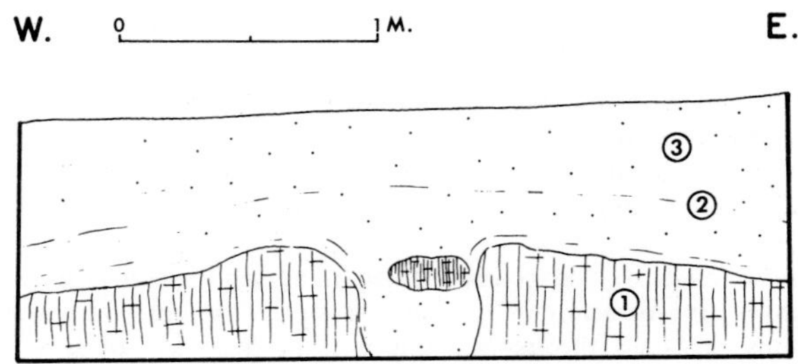

Figure 29. Profile of Trench 4, Site E71K14, Area A.

1. Brown (10YR 5/3), sandy silt; unconsolidated, slightly wet; unstratified with coarse, angular blocky structure; calcareous. Small channel cut in the middle of the section filled with reworked dune sand; thin (less than 0.5 cm), sandy silt layers and larger oval silt pebble.

2. Yellowish, medium and coarse-grained, reworked dune sand with thin streaks of sandy silt; loose, single-grain structure; weak traces of stratification; calcareous; slightly wet at the base.

3. Yellowish, medium and coarse-grained dune sand; weak traces of stratification; loose; extremely thin laminae of silty sand (up to 2 mm thick) in places; calcareous.

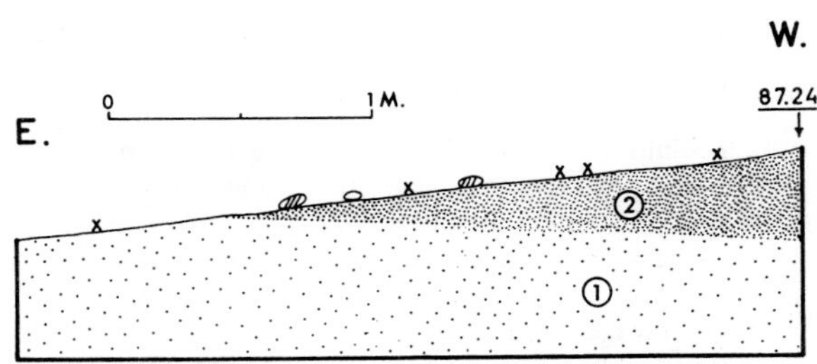

Figure 30. Profile of Trench 5, Site E71K14, Area A.

1. Yellowish-gray, medium and coarse-grained dune sand, unstratified; loose, single-grain structure; calcareous.

2. Grayish, fine to coarse-grained sand; unstratified; cemented root drip casts in places near the top or on the surface; $CaCO_3$ content slightly above 9%.

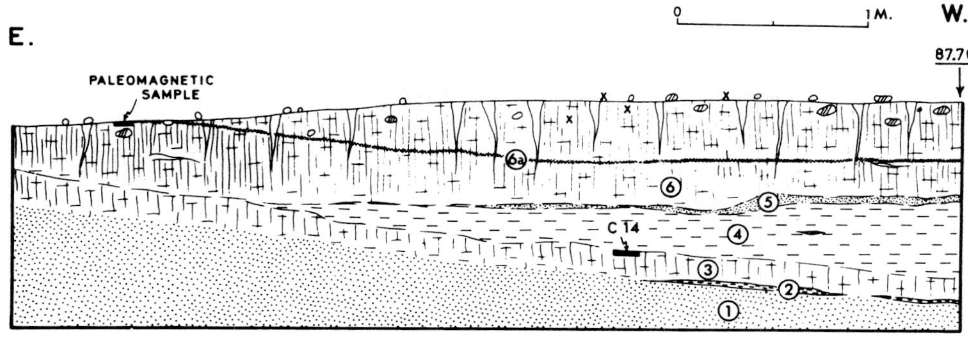

Figure 31. Profile of Trench 1, Site E71K14, Àrea A.

1. Grayish, fine to coarse-grained dune sand; unstratified; cemented by calcium carbonate (*ca.* 9%); root drip casts seen, in places, near the top.

2. Light gray (10YR 7/1), silty diatomaceous sediment with small admixture of medium and coarse-grained sand. Contains very numerous diatomites and therefore also called lower diatomite. Consolidated; highly calcareous; light.

3. Very dark gray (10YR 3/1), sandy silt; cemented; unstratified with medium, angular blocky structure; calcareous. A very thin layer of carbonaceous sand just above this sandy silt and below the overlying diatomaceous layer gave a radiocarbon date of 10,740 BC ±240 (I-3421).

4. Light gray (10YR 7/1), diatomaceous sediment (upper diatomite) with small admixture of medium and coarse-grained sand; contains very numerous diatoms; consolidated to cemented; highly calcareous. Thin and short lenses of medium-grained sand occur more or less frequently within this layer. In the western part of the section, this diatomaceous sediment interfingers with a layer of medium-grained, yellowish, loose beach sand (4a) containing numerous calcareous root casts in its upper part.

5. A thin layer of medium-grained, grayish, loose, calcareous sand.

6. Dark, grayish-brown (10YR 4/2), sandy silt; unstratified; cemented; medium; angular blocky structure. Near the middle of this layer, a very pronounced reddish-brown horizon of fired silt was observed.

6a. A sample of this fired silt was collected for future paleomagnetic dating. A cultural layer highly abundant in chipped stone artifacts and faunal remains occurred in the upper 15 cm of the silt. Numerous artifacts and stones, mostly burned, littered the surface of the area. A well-developed network of dehydration cracks is observed on the surface as well as in the sections down to the base of the silt.

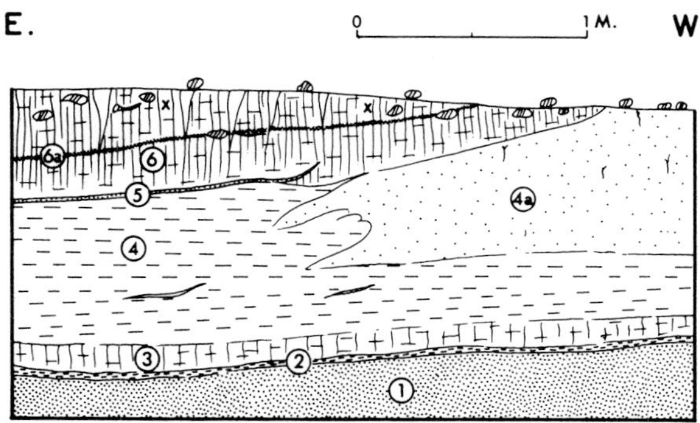

Figure 32. Profile of Trench 2, Site E17K14, Area A. (See Figure 31 for explanation of units.)

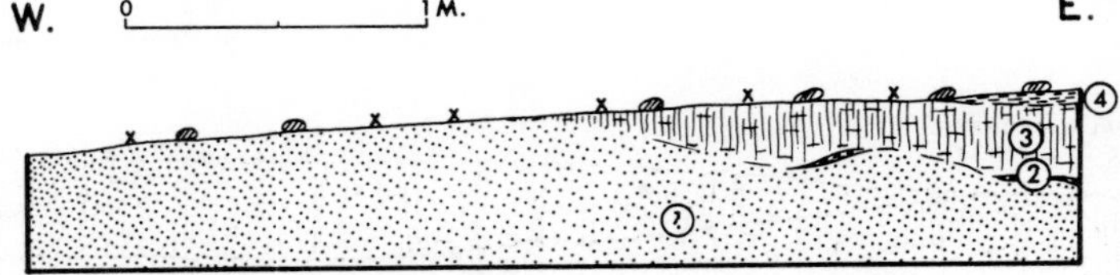

Figure 33. Profile of Trench 3, Site E71K14, Area A.

1. Same as (1) in Trenches 1 and 2.
2. Same as (2) in Trenches 1 and 2.
3. Same as (3) in Trenches 1 and 2.
4. Same as (4) in Trenches 1 and 2. The surface of this trench, as well as the surface of the whole area, was littered by heavily concentrated stone artifacts, burned stones, and strongly weathered fossil bones.

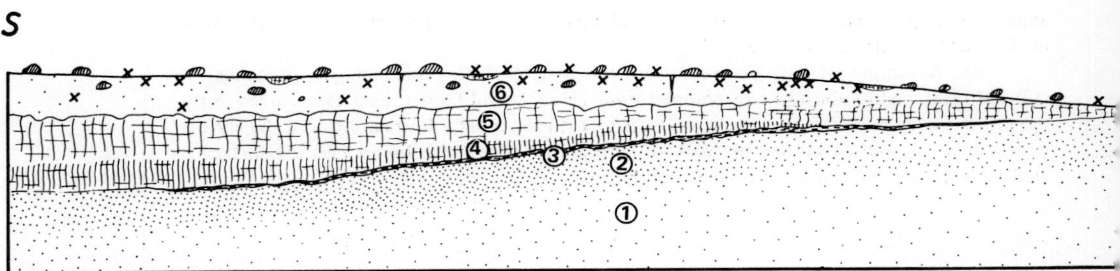

Figure 34. Profile of Trenches 1 and 2, Site E71K14, Area D.

1. Yellowish, medium to coarse-grained dune sand; unstratified; carbonaceous; consolidated to loose near the bottom of the trench; limonitic oxidation stains dispersed within the unit in a form of semivertical root traces. A single blade found near the middle of this unit.

2. Grayish, fine to coarse-grained dune sand; unstratified; cemented by heavy contents of calcium carbonate, clearly truncated at the northern end of the trench. Numerous root drip casts. Sterile.

3. Light gray (10YR 7/1), diatomaceous, silty and fine-grained sandy sediment; unstratified; unconsolidated to loose; highly calcareous; contains diatoms. Culturally sterile.

4. Very dark gray (10YR 3/1), sandy silt with medium, angular blocky structure; unstratified; consolidated; calcareous; sterile; grades into (5).

5. Gray, silty sand or sandy silt with small, angular blocky structure; unstratified; unconsolidated to consolidated in places; calcareous; sterile.

6. Light, grayish silt and fine to medium-grained diatomaceous sandy sediment (pond sediment); unstratified; loose to unconsolidated; highly calcareous, contained very numerous fresh stone artifacts, burned stones, and rare bones concentrated in a 10 cm layer in the top; single artifacts dispersed down to the base. Surface eroded and littered with extremely dense concentration of stone artifacts visibly windworn. Numerous small and flat swales in the surface filled with dark, grayish-brown (10YR 4/2), powdered silt in which traces of the burned layer were observed in the form of concentrations of baked and hardened silt. In a few places the uneroded surface of the described fine-grained pond sediment shows traces of burning in the form of a fired, pinkish, hardened surface evidently associated with the burned layer in the silt. A sample for paleomagnetic dating was collected from the top of the burned pond sediment.

7. Brownish, coarse-grained, reworked dune sand; cemented; unstratified; contained numerous washed-down and waterworn stone artifacts but no bones. Calcareous; separated from the underlying sediment by a clear truncation.

8. Dark, grayish-brown (10YR 4/2), slightly sandy silt with medium, angular blocky structure; unstratified; cemented to consolidated. Numerous dehydration cracks on the surface down to the bottom. Sterile.

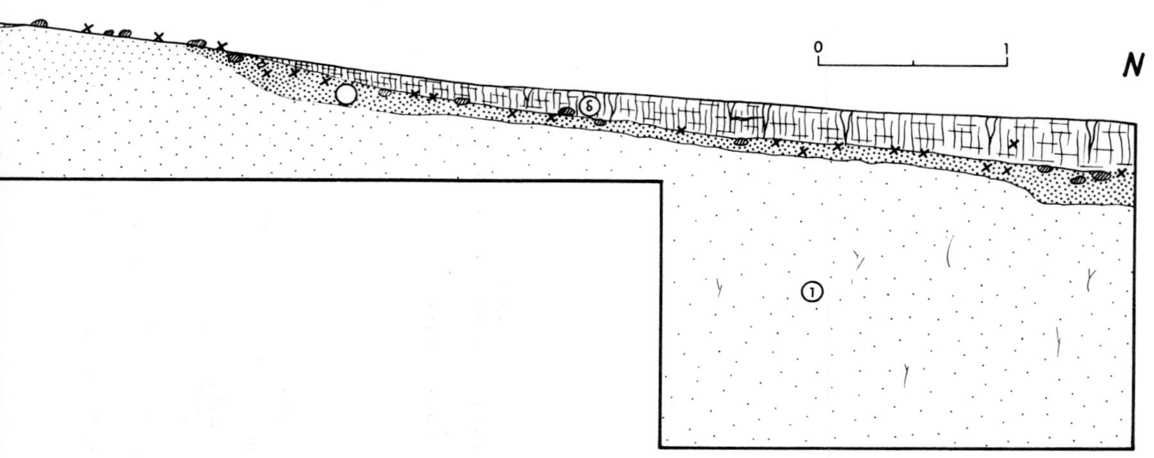

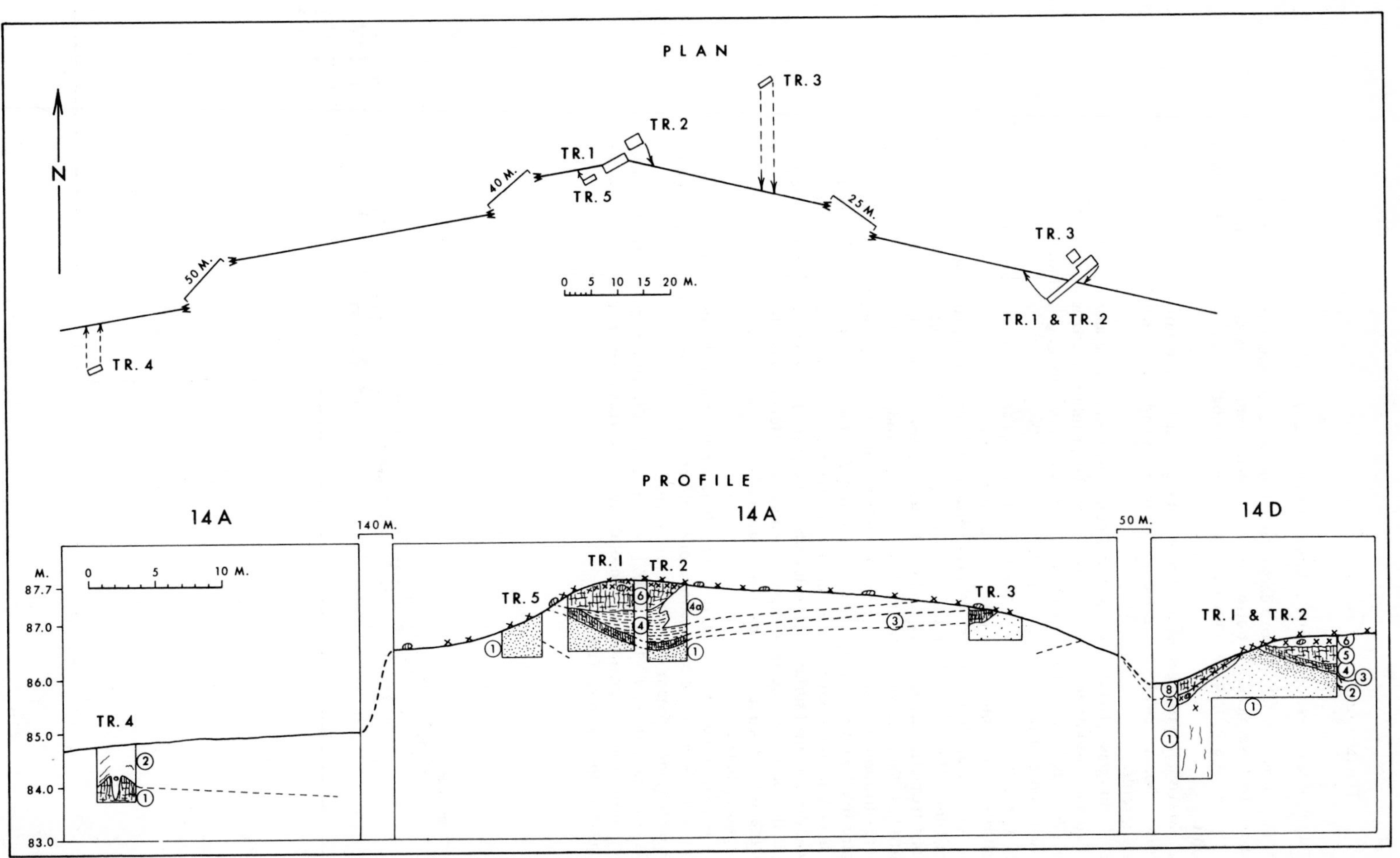

Figure 35. Site E71K14, cross-section through Areas A, B, D. (For sediment explanation see detailed profiles of Trenches 1–4 at Site E71K14A and 1 and 2 at Site E71K14D.

(Site E71K15). The entire site area was collected, and seven trenches were excavated (Figures 36–37).

Another site was located 150 m to the south on a similar circular sand mound. It was designated as Site E71K15B, but was not collected.

Other Sites

North of Sites E71K12 and E71K13, at the edge of wadi No. 6, were two surface concentrations. They were recorded as Sites E71K7 and E71K11. Neither site was collected. Both of the sites, together with Sites E71K14 and E71K15, seem to represent the same industry. Sites E71K12 and E71K13 are both different from each other and different from the industry at Sites E71K14 and E71K15.

Discussion of the Stratigraphy at Wadi No. 6

The trenches and exposures in this area revealed a complex stratigraphy. The lower sediment exposed was a brownish silt covered by dune sand in which there were three lenses of the same silt. The silt layers within the dune were observed in several areas, particularly at Site E71K13 below the occupation horizon, where they were relatively thick (*ca*. 20 cm).

In most areas the dune sand is loose and stratified, but where the upper part has not been removed by deflation the top of the sand unit is cemented by a high concentration of calcium carbonate reaching a value of 10% of the sediment. Granulometric analysis shows that the cemented zone of the dune also contains more fine grains and a relatively high count (*ca*. 70%) of fine sand and silt-sized particles (below 0.2 mm). In several exposures and trenches the top of the sand unit is presumably marked by a weak soil of the aridisol or ustalf groups characterized by streaks of pale orange illuvial stains (B horizon), denser in the upper part and extending down at least 1.20 cm. Some of these stains appear to follow plant roots. In this stained horizon the dune stratification is completely destroyed. The artifacts at Sites E71K12 and E71K13 were distributed within the whole thickness of this illuvial stained zone. The uppermost part of this soil was subsequently marked by a heavy concentration of calcium carbonate connected with the same overlying ponds.

Over the dune sand, in what is a group of topographic lows forming a series of separate small basins, are the remnants of a sequence of pond sediments interrupted by a layer of silt. Subsequent erosion, both fluvial and recent aeolian, has reversed the topography, leaving the remnants of the basin floors at a higher elevation today. At the base of the pond sequence are thin patches (2–4 cm thick) of a fine, light gray, calcareous sand (previously called "Lower Diatomite"—Wendorf *et al*. 1970), containing about 60% silt-sized particles and 13 percent fine sand grains. Overlying these patches are a silt layer from 20 cm to 30 cm thick. This silt differs from both the lower silt and the final silt in this sequence by having 10% less silt-sized and 10% more very fine sand-sized particles.

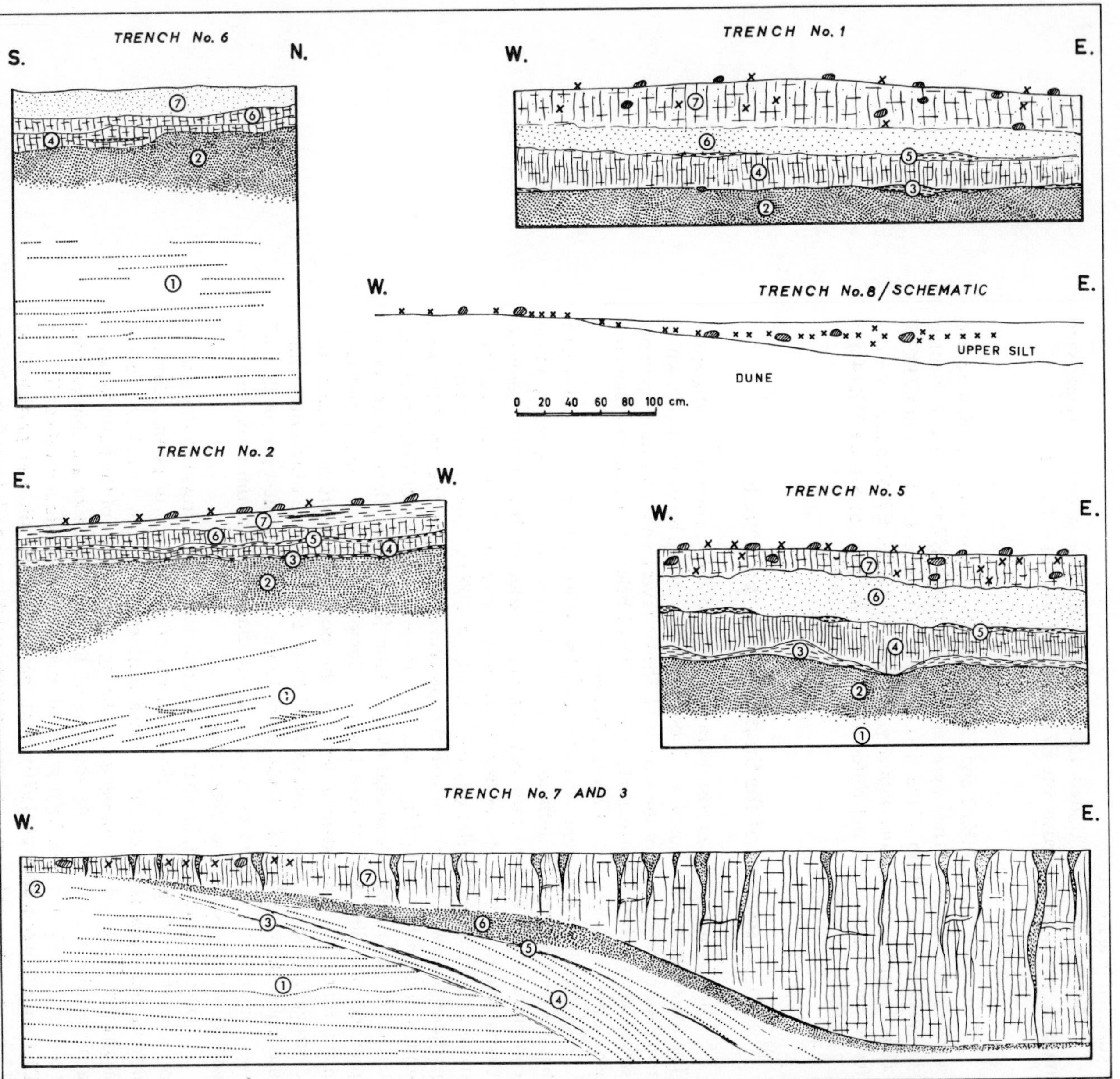
TRENCH No. 6
S.
N.
TRENCH No. 1
W.
E.
TRENCH No. 8/SCHEMATIC
W.
E.
UPPER SILT
DUNE
0 20 40 60 80 100 cm.
TRENCH No. 2
E.
W.
TRENCH No. 5
W.
E.
TRENCH No. 7 AND 3
W.
E.

Figure 36. Profiles of Trenches at Site E71K15.

Trenches 1 and 5

1. Yellowish, medium and coarse-grained dune sand; unstratified; loose; calcareous; sterile.
2. Gray (10YR 5/1), fine to coarse-grained dune sand; unstratified; cemented; highly calcareous; numerous traces of root drip casts. Sterile.
3. Light gray (10YR 7/1), silty, sandy diatomaceous sediment; unstratified; unconsolidated; highly calcareous. Sterile.
4. Very dark gray (10YR 3/1), sandy silt with medium blocky structure; unstratified; consolidated to cemented; calcareous. Sterile.
5. Light gray (10YR 7/1), sandy diatomaceous sediment; unstratified; unconsolidated to loose when exposed; highly calcareous. Sterile.
6. Grayish, medium and fine-grained sand, slightly diatomaceous; unstratified; consolidated to unconsolidated and loose when exposed down the slope; highly calcareous. Diatoms present. Culturally sterile.
7. Grayish-brown (10YR 5/2), to light grayish-brown (10YR 6/2), sandy silt; calcareous; powdered and entirely loose; unstratified; contained numerous stone artifacts, burned stone, and a few bones throughout layer.

Trenches 2 and 6

1. Yellowish, medium and coarse-grained dune sand; stratified with clear foreset dip toward the river, limited cross-lamination in places, passed into unstratified dune sand toward the top; loose, single-grain structure; calcareous. Culturally sterile.
2. Gray (10YR 5/1), fine to coarse-grained dune sand; unstratified; cemented, numerous root drop casts throughout the layer; highly calcareous. Culturally sterile.
3. Light gray (10YR 7/1), diatomaceous sediment same as (5) in trenches 1 and 5.
4. Very dark gray (10YR 3/1), sandy silt same as (4) in trenches 1 and 5.
5. Light gray (10YR 7/1), diatomaceous sediment same as (5) in trenches 1 and 5, passed into more silty and more grayish sediment toward the top (6).
6. Grayish, medium and fine-grained sediment same as (6) in trenches 1 and 5, passed into more medium-grained sand down the slope toward trench 6.

Trenches 3 and 7

1. Yellowish, medium and coarse-grained dune sand; stratified with a slight dip toward the river; loose; calcareous. Sterile.
2. Yellowish, medium and coarse-grained dune sand; unstratified; passing down to (1); loose; calcareous. Sterile.

3–5. Medium and coarse-grained dune sand, foreset-dipped, interstratified with continuous laminae of brownish sandy silt. This unit truncates underlying stratified sands. Passed into (6); loose to consolidated near the top; calcareous.

6. Gray (10YR 5/1), fine to coarse-grained dune sand with root drip casts; unstratified; cemented; grades down to stratified dune sand with silt streaks; highly calcareous. Sterile.
7. Dark, grayish-brown (10YR 4/2), sandy silt rather unconformably overlying cemented top of the dune; cultural horizon with waterworn chipped stone artifacts and burned stones within upper 15 cm of unit. Coarse to medium, angular blocky structure. Numerous wide and deep dehydration cracks filled with yellow dune sand cut this silt vertically. Unstratified; calcareous.

Trench 8

Shallow trench cut for the purpose of linking surface material with that occurring *in situ* in the uppermost part of the silt showed that the artifacts continued to occur in a 10 cm layer within the silt. The redeposited, cultural layer showing high silt polishing, is covered by a very thin layer of sandy silt.
Schematic cross-section at Site E71K15A:

1. Stratified dune.
2. Upper part of the dune cemented by calcium carbonate with numerous root casts.
3. Nilotic sandy silt with a thick layer of diatomaceous fine sands below and above.
4. Medium and fine-grained diatomaceous pond sand.
5. Powdered upper silt with cultural remains throughout the layer.
6. Foreset-dipped dune sand interstratified with thin streaks of sandy silt.
7. Same as (2).
8. Nilotic sandy silt with waterworn artifacts near the top.

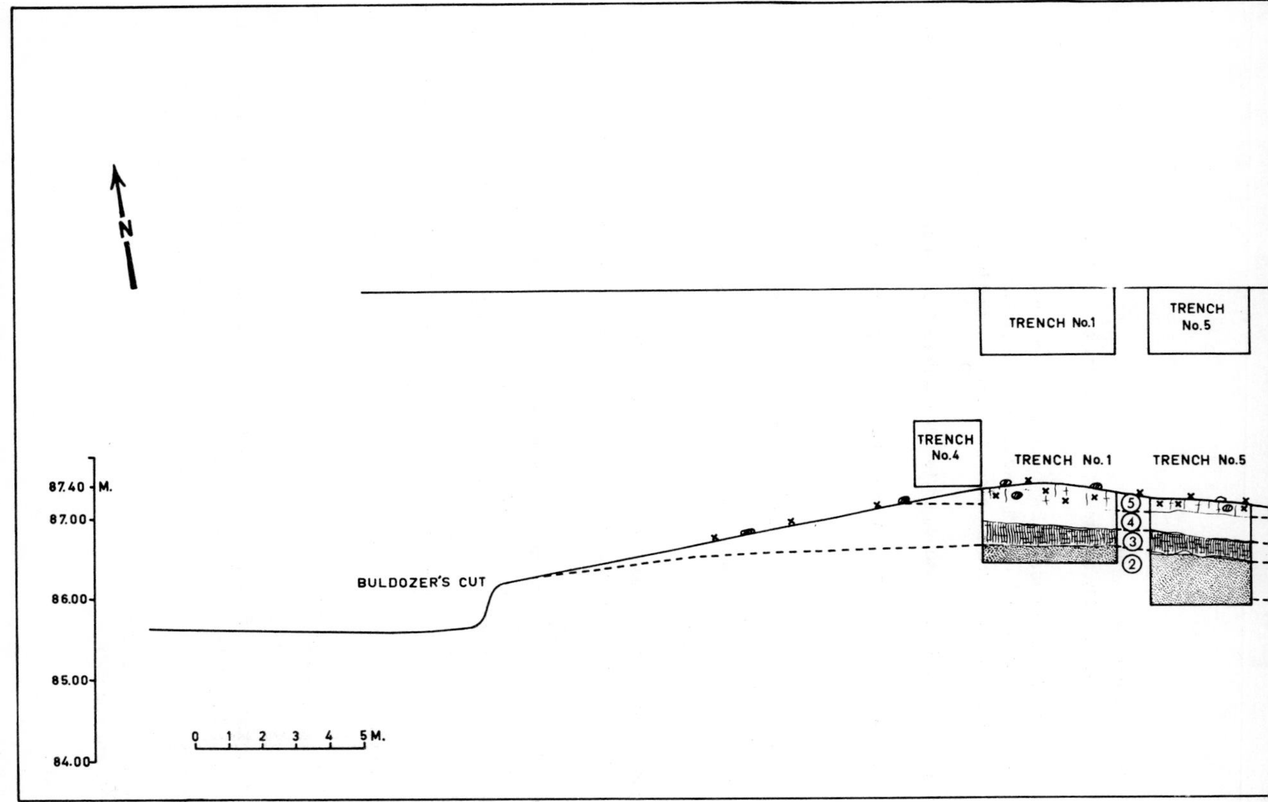

Figure 37. Cross-section throughout Site E71K15. (For sediment explanation, see Figure 36).

Above the silt layer, where traces of the basins are preserved, are pond sediments that differ slightly from basin to basin. One of the basins (Site E71K14A) is a light gray, highly calcareous, diatomaceous sediment containing more than 50% silt-sized particles and about 25% very fine sand grains. This pond is bordered to the west by a loose dune sand that interfingers with the upper part of the diatomaceous sediment.

An analysis of the diatoms from this unit by W. Przybylowska disclosed the presence of 46 species. The specimens were badly crushed and damaged, which prevented a statistical treatment and made possible only an approximate evaluation.

In all samples the fauna were basically the same. All were cosmopolitan, and they included three species that may have slight tropical affinities (*Navicula cuspidata*, *Gomphonema lanceolatum*, and *Ephitemia sorex*). This contrasts with the Holocene diatom fauna from the Fayum (Abdel Alem 1958), where tropical fauna are well represented. One species (*Melosira granulata*) prefers deep water and was present in the lowest sample only; much more common was

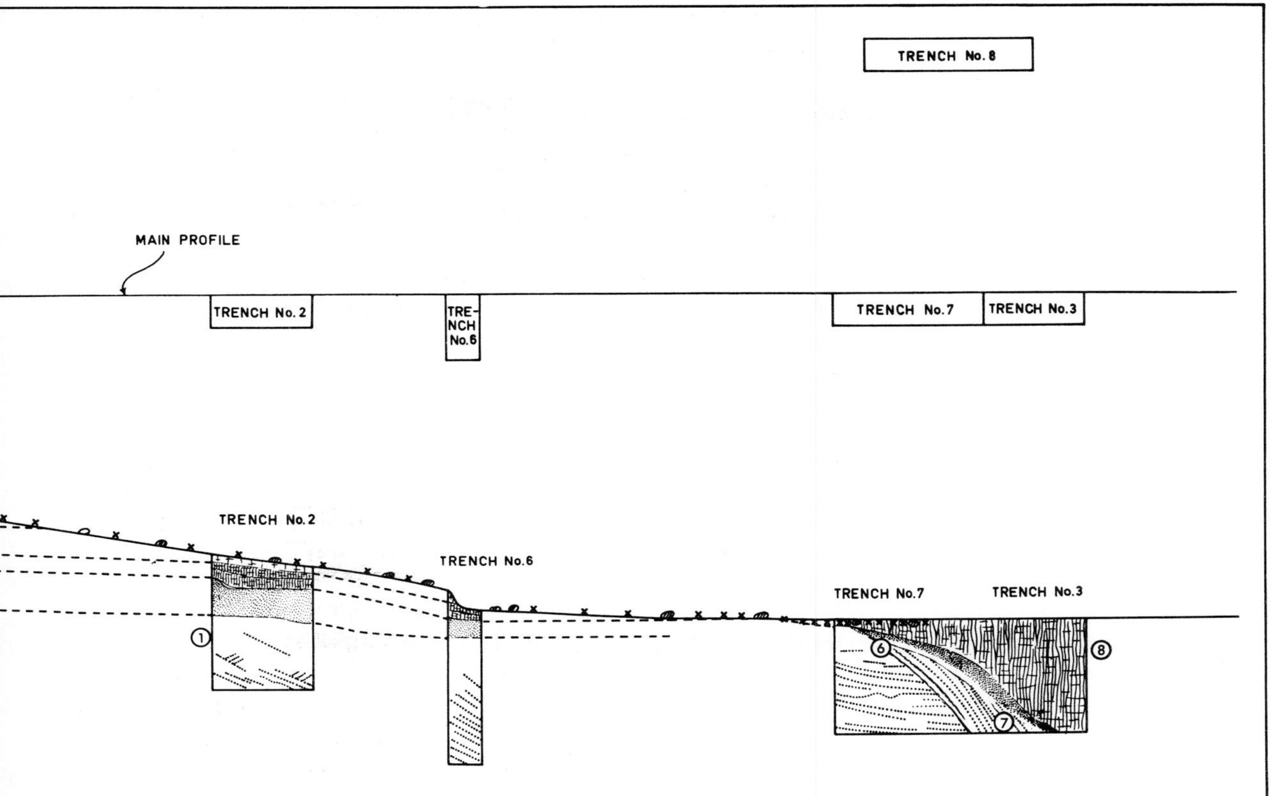

Coconeis placentula, a littoral form found throughout the sediment. All but one of the diatom types were alkalibiontic, alkaliphilic, or indifferent, strongly suggesting a shallow, highly alkaline pond environment.

A preliminary analysis of pollen from the diatomaceous sediment by M. J. Dabrowski of the Polish Academy of Sciences resulted in the following:

1. The diatomaceous sediments yielded a fair amount of pollen grains, all of them in a fossil state.
2. The pollen assemblages from all the diatomaceous layers include an amount of boreal types presumably representing long-distance transport.
3. None of the pollen spectra included aquatic plants, suggesting an absence of permanent or longstanding water bodies.
4. The remaining elements suggest a grassland environment.
5. Scattered through the pond sediments were low frequencies of a large-grass, cereal-type pollen grain. These cereal-type grains suddenly became numerous (around 10–15% of the total pollen) near the top of the sequence.

6. Dr. Dambrowski tentatively identified the large cereal-like pollen as barley.

A sample of carbonaceous sand at the base of the diatomaceous unit yielded a radiocarbon date of 10,740 BC ±240 years (I-3421).

In two adjacent basins (E71K14D and E71K15), in the same stratigraphic position, the pond sediment is a very fine calcareous sand containing between 29% and 55% very fine sand grains. These basins may be less deep than the one at Site 14A.

The sequence continued with a reoccupation of the area during a temporary dry phase of the pond at Site E71K14D. Here the artifacts occurred in the uppermost part of the fine calcareous sand unit.

The pond sequence at this site is terminated by the deposition of an upper silt unit accompanied by a pronounced erosion that partially destroyed the previous morphology of the landscape. The upper silt is preserved in large remnants up to 50 cm thick that mantle the tops of most of the mounds and partially protect them from deflation. It also occurs in thicker sections on both sides of the dune field. The upper silt is a dark, grayish brown and contains over 70% silt-sized particles. Its granulometric composition is closely similar to that of the lower silt.

Near the center of the silt remnants was a burned layer of reddish-pink color, probably attributable to a widespread brush fire. Traces of this event in the same stratigraphic position were noted as far south as Deir El-Fakhuri and northward on both the east and west banks to the Dishna area at the Qena Bend of the river, a distance of over 200 km. A radiocarbon sample of carbonaceous sand from the top of this burned horizon at a locality near Kumbelat yielded a date of 10,550 BC ±230 years (I-3424).

At Sites E71K14A and E71K15 the occupation horizon occurred at the very top of the upper silt unit, and at E71K14A it was above the burned layer. No burned layer was recorded at Site E71K15. The occupation at E71K14D was covered by thin patches of silt with traces of the burned layer. Thus the occupation at these localities occurred before (E71K14D) and after (E71K14A) the brush fire event.

To summarize, the sequence of events discernible in the Wadi No. 6 area is as follows:

1. Deposition of lower silt together with formation of dunes.
2. Possible development of an aridosol or ustalf-like soil over the dunes, accompanied by a much lower Nile level. The occupations of Sites E71K12 and E71K13 possibly occurred during this event.
3. Initial development of ponds, followed immediately by deposition of silt with a rising Nile level.
4. Second and more prolonged phase of ponding, possibly accompanied by a slight reduction in the level of the Nile. Occupation at Site E71K14D.
5. Rise in the Nile and deposition of the upper silt, accompanied by fluvial erosion.

6. Brush fire near the end of the upper silt aggradation; occupation at Sites E71K14A and E71K15.
7. Recession of the Nile.
8. Development of the modern topography through aeolian deflation.

Sites Near Thomas Afia Village

Just north and northeast of the village of Thomas Afia and 2 km north of the monastery at Deir El-Fakhuri is another extensive sandy area, roughly triangular in outline and nearly 1 km on a side. The landscape is generally flat with several large, shallow, wind-scoured depressions dotting the surface. West of the sand field there is an extensive surface of silt that overlaps the sand. The western portion of the sand field also has several flattish remnants of pond sediments that cover the sand.

Extensive areas of occupation debris also occurred in this western portion of the sand field on the deflated sand surface or eroding from beneath the remnants of the pond sediments. Several distinct, dense, and separate concentrations of lithic artifacts were recognized in this area (Figure 38). These were grouped arbitrarily into two main sites: E71K6 and E71K18. Each of these was further divided into areas representing distinct concentrations. Each of these areas is probably a separate occupation and could be regarded as a separate site.

E71K6

This site was a scattered concentration of artifacts covering an oval area about 20 m by 20 m located adjacent to a remnant of pond clay. The fresh appearance of the artifacts suggested that they had been exposed only recently. The site area was totally collected, and a trench 1 m by 3 m was dug at the edge of the adjacent remnant (Figure 39).

E71K6B

This was a large, dense concentration of totally deflated artifacts covering a roughly oval area some 45 m by 60 m. A rectangular area 10 m by 20 m near the center of the concentration was fully collected.

E71K6C

This was a very large, dense concentration of artifacts on the surface of an area near the north edge of the sand field that had been partially disturbed by heavy equipment. All of the artifacts were collected from two separate areas. Area 1 was roughly trapezoidal in outline and approximately 18 m by 8 m in size; Area 2 was rectangular in outline and 6 m by 7 m in size.

E71K6D

Here there occurred a large, oval, scattered concentration of artifacts in an area 35 m by 40 m in size. All were on the deflated sand surface. It was not collected.

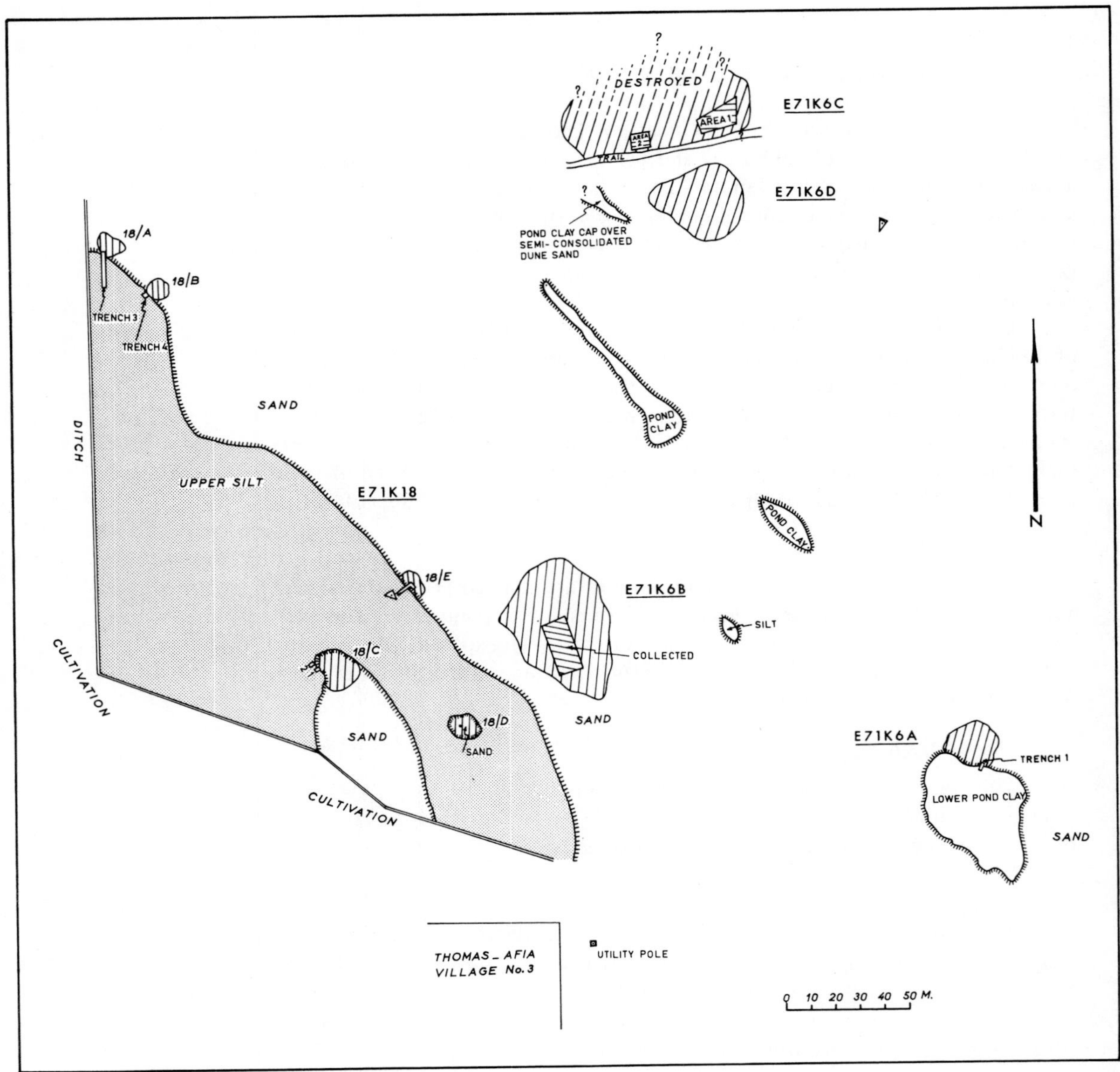

Figure 38. Map of area north of Thomas Afia Village showing locations of Sites E71K6 and E71K18.

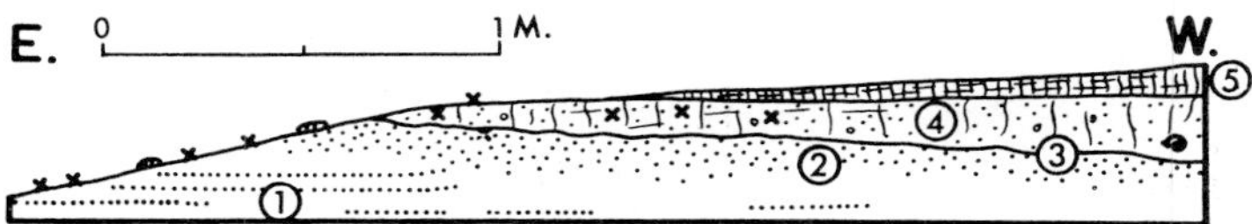

Figure 39. Profile of Trench 1, Site E71K6, Area A.

1. Yellowish dune sand, loose, with traces of stratification at the base of the trench.
2. Cemented, highly calcareous dune sand.
3. Discomformity.
4. Light gray (10YR 7/2), sandy silt with small clay pebbles, occasional snails, and cultural material (lower pond sediment). The deposit is conformably overlain by gray silt containing rare snails; sterile. Surface deflated.

Site E71K18

This site had five distinct small, dense concentrations, all nearly circular in outline and ranging from 9 m to 15 m in diameter. Three of these concentrations (A, B, and E) were located along the low contact between the sand field and the silt cover that bordered the sand field along its western edge. Two other concentrations (C and D) were exposed by wind deflation in the silt mantle (Figure 40). Trenches were dug at four of the concentrations (all but D).

A trench 9 m long and 2 m wide dug at Site E71K18A disclosed the most complete stratigraphic sequence (Figure 41). The basal unit is a light, brownish-

Figure 40. View of area in vicinity of Thomas Afia Village, looking west. Vehicle is on silt of Sahaba–Darau aggradation. Site E71K18, Area C was immediately behind photographer.

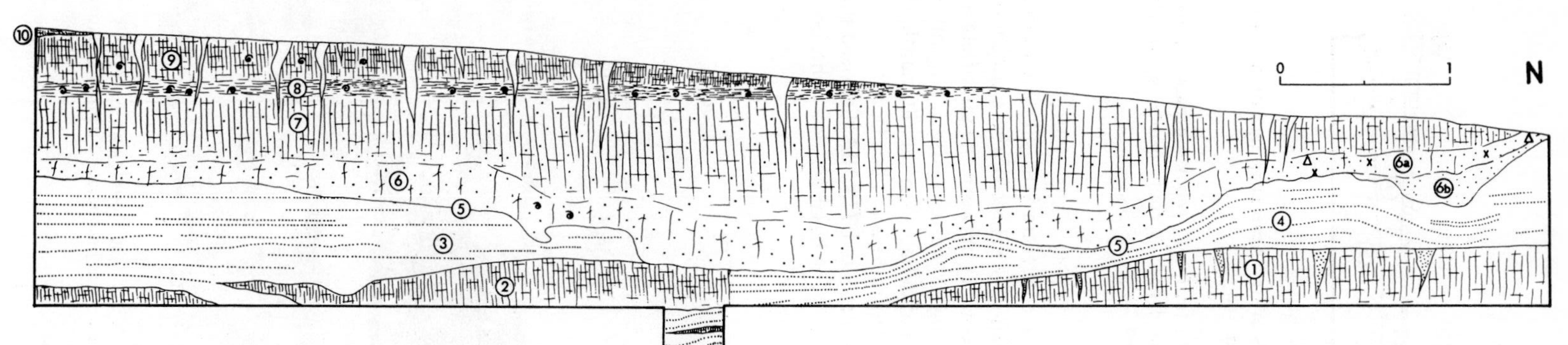

Figure 41. Profile of Trench 3, Site E71K18, Area A.

1. Light, brownish-gray (10YR 6/2), consolidated to cemented, calcareous silt with medium, angular blocky structure and fossil desiccation cracks filled with reddish, loose dune sand.
2. Same silt as (1).
3. Yellowish stratified medium and coarse sand, possibly reworked dune sand.
4. Same as (3).
5. Surface of erosion.
6. Pinkish-gray (7.5YR 7/2), cemented, sandy silt with clay pebbles and snails; highly calcareous with coarse blocky structure. Much occupational debris at the eastern end of the trench (6a). Occasional pockets of reworked sand (6b). "Lower pond deposit."
7. Pinkish-gray (7.5YR 6/2), unstratified, cemented, sandy silt with medium, angular blocky structure; contains rare snails; culturally sterile; calcareous. "Middle pond sediment" with Nile silt admixture.
8. Light gray (10YR 7/1), stratified diatomite with numerous snails; highly calcareous; becomes gradually thinner toward the east.
9. Light gray (10YR 6/1), cemented, sandy silt; unstratified with medium to small, angular blocky structure, contains numerous snails; highly calcareous. "Upper pond sediment." Surface deflated with several deep dehydration cracks. Culturally sterile.
10. Dark gray (10YR 4/1), unstratified consolidated Nile silt; calcareous; highly eroded, preserved as a thin veneer at the western corner. Sterile. "Sahaba silt."

gray, cemented and calcareous silt with desiccation cracks filled with reddish sand, possibly aeolean. The upper surface is eroded and truncated. Overlying the basal silt is a reworked dune sand deposited simultaneously with another silt unit, which, in turn, is covered by a dune or reworked dune sand. A pronounced erosional unconformity separates these two supposedly reworked sands from an overlying pond sediment of light gray color. This pond sediment contains very small, rolled clay pebbles, a heavy concentration of sand, and a clay or silt mixture. It is highly calcareous and contained concentrations of snails and cultural debris. The underlying sand rises steeply eastward, indicating a nearby shore. The artifacts were concentrated in the area immediately adjacent to this shore.

Above this light-gray pond sediment and separated from it by an erosional surface is a light, pinkish-gray, silty pond clay containing, in places, rolled pebbles of the underlying light gray pond sediment as well as sand and rare snails. The base of this sediment generally follows the outlines of the depression previously partially filled by the earlier sediment. Above the pinkish pond clay is a thin (10 cm) layer of finely stratified light gray diatomite with a heavy concentration of snails. The diatomite unit can be seen along the entire face of a low silt scarp, a distance of over 200 m, and in the ditch that borders the cultivated area. Here the diatomite reached a maximum observed thickness of 30 cm (Figures 42–45).

A preliminary pollen analysis by N. Frederiksen of a sample from the middle of the diatom unit yielded sparse pollen. The most numerous grains were of the grass family plus a smooth, elongate type that could be a palm (but definitely not a date palm). There was also an indication of a pond weed (*Sparagarium*).

Overlying the diatomite is a light, brownish-gray, silty pond clay with sand admixture. This, in turn, is covered by a dark gray, calcareous upper silt unit.

Discussion of Stratigraphy at Thomas Afia Village

The stratigraphic sequence in the trenches and cuts at Sites E71K18 and E71K6 suggests the following dynamic interpretation of events:

1. Deposition of lower silt.
2. Drying of lower silt, formation of desiccation cracks, and filling with dune sand.
3. Reworking of dune sand simultaneously with deposition of additional lower silt layers; events 1, 2, and 3 may represent a short interval and most likely are contemporary with the maximum of aggradation and dune sedimentation at the Deir El-Fakhuri area; but here, as a result of a slightly lower elevation (about 84 m versus 87 m above sea level at Deir El-Fakhuri), the dunes were subjected to greater stream velocity.
4. Erosion of the reworked sand sediments and deepening of previously existing depression.

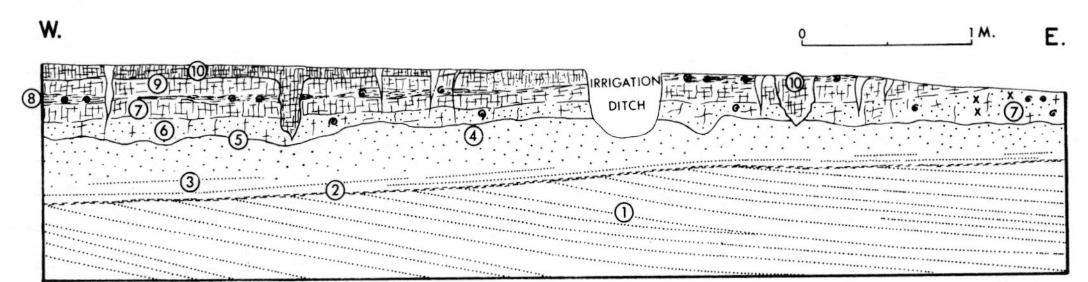

Figure 42. Profile of Trench 6, Site E71K18, Area E.

1. Yellowish, stratified, medium and coarse-grained dune sand with slight inclination of laminae toward the east; loose-grain structure, sterile, truncated at the top. Calcareous.

2. Grayish, thin layer of sandy silt.

3. Yellowish, medium and coarse-grained stratified sand with a noticeable dip toward the west, conformable with sandy silt layer; loose; calcareous; passes into unstratified same sand with extensive limonite oxidation staining (4).

5. Sharp unconformity.

6. Light gray (10YR 7/3), cemented, sandy silt with clay pebbles and numerous snails; highly calcareous with coarse blocky structure. Contains occupational debris at the eastern end of the trench. "Lower pond deposit."

7. Gray (10YR 5/1), unstratified, cemented, sandy silt with medium blocky structure; contains rare snails. Culturally sterile. "Middle pond sediment" with Nile silt admixture.

8. Light gray (10YR 7/1), stratified diatomite with numerous snails. Eroded and thinning in places. Highly calcareous. At Trench 5 grades up into fine loose sand.

9. Light gray (10YR 6/1), unstratified, cemented, sandy silt with medium blocky structure; highly calcareous; culturally sterile. "Upper pond sediment."

10. Dark gray (10YR 4/1), unstratified consolidated Nile silt with medium, angular blocky structure; calcareous; sterile; numerous desiccation cracks, some of which are filled with same silt.

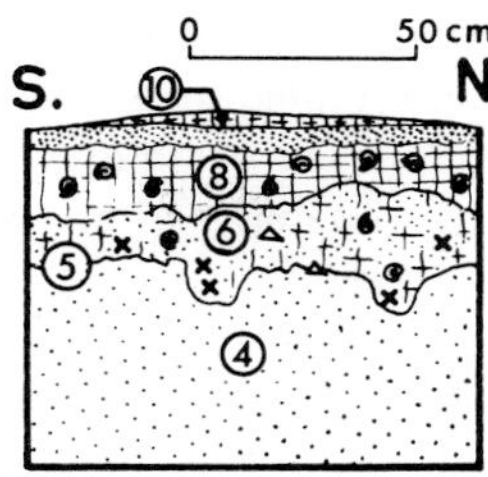

Figure 43. Profile of Trench 5, Site E71K18, Area E. (For description of sediments see Figure 42.)

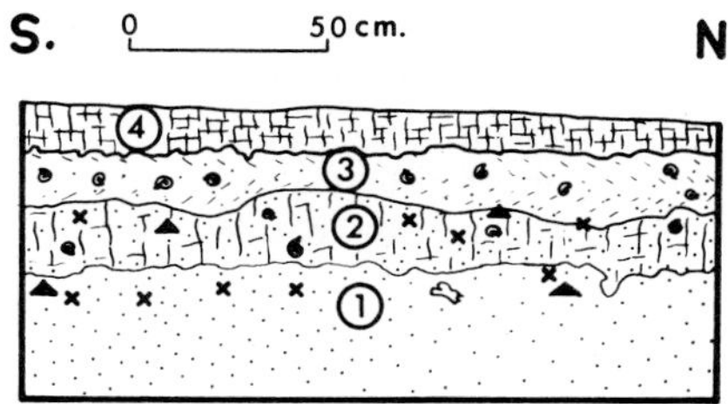

Figure 44. Profile of Trench 2, Site E71K18, Area C.

1. Yellowish, unstratified, coarse and medium-grained sand with limonite oxidation stains; loose-grain structure; highly calcareous. Sterile.

2. Light gray, cemented, sandy silt with numerous clay pebbles, artifacts and snails; unstratified; highly calcareous; separated from underlying sand by a sharp unconformity. "Lower pond sediment."

3. Light, yellowish, medium and coarse-grained, consolidated sand; unstratified; highly calcareous; contains numerous snails. Possibly shore sand.

4. Dark gray (10YR 4/1), consolidated Nile silt separated from underlying sand by sharp unconformity. Highly calcareous with medium angular blocky structure. "Sahaba silt."

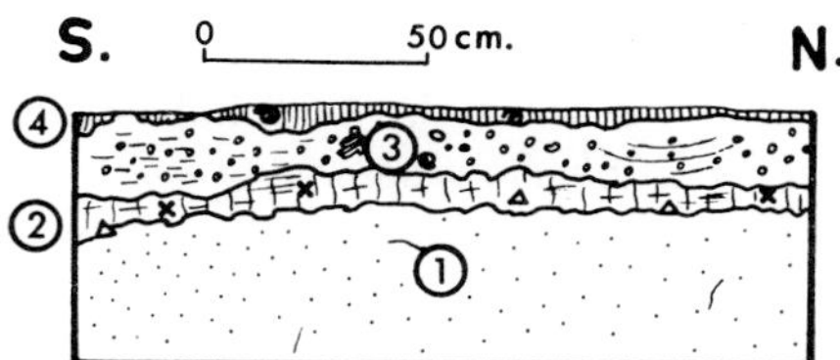

Figure 45. Profile of Trench 4, Site E71K18, Area B.

1. Yellowish, consolidated, medium and coarse-grained sand with extensive limonite staining; unstratified; calcareous.

2. Gray, consolidated to cemented, sandy silt with medium, angular blocky structure; contains numerous artifacts and occasional snails. Separated from underlying sand by sharp disconformity. "Lower pond sediment."

3. Grayish, unsorted, rounded pellets of sandy silt in sandy matrix; consolidated to cemented; calcareous, separated from (2) by an erosional surface. Reworked dry pond sediment.

4. Light gray (10YR 7/1), stratified diatomite with numerous snails; fills micro-channels and small depression on the surface of (3). Highly calcareous.

5. Deposition of lower pond sediment in a shallow swamp due possibly to seepage; this swamp dried and refilled seasonally, as is shown by the presence of rolled pebbles of the same clay; occupation of adjacent dune hummock.

6. Drying of the shallow swamp and subsequent erosion of the lower pond sediment.

7. Refilling of the renewed concavities with pinkish pond sediment, more silty than the lower pond sediment and containing stringers of Nile silt.

8. Deepening of the pond, possibly contemporaneously with a lowering of the level of the Nile, and deposition of the diatomite. The presence of the diatomite without traces of Nile silt implies deeper water that was not enriched by Nile flood water. This situation may suggest reduced evaporation accompanied by a slightly lower Nile level.

9. Deposition of the uppermost pond clay containing Nile silt and indicating a rising level of Nile floods.

10. Deposition of the upper silt at an elevation of about 85 m; this silt almost certainly represents the same aggradational event as the upper silt at Deir El-Fakhuri.

All five sites occupied at Site E71K18 are associated with the lowermost pond and swamp sediment and may be regarded as of the same age. They also appear to be of the same industry. The limited size of the concentrations suggests nuclear family units occupying low sand knolls at the edge of a fairly large, swampy pond.

The occupation at Site E71K6A belongs to an entirely different industry, although the artifacts occurred in the same lowermost pond sediment and in the same microenvironmental setting. The other sites at E71K6 are all surface, and their original stratigraphic positions are not known, although the assemblage at E71K6B belongs to the same industry as that found in the five concentrations at E71K18.

The cultural layers from the trenches at Site E71K18 yielded fish and mammal remains at all localities and bird bones at two. Locality A contained at least seven individual fish of *Clarias* sp. with reconstructed lengths ranging from 15 cm to 80 cm. Locality B had at least 15 individuals. All but one were *Clarias* sp.; the other was possibly *Heterobranchus* sp. Localities D and E had at least one specimen each of *Clarias* sp. between 35 cm and 50 cm in length. Locality C also yielded fish, but it was not identified.

Mammal remains were less numerous, but *Bos primigenius* was present at all but Locality A. *Alcelaphus buselaphus* (hartebeest) was present at all localities. Other remains included *Gazella rufifrons*, *Lepus capensis*, and *Nesokia indica*, all present in small quantities and without evident pattern. The bird bones were not identified.

Sites Near No. 4 Village

At the north edge of the reclaimed area, some 1500 m north of the Wadi No. 6 area, at the western edge of the cultivated silt, and just south of No. 4

Figure 46. View of Site E71K9 looking west. Site is located on low knoll where figures are excavating and extends beyond left edge of picture.

Village is an irregular sandy area 300 m by 600 m that was not leveled. The northern and southern edges of the sandy area are bordered by cultivated silts. To the west the landscape rises rapidly to the gravel foothills. The center of the sandy area is occupied by an elongated, steep mound with a maximum elevation just about 87 m, about 2 m above most of the surrounding sands. The landscape is slightly rolling and was strongly deflated in recent times.

Three sites were recorded here: E71K8, E71K9, and E71K10. Sites E71K9 and E71K10 were both composed of more than one concentration.

E71K8

The occupation here was represented by a thin, irregular, oval (about 60 m in diameter) concentration of artifacts entirely on the sand surface. Most of the artifacts were eolized; however, a few were very fresh and appeared to be weathering from thin lenses of silt within the dune sand. Two trenches, each 1 m by 2 m, were cut in the area where the fresh artifacts occurred; however, neither yielded any material *in situ*.

E71K9

There are two localities at this site (Figure 46). The first was a large, dense concentration, 120 m long and 30 m wide, on the crest of a flat, elongated dune knoll at the eastern edge of the sandy area and immediately adjacent to the cultivated silt. The site was divided into five arbitrary rectangular areas, each 20 m by 30 m, designated Areas A–E. Within these areas all artifacts on the surface were collected. Two small trenches, each 2 m by 4 m, were dug near the northern and northeastern edges of the concentration. They revealed the presence of a rich cultural horizon throughout a sand layer, from 10 cm to 40 cm thick, resting on a dense brown silt (Figure 47).

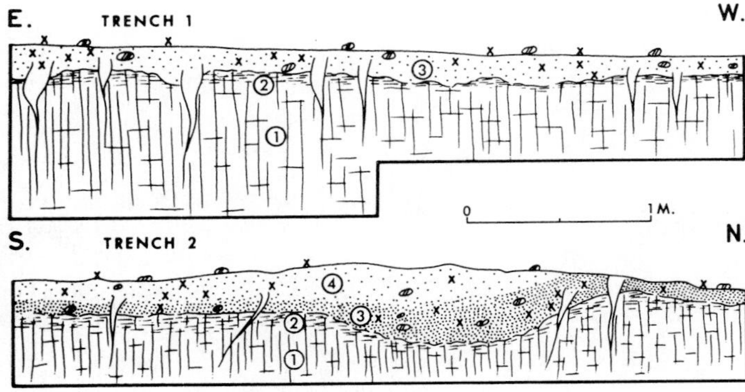

Figure 47. Profile of Trenches 1 and 2, Site E71K9.

1. Brown (10YR 5/3), consolidated, unstratified, slightly sandy Nile silt with medium, angular blocky structure; calcareous; sterile.

2. Same as (1), weathered and loose to consolidated with small, angular blocky structure in places; unstratified; calcareous.

3. Yellowish-brown, coarse and medium dune sand; loose to consolidated with numerous artifacts throughout and dehydration cracks protruding into the silt. Surface deflated.

4. Yellowish, coarse and medium-grained, loose dune sand with artifacts; unstratified; grades down into (3). Calcareous. Deflated.

The second locality assigned to this site (E17K9X) was a dense oval concentration, 15 m by 25 m, entirely on the sand surface of a low, rounded knoll located 80 m southeast of the main concentration at K9 (Figure 48). The site was totally collected. A trench 2 m wide and 14 m long was dug from the center of the concentration to beyond its western edge. No material was found *in situ*.

E71K10

This site is also comprised of two localities (A and B). The two localities are adjacent to each other on low sand knolls near the northern and eastern edges of the sandy area. To the west of Locality B, there is a shallow swale bounded on the east by the dune sand and on the west by the low footslope of the gravel hills. The swale contains a thin veneer of silt, and numerous *Cleopatra bulimoides* shells were found eroding from the silt. These, together with small fragments of charcoal found with the shells, were collected for radiocarbon dating.

Discussion of Stratigraphy Near No. 4 Village

The series of trenches and exposures reveal the following sequence of events in this area. The lowest unit is a brown, hard, calcareous silt with a weathered softer horizon at the top. At Site E71K9X the top of the silt has large, vertical desiccation cracks filled with sand. In a small erosional depression in the silt, there is a series of silty pond sediments containing a strong admixture of sand. At the base of this series of pond sediments are several calcareous root

Figure 48. Excavation of trench at Site E71K9X, looking southwest. Occupation debris here was entirely on surface and extended from the upper end of the trench and mostly beyond the left edge of the picture.

casts; one of these yielded a radiocarbon date of 14,880 BC ±290 years (I-3420). The pond sequence is terminated by the deposition of aeolean dune sand with streaks of silt.

At Site E71K9 the dune sand shows well-marked desiccation cracks posterior to the dune deposition. These cracks carry downward into the underlying silt. The occupation at this site occurred during the deposition of the sand and before the formation of the desiccation cracks. Because the site is situated near the eastern edge of the dunes, it may have been occupied near the end of the period of dune deposition, assuming an easterly movement of the dunes.

The top of the sand, although extensively deflated, still shows traces of a red-brown soil, and the dune stratification has been destroyed in the upper part of the unit.

In the area north and east of Sites E71K9X and E71K9, where the dune sand surface is slightly lower than at both these sites, thin patches of dark gray, silty sand could be observed. This silty sand contained numerous fresh shells of *Lanistes carinatus* and rolled *Cleopatra bulimoides*. In a small depression formed between the dune at Site E71K10 and the low footslopes of the gravel hills is a more extensive but thin layer of silty sand that contained numerous rolled *Cleopatra bulimoides* and small pieces of charcoal. At the time this locality was studied, the silty sand units were believed to be equivalent to the upper silt units recorded from the other areas at Isna. The radiocarbon date on the charcoal is 8450 BC ±470 years (I-3428), and the shell dated 7380 BC ±160 years (I-3422). If correct, these dates exclude a correlation with the upper silt units and suggest either a later episode of a high Nile level (possibly the Arkin aggradation) or that the sandy silt represented a later swamp deposit. This question cannot be resolved without additional field work.

Site E71K9 yielded numerous mammal remains. The most common was hartebeest, followed by *Bos primigenius.* There were also a *Gazella rufifrons,* several possible *Lepus capensis,* and a *Hyaena hyaena.* Fish remains were very scarce, and all were assigned to *Clarias* sp.

Site E71K10 yielded only three bones from the surface. Two of them were hartebeest and the third a *Bos primigenius.*

In summary, the events at No. 4 Village were as follows:

1. Deposition of an old silt unit with desiccation cracks at Site E71K9X.
2. Erosion of the old silt unit.
3. Formation of thin pond sediments in the eroded depressions.
4. Deposition of aeolean sand accompanied by high Nile levels; occupation at Site E71K9.
5. Desiccation and cracking of wet dune sand and underlying lower silt unit.
6. Presumed formation of soil over the dunes.
7. Deposition of silty sands containing swamp and river shells.

Miscellaneous Sites in the Reclamation Area

Several isolated sites were recorded in three widely separated, undestroyed sections within the limits of the general Isna reclamation project area. Three sites (E71K19, E71K20, and E71K21) are located between 1 km and 2 km southwest of the monastery at Deir El-Fakhuri on flat sandy areas at elevations about 87 m above sea level.

E71K19

This is a widely scattered site that appears to be deflated on the surface of an aeolean sand. All of the artifacts were badly eolized, and the site has not been collected. A preliminary inspection of the tools suggests that this site belongs to the same industry as that represented at Sites E17K14 and E71K15.

E71K20 and E71K21

Both of these sites are situated in the far southwest corner of the reclamation area, and both are on the exposed surface of an aeolean sand. Of the two, only E71K20 has been collected. It appeared to comprise two distinct, dense concentrations. Area A was an irregular elongated oval 27 m by 8.5 m. Area B was located about 6 m to the south; it was roughly circular in outline and measured 21 m by 16 m. Near the northern edge of this concentration were numerous firecracked rocks, possibly indicating a deflated hearth. A few artifacts had canker adhering to their surfaces, and a few others appeared to be fresh; however, most of the material was eolized. Several test pits were dug in the vicinity of the fresh artifacts in both concentrations, but no trace of a cultural layer was found.

To the northeast of the concentrations, just beyond the edge of concentration A, a contact between the underlying dune sand and an overlying upper silt was preserved. When first observed, a series of burned areas were noted on the surface of the dune sand near the contact with the silt; however, subsequent grading of a trail in this area removed all traces of the burned areas before they could be mapped. A trench 3 m long and 2 m wide was dug in this area after the grading of the trail, but no traces of occupation were noted. These burned areas were possibly connected with the occupation of Area A; however, no artifacts were recovered from them.

The surface collections from Site E71K20 were closely similar to material from Gebel Silsila, Site 2B, Area II(B) at Kom Ombo (Phillips and Butzer, in press). This site yielded radiocarbon dates of 13,360 BC ±200 years (Y-1376) on charcoal (Reed 1965) and 12,440 BC ±200 years (I-5180) on *Unio* shell (Phillips and Butzer, in press). The last date, considered more accurate by Phillips and Butzer, may suggest the sand unit in this particular area was deposited before 13,000 BC.

Another group of five sites, recorded as Site E71K17, Areas A, B, and C, E71K16, and E71K15B, were located some 1.5–3.0 km north of the Deir El-Fakhuri Monastery and about 500–1000 m west of Site E71K18 in prominent dune sand areas. In all cases the cultural materials were widely scattered, and all were heavily windworn. These sites have not been collected, but preliminary inspection suggest that they also belong to the same industry as that represented at Sites E71K14 and E71K15. This Isnan industry was clearly the most common in this area; it was represented at more than 14 localities, most of which were dense and covered very large areas.

General Reconstruction of the Fossil Landscape in the Isna Area

The sequence in this area began during the aggradation of the older silts when a large dune field, approximately 10 km long and less than 1 km wide, developed along the west bank of the Nile floodplain. This dune field was bordered on the east by the Nile silt plain and on the west by the rapidly rising footslopes of the gravel hills that extend westward to front the Eocene escarpment (Figure 49). The older silts are still exposed on the surface for an extensive area about 2 km wide on the west bank at Isna. The top of these older silts is about 85 m above sea level, or 5 m above the modern Nile floodplain. A steep step terrace edge marks the eastern limit of these older silts and separates them from the modern floodplain.

The several radiocarbon dates of around 15,000–16,000 BC obtained on charcoal and shells associated with occupations near the end of this depositional period are comparable with those obtained from the top of the older silt in the El-Kilh area and strongly suggest that they belong to the same episode of aggradation.

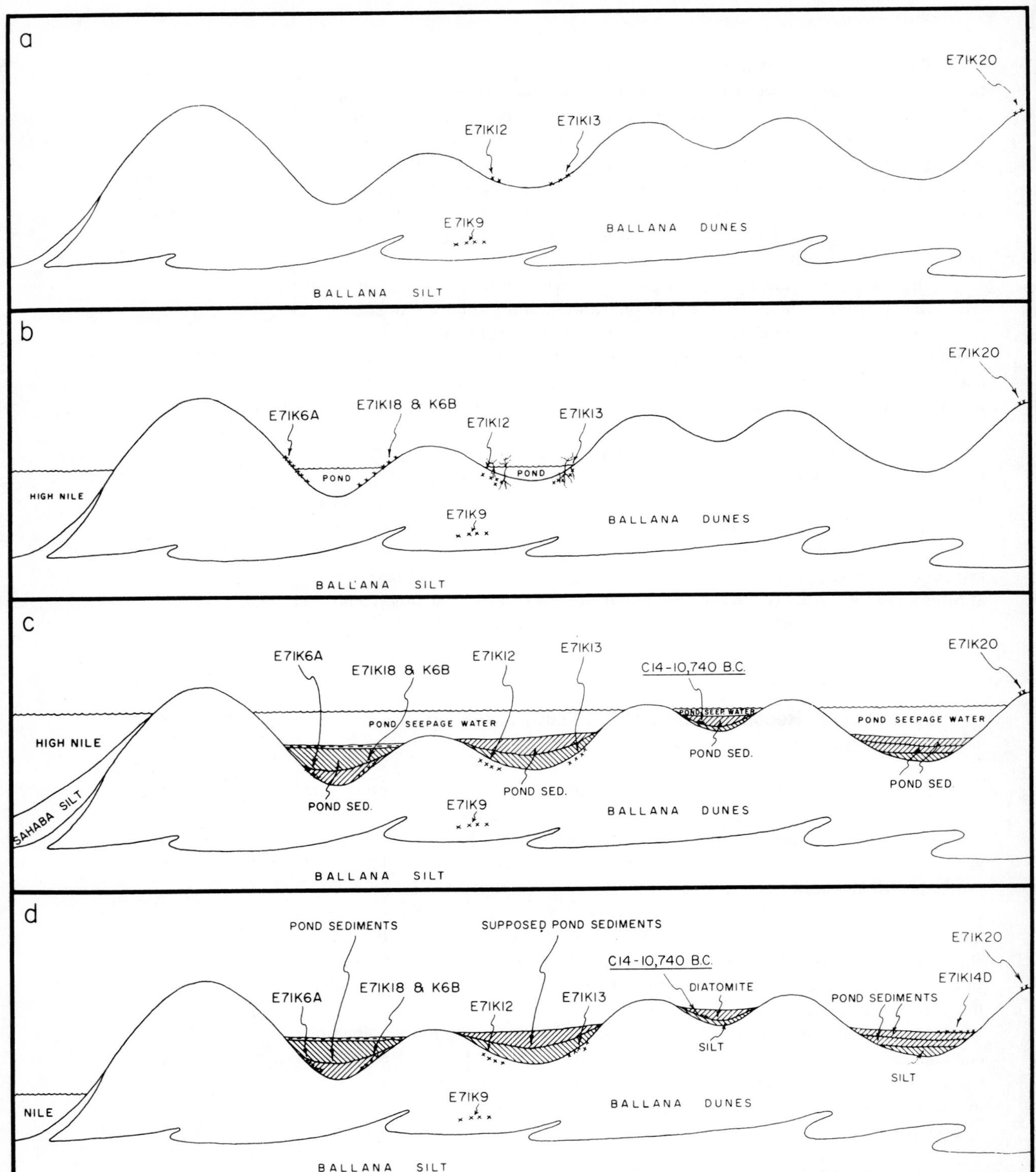

a
E71K20
E71K12
E71K13
E71K9
BALLANA DUNES
BALLANA SILT
b
E71K20
E71K6A
E71K18 & K6B
E71K12
E71K13
POND
POND
HIGH NILE
E71K9
BALLANA DUNES
BALLANA SILT
c
E71K6A
E71K18 & K6B
E71K12
E71K13
C14-10,740 B.C.
E71K20
POND SEEP WATER
POND SEEPAGE WATER
POND SEEPAGE WATER
HIGH NILE
POND SED.
POND SED.
POND SED.
POND SED.
SAHABA SILT
E71K9
BALLANA DUNES
BALLANA SILT
d
POND SEDIMENTS
SUPPOSED POND SEDIMENTS
E71K20
C14-10,740 B.C.
E71K14D
E71K6A
E71K18 & K6B
E71K12
E71K13
DIATOMITE
POND SEDIMENTS
SILT
SILT
NILE
E71K9
BALLANA DUNES
BALLANA SILT

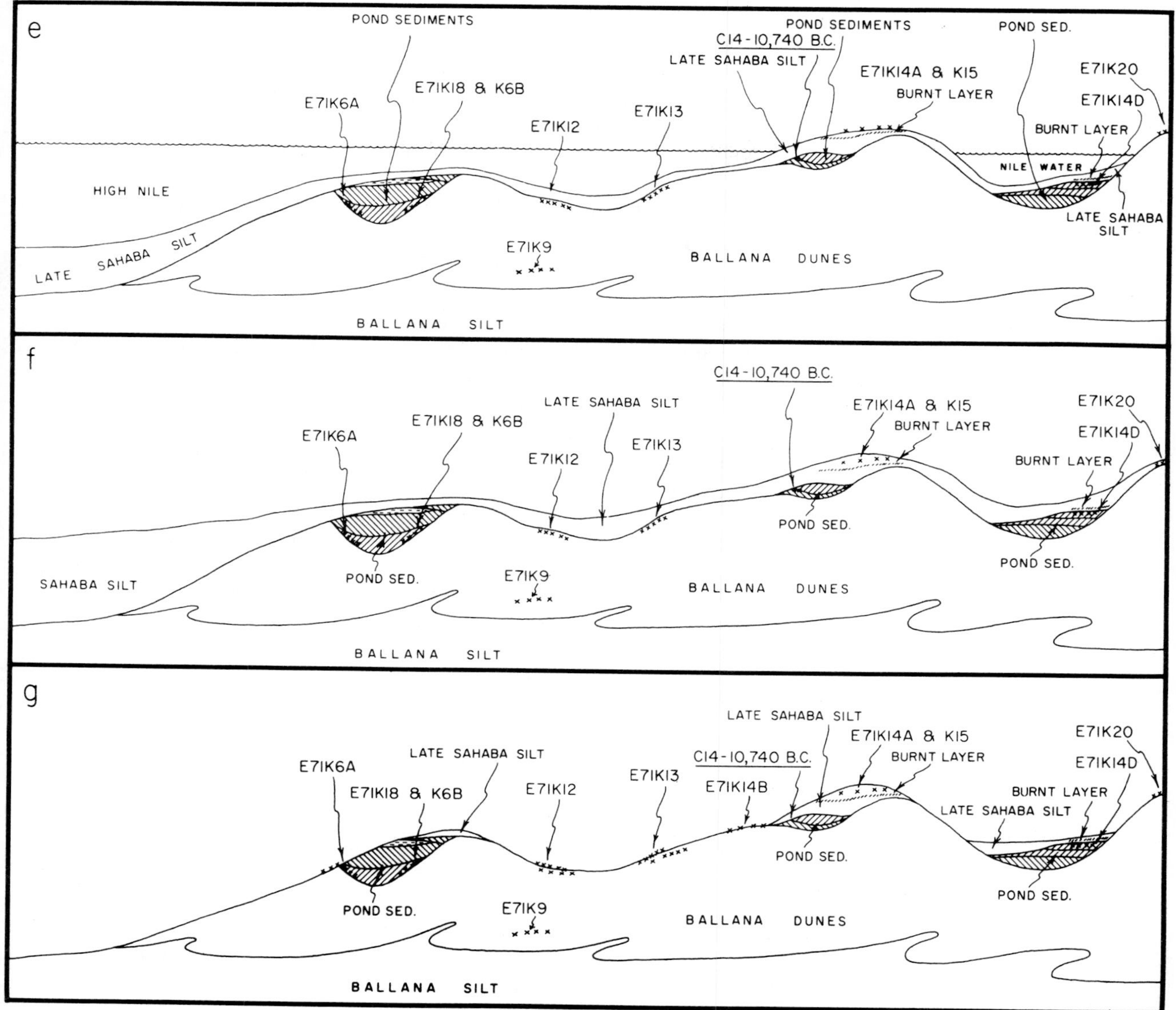

Figure 49. Idealized reconstruction of evolution of the landscape at Isna.

a. Landscape during interval of downcutting that followed the Ballana–Masmas aggradation (*ca.* 15,000–12,000 BC).

b. Initial ponding episode during early phase of Sahaba–Darau aggradation (*ca.* 12,000–11,200 BC).

c. Later Sahaba–Darau aggradation and related seep-ponding during seasonally high Nile levels (*ca.* 10,700 BC).

d. End of ponding episode during low Nile phase of Sahaba–Darau aggradation (*ca.* 10,600 BC).

e. Late Sahaba–Darau period, landscape eroded, primarily by Nile floods (post 10,500 BC).

f. Final Sahaba–Darau (*ca.* 10,000 BC).

g. Modern landscape eroded by wind action.

The oldest occupation noted from the Isna area is contemporaneous with the end of the period of simultaneous dune formation and silt accumulation. Most of these settlements were located at the eastern edge of the dune field where it abutted the floodplain. Many of the sites contained evidence of extensive fishing activity (especially E71K3).

There followed a period when the level of the Nile fell to an unknown elevation, the dunes were covered by vegetation, and possibly a soil developed whose Bc horizon in places achieved a thickness of more than one meter. During this presumably long episode the dunes were occasionally occupied (Sites E71K12 and E71K13), and the sites that are known from this period are not located at the edge of the dunes but farther back near the center. The limited faunal remains these sites prohibit an evaluation of their economic base.

The duration of this episode is unknown, but it was terminated by a gradual rise in the level of the Nile that caused the formation of numerous seepage ponds in the topographic lows in the sand field. Most of the ponds were situated in back of the high dune ridge that fronted the floodplain. They were bounded by a dune ridge on the east and the rapidly rising footslopes of the escarpment on the west. These ponds were probably ephemeral and shallow, as is shown by the diatom and pollen analyses. The adjacent dune shores were frequently occupied by groups that seem to have preferred nuclear family settlement units. Most of these occupations were for a considerable period, judging by the number of tools present (E71K18 and E71K6B); however, a few were of short duration (E71K6A).

During periods of unusually high floods, the ponds received small amounts of Nile water influx, and at one point a major intrusion of Nile floods occurred, possibly over a period of several years. This resulted in the deposition of the middle silt layer.

A slight reduction in the Nile flood level occurred again, but not to a level sufficient to end the seepage of water into the ponds, which again formed and continued to exist for some time. The adjacent shores of these ponds were occasionally occupied. There is evidence to indicate that grasses were gathered extensively at this time, suggesting that some of the occupations occurred during the summer, when some of the ponds were dry but the grass seeds would have been mature (Site E71K14D).

There followed a period when the level of the Nile rose gradually, permitting the floods to break through the dune barrier and spill water into the ponds; at its maximum it rose over the dunes to an elevation of 87.7 m above sea level, or almost 8 m above the modern floodplain. Near the end of this period of maximum Nile floods, a widespread brush fire swept over the dry vegetation that bordered the valley on both sides. Traces of this brush fire were noted at three localities near Isna (E71K22, E71K14A, and E71K14D), and downstream for a distance of 200 km. The single radiocarbon date obtained on carbonates from the base of the diatomaceous unit above the middle silt at Site E71K14A, around 10,700 BC, would suggest that the overlying upper silt unit is comparable with the end of an aggradational event known in Sudanese Nubia as the Sahaba, which elsewhere has been dated around 10,000 BC.

Following the aggradation represented by upper silts, the Nile declined again to an unknown level. A subsequent dated episode of higher Nile levels was recorded near Village No. 4. Here there accumulated a silty sand sediment containing rich molluscan fauna requiring some moving water, possibly of Nile origin. Two dates around 8000 BC are recorded for this area.

Presumably the present topography of scattered hillocks, flattish sand areas, and extensive silt plain resulted from several factors: first, water erosion of the dune ridge during the maximal phase of the upper silt aggradation; second, the subsequent deflation of the softer sediments following the recession from the upper silt maximum; and third, the leveling activities conducted during the modern reclamation program.

Geology of the Dandara Area

BAHAY ISSAWI

Dandara is located on the Nile bank 8 km west of Qena. In the vicinity of Dandara, the Nile flows in an east–west direction, a unique trend in the river's course. Past Dandara, the river runs for a short distance, 4 km, from north to south; it then resumes its east–west trend till Nag Hammadi where it again turns north.

The floodplain in the Dandara area is triangular in shape with the apex located just west of Dandara and the base located 3 km to the south and extending 8 km in an east–west direction. On both sides of the base of the triangle, the floodplain abuts the river to the north and the desert edge to the south. On the opposite side of the river the edge of the desert continues immediately adjacent to the Nile, for a distance of 11 km before another patch of irrigated floodplain occurs to mark the western and southern side of the Nile.

Southward the floodplain terminates in a piedmont surface that is very irregular in outline before the scarp is reached. The scarp here is a part of a major promontory that fills the Qena Bend. The promontory is a very intricate mass of limestone, highly irregular, with several embayments, indentations, spurs, and points. The highest part of this mass is 526 m above sea level and rises about 400 m above the floodplain. The Limestone Promontory is highly dissected by wadis that generally run in a north–south direction along the face of the promontory, crossing the piedmont surface before fanning out near the floodplain. The wadis are mostly dry; they never contain any water except during cloudbursts, which are rare.

The piedmont slopes northward to the Nile and is covered with limestone gravels that increase in size near the scarp. The piedmont is dissected by the wadis into subparallel ridges delineated north–south. The relief of the piedmont is low, ranging from 200 m above sea level near the scarp face to 100 m near the floodplain. The width of the piedmont surface varies from a few kilometers southeast of Dandara to 20 km at its southwestern extremity.

The bajada surface is very thin, ±1 km, indicating a youthful physiography, since the zone of planation is much wider than the zone of deposition. The bajada surface is covered by a thin veneer of loose gravels overlying a relatively thick section of proto-Nile silt.

The oldest exposed rocks in the area crop out at the base of the Limestone Promontory and belong to the Esna Shale (Said 1962 and Faris 1947). The thickness of this unit is 40 m. It is formed mainly of gray, paper-like shales, including marl bands that increase in thickness and number toward the top. Overlying this unit rests, conformably, a massive limestone section with flint bands. It measures about 350 m in thickness and is part of the Thebes Formation. Both units are highly fossiliferous, indicating their age as Lower Eocene. The lower beds of the Esna Shale may belong to the Upper Paleocene.

On the western side of the promontory, Faris (1947) records older units below the Esna Shale. He describes a chalk section 8 m thick and a lower section of Dakhla Shale 40 m in thickness. Both these units belong to the Paleocene.

Quaternary deposits include Nile sediments, wadi deposits, gravel sheets, and deflated sands. These cover the bedrock along the piedmont surface and, with the exception of the Nile sediments, the face and top of the Limestone Promontory.

Structurally the area dips gently to the northwest—3° on the average. Recently El-Hinnawi and El-Deftar (1970) mapped several small faults at the scarp face trending northeast to north–south and southwest. A major fault at the western side of the Limestone Promontory trending north–northeast was also recorded. Most probably this fault crosses the Nile east of Dandara and runs along Wadi Qena in the Eastern Desert.

Survey of the West Bank from the Valley of the Kings to Gebel El-Duqm

In mid-January 1968 a three-day survey was conducted along the west bank of the Nile from just north of the Valley of the Kings to the north end of Gebel El-Duqm, a distance of 60 km (Figure 50). Five localities were recorded, and three samples for radiocarbon dating were collected. The amount of time spent in the area permits only preliminary observation on the cultural and stratigraphic sequence; however, several of the sites record traces of archaeological materials that are earlier than those recovered elsewhere.

Site E6101 is located 7 km southeast of Dandara on a low knoll standing 8 m above the floodplain near the western edge of the cultivation. A quarry pit in the top of the knoll exposed a section about 3 m thick (Figure 51). At the base is a unit of light brown, soft, calcified, fine sand or coarse silt with moderate prismatic structure and a few lenses of grit and small pebbles. Plant casts were observed. This unit is more than 2 m thick (base unexposed). Near the bottom of the exposed section is a single core *in situ*. These sandy silts seem to be equivalent to the old silts noted across the river and named the Dandara Formation.

Unconformably overlying the basal silt is a layer of pebble and gravels in a sandy matrix grading up to a pale brown clay or coarse silt with dispersed grit and pebbles. It shows a coarse, blocky and weak, fine, platy to crumbly structure. The unit is calcified, and carbonate nodules were observed. Eolized and slightly rolled Acheulean handaxes were recovered both from the erosional surface between this unit and the underlying silt, and throughout the pebble and gravel layer.

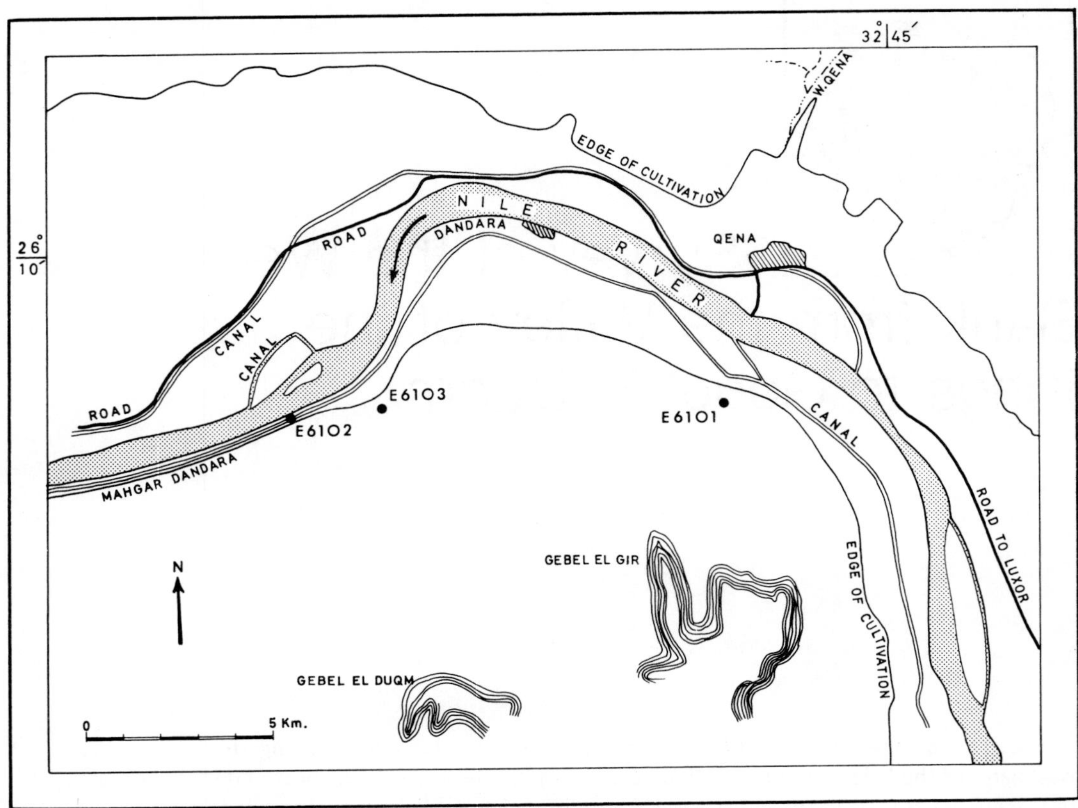

Figure 50. Map of Nile Valley at Qena Bend showing locations of sites recorded during West Bank survey near Dandara.

Above an obscure contact is a pale, brownish-yellow, pebbly, silty sand with coarse to moderate prismatic structure.

Numerous Acheulean handaxes, together with elongated, very large Levallois cores and a chipped stone celt, all made of Eocene flint, occurred on the surface and down the slope of the hill.

A second site (E6103) displaying similar old silts was found 6 km southwest of Dandara just beyond Wadi Ahu Subai. The site occurred where a large and prominent erosional remnant about 15 m high was preserved adjacent to the cultivation (Figure 52). A large quarry pit has been dug into the north face of the remnant. The bulk of the remnant is composed of two units of silt (Figure 53). The lower is a gray-colored, fine, sandy silt. Conformably overlying it is a brown silt with several layers of freshwater limestone near the top. A sample of the uppermost limestone yielded a radiocarbon date of more than 39,900 years BP (I-3424). About 2 m below the limestone layers was a burned area, which was collected for paleomagnetic dating. A thick, red soil is preserved on the eroded surface of the brown silt above the freshwater limestone layers. The two silt units are identified as the Dandara Formation.

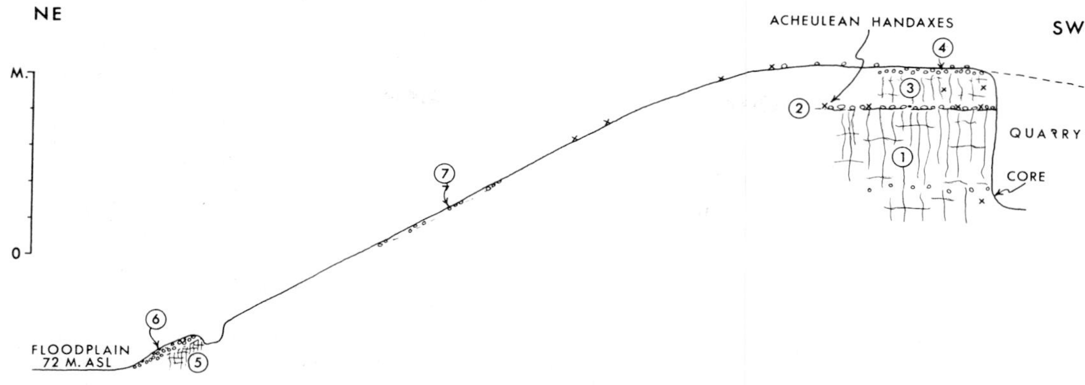

Figure 51. Schematic profile of Site E6101 (from field notes of C. Vance Haynes).

1. Light brown, very calcareous, fine sand and coarse silt with moderate or coarse prismatic structure and few dispersed grit and small pebbles. Lamination obscure. Becomes less calcareous and more clayey to southeast. Dandara Formation.
2. Pebbles and gravels in a sandy matrix with Acheulian artifacts in a layer unconformably overlying (1).
3. Pale brown, clayey, fine sand or coarse silt with dispersed grit and pebbles; angular blocky and fine platy to crumbly structure. Consolidated, soft; irregular carbonate nodules; calcareous; contains a few Acheulian artifacts.
4. Pale, yellowish-brown, pebbly, silty sand with moderate coarse prismatic structure and vesicular horizon beneath surface pebble layer.
5. Mottled red brown to pale olive, very calcareous, sandy, stony mudstone with carbonate veins and irregular nodules; strong, coarse blocky structure. Upper surface erosional. Contains root drip casts.
6. White, calcareous, clayey, pebble–cobble gravel cemented with calcium carbonate. Local chert, pebbles, and cobbles mostly angular to subangular. A few well-rounded quartz pebbles.
7. Pale, yellowish-green, firm, friable, pebbly sand and silt sand down the slope with dispersed pebbles and pebble lag on surface.

Banked against the east slope of the silt remnant is a 5 m thick unit of loose, pale yellow, coarse fluvial sand. Included within this unit was a thin layer of consolidated sand with arenaceous casts of shells of *Unio abyssinicus* and *Aspatharia caillaudi.* At the top of this sand unit is a red soil that may be correlative with the one noted at the top of the silt remnant. This fluvial sand is believed to be equivalent to the Qena sands across the river.

Both the silt and sand units are mantled by a thick veneer of locally derived gravels and cobbles in a sand matrix. Within these gravels, redeposited on the eastern slope of the remnant, was an extensive concentration of slightly rolled artifacts, including a high frequency of Levallois flakes and cores together with several bifacial foliated points, picks, cleavers, handaxes, and sidescrapers. The collection seems to be related to the Sangoan assemblages to the south.

The southernmost site recorded on the survey of this stretch is designated E71C2 (Figure 54). It is located on a broad sand plain near the village of Nag El-Zamami. The site consists of two main parts. The first comprised five separate, totally deflated, badly scattered concentrations (A–E) on the surface of an

Figure 52. Site E6103, looking southwest from edge of floodplain to remnant of Dandara Formation. Occupation here was at foot of hill, near where figure is standing.

extensive area of dune sand on which patches of silt are preserved (Figures 55 and 56). The second part was a single thin, widely dispersed concentration of artifacts on the surface of a silt and fluvial sand knoll located between the dune sand located between the dune sand and the cultivation. Except for a few small test pits, no trenches have been dug, and the stratigraphy is reconstructed on the basis of surface observations (Figure 57).

Toward the west, not far from the limestone escarpment of the Gebels, is a low bluff of old silts, possibly the Dandara Formation. Between the silt bluff and the first part of the site, the surface of the plain is mantled with gravel; however, in the vicinity of the first part of the site the area is swept clean of gravel, and few stones appear except where the artifacts occur. All of the artifacts rested on the deflated surface of a pale yellow, coarse, aeolean sand, except in one area where a small, rock-lined hearth was still partially *in situ* about 10 m outside of the concentration at Area E toward the river. Burned *Unio* shell from this hearth yielded date of 14,880 BC ±300 years (I-3427). Because the hearth was not directly associated with a concentration, the date may not apply to the assemblages occurring on the surface.

The surface concentrations may be contemporary with the postdune silt accumulation. The five surface concentrations in this part of the site were all an elongated oval in outline and between 20 m and 50 m in length, with the long axes generally parallel with the river. They occupied the tops of low knolls standing slightly above the surrounding plain. In the shallow swales between several of the concentrations were patches of silt up to 50 cm thick. Several test

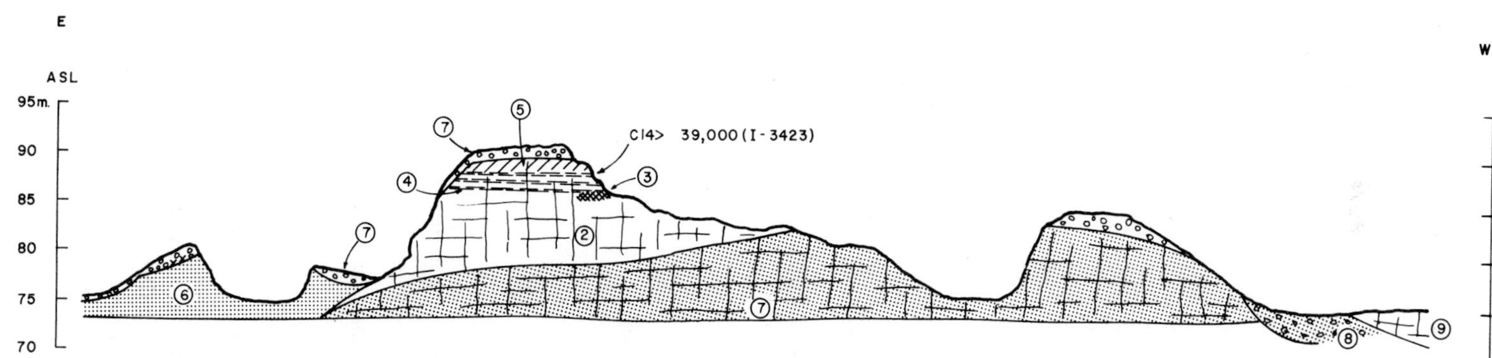

Figure 53. Schematic profile of Site E6103 (from field notes of C. Vance Haynes and Fekri Hassan).

1. Brownish, sandy silt with medium angular blocky and platy structure. Sterile; cemented; calcareous. Dandara Formation.
2. Brownish silt with blocky and platy structure, contains numerous calcium carbonate concretions. Dandara Formation.
3. Burned area.
4. Layers of fresh water limestone. The top layer gave a radiocarbon date of more than 39,900 BP (I-3423).
5. Deep red soil.
6. Coarse sand with bed containing *Asphataria* and *Unio* shells. Qena Formation.
7. Gravel, pebbles, and cobbles in a matrix of coarse sand containing slightly rolled artifacts of Sangoan–Lupemban appearance. Slopewash.
8. Coarse fluvial sand with metamorphic and igneous cobbles.
9. Young, cultivated Nile silt.

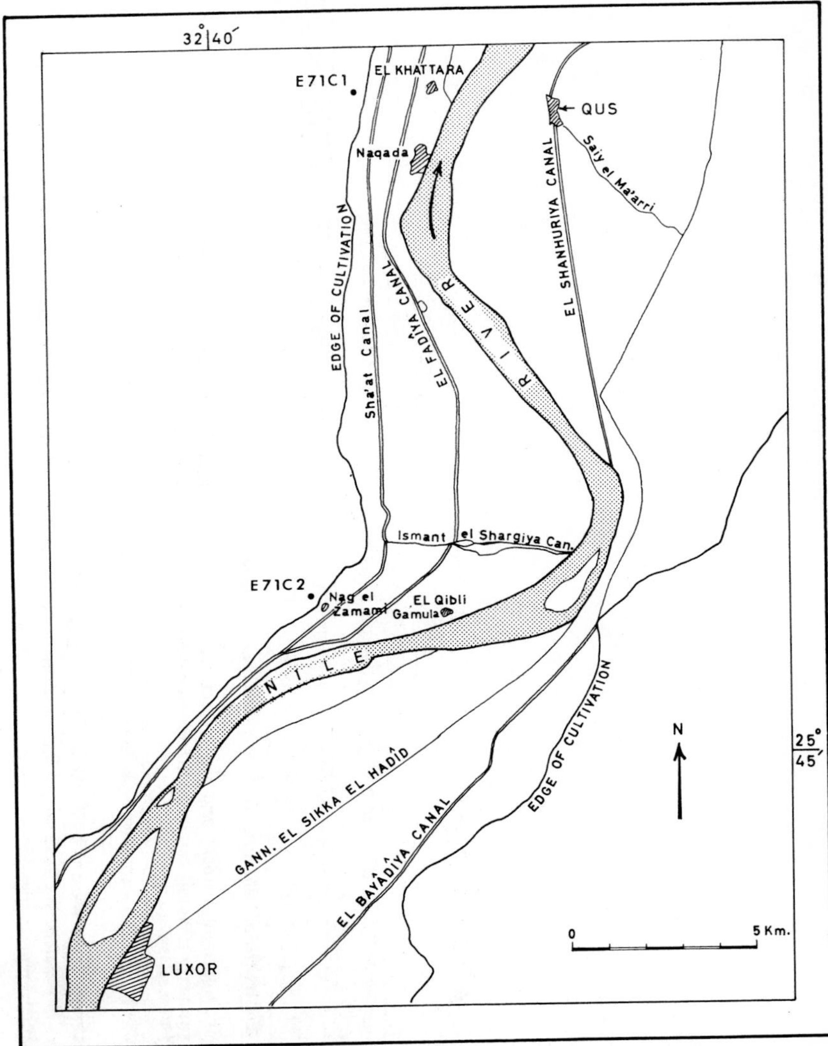

Figure 54. Map of area immediately north of Luxor showing locations of sites recorded. Site E71C1 is Predynastic.

pits were dug along the margins of these silt patches in an attempt to find *in situ* artifacts, but all were unsuccessful.

A more extensive area of silt, presumably equivalent to the patches preserved at the first part of the site, occurs some 330 m to the southeast between the aeolean sand plain and the cultivation. Here a silt knoll stands 5 m above the floodplain and just slightly lower than the level of the sand plain and separated from it by an eroded area. On the top of this knoll was a dispersed concentration of lithic artifacts (E71C2, Area F).

Figure 55. Site E71C2, looking northwest. Burned *Unio* from hearth in foreground yielded radiocarbon date of 14,880 BC ±300 years (I-3427).

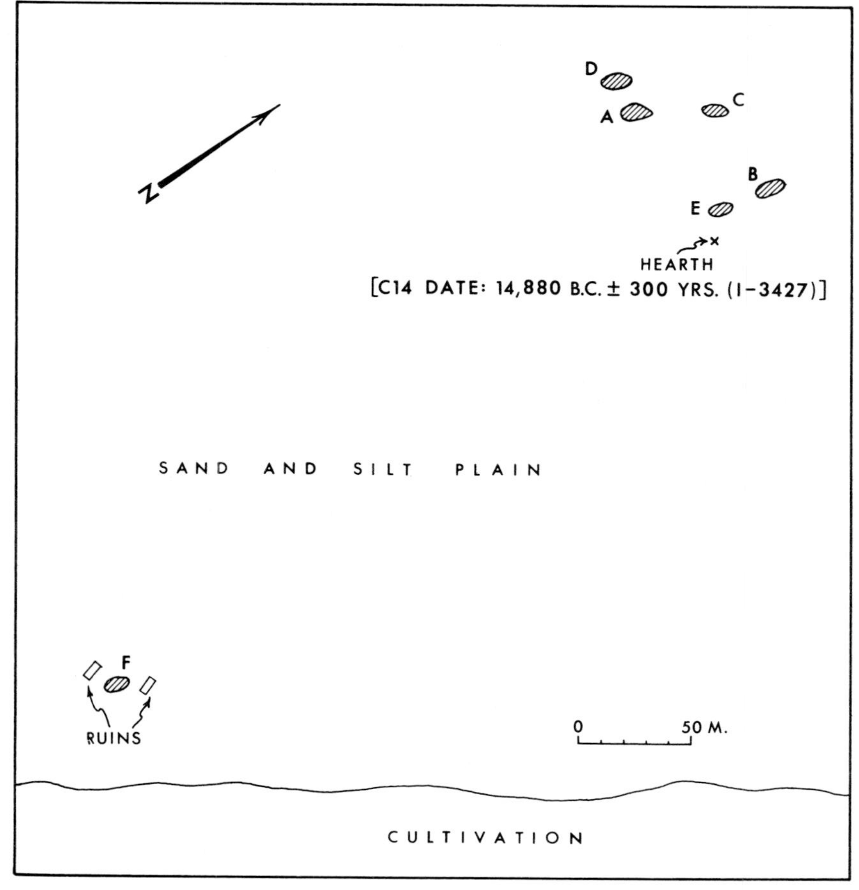

Figure 56. Map of Site E71C2 showing areas of concentration and location of dated hearth.

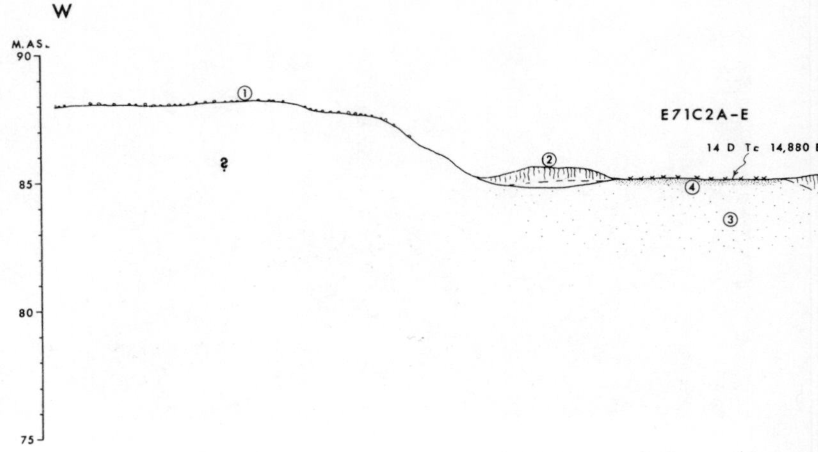

Figure 57. Schematic profile of Site E71C2 near Ez El-Zamami, Luxor.

1. Gravel and pebble lag.
2. Silt with angular blocky structure in patches over the dune.
3. Dune sand.
4. Reddish soil (?).
5. Sahaba silt with angular blocky structure; cemented; calcareous.
6. Silt of modern floodplain.

About 5 km south of site E6101, where the dirt trail crosses a wadi just above the area of cultivation, and across from the village of Kumbelat, the side erosion of the wadi has exposed a series of exposures that permit a reconstruction of the stratigraphic sequence in this area (Figure 58). The oldest exposed unit is a pale brown, silty sand about 3 m thick (base unexposed), on the top of which is developed a thick, red soil truncated by an erosional surface. This unit appears to be the Dandara Formation. On the eroded surface of the pale brown silt is a thin layer of pebbles and gravels. Overlying these, in turn, is a very light gray, consolidated, medium-grained sand, which appears to be of aeolean origin. The top of the sand unit is eroded. A brown, clayey silt with strong prismatic structure and calcium carbonate coating unconformably overlies the sand. The silt unit is about 1 m thick and at its maximum is 5 m above the floodplain. At the base of the silt is a burned layer up to 10 cm thick. The effects of the fire are evident on the underlying sand. The burned silt displayed casts of a thick mat of vegetation. A sample of carbonaceous sand from the sand and silt unit yielded a radiocarbon date of 10,550 BC ±230 years (I-3424). A second sample for paleomagnetic dating was collected from the exposed burned surface of this sand.

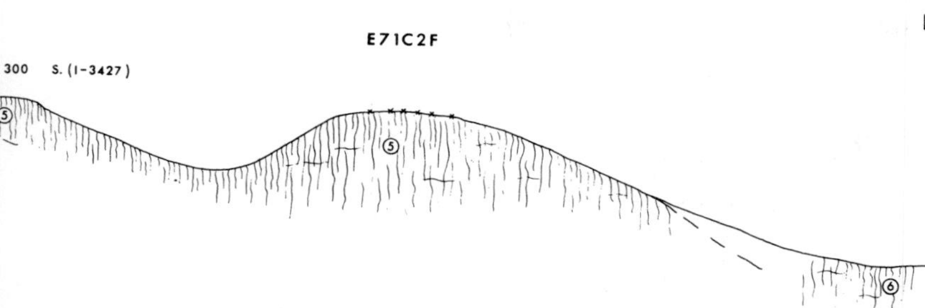

Above the silt is a veneer of pebbles and gravels in a fine sand matrix, possibly of wadi origin. Another phase of wadi activity was recorded down the section toward the river, where a small wadi channel fill occurs. It consists of unsorted gravels and pebbles in a coarse sand matrix.

The radiocarbon date and the general stratigraphic situation suggests a correlation of the upper silt unit with the final phase of the Sahaba Formation in Nubia and of the Darau member of the Gebel Silsila Formation in Kom Ombo. In this context the underlying dune sand should be considered to be the lithostratigraphic equivalent of the Ballana Formation in Sudanese Nubia.

Some 2.5 km west of Site E6103, the river has cut into the Mahgar Daridera Canal. Just 200 m beyond the breached area, in the side walls of the abandoned canal, a number of artifacts were collected from a deeply buried living surface cut by this canal (Figures 59 and 60).

At the base is a series of soft, friable, pale yellow fluvial sands with interbedded lenses of coarse gravels; the series is about 9 m thick (Figure 61). At the top of this fluvial unit is a weak orange paleosol with artifacts on its surface and within the soil. The contours of this buried soil suggest that the settlement was located on a small, low knoll, most of which was destroyed by the excavation of the canal. The occupation surface is buried beneath a unit of brown, clayey silt from 2 m to 3 m thick. The base of the silt alternates with layers of gravel and fluvial sand. The top of the silt is eroded and covered by a thick (up to 4 m) unit of soft, tan sand with interbedded layers of chert gravels.

The lower gravel and sand beds seem to record channel deposits that were subsequently exposed as a result of a major decline in the level of the river. On the exposed surface of these channel deposits, a thin, arid soil developed and a

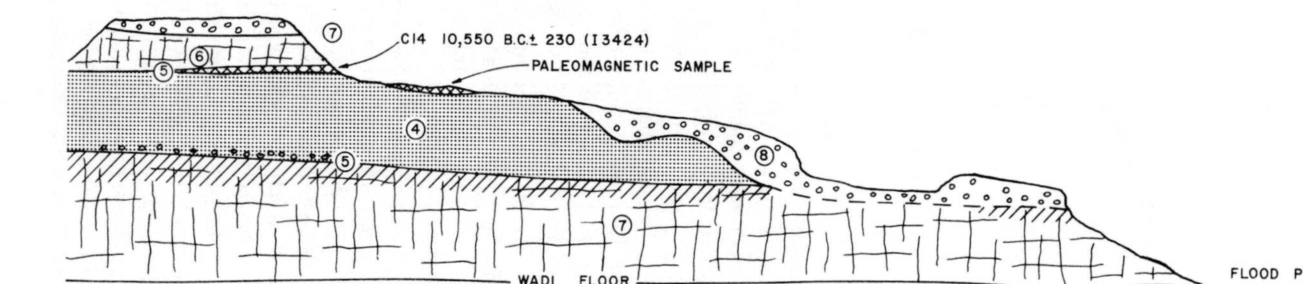

Figure 58. Schematic section of wadi across from Kumbelat (from field notes of C. Vance Haynes).

1. Pale brown, silty sand with medium angular blocky structure.
2. Deep red soil.
3. Pebbles and gravels on an erosional surface.
4. Very light gray, medium and coarse-grained sand; cemented. Ballana dune.
5. Burned red layer with radiocarbon date of 10,550 BC ±230 (I-3424).
6. Brown, clayey silt with medium prismatic structure and calcium carbonate coating. Sahaba silt.
7. Friable, silty, fine, angular pebble gravel interbedded with fluvial sand.

Figure 59. View of Mahgar Daridera Canal showing Site E6102. Traces of living surface exposed about halfway up the walls of the canal on both sides.

Figure 60. Site E6102. Figures are standing on living floor.

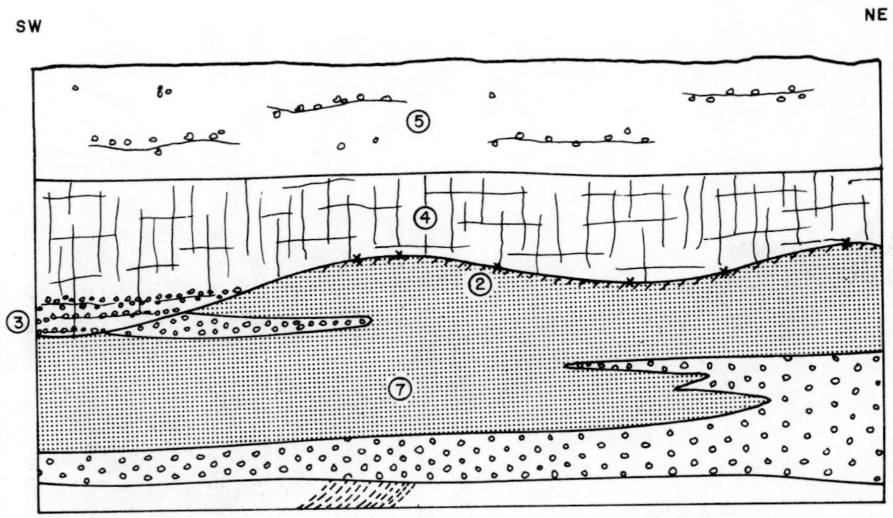

Figure 61. Profile of west face of Mahgar Daridera Canal at Site E6102 (from field notes of C. Vance Haynes).

1. Soft, friable, pale yellow sand with layers and lenses of coarse gravel.
2. Weak orange paleosol developed on an erosional surface. Late Paleolithic artifacts within the soil and on its surface. Truncated at southwestern end.
3. Stratified sand and gravel conformably (?) covered by (4).
4. Brown, clayey silt.
5. Tan, soft sand with layers of chert gravel.

settlement was located. Later this soil was partially eroded by the rising river and an adjacent minor channel and, finally, covered by floodplain sediment. Following the silt sedimentation the entire area was mantled by a thick cover of wadi and slopewash gravels.

A small collection of artifacts were recovered from the occupation surface by test quarrying along the exposed face of the canal. The collection is of early Late Paleolithic aspect but, unfortunately, not closely comparable with other known assemblages along the Nile. No charcoal or other datable material was recovered; however, the overlying silt appears to be comparable with the upper silts recorded elsewhere along this stretch of the river and equated with the Sahaba Formation.

Summary of Events in the Dandara Area

The following sequence of events is suggested by the stratigraphic observations recorded along the west bank of the river between Luxor and Dandara:

1. Deposition of two different units of old Nile silts, older than 40,000 BC and possibly contemporaneous with Middle or Late Acheulean.

2. Development of a thick, red soil at the top of the uppermost Dandara silt.

3. Deposition of another sedimentary unit, a massive bulk of coarse sands overlying the Dandara silts. There is no archaeology in direct association; however, a Sangoan-related industry was found above it in secondary position.

4. Sedimentation of the older gravels and fluvial sands in the channel at the base of the Mahgar Canal, possibly representing main channel facies of the Debeira–Jer or Ballana–Masmas aggradations.

5. On the basis of observations farther south in the Isna area, the final phase of what seems to be the same aggradation was accompanied by the deposition of extensive dune fields along the west bank of the river. The radiocarbon date of 14,880 BC (I-3427) at Site E6102 suggests general contemporaneity of this hearth with the final phase of this event or immediately afterward.

6. A major decline in the level of the Nile is recorded at the Magahar Canal section, where the top of the earlier channel sediments was exposed for settlement and development of the soil.

7. Another Nilotic aggradation occurs with the deposition of the Sahaba silts, remnants of which were observed at several places.

8. A burned layer, possibly near the end of this Sahaba event, is seen at Kumbelat and yielded a radiocarbon date around 10,500 BC.

9. A subsequent decline in the level of the Nile and the dissection of the landscape by wadis is undated.

Geology of the Dishna-Makhadma Area

BAHAY ISSAWI

Dishna is located on the Nile 30 km west of Qena, on the northern part of the Qena Bend, facing the Eastern Desert.

Near Dishna the Nile flows from east to west, a peculiar trend in the course of the river. However, 30 km west of Dishna it changes its course to the northwest, one of the main trends of the river.

At Dishna the floodplain of the river is confined mainly to the northern part of the valley; its average width is 7 km. A piedmont follows the floodplain northward to an immense cliff marking an extensive plateau farther north. The relief of the piedmont is low, ranging from 100 m near the cultivation edge to 200 m at the footslope of the northerly plateau. The piedmont has different widths, depending on the undulations in the plateau face. Opposite Makhadma, the piedmont stretches 20 km before reaching the plateau, while at Dishna, slightly to the northwest, a nearly vertical cliff rises over the cultivation edge.

The distinction of the piedmont in the Dishna area into pediment and bajada is difficult because of the concealed nature of the former. However, near the plateau, the equivalent of the pediment is densely covered by limestone gravels that decrease in size as one proceeds southward toward the Nile. Next to the cultivation, the bajada part of the piedmont is characterized by the presence of well-displayed yardangs cut in the relatively loose silt. The yardangs acquire different irregular shapes and rise several meters above the surrounding surface.

The plateau surface rises 300 m, on the average, above the floodplain. It stretches farther north and east and terminates suddenly overlooking Wadi Qena.

In sharp contrast with the uniform, flat-topped rock wall of the Limestone Plateau are the serrated and multicolored igneous and metamorphic peaks on the other side of Wadi Qena. Between these features lie broad plains out of which rise tabular outliers of brown sandstone.

The plateau surface is dissected by several major wadis that cut into the plateau for considerable distances—from 25 km at the wadis opposite Dishna to 85 km at Wadi Qasab and Wadi Abu Nafukh northwest of Dishna. The drainage pattern over the plateau is subparallel, and most of the wadis continue over the piedmont surface to the Nile. However, owing to the extensive cultivation of the floodplain, the channels of the wadis are not easily recognizable in the cultivable area. Over the piedmont surface the incision of the wadis is in the range of 6 m.

The area under consideration is among the least-known areas in Egypt. Outside the early work of Hume (1911, 1965), practically nothing has been published on the area.

The plateau surface and the scarp face north of the Nile at Dishna are formed of alternating thick- and thin-bedded limestone. The total thickness of the limestone sequence is about 225 m. The limestone is hard, interbedded with marl and cherty bands at the summit. Nummulitic bands and oyster banks of the multicostata type are common in the section. Nodular, hard limestone makes a distinct, precipitous cliff overlying soft, argillaceous, slope-forming limestone beds. Flint bands are common, increasing toward the top, while thin shale intercalations are seen near the base of the cliff. Pinkish ferrugineous bands are of minor importance. The limestone is crystalline in places, occasionally siliceous and rarely dolomitic. The sequence of limestone beds is weathered to an earthy grayish to brownish color, whereas on a fresh surface the limestone is mainly white.

Hume (1911, 1965), on paleontological grounds, considers this section to be of Lower Eocene age. He assigns the term *Serrai Limestone* to this sequence, which can be correlated with Said's Thebes Formation (1960).

Older units are exposed on the eastern side of the plateau surface along Wadi Qena. Here, Hume (1911), Said (1962), El-Akkad and Dardir (1966), and Issawi (ms.) describe a thick section of sediments belonging to the Cenomanian, Turonian, Campanian, Maestrichtian, Paleocene, and Lower Eocene.

Quaternary deposits, mainly silt, sand, and gravel sheets, cover the surface of the piedmont. These may assume different thicknesses, depending on the exhumed pre-Quaternary surface. Owing to the cut of the bajada by several wadis, a considerable thickness (6 m) of silt is exposed. Over the bajada surface an irregular yardangs, formed mainly of silt, assumes an average height of 4 m; hence, the thickness of the silt in the Dishna area may be in the range of 10 m.

The outcroppings of the old sediments in Wadi Qena may be interpreted as due to structural lines that control the trend of the geomorphic features in the area. Youssef (1968) reports on a major fault trending north-northeast–south-southwest along Wadi Qena, while El-Hinnawi and El-Deftar (1970) consider the northern part of the Nile bend at Qena as due to a major fault trending east-northeast–west-southwest. The latter fault crosses the Nile west of Dishna and continues on the Western Desert to bound the huge promontory of the western Limestone Plateau that protrudes to fill the western side of the Qena Bend. Whether there is a horizontal movement along this fault or not is not certain. Other minor faults, mostly parallel to the Wadi Qena Fault, have been noticed in the plateau surface opposite Dishna, while strike faults parallel to the scarp face are common.

Folds are of relatively less importance than faults. The folds are evident only on the plateau surface. They are shallow and of limited extension, and their trend is oblique to the strikes of the major faults—north-northwest–south-southwest and north-northeast–south-southwest. The flanks of the folds dip with an average angle of 4°, though higher angles, up to 30°, are known near fault lines.

Quaternary Geology and Archaeology of the Makhadma Area

Most of the survey undertaken by the Combined Prehistoric Expedition was along the west bank; however, in the area north of Luxor a short section of the east bank was also examined. This survey yielded sites in two localities. One of these was located downstream from Qena about 10 km, almost opposite the temple of Dandara and near the small modern community of El-Makhadma. The floodplain here is narrow, bounded by rolling, sandy hills capped with a thick cover of gravels, pebbles, and boulders, and standing from 20 m to 30 m above the Valley plain. Farther back from the river these rolling hills abut directly against the Eocene cliffs.

Between the Qena hills and the modern floodplain is a narrow belt of older Nile sediments partially covered by sheet wash gravels. Most of these older silt remnants have been destroyed through modern quarrying by the local population in search of salts.

E6104

Immediately northwest of the village of Makhadma, no more than 300 m distant from the edge of the community, a rounded hill projected into the floodplain (Figure 62). Numerous quarry pits had been dug here in the southern footslope of the hill. On examination of these quarry pits, numerous fresh artifacts were noted in the walls of the pits and spoil dumps nearby. Further search disclosed that except in the quarried areas there were few artifacts on the surface, and most of these were rolled.

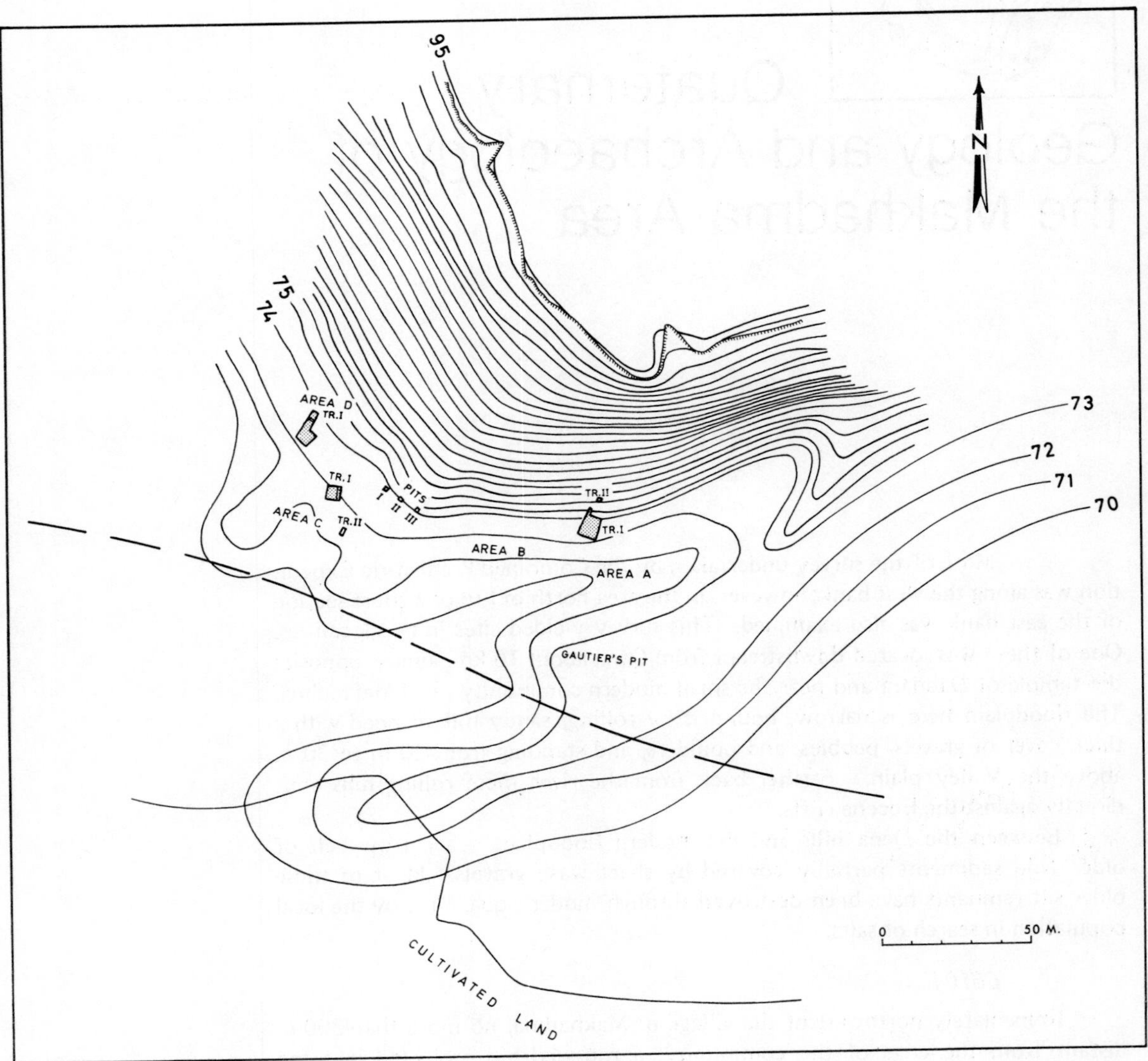

Figure 62. Map of Site E6104, near El-Makhadma.

The site was divided into four areas (A–D), roughly corresponding to the localities where the artifacts appeared to be most common. A series of trenches and pits were dug in all areas except B, which had been badly destroyed. These trenches disclosed a complex stratigraphy (Figures 63–65).

At the base is a dark, grayish-brown, high calcareous silt with coarse sand admixture. A pronounced disconformity separated it from the overlying sediments. The silt, tentatively identified as an equivalent of the oldest silts found near Dandara, is covered by a thick slopewash of sand, gravel, and boulders evidently derived from the top of the nearest sandy hill. The slopewash ranges in color from pale yellow to light yellowish-brown and might be divided into three stratigraphic zones, each grading imperceptibly into the next. The lower part, the thickest, contained moderate quantities of boulders together with abundant pebbles in the sand matrix. The boulders become significantly more numerous and larger (up to 40 cm in diameter) in the middle portion of the sediment. The upper part is loose, composed mostly of fine-grained sand with no boulders and only a few quartz pebbles. Traces of wavy stratification generally following the line of the slope were noted. A possible weak soil formation, indicated by numerous iron stains, may have developed in the uppermost part of the sediment.

Through the lower two zones of the slopewash were numerous badly rolled artifacts of Middle Paleolithic appearance. The uppermost 30 cm of the unit, however, contained a very fresh early Late Paleolithic assemblage confined to a restricted area in the eastern part of the site (Areas C and D).

Above the slopewash is a massive, brown, highly calcareous and firmly salt-cemented silt. This silt has been essentially destroyed by recent quarrying in the lower part of the footslope; however, a few patches remained higher up the slope. At the east end of the site, these silt remnants were even more extensive, but the highest part of the slopewash was not present. The silt rested directly on a slopewash sediment composed almost entirely of boulders with numerous Middle Paleolithic artifacts.

The upper silt reaches a maximum thickness of 40 cm and contains a thick, burned layer composed of lumps of burned silt in an ash matrix. This burned layer could be traced both up and down the valley for several kilometers wherever patches of the upper silt were preserved. It presumably recorded a widespread brushfire.

Immediately above the burned layer was a poorly defined occupation horizon. At the uppermost edge of this silt, charcoal was collected, presumably connected with this occupation; but the exact relation of the charcoal with the burned layer could not be established. It yielded a radiocarbon date of 11,430 BC ±770 years (I-3440).

Some 40 m downslope, in a quarry pit, the upper silt is covered by coarse, poorly sorted fluviatile sand with numerous bands of Nilotic mollusks (*Valvata nilotica*, *Gyraulus costulatus*, *Bulinus truncatus*, and *Corbicula vara*). This fluvial sand and its associated fauna possibly represent part of a sand bar or a levee away from the main channel.

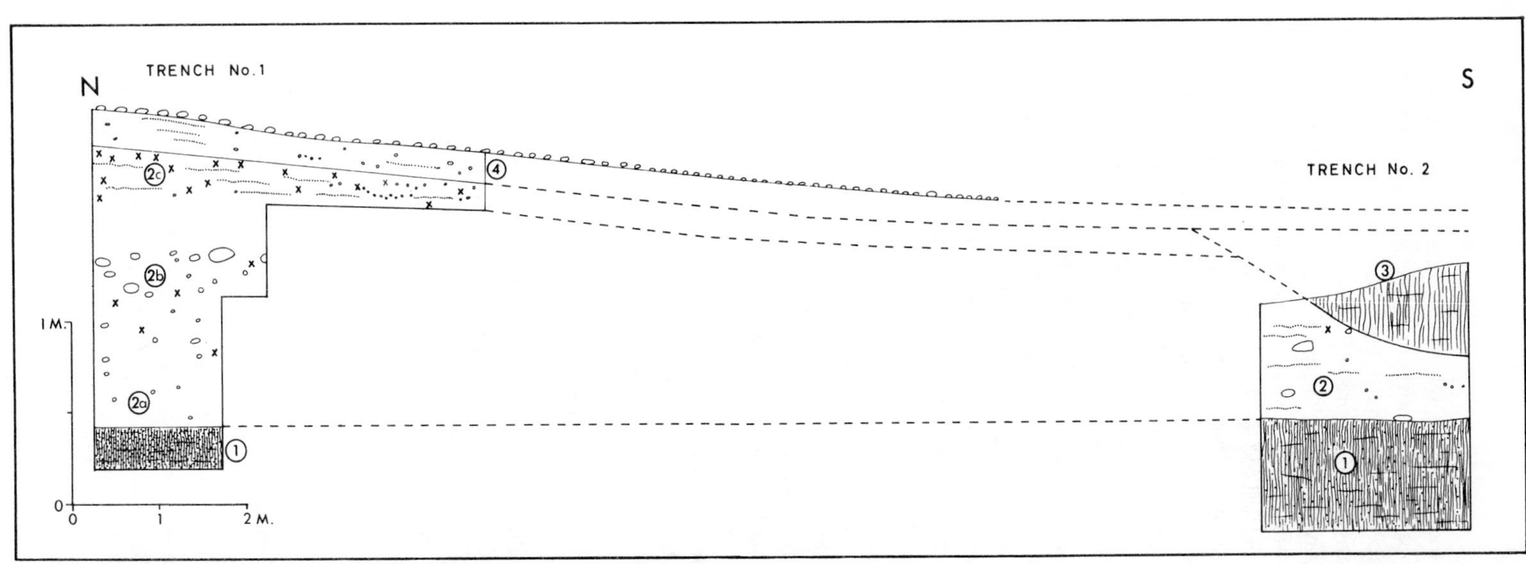

Figure 63. Profiles of Trenches 1 and 2, Site E6104, Area C.

1. Dark, grayish-brown (10YR 4/2), sandy silt with high admixture of coarse quartz sand; unstratified, cemented; coarse, inconspicuous blocky structure; highly calcareous. Surface almost horizontal, clearly erosional. Sterile. Possible Dandara sandy silt.

2. Brown (10YR 5/3), unsorted sand; stratified in places; dips conformable to the slope. Contains numerous pebbles and cobbles, rounded to subrounded. The amount of pebbles and cobbles, considerable at the base (2a), increases toward the middle part of the unit (2b) and decreases gradually higher up. Near the top the sediment contains only rare gravels (2c). Rolled Middle Paleolithic artifacts throughout 2a and 2b with clear concentration in the middle part of the unit. Early Late Paleolithic cultural layer at the top of this unit within the finest part of the sediment. Slightly consolidated to cemented near the bottom; highly calcareous. Slopewash.

3. Brown (10YR 5/3) silt, unstratified with medium, angular blocky structure, partially destroyed by quarrying activities. Cemented, highly calcareous. Disconformable with (2). Sterile. Possible Sahaba silt.

4. Light, yellowish-brown (10YR 6/4), unsorted sand with pebbles and gravels of local derivation; traces of stratification in places conformable to the slope. Loose, single-grain structure; contained very rolled Middle and Late Paleolithic artifacts. Disconformably overlies (2) and (3); highly calcareous. Surface paved with small pebbles and gravels. Upper slopewash.

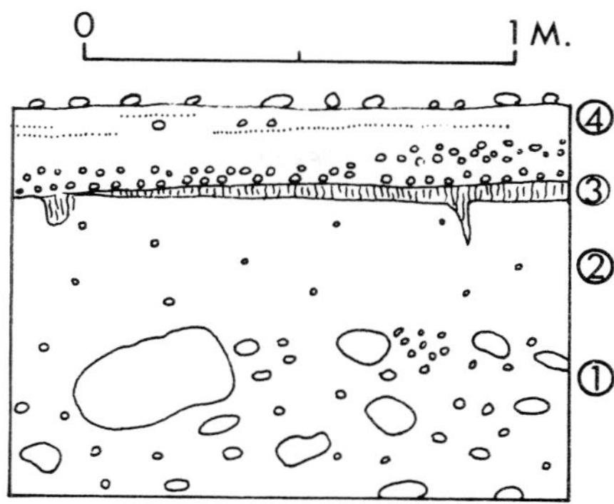

Figure 64. Profile of Pit 2, Site E6104, Area C.

1. Light, yellowish-brown (10YR 6/4) to pale yellow (2.5Y 8/4), unsorted, fine to medium-grained sand with gravel, pebbles, cobbles, and occasional boulders; cemented; calcareous; contains numerous rolled Middle Paleolithic artifacts. Lower slopewash.
2. Light, yellowish-brown (10YR 6/4) to pale yellow (2.5Y 8/4), unsorted, fine to coarse-grained sand with rare pebbles and fresh artifacts of early Late Paleolithic age. Generally unstratified; calcareous; consolidated. Upper part of the lower slopewash.
3. Yellowish-brown (10YR 5/4), sandy silt with small quartz gravels; loose; calcareous. Sahaba silt, possibly slightly redeposited.
4. Light, yellowish-brown (10YR 6/4), unsorted fine to coarse-grained sand with gravels and small pebbles concentrated mainly at the base. Upper part contains less gravel and pebbles and shows traces of stratification conformable to the slope. Loose, calcareous. Surface paved with gravel and pebbles. Contained rolled artifacts.

The entire site area is mantled by a thin veneer of loose, light, yellowish-brown, high calcareous sheet wash composed of very fine sand with small quartz gravels and pebbles. The sheet wash is stratified in places and contained rare heavily rolled artifacts.

Associated with the early Late Paleolithic occupation near the top of the slopewash in Trench 1, Area C were several fragments of a molar, probably hartebeest. No other faunal remains were found.

The upper silt in Trench 1, Area A, yielded a small series of mollusks of the following species: *Valvata nilotica*, *Gyraulus costulatus*, *Bulinus truncatus*, and *Gabiella senaariensis*.

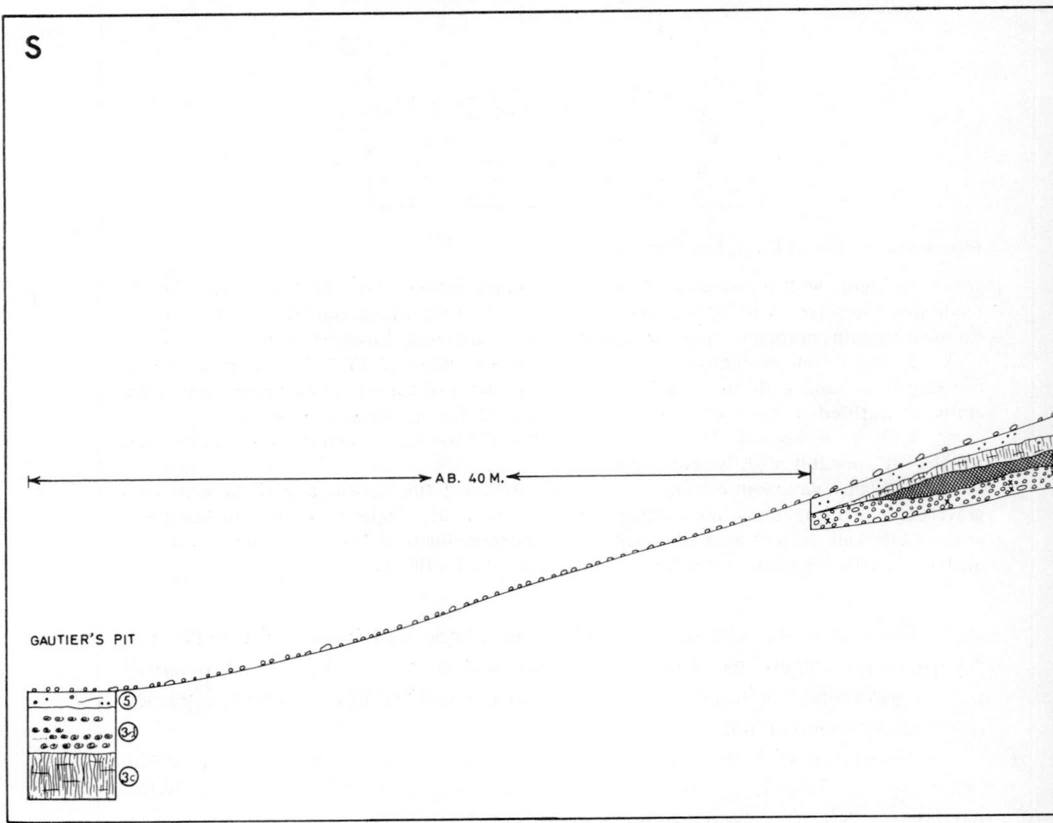

Figure 65. Profile of Trenches 1 and 2 and Gautier's Pit, Site E6104, Area A.

1. Light, brownish-gray (2.5Y 6/2) to yellowish-brown (10YR 6/4) or yellow (10YR 7/6), unsorted sand with numerous gravels, pebbles, and cobbles subrounded to rounded, of local derivation, and heavily rolled Middle Paleolithic artifacts. Loose to consolidated; unstratified; calcareous. Lower slopewash.

2. Lumps of baked silt mixed with loose ash. Probably washed, burned layer.

3. (a) Very dark, grayish-brown (10YR 3/2), slightly sandy silt, loose, unstratified but with thin laminae of very small lumps of baked silt. Contained relatively rare Late Paleolithic artifacts slightly silt polished. Calcareous. (b) Very dark, grayish-brown (10YR 3/2), sandy silt, very loose, powdered; contains concentration of white calcium carbonate. Culturally sterile; calcareous, unstratified. Charcoal sample collected from the thin wedge of silt containing small lumps of baked silt at Trench 2 gave a date of 11,430 BC ±770 years (I-3440). (c) Brown (10YR 5/3), sandy silt, unstratified, with medium angular blocky structure; calcareous. (d) Grayish, stratified, poorly sorted fluviatile sand with heavy mineral and mica concentration. Contains numerous bands of Nilotic mollusks (*Valvata nilotica, Gyraulus*

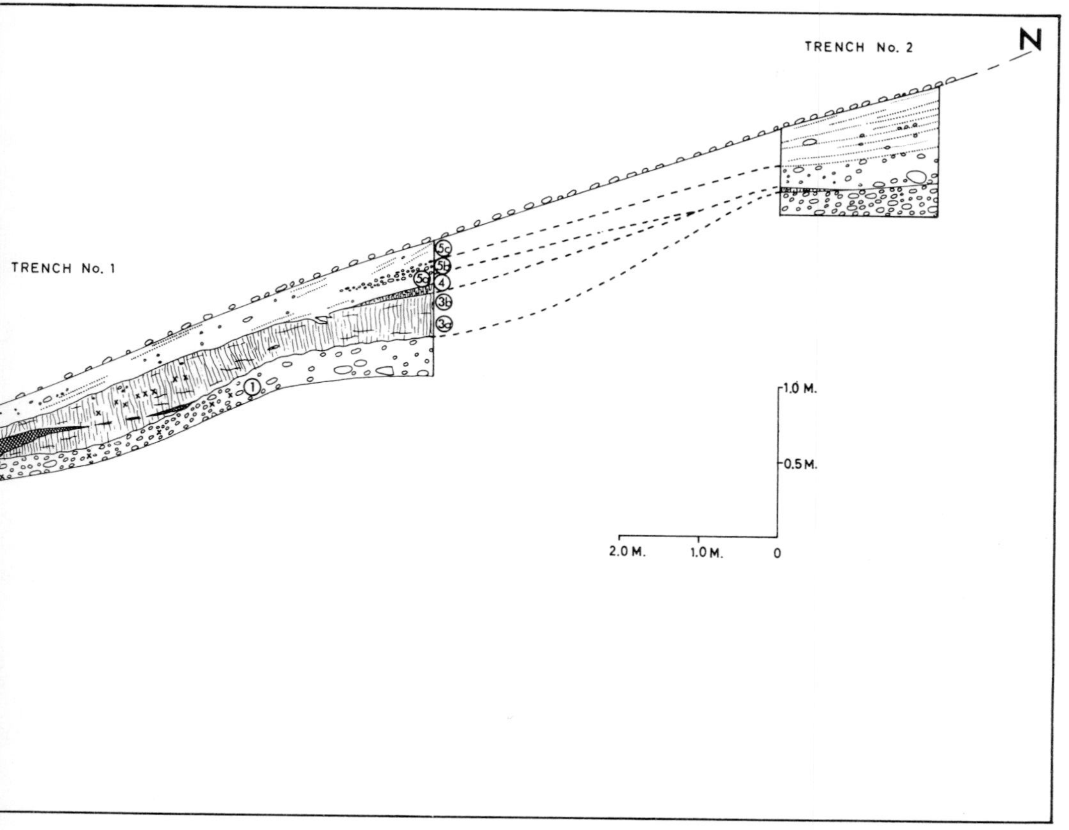

costulatus, *Bulinus truncatus*, *Corbicula vara*). Disconformable with (3c). Loose, calcareous, culturally sterile. Possible Sahaba.

4. Light, yellowish-brown to very pale brown (10YR 7/3–6/3), silty sand, unstratified; loose, contains well-rolled quartz pebbles; calcareous, sterile. Lower part of the upper slopewash.

5. (a) Very pale brown (10YR 7/4), unsorted, fine to coarse-grained sand; unstratified; loose; contains rare well-rolled gravels and pebbles; calcareous. A few rolled artifacts within this unit. Lower part of the upper slopewash. (b) Lense of gravel, pebbles, and occasional cobbles in a matrix of coarse sand. Loose, calcareous, unsorted and unstratified; a few rolled artifacts within the unit. (c) Very pale brown (10YR 7/4), unsorted sand with traces of stratification conformable to the slope inclination in upper part and up the slope. Contains gravel, pebbles, and occasional cobbles; calcareous; loose. A few well-rolled artifacts within the unit. Upper slopewash.

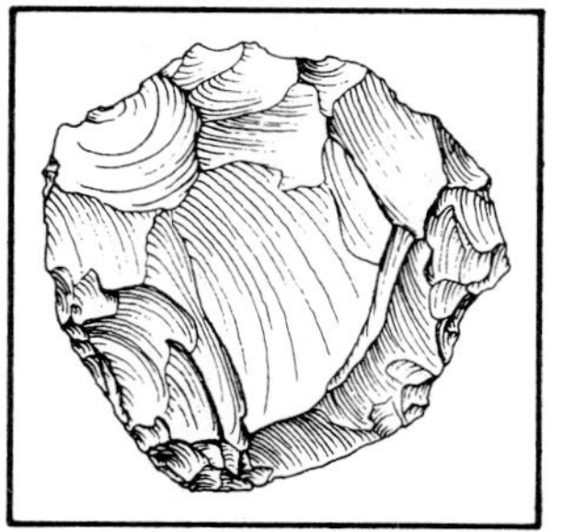

Pleistocene Stratigraphy and Archaeology of the Dishna Area

Introduction

The second area on the east bank where prehistoric sites were recorded is near the point where the Nile discontinues the westward direction of the Qena Bend and resumes its generally northward trend (Figure 66). Here there is a prominent gebel (El-Tarif) with near-vertical cliffs of Thebes Limestone that projects into the Valley to abut directly against the river, leaving no floodplain. Just east of this, near the town of Dishna, is a broad reentrant where a relatively thick section of Nile silts and playa deposits is preserved. At the western edge of this reentrant are numerous Late Paleolithic sites exposed as a result of erosion and dissection of the older silts by modern wadi activity and deflation (Figure 67). The silt remnants stand as a series of low yardangs fringing the cultivation. Several of the yardangs are capped by crusted, fine-grained playa sediments, and between them are modern wadi channels partially filled with sand and gravels (Figure 68).

Behind the yardangs, toward the Eocene cliffs, the ground rises gradually to the foot of the cliffs. These higher slopes consist of older wadi sediments covered by patches of playa and a more recent loess-like wadi wash. Along the northwestern edge of the yardangs, the older wadi sediments and the silts interfinger in a complex relationship that will be discussed in detail in subsequent sections.

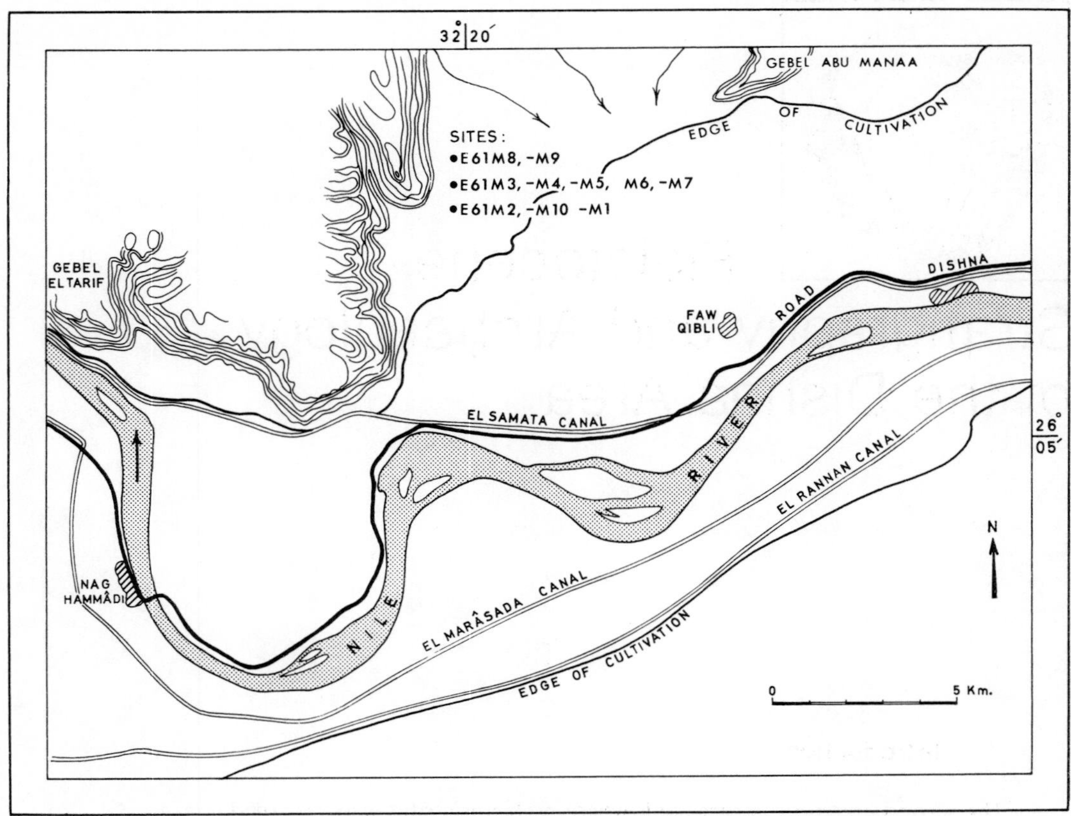

Figure 66. Map of Dishna area showing locations of sites studied.

Older Units

Although no effort was made to study the older units in this area in detail, several sections were observed east of the main concentration of sites, between Wadi Qena and an unnamed small wadi west of Abu Manaa. The oldest exposed unit of fluviatile sediments forms low benches (8–15 m above the modern floodplain). This sediment is better represented along the west bank between Dandara and El-Marashda. It is a gray, poorly sorted, compact and massive silty sand with occasional gravel bands (of Eocene and Precambrian derivation) and lenses of coarse sand. It has been named the Dandara Formation (Said *et al.* 1970). The Dandara silt is usually unconformably overlain by a thick (*ca.* 1 m) bed of gravel and cobble rubble that has a reddish sand matrix. These gravels are derived from the Precambrian exposures to the east and are indistinguishable from the recent

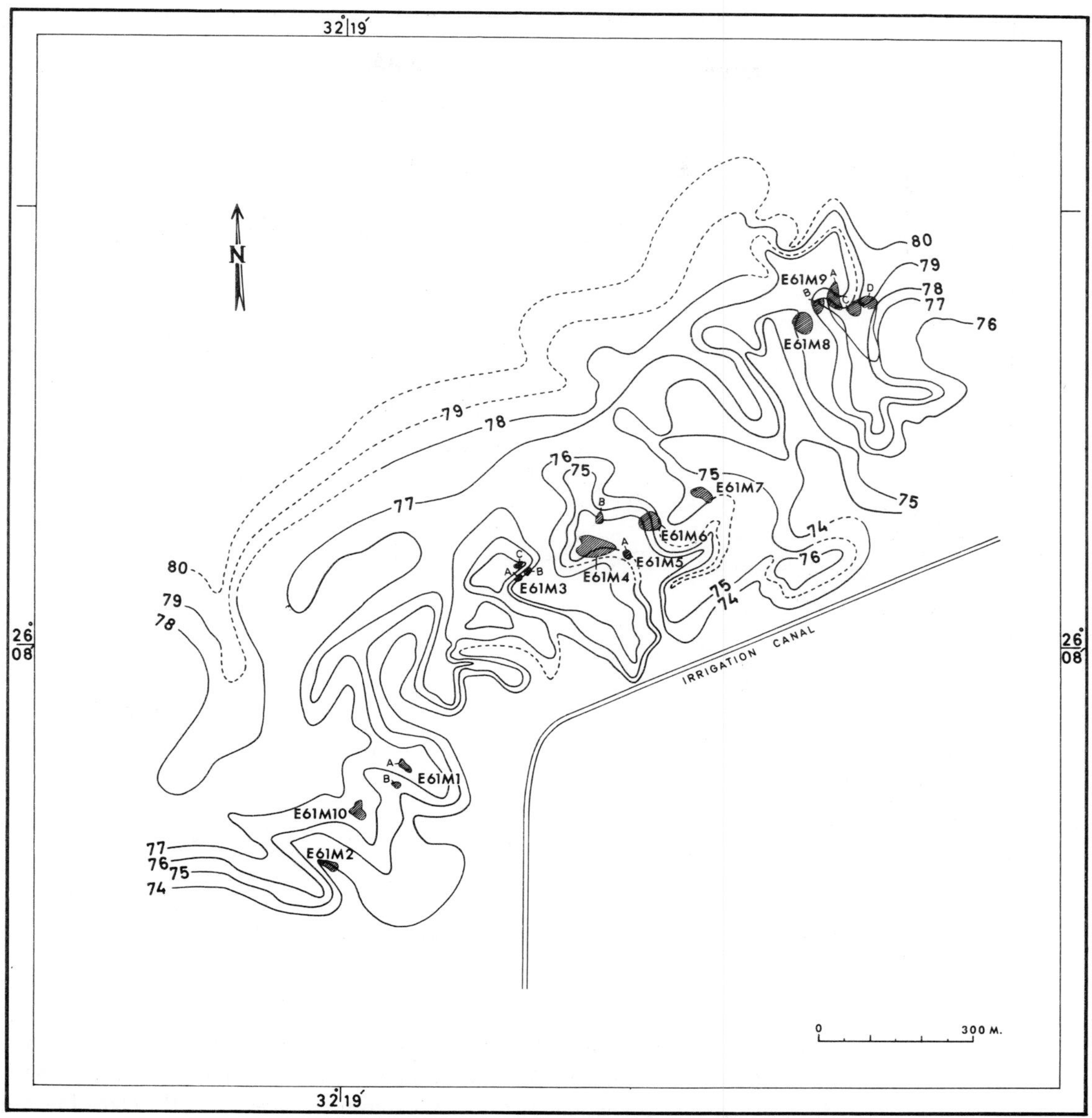

Figure 67. Detail map of site cluster near Dishna showing locations of sites studied.

gravel beds that cover the floors of the modern wadis in the Eastern Desert. The surface of the silt below the gravel veneer is altered by a thick (*ca.* 1 m), red soil.

As suggested by the stratigraphy observed along the west bank at Site E6103, the Dandara silts are covered by similar massive sands; however, the

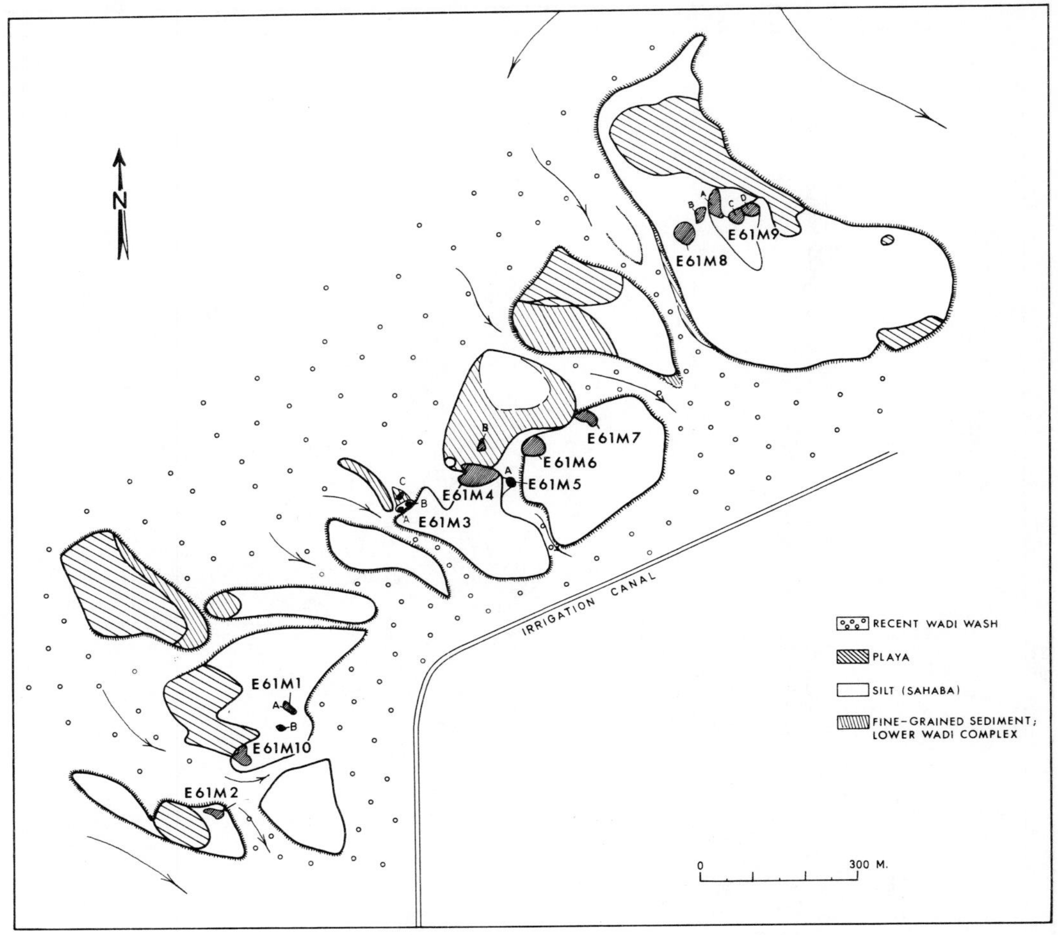

Figure 68. Detail map of site cluster near Dishna showing surfacial geology.

stratigraphic relationship between these two units was not determined by our observations on the east bank. No localities were examined in this area, where the two deposits occur together. Very extensive exposures of the Qena Formation occur along all of the wadis that have their confluence in the lower basin of Wadi Qena, as well as westward from there to Abu Manaa. The Qena Formation is a unit made up of alternating beds of cross-bedded coarse sand and thin beds of grits and gravels that are occasionally consolidated. It is capped by a gravel and cobble veneer in a red soil matrix, presumably the same gravel veneer observed overlying the Dandara Formation. A single slightly worn flake was recovered from near the top of the massive sand unit below the rubble cap of the quarry face at Abu Manaa Bahari.

Later Stratigraphy

A series of ten sites were found near the Eocene escarpment at the western edge of the reentrant at Dishna (Figure 69). Most of the sites were both exposed on the surface and partially *in situ* within an isolated and dissected remnant of silt covering an area 1700 m long and 400 m wide. On the east the silt remnant is bordered by a large wadi and on the west it almost abuts the cliff; to the south it dips beneath the modern floodplain. A pediment and wadi gravel occupy the area between the silt island and the cliffs to the north. The sites occur in three distinct clusters, each containing several concentrations. The basic stratigraphy at all localities is essentially the same, however, and this will be described initially.

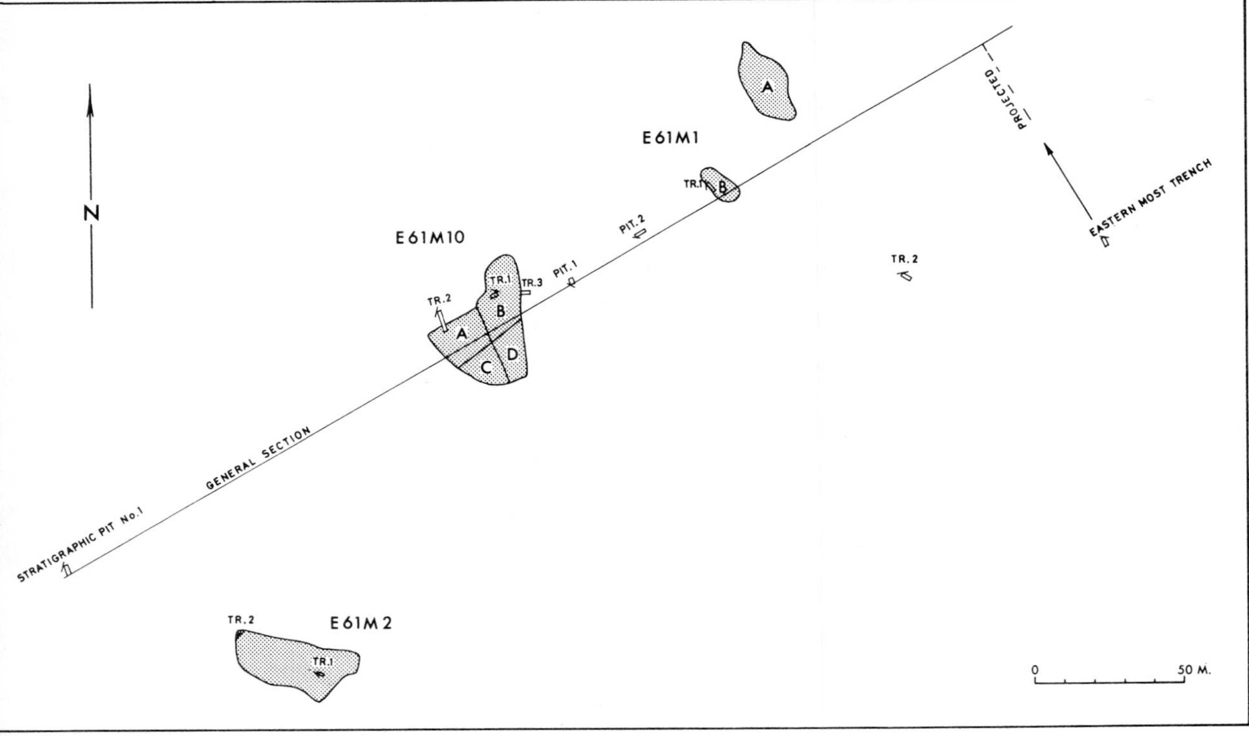

Figure 69. Map of Sites E61M1, E61M2, and E61M10 showing areas of concentrations.

Figure 70. Excavation of stratigraphic Pit 1 near Dishna.

At the base of the section here, exposed in only one trench (Site E61M5, Trench 5), is a wadi sediment composed of two units. The lower is an unsorted unit of locally derived Eocene and Precambrian pebbles and gravels in a matrix of fine pale yellow (5Y 8/3) sand. It is unconformably covered by a unit of pale yellow (5Y 8/3), fine, stratified sand and pea gravels. Both units are highly calcareous and contain abundant sodium chloride.

Unconformably above the wadi sediment is a layer of silt about 60 cm thick. This silt is exposed in Trench 5 and in Trench 1 at Site E61M5, Area B. The silt is dark, yellowish brown (10YR, 4/4), with slickensides, highly calcareous, and contains abundant salts. At Trench 1 in Area B the silt is slightly lower and forms a small depression. Here the silt is wet owing to the capture of subsurface water in the basin, and the salts have been leached from it, but it is still highly calcareous. The wet silt is yellowish brown in color (10YR 5/4).

Above these silts is a second complex of wadi sediments. These sediments are exposed in several trenches and pits (Stratigraphic Pits 1 and 2; E61M2, Trench 2; E61M10, Trench 1; E61M3, Area A, Trench 1; E61M3, Area C, Trench 1; E61M5, Area A, Trenches 2 and 5; E61M5, Area B, Trench 1; E61M9, Area C, Trench 1).

The most complex picture was recorded at Stratigraphic Pit 1 (Figures 70 and 71), located at the western edge of the area in a small wadi north of Site E61M2. The lowest exposed stratum of this wadi sequence is composed of unsorted pebbles, gravels, and cobbles ranging in size from 0.5 cm to 15 cm in

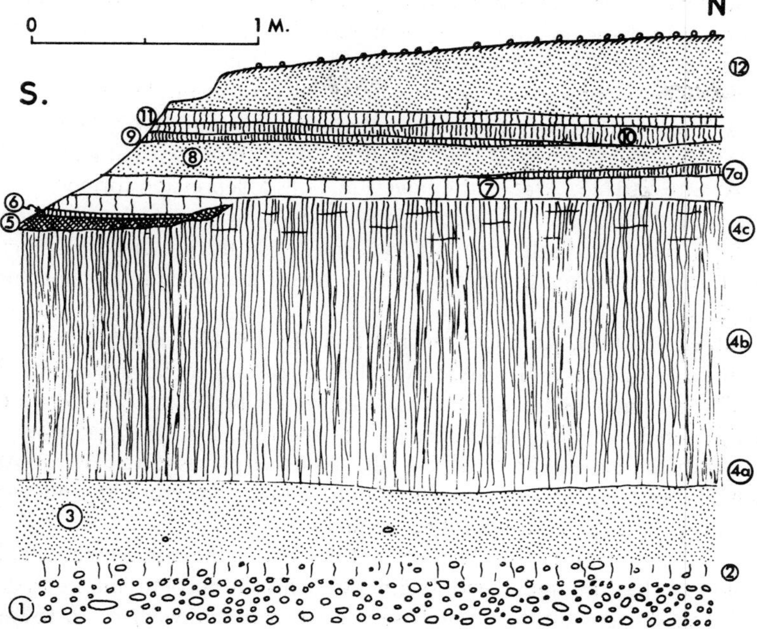

Figure 71. Profile of Stratigraphic Pit 1 near Site E61M2.

1. Gravel, pebbles, and cobbles subrounded to rounded of local derivation. Eocene Limestone and chert in a matrix of light gray (2.5Y 7/2), unsorted sand. Contained rare, very rolled, artifacts of unknown age. Calcareous; unstratified; rare manganese stains throughout the layer. Grades to (2).

2. Same as (1) but containing much less pebbles and gravels.

3. Light gray (2.5Y 7/2), fine and medium-grained sand with traces of gley and manganese stains. Unstratified; cemented; calcareous; grades down to (2).

4. (a) Light, brownish-gray (2.5Y 6/2), clayey silt with slickensides; medium prismatic structure; unstratified; cemented; calcareous. (b) Same as (4a) but with numerous gypsum crystals between the cracks. (c) Dark gray (10YR 4/1), clayey silt slightly less cemented. Numerous gypsum crystals and salt concentrations; unstratified; calcareous.

5. Very light, pinkish-white (7.5YR 8/3), powdery material; ashy, slightly calcinated. Burned layer.

6. Dark gray (10YR 4/1), carbonaceous sand on top of the burned layer.

7. Pale brown (10YR 6/3), fine, silty sand; unstratified; consolidated; calcareous. Playa. (a) Same as (7) but slightly more silty. Playa

8. Light gray (1.5Y 7/2), sandy silt; unstratified; calcareous; consolidated. Playa.

9. Pale brown (10YR 6/3) silt; unstratified; calcareous; consolidated. Playa sediment with Nile silt.

10. Same as (9) but slightly darker.

11. Brown (7.5YR 6/2) silt; unstratified; consolidated; calcareous. Nile silt.

12. Light brown (7.5YR 6/4), silty sand, salt crusted at the top. Cemented; unstratified; calcareous, with concentration of salt throughout the layer. Playa sediment.

diameter and of local derivation, mainly limestone, chert, and flint, rounded to subrounded in shape, in a very fine, light gray (2.5Y, 7/2) sand matrix. Included in the gravel were a few rolled artifacts. This stratum grades up to a compact, very fine, highly calcareous, light gray sand with traces of gley and a few small pebbles. The stratification, if present, is masked. At Site E61M2, Trench 2 a few fresh artifacts were recovered from near the top of this fine, light gray sand unit.

At Site E61M5, Area B the lower unit fills a depression formed in the top of the underlying silt. The upper strata here contain a higher frequency of gravels. A clear, hard salt crust is also formed near the present top of this unit. Above the salt crust and just below and on the surface was a small concentration of artifacts.

At Site E61M9, Area C, Trench 1 and Site E61M, Area A, Trench 1, this upper wadi complex is represented by only the gravel, pebble, and cobble strata.

The terminal phase of this wadi section is represented at Site E61M3, Area C, Trench 1, where the upper part of the fine, light gray sand unit interfingers with the base of an overlying silt. At other places (Site E61M3, Area A, Trench 1), the basal part of this silt contains a high admixture of sand, together with a few pebbles and, rarely, rolled artifacts.

The main stratigraphic feature of this area is the silt remnant that conformably overlies the upper wadi sediments. This silt becomes markedly thicker toward the river (greater than 3 m, base not exposed) and wedges out toward the cliffs. In the pit closest to the cliffs (Stratigraphic Pit 2), it has a thickness of only 60 cm (Figure 72). The silt is preserved to a maximum elevation of slightly more than 76 m above sea level, or about 4 m above the modern floodplain. It is calcareous, ranges in color from dark brown to brown (10YR, 4/3–5/3), is massive, with slickensides, and frequently displays a salt crust near the top. In places the main body of the silt also contains one or more layers of gypsum crystals. Today the levee remnant has a slight slope toward the cliffs (which is not evident on our topographic map owing to the broad contour interval) and toward the river (Figure 73).

At several sites (Stratigraphic Pits 1 and 2, and Site E61M9, Area C, Trench 1), the silt has a distinct burned layer about 5 cm thick and from 4 cm to 26 cm below the top of the silt. The burned layer appears as a hard, red, oxidized clay horizon that extends over a considerable area and could be observed in several places on the eroded surface.

At Site E61M3, Area A, Trench 1, the upper part of the silt contains scattered pebbles, possibly of Nilotic origin, and rolled artifacts. At almost all localities the upper 10 cm of this silt was weathered and appeared as a fine powder. Most of the archaeological materials occurred in this upper part of the silt; within and below the fine, powdered zone; and below, within, and above the burned layer.

Above the silt is a series of sediments believed to represent accumulation in a playa. These playa sediments are intercalated with thin layers of silt. They are best represented at Stratigraphic Pits 1 and 2, where they achieve a thickness of

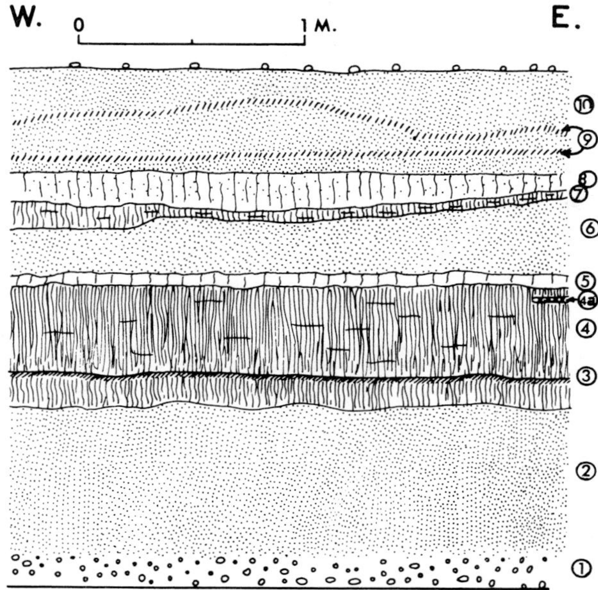

Figure 72. Profile of Stratigraphic Pit 2, northwest of Site E61M3.

1. Pebbles and gravels, rounded to subrounded, of local derivation in a matrix of pale yellow (2.5Y 7/4), fine to medium sand; contains salt; cemented; unstratified.

2. Pale yellow (2.5Y 7/4), fine and medium-grained sand with occasional small gravels and pebbles; unstratified; cemented; highly calcareous.

3. Salt crust within silt unit.

4. Dark, grayish-brown (2.5Y 4/2), clayey silt; cemented; unstratified with angular prismatic structure more pronounced in its upper part. (a) Burned silt.

5. Pale brown (10YR 6/3), fine, silty sand; cemented or consolidated; unstratified; highly calcareous. Playa with silt admixture.

6. Light, yellowish-brown (10YR 6/4), fine, silty sand; unstratified; cemented or consolidated; calcareous. Playa sediment.

7. Yellowish-brown (10YR 5/4) silt with medium prismatic structure; unstratified; cemented; highly calcareous.

8. Light, brownish-gray (10YR 6/2), fine, silty sand containing salt; unstratified; cemented; highly calcareous. Playa with Nile silt admixture.

9. Salt crusts.

10. Light, yellowish-brown (10YR 6/4), silty sand; unstratified; cemented; highly calcareous; contains silt; pebbles and gravel on the surface.

about 1 m. The playa sequence is composed of two layers of playa separated by a thin (10 cm) silt layer, followed by a layer of silt and playa sediment up to 15 cm thick, and, in one profile (Stratigraphic Pit 1), a second layer of silt. This sequence has been named the Dishna Formation (Said *et al.* 1970).

The lower playa sediments are composed of a very fine, light gray (2.5Y, 7/2), unstratified, silty sand that is highly calcareous and unconsolidated and

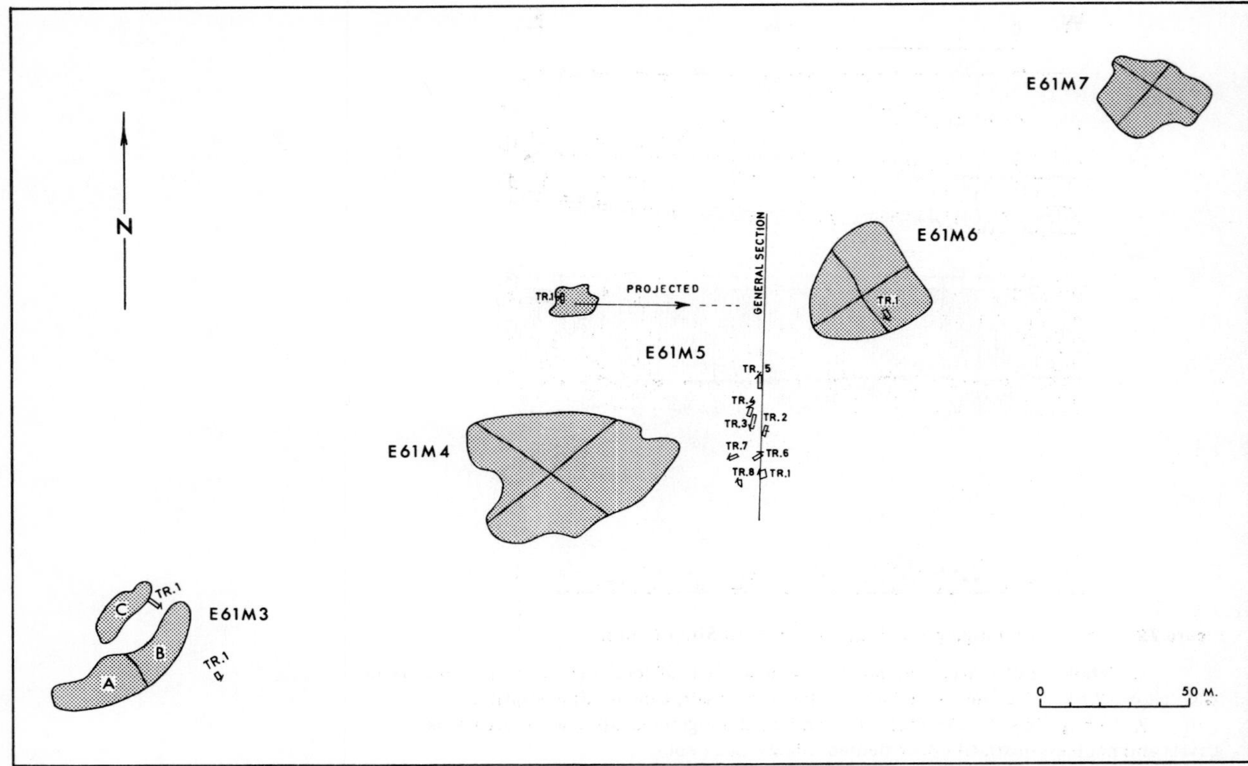

Figure 73. Map of Sites E61M3, E61M4, E61M6, and E61M7. Shaded area indicates extent of concentrations.

contains abundant salt. The upper playa sediments contrast markedly with the lower unit. They are light, yellowish brown to light brown (10YR, 6/4–7.5YR, 6/4) in color and composed of unstratified (or masked), silty sand that is also highly calcareous with concentrations of salt. At Stratigraphic Pit 2 there are two salt crusts, each from 2 cm to 4 cm thick, one near the bottom and the other near the middle of the unit. At Stratigraphic Pit 1 the upper playa sediment is capped by a salt crust. The upper playa also occurs at Sites E61M9 and E61M10. In both instances it forms a layer less than 25 cm thick and is capped by a salt crust. No artifacts occurred within the playa sequence at any locality.

Following the playa there was a period of erosion and dissection during which the present topography was formed. One of the factors of erosion was a pronounced wadi activity. The wadis cut through the silt island, in some instances leaving a series of sediments. These are best represented at Site E61M5, particularly the trenches located in the wadi bed (Trenches 3 and 4). The wadi sediments rest unconformably on the eroded surface of the silt and are composed of several strata. The lowest unit is a light, yellowish-brown (10YR, 6/4), unsorted, coarse sand with pebbles and gravels. It is consolidated, highly calcareous, and rich in salts. Unconformably above this is a similarly colored, powdered, fine-grained sand with occasional gravels. It is highly calcareous and also contains salt. An erosional surface separates this unit from an overlying stratum of very pale brown (10YR, 7/4), horizontally stratified, unsorted, coarse-grained sand and pea gravels. It is also highly calcareous and rich in salt. Throughout most of the area, and not only in the wadi beds, the surface is littered with gravels and pebbles.

The Dishna Sites

The archaeological sites recorded at Dishna occur in three groups. The southernmost group is composed of three sites: E61M1, E61M2 and E61M10 (Figure 69).

Site E61M2 is the farthest south. It consists of an elongated, roughly oval concentration 17 m by 40 m in size. Two trenches were dug here. Trench 1, located near the center of the concentration, was 1 m by 2 m in size and 1.5 m deep (Figure 74). It disclosed a few artifacts in the powdery weathered silt

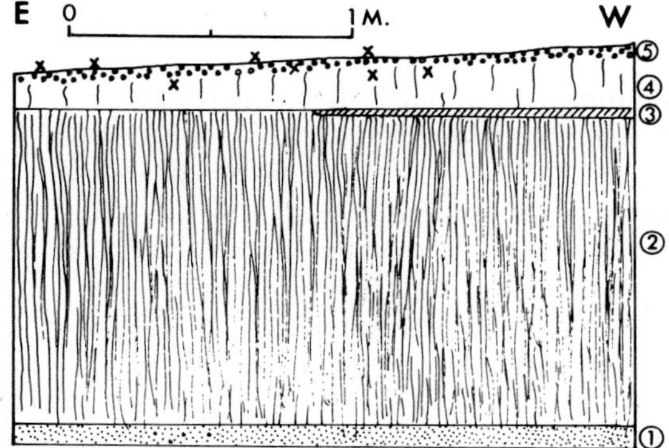

Figure 74. Profile of Trench 1, Site E61M2.

1. Light gray (2.5Y 7/2), silty sand with gley staining; calcareous; unstratified; consolidated to cemented. Fine-grained wadi deposit.
2. Light, brownish-gray (2.5Y 6/2), clayey silt with slickensides and medium prismatic structure; unstratified; calcareous; cemented, less cemented at the top. Crystals of gypsum throughout the unit.
3. Salt crust.
4. Pale brown (10YR 6/3) silt; loose, powdered structure; unstratified; calcareous; contains rare, almost fresh (silt-polished) artifacts at the very top.
5. Light gray (2.5Y 7/2), unsorted sand with numerous small gravels and concretions of calcium carbonate. Slightly rolled artifacts within the unit and on the surface. Surface wadi wash.

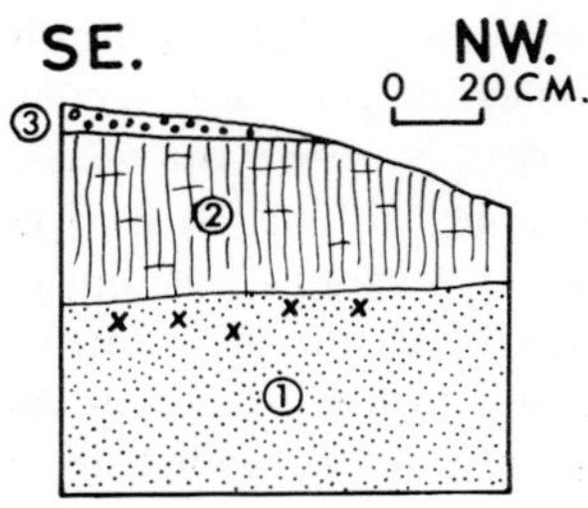

Figure 75. Profile of Trench 2, Site E61M2.

1. Light gray (2.5Y 7/2), silty sand with gley staining; calcareous; unstratified; cemented. Contains cultural layer with numerous fresh artifacts near the top. Fine wadi deposit.

2. Light, brownish-gray (2.5Y 6/2), clayey silt with slickensides and medium prismatic structure; unstratified; calcareous; cemented. Crystals of gypsum throughout the unit. Sahaba silt.

3. Light gray (2.5Y 7/2), unsorted sand with gravels. Surface wadi wash.

above the salt crust that separates the powdered from the consolidated portions of this silt. Most of the artifacts were on the surface. The second trench, located at the edge of the low wadi escarpment, was only 1 m^2 and about 1 m deep (Figure 75). It yielded a few artifacts near the top of the fine-grained wadi sediment just below the silt unit. The artifacts were too few to permit industrial identification.

About 100 m northeast of Site E61M2 is another large, dense concentration, irregular in outline and 30 m by 45 m in size. It was designated as Site E61M10 and arbitrarily subdivided into four more or less equal quadrants (Areas A–D). Some of the surface artifacts were eolized; however, many were fresh and apparently had been exposed only recently. They occurred on the slightly sloping surface of the exposed silt.

Three trenches were dug. Trench 1 (1 m by 2 m in size and 2.3 m deep) was dug in Area B, near the upper (northern) edge of the concentration (Figure 76). Here the artifacts occurred in the cemented silt between 40 cm and 50 cm below the surface and just above a layer of gypsum crystals.

Trench 2 was dug at the northern edge of Area A. It is 7 m long, 1 m wide, and 70 cm deep at its lowest point (Figure 77). Here the artifacts were found just below the surface of the silt and partially covered by the playa sediment. From 20 cm to 30 cm below this occupation horizon was another zone containing a few rolled artifacts.

Trench 3 (1 m by 3 m in size and 2 m deep) was dug just beyond the eastern edge of Area B. It was excavated in an effort to relate the occupation at Site E61M10 with that at E61M1; it did not yield any artifacts. Here the occupation horizon was already eroded and completely exposed on the surface.

Site E61M1 contains two distinct concentrations located between 75 m and 100 m northeast of Site E61M10. Area A is larger but thinner and is totally

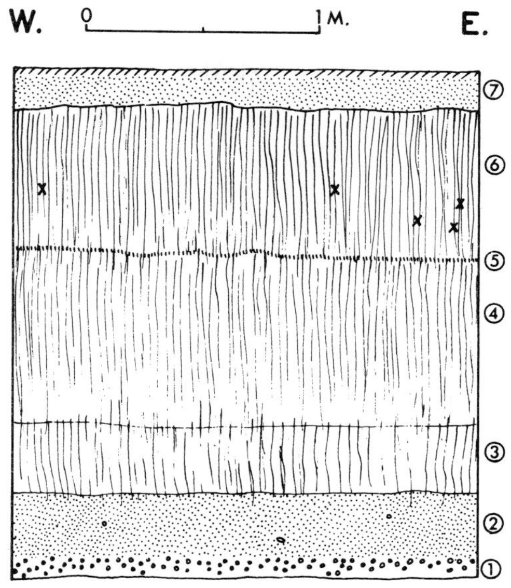

Figure 76. Profile of Trench 1, Site E61M10.

1. Light gray (2.5Y 7/2), fine and medium-grained sand with gravels and pebbles of local derivation, rounded and subrounded. Unstratified; calcareous; cemented.

2. Very pale brown (10YR 7/3), fine and medium-grained sand; unstratified; calcareous; cemented.

3. Light, yellowish-brown (10YR 6/4), clayey silt with slickensides; grades up into 4; unstratified; calcareous; consolidated to cemented.

4. Gray (rY 6/1), clayey silt with slickensides; unstratified; consolidated; calcareous.

5. White layer of gypsum crystals.

6. Brown (10YR 6/3), clayey silt, weathered with angular, prismatic medium structure; unstratified; calcareous; contains cultural layer near the base, slightly above the layer of gypsum needles (5). Contains small Nilotic mollusks.

7. Very pale brown (10YR 8/4), silty sand or fine sand; cemented; unstratified, with salt crust at the top. Playa sediment.

on the surface. It is an elongated oval 15 m by 30 m in size. No trenches were dug.

Area B at Site E61M1 is a small, oval concentration, totally subsurface, that has been almost entirely destroyed by native salt-quarrying activities. The artifacts were found in the back dirt of the numerous pits. One trench, 1 m by 2.5 m in size and about 3 m deep, was dug in the small undisturbed area near the southwestern edge of the concentration (Figure 78). Artifacts occurred from just below the top of the silt to a depth of 25 cm.

A series of pits and trenches were excavated between this site and E61M1 in an attempt to establish the stratigraphic relationship between the two sites,

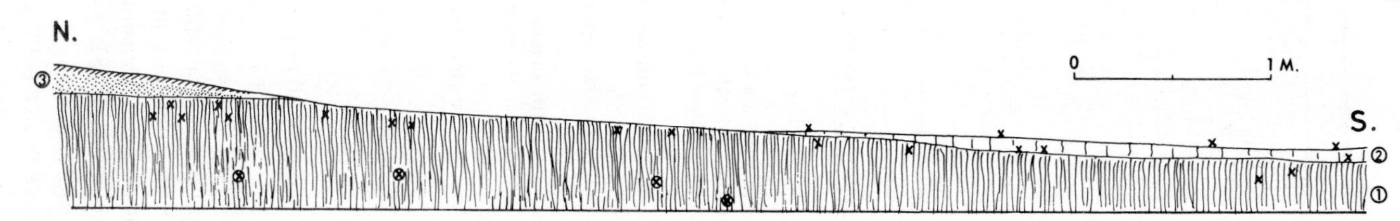

Figure 77. Profile of Trench 2, Site E61M10.

1. Same as (6) in Trench 1. Fresh, slightly silt-polished artifacts near the top. Less numerous rolled Late Paleolithic artifacts at the base of the trench.
2. Loose, powdered silt with a few fresh artifacts; very recently wind eroded.
3. Same as (7) in Trench 1.

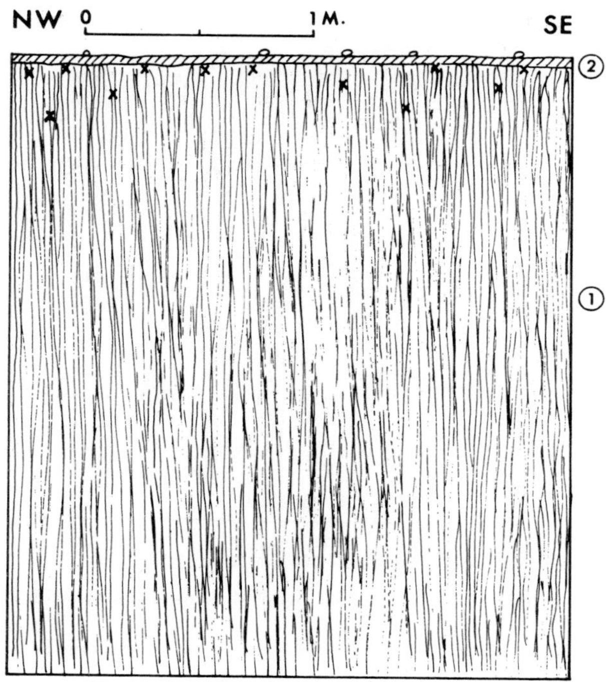

Figure 78. Profile of Trench 1, Site E61M1, Area B.

1. Clayey silt with slickensides throughout the unit; dark, grayish brown (10YR 4/2) in the upper part passing into brown (10YR 5/3) near the bottom. Unstratified; cemented or consolidated; prismatic structure more noticeable in its upper part. Contains Sebilian cultural layer at the very top down to 30 cm below the surface. Highly calcareous. Sahaba silt.

2. Salt crust.

without conclusive results (Figures 79 and 80). For stratigraphic purposes two other trenches were dug down the eroded slope of the silt southeast of Site E61M1. Both of these trenches and those between E61M1 and E61M10 disclosed only the massive silt unit with occasional layers of gypsum crystals.

The middle group of sites at Dishna comprises five sites; two of these contain more than one concentration (Figure 70). Site E61M3 now appears to have two oval concentrations the smaller 8 m by 25 m and the larger 15 m by 60 m. The larger one was arbitrarily subdivided into two areas (A and B). The occupation was almost entirely on the surface, and it appears likely that recent wadi activity may be largely responsible for the discontinuous distribution of the artifacts today (Figure 81).

Two trenches were dug. The first, between Areas B and C, is 1 m wide, 1.6 m long, and 1.5 m deep. No artifacts were found *in situ*. The second trench was located 15 m southeast of Area B and outside the concentration of artifacts.

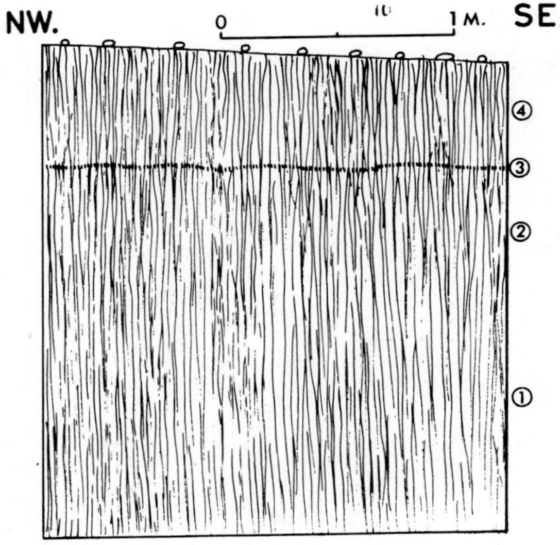

Figure 79. Profile of Pit 1, between Sites E61M1 and E61M10.

1. Brown (10YR 5/3), clayey silt with slickensides; unstratified; consolidated; calcareous.

2. Light, brownish-gray (2.5Y 6/2), clayey silt with pronounced slickensides; unstratified; highly calcareous; consolidated.

3. Layer of gypsum crystals.

4. Dark, grayish-brown (10YR 4/2), clayey silt with angular blocky structure; unstratified; cemented; contains concentrations of calcium carbonate and salt. Sterile. Numerous gravels and pebbles on the surface.

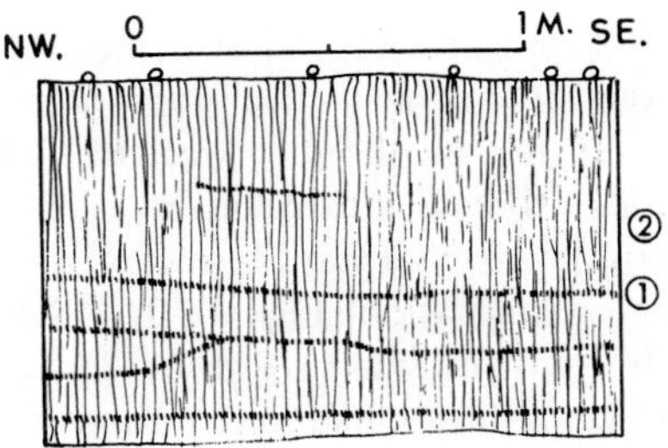

Figure 80. Profile of Pit 2, between Sites E61M1 and E61M10.

1. Layers of gypsum crystals.

2. Clayey silt, grayish brown (10YR 5/2) in the upper part passing into yellowish brown (10YR 5/4) near the bottom of the trench. Numerous slickensides throughout the unit; unstratified; consolidated to cemented with more pronounced angular blocky or prismatic structure near the top. Sterile; pebbles and gravels on the surface.

It is 80 cm wide, 2 m long, and 2.5 m deep. A few fresh artifacts were recovered from the powdered silt unit at the very top of the section, just above a salt crust.

About 100 m northeast of Site E16M3 was another very large and rather thin concentration of artifacts entirely on the surface—Site E61M4. The concentration was an irregular oval 45 m by 60 m in size, which was arbitrarily subdivided into four quadrants. The artifacts were found on the north slope of the silt island and occurred not only on the eroded surface of the silt but also on the surface of a fine wadi sediment that outcropped near the base of this slope.

Two separate concentrations were present at Site E61M5, the first one only 15 m east of Site E61M4. This concentration (Area A) was a very small oval 15 m in diameter. It was situated in a modern wadi bed on a small, flat remnant connected with the main silt island. The presence of the concentration was revealed by recent extensive salt-quarrying activities in the area. A few slightly polished artifacts occurred on the contact between a powdered, brownish-yellow silt and an overlying very pale brown, coarse, unsorted wadi sand. A distinct salt crust separates the powdered silt from the underlying dark brown, massive, unweathered silt.

Northwest of Area A a distance of 75 m was another small, very thin, irregular oval concentration 15 m in diameter (Area B). The concentration occurred on the surface and slightly subsurface in an extensive exposure of wadi sediment that stratigraphically underlies the massive silt island. A few of the artifacts were fresh and seemed to be *in situ* within the wadi sediment. In this area the wadi sediment forms an extensive flat with a gentle slope toward the southeast.

A series of nine trenches were dug to determine both the stratigraphic relationships of the two concentrations at Site E61M5 and the local sequence of events in this area. The oldest deposits are found in Trench 5 (Figure 82). These are wadi sediments consisting of pebbles, gravels, and sands below a layer of silt. The silt, in turn, is covered by a second series of wadi sediments of gravels and fine-grained sands with occasional pebbles. The occupation at Area B was in the top of this second series of wadi sediments just above a salt crust. The massive silt unit stratigraphically overlies these wadi sediments in Trench 2, located 70 m to the southeast (Figure 82). The slightly polished artifacts found in Area A occurred on the contact of this massive silt and the covering third and most recent series of wadi sediments. These most recent wadi sediments are best represented in Trenches 3 and 4 in the bed of the wadi (Figure 83). Three units were recorded. Rolled artifacts occurred in the lowest unit. The occupation at Area A cannot be regarded as *in situ* (Figures 84, 85, and 86).

Northeast of Site E61M5, Area A a distance of 40 m, on the northwestern slope of another silt remnant, was a large, thin concentration (E61M6) almost circular in outline and 40 m in diameter. Site E61M6 was arbitrarily subdivided into four quadrants. One trench 1 m by 2 m in size and 1.3 m deep was dug near the southern edge of the concentration (Figure 87). Almost all of the site had been deflated and was on the surface; however, there were a few fresh arti-

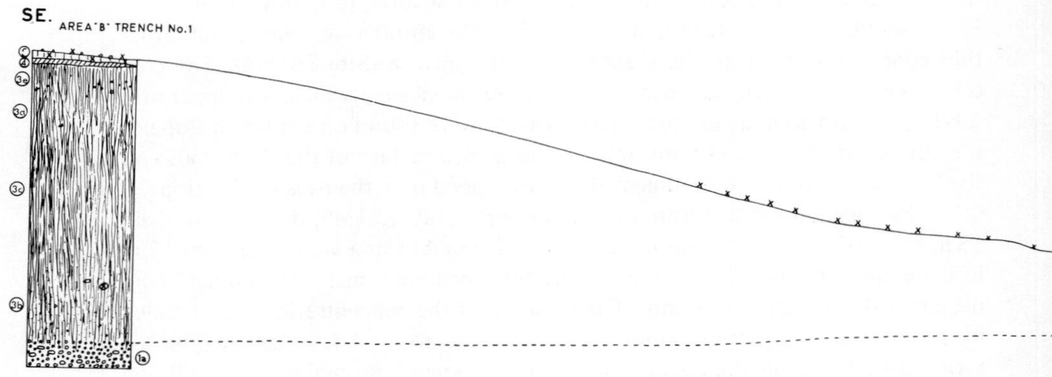

Figure 81. Profile through Site E61M3, Areas B and C.

1. Gravels, pebbles, and cobbles subrounded to rounded of local derivation, composed mainly of Eocene cherts and limestones, in a matrix of light, yellowish-brown (10YR 6/4), fine to medium-grained sand with gley and manganese stains. In Area C, a single, very rolled, Levallois core was found in this unit. At Trench 1 in Area B the unit is more stony and grades up into very sandy silt. Consolidated to cemented; calcareous; unstratified.

2. Light, yellowish-brown (10YR 6/4), fine to coarse-grained sand with single, well-rolled pebbles and occasional cobbles; cemented; calcareous.

facts in the very top of a powdered, light, brownish-gray silt just above a salt crust that separated this powdered silt from the underlying massive silt.

Site E61M7 was located 85 m northeast of Site E61M6. Both sites are situated on the northwestern slope of the same silt island. The concentration of Site E61M7 was an irregular oval in outline and about 30 m in diameter. The site was entirely on the surface, and no trenches were dug.

The third group of sites is located about 400 m to the northeast of Site E61M6 and separated from it by a large, flat wadi (Figure 88). The westernmost of these sites is designated E61M8 (Figure 89). It is a large, rough erosional hillock of silt. A few fresh artifacts were found in a thin layer of powdered silt, but most of the site was exposed on the surface. Two trenches were dug. The first (1 m by 3.5 m in size and 50 cm deep) was excavated near the center of the concentration (Figure 90). The second was placed just west of the concentration, and it is 1 m wide, 5 m long, and 70 cm deep (Figure 91).

The last site in this group (E61M9) was semiarbitrarily divided into four areas (A–D), following the outline of the denser occurrences of artifacts. It

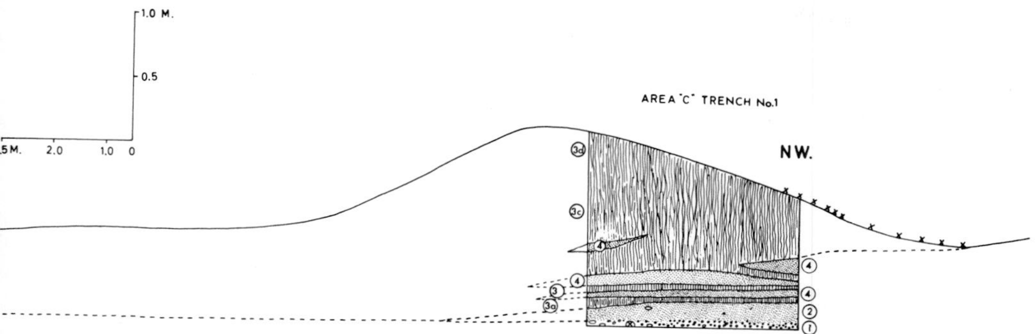

3. (a) Lenses of brown (10YR 5/3), sandy silt; unstratified; calcareous; cemented. (b) Brown (10YR 5/3), very sandy silt containing rare pebbles and rolled artifacts. Cemented; calcareous; unstratified. (c) Brown (10YR 5/3), clayey silt with slickensides; unstratified; calcareous; cemented. (d) Grayish-brown (2.5Y 5/2), clayey silt with slickensides and angular prismatic structure; unstratified; cemented. (e) Same as (3d), but with rare pebbles and rolled artifacts of Late Paleolithic appearance.

4. Salt crust.

5. Powdered, loose silt with rare fresh artifacts slightly silt polished.

should be noted that artifacts were present throughout this area and beyond; thus the areas do not define the occupation limits. The site is a very large (120 m in diameter), dense occupation area, and certainly represents multiple settlements. The occupation was partially exposed by erosion; however, an unknown part of the site is still buried within silts, which, in turn, are covered by playa sediment capped by a very hard salt crust.

Two trenches were excavated at Area C. Trench 1, located in an uneroded area, was 2 m wide, 5 m long, and nearly 2 m deep (Figure 92). At the base is a layer of unsorted pebbles, gravels, and cobbles of local origin in a matrix of pale, olive-colored sand with manganese stains. This sand is highly calcareous and lacked salt. It is conformably overlain by massive, olive-gray silt with slickensides About 25 cm below the top of this silt is a distinct burned layer about 5 cm thick composed of lumps of baked silt and ash. Traces of this distinct burned layer were observed throughout this area in the same stratigraphic position. Above the burned layer the silt is weathered and gray in color. Slightly silt-polished artifacts occurred in the silt to a depth of 70 cm, or 50 cm below the

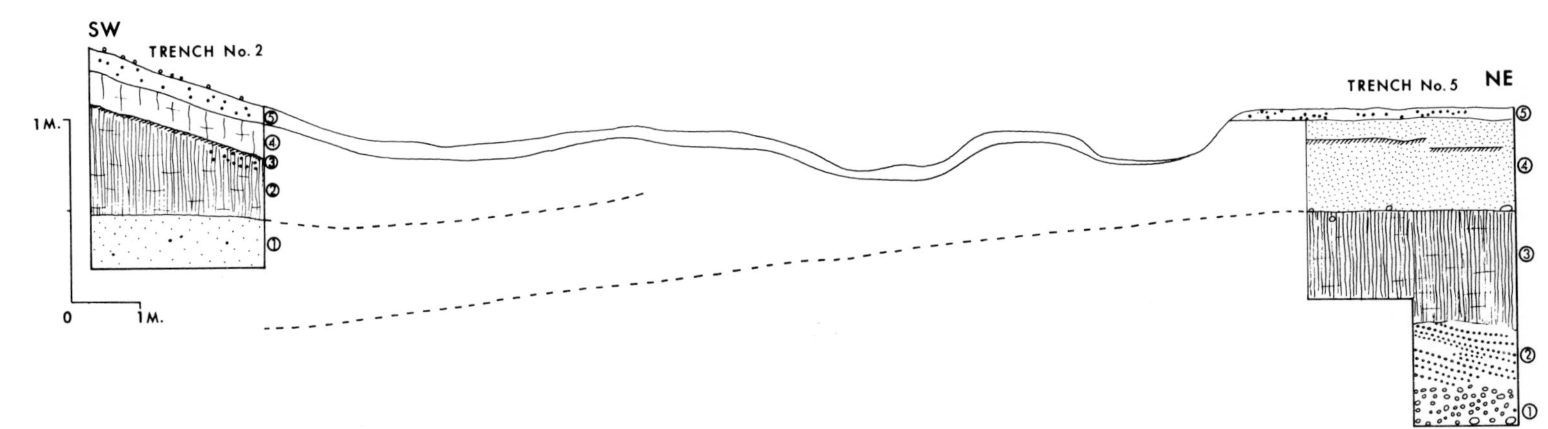

Figure 82. Profile of Trenches 2 and 5, Site E61M5, Area A.

Trench 2

1. Light, yellowish-brown (10YR 6/4), unsorted, fine to coarse-grained sand with occasional gravels and pebbles of local derivation; unstratified; cemented; calcareous. Wadi deposit.
2. Light, yellowish-brown (10YR 6/4), clayey silt with slickensides; cemented to consolidated with medium prismatic structure and a few gravels at the top. Cemented; calcareous; unstratified.
3. Salt crust.
4. Light, yellowish-brown, loose, powdered silt.
5. Coarse, unsorted sand with gravel and pebbles. Wadi deposit.

Trench 5

1. Unsorted gravels, pebbles, and cobbles in a matrix of pale yellow (5Y 8/3); fine to coarse sand. Gravels, pebbles, and cobbles of local derivation subrounded to well rounded. Cemented; highly calcareous. Wadi deposit.
2. Pale yellow (rY 8/3), cross-bedded, fine sand with interbedded pea gravel. Consolidated; highly calcareous. Wadi deposit.
3. Dark, yellowish-brown (10YR 4/4), clayey silt with slickensides and medium prismatic structure at the uppermost part. Cemented; unstratified; highly calcareous; truncated at the top.
4. Very pale brown (10YR 8/3), fine to medium-grained sand with a few pebbles and cobbles at the base on the silt erosional surface. Salt crust in top part. Cemented; unstratified; highly calcareous. Suspended wadi sediment.
5. Recent wadi wash.

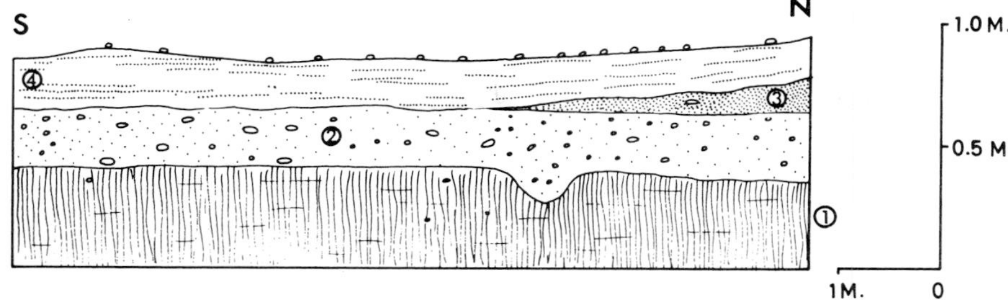

Figure 83. Profile of Trenches 3 and 4 (combined), Site E61M5, Area A.

1. Dark, yellowish-brown (10YR 4/4), clayey silt with slickensides and occasional pebbles near the top. Medium prismatic structure; unstratified; cemented; calcareous.

2. Light, yellowish-brown (10YR 6/4), unsorted sand with pebbles and gravels; unstratified; consolidated; calcareous. Wadi sediment.

3. Light, yellowish-brown (10YR 6/4), fine to medium-grained sand with very occasional pebbles; loose; unstratified; calcareous. Wadi deposit.

4. Very pale brown (10YR 7/4), coarse, stratified sand with lenses of pea gravel; loose; calcareous. Recent wadi deposit.

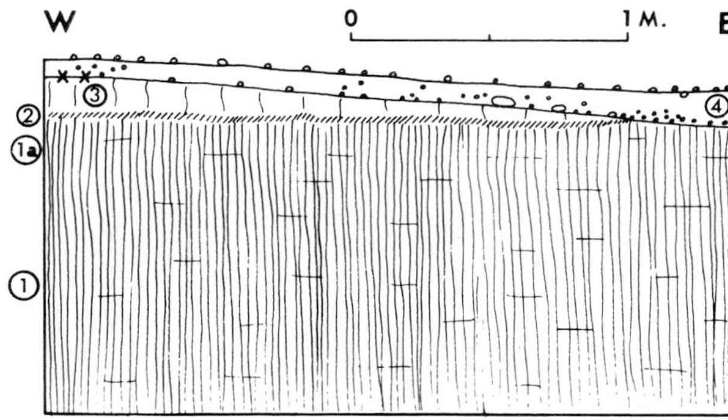

Figure 84. Profile of Trench 1, Site E61M5, Area A.

1. Brown (10YR 4/3), clayey silt with slickensides; cemented to consolidated; unstratified; highly calcareous. (a) Light, yellowish-brown (10YR 6/4), clayey silt with slickensides and medium prismatic structure; cemented; unstratified; calcareous.

2. Salt crust.

3. Light, yellowish-brown (10YR 6/4) loose, powdered silt; unstratified; calcareous.

4. Very pale brown (10YR 7/4), coarse sand with gravels, pebbles, and slightly rolled artifacts. Recent wadi sediment. Fresh artifacts at the contact with underlying powdered silt.

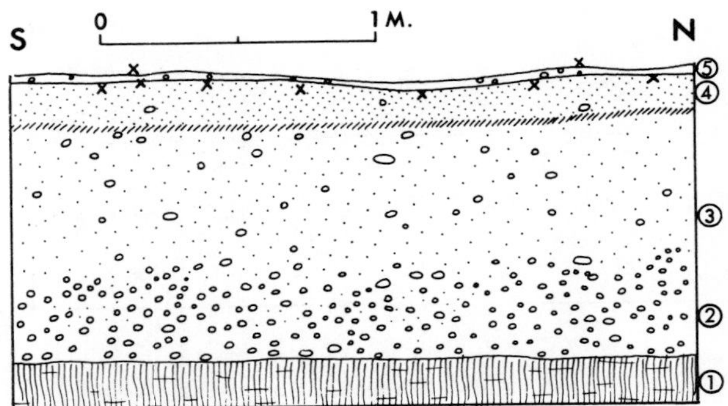

Figure 85. Profile of Trench 1, Site E61M5, Area B.

1. Yellowish-brown (10YR 5/4), clayey silt with slickensides; wet (high water table); consolidated; unstratified; highly calcareous; truncated by overlying gravels.
2. Gravels, pebbles, and rare cobbles in a matrix of pale brown (10YR 6/3), unsorted sand; consolidated to cemented; unstratified; highly calcareous. Wadi deposit.
3. Same as (2) but less rich in pebbles and cobbles, which gradually diminish toward the top. Salt crust in the upper part. Wadi deposit.
4. Same as (3) but less rich in pebbles and cobbles. Cultural layer of rare fresh artifacts in upper 5 cm and on the surface. Wadi deposit.
5. Recent wadi wash.

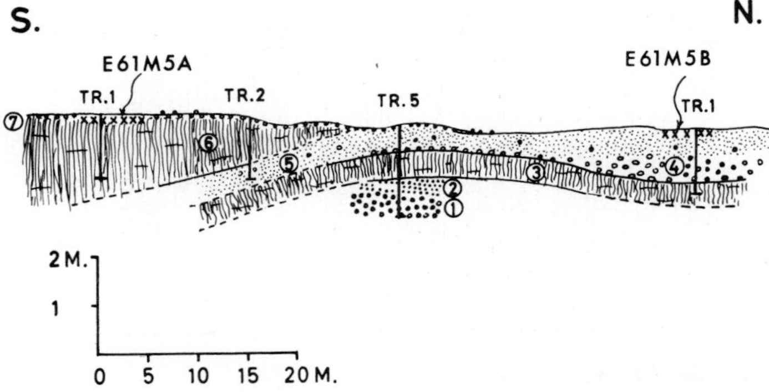

Figure 86. Schematic cross-section through Site E61M5, Areas A and B.

1. Lower wadi pebbles and cobbles.
2. Lower wadi stratified sands and pea gravels.
3. Nile silt.
4. Upper wadi pebbles and cobbles in a sand matrix.
5. Upper wadi sands with occasional pebbles and gravels.
6. Nile silt.

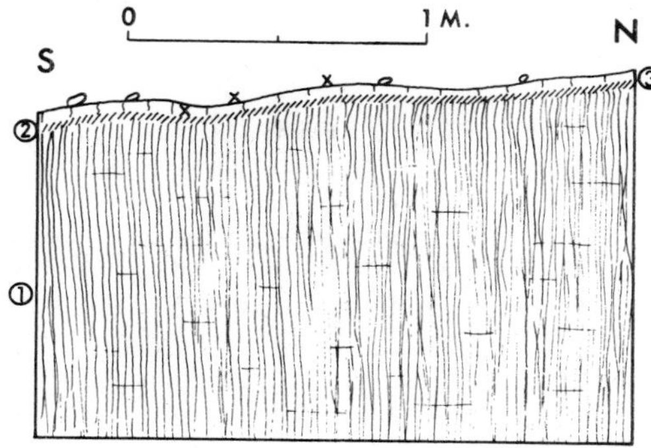

Figure 87. Profile of Trench 1, Site E61M6.

1. Light, brownish-gray (2.5Y 6/2), clayey silt with slickensides gradually becoming browner toward the base (10YR 5/3); cemented at the top and consolidated to cemented near the base of the trench. Prismatic structure clearer near the top. Unstratified; highly calcareous.

2. Salt crust.

3. Light, brownish-gray (2.5Y 6/2), powdered, loose silt with a few fresh artifacts at its very top. Surface covered by eolized artifacts and occasional gravels. Unstratified; calcareous.

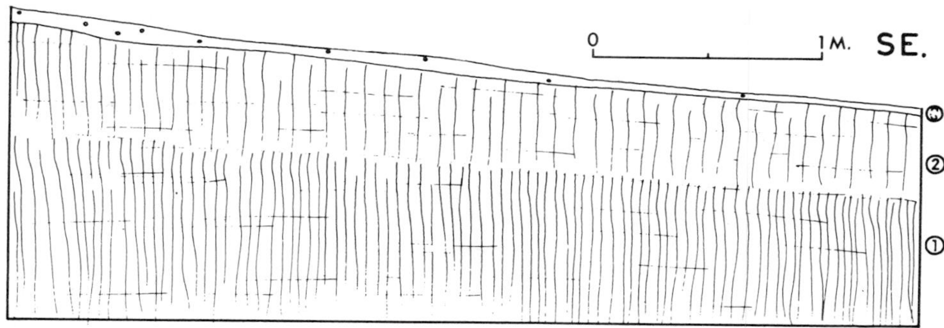

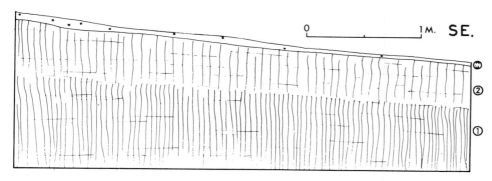

Figure 88. Profile of Easternmost Trench, south of Sites E61M2, E61M3, and E61M1.

1. Dark brown (7.5YR 4/2), clayey silt with slickensides and sand admixture near the bottom of the trench; unstratified; consolidated; calcareous; wet; passes into (2).

2. Dark, yellowish-brown (10YR 4/4) silt with slickensides; consolidated; wet; calcareous; unstratified.

3. Brown (10YR 4/3), powdered, loose silt with rare pebbles and gravels. Modern wash.

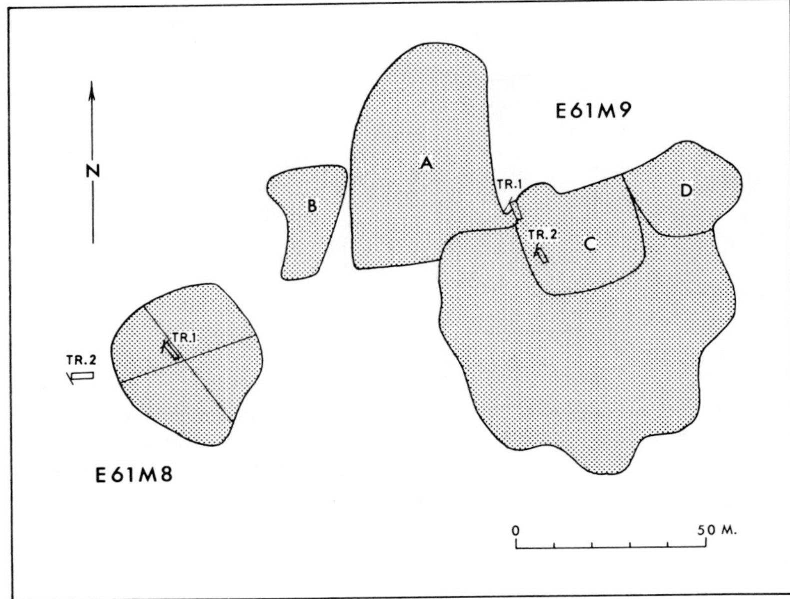

Figure 89. Map of Sites E61M8 and E61M9 showing areas of concentrations and areas collected.

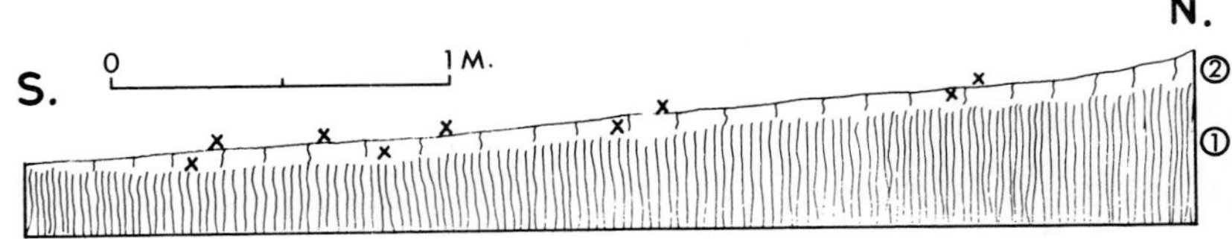

Figure 90. Profile of Trench 1, Site E61M8 (for description of units see Figure 86).

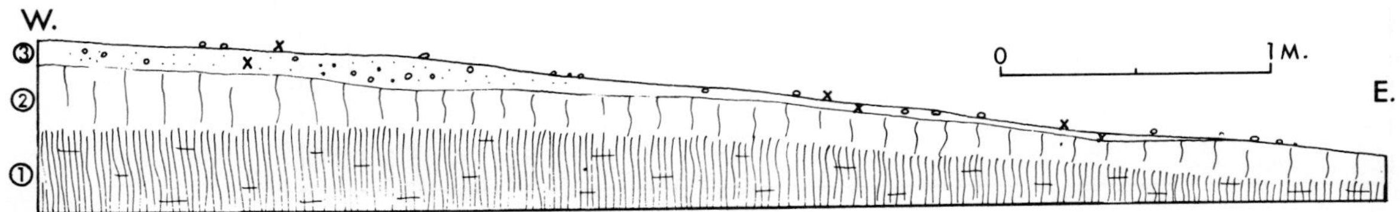

Figure 91. Profile of Trench 2, Site E61M8.

1. Grayish-brown (2.5Y 5/2), clayey silt with slickensides and medium prismatic structure in its upper part; unstratified; consolidated to cemented; calcareous. Near the top a single, fresh, Late Paleolithic flake.

2. Same as (1) but light, brownish gray (2.5Y 6/2); loose structure. Unstratified, highly calcareous. In Trench 1 a few artifacts at the very top of this unit, just below the surface.

3. Very pale brown (10YR 7/3), unsorted sand with small gravel, pebbles, and slightly rolled artifacts; loose; unstratified; calcareous. Recent wadi wash.

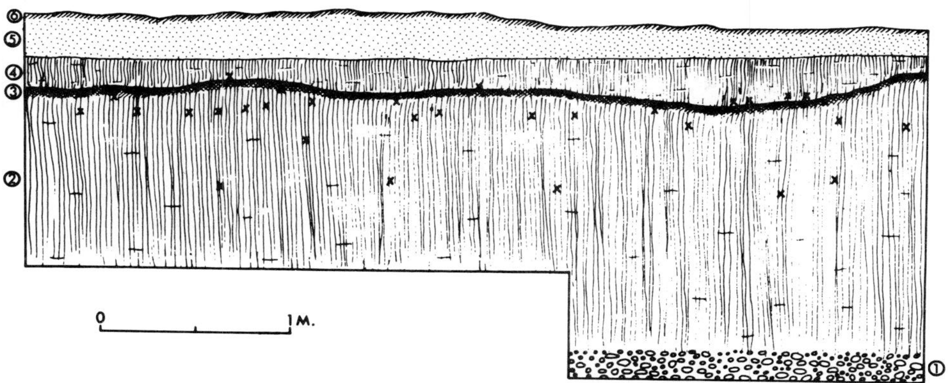

Figure 92. Profile of Trench 1, Site E61M9, Area C.

1. Gravel, pebbles, and cobbles subrounded to rounded of local derivation, mainly Eocene, chert and limestone in a matrix of pale olive (5Y 6/3), fine and medium-grained sand with gley and manganese stains. Unstratified; consolidated; calcareous.

2. Olive-gray (5Y 5/2), clayey silt with slickensides; consolidated to cemented with medium prismatic structure; highly calcareous. Burned layer (3) on top down to *ca.* 5 cm. Contains slightly silt-polished artifacts down to 50 cm from its top.

3. Baked silt lumps; ash; burned silt and heated chert artifacts. Burned layer.

4. Gray (5Y 5/1), clayey silt with slickensides; consolidated to cemented; unstratified.

5. Light, yellowish-brown (10YR 6/4), fine and medium-grained sand; unstratified; cemented; highly calcareous with salt concentration. Playa sediment.

6. Salt crust.

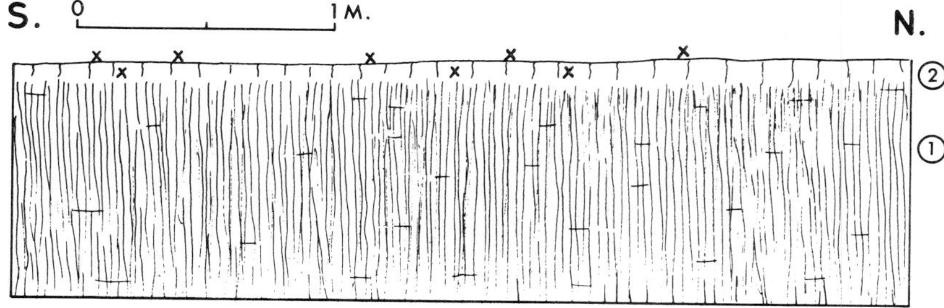

Figure 93. Profile of Trench 2, Site E61M9, Area C.

1. Olive-gray silt (5Y 5/2), same as (2) in Trench 1, slightly wet near the bottom of the trench.

2. Powdered, loose silt with a few fresh artifacts at the very top.

Trench 2 is slightly below Trench 1, and its surface is at the level of the middle part of unit 2 in Trench 1. Numerous artifacts on the surface between the trenches come from eroded units 2–4.

burned layer. They also occurred in the burned layer and just above it. The greatest number were immediately below the burned layer. Many of the artifacts just below and in the burned layer were heat cracked. The entire occupation spans nearly 60 cm, all within the silt. Above the silt is a layer of very fine-grained, light, yellowish-brown sediment that is highly consolidated, calcareous, and rich in salt. A salt cap 5 cm thick covers the surface of this upper playa deposit.

Trench 2 was located within an eroded portion of Area C in an area of dense artifact concentration on the surface. It was 1 m wide, 3.5 m long, and 1 m deep (Figure 93). It yielded a few fresh artifacts in the weathered part of the silt, apparently below the burned layer, which was not preserved in this portion of the site.

General Reconstruction of the Fossil Landscape at Dishna

The development of the landscape at Dishna began with the deposition of the first cycle of wadi sediments, which record torrential discharge from the adjacent plateau of the Eocene Thebes Formation (Figure 94). This discharge was part of a larger wadi system running from the plateau surface down through the sands and gravels of the Qena Formation to the Nile river. Today this system is represented by Wadi Abu Manaa, which borders the eastern edge of the pronounced silt remnant on which most of the sites were found.

There followed a short period of high Nile floods during which a relatively thin deposit of silt was laid down over the earlier wadi sediments. This silt was observed in only two narrow trenches; therefore we cannot determine if the silt

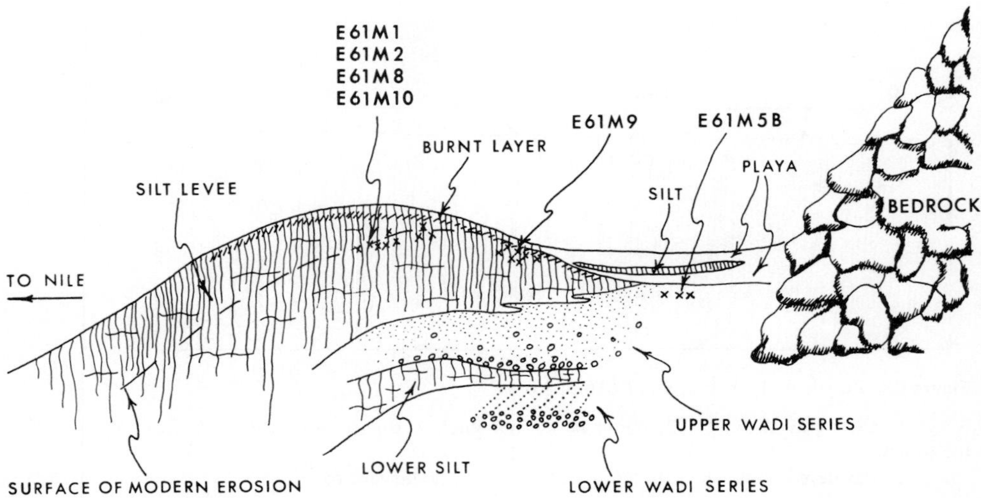

Figure 94. Schematic reconstruction of sequence of sedimentation and archaeological associations at Dishna.

and wadi sediments interfinger. Also, we cannot estimate the full thickness or massiveness of this silt unit toward the river; however, it seems to be slightly lower in elevation than the maximum of the extensive episode of siltation that occurred later. There is no archaeological or other evidence available on which to determine the age of this silt.

Another series of wadi sediments lies unconformably over this earlier silt. It also records torrential flow at the beginning, with constantly reducing velocity toward the top. The very fine matrix, with a few pebbles in places, seems to indicate a rising base of erosion and the deposition of suspended, very fine silt particles in a blocked basin. An occupation occurs near the end of this wadi deposition, suggesting that the water body in the blocked basin was seasonal. The upper part of this fine wadi sediment interfingers with the base of the overlying silt, indicating that the obstruction of the wadi mouths and the creation of a blocked basin was probably a result of the deposition of silts at a high level along the extreme edge of the floodplain. The interfingering of Nile silts with fine-grained wadi sediments indicates that the wadis were not active during the periods of maximum Nile flood but were active during other times of the year. Presumably, therefore, most of the local rainfall (which was probably more than today) occurred during the winter months, if the Nile flood maximum was in late summer, as it is today.

The second episode of silt deposition resulted in a thick and massive silt wedging toward the cliffs. The preserved remnant appears to have been a large floodplain levee, with its western tip abutting the projecting escarpment of the Thebes limestone. It may have arched around the mouth of the entire reentrant, touching another projecting escarpment at Abu Manaa on the east.

No wadi gravels were noted within the massive silt, except at the beginning. The most distinctive event during the deposition of the massive silt occurred near the end, when a widespread burning of the margin of the floodplain occurred. Traces of burning in the same stratigraphic position have been observed at several localities along both banks of the river from Isna on the south to Dishna, a distance of more than 150 km. This burning has been referred to as a brush fire (Said *et al.* 1970); however, it seems likely that dense, marshy aquatic and floodplain vegetation was responsible because the thickness and color of the burned layer would suggest a high temperature for a long period. Thin savanna vegetation would not be sufficient to burn for the long time and at the high temperature required. Our reinterpretation of this event was stimulated by observations in the Fayum depression, where numerous consecutive burned layers were observed along the fossil shore of fluctuating Lake Moeris.

The main series of occupations in the Dishna area occurred during the formation of the massive silt levee but after its shape had already been achieved. The sites located along the ridge of the silt remnant do not show any traces of the burned layer, which suggests that it had been removed by subsequent erosion and that these sites (E61M1; E61M2; E61M10; E61M3; E61M4; E61M5, Area A; E61M6; and E61M7) were occupied before the burning occurred. The earlier part of Site E61M9, and possibly E61M8, may also belong to this general period. Between these sites there is no stratigraphic evidence to support chronological seriation. All but one (Site E61M1, Areas A and B) belong to the same industrial tradition, and possibly are a quarry facies of the Isnan industry, represented at Sites E71K14 and E71K15 in the Isna area. The exceptional site is assigned to the Sebilian.

On the basis of the burned layer and similar geomorphic position, the episode of siltation that was responsible for the deposition of the massive levee may be regarded as contemporaneous with the upper silt aggradation at El-Kilh, Isna, and Makhadma. This correlation is reinforced by the similarities of the archaeology.

A fossil salt crust below the top of the silt at Stratigraphic Pit 2 may indicate a period of increased local rainfall immediately following the end of siltation and the development of the silt levee. The salt crust indicates that the silt surfact behind the levee was exposed.

The formation of the salt crust was followed by the development of a playa in this basin formed behind the levee. The source of the water in the playa must have been mostly seasonal wadi flow from the adjacent area, which carried water into the blocked basin. This wadi flow must have been responsible for the transportation of the sediment into the playa. The fine-grained, silty playa sediments were presumably in suspension in the basin.

The playa event was interrupted by a short period of high floods that overflowed the levee and deposited thin, homogeneous layers of silt over the lower playa sediments. The unmixed character of some of these silt layers indicates that the deposition of these silts occurred in a dry basin. While some of the silt layers are unmixed and homogeneous, others are mixed with playa sediments, possibly owing to the renewal of playa sedimentation (seasonally?) and rewashing of the freshly deposited silt.

This event of higher Nile floods recalls the previously recorded series of unusually high post or terminal Sahaba floods in Nubia and the Darau Member in Kom Ombo, which have been dated by five radiocarbon determinations ranging from 9,250 to 10,070 BC (de Heinzelin, in Wendorf 1968; Butzer and Hansen 1968; Wendorf *et al.* 1970). The similarity in stratigraphic position suggests a similar age for this event at Dishna.

Conditions of playa sedimentation continued after this brief period of siltation and led to deposition of the upper playa sediments. It is likely that the playa was seasonally dry, for in some places two separate salt crusts were formed; the upper one may date after the playa. The wadi activity and formation of the playa suggest a higher rainfall than occurs today, and compared with the conditions during the main silt deposition and formation of the levee, but it does not exclude general arid conditions. There is no evidence of occupation with either playa sediment.

It now seems likely, if the correlation with the high floods just discussed is correct, that the playa sediments of the Dishna Formation are slightly earlier than previously stated (Said *et al.* 1970). In chronological position they are probably contemporary with the final silts of the Sahaba Formation in Sudanese Nubia and the Darau Member siltation at Kom Ombo. At lower elevations the final high flood silts cannot be distinguished; there they may form the top part of the Sahaba silts.

The next event recorded in the sequence is wadi erosion of the levee, resulting in breaching of the levee in several places and rejuvenation of the main wadi beds. This must have been accompanied by a lowering of the base of erosion due to a much lower Nile. During the course of this erosion, the levee was dissected by numerous small wadis that were part of the main wadi system, leaving a landscape essentially like that of today. The age of this renewed wadi activity is unknown, but it is certainly not recent.

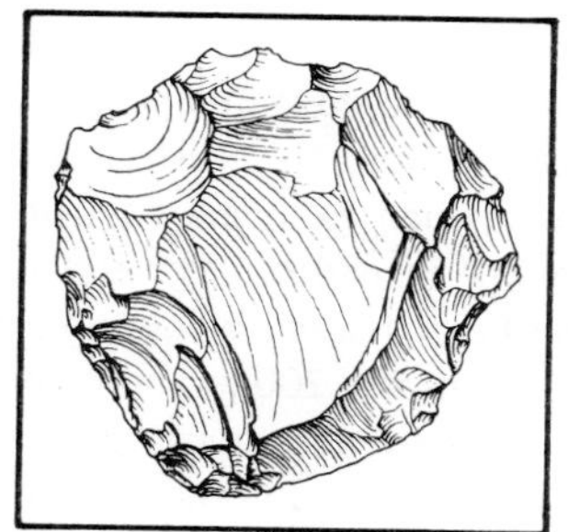

Geology of the Fayum Depression

BAHAY ISSAWI

The Fayum Depression is one of the major oases of the Western Desert. It is usually looked upon as a part of the Nile Valley rather than a part of the desert. This is because of the fact that the Fayum is located near the Nile, 60 km southwest of Cairo, and also due to its connection with the Nile through the Bahr Youssef canal. The major difference between the Fayum and similar depressions of the Western Desert is the Nile silt that covers the floor of the Fayum Depression and is not found in any other depression in the desert.

The Fayum Depression covers an area of 12,000 km^2, with a general slope to the northwest where Lake Qarun is located. The lower part of the Fayum Depression, Lake Qarun, has an elevation of 44 m below sea level. The lake is bounded on the north by a huge, vertical scarp that nearly encircles the depression in a broad arc open toward the east. Through this opening the Bahr Youssef Canal enters the depression.

The northern part of this arc-like scarp attains the highest elevation above the floor of the depression, 300 m, and is a nearly vertical wall made of several steps overhanging each other. The steps vary in width from a few tens of meters to a little less than a kilometer before the top of the scarp is reached. The steps mark the more resistant, hard limestone beds intercalated in a softer shale sequence. The top of the scarp is capped by a basalt sheet striking in an east–west direction.

The western and southern scarps are much lower and dissected than the northern one. Several indentations alternating with projecting spurs and promontories characterize the southwestern part of the scarp. Both the western and southern scarps overlook another depression, Rayan, which is separated from the Fayum Depression by a topographic saddle 15 km in width. The Rayan Depression is an elongate north-northwest–south-southeast feature assuming an elevation of 43 m below sea level. The surrounding scarps rise 200 m above the Rayan floor. In contrast to the Fayum Depression, where the lowest part is occupied by Lake Qarun, the lowest part of Rayan is covered by salt incrustation, sabakha, and sand dunes. These deposits are also common near the northern part of Lake Qarun.

The floor of both depressions rises gradually toward the adjacent scarps, forming undulating, dissected pediplains that are mostly covered by deflated sand. The elevation of these surfaces varies from 0 to +50 m above sea level. The pediplains are formed by several rock-cut pediments overhanging each other, covered mostly by deflated sand. Coming out of this sand are hard limestone knobs and patches, giving the area its peculiar type of landscape.

The surface of the pediplains is also littered by several monadnocks near the surrounding scarps, while mesas and buttes are not so common. These features assume considerable heights above the nearby surfaces from 80 to 100 m.

The stratigraphy of the Fayum area has been dealt with by Beadnell (1905) and reviewed by Said (1962). The succession of rocks exposed at the Fayum area is as follows (from top to base):

Quaternary deposits	
Pliocene sandstone	
Lower Miocene sand and gravel	
Basalt	Oligocene
Gebel Qatrani Formation	
Qasr El-Sagha Formation	
Birket Qarun Formation	Upper Eocene
Ravine beds and Wadi Rayan Formation	Middle Eocene

The oldest rock units, the Wadi Rayan Formation and Ravine beds, belong to the Middle Eocene; they crop out at the scarps surrounding the depression and partly forming its floor.

The Rayan Formation is made of hard limestone that is highly fossiliferous, including *Nummulites gizehensis*, *Ostrea* sp., and others, with shale and marl intercalations.

The thickness of this unit is 130 m. The ravine beds that conformably overlie the Rayan consist of gypseous shale, marl, and limestone, attaining a thickness of 50 m. Vertebrate remains, *Zeuglodon* sp., were collected from the lower ravine beds.

The Upper Eocene section, Birket Qarun Series, and Qasr El-Sagha Formation (Beadnell 1905) are distinguished in the northern part of the area, forming most of the scarp face and the low-lying pediplain surface. The section is made of hard, brownish limestone, shale, and marl bands. Sandstone beds are common in the upper part of the section. The beds are highly fossiliferous, including both invertebrate and vertebrate remains. Similar beds are exposed all the way between the Fayum and Cairo, they are well displayed at Mokattam Hill and also at Bahariya Oasis. The thickness of Birket Qarun is 50 m, while the overlying Qasr El-Sagha is 180 m thick.

The Oligocene beds of the Gebel Qatrani Formation are exposed in the northern part of the Fayum Depression, overlying Qasr El-Sagha, and are formed of variegated sandstone with alternating shale and calcareous grit beds. The thickness of this Oligocene unit varies from 250 m at Gebel Qatrani to less than 4 m in the eastern part of the depression, where it is covered by gravel sheets. These gravel sheets are, again, well developed in the southern part of the depression, El-Gharag El-Sultani, and may be of Oligocene age or younger. From the Gebel Qatrani Formation extensive vertebrate remains were obtained including *Arsinoitherium zitelli* and *Moeritherium* sp.

To the Oligocene also belong the extensive basalt sheets on the rim of the northern scarp. These may assume a tubular shape and have a thickness of 40 m, striking either east–west or east-northeast–west-southwest.

The Lower Miocene beds are made of alternating sand and gravel beds overlying the basalt on the northern scarp. The Lower Miocene beds dip gently to the north and include fossil wood and freshwater shell. The thickness of this unit averages 20 m.

The Pliocene beds are ill defined in the Fayum area. Probably some of the fossiliferous sandstone beds between the Nile and the depression may belong to this system.

The Quaternary deposits are well developed in the area, mostly covering extensive parts of the floor of the depression. Freshwater lake deposits, diatomites, silt, gravel sheets, and deflated sands are the types of sediments dating from the Quaternary. The recorded thickness of the Quaternary sediments is 20 m at the minimum.

Structurally the Fayum Depression is surrounded by a great number of faults, most of which trend northwest–southeast. The major faults of this trend are located along both sides of the Rayan Depression. Associated with the major faults are small antithetic faults of the same trend.

The beds are generally horizontal or slightly dipping (2–3°) to the northwest except near fault planes. Small, shallow folds are known from the surrounding scarps. Fold axes tend to be oblique or perpendicular to the strike of the main faults.

Reefal basin-like structures are very common at the southern and southwestern part of the Fayum Depression. These were for some time looked upon as true structural basins, but recent investigation of the area has revealed the reefal nature of the beds; this explains their dipping inward, since the growth of the reef is accomplished from the peripheries upward.

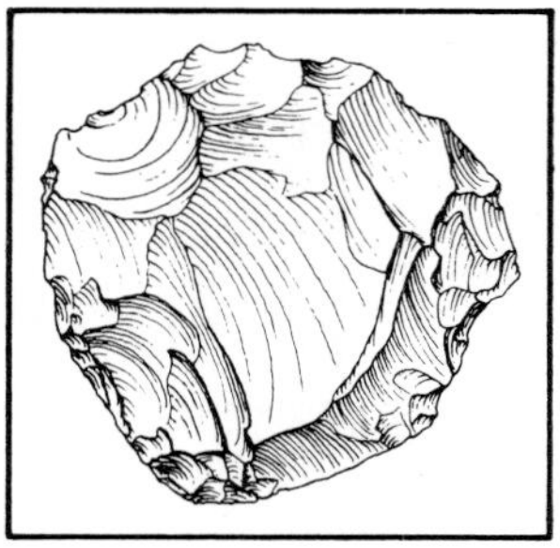

Archaeology and Pleistocene Stratigraphy of the Northern Fayum Depression

Introduction

As part of the study of the Quaternary geology and archaeology of the Nile Valley, a brief survey and a series of test excavations were conducted during the winter of 1969 in the area along the north rim of the Fayum Depression between Kom Aushim and Qasr El-Sagha (Figures 95 and 96).

The origin of the Fayum Depression and its Quaternary history have attracted the attention of scientists for a long time. Herodotus mentioned the presence of an extensive lake in the depression (Lake Moeris) when he visited Egypt around 450 BC. He described an artificial lake 3600 furlongs in circumference and 50 fathoms deep. According to Herodotus, water from the Nile flowed into the lake six months of each year and from the lake to the Nile during the other six months.

One of the first modern scholars to speculate on the history of the Fayum Depression was Jomard, who accompanied Napoleon on his expedition to Egypt in 1798. He identified Herodotus' Lake Moeris with modern Birket Qarun (Jomard 1918), not knowing that the actual elevation of the modern lake and the depth of the depression below the level of the Nile make it impossible for water to flow from the lake into the Nile. Linant de Bellefonds (1843) rejected Jomard's hypothesis on the basis of the very different elevations of the Nile and the lake and the presence of archaeological remains believed to be of ancient Egyptian age on the floor of the depression. He proposed that Lake Moeris

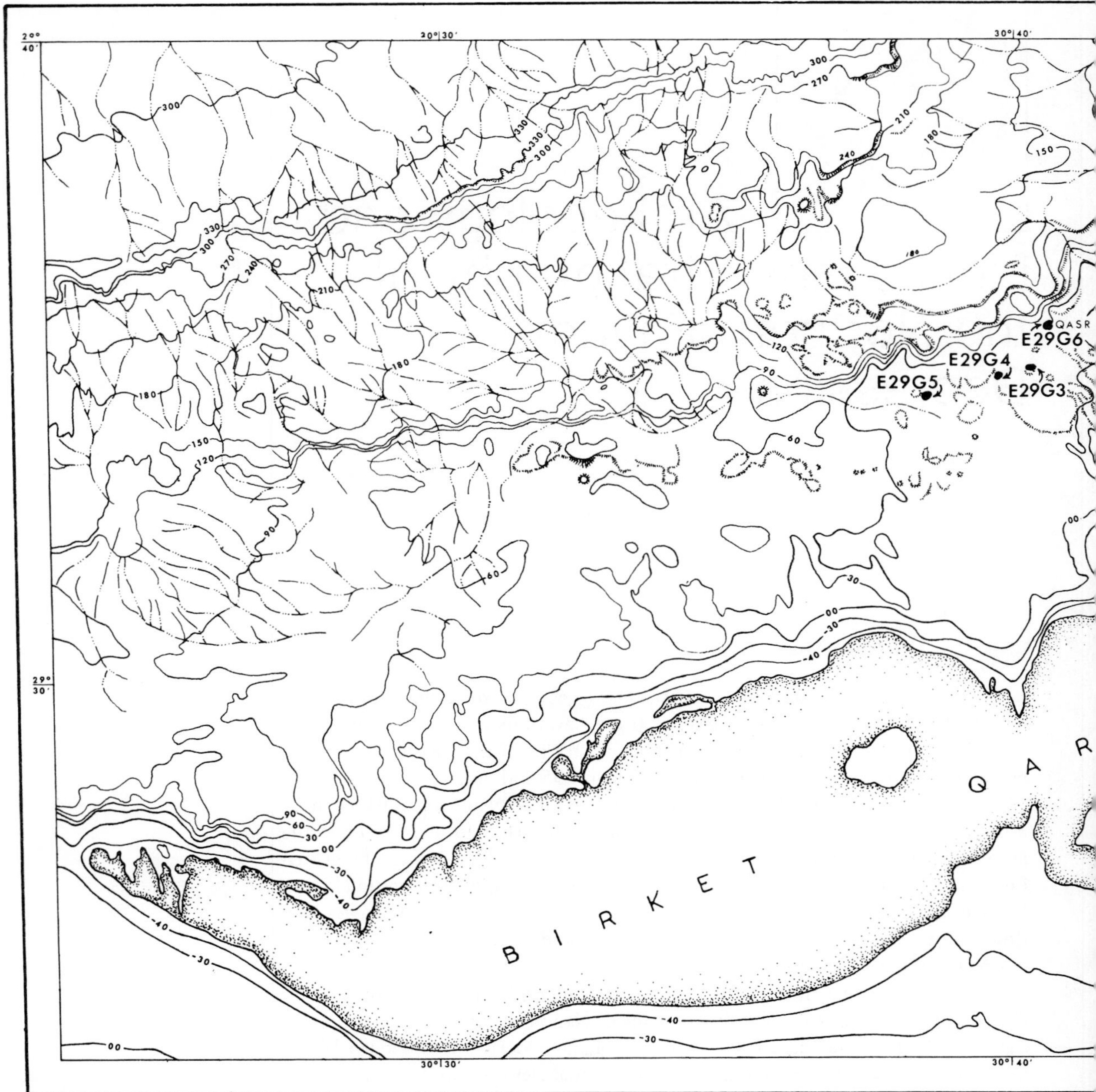

Figure 95. Map of Fayum Depression showing location of sites investigated.

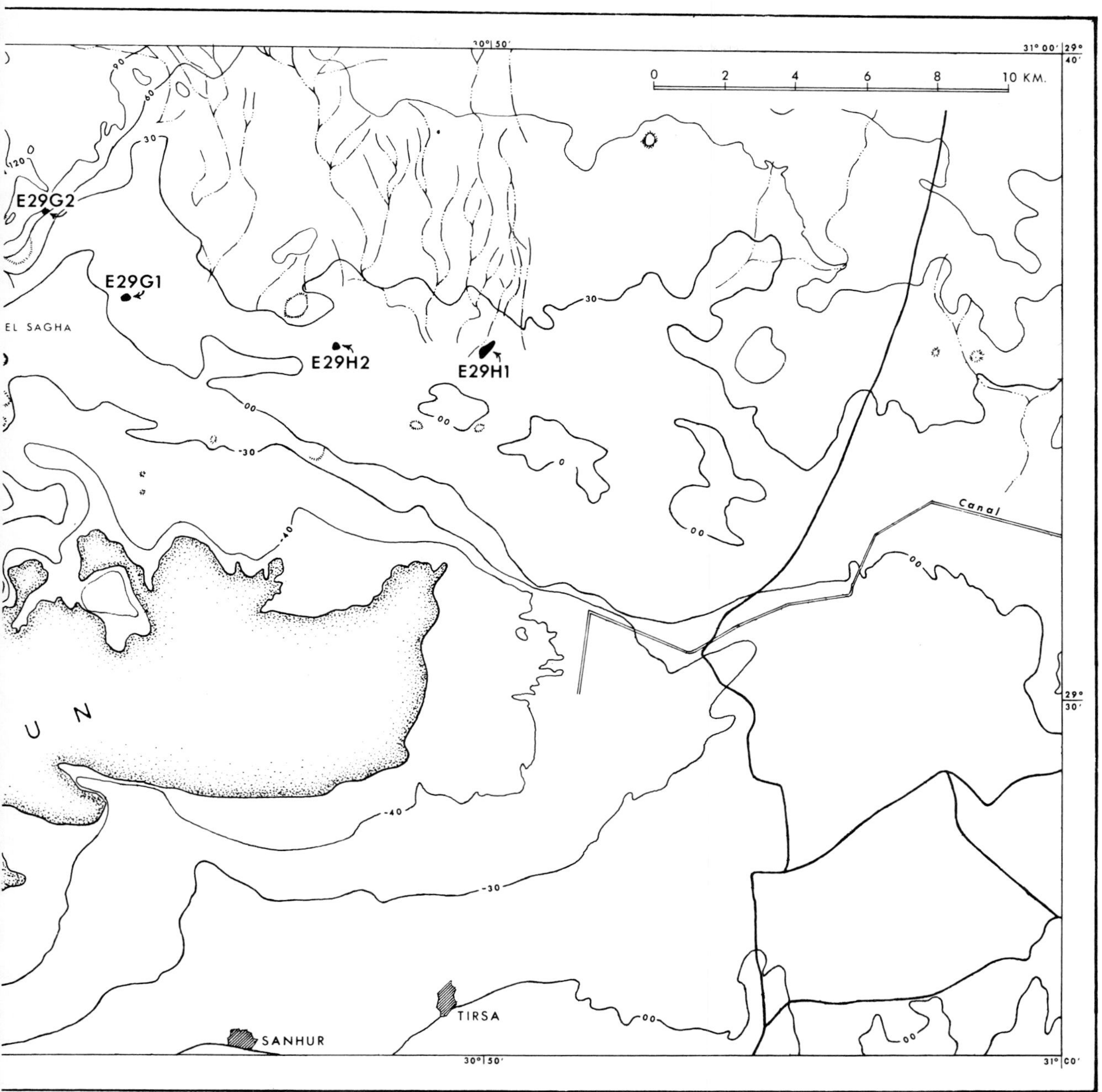

30°|50′
31° 00′ 29° 40′
0 2 4 6 8 10 KM.
E29G2
E29G1
EL SAGHA
E29H2
E29H1
Canal
29° 30′
U N
TIRSA
SANHUR
30°|50′
31° 00′

Figure 96. General view of landscape along northwest edge of Fayum Depression. Note vegetation casts in foreground. Figure is pointing to casts of trees.

existed at the southeastern section of the depression, where large embankments occurred. This hypothesis was refuted by a number of scholars, both archaeologists and geologists, working in the area in the late nineteenth century (Whitehouse 1882; Schweinfurth 1886; Petrie 1889; and Brown 1892), who showed that the embankments were natural and that the ruins on the floor of the lake were of Ptolemaic and Roman age rather than ancient Egyptian. Most of these scholars held

> that a natural high-level lake, communicating freely with the Nile, had existed within the Faiyum from prehistoric times, filling the entire depression to a level of about 25 m above the present Mediterranean level, and that what the "King Moeris" of Herodotus did was not to construct an artificial lake, but to reclaim from this natural lake a relatively small tract of land some 100 sq km in area around the site of the present town of Madinet el Faiyum, where the depth of the lake was smallest . . . [Ball 1939: 182].

According to this interpretation, these changes were achieved by the construction at the Fayum entrance near Lahun of a series of embankments and dams that regulated the flow of Nile water into and out of the depression.

The topography and older geology of the depression were first extensively investigated by Beadnell (1905), who proposed a series of tectonic movements and accompanying wind deflation to account for the origin of the depression in Pliocene and early Pleistocene times.

The next significant work was by G. Caton-Thompson, E. W. Gardner, and S. A. Huzayyin, who in a series of publications (1926, 1929, 1932, 1934, 1937) gave the results of their archaeological excavations and related geological studies. They concluded that two lakes, both communicating with the Nile, had succeeded each other in the depression. The earliest lake was of Pleistocene age and reached a maximum elevation of 34 m above sea level. The age of that lake was determined primarily on the basis of rolled "Levalloisian" tools associated with *Corbicula* shells in gravel deposits resting on bedrock in the eastern part of the depression. The Pleistocene lake, according to these authors, either disappeared or shrank to a much smaller size. The lacustrine deposits at the 22 m level, previously believed to have been associated with historic Lake Moeris, were regarded by Caton-Thompson and Gardner as a stage in this shrinking Pleistocene lake.

The second lake, according to Caton-Thompson and Gardner, rose to a level of 18 m. Along the retreating shores of this lake, successive communities of early pottery-using Neolithic and subsequent people lived. In addition to the 18 m stage, these authors record stages at 10 m to 6 m, at 4 m, and at –2 m.

A number of archaeological sites were located with each of these levels in the second lake, beginning with the 10 m–6 m stage. The earliest settlements are called Fayum A and contain pottery, bifacial tools, and concave base arrowheads. These communities were fully developed Neolithic societies depending on wheat and barley agriculture and domestic animals as well as fishing and hunting. The age of the Fayum A settlements was estimated to be around 5000 BC, a date that may be slightly too old. There are now four radiocarbon dates from Fayum A sites which range between 4400 and 3860 BC.

The settlements associated with the 4 m and –2 m stages were termed Fayum B and described as a "lingering mesolithic group, some unprogressive tribe [Caton-Thompson and Gardner 1934]." All of the sites of the Fayum B group were surface concentrations of worked stone and contained occasional bifacial specimens similar to those from Fayum A sites.

Caton-Thompson and Gardner also found Old Kingdom pottery and artifacts (third to sixth dynasties) at –2 m and believed that the lake never again rose above this level. According to this interpretation, the historic Lake Moeris could not have discharged into the Nile as described by Herodotus, nor could there have been any artificial lowering of the lake and subsequent reclamation by "King Moeris" or by Ptolemy Philadelphus.

At about the time that Caton-Thompson and Gardner were working in the Fayum, a geological and archaeological survey was being conducted along the adjacent Nile and the Nile–Fayum divide by Sandford and Arkell (1929). They concluded that the Fayum Depression was the result of fluviatile erosion that occurred up to Pre-Mousterian times, when drainage was passing through the Hawara Channel into the Nile. They postulated that their Mousterian Nile Terrace at 36 m above sea level near Beni Suef is continuous with their lake terrace at 34 m in the Fayum Depression. In addition, their Sebilian Nile Terrace at 31 m was believed to correspond with a lake terrace at 28 m.

Sandford and Arkell traced two other terraces within the Fayum, one at *ca.* 22 m, believed to date from Late Sebilian times, and another at 18 m, considered to date from the Neolithic. Both of these were believed to relate to Nile Valley terraces, but the connection could not be traced.

The diverse interpretations of the origin of the Fayum Depression led the Geological Survey of Egypt to sink several boreholes in the Hawara Channel in 1934 to determine the depth of the bedrock sill separating the Nile from the Fayum. The results of this work show that the sill is at an elevation of 17 m below sea level, which indicates that the depression could not have been formed by fluviatile action, at least not at its lower levels (Little 1936). It was also recorded that supposed lacustrine beach gravels were present up to elevations between 42 m and 44 m above sea level in the eastern part of the depression, and that an extensive shoreline at 22 m preserved as a bank in the western part of the depression, and known as Gisr El-Hadid, contained pottery (Little 1936).

The next important synthesis of the area was by Ball (1939), who attempted to integrate the diverse opinions and data on the origin and history of the Fayum. He closely followed Sandford and Arkell's terrace sequence along the Nile and in the Hawara Channel, but he rejected their hypothesis of a fluviatile origin for the depression. He suggested instead that it was hollowed out by wind deflation in Early Pleistocene times and remained separate from the river up to the later part of the Early Paleolithic, when gravels and sands, believed to be a beach deposit, were laid down at an elevation between 42 m and 44 m above sea level. The dating of this event was correlated with Sandford and Arkell's 42 m Nile terrace at Beni Suef, which is reported to contain Acheulean artifacts. By Mousterian times, according to Ball, the level of the lake had fallen to 34 m above sea level (the Caton-Thompson and Gardner "Pleistocene lake") and was still connected with the Nile, through the Hawara Channel, and with the 36 m Mousterian terrace of Sandford and Arkell. At the beginning of the Late Paleolithic, the lake level had fallen to 28 m, to correlate with the Sebilian river terrace at 31 m. Ball postulated that the lake level then fell to 22 m, remained constant for a period during the Middle Sebilian, fell again to –5 m, and then rose again to about 18 m by the beginning of the Neolithic, all based on the Nile terrace sequence of Sandford and Arkell and on the 18 m "white sand terrace" of Caton-Thompson and Gardner. Finally, Ball postulated that the lake fell again during the Fayum A Neolithic to 10 m above sea level, and then fell to –2 m during the Fayum B occupation, where it remained stationary through early Dynastic times.

To explain Herodotus' account of Lake Moeris, Ball postulates extensive hydrologic engineering works to deepen and widen the Hawara Channel during the twelfth dynasty, probably during the reign of Amenemhat I. This caused the level of the lake to rise to 10 m above sea level and placed the lake and the river in hydrologic equilibrium. According to his calculations, there was an annual fluctuation of about 2.5 m due to the influx of Nile floodwater, the return flow, and evaporation.

A rise to about 20 m is suggested for the time of Herodotus; but 150 years later, according to archaeological evidence and written records, the construction of the embankment called Gisr Bahlawan during the reign of Ptolemy I (323–285 BC) caused the level of the lake to fall, and by 280 BC the lake had sunk to 2 m below sea level, where it remained throughout the Ptolemic period. By the second century AD the lake had fallen to −7 m, according to archaeological evidence. By the thirteenth century, during the governorship of Nabulsi, the lake is described as being at essentially the same level as it is today.

A year after Ball's publication appeared, Shafei (1940), whose main concern was to establish the margins of the lake from Old Kingdom through medieval times, concluded that the lake reached its highest elevation around the fourth dynasty of the Old Kingdom, when it stood slightly below the foot of the Qasr El-Sagha Temple, a conclusion with which the present authors are in agreement, in contrast to the position held by previous students of the subject.

Recent Work in the Northern Fayum

In January and February 1969 a survey was conducted along the north rim of the Fayum Depression, and test excavations were made at eight sites ranging in age from Terminal Paleolithic to Old Kingdom.

Beyond a brief visit to Kom K ridge, on which occur the deposits of the 34 m beach of Caton-Thompson and Gardner (1934: 50), no attempt was made to study the older Pleistocene deposits in the depression. Our impression of these older deposits, based on this brief visit, is that they are possibly of fluvial rather than lacustrine origin. They are composed of a mixture of pebbles and sand containing *Corcibula*, rare *Unio*, and few water-worn artifacts, including Levallois flakes and cores. Because of their paucity the artifacts can not be related to any specific archaeological entity. The gravels vary in thickness from a few cm to nearly 3 m, according to Caton-Thompson and Gardner (1934: 50). The shells of *Corbicula* are disarticulated but intact and show no evidence of rolling, while the gravels are Nilotic in aspect and are rounded to subrounded. Little (1936) describes similar deposits up to 44 m above sea level. These skirt the depression toward the east along the Nile–Fayum divide.

It has been postulated (Said *et al.* 1972a; 1972b) that these deposits may have been laid down by Nile distributaries that formerly flowed through a shallow basin within the eastern part of the Fayum Depression.

The lacustrine deposits of the Fayum Depression occur in a sequence of deep and shallow water sediments, as well as shore features, which appear to record at least four succeeding episodes of lake aggradation and recession. This sequence can be reconstructed only from the stratigraphic, radiocarbon, and archaeological evidence; the modern geomorphology of the basin has been so dissected by deflation that most clues to its complex history have been obscured. Previous reconstructions based mainly on level of occurrence have been misled by the absence of firm, large-scale stratigraphic data and by the complex history of the basin. During the course of our work, more than a kilometer of sections were drawn from 46 excavated trenches. These led to the recognition of four succeeding lakes within the depression. These lakes have been given names (Said *et al.* 1972a) and will be discussed in the following sections.

The Oldest or Paleomoeris Lake

Site E29G1

Lacustrine deposits belonging to this phase have been found at only one site—E29G1, Area F. This site, probably Caton-Thompson and Gardner's Site Z1 (1934: Plate CIX) comprised a series of more than six concentrations, together with a broadly scattered veneer of other artifacts, along the east slopes of two large, deflated basins (Figure 97). The exposed portion of the site is about 700 m long and 120 m wide, and the occupied areas range from 15 m to slightly less than 20 m above sea level. The basins are entirely surrounded by lacustrine sediments, but low bedrock remnants protrude from the lake sediments on both the east and west sides of the basins and separate the deflated area into the two basins. A low, dry masonry stone wall has been built between two of the bedrock outcrops, possibly as a recent game trap. The floors of the basins are formed by firmly cemented diatomite, which have prevented further deflation. A small but prominent inselberg of lacustrine sediment is preserved at the east edge of the south basin.

Site E29G1 has obviously been occupied numerous times. From the dip of the surrounding lacustrine sediments, we may infer that the bedrock outcrops and the earlier deposits had the same geomorphic relationship during the time of occupation that they have today. The result was a particularly favorable locality for fishing. The bedrock outcrops would have served as a natural sill behind which fish would be trapped during the low-water stage each year. The Terminal Paleolithic and later people in the Fayum obviously took frequent advantage of this situation.

According to calculations by Ball (1939: 205), the lake would be lowest near the end of May, when both the river and the lake would have fallen to their minimum. If this held true during the Terminal Paleolithic period, then most of the occupations at this site probably occurred during the late spring. This inference of occupation during the annual low-water phase is further supposed by the occurrence of the occupation floors within organogenic swamp sediments, and almost always associated with a swamp species of snails, *Pila ovata.*

Area F, in a series of five trenches leading out from a large, protruding remnant butte standing 20 m above sea level, disclose a complex stratigraphy, of which four units belong to the oldest lake (Figure 98). At the base is a pale yellow (2.5y, 7/4), cemented, fine and medium-grained sand with a dip of 10–15° toward the center of the basin (Figure 99). The trenches disclosed a thickness of 25 cm, base unexposed. Above it is a white (2.5y, 8/2), cemented diatomite, about 20 cm thick, with rare snails and a blocky structure. Above the diatomite is a thin layer of pale yellow (5y, 7/3), almost horizontally stratified, fine-grained sand with foreset dip and small snails (Figure 100). It ranges from 25 cm to more than 1 m in thickness, becoming thicker toward the edge of the basin. A second layer of diatomite ends the sequence of deposits assigned to the oldest or "Paleomoeris" lake. A breccia of small snail shells occurs at the base of the diatomite (Figure 101). At the top it has a deep fossil network of dehydration or desiccation cracks. The top of the diatomite also shows traces of fire, and in places powdered burned swamp sediment fills the desiccation cracks (Figure 102). In other places these cracks may be filled by the lacustrine sediments of the succeeding lake. Wind deflation has removed the overlying lake sediments over a large area of the site down to the hard surface of this deeply cracked diatomite, leaving a basin (identified as the South Basin at Site E29G1) surrounded by outcrops of limestone bedrock and later lake deposits (Figure 103).

The top of this deeply cracked diatomite is between 10 m and 11 m above sea level (Figure 104). The maximum stand of the lake is unknown, since the diatomite is a deep water formation, but this sequence of sediments seems to record an aggrading lake followed by a decline to below 10 m and a burning of the dry aquatic vegetation, possibly through natural causes. No evidence of human activity was noted.

The Premoeris (Terminal Paleolithic) Lake

Unconformably above the burned and cracked diatomite at Site E29G1, Area F is another series of lacustrine sediments. Immediately above the diatomite is a light, yellowish-brown (2.5y, 6/4), cemented and horizontally stratified, fine to medium-grained sand with oxidation stains. Near the top there are several thin layers of concentrated small snail shells. This unit is about 3 m thick and eroded, and shallow swales occur in the base of the overlying unit. In these swales are pockets of small snails evidently washed from the upper part of the lower unit. The overlying sediment is another unit of fine sand, ranging in color from yellow (10 YR, 7/8 and 2.5y, 7/6) to pale yellow (2.5y, 8/4), consolidated, nearly 5.5 m thick, and with topset and backset stratification at the base and foreset dip with increasing inclination toward the top. This unit is interrupted by eight separate beds of organogenic, powdery swamp sediments ranging from 1 cm to 30 cm in thickness and from grayish brown (2.5y, 5/2) to very dark grayish-brown (2.5y, 3/2) in color. These swamp sediments are reworked in places (with fine stratifaction), and some show traces of burning. A few reworked stone artifacts occurred with the third through fifth layers (from the bottom). These artifacts possibly represent a single reworked occupation. A fragmentary human skull and numerous fishbones were also present. At the top of the unit is another very dark gray (2.5y, 3/0), silty and powdery swamp sediment, cracked, with small blocky texture, and eroded at the surface.

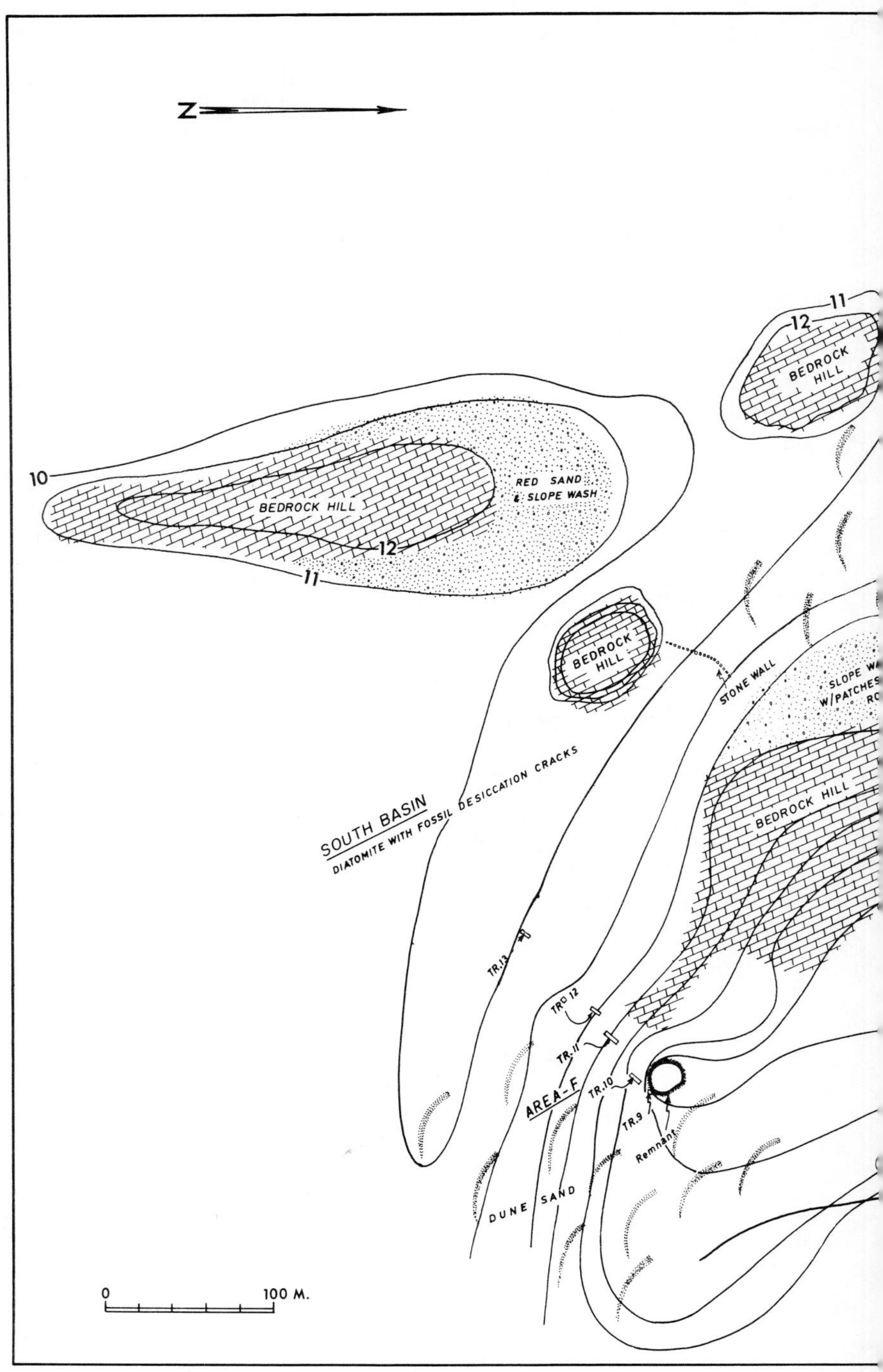

Figure 97. Map of Site E29G1 showing location of Areas A–F.

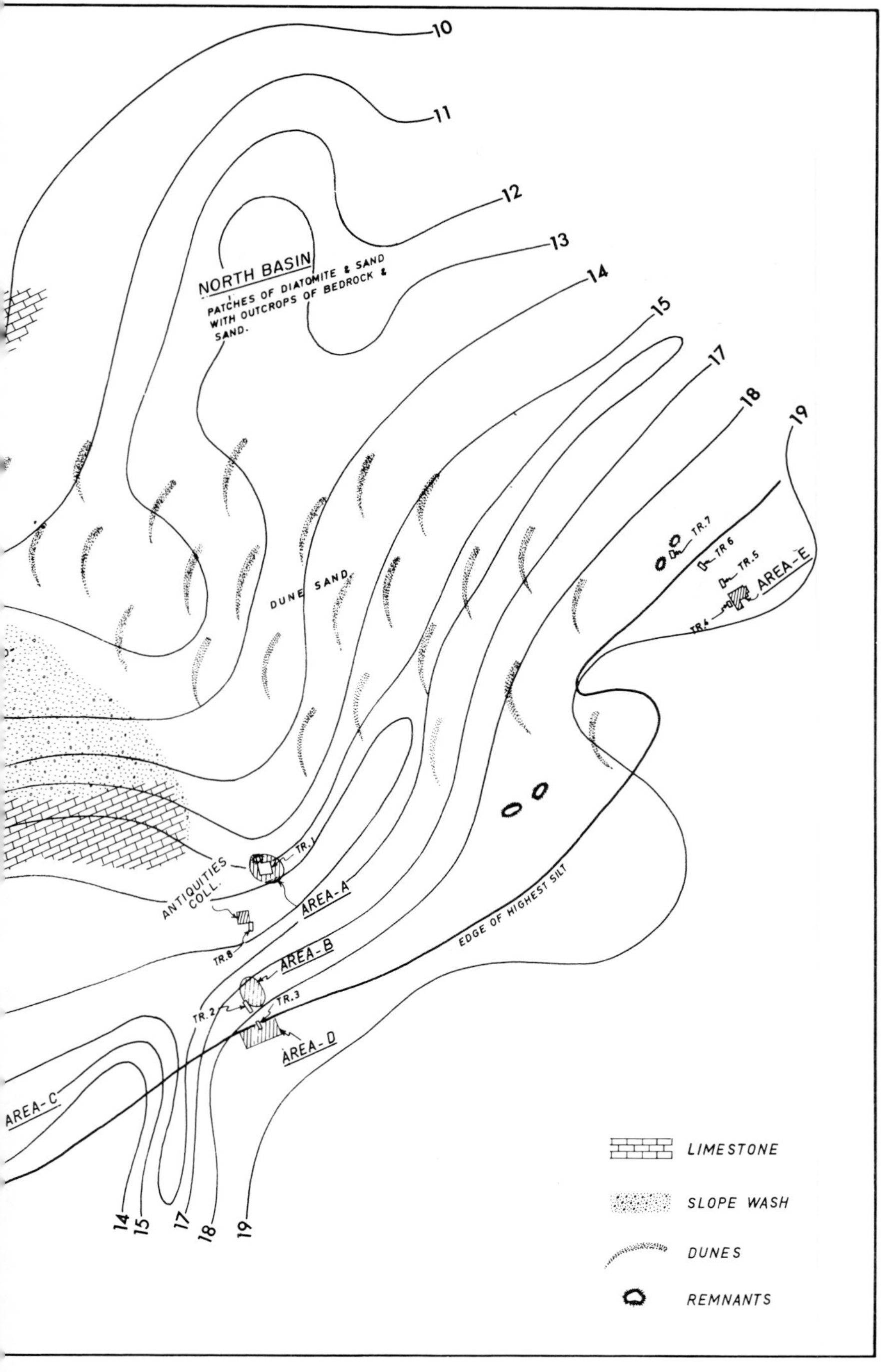

10
11
12
13
14
15
17
18
19
NORTH BASIN
PATCHES OF DIATOMITE & SAND WITH OUTCROPS OF BEDROCK & SAND.
DUNE SAND
TR.7
TR.6
TR.5
AREA-E
TR.4
TR.1
ANTIQUITIES COLL.
AREA-A
TR.8
AREA-B
TR.2
TR.3
AREA-D
AREA-C
EDGE OF HIGHEST SILT
14
15
17
18
19
LIMESTONE
SLOPE WASH
DUNES
REMNANTS

Figure 98. Site E29G1, Area F, showing remnant of Premoeris silts interspersed with thin zones of swamp sediment.

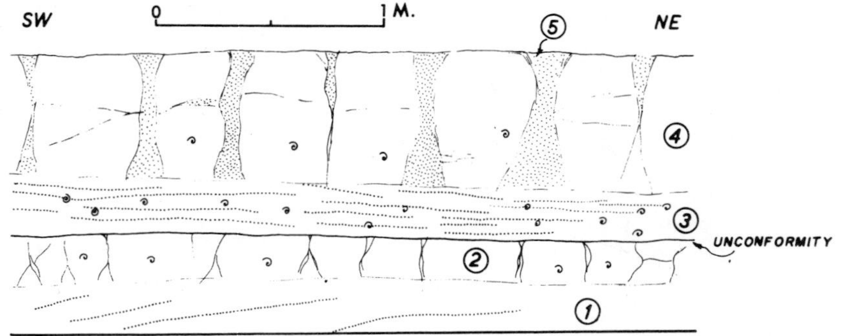

Figure 99. Profile of Trench 13, Site E29G1, Area F.

1. Pale yellow (2.5Y 7/4), fine and medium-grained sand; stratified, with small dip toward the center of the basin; cemented; calcareous.

2. White (2.5Y 8/2) diatomite with irregular coarse blocky structure and rare small lacustrine snails; cemented; highly calcareous; unstratified.

3. Pale yellow (5Y 7/3), fine-grained sand almost horizontally stratified and with numerous small lacustrine snails; loose to consolidated; calcareous.

4. White (2.5Y 8/2) diatomite with an extensive polygonal network of fossil desiccation cracks down to its base; coarse, angular blocky structure; unstratified; highly carbonaceous; cemented. Small snails dispersed within its lower part.

5. Pale yellow to greenish, fine and medium-grained lacustrine sand filling dehydration cracks in the diatomite.

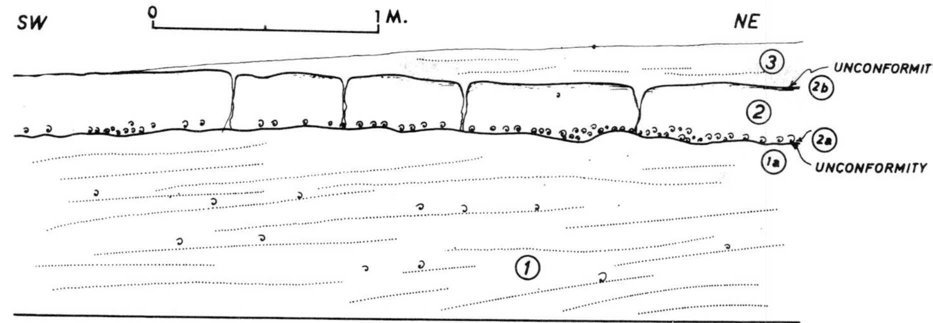

Figure 100. Profile of Trench 12, Site E29G1, Area F.

1. Pale yellow (2.5Y 7/4), fine and medium-grained, foreset-bedded sand with numerous small snails containing mainly *Planorbis mareoticus, Bulinus truncatus, Melanoides tuberculata*, and *Bitynia* sp. Cemented; highly carbonaceous.
2. Same diatomite as (4) in Trench 13 but with a clear layer of small lacustrine snails, of essentially the same complex at the base.
3. Light, yellowish-brown (2.5Y 6/4), fine and medium-grained sand resting unconformably on (2). Horizontally stratified; cemented; calcareous.

Around the base of the wind-scoured remnant are deep, deflated pockets (2 m) that are filled with loose, coarse-grained, aeolean sand and blocks of cemented older sand units fallen from the remnant.

It is most fortunate that the distinctive bands of swamp sediment can be traced on the surface to adjacent areas of the site (A to E). Because of this it is possible to correlate the long sequence at Area F with these other areas, where significant archaeological material occur (Figures 105 and 106). At Area A, Trench 1 (Figure 107), unconformably above a unit of white, highly cemented, horizontally stratified, fine to medium-grained sand, is a yellow (2.5y, 7/6), almost horizontally stratified, fine to medium grained sand with visible oxidation stains and with three thin (1–2 cm), organogenic, gray (2.5y, 5/0) and dark gray (2.5y, 4/0) banks of swamp sediments. The lowest, at an elevation of 15 m above sea level, contained numerous fishbones, chipped stone, and charcoal. A sample of the latter yielded a radiocarbon date of 6150 BC ±130 years (I-4128). This level seemingly correlates with the lowest gray-colored, powdery level at Area F.

Upslope from Trench 1 at Area A to Area B are six more bands of swamp sediment exposed on the surface and in the excavated trenches (Figures 108 and 109). The uppermost band in Area B, at an elevation slightly above 17 m above sea level, also contained numerous fishbones and chipped stone artifacts. Near the top of this series are 2 thin (5–15 cm) layers of clayey, sandy silt ranging in color from pale yellow (2.5y, 8/4) to light yellowish brown (2.5y, 6/4). An unconformity separates the uppermost of these from the overlying sand, which is pale yellow (2.5y, 8/4) in color, almost horizontally stratified, and visibly less cemented than the underlying sand and silt series (Area D). This weakly

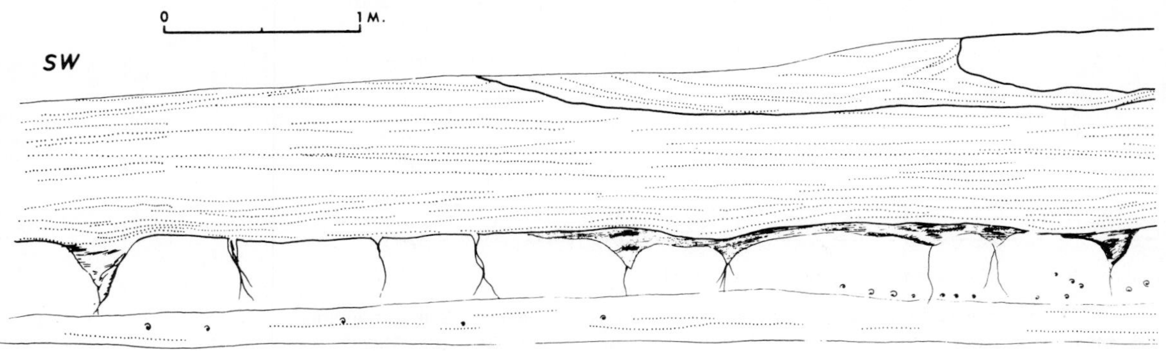

Figure 101. Profile of Trench 11, Site E29G1, Area F.

1. Same as (1) in Trench 12.

2. Same diatomite as (2) in Trench 12 and (4) in Trench 13. Dehydration cracks filled with burned swamp sediment.

3. Diatomite shows numerous traces of heat on its surface.

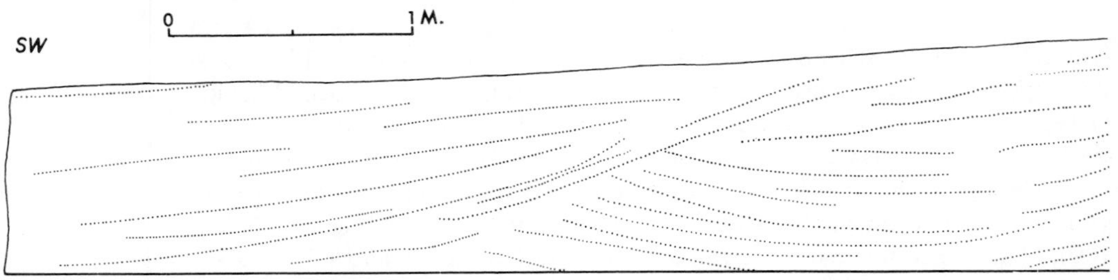

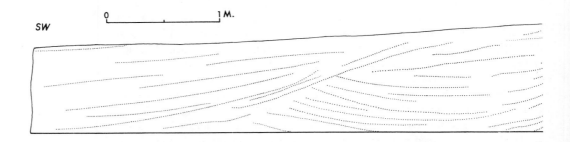

Figure 102. Profile of Trench 10, Site E29G1, Area F.

1. Yellow (10YR 7/8), fine and medium-grained sand with minimal backset dip; cemented; calcareous.

2. Pale yellow, fine sand with thin lamina of snails on a minor erosional surface. Small channels eroded in (1). Traces of almost horizontal bedding; cemented; calcareous.

3. Stratified, fine to medium-grained sand; cemented.

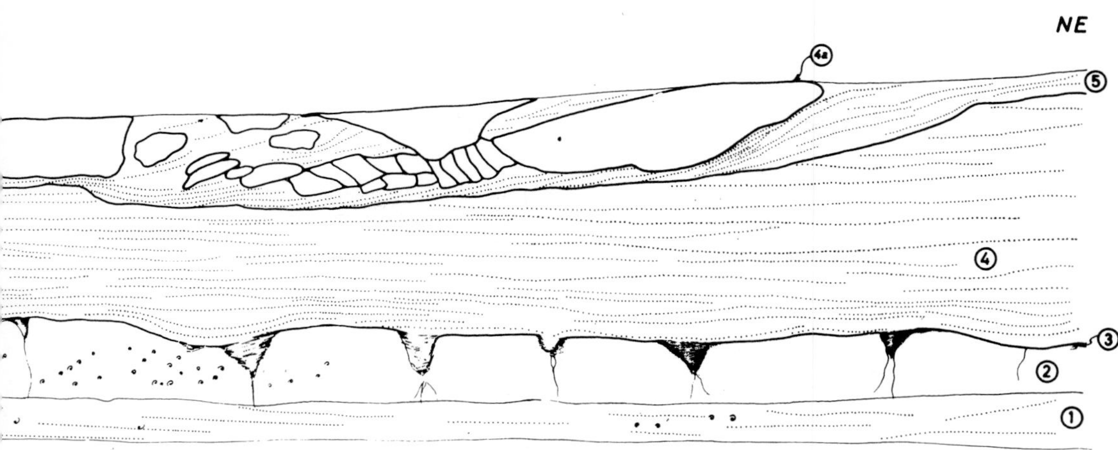

4. Light, yellowish-brown (2.5Y 6/4), almost horizontally stratified sand with numerous oxidation stains dispersed throughout the unit; cemented; calcareous. (a) Boulders of cemented lacustrine sand fallen from wind-eroded, cliff-like face of the remnant at Area F.

5. Coarse-grained, loose, modern eolian sand.

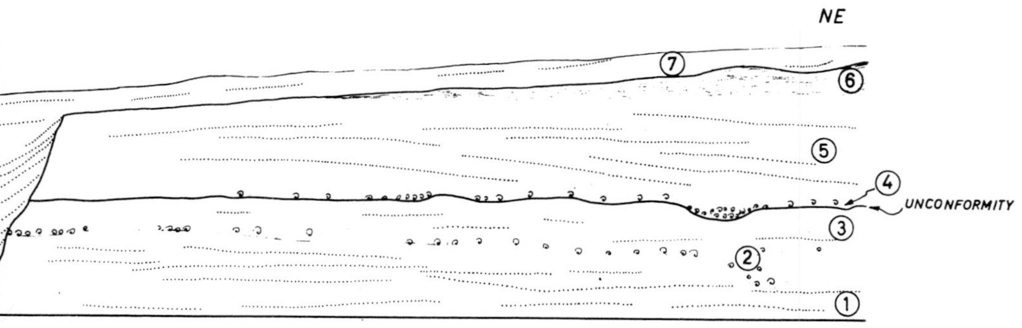

4. Thin layer of small lacustrine snails on an erosional surface developed in (3). Concentrations of snails in form of breccia in shallow erosional depressions.

5. Yellow (10YR 7/8), fine and medium-grained sand with noticeable backset dip; cemented; calcareous.

6. Dark, grayish-brown (2.5Y 4/2), loose, powdery, swampy sediment in a sandy matrix.

7. Modern eolian coarse sand.

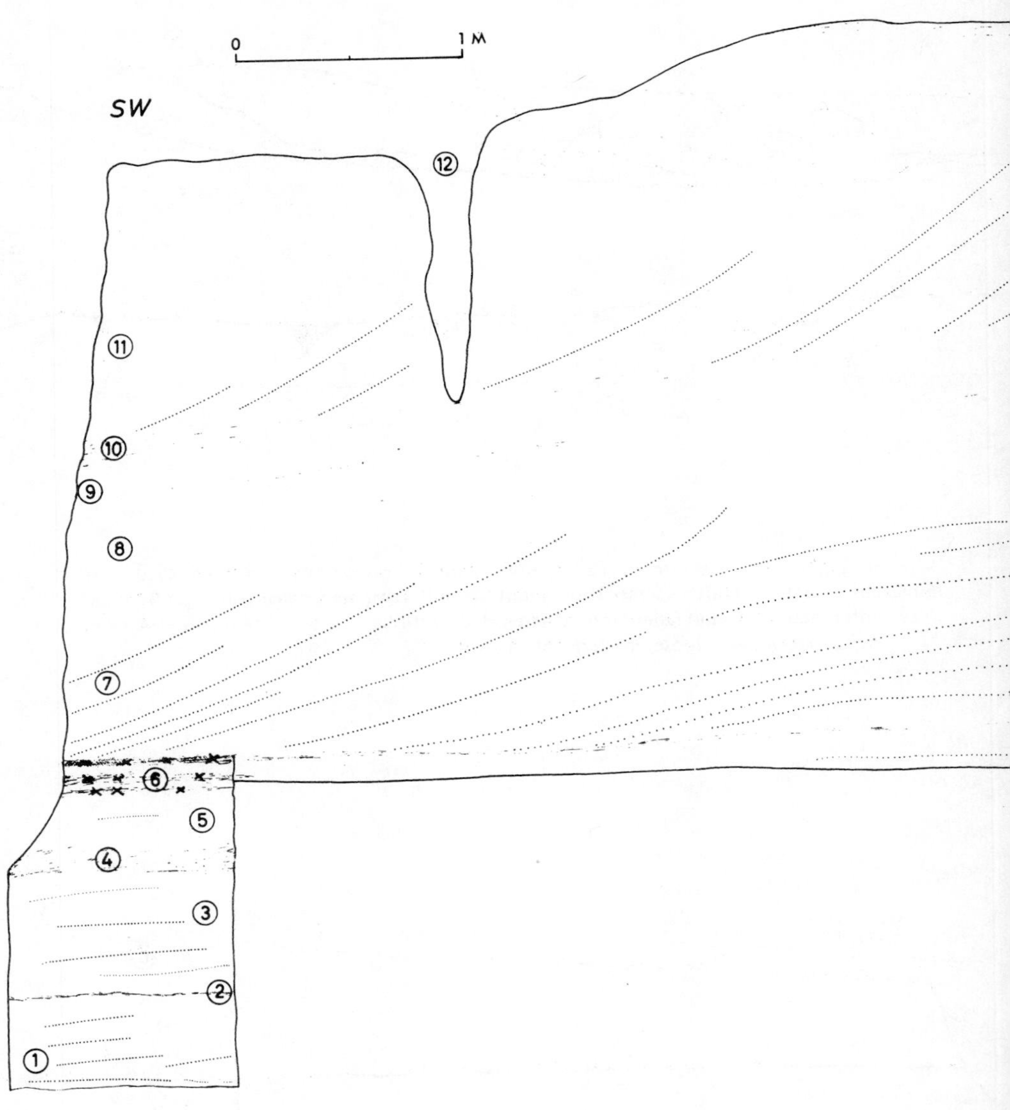

0
1 M
SW
⑫
⑪
⑩
⑨
⑧
⑦
⑥
⑤
④
③
②
①

Figure 103. Profile of Trench 9 and adjacent silt remnant at Site E29G1, Area F.

1. Pale yellow (2.5Y 8/4), medium and fine-grained sand with traces of bedding; cemented; calcareous.

2. Grayish-brown (2.5Y 5/2), powdery, swampy sediment.

3. Pale yellow (2.5Y 8/4), fine and medium-grained sand with iron stains; inconspicuous bedding; cemented; carbonaceous.

4. Very dark, grayish-brown (2.5Y 3/2), powdery, loose, swampy sediment.

5. Pale yellow (2.5Y 8/4), medium and fine-grained sand with traces of bedding; cemented; calcareous.

6. Very dark, grayish-brown (2.5Y 3/2), powdery, loose, swampy sediment interbedded with cemented sand. Contains rare chipped stone artifacts, animal and fish bones, and fragments of human skull.

7. Yellow (2.5Y 7/6), fine and medium-grained sand, foreset bedded with the bedding inconspicuous in places. Cemented; carbonaceous.

8–10. Grayish-brown (2.5Y 5/2), powdered, loose, swampy sediment interbedded with unstratified, yellow, cemented sand.

11. Pale yellow (2.5Y 8/4), fine and medium-grained sand, foreset bedded, with lamination hardly noticeable at the top. Cemented; calcareous.

12. Rain erosion holes.

13. Very dark gray (2.5Y 3/0), silty swamp sediment; consolidated; unstratified; carbonaceous.

Figure 104. General cross-section at Site E29G1, Area F.

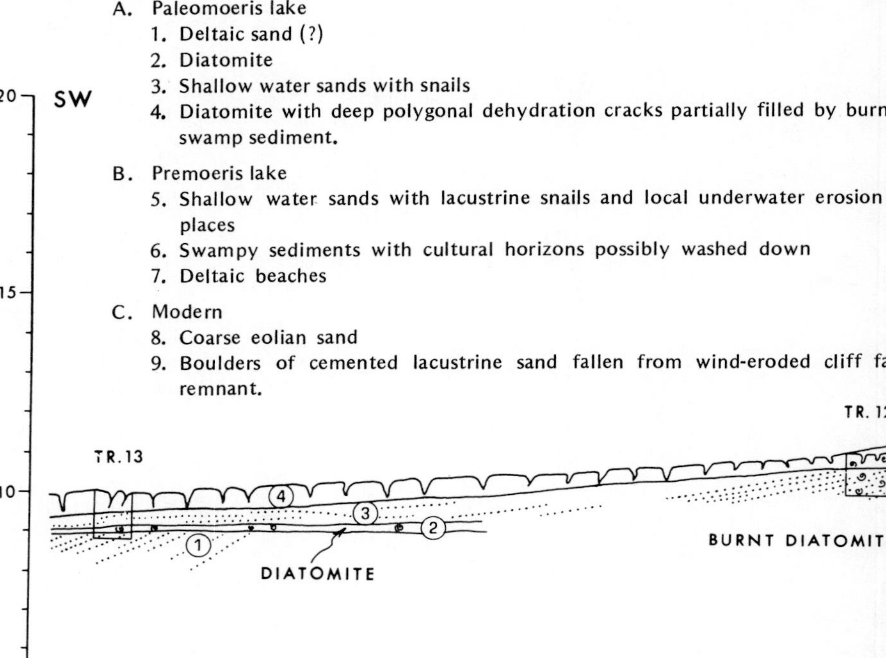

Figure 105. Site E29G1, Area A, looking east. Area F is just over hill beyond vehicle, around prominent remnant in center skyline.

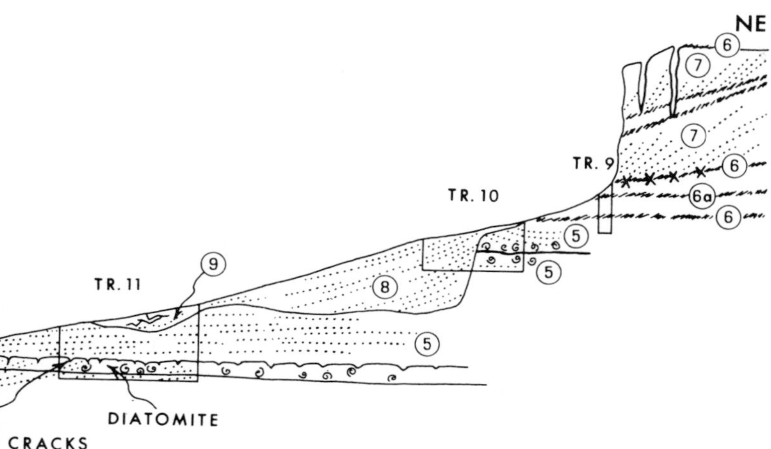

Figure 106. Site E29G1, Area A. Figure is pointing to a line of swamp sediment of Premoeris Lake.

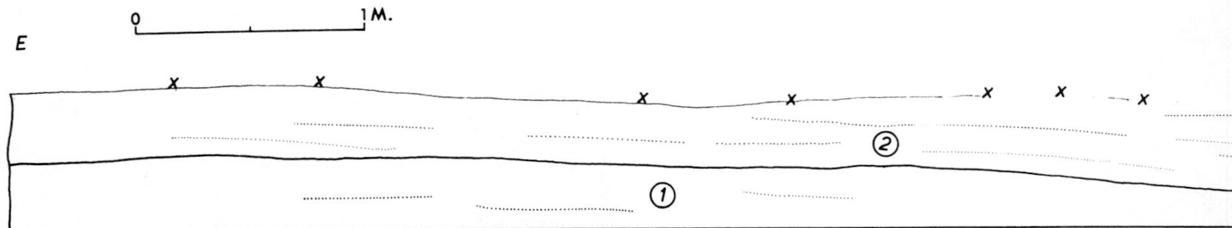

Figure 107. Profile of Trench 1, Site E29G1, Area A.

1. White (2.5Y 8/2), fine and medium-grained sand with inconspicuous foreset-bedded stratification dipping slowly toward the basin; cemented; calcareous, separated by clear erosional surface from the overlying sediment.

2. Yellow (2.5Y 7/6), fine and medium-grained sand; stratified with slight dip toward the basin and numerous elongated, almost vertical, root-like oxidation stains. Cemented; calcareous.

3, 5, 7. Gray (2.5Y N5) to dark gray (2.5Y N4), powdered, loose, swampy sediments conformably intercalating with lacustrine sands (4,6). Lowest layer contains numerous chipped stone artifacts with plentiful fishbones and charcoal. A charcoal sample from this layer (3) gave a radiocarbon date of 6150 BC ±130 years (I-4128).

4, 6. Yellow (2.5Y 7/6), fine and medium-grained sand with inconspicuous lamination and a small dip toward the basin; cemented; calcareous; sterile.

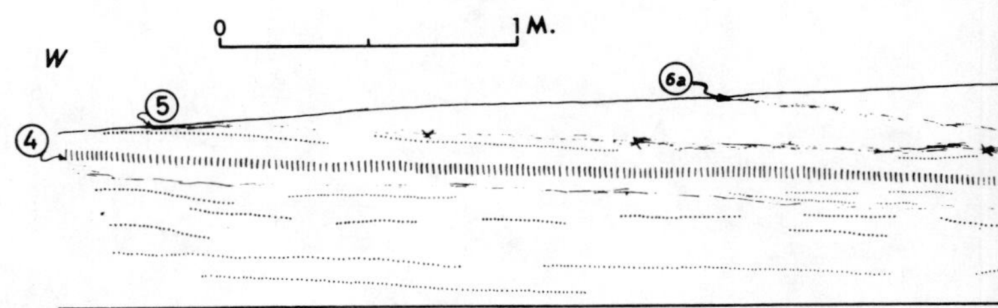

Figure 109. Profile of Trench 2, Site E29G1, Area B.

1. Pale yellow (2.5Y 8/4), fine and medium-grained sand with slight backset bedding; cemented; calcareous.

2. Dark gray (2.5Y N4), powdered, loose, swampy sediment with lamination and traces of washing in places.

3. Pale yellow (2.5Y 8/4), fine and medium-grained sand with conspicuous stratification conformable with (2) and (4). Cemented; calcareous.

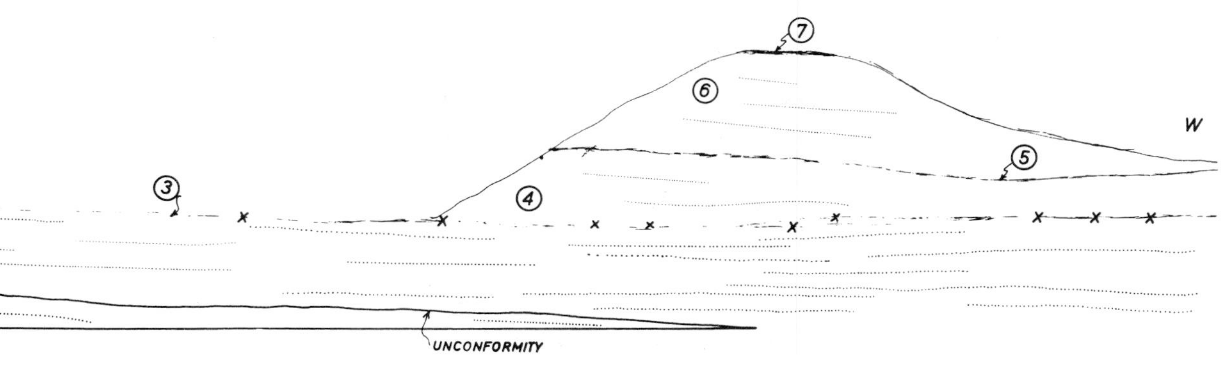

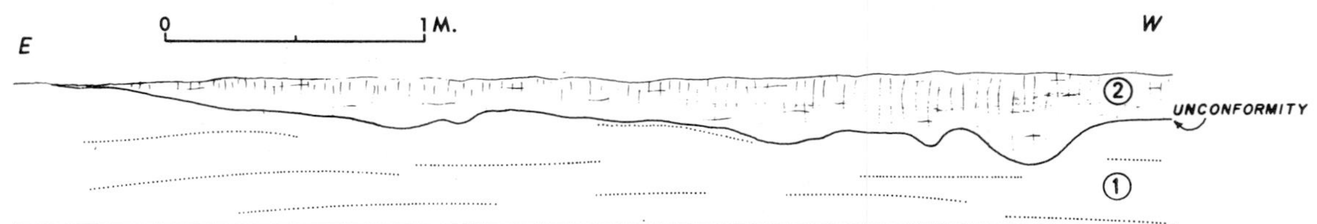

Figure 108. Profile of Trench 8, Site E29G1, Area A. White (2.5Y 8/2), fine and medium-grained sand with inconspicuous stratification and a slight dip toward the basin. Large depression filled by very dark gray (2.5Y N3), powdery, swampy sediment (2) eroded in its surface. Traces of lamination and washing within the depression fill.

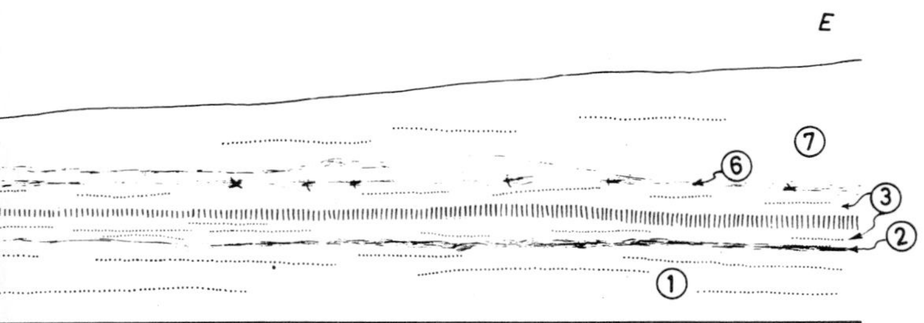

4. Pale yellow (2.5Y 8/4), heavily sandy silt or silty sand with irregular blocky structure; cemented; calcareous.

5–6a. Dark gray (2.5Y N4), powdery, loose, swampy sediments with Terminal Paleolithic chipped stone artifacts and fishbones in lowermost layer (5). Washed and interbedded with cemented yellow sands.

7. Pale yellow (2.5Y 7/4), fine and medium-grained sand with very inconspicuous backset bedding. Cemented; carbonaceous.

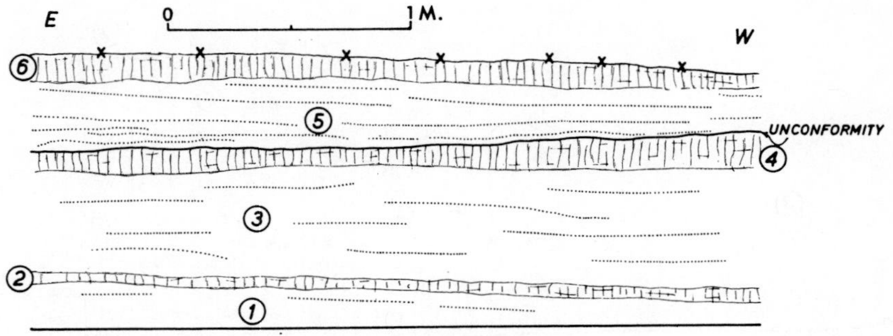

Figure 110. Profile of Trench 3, Site E29G1, Area D.

1. Yellow (2.5Y 7/8), fine and medium-grained sand with light foreset bedding and small oxidation stains; cemented; carbonaceous.

2. Light, brownish-gray (2.5Y 6/2), sandy silt or silty sand with irregular blocky structure and small particles of charcoal. A single stone artifact within the unit. Cemented; unstratified; carbonaceous.

3. Yellow (2.5Y 7/8), fine and medium-grained sand with inconspicuous stratification and slight dip toward the basin. Conformable to (2) and (4). Cemented; carbonaceous.

4. Light, yellowish-brown (2.5Y 6/4), sandy silt with irregular medium blocky or prismatic structure. Top truncated. Cemented; unstratified; carbonaceous.

5. Pale yellow (2.5Y 8/4), fine and medium-grained sand with slight foreset bedding; consolidated; carbonaceous.

6. Light, yellowish-brown (2.5Y 6/4), sandy silt with irregular blocky structure; unstratified; cemented; carbonaceous. Numerous Neolithic and younger artifacts with heavy sandblast on the surface.

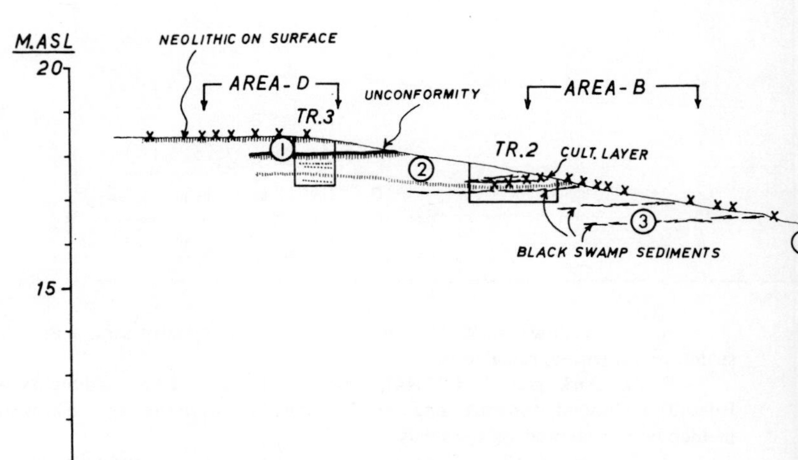

cemented sand is, in turn, conformably overlaid by light, yellowish-brown (2.5y, 6/4), cemented silt with blocky texture (Figure 110). On the surface of this silt, at an elevation of 18.5 m above sea level, were numerous highly wind-polished artifacts, including bifacial tools. Similar artifacts occurred on the slope below at a lower elevation, mixed with artifacts from the exposed cultural layers of earlier date. The artifacts presumably had been dropped from a higher surface that has since been destroyed (Figure 111).

At the north edge of the site was Area E (Figure 112), a small concentration indicated by a few very fresh flakes that were eroding from the top of lacustrine sediments (Figures 113 and 114). Deflation here had exposed only a very limited part of the top of the cultural layer. A large, L-shaped trench (9 m by 12 m) was dug to expose the concentration, and four smaller trenches were cut for stratigraphic purposes (Figure 115).

Figure 111. General cross-section of Site E29G1, Areas A, B, and D.

A. Possible Paleomoeris Lake
   4. Shallow water sand or a part of the deltaic beach structure
B. Premoeris Lake
   2. Shallow water sands and silts
   3. Swampy sediments with cultural layers at the base and in the upper part of the series
C. Possible Protomoeris Lake
   1. Shallow water sands and silts with eolized Neolithic and younger artifacts on deflated surface

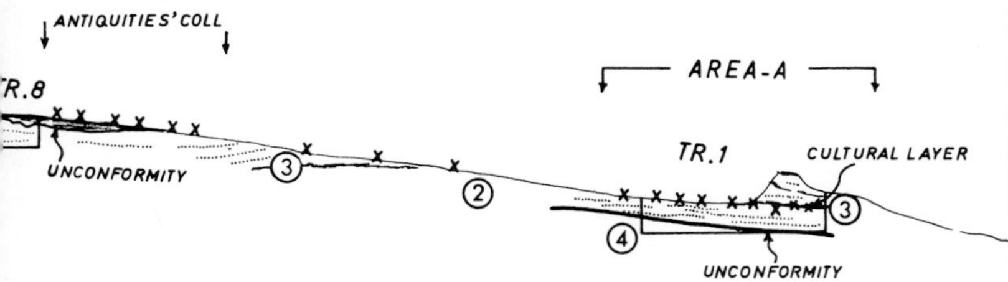

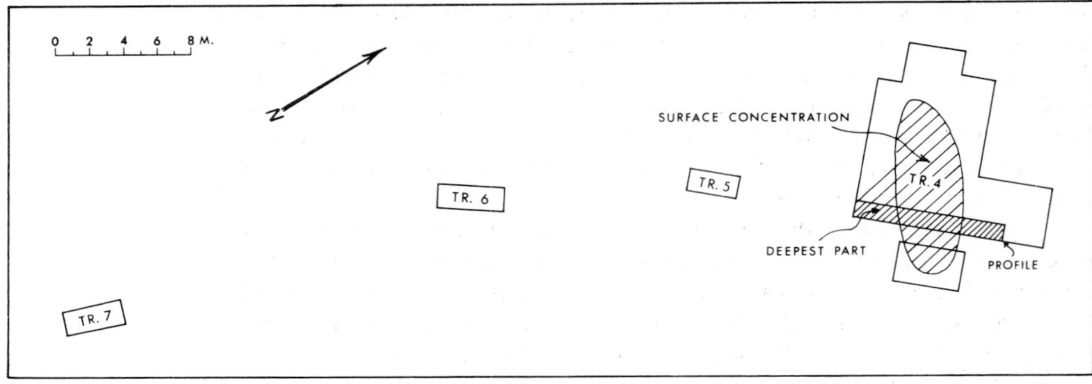

Figure 112. Map of Site E29G1, Area E showing location of trenches.

Figure 113. Site E29G1, Area E, looking east. Buried living floor occurred just behind figures at screen.

Figure 114. View of east wall of trench at Site E29G1, Area E. Figure is pointing to living floor.

Underlying the cultural layer is a thick (1.10 m, base unexposed), yellow (10 yr, 7/6), fine to coarse-grained sand, cemented and clearly stratified to expose the foreset beds with considerable dip. This sand also has heavy oxidation stains (Figure 116).

Unconformably above is the cultural layer, a pale yellow to gray (5y, 7/3 and 2.5y, 6/0), sandy silt and fine, powdered swamp sediment subdivided into at least three conspicuous layers (Figure 117). The sublayers are darker in color and contained fishbone breccia in places, concentrations of complete and burned *Pila ovata* snail shells, and relatively rare chipped stone artifacts. The artifacts and fishbones occurred not only in the darker sublayers but also in the light sand lamina that separate the darker layers. The cultural layer throughout is firmly cemented and could be excavated only with heavy picks. It had clearly been repeatedly rewashed on a flat shallow water and beach area. Burned *Pila ovata* shell from this cultural layer yielded a radiocarbon date of 5190 BC ±120 years (I-4129).

The cultural layer is covered by a light, yellowish-brown (2.5y, 6/4), sandy silt. Slightly beyond the area of the concentration, in trench 7 (Figure 118), is a fine, silty sand and a fine to medium-grained, cemented sand; these are separated by an unconformity. Both of these sand units, and certainly the upper one, overlie the sandy silt that covers the cultural layer. A grinding stone and matching

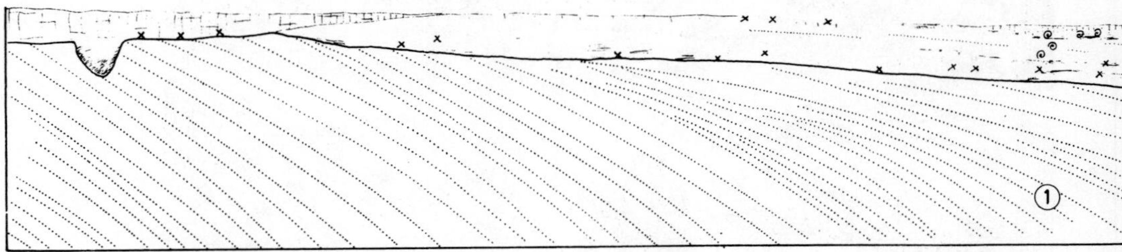

Figure 115. Profile of Trench 4, Site E29G1, Area E.

1. Yellow (10YR 7/6), fine to coarse-grained sand with conspicuous foreset bedding, truncated at the top; cemented; calcareous, with heavy oxidation stains throughout the unit.

2. Gray (2.5Y N6), loose, powdered, swampy layers intercalated with pale yellow (rY 7/3), cemented sand layers resting unconformably on (1). Numerous small underwater erosion channels and swales filled by swampy sediment are recorded in the trench. Cultural material in the form of relatively rich chipped stone artifacts and numerous fishbones as well as bone artifacts occurred throughout the series, concentrated mostly within the swampy layers and lenses. Fishbone breccia in lenses dispersed within the unit. Burned and unburned *Pila ovata* shells were found in concentrations or in erosional swales. A sample of burned shells gave a radiocarbon date of 5190 BC ±120 years (I-4129). Single occupation or several repeated occupations washed and redistributed by waves and/or seasonal inundations in the shallow water/swampy areas. Cemented to loose; carbonaceous.

3. Pale yellow (2.5Y 7/4), fine to coarse sand conformably overlying (2) with slight dip toward the basin; cemented; carbonaceous.

4. Light, yellowish-brown (2.5Y 6/4), sandy silt unconformably overlying (2) and (3). At the northeastern corner of the trench, contained stone artifacts eroded from cultural layer showing a clear silt sheen. Surface deflated. A few heavily windworn bifacial artifacts on the surface. Cemented, with angular medium blocky structure; carbonaceous.

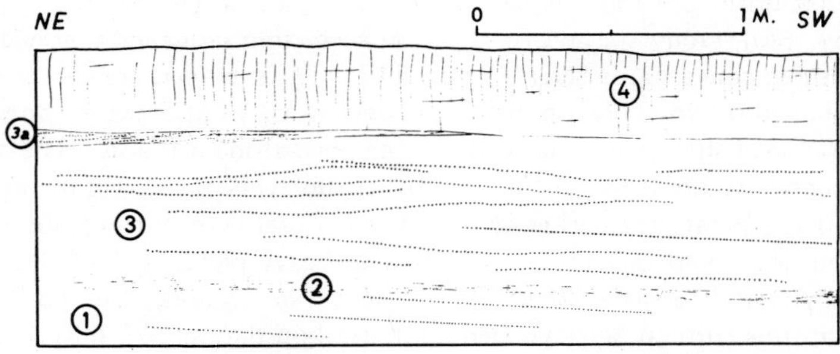

Figure 116. Profile of Trench 5, Site E29G1, Area E.

1–3. Yellow (2.5Y 7/8), fine to coarse-grained sand; stratified, with a slight dip toward the basin; cemented; carbonaceous; numerous oxidation stains; sterile.

2. Gray (2.5Y N5), powdered, loose, swampy sediment with rare artifacts and fishbones, conformable with (1) and (3).

3a. Fine, stratified sand; consolidated to loose, seems to grade down into (3).

4. Same sandy silt as (4) in Trench 4.

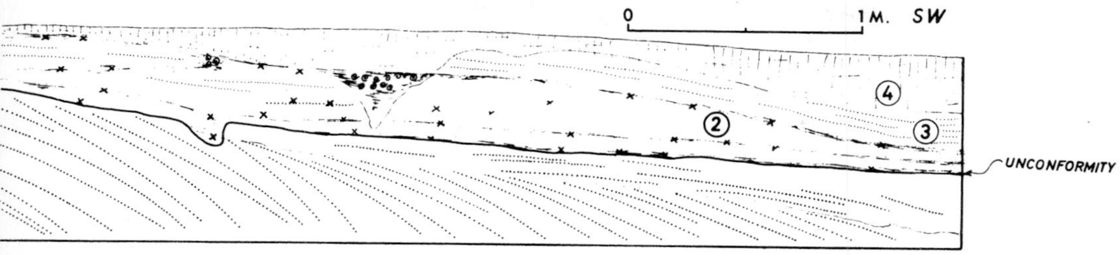

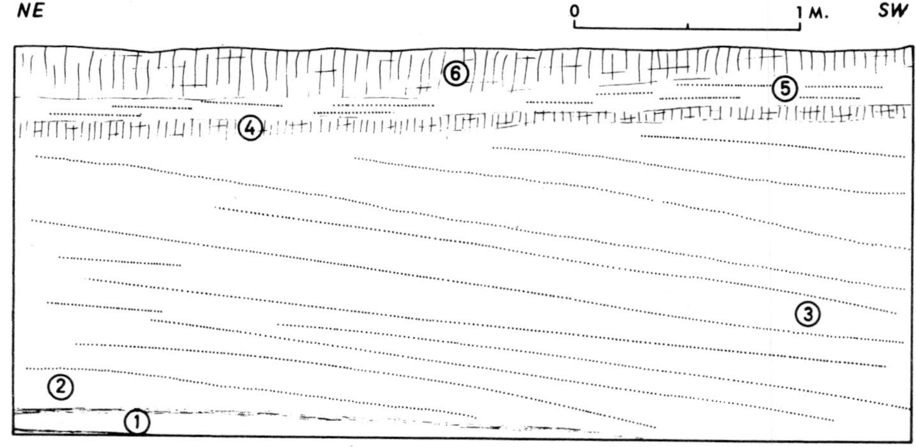

Figure 117. Profile of Trench 6, Site E29G1, Area E.

1. Same sand as (1) in Trench 5.
2. Gray, powdered, loose, swampy sediment with very rare artifacts and fishbones, same as (2) in Trench 5.
3. Yellow (2.5Y 7/6), fine to coarse-grained, foreset-bedded sand; cemented; calcareous.
4. Light, yellowish-brown (2.5Y 6/4), very sandy silt with medium angular blocky structure; cemented; carbonaceous.
5. Yellow (2.5Y 7/6), fine to medium-grained sand conformable with (4) and (6); cemented; carbonaceous.
6. Same sandy silt as (4) in Trench 5.

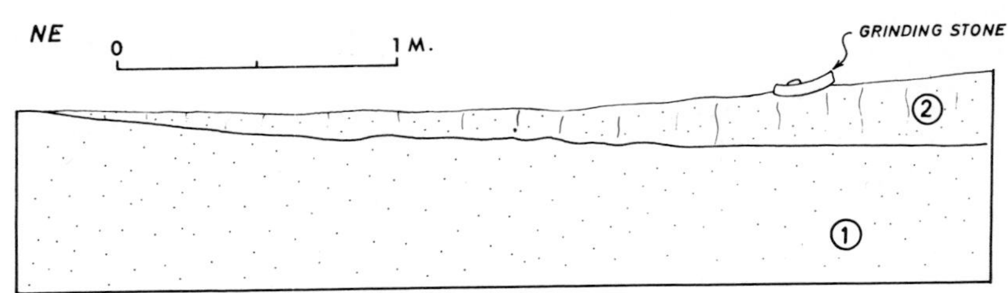

Figure 118. Profile of Trench 7, Site E29G1, Area E.

1. Pale yellow (2.5Y 7/4), fine and medium-grained sand with stratification entirely masked; contains numerous oxidation stains; cemented; carbonaceous. Clearly truncated.

2. Light gray (2.5Y 7/2), silty sand separated from (1) by clear erosional surface; cemented; unstratified; carbonaceous. Large grinding stone with its grinder still in place is eroding from this unit.

grinder, resting together in operating position, were found firmly embedded in the upper silty sand unit at this trench.

The pronounced unconformity that underlies the cultural layer at Area E, and below the silt cap at Area D, seemingly records an important event in the history of the lake (Figure 119). The radiocarbon date of 5190 BC, if correct, indicates a high lake stand—around 19 m—at that time. Site E29G3, Area A will be discussed later; however, a cultural layer at an elevation of 12 m, associated with a clear recessional phase and dated 5550 BC, indicates a major drop in the level of the lake to considerably below 12 m between 5200 and 5600 BC. This decline in lake level separates our Premoeris and Protomoeris lakes, and therefore the occupation at E29G1, Area E has to be assigned to the later of these aggradations, or the Protomoeris lake.

Site E29H1

Other occupations of the Premoeris Lake occur at Sites E29H1 and E29G3. Site E29H1 is probably the unnamed Fayum B site at the north edge of "X Basin" of Caton-Thompson and Gardner (1934: Plate CIX). The site was a vast scatter of artifacts on the gently sloping expanse of lacustrine sediments that overlook X Basin on the north side (Figure 120). The floor of the basin is covered by a thick layer of diatomite, which has inhibited further deflation. Artifacts occurred most commonly in an oval area 300 m by 540 m; however, careful surface examination disclosed that the artifact-littered area consisted in reality of two groups, one inside the other (Figure 121). The smaller, an elongated oval about 300 m long and 100 m wide, contained several separated concentrations on the surface, together with a thin scatter of other artifacts of Terminal Paleolithic age mixed with later artifacts. A distinct difference in surface weathering distinguished many of the Terminal Paleolithic artifacts from those of later type. Most of the Terminal Paleolithic artifacts were fresh or almost

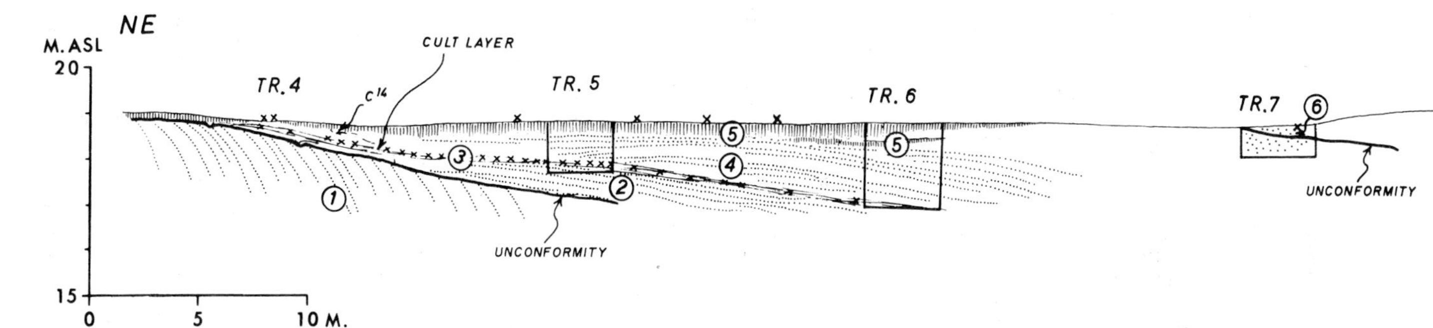

Figure 119. General cross-section of Site E29G1, Area E.

A. Possible Premoeris Lake
   1. Deltaic beach structure
B. Protomoeris Lake
   2–5. Shallow water sands (2/4); washed, swampy sediments with occupation remains (3); sandy silts (5).
C. Moeris Lake
   6. Silty sands

Figure 120. View of Site E29H1 before excavation. Figure is near center of surface concentration. Artifacts occurred below surface in trench excavated to right of figure.

fresh, and in this area fossil bone and bone tools occurred on the surface. The artifacts of later type, however, were uniformly heavily eolized.

Three surface concentrations of Terminal Paleolithic artifacts were collected and designated areas A–C. Areas A and C were partially excavated; Area B, a 10 m by 10 m square, was surface collected, but no trench was dug.

Beyond the limits of the smaller group of concentrations, composed primarily of Terminal Paleolithic artifacts, was a thinner scattering composed entirely of later tools, grinding stones, and a very few potsherds, all heavily wind polished. No fossil bone occurred in this larger area.

A series of 18 trenches were dug across the site and toward the basin, covering a distance of 540 m. In addition, the deflation has truncated most of the lake sediments, exposing clear-cut stratigraphy, which aided the efforts to follow and connect the observed units and facilitated the reconstruction of events at this locality.

The partially exposed stratigraphy disclosed a belt of sandy sediments across the center of the site. The Terminal Paleolithic artifacts were confined to this belt. Further excavation defined the belt as the oldest unit within a long sequence of lacustrine sediments.

At the base of the oldest series of exposed sediments is a sequence of pale yellow to yellow (2.4Y 7/4 and 7/6), foreset-bedded, medium to coarse-grained, cemented sands with three intercalating thin layers of very dark gray and black

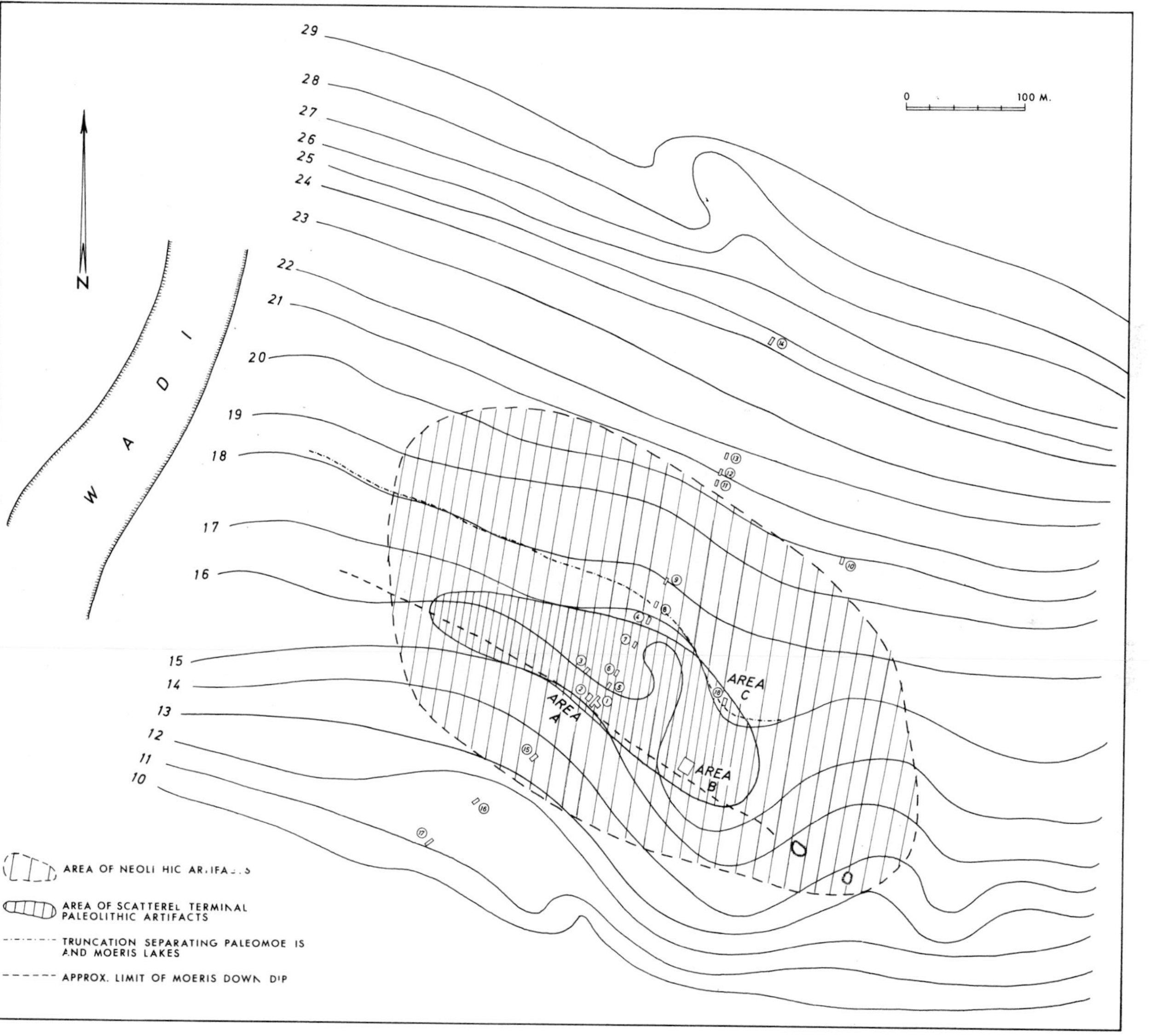

Figure 121. Map of Site E29H1, Fayum.

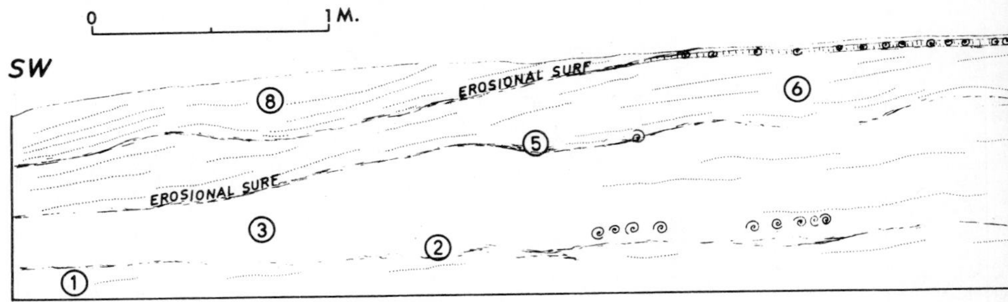

Figure 122. Profile of Trench 4, Site E29H1.

1. Light gray (2.5Y 7/2), fine and medium-grained sand; stratified, with a slight dip toward the center of the basin. Cemented by heavy contents of calcium carbonate.

2. Lenses of very dark gray (10YR 3/1), powdered, loose, very fine swamp sediment deposited on an erosional surface. Concentration of *Pila ovata* in places within the sediment or just above. Shells sometimes broken but usually intact. In places traces of minor erosion or washing.

3. White, fine and medium-grained sand with traces of wavy stratification and slight dip toward the center of the basin. Rare shells of *Pila ovata* dispersed throughout the layer. Cemented; highly carbonaceous. A few fresh artifacts at the very top of this unit.

4. Grayish, thin layer of sandy silt with blocky structure; cemented; unstratified; calcareous.

5. Black (10YR 2/1), powdery, fine swamp sediment; rare *Pila ovata*. Clearly truncated in places.

6. Pale yellow (2.5Y 7/4), fine and medium-grained sand; stratified conformably with underlying erosional surface; cemented; highly calcareous.

7. Blackish, sandy silt with prismatic or blocky structure and very numerous *Pila ovata* shells intact in most cases. Truncated at the southwestern end of the trench.

8. Light gray (2.5Y 7/2), fine and medium-grained sand; stratified, with lamination conformable to the underlying minor erosional suraface; cemented; highly calcareous.

(10YR 3/1 and 2/1), powdered, loose swamp deposits, in places grading into sandy silt. Here and there these layers contained very dense concentrations of intact shells of *Pila ovata*. Two fresh cores were found just below the middle layer (Figure 122).

Downslope the three swampy layers merge and are, in turn, covered by a massive deltaic top and foreset-bedded body of medium and coarse-grained, yellow to almost white (10YR 8/6, 8/8; 2.5Y 8/2) sands (Figures 123–125). These sands are cemented at the top to almost loose at the bottom, and have oxidation stains in places. They also contained very rare snails. The occupation floor, now deflated, almost surely was on a surface of the topset beds of this unit. A cultural layer reworked by the lake waters, from 10 cm to 20 cm thick with the upper part at an elevation almost 15 m above sea level, occurs within the foreset bedding of this deltaic type of structure (Figure 126). The cultural layer is a very pale brown (10YR 8/3), loose, medium and coarse-grained sand, with traces of stratification within the layer (Figure 127). Just below and above the

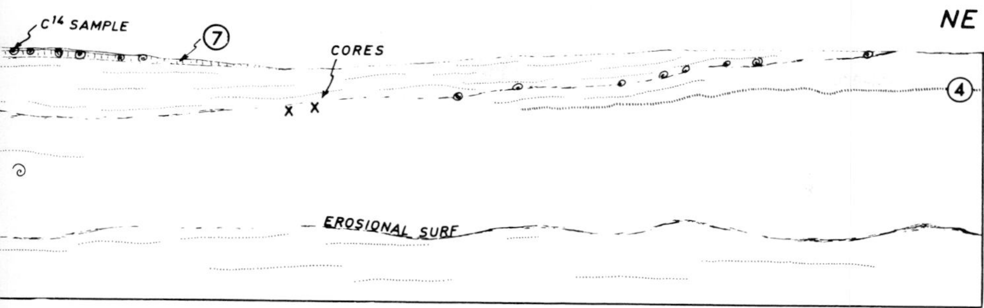

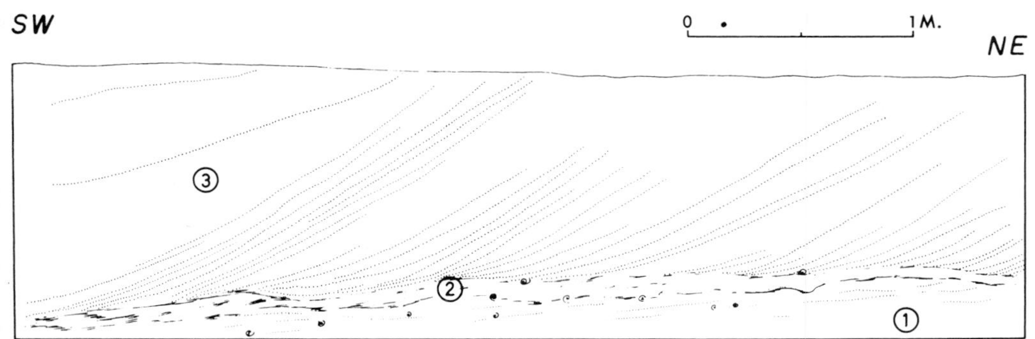

Figure 123. Profile of Trench 7, Site E29H1.

1. White (2.5Y 8/2), fine and medium-grained sand with strata dipping slightly toward the basin. Small lacustrine snails dispersed throughout the layer; cemented; highly calcareous.

2. Dark gray (2.5Y N4), powdery swamp sediment with pale yellow (2.5Y 7/4) interbeds of fine and medium-grained sand. Intact or slightly damaged shells of *Pila ovata* in places. Slight dip toward the basin. Cemented; calcareous.

3. Yellow (10YR 8/6), foreset-bedded, medium and coarse-grained sand of the base of the deltaic beach complex resting on (2). Cemented; highly calcareous.

Figure 124. Profile of Trench 6, Site E29H1. Yellow (10YR 8/6), fine to coarse-grained sand with short series of foreset beds and minor erosional phenomena in places and a topset bed passing slowly into foreset bed in the upper part. Cemented; calcareous.

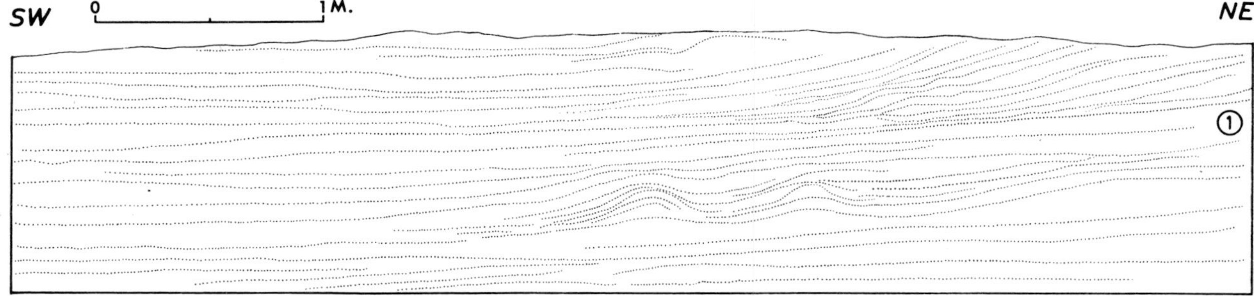

Figure 125. Profile of Trench 5, Site E29H1. Yellow (10YR 8/6), fine to coarse-grained sand with foreset-bedded stratification; cemented; calcareous.

Figure 126. Site E29H1. Figure is pointing to line of charcoal and Terminal Paleolithic debris. Charcoal yielded radiocarbon date of 6120 BC ±115 years (I-4126).

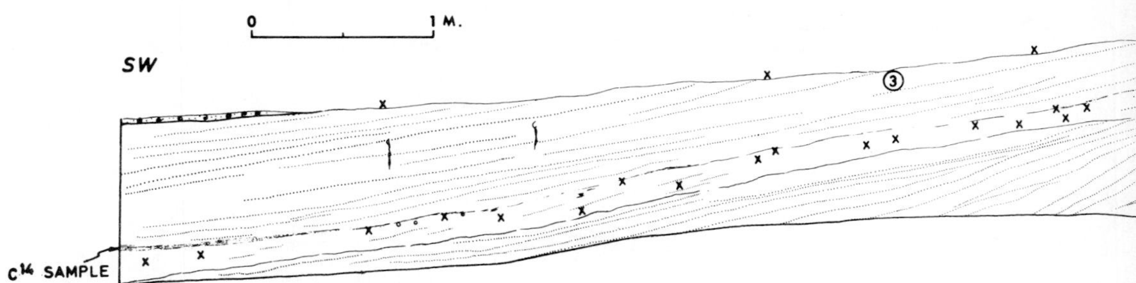

Figure 127. Profile of Trench 1, Site E29H1.

1. Yellow (10YR 8/8), fine and medium-grained sand; stratified; clear foreset bedding at the base and topset beds passing into foreset beds near the top. Root drip casts numerous in upper part of this unit. Cemented; oxidation staining observed throughout the layer.

2. Very pale brown (10YR 8/3), fine and medium-grained sand with lenses and patches of powdered charcoal, bones, and chipped stone artifacts. Loose to consolidated; calcareous. A charcoal sample from this layer collected at the southwest corner of the trench gave a radiocarbon date of 6120 BC ±115 years (I-4126).

3. Same as (1). Dispersed artifacts on the surface.

4. White, loose, fine sand separated from underlying unit by an erosional surface; small, shallow channel cut in (3) and filled with loose sand and small pebbles of cemented units (1) and (3) observed along the southwestern edge of the trench. Contained very numerous shells of *Planorbis mareoticus*, *Bulinus truncatus*, *Melanoides tuberculata*, and *Bitynia* sp.; traces of stratification observed in places; calcareous.

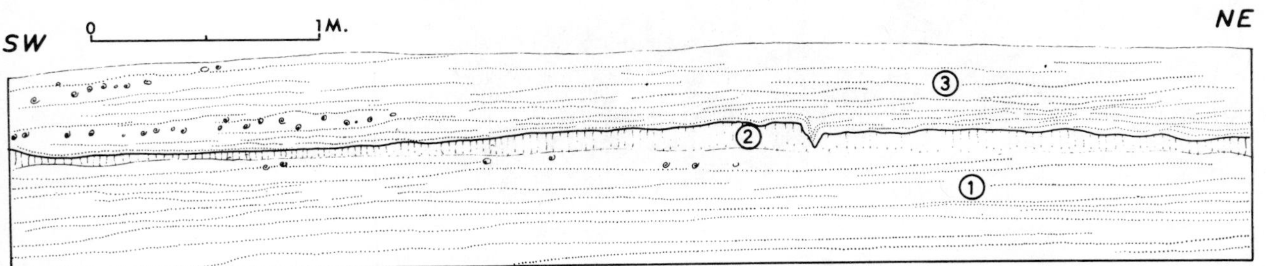

Figure 128. Profile of Trench 15, Site E29H1.

1. Pale yellow (2.5Y 8/4), fine sand; stratified; slight dip toward the center of the basin. Layers of small lacustrine snails in places, more numerous near the top, with *Planorbis mareoticus*, *Bulinus truncatus*, *Melanoides tuberculata*, and *Bitynia* sp.; cemented; calcareous; oxidation stains observed throughout the unit.

2. Conformably overlying light gray (5Y 7/2), very sandy silt with medium prismatic structure and fossil dehydration cracks down to the base filled with overlying sediment. Surface clearly truncated. Cemented; unstratified; highly calcareous.

3. Very pale brown (10YR 7/3), loose, fine sand with numerous thick layers of small lacustrine snails same as in (4) in Trench 1. Stratified, with wavy lamination and small dip toward the center of the basin. Thin laminae of iron and manganese concentration throughout the unit. Calcareous.

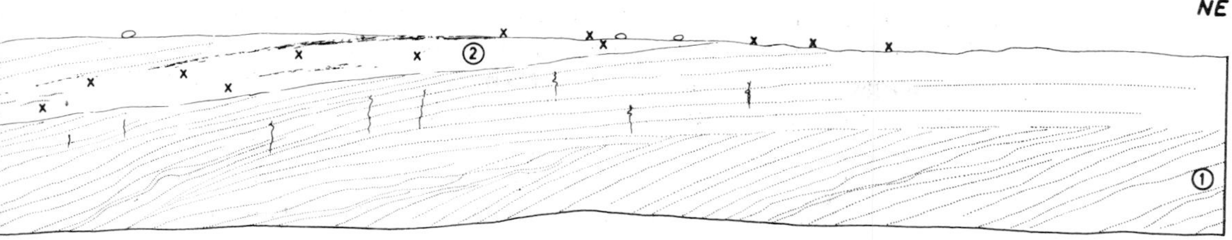

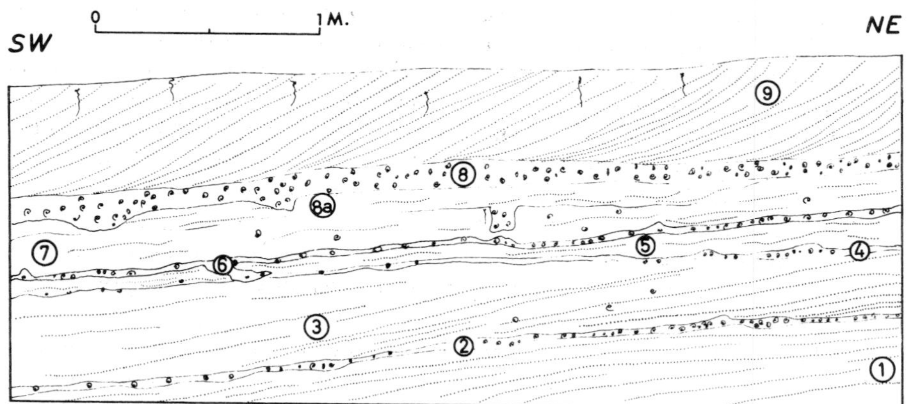

Figure 129. Profile of Trench 16, Site E29H1.

1. Pale yellow (2.5Y 8/4), fine and medium-grained sand; stratified with clear foreset dip; cemented; calcareous.
2. White (2.5Y N8) layer of snails in a diatomaceous matrix. Contains *Planorbis mareoticus*, *Bulinus truncatus*, *Melanoides tuberculata*, and *Bitynia* sp. Consolidated; calcareous; unstratified.
3. Pale yellow (2.5Y 8/4), fine and medium-grained, foreset-bedded sand with rare lacustrine snails containing previously mentioned species. Cemented; calcareous; dispersed oxidation stains.
4. Same as (2).
5. Same as (3).
6. Same as (2).
7. Same as (3).
8. Same as (2). (a) White (2.5Y 8/2), fine sand with wavy foreset bedding and small pockets with lacustrine snails. Cemented; calcareous.
9. Yellow (10YR 8/8), medium-grained sand, foreset bedded, resting on (8). Numerous root drip casts observed in upper part. Cemented; calcareous, with oxidation coloring throughout the unit.

cultural layer are calcareous root casts, evidence for the presence of beach vegetation. Numerous lenses of charcoal and charcoal powder occurred in the cultural layer, together with chipped stone artifacts, numerous fish, and a few mammal remains. A sample of charcoal from the top of this reworked layer gave a radiocarbon date of 6120 BC ±115 years (I-4126).

Still farther downslope this deltaic structure of sands is conformably overlain by a unit of light gray (5Y 7/2), very sandy silt with numerous fossil desiccation cracks and with a pronounced unconformity separating it from the overlying sediments (Figure 128).

Above the sandy silt is a series of loose sands containing numerous small snails (*Planorbis mareoticus, Bulinus truncatus, Bitynia* sp., and *Melanoides tuberculata*). The snails become more numerous downslope, where they form breccia layers in a cemented, white (2.5Y 8/0), diatomaceous matrix separated by layers of medium-grained sand (Figure 129).

These snail breccia layers are, in turn, conformably overlain by foreset-bedded, medium-grained, cemented sands colored by yellow oxidation stains (10YR 8/8). These sands also contain calcareous root casts (Figure 130). Near the bottom of the basin, the stratification of these sands destroyed near the top of the unit, where there occurs a red (7.5YR 6/8), sandy, soil-like sediment containing fishbones. The reddish color is intense near the top and grades into the underlying foreset-bedded sand. The red, soil-like sediment is unconformably covered by sandy, white (7.5YR 8/0), cemented diatomite with desiccation cracks. The diatomite forms the floor of the basin.

Upslope from Area A and the earlier deltaic beach deposits is a filled subbasin separated from the underlying deltaic deposits by a very pronounced truncation. The subbasin abuts a fossil slopewash that covers the Eocene shales that form the margin of the Fayum Depression in this area, and thus the subbasin forms the upper edge of the lacustrine sediments here. At the base of the deposits in the subbasin, just above the truncation, is a pale yellow (5Y 7/4 to 2.5Y 8/4), unstratified, coarse sand containing very numerous crushed shells of *Pila ovata* undoubtedly derived from beds of the same kind of snails within the underlying deltaic deposits (Figure 131). At Area C, at an elevation of about 17 m above sea level, this coarse sand grades up into medium to coarse, stratified sand with a slight dip toward the center of the subbasin (Figure 132). The laminae of this stratified sand are wavy in places and contained thin lenses of fishbones together with small snails. Near the top of this unit is a supposedly slightly reworked Terminal Paleolithic occupation. The artifacts were fresh and very numerous and were accompanied by a few fishbones.

Elsewhere at this site (Trench 8, Figure 131), the coarse sand at the base of the deposits in the subbasin is covered by a pale yellow (5Y 7/3), cemented, sandy silt with angular blocky structure, the first of a thick (more than 6 m) series of alternating layers of silty sands, sandy silts, and blackish, powdery swamp

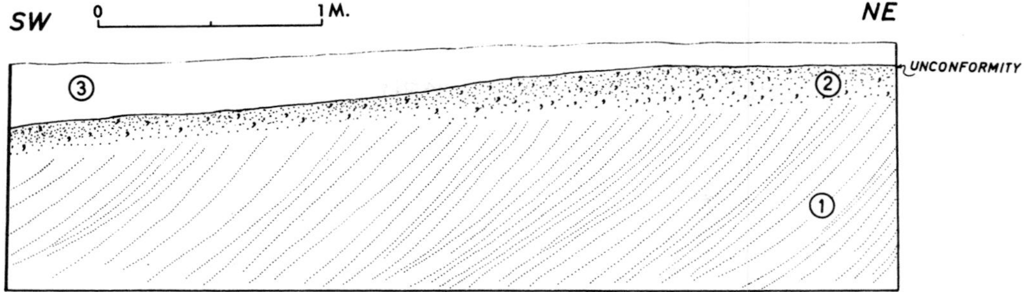

Figure 130. Profile of Trench 17, Site E29H1.

1. Brownish-yellow (10YR 6/6), fine and medium-grained, foreset-bedded sand with stratification disappearing near the top. Oxidation stains observed throughout the layer. Cemented to consolidated; calcareous.

2. Reddish-yellow (7.5YR 6/6), fine and medium-grained sand with rare fishbones; unstratified; intensively colored in its upper part and gradually paler near the base. Loose to slightly consolidated with heavy iron components. Possible soil.

3. White (7.5YR N8), sandy diatomite unconformably overlying (2); cemented; unstratified, with a network of dehydration cracks on the surface; highly calcareous.

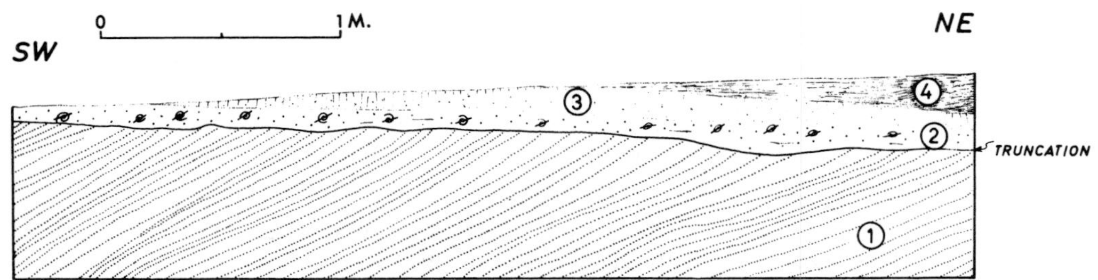

Figure 131. Profile of Trench 8, Site E29H1.

1. Pale yellow (2.5Y 8/4), fine and medium-grained sand with foreset bedding; cemented; calcareous; heavily truncated at the top.

2. Pale yellow (5Y 7/3), coarse sand with very numerous small fragments of crushed shells of *Pila ovata*. Traces of inconspicuous lamination with a small dip toward the subbasin and conformable with the truncation. Loose to consolidated; calcareous.

3. Pale yellow (5Y 7/3), sandy silt with angular medium blocky structure; cemented; unstratified, with a dip conformable to the truncation and underlying coarse sand.

4. Dark gray (5Y 4/1), very fine, swampy sediment; loose, powdered, very light, with irregular lump structure in places and traces of dried roots. Unstratified; truncated by deflation at the surface.

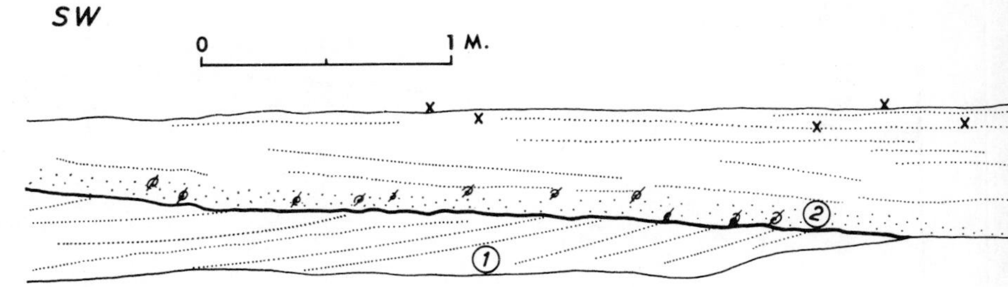

Figure 132. Profile of Trench 18, Site E29H1.

1. Pale yellow (2.5Y 8/4), fine and medium-grained sand with foreset bedding; cemented; calcareous; truncated at the top.

2. Pale yellow (2.5Y 8/4), coarse sand with numerous crushed small fragments of *Pila ovata* shells; unstratified, with a dip conformable to the truncation toward the subbasin. Grades up into coarse sand with wavy lamination and the dip conformable to the truncation. In places, thin lenses of fishbones and small lacustrine snails.

3. Cultural layer with very numerous fresh artifacts and rare animal and fish bones dipping conformably toward the subbasin. Farther to the northeast this sediment, together with the cultural layer is, in turn, covered by sandy silt and black, swampy sediment.

sediments, frequently burned (Figure 133). As the subbasin filled and decreased in size, the dip of these swampy sediments increased (Figures 134-139).

The radiocarbon date of 6150 BC associated with the cultural layer at Area A indicates that the deltaic deposit there was formed during the Premoeris lake, when that lake stood at around 15 m above sea level, the same level and age as the occupation at Site E29G1, Area A. If this conclusion is correct, then the unconformity that separates these earlier deltaic deposits from the series of deep water diatomaceous sediments downslope and from the swampy deposits in the subbasin presumably records the recession separating the Premoeris and Protomoeris lakes (Figure 140).

The occupation at Area C, which occurred at an elevation of about 17 m above sea level around the edge of the filling subbasin, was contemporary with the already rising Protomoeris lake. There is no radiocarbon date associated with Site E29H1, Area C; however, if the date of 5190 BC at E29G1, Area E (which, incidentally, is at about the same elevation (*ca.* 19 m) and is also believed to be associated with the Protomoeris lake) is correct, then the occupation at Area C occurred around 5200 BC.

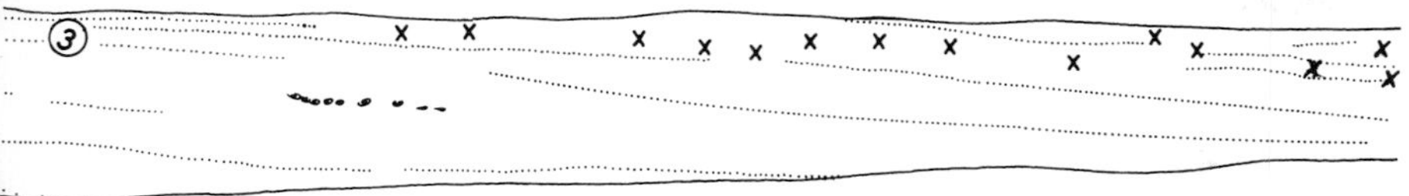

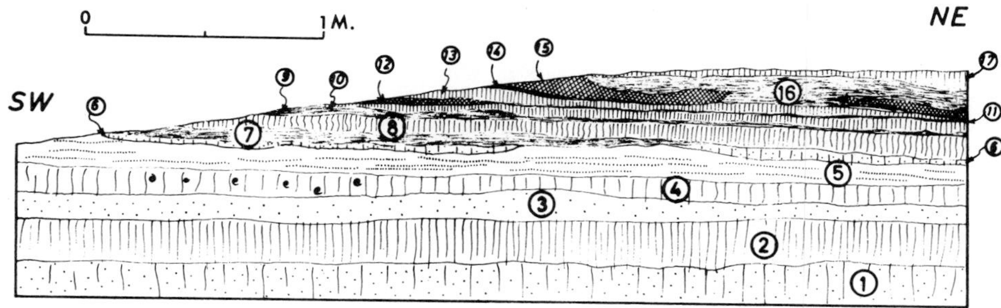

Figure 133. Profile of Trench 9, Site E29H1.

1. Light gray (2.5Y 7/2), silty sand with irregular, coarse blocky structure; unstratified; cemented; calcareous.

22. Gray (5Y 5/1), sandy silt with irregular, coarse blocky structure; cemented; unstratified; calcareous.

3. White (5Y 8/2), fine sand; unstratified; cemented; calcareous.

4. Light gray (5Y 7/2), sandy silt with rare lacustrine snails dispersed throughout the layer; cemented; unstratified; calcareous.

5. White (5Y 8/2), fine sand, stratified, with a small dip toward the subbasin; cemented.

6. Light gray (5Y 7/2), sandy silt with inconspicuous small blocky structure; cemented; unstratified; calcareous.

7. Very dark gray (10YR 3/1), loose, powdered, swampy sediment with traces of burning in places; unstratified; loose, calcareous.

8. Gray (5Y 6/1) silt with medium angular blocky structure; unstratified; cemented; highly calcareous.

9. Very dark gray (10YR 3/1), loose, powdered, fine, swampy sediment with traces of burning in places; unstratified; calcareous.

10. Silt, same as (8).

11. Very dark gray, swampy sediment, same as (9).

12. Extensive traces of burning within very dark gray, swampy sediment.

13. Silt, same as (8).

14. Very dark gray, swampy sediment, same as (9).

15. Very extensive areas of burned, swampy sediment.

16. Very dark gray, swampy sediment.

17. Silty clay, same as (8).

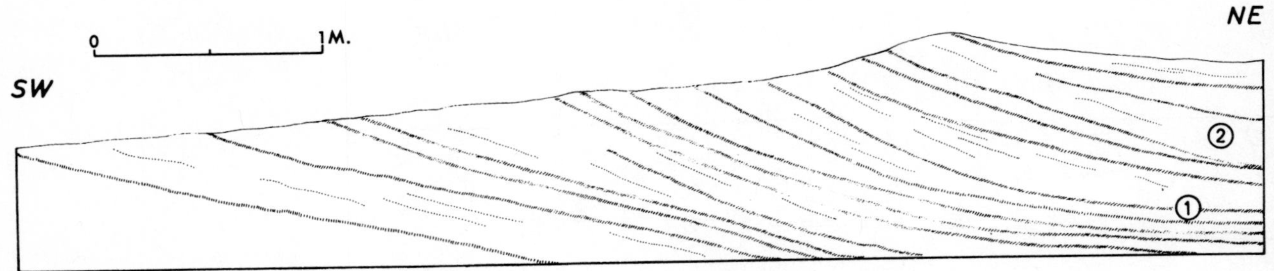

Figure 134. Profile of Trench 10, Site E29H1.

1. Light gray (2.5Y 7/2), sandy silt layers with carbonate concentrations; cemented. Blocky structure in places. Dip toward the center of the subbasin.

2. Yellow (2.5Y 8/6), fine and medium-grained sand with traces of lamination conformable to the dip of (1). Cemented; carbonaceous.

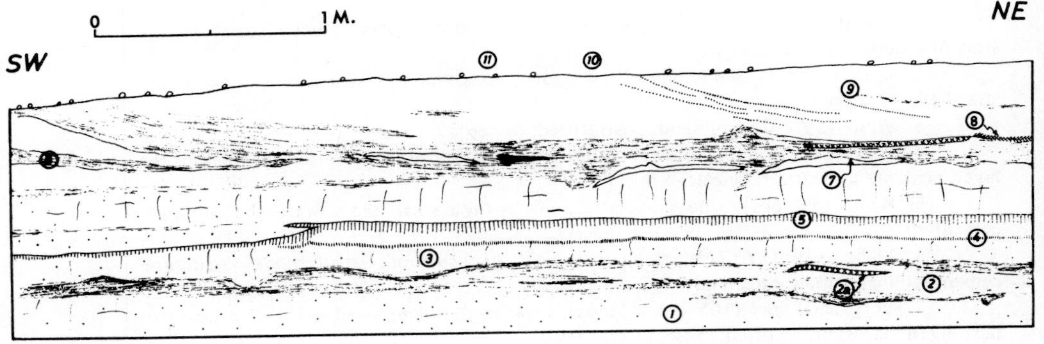

Figure 136. Profile of Trench 11, Site E29H1.

1 and 3. Light gray, sandy silt (2.5Y 7/2) with coarse irregular blocky structure; cemented; unstratified; carbonaceous.

2 and 6. Dark gray (10YR 4/1) to very dark, grayish-brown (10YR 3/2), loose, powdered, swampy sediment; unstratified; carbonaceous; burned in places.

2a. Lens of baked sand.

4 and 5. Thin layers of gray (10YR 5/1), sandy silt with irregular medium blocky structure; cemented; carbonaceous; unstratified.

7. Lens of fine and medium-grained sand; redeposited.

8. Baked sand.

9 and 10. Yellowish, fine and medium-grained sand with lens of loose, dark gray, swampy sediment. Stratified, with the dip toward the center of the subbasin. Cemented; calcareous.

11. Pebbles and gravels. Sheet wash.

Figure 135. Site E29H1, view upslope (north). Occupation area was at left edge of picture and exposed in trench where left figure is standing.

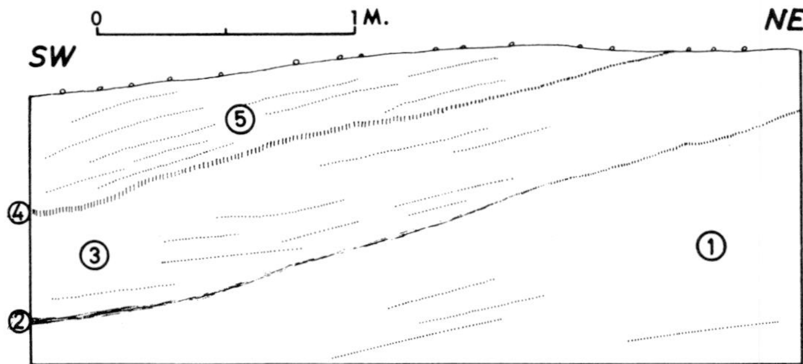

Figure 137. Profile of Trench 12, Site E29H1.

1. Very pale brown (10YR 7/3), fine and medium-grained sand with traces of bedding in places conformable to the overlying units and toward the center of the subbasin. Cemented; highly carbonaceous.

2. Very dark, grayish-brown (10YR 3/2), loose, powdered, swampy sediment; burned. Grades up the slope into silty sand with small angular blocky structure. Top of the silty sand at the northeastern corner of the trench slightly truncated. Dip toward the center of the subbasin.

3. Very pale brown (10YR 7/3), fine and medium-grained sand with stratification conspicuous in places and conformable with the general tendency of the dip toward the center of the subbasin. Cemented; carbonaceous, with manganese and iron stains near the base.

4. Grayish-brown (2.5Y 5/2), sandy silt with blocky structure; cemented; unstratified; becoming thinner up the slope; calcareous.

5. Yellow (2.5Y 7/6), fine and medium-grained, cemented sand with stratification conformable with underlying units. Calcareous.

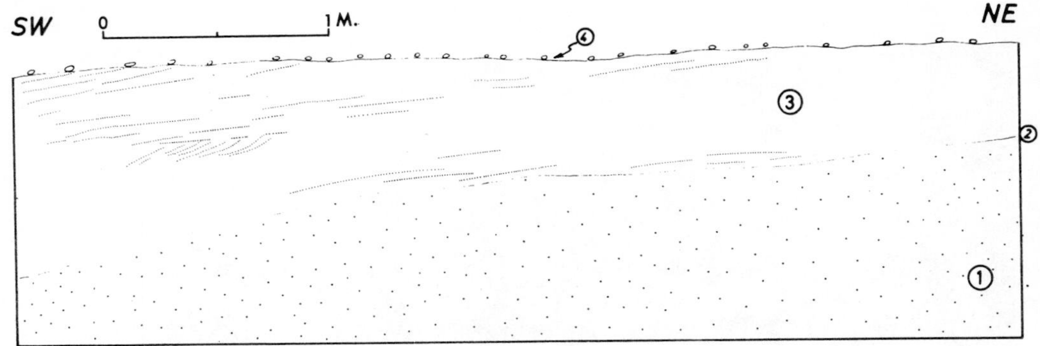

Figure 138. Profile of Trench 13, Site E29H1.

1. Light gray (2.5Y 7/2), fine and medium-grained sand with inconspicuous stratification and heavy carbonate content. Cemented.

2. Distinct color boundary between (1) and (3).

3. Brownish-yellow (10YR 6/6), fine and medium-grained sand, stratified, with the dip toward the center of the subbasin and cross-bedded lenses in places. Oxidation and manganese staining throughout the unit. Cemented; carbonaceous.

4. Pea gravel. Modern sheet wash.

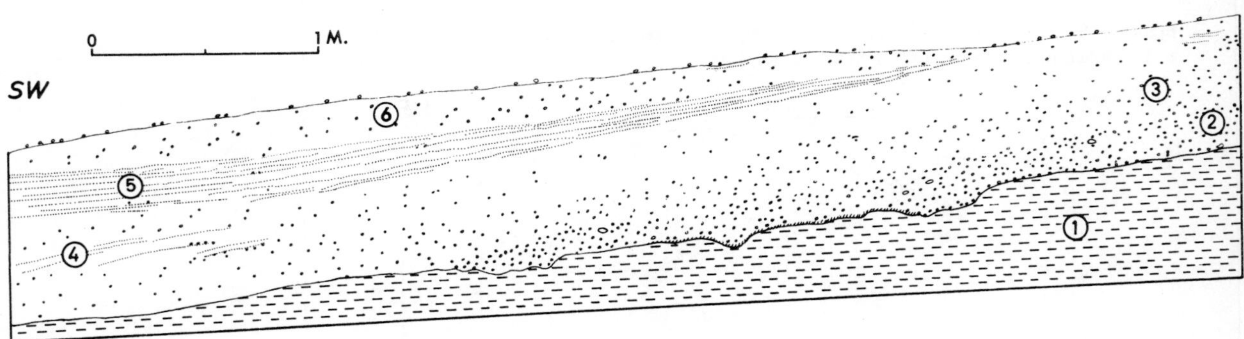

Figure 139. Profile of Trench 14, Site E29H1.

1. Light, yellowish-brown (2.5Y 6/4), weathered Upper Eocene shale; loose to consolidated. Concentration of gypsum and calcium carbonate in lenses on the contact with (2).

2. Unsorted gravels and pebbles up to 6 cm in diameter in a coarse sand matrix. Gravels and pebbles of local derivation mostly subrounded. Cemented; unstratified; carbonaceous.

3. Unsorted gravel and pebbles in a yellow (2.5Y 7/8) sand matrix with lenses of stratified pure sand in places (4). Contains gradually less pebbles than (2). Slopewash.

5. Yellow (2.5Y 8/6), medium and coarse-grained lacustrine sand. Stratified, with the dip conformable down the slope and rare small gravels dispersed throughout the unit. Loose; carbonaceous.

6. Yellow (2.5Y 7/8), unsorted sand with numerous unsorted gravels and small pebbles. Generally unstratified but with traces of lamination at the top; consolidated; carbonaceous. Gravels and pebbles subrounded. Recent slopewash.

It seems likely that the subbasin contained water only during the periods of seasonal high-water levels and only after the lake had risen to around 15 m. The deep water sediments, seemingly contemporaneous with the subbasin, were formed near the center of X Basin.

The water-laid sediments of the Protomeris lake in the subbasin (Trench 14) reached a maximum elevation of 24.5 m above sea level. These may represent the highest seasonal levels reached by this lake or rare storm levels, but there can be no doubt that the lake reached a maximum of at least 23 m during this period. It seems that the lake did not stand at this level for long, since there are no well-developed beach features around the subbasin.

The soil-like deposit at about 9 m above sea level in Trench 17 presumably records the recession separating the Protomoeris and Moeris lakes, and the overlying diatomite that forms the floor of X Basin would represent the subsequent deep water facies of the succeeding Moeris Lake. It is evident that the shallow water and beach deposits of the Moeris Lake were once occupied by man; this accounts for the numerous heavily eolized stone tools of later type that occurred scattered over the surface of the site. However, these later deposits had been entirely removed by deflation and the artifacts dropped from a considerable height to their present position.

Site E29G3

Another locality with deposits and associated cultural material that evidently dates with the recession of the Premoeris lake is designated Site E29G3, possibly Caton-Thompson and Gardner's Site R (1934: Plate CIX). This site is located about 1.2 km southwest of the Old Kingdom temple of Qasr El-Sagha and just immediately west of the famous stone-capped "L-shaped mound." Several prominent remnant buttes of lacustrine sediments dot the area in and around the site (Figure 141). When first visited it appeared to be an extensive but dense concentration of lithic artifacts, bones, and pottery occupying a roughly oval area about 100 m long and 60 m wide just west of a prominent and partially stone-capped butte some 80 m west of the L-shaped mound. Examination disclosed numerous artifacts eroding from lacustrine sediments around the northwest side of this butte, and at least 17 hearths in two or three clusters, some of them partially deflated and exposed on the surface of the site, others still *in situ*, and all of them at elevations ranging from 13 m to almost 15 m above sea level. The pottery of this locality is similar but not identical to that recovered from the type Fayum A communities (Kom W and Kom K). Fiber temper occurs, but does not predominate. Many of the vessels are sand tempered, and the sherds seem to be from smaller vessels than those at the type sites. The lithic artifacts have not yet been studied in detail, but the collections include numerous concave base arrowheads and large bifacial pieces, together with cylindrical, double-pointed bone shafts, all typical of Fayum A. For this reason the site is placed within the Fayum A complex.

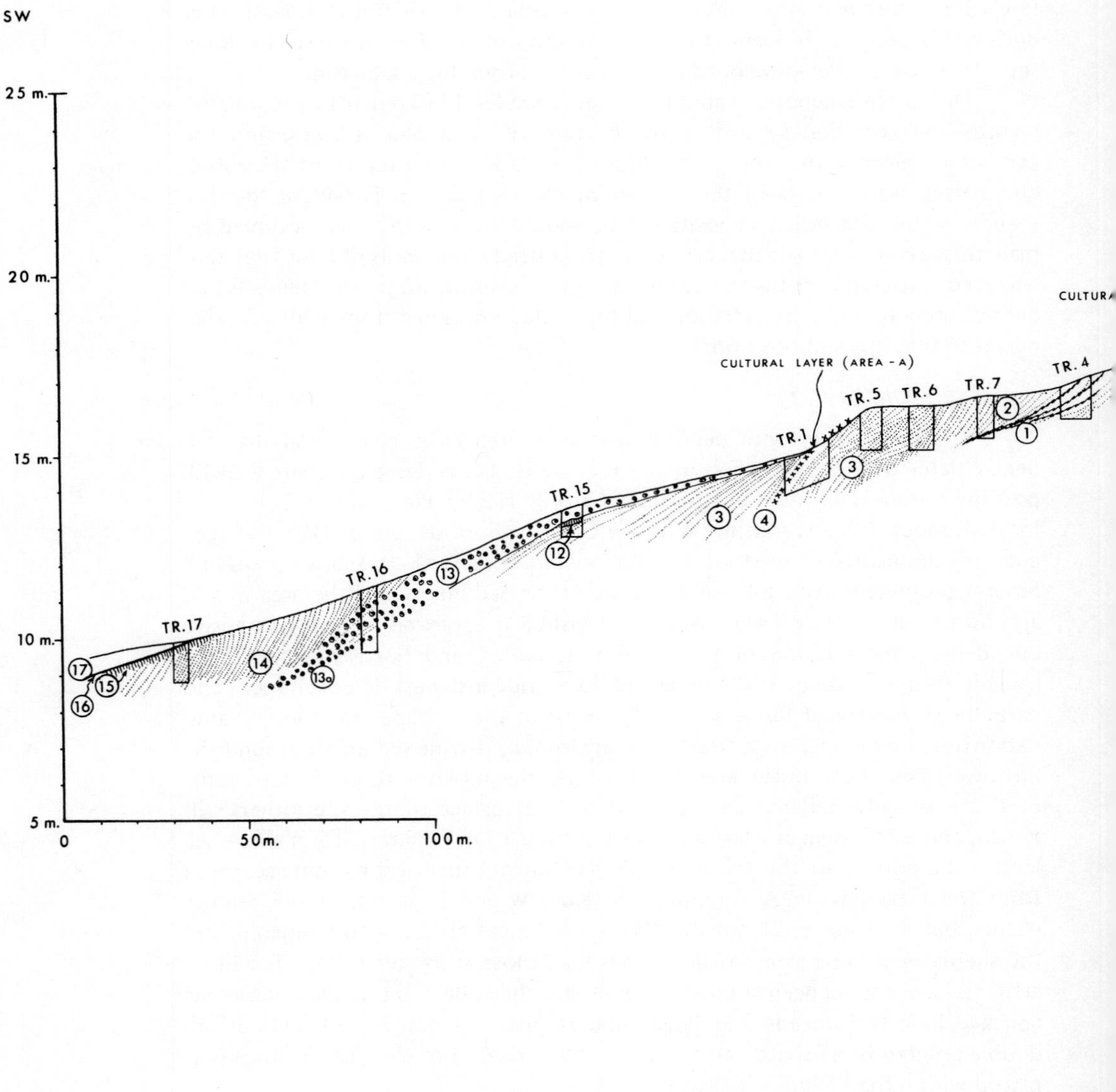

SW
25 m.
20 m.
15 m.
10 m.
5 m.
0
50m.
100m.
CULTURAL LAYER (AREA - A)
TR.17
TR.16
TR.15
TR.1
TR.5
TR.6
TR.7
TR. 4
1
2
3
3
4
12
13
13a
14
15
16
17

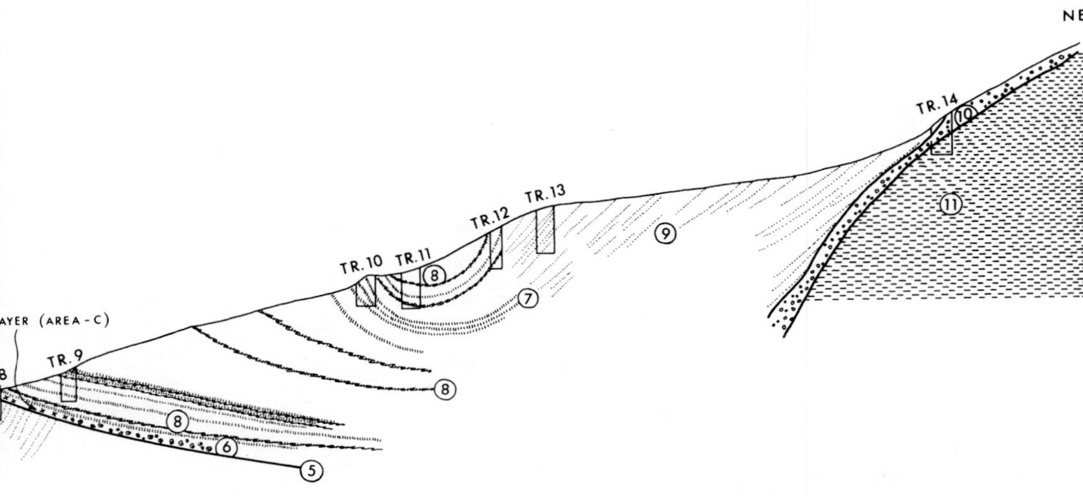

Figure 140. General cross-section of Site E29H1.

A. Premoeris Lake
  1. Sands of the deltaic beach
  2. Dark swamp layers with *Pila ovata*
  3. Deltaic beach
  4. Cultural layer with a radiocarbon date of 6120 BC ±115 years

B. Protomoeris Lake
  5. Pronounced erosional surface
  6. Coarse sand with crushed *Pila ovata* shells and younger occupation above in stratified sands at the edge of the subbasin
  7 and 8. Intercalated beds of sandy silts or silty sands and dark, loose swamp sediments burned in places
  9. Beach sands
  10. Older slopewash
  11. Upper Eocene shale
  12. Sandy silt with dehydration cracks
  13. Fine sand with numerous small snails grading down the slope into diatomaceous sediment with snail breccia
  14. Deltaic sands
  15. Soil (?)
  16. Pronounced erosional surface

C. 17. Diatomite

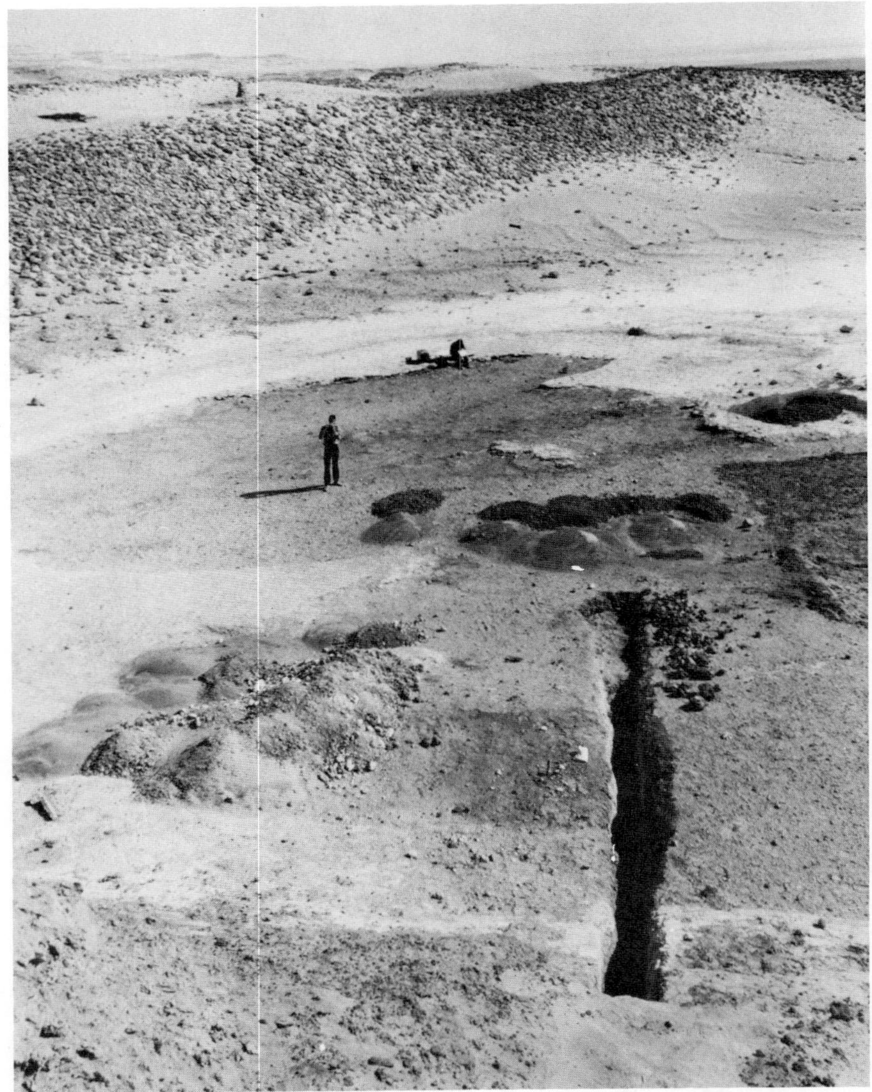

Figure 141. Site E29G3, Area A, looking toward slab-armored "L-shaped mound." Site was exposed in dark-colored deflated area where figure is standing.

Within the arms of the L-shaped mound, and separated from the main concentration of artifacts and hearths by a large remnant butte, was an eroded area some 30 m in diameter (Figure 142). In the bottom of this eroded area were found a few other artifacts distinctly different from those around the hearths but similar to the Terminal Paleolithic artifacts found *in situ* at Sites E29G1 and

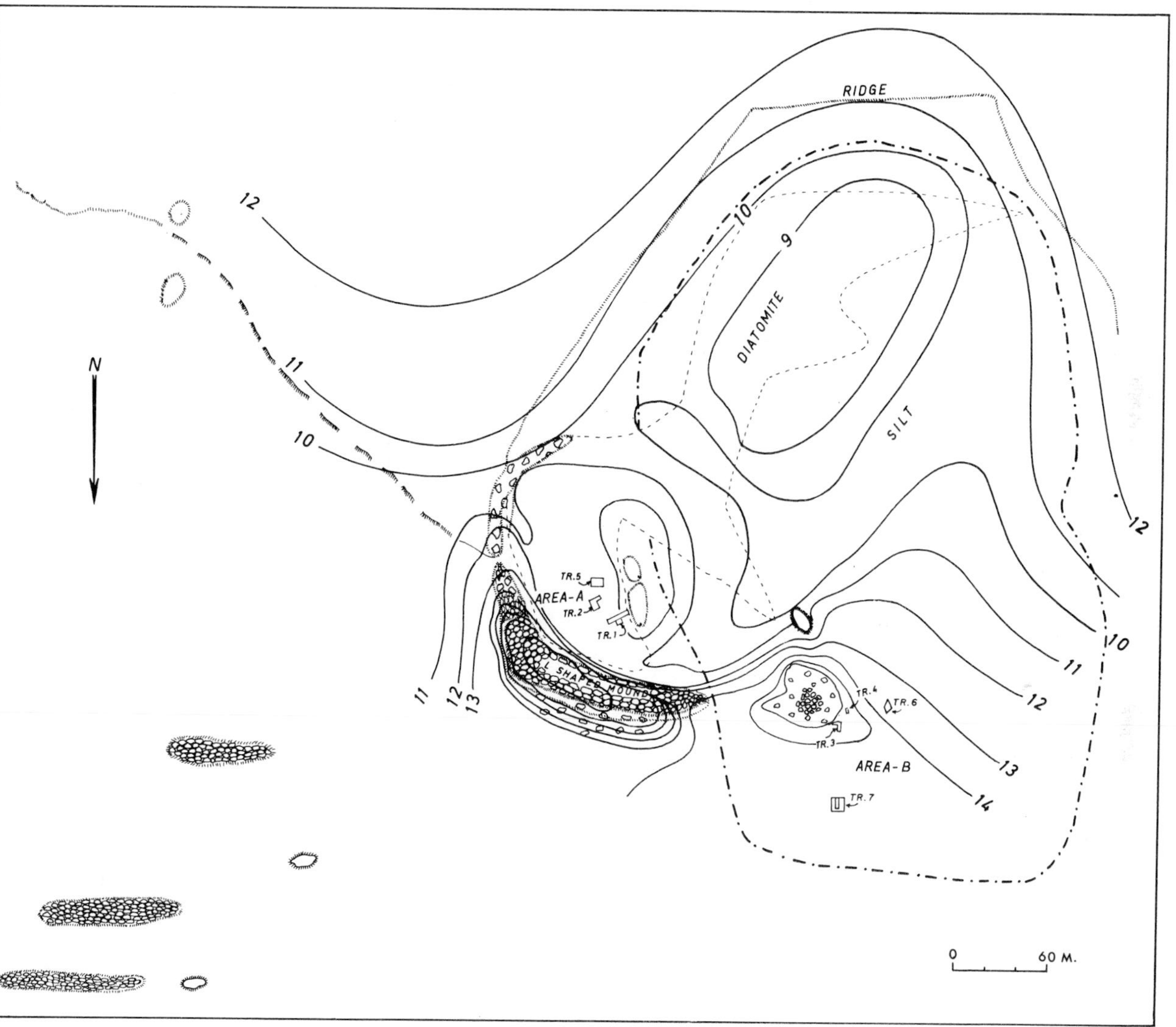

Figure 142. Map of Site E29G3 showing locations of armored mounds and Areas A and B.

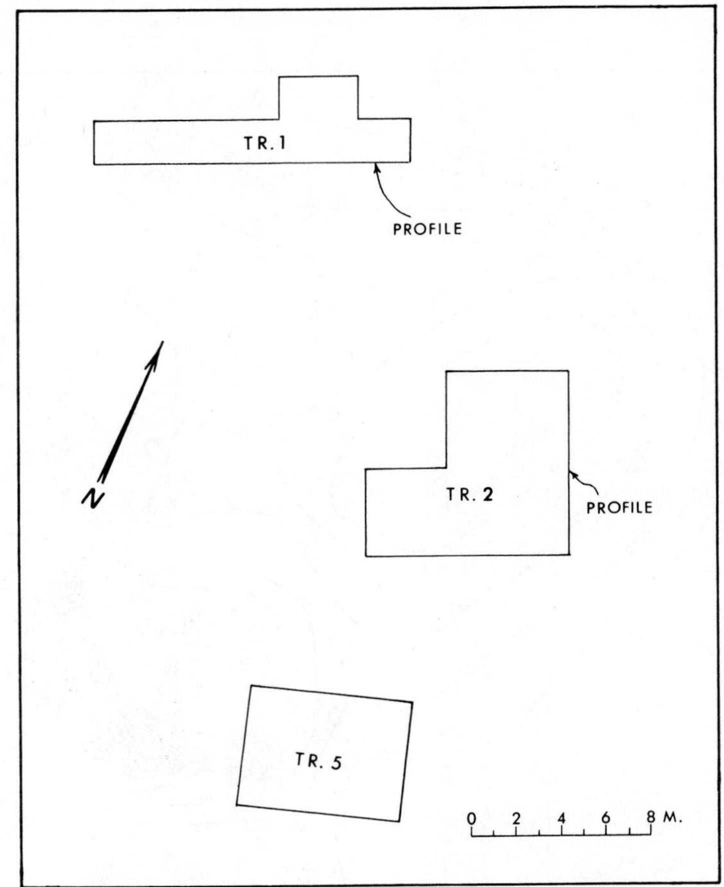

Figure 143. Map of Area A at Site E29G3 showing relative positions of excavated trenches.

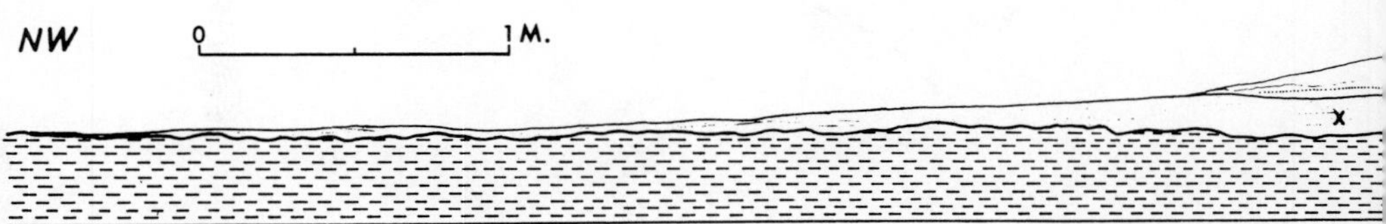

Figure 144. Profile of Trench 2, Site E29G3, Area A.

1. Weathered Upper Eocene shale.

2. Dark, grayish-brown (2.5Y 4/2), powdered, loose, swampy sediment; unstratified; with numerous chipped stone Terminal Paleolithic artifacts, bones, and traces of burning in places. Calcareous. A charcoal sample from this layer gave a radiocarbon date of 5550 BC ±125 (I-4130).

E29H1. This portion of the site was designated as Area A (Figure 143), and three trenches were dug: 1, 2, and 5. The large concentration to the west of the butte was designated as Area B, and four trenches were dug: 3, 4, 6, and 7.

The artifacts found on the surface at Area A occurred in an eroded area between Trenches 1 and 2, resting on Eocene shale. Around the eroded area to the southwest, however, was a thin veneer of lacustrine sediments from which were eroding fresh but slightly silt-polished artifacts, charcoal, and a few fishbones. Toward the west, near the base of the remnant butte, were other rolled and heavily chemical-weathered artifacts of similar type eroding from the surface of a gravel wadi fill. Trenches 1 and 2 yielded the basic stratigraphic evidence at this locality (Figures 144 and 145).

At the base of Trench 2 is a weathered Eocene shale covered immediately by a thin cultural layer of dark, grayish-brown (2.5Y 4/2), loose, powdery, unstratified swamp sediment, with traces of burning in places and with fresh stone artifacts, a few bones, and flecks of charcoal. This unit reaches a maximum thickness of 20 cm. A sample of charcoal from this unit at Trench 5 yielded a radiocarbon date of 5550 BC ±125 years (I-4130). It is at an elevation of 12.2 m above sea level.

The top of the swamp sediment is eroded, and small erosional channels and swales are carved in the top of the unit and filled by loose, stratified, very pale brown (10YR 7/4) fluvial sand, which, in turn, is covered by a white (2.5Y 8/2) diatomite whose top is eroded.

A slightly different and more complex sequence is preserved at Trench 1, which extends into the base of the remnant butte (Figure 146). Here, above the weathered Eocene shale, there is a thin layer of cemented, yellow (2.5Y 8/6), stratified, fine, silty sand sloping toward the southwest, following the inclination

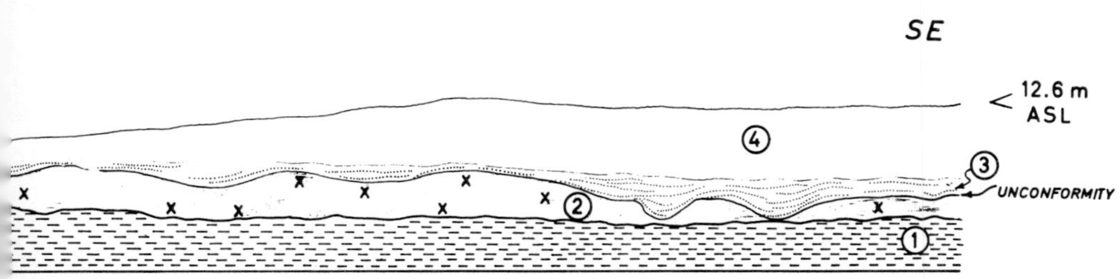

3. Very pale brown (10YR 7/4), coarse sand with gravels in eroded swales and depressions cut in the upper part of (2). Loose; stratified, conformable to the erosional surface. Same as (7) in Trench 1.

4. White (2.5Y 8/2) diatomite, same as (8) in Trench 1.

Figure 145. Profile of Trench 1, Site E29G3, Area A.

1. Pale yellow (5Y 7/3), weathered Upper Eocene shale; consolidated to loose.

2. Yellow (2.5Y 8/6), fine, silty sand; stratified, with noticeable dip toward the basin; cemented; carbonaceous.

3. White (2.5Y 8/2) diatomite conformably overlying (2), truncated by (5). Cemented; unstratified; highly carbonaceous.

4. Dark gray (2.5Y N4), laminated, powdered, loose, swampy sediment in a small channel cut into (3). Contains rare fresh Terminal Paleolithic stone artifacts. Carbonaceous. Equivalent to (2) in Trench 2.

5. Light, yellowish-brown (2.5Y 6/4), disintegrated Eocene shale with numerous limestone pebbles and gravels subrounded to well rounded. Unstratified; cemented to consolidated; calcareous. Wadi fill. Grades into (6).

6. Gray (5Y 6/1) wadi fill with darker lenses and laminae containing reworked swampy sediment in a matrix of disintegrated shale. Numerous Terminal Paleolithic stone artifacts slightly rolled and heavily patinated in the top part of the unit. Surface clearly eroded, with small channels and swales. Cemented; carbonaceous.

7. Very pale brown (10YR 7/4), coarse sand with gravels; stratified, conformable to the eroded surface of (6). Concentrations of pea gravels in shallow channels and small swales. Loose, contains rather rare weathered and rolled Terminal Paleolithic stone artifacts. Carbonaceous.

8. White (2.5Y N8) diatomite; unstratified; highly carbonaceous; eroded at the top.

9. Light gray (2.5Y 7/2), silty sand rich in small lacustrine snails containing *Bulinus truncatus* (Audoin), *Bithynia conollyi* (Gardner), *Planorbis planorbis* (Linneaus), and *Lymnea* sp. Coarse irregular blocky structure. Cemented; calcareous; unstratified.

10. Pale yellow (2.5Y 7/4), medium to coarse-grained, foreset-bedded sand with a layer of numerous fishbones and charcoal particles at the base. A charcoal sample from this layer gave a radiocarbon date of 3210 BC ±110 (I-3469). Cemented; carbonaceous.

11. Pale yellow (2.5Y 7/4), medium to coarse-grained sand unconformably overlying (10).

12. Yellow (2.5Y 8/6), medium to coarse-grained sand unconformably over (11). Foreset bedded; contains one minor erosional surface within the unit. Cemented; calcareous.

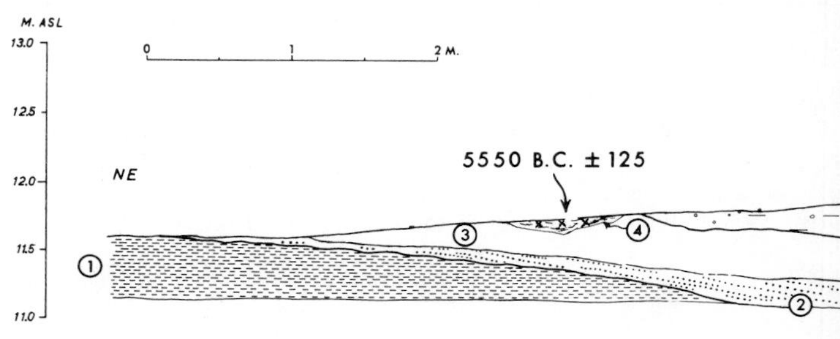

Figure 146. Site E29G3, Area A, looking toward remnant of deltaic sediments of Lake Moeris. Charcoal from this remnant derived from an unidentified occupation at a level just above head of figure standing at right gave a radiocarbon date of 3210 BC ±110 years (I-3469). Charcoal from the Terminal Paleolithic occupation in dark layer where figures are screening at left yielded a radiocarbon age of 5550 BC ±125 years (I-4130).

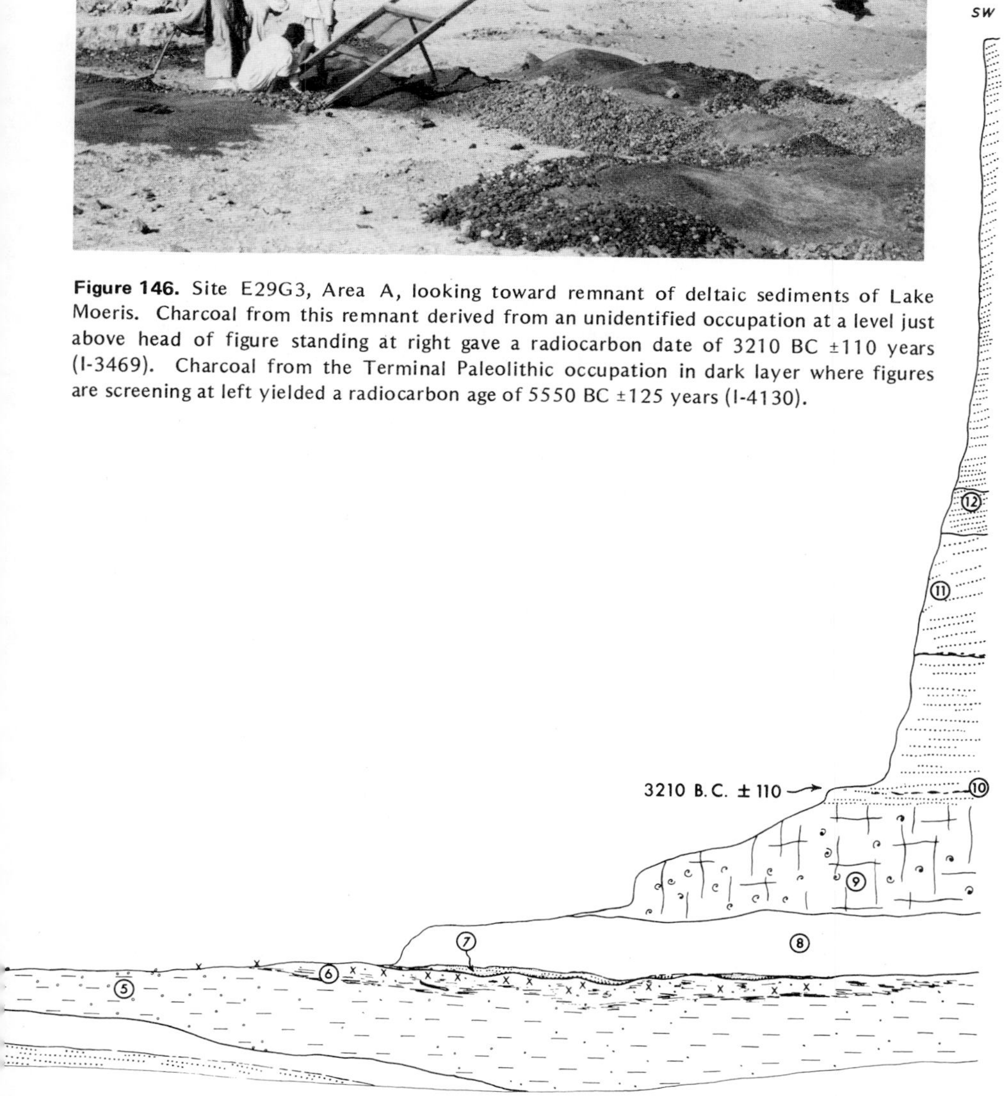

SW
12
11
3210 B.C. ± 110
10
9
7
8
6
5

of the bedrock surface. This silty sand is covered by white (2.5Y 8/2) diatomite that is eroded at the top. In a pocket near the northeastern edge of the trench is an inconspicuously stratified, dark gray (2.5Y 4/0), powdery swamp sediment containing a few artifacts.

Beyond this pocket, toward the remnant butte, a large part of a wadi fill was exposed in a clear-cut channel. It consists of redeposited, disintegrated, olive-yellow (2.5Y 6/4) bedrock shale with numerous rounded to subrounded limestone pebbles. At the very top of this unit, the wadi fill grades into essentially the same sediment, grayish in color (5Y 6/1) and containing reworked swamp sediment in a matrix of disintegrated shale and limestone pebbles together with numerous rolled and chemically weathered stone artifacts of Terminal Paleolithic character. The top of the wadi fill is eroded, and numerous small channels and swales were carved in it and filled with a very thin layer of small pebbles and rolled and weathered artifacts at the base, as well as stratified, loose, yellow (10YR 7/4) fluvial sand. Above the fluvial sand is a white diatomite, the same unit that covers the fluvial sand and cultural layer in Trench 2.

The diatomite is separated from the overlying unit by an unconformity. Above the diatomite is a light gray (2.5Y 7/2), sandy silt with numerous small snails. This, in turn, is covered by a pale yellow (2.5Y 7/4), fine to medium-grained sand, containing near the bottom, at an elevation of about 13.5 m, a thin layer with fishbones and charcoal. Charcoal from this layer, presumably washed down from a higher, unknown settlement, was dated by radiocarbon at 3210 BC ±110 years (I-3469). The longitudinal profile of this remnant discloses a pronounced dip toward the center of the basin (southeast) but does not indicate the height of the settlement from which the charcoal was derived.

A second thin layer of fishbones and charcoal occurred at the base of the next overlying unit, but it failed to yield sufficient charcoal for a date. A surface of erosion separates the two units. The overlying bed is a pale yellow (2.5Y 7/4), stratified and cemented, fine to medium-grained sand with foreset dip. Another unconformity separates this sand from a thick (4 m +) bed of pale yellow (2.5Y 8/6), foreset-bedded grading to topset sand. It is interrupted near the base by a slight unconformity. The top is at an elevation of slightly more than 20 m above sea level, about the same elevation as the top of the adjacent stone-capped L-shaped mound.

At Area B (Figure 147) the trenches were shallow and did not record as long and as clear a sequence as that in Area A. The main purpose of these trenches was to establish the stratigraphic position of the *in situ* pottery occupation (Fayum A) and to collect a charcoal sample for radiocarbon dating.

The bottom layer at Trench 3, dug at the base of a stone-capped remnant, is a cemented, pale olive (5Y 6/3), sandy silt with a cultural layer in the upper part, at an elevation of about 15 m above sea level (Figure 148). The cultural layer contained abundant pottery, chipped stone artifacts, and fish and animal bones. This sandy silt is more sandy in Trench 4 and has a light, brownish-gray color (2.5Y 6/2). It seems to be equivalent to the light gray, sandy silt above the

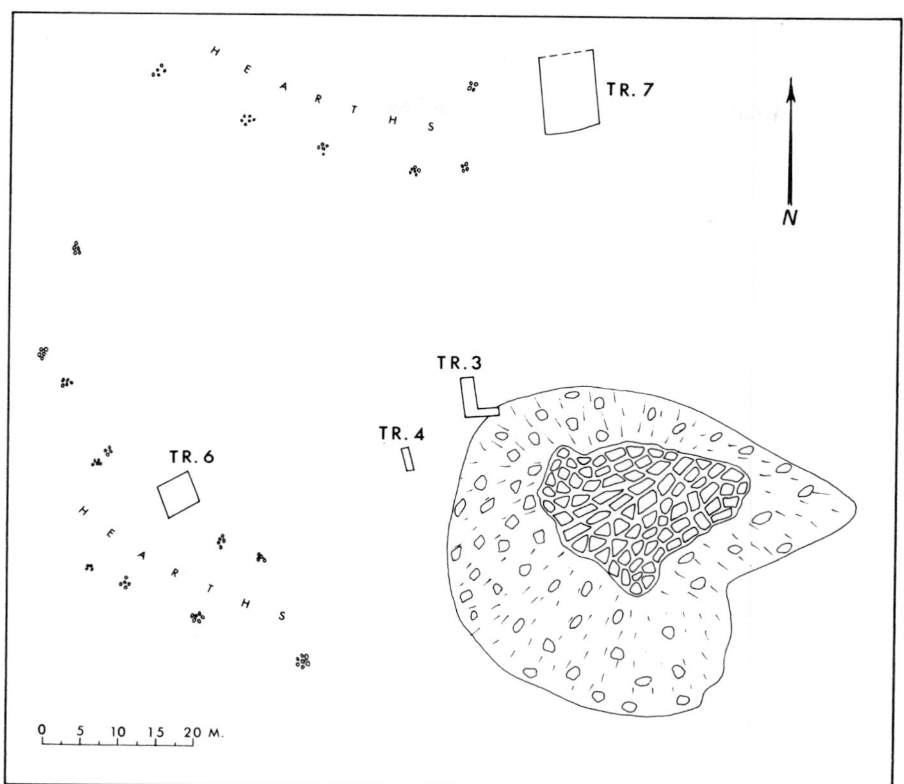

Figure 147. Map of Area B, Site E29G3.

upper diatomite at Area A (Figure 149). A sample of charcoal from the cultural layer in Trench 4 gave a radiocarbon date of 3910 BC ±115 years (I-4131).

Above the sandy silt is a stratified, cemented, pale yellow (2.5Y 7/4), fine to medium-grained sand covered, in turn, by a silty layer and a yellow (2.5Y 7/6) sand with many flat sandstone slabs on the eroded surface.

The sequence of deposits at Site E29G3 records a complex history for this area. The oldest lacustrine sediments were sands grading into a diatomite that marked a deep water stage preceding the Terminal Paleolithic occupation at Area A. A decline in lake level must have occurred to expose the surface of these deep water sediments and thus permit the deposition of organogenic swamp sediments near the shore.

The low lake level also exposed an outcrop of Eocene bedrock that stood slightly over 12 m above sea level. This outcrop probably retained a small pool of water following the high-water stage each year and encouraged the Terminal Paleolithic people to settle along the swampy shore, where they could harvest the fish trapped in the pool.

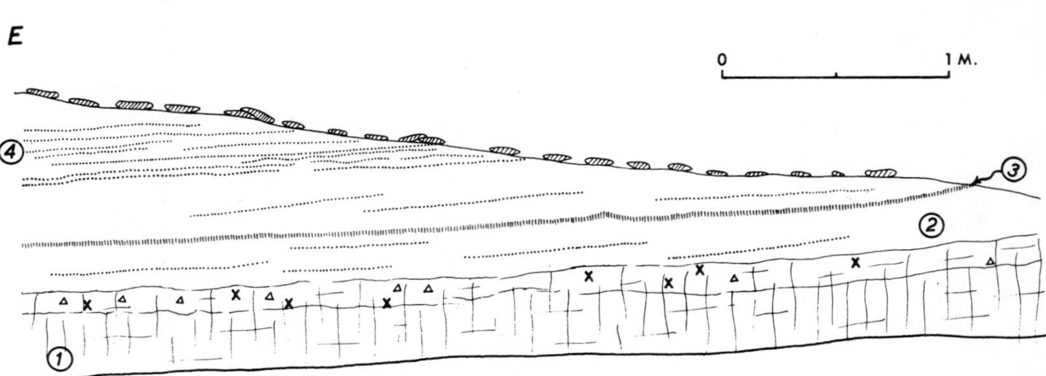

Figure 148. Profile of Trench 3, Site E29G3, Area B.

1. Pale olive (5Y 6/3), sandy silt or silty sand; unstratified or with masked stratification and inconspicuous blocky structure; cemented; highly calcareous. Contained occupational debris with numerous chipped stone artifacts, pottery, and bones within upper 10 cm.

2. Pale yellow (2.5Y 7/4), almost horizontally stratified fine to medium-grained sand; cemented; calcareous.

3. Thin layer of sandy silt with angular blocky structure.

4. Yellow (2.5Y 7/6), medium to coarse-grained, slightly foreset-bedded sand; deflated, with a pavement of lag sandstone slabs.

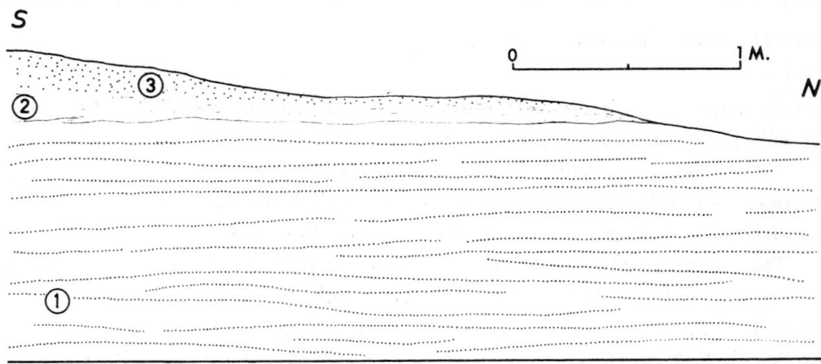

Figure 149. Profile of Trench 4, Site E29G3, Area B.

1. Light, brownish-gray (2.5Y 6/2), fine, silty sand with almost horizontal stratification; cemented; calcareous.

2. Cultural layer; gray, unstratified, fine, silty sand or sandy silt with charcoal and numerous artifacts. A charcoal sample from this layer gave a radiocarbon date of 3910 BC ±115 (I-4131).

3. Fine, silty sand; unstratified; cemented.

A further decline in the lake to an unknown level led to pronounced erosion and formation of a wadi, which near the end of its existence cut across and redeposited part of the occupation debris of the settlement. Because of the radiocarbon date of 5550 BC associated with the Terminal Paleolithic occupation of Area A, this decline is believed to be the same as the one that separated the Premoeris and Protomoeris lakes. The underlying diatomite, then, may represent a deep water sediment of the Premoeris lake.

The thin layer of sand that fills the small channels and swales at the top of the wadi fill may record the first phase of a rapidly rising lake, while the upper diatomite presumably was deposited as a deep water sediment during the maximum phase of this succeeding Protomoeris lake.

The entire sequence of lacustrine sediments, which lie above the upper diatomite and are separated from it by a surface of erosion, seems to represent the Moeris Lake, according to the associated cultural materials and radiocarbon dates. These upper deposits record, at the beginning, fairly deep water, which must have been seasonally exposed for settlement by Fayum A people, no doubt attracted by the same feature of seasonal ponding that brought the earlier Terminal Paleolithic group. Eventually this settlement was covered by a progressive deltaic structure that was building, in a rising lake, from the basin and being fed primarily by aeolean sands blown from the adjacent desert plateau into the depression.

Near the maximum of the Moeris Lake, stone slabs were laid in selected places on the surface of these deltaic sands. The purpose of these slabs is not clear, but they could have been placed along the shore to assist in landing or unloading boats in connection with the nearby Old Kingdom temple of Qasr El-Sagha. Subsequent decline of the lake led to pronounced deflation of the soft, sandy delta deposits, except in the places where the stones had been laid. These stone-capped areas now stand as prominent mounds protruding from the floor of the basin.

Site E29H2 (Kom W)

One of the largest Neolithic settlements in northern Egypt undoubtedly is the low knoll known as Kom W (Caton-Thompson and Gardner 1934: 22–37), located near the northern edge of the Fayum Depression about midway between, and slightly north of, the two large subbasins known as Z Basin and X Basin. Caton-Thompson and Gardner excavated most of the site in 1925 and 1926. They reported it to be essentially an unstratified site "in which stratification could be claimed only at certain points [1934: 24]." It was the type locality for the Fayum A complex.

When first seen in 1969 the site appeared as a low, elongated mound about 200 m long, 175 m wide, and standing some 3 m higher than the surrounding deflated lacustrine sand plain. The highest point of the mound is 20.6 m above sea level. The surface was paved with potsherds and stone artifacts, and the back-dirt fill strips of Caton-Thompson and Gardner were still evident.

For stratigraphic purposes two small trenches were dug near but just beyond the southwest corner of Caton-Thompson and Gardner's excavated area. Trench 1 was placed just outside of the south end of their "Strip Q" and was 3.5 m long, 3 m wide, and 2.5 m deep (Figure 150). Trench 2 was 7 m long, 1.5 m wide, and 2.3 m deep, and was situated at the southwest corner of "T Strip" parallel to the long axis of the mound and extending toward the basin (Figure 151). Both trenches disclosed several distinct cultural layers to a maximum depth of 1.40 m, separated from each other by fluvial sand.

In Trench 1, at the base, is a thick unit of horizontally stratified, medium to coarse-grained, yellow (10YR 7/6) lacustrine sand with a 30 cm salt-cemented band near the top. This band is very pale brown (10YR 8/4) in color, and the stratification is concealed by the heavy salt concentration. At the top of this unit is a second thin (1-2 cm) band, pale yellow (2.5Y 7/4) in color and partially destroyed by the overlying cultural layer. Possible traces of occupation occurred in the upper part of this unit, but there was no distinct cultural layer.

The lowest cultural layer has an irregular surface, and part of a pit was exposed at the southwest corner. It yielded chunks and powdered charcoal, numerous potsherds, stone artifacts, and numerous fragments of fish and animal bone. A radiocarbon date on charcoal from this lowest cultural layer is 3860 BC ±115 years (I-4127). The deepest exposed part of the cultural pit is 17.2 m above sea level, indicating that the lake was below this level at that time.

Above the lowest cultural layer dense occupation debris occurred throughout the section, mixed with lacustrine sand. At least three distinct cultural layers are present; however, the section is subdivided by the geological phenomena—salt crusts, salt cementation, and stratified lacustrine sands.

Trench 2 was evidently dug just beyond the dense occupation area. It shows a thick (2 m, base unexposed) series of topset deltaic sediments with occasional snails, and stringers of washed-in cultural material within the sand laminae. The lowest washed-in cultural evidence occurs at an elevation of 16.8 m above sea level. Above this there are several dispersed cultural horizons. At the top of the section is a unit of unstratified lacustrine sand with salt crust near the middle and dense, evenly spread occupation debris throughout. There are occasional lenses of sterile lacustrine sand, and at the top in the northeast corner is a burned clay feature with a clear charcoal-blackened layer (10YR 2/1). Numerous windworn artifacts formed a pavement on the surface. The maximum elevation of occupation at the site probably is slightly more than 20 m above sea level.

These trenches show convincingly that Kom W was occupied during a period of slowly rising lake levels. It is possible that the locality might have been seasonally inundated and repeatedly reoccupied during low-water phases. On the other hand, the site may have been flooded only during years of exceptionally high water, which might explain the occupants' tenacity in staying at this particular place. The locality has no evident advantage over other sections of the shoreline. The hill or kom was not a natural high point, but is a recent feature

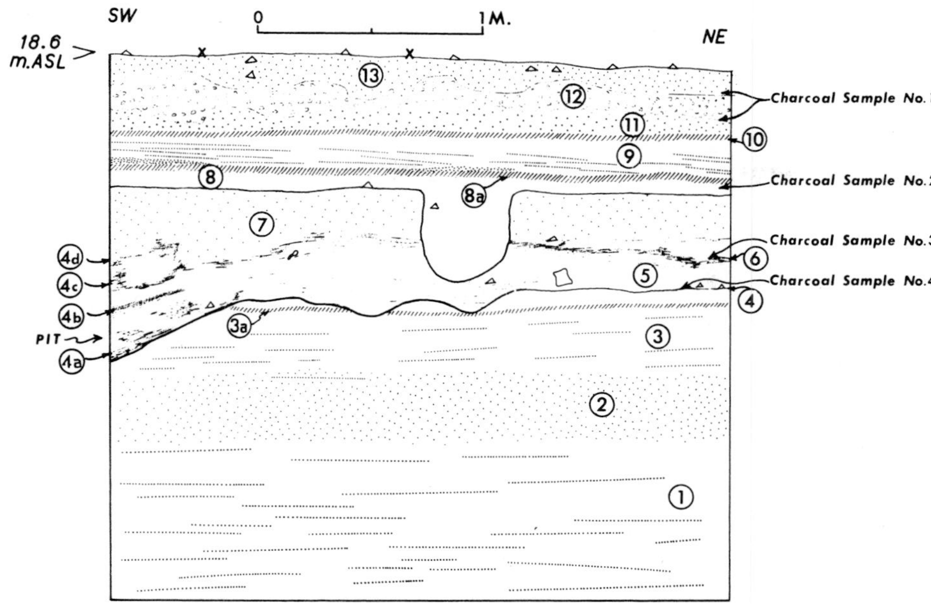

Figure 150. Profile of Trench 1, Site E29H2.

1. Yellow (10YR 7/6), fine to medium-grained sand with horizontal or almost horizontal conspicuous stratification. Contains dispersed manganese stains. Cemented; calcareous. Sterile (?).

2. Same as (3) but with stratification masked by salt crust and slightly lighter brown (10YR 8/4) color. Contains dispersed fishbones. No traces of occupation.

3. Very pale brown (10YR 7/4), fine and medium-grained sand with conspicuous stratification and heavy salt content. Cemented; calcareous. Sterile (?). (a) Salt crust. Possible occupation (?).

4. Brown (10YR 5/3), fine to coarse-grained sand with heavy content of charcoal, burned bones, and potsherds. A charcoal sample from this layer gave a radiocarbon date of 3860 BC ±115 (I-4127). Base clearly marked by surface of human activity.

4a. Dark lense of charcoal at the base of pit fill. (b) Burned, silty sand within pit fill. (c) Lens of charcoal. (d) Baked, silty sand.

5. Thick and extensive lens of fine and medium-grained, very pale brown (10YR 7/4) sand cemented by heavy salt content. Charcoal particles rare; traces of occupation less intense.

6. Layer of heavy concentration of charcoal; burned bones and potsherds in a matrix of brown sand (10YR 5/3). Cemented; calcareous.

7. Yellow (10YR 8/6), fine and medium-grained sand with traces of occupation; cemented; unstratified; calcareous.

8. Very pale brown (10YR 7/3), fine to coarse-grained sand with numerous occupation debris and a man-dug pit. (a) Salt crust with traces of occupation.

9. Yellow (10YR 8/6), fine and medium-grained sand with conspicuous horizontal bedding and occupational debris.

10. Salt crust with traces of occupation.

11. Very pale brown (10YR 8/4), coarse sand; unstratified; loose, much occupational debris.

12. Very pale brown (10YR 7/3), coarse sand; salt crusted; rich in artifacts and faunal remains; cemented; unstratified; calcareous.

13. Light, yellowish-brown (10YR 6/4), fine, loose sand rich in occupational debris; unstratified; calcareous.

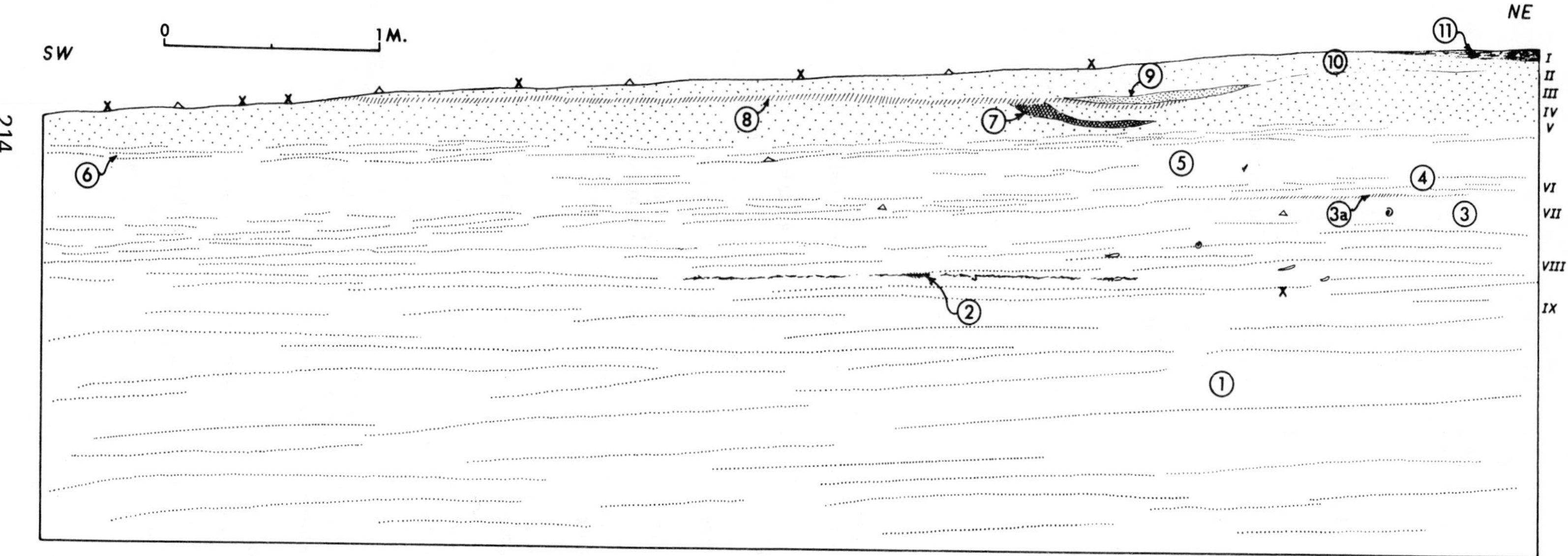

Figure 151. Profile of Trench 2, Site E29H2.

1. Stratified, fine and medium-grained sand with slight dip toward the basin; cemented to consolidated; carbonaceous. Contains washed-in stone artifacts, pottery, and bones down to 20 cm below charcoal lens (2).
2. Thin lens of charcoal with occasional potsherds.
3. Unstratified, fine and medium-grained sand with stone artifacts, pottery, bones, and small lacustrine shells. Consolidated.

3a. Salt crust.

4. Very pale brown (10YR 7/4), fine and medium-grained, stratified sand with minimal dip toward the basin; cemented to consolidated; calcareous. Contains washed-in artifacts.
5. Very pale brown (10YR 7/4), fine and medium-grained sand cemented by salt; stratification very inconspicuous; contains artifacts.
6. Stratified sand; no traces of occupation.
7. Burned clay structure.
8. Salt crust with artifacts.
9. Lenses of sterile, loose, lacustrine sand.
10. Loose, powdered, fine sand with numerous artifacts.
11. Black (10YR 2/1), loose sand with charcoal admixture and artifacts.

due entirely to the deflation of the surrounding sands and the protective pavement of cultural debris that has resisted the deflation at the site.

Site E29G4

About 700 m west of Site E29G3 is a prominent sand remnant like the smaller ones at E29G3. On top of this remnant there was a dense concentration of stone artifacts and potsherds, all eolized. It was designated E29G4 (Figure 152). The sherds at this site are slightly better made than those at E29G3 or at E29H2 (Kom W). They are sand tempered rather than fiber tempered but undecorated, with simple, direct rims. They might be classified as Predynastic.

A surface collection was taken from a rectangular area 30 m long and 15 m wide (450 m^2). A trench 9 m long and 2 m wide was dug at the southeastern edge of the concentration where a few very fresh artifacts were found (Figure 153).

The trench reveals a distinct cultural layer buried in foreset-bedded deltaic sands with occasional thin layers of sandy silt. The cultural layer is gray (2.5Y 6/0) in color and between 8 cm and 5 cm thick.

The cultural layer and artifacts present a washed-down horizon from an unknown but not necessarily much higher level. Since the highest point where

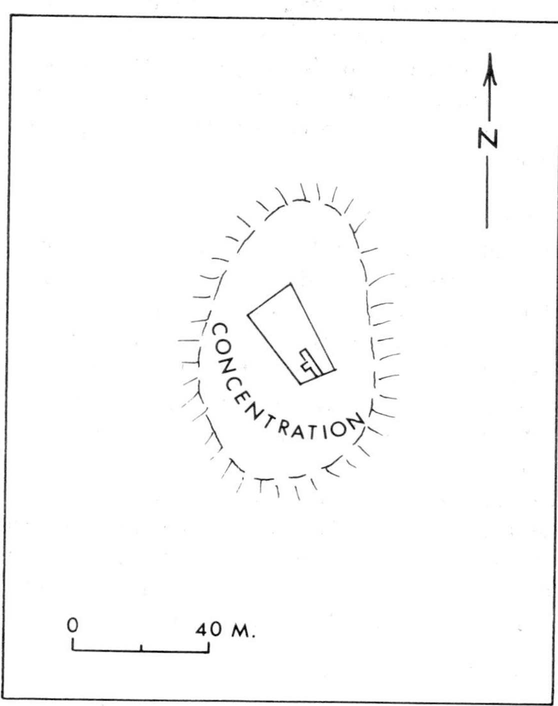

Figure 152. Schematic map of Site E29G4 showing area collected and position of Trench 1.

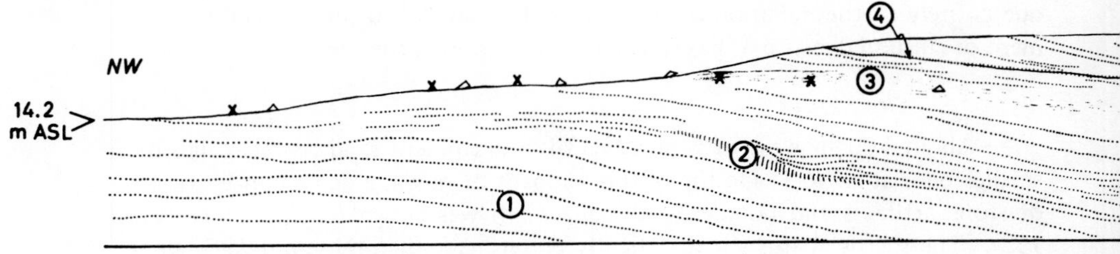

Figure 153. Profile of Trench 1, Site E29G4.

1. Pale yellow (2.5Y 8/4) to yellow (2.5Y 7/6), medium to coarse-grained sand, generally foreset bedded with occasional local cross-bedding. Oxidation dispersed in layers. Loose to consolidated. Carbonaceous.

2. Light, yellowish-brown (2.5Y 6/4), very sandy silt grading into sand. Consolidated; carbonaceous.

3. Gray (2.5Y N6) cultural layer with charcoal, stone artifacts, and pottery; slightly washed; conformable to general bedding. Loose; carbonaceous.

4. Yellow (2.5Y 7/6), stratified, fine and medium sand, foreset bedded, with occasional cross-bedding. Surface deflated.

artifacts in the cultural layer occurred is 14.4 m above sea level, the level of the original occupation surface was probably not more than 16.5 m. The significance of the observation is the indication of lake level at least 4 m lower during the Predynastic period than during the latest part of the Fayum A occupation at Kom W. The difference, however, may be only seasonal, with the Predynastic occupation occurring during the maximum low stage, possibly following an unusually low flood.

Site E29G5

Another late site (E29G5) was found about 2 km southwest of Site E29G4. The scattered concentration covered an area 150 m by 200 m in size at an elevation of 13.4 m above sea level. It was located in a small semibasin near the edge of a deltaic, foreset-bedded mass of sandy lake sediments. The artifacts were eroding from the top of a deeper water sediment of light, yellowish-brown (2.5Y 6/4), sandy silt covered by an overlying light gray (2.5Y 7/2), silty sand. A small trench 3.5 m long and 1 m wide was dug near the center of the concentration (Figure 154).

The *in situ* artifacts included potsherds with everted rims, a bronze harpoon, animal bones, and charcoal. The harpoon and pottery indicate an Old Kingdom age for the occupation. Unfortunately there was no means of estimating the water level at the time of occupation. The artifacts had been dropped or washed into the bottom sediments below the water of unknown depth.

Site E29G6 (Qasr El-Sagha)

Just below the famous Old Kingdom temple of Qasr El-Sagha is a broad bench of deltaic topset and foreset-bedded sands. This bench preserves one of

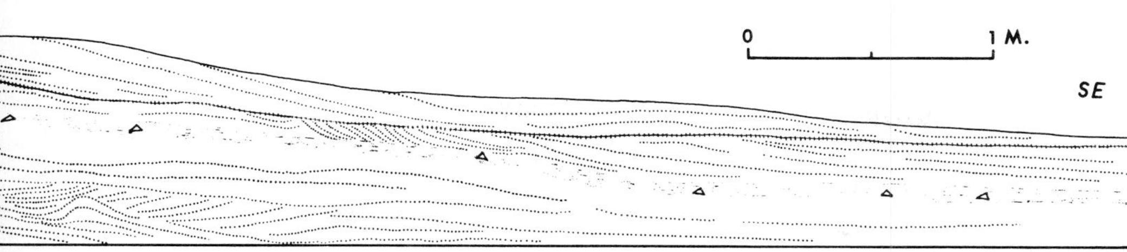

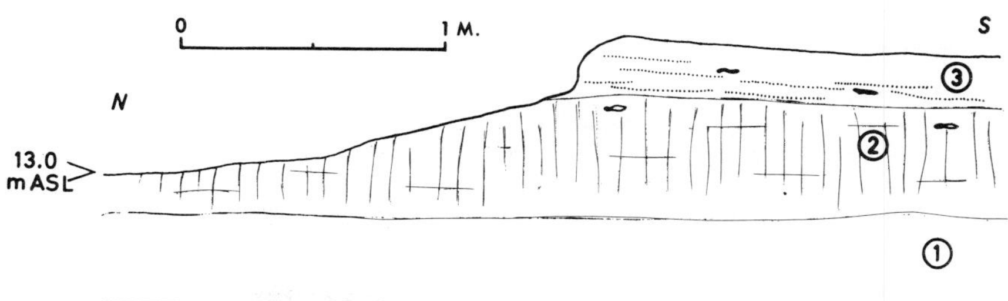

Figure 154. Profile of Trench 1, Site E29G5.

1. Light gray diatomite with coarse angular blocky structure; unstratified; cemented; highly carbonaceous.

2. Light, yellowish-brown (2.5Y 6/4), sandy silt with coarse angular blocky structure; unstratified; highly calcareous. Contains occasional animal bones and charcoal in upper 10–20 cm. Cemented.

3. Light gray (2.5Y 7/2), silty, fine sand with traces of stratification; contains some charcoal and animal bones; cemented; calcareous.

the more extensive sections of Moeris lake deposits. West of the temple, along this bench and above it for several hundred meters, is scattered debris of a very extensive Old Kingdom occupation. In front of the temple and from 10 m to 13 m lower are numerous elongated and rectangular sand remnants that have been capped with sandstone slabs. Two of the longest of these, on either side of the temple, are paved with sandstone and limestone slabs, in place still closely fitted together. Another elongated mound is located in front of the temple but beyond the two longer stone-paved mounds, and is covered by large, irregular blocks of unshaped dolorite that was quarried some 6 km away on the plateau (Caton-Thompson and Gardner 1934: 136–138).

The purpose of these stone-capped and paved mounds has long been disputed. Caton-Thompson and Gardner believed they represented either defensive constructions (ibid., p. 134) or, in the case of the dolorite, a dump (ibid., p. 137). This view was strongly influenced by their interpretation of the lake level during Old Kingdom times. Earlier, Baedeker (1929: 209) referred to an ancient quay in the vicinity of Qasr El-Sagha Temple, possibly referring to

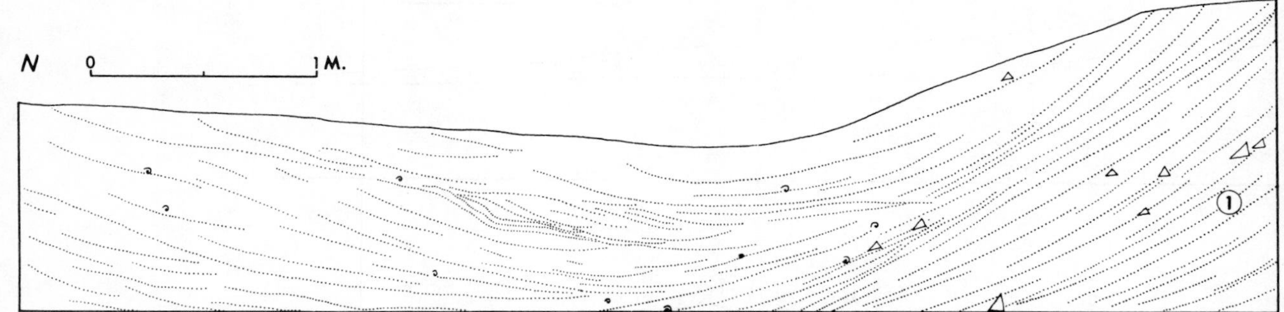

Figure 155. Profile of Trench 1, Site E29G6. White (10YR 8/1) to yellow (10YR 7/6), stratified, silty sand filling fossil channel in the deltaic beach of Lake Moeris. Cemented. Contains very numerous Old Kingdom potsherds, fired brick, and small lacustrine snails, including *Bulinus truncatus* (Audouin), *Lymnea lagotis* (Schrank), *Cleopatra bulimoides* (Oliver), and *Planorbis* throughout the unit. Calcareous.

these structures. A similar view was held by Shafei (1940), who also postulated that they were quays, following his observation of a high lake during the Early Dynastic period. Our investigations did not conclusively establish the purpose of these stone-covered ramps and mounds, but they do indicate that these features were along the shore of Lake Moeris during Old Kingdom times.

Two trenches, together with several natural sections along the wadis dissecting the deltaic bench, provided the stratigraphy for this area. Trench 1 was cut across a small filled channel within the bench at an elevation of about 18.5 m above sea level (Figure 155). It yielded numerous Old Kingdom potsherds, a fired brick, and snail shells, with *Bulinus truncatus* (Audouin) and *Lymnea lagotis* (Schrank) most common and *Cleopatra bulimoides* (Oliver) and *Planorbis* less frequent. The sherds occurred toward the bottom of the trench (1.5 m) in a matrix of stratified white to yellow (10YR 8/1 to 7/6), cemented, silty sand. The channel appears to have been formed during seasonal lake fluctuation, and the artifacts were washed in from a higher level.

Trench 2 was a small pit 2.6 m long and 1 m wide cut into the top and side of the elongated stone-paved ridge at the foot of Qasr El-Sagha Temple at an elevation of 22.3 m above sea level. This trench disclosed a rich culture layer, light brownish gray in color (2.5Y 6/2), 12 cm thick, and 52 cm below the base of the stone pavement (Figure 156). It contained numerous Old Kingdom potsherds and charcoal (Figure 157). Between the stone pavement and the cultural layer is a yellow (2.5Y 7/6), medium to coarse-grained sand, loose and poorly stratified. The cultural layer is on top of a light, yellowish-brown (2.5Y 6/4), unstratified, silty sand, which, in turn, overlay a unit of yellow (2.5Y 7/6), loose, coarse to medium-grained sand. The source or origin of the upper loose sand is unknown. It may be of lacustrine origin or an intentional dump at the time the stone pavement was constructed.

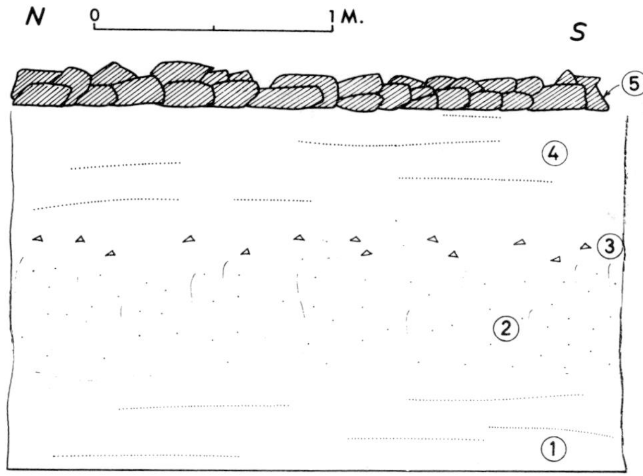

Figure 156. Profile of Trench 2, Site E29G5.

1. Yellow (2.5Y 7/6), coarse to medium-grained, inconspicuously stratified sand. Loose, calcareous.
2. Light, yellowish-brown (2.5Y 6/4), silty sand; unstratified; loose to consolidated; calcareous.
3. Light, brownish-gray (2.5Y 6/2) cultural layer in a sandy matrix. Contains charcoal and Old Kingdom pottery. Loose, calcareous.
4. Yellow (2.5Y 7/6), medium and coarse-grained sand; loose, with very inconspicuous stratification; carbonaceous.
5. Boulders and slabs of sandstone laid by man.

Figure 157. Site E29G6 below Qasr El-Sagha showing level with Old Kingdom artifacts buried in beach deposits of Lake Moeris.

The complete section measured by Albritton (in Said *et al.* 1971) is as follows:

Top	*Thickness in meters*
9. Sand, fine, compact, yellowish-brown; 7 cm black, carbonaceous layer at base. Stands as hummocks.	2
8. Sand, medium-grained, friable, light brown; caliche nodules and calcareous casts of plants at top. Contained abundant Old Kingdom potsherds.	1
7. Sand, fine and silty toward base, coarse, with rock fragments toward top; olive gray with brownish mottling. Casts of plant stems at top.	2
6. Sand, medium, silty, hard. Fills channel in older beds. Contains abundant snails: *Bulinus truncatus* (Audouin) and *Lymnea lagotis* (Schrank), the two most abundant, and less commonly *Cleopatra bulimoides* (Oliver) and *Planorbis*. Abundant Old Kingdom potsherds and one fired brick.	0–2
5. Sand, medium-grained, reddish brown, friable except at top, where cemented by carbonate to form trapezoid concretions and casts of stems.	1
4. Sand, fine, very light gray to pale olive with brownish mottlings; pulverent; bedded in units 7–60 cm thick.	4.5
3. Silt and clayey silt interbedded, brownish gray, bedded in units 7–30 cm thick. Clayey silt with desiccation cracks, upper surface scoured, with concentrations of small gastropolis in silty lenses: *Bulinus truncatus* (Audouin), *Bithynia conollyi* (Gardner), *Planorbis planorbis* (Linneaus), and *Lymnaea* sp.	4.5
2. Sand, fine, brownish gray. Laminated. Root casts.	1
1. Diatomite, gray, calcareous; evenly bedded in units 2–15 cm thick. Dessication-cracked, gastropod shells concentrated along bedding surface. Base not exposed.	1

The highest potsherds buried in the sediment occurred at an elevation of about 22 m above sea level (Figure 158). There can be no doubt that the level of the lake during the Old Kingdom was about 22–23 m above sea level, with seasonal variation. In view of this it seems highly probable that the stone-capped and paved mounds and ridges and the dolorite ridge represent the landing facilities for an extensive harbor presumably connected with the dolorite quarries at Gebel El-Qatrani, believed to be the source of the dolorite used in the pyramids (Lucas 1926). A road connecting the quarries and the escarpment

Figure 158. Closeup of Site E29G6, with numerous Old Kingdom potsherds buried within Lake Moeris sediments.

above the harbor facilities was traced by Caton-Thompson and Gardner (1934: 136–138). The extensive settlement and the temple at the shore of the lake were parts of this harbor complex, and Lake Moeris was at its highest level during this period.

If we accept Ball's calculation (1939: 204) of the lake level during the reign of Amenemhat I, then at that time the lake was declining from its previous maximum, possibly owing to siltation of the Hawara Channel. Furthermore, the hydroengineering activities assigned to his reign might have been efforts to retard this decline by removing the silts blocking the channel and building the embankment at Gisr Godalla.

A detailed study of diatoms from an exposed, thick, diatomaceous bed at an elevation about 1 m below sea level and located near Um El-Atl in the northeast portion of the depression (Alem 1958) showed a dominant complement of cosmopolitan diatoms (to 70%), with a considerable frequency of tropical forms together with rare types that prefer colder conditions. A vast majority of the diatoms were derived from the Nile (ibid., p. 238). At the base of his sampled profile, deeper water forms are more common, and toward the top they are replaced by littoral or shallow water species, suggesting a decline in the lake level. Alem (ibid., p. 240) concluded that water temperatures ranged between 15° and 30° C, about the same as today, and that rainfall and other climatic parameters were similar to present conditions.

The stratigraphic position of the profile sampled by Alem is unknown; however, it may possibly be attributed to the Moeris Lake because of the thickness of the diatomaceous beds, which suggests a long period of sedimentation.

Summary of the Holocene Lacustrine Events in the Fayum Depression

The series of excavations and the resulting environmental, archaeological, and radiocarbon data show a very complex and not entirely understood series of lake aggradations and recessions during the Holocene in the Fayum Depression. This series of lakes is derived entirely from the Nile and undoubtedly reflects changes in the level of the river. Unfortunately, however, there is almost no information available on the river regimen in this area for that period.

Reported lacustrine deposits believed to be of Pleistocene age have not been examined in sufficient detail to permit a definitive statement; however, the appearance of the gravels previously attributed to a Pleistocene lake, together with numerous *Corbicula* shells, would suggest a fluvial rather than lacustrine environment and a Nilotic provenience.

The age of this event is not clearly known. The derived artifacts associated with the gravel, among which are rolled Levallois cores and flakes, may be of Middle Paleolithic age or later; the Levallois technique survives well into the Late Paleolithic along the Nile. The so-called Late Pleistocene gravels, which occur at elevations over 30 m above sea level, or around 80 m above the present lake level, skirt the north and eastern edges of the depression as well as the Fayum entrance. If these gravels do indeed represent Nile tributaries (Said *et al.* 1971) and date prior to the presence of a lake in this area, then either the depression was wind excavated following the deposition of these gravels, or else there was a barrier that separated these tributary beds and the depression. In the latter event the depression must have been smaller than today and must have resembled Wadi Rayan, a dry depression that abuts the Fayum on the south. The answer to this question may be buried below the modern lake of Birket Qarun.

The oldest definite lacustrine deposits found (Paleomoeris Lake) were seen at only one locality (E2961, Area F) and were represented only by fluvial sands and diatomites (Figure 159). These undoubtedly represent deep water sediments, and no information is available on the shore or lake level during this period. Judging from the thickness of the diatomites, this lake had a long history. No radiocarbon dates are available, but probably did not precede the subsequent lake by a significant interval. A date around 7000 BC is estimated.

If this estimate is correct, the maximum of this Paleomoeris Lake may possibly be contemporaneous with a relatively high level of the Nile, known as the Arkin Aggradation, the maximum of which is dated slightly before 7000 BC (Wendorf, Schild, and Said 1970: 70).

The deep fossil dehydration cracks in the top of the upper diatomite unit assigned to the Paleomoeris Lake show that the lake level during the following recession sank at least to below 11 m above sea level and possibly much lower.

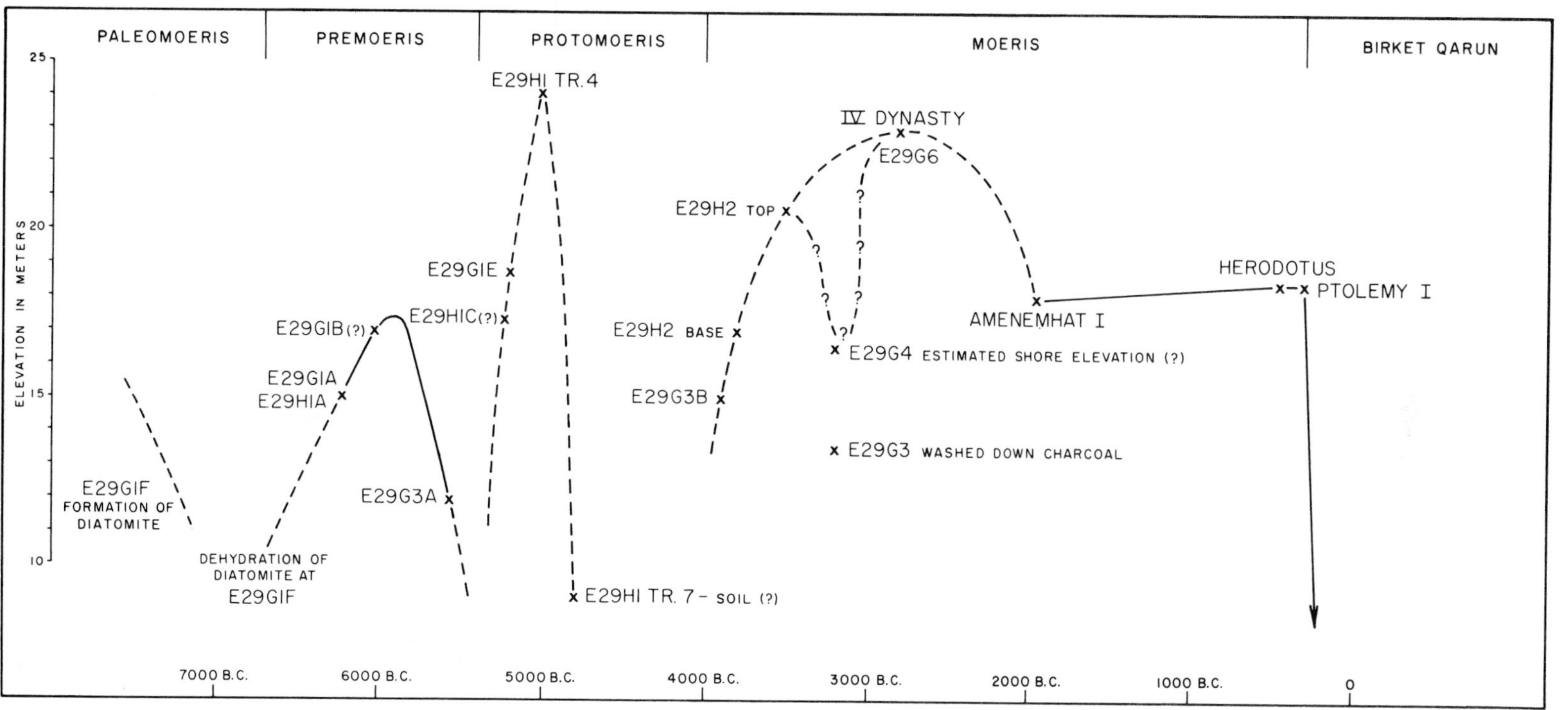

Figure 159. Summary diagram of indicated fluctuations in lake levels at Fayum.

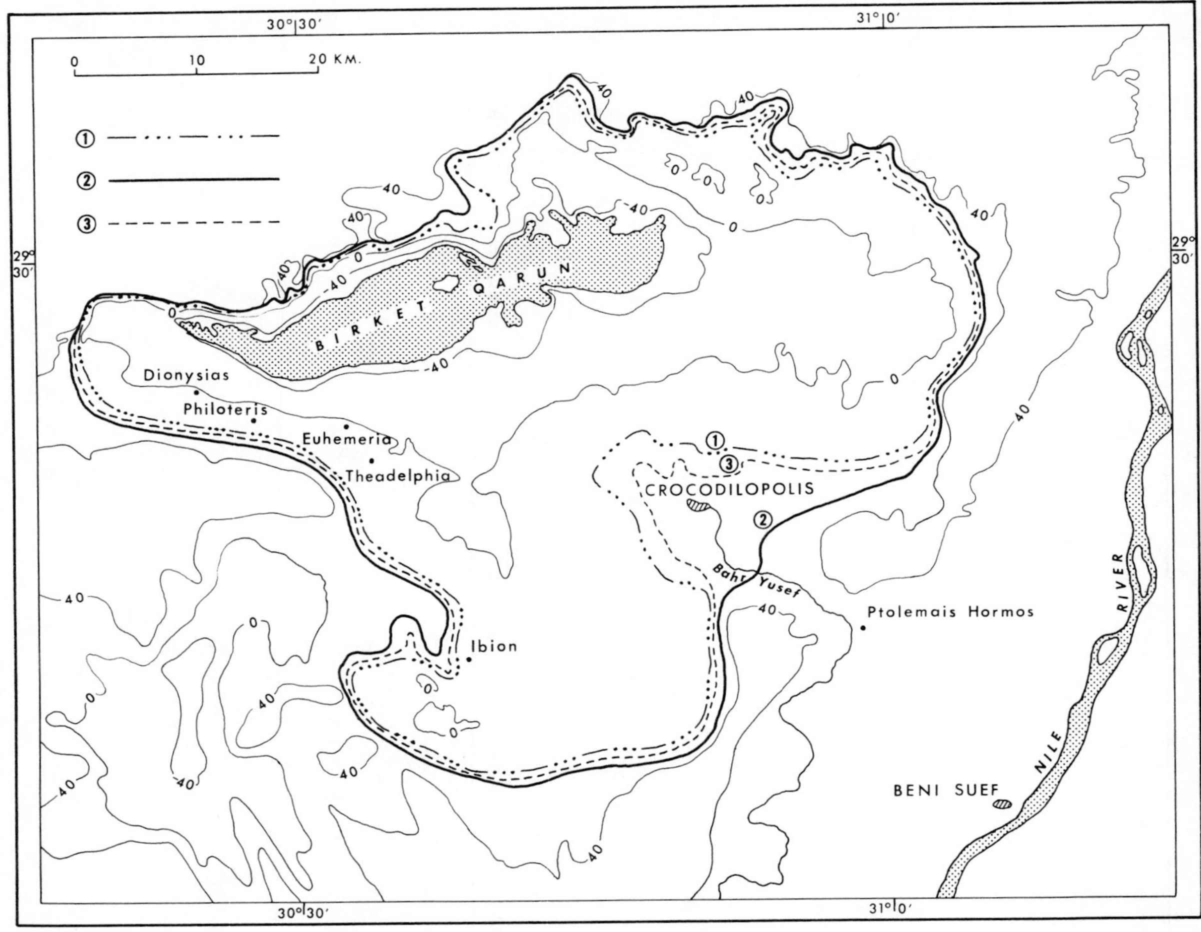

Figure 160. Map of Fayum Depression indicating extent of earlier lakes:

1. Maximum extent of Premoeris Lake
2. Maximum extent of Protomoeris Lake
3. Maximum extent of Moeris Lake

The succeeding Premoeris Lake is much better documented. Deposits of this lake occur at three localities (E29G1, Areas A and B; E29G3, Area A; E29H1, Area A). At all these localities there are archaeological materials in direct association, and two of them (E29G1, Area A and E29H1, Area A) show the same radiocarbon age (6150 and 6120 BC) and the same elevation (15 m above sea level). The occupation at Site E29G1, Area B at 17 m above sea level suggests that the maximum of the Premoeris Lake probably exceeded the 17 m level (Figure 160). All three sites yielded evidence of seasonal fluctuations, but the precise place of the occupations within these seasonal variations cannot be assigned with certainty, although it is suggested that they occurred during a low-water phase and repeatedly utilized localities where bedrock outcrops facilitated fishing.

There is an indication that this Premoeris Lake may also be correlated with a short-lived episode of aggradation reported from along the Nile south of Luxor and published as the Elkab Formation (Vermerrsch 1970: 48–51). Three radiocarbon dates—6400 BC ±160 years (LV 393), 6040 BC ±150 years (LV-464), and 5980 BC ±160 years (LV 465), the last one near the top—are reported from this Elkab Formation. Another radiocarbon date from Sudanese Nubia also records the first Post-Arkinian high Nile level there at Site D1W-51 in 5750 BC ±120 years (WSU-176) (Schild, in Wendorf 1968: 654). This series of dates strongly suggests that the end of this high Nile interval occurred around 6000 BC or slightly later.

The radiocarbon date of 5550 BC and the elevation of 12 m at Site E29G3, Area A indicate that the maximum lake level sank well below 12 m above sea level during the recession of the Premoeris Lake. There is firm evidence that during this recession the edge of the basin was being actively dissected, and the resulting wadi channels were subsequently filled. The wadi fill shows the presence of significant local rainfall at this time, and also that the base of erosion was rising during the sedimentation of the fill. The rapidity of these events indicates that no great span of time is involved for the period of recession.

Deposits of the following Protomoeris Lake occur at two localities: E29H1, Area C and E29G1, Area E. Only one radiocarbon date (on burned shell) is associated with this event, and it indicates a high lake level (above 19 m) around 5190 BC. The stratigraphic sequence in the subbasin at Site E29H1 shows that this lake was possibly the highest of all, at 24 m above sea level.

The only evidence of a very high Nile at this time is at Catfish Cave in Egyptian Nubia (Wendt 1966), where silts at 18 m above the floodplain are associated with a radiocarbon date of 5110 BC ±120 years (Y-1644). This date closely agrees with the date for the Fayum from near the top of this Premoeris Aggradation.

The red soil (?) at an elevation of 9 m above sea level in X Basin may confirm that the lake must have shrunk to well below 9 m during the succeeding recession. Furthermore, a long time span must be represented between the Premoeris Lake and the succeeding Moeris Lake. This long interval of a very low lake level (or possibly no lake at all!) may explain the perplexing absence of any archaeological remains dating in the interval between 5000 and 4000 BC when already well-developed Neolithic communities first appear along the lake shores.

The deposits of the rising Moeris Lake occur with pottery and artifacts of the Fayum A people. The lowest elevation (around 15 m above sea level) and the earliest date (3910 BC ±115 years) occur at Site E29G3, Area B. Two meters higher, at Site E29H2 (Kom W), the occupation is dated 3860 BC ±115 years. The dates and the elevation would suggest that the first site is slightly older; however, the standard error overlaps; and the difference in elevations is probably within the seasonal fluctuation of the lake.

The ceramics at these two sites, while within the same general tradition, are not identical. Those at E29G3 are rarely fiber tempered and tend to be from smaller vessels. This may indicate a seasonal activity connected with the low lake stage, while Kom W may represent a permanent village type of settlement. The differences may also be accounted for as reflecting minor cultural variations between communities. This question might be resolved by detailed analysis of the faunal material from the two sites, but our data are not adequate for this purpose.

The Moeris Lake was slowly but persistently rising throughout the period of the Fayum A Neolithic, and near the end of the occupation at Kom W the lake probably stood at an elevation slightly over 20 m above sea level.

A minor decline or an unusual series of low floods made it possible for a Predynastic settlement to occur on an exposed surface of a forming deltaic bench at an estimated elevation of around 17 m above sea level (E29G5). Following this brief event the lake continued to rise and reached its maximum around 23 m above sea level during the Old Kingdom, about 2800 BC. It seemingly stood at near this elevation for a considerable period, judging by the elaborate harbor facilities that were constructed along the north shore of the lake below Qasr El-Sagha Temple.

If the correlation of the diatomaceous bed studied by Alem with the Moeris Lake is correct, then the climatic conditions at this time were very close to those prevailing today.

The later history of the lake has been traced by Ball (1939) and Shafei (1940), who concluded that during the reign of Amenemhat I the maximum lake level stood around 18 m above sea level. If so, following the Old Kingdom maximum the lake shrank, and possibly the engineering activities attributed to Amenemhat's reign were concerned mainly with the prevention of further decline in the lake.

The decline to the modern lake of Birket Qarun may be attributed to the barrage at Lahun constructed by Ptolemy I, who lowered the level of the lake in order to reclaim the silt fan beyond the entrance to the Fayum Depression. Deprived of most of the annual influx of Nile flood water, the lake rapidly shrank to below sea level through evaporation. The Moeris Lake seems to have been the most stable and to have survived for the longest period—almost 4000 years. The duration of the lake is reflected in the massive deltaic, desert-fed, sandy benches that occur along almost the entire north edge of the lake.

PART 2

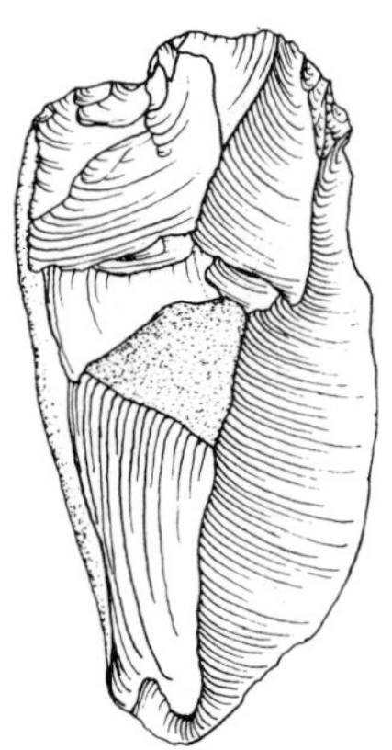

Synthesis

The Older Nilotic Deposits

Although the emphasis of the work since 1966 has been on the later Pleistocene events in the Nile Valley, some data have been acquired that pertain to the earlier history of the river. It seems that the silts and sandy silts assigned to the Dandara Formation, according to the heavy mineral analyses, reflect a regimen not unlike that of today, with considerable water flow from the area of the Blue Nile and Atbara basins. Heretofore the oldest sediments attributed to the modern regimen were recognized within the Korosko Formation (Butzer and Hansen 1968: 435), the upper part of which is radiocarbon dated at 25,250 BC ±1000–900 years (I-2061). This is almost certainly more recent than the Dandara Formation, dated at more than 39,000 BP, which elsewhere underlies the Late Acheulean. Deposits similar to the Dandara Formation have been noted downstream near Badari and described as "brown soil with calcareous precipitate [Butzer 1959: 62 and personal communication]," but they were not dated. The exact age of the oldest silts at Dandara is still unknown, but it is clearly pre-Late Paleolithic; and for this reason our earlier concept of a comparatively recent age for the origin of the Nile in the modern sense, with headwaters derived mainly from the Ethiopian highlands, must now be abandoned. It would also seem appropriate to suggest that the adjustment to the Nilotic microenvironment by Paleolithic man must have occurred at a much earlier date than formerly believed (Wendorf 1968: 1054).

Most exposures displaying the primary or fossil surface of the oldest silts at Dandara have a distinct red soil preserved at the top of the unit. It is interesting to note that this soil has never been found under the Qena sands, which may suggest a partial or entire correlation with the red soil found over the sandy hills at Dandara. Although the precise environment in which this soil formed is not known, the soil does serve as evidence for a major period of lower river levels accompanied by local precipitation and vegetation.

It seems particularly appropriate to emphasize that the sequence of these earlier Nile deposits is not clearly established. A number of separate episodes of aggradation could well be included in the silts that have been grouped into the Dandara Formation. Nor are we completely satisfied with the proposed Dandara and Qena sequence. In one locality the Dandara silts are overlain by gravels and sands locally derived from the Eastern Desert and initially identified as the Qena Formation. It seems possible, however, that these sands and gravels may not be equivalent to the thick suite of similar gravels and sands in the type locality for the Qena Formation, and that two different episodes may be represented. In any event, the thick beds of sands and gravels of the Qena Formation seemingly record an interval of heavy rainfall in Egypt accompanied by a markedly different Nilotic regime from that which prevailed previously, when the bulk of the water was derived from the Abyssinian plateau. A thick, red soil, possibly correlative with the one previously noted on the Dandara Formation, also occurs at the top of the subsequent sands. No distinct archaeological materials were recovered from this unit, nor is any other means of direct dating available.

A thick mantle (50 cm–1 m), composed mainly of locally derived Eocene pebbles and cobbles embedded in a red clay matrix, covers the eroded surface of the Qena sands as well as the exposed oldest silts. Extensive sheets of these gravels occur on the tops of the rolling hills of the Qena Formation west of Wadi Qena and, secondarily, as a slopewash down the sides of the hills. The gravels are wadi-like in character and indicate a sizable stream velocity and, thus, presumably heavy seasonal rains at the time of their deposition. The positions of these gravels were not mapped; therefore it cannot be determined if they were laid down as an extensive sheet wash or in a complex series of wadi beds; however, the latter seems more likely. A long period of erosion must have followed the deposition of the gravel mantle. It was during this period of erosion that the modern rolling topography was formed and the morphology of the overlying presumed wadi beds was inverted.

Chronologically, the next record concerning the Nile is a thick unit of slopewash along both sides of the river. This slopewash, composed mainly of gravels, pebbles, and cobbles from the gravel mantle covering the Qena hills, contains at its base numerous derived artifacts of Middle Paleolithic aspect. Proceeding upward in this unit, the deposit becomes clearly more colluvial, and both the frequency and the size of the gravel significantly diminish. Near the top it becomes a true colluvium, and at one locality (Site E6104) an extensive settlement (or several settlements) was found *in situ*. The artifacts were fresh and clearly untransported. Site E6104 is both technologically and typologically early Late Paleolithic (see Table 1). On the basis of its archaeological contents (Figures 161–163), the date for the later part of this slopewash is probably around 20,000 BC or slightly before. The episode of slopewash seems to have been a continuous one throughout the period of sedimentation with no evident breaks. Unfortunately there is no basis for relating this unit with the proper Nile sediments, but it is presumably of about the same age as the Nilotic Korosko Formation in Nubia (Butzer and Hansen 1968: 87–97), dated by radiocarbon around 25,000 BC, and it may represent an episode contemporaneous with the downcutting that must have separated the Korosko and Masmas Formations of Butzer and Hansen (1968).

The slopewash undoubtedly indicates somewhat greater rainfall than today, for similar sediments are not developing under present climatic conditions. The intensity of the rainfall seems to have progressively declined toward the top; however, this decline in the velocity of the water discharge that promoted the formation of the slopewash may be due to simple reduction in intensity or to a change in the seasonal pattern of the precipitation, or even to the development of a vegetation cover sufficient to retard the surface runoff.

Table 1. Main Typological Indices at Site E6104, Area C

Endscrapers	1.0
Transverse scrapers	.5
Sidescrapers	.5
Notches and denticulates	53.9
Truncations	1.1
Retouched flakes	36.7
Retouched bladelets	4.7
Varia	2.1

If the postulated, but not demonstrated, correlation of the slopewash with the early Korosko Formation or the preceding downcutting is correct, then it follows that a pattern of local rainfall both greater and more persistent than today was present at a time when it seems likely that greater precipitation occurred in sub-Saharan Africa. It should be noted, however, that adequate chronological controls are not available for either the Korosko Formation or the described slope sediments. No traces of the Korosko Formation have been found north of the Kom Ombo area.

Undoubtedly a long series of events is missing in the sequence, as it is now known, between the gravel and cobble mantle covering the sandy Qena hills and the slopewash episode. This lack of information is largely a result of the expedition's emphasis on the archaeological problems of the Late Paleolithic. The main concern was with the interval after 20,000 BC, and no attempt was made to compile a complete geological sequence for the earlier periods.

Rethinking the Dibeira-Jer and Ballana Formations of Nubia

As originally conceived by de Heinzelin (1968: 46), the Dibeira-Jer Formation represented the first episode of silt deposition by the modern Nile

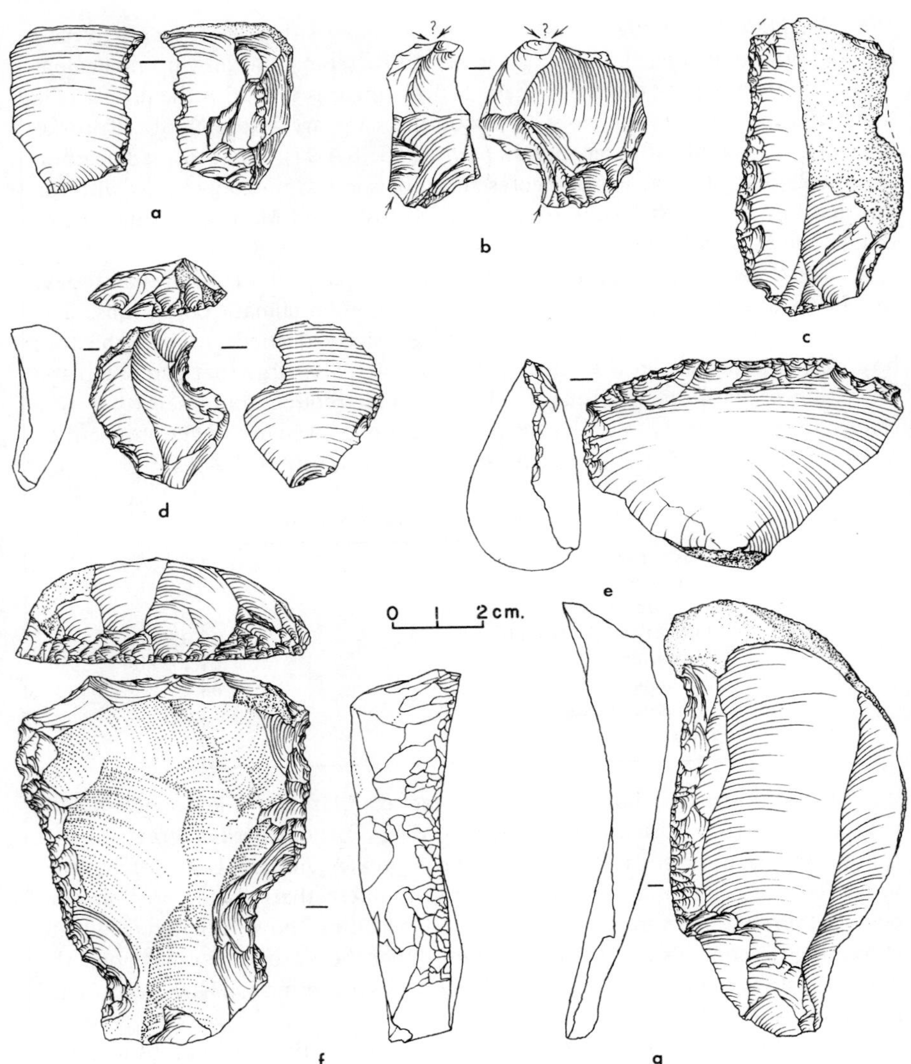

Figure 161. Tools from Site E6104, Areas C and D: (a) denticulated flake; (b) burin; (c and g) simple sidescraper; (d) composite tool; (e) transverse scraper, slightly denticulated; (f) endscraper on bilaterally retouched and notched flake (made on reused Levallois flake).

regime, with the major flow derived from the Ethiopian and East African headwaters. According to this view, the Nile Valley from the Batn El-Hajar northward was drained by a local stream before major tectonic activity created a link between this "Egyptian Nile" and the Sudanese basin to the south. The earliest "true Nile" silts, the Dibeira-Jer, were reported to occur up to 36 m above the

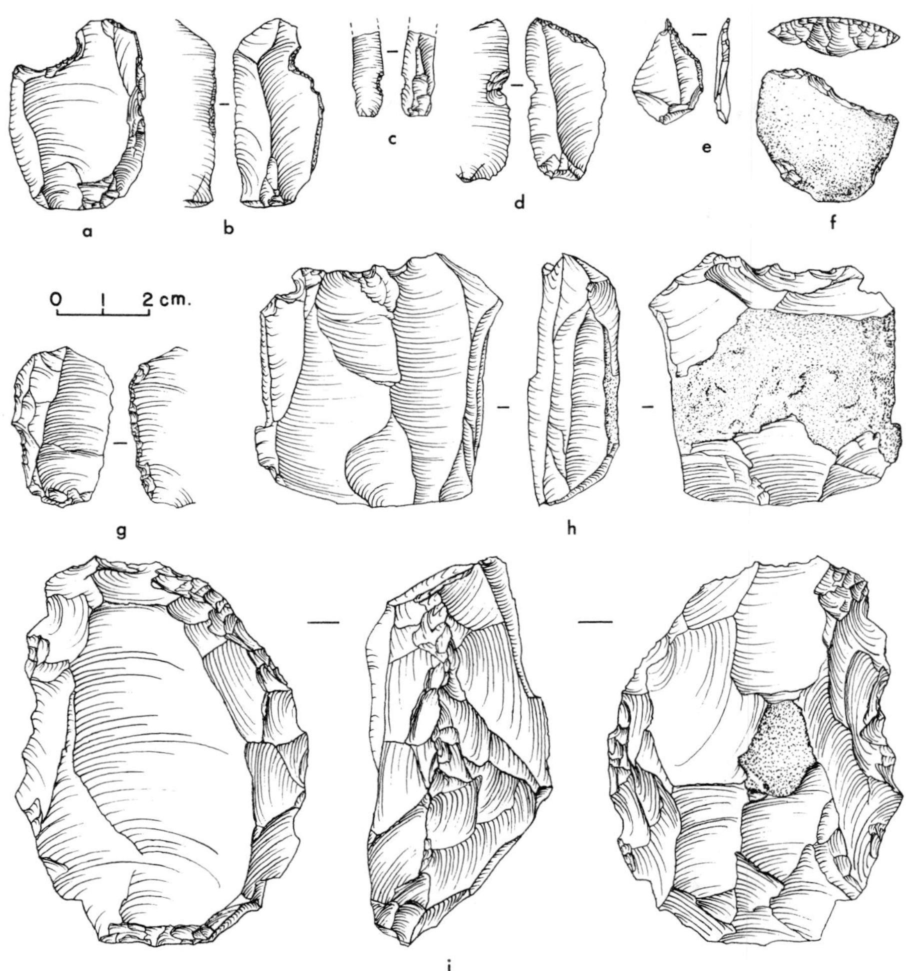

Figure 162. Tools and cores from Site E6104, Area C: (a) (d) notch on retouched flake; (b) notch on retouched blade; (c) notch on bladelet; (e) groover; (f) concave oblique distal truncated flake; (g) retouched flake; (h) opposed-platform core; (i) Levallois flake cores.

modern floodplain, to a maximum elevation of 157 m above sea level in the vicinity of Wadi Halfa in the Sudan. They were followed by a major interval of erosion in which extensive dunes were formed, and a second episode of aggradation, in two phases, both termed the Sahaba Formation.

The recent work in Upper Egypt has suggested several significant revisions in this perhaps too simple reconstruction of the history of the Nile. Probably the most significant, as already noted, is the recognition (Butzer and Hansen 1968: 78ff, 264, 453ff; Said *et al.* 1970: 44ff) that the Ethiopian Nile is far older than

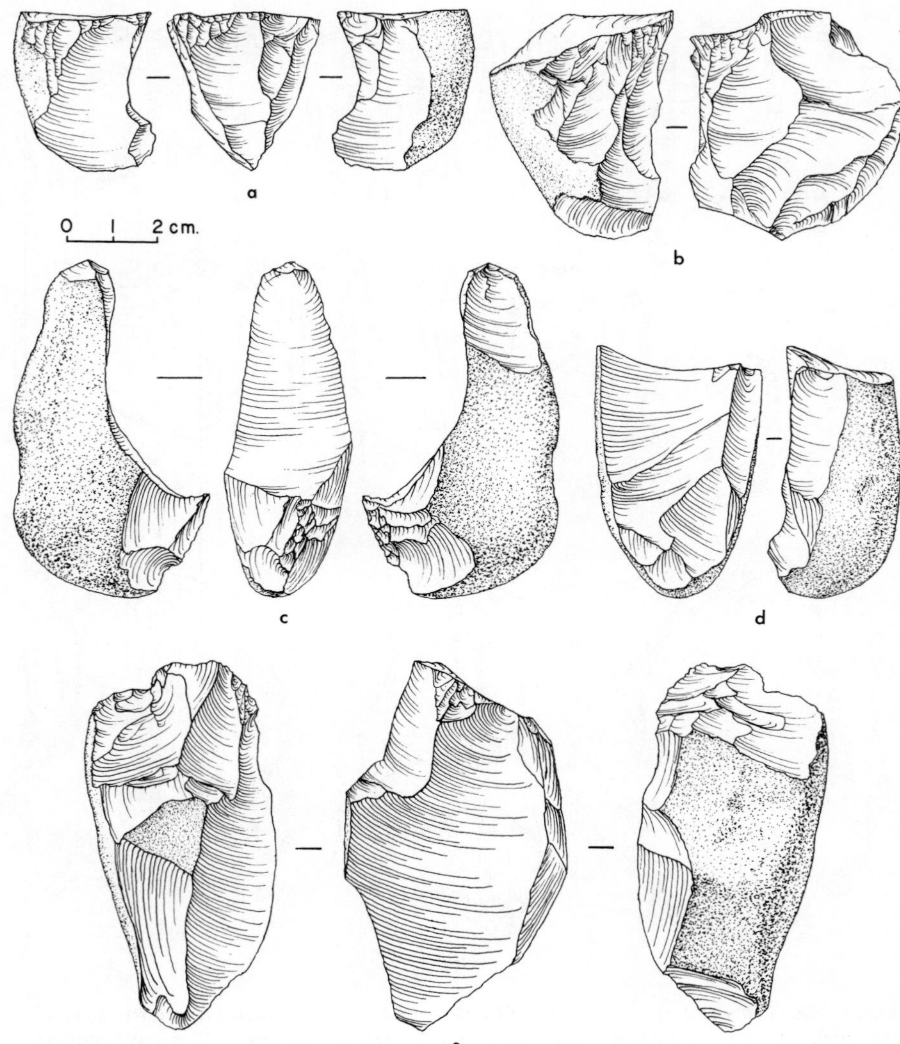

Figure 163. Cores from Site E6104, Areas C and D: (a and e) single platform; (b) opposed platform; (c) flake showing clear traces of side preparation; (d) single platform, rejuvenated.

previously stated (at least Late Acheulean, and probably older); as a consequence many of the older but undated silt remnants in Sudanese Nubia, which were previously assigned to the Dibeira-Jer Formation on the basis of elevation, may represent pre-Dibeira-Jer aggradations.

While the Egyptian data on this point are convincing, there were also some indications of a pre-Dibeira-Jer age for the modern Nile from the work in Nubia.

Clues suggesting this interpretation were indicated at an Acheulean site, Arkin 14 (Chmielewski 1965 and 1968: 125–133), and from a reexamination of some of the sections of Dibeira-Jer deposits in Nubia. The Upper Egyptian data also strongly support the interpretation that another episode of aggradation occurred between the Dibeira-Jer and the Late Sahaba, an event that was also tentatively suggested by de Heinzelin (1968: 49). The basic evidence is as follows:

1. The implied type locality for the Dibeira-Jer Formation in Sudanese Nubia is Site 1017 in the Khor Musa, just south of Wadi Halfa. This site contained a living floor of the Khormusan industry at an elevation between 147 m and 148 m above sea level, or about 26 m above the floodplain. Charcoal from this layer yielded a revised radiocarbon date of 18,950 BC ±280 years (WSU-203, Chatters 1968). This is the only date definitely associated with Nile sediments of the Dibeira-Jer Formation; and if the date is correct, it conclusively confirms that Nile sedimentation was occurring at least up to 148 m above sea level around 19,000 BC.Recently, however, this date has been revised, as will be discussed later.

2. In the same vicinity, and also in another locality across the river, there are beach lines at an elevation of 157 m that were assigned to the Dibeira-Jer maximum solely on the grounds that they represented the highest observed siltation and, therefore, must record this earliest true Nile event.

3. Another series of localities (Sites 443, 1014, 1018, 1020, and 2014) with Nile fluvial deposits believed by de Heinzelin to be the Dibeira-Jer Formation is also in the Khor Musa, but separated from the type locality by some 2 km of extensively eroded area. The oldest fluvial deposits here reach an elevation of 153 m above sea level and are separated from a subsequent dune by a pronounced erosional surface. Between the deposition of the older fluvial deposits and the dune, there is a decline in the level of the Nile, and wadi sediments were deposited in the eroded channel up to 143 m above sea level. These wadi deposits indicate that the Nile fell more than 10 m during this recession. The dune that overlies the wadi sediments seemingly interfingers (at Site 1020) with a silt in which a vertisol developed at a maximum elevation of 146 m above sea level, or some 25 m above the modern floodplain. Archaeological materials of the Halfan industry on and in this vertisol (at Site 2014) yielded a radiocarbon date of 17,200 BC ± 375 years (WSU-332). A second radiocarbon date, 14,550 BC ±500 years (WSU-201), was obtained from Site 443 at the top of the dune sand. This second date is regarded as minimal by the laboratory because of sample size. The dune sand in the Khor Musa was assigned to the recessional event of the Ballana Formation by de Heinzelin (1968).

4. At the type locality of the Ballana Formation, Site 8859, just across the Sudanese–Egyptian frontier, the Ballana dune sand clearly interfingers with silt at an elevation of about 136 m above sea level, or 16 m above the floodplain. Charcoal from the Halfan occupation below the upper layer of interfingering silt dated 16,650 BC ±550 years (WSU-318).

5. Further evidence of Nile sedimentation during this interval is provided by Site ANW-3, on the west bank of the river opposite the Khor Musa. Here the

deflated surface of fluvial Nile sediments reaches an elevation of up to 140 m above sea level, or some 19 m above the modern floodplain, where it occurs with a late Khormusan industry and a radiocarbon date of 15,850 BC ±500 years (WSU-215). A clear erosion separates the fluvial sediments with the archaeological materials from an older but undated silt assigned to the Dibeira-Jer Formation. The younger fluvial sands were assigned to the early part of the succeeding sub-Sahaba aggradation.

6. Slightly farther north from Site ANW-3 at Colorado site GB27 (de Heinzelin 1968: 32, Atlas Fig. 33; Irwin, Wheat, and Irwin 1968: 30, 110), between 17 m and 19 m above the Nile floodplain, there is a series of silt units that seem to record the same episode of Nile sedimentation. However, a series of conflicting radiocarbon dates was obtained from these silts: 4,200 BC ±300 years (I-864); 7,325 BC ±600 years (GXO-122); and 16,155 BC ±1,200 years (I-863). The associated industry favors the oldest of these dates; it certainly is much older than either of the two younger dates.

7. The same aggradation occurs at Kom Ombo, where the Masmas Formation of Butzer and Hansen (1968: 103–105) has radiocarbon dates of 16,350 BC ±300 years (I-2060) and 15,150 BC ±400 years (I-2178)

8. This episode of aggradation was also possibly recognized by de Heinzelin (1968: 47) as an early unit of the Sahaba aggradation, based on Sites 443 and ANW-3, but he failed to relate this aggradation to an extensive period of dune deposition. Instead, the deposition of the Ballana dunes was considered as an earlier event, an arid interval separating the Dibeira-Jer and the first phase of the Sahaba aggradations.

9. In Upper Egypt several sections were recorded where the final stages of an aggradation of Nilotic floodplain silt interfinger with extensive dune fields and, according to the radiocarbon dates, closely coincide with the interval of dune and silt deposition noted in Nubia. The combined silt and dune deposits in Upper Egypt, however, occur at a much lower elevation relative to the modern floodplain. A series of nine radiocarbon dates was obtained from the top of the silts and the interfingering dunes. These dates range from 16,070 BC (E71K1) to 14,880 BC (E71K9X and E6102), and closely agree with the dates from Nubia ranging from 17,200 BC to 14,550 BC, all obtained from dune sand and fluvial deposits.

The combined evidence strongly suggests that this was an interval, dating between 17,000 BC and 15,000BC, when a major episode of Nile aggradation accompanied dune migration. The stratigraphic and chronologic evidence shows clearly that the dune migrations and the maximum of this aggradation were occurring together. We wish to propose, therefore, a significant revision in the stratigraphic terminology. The deposits of dune and interfingering Nile sediments, previously regarded as two separate formations, are now understood as different lithological facies of the same chronological episode. The episode of simultaneous dune sedimentation and silt accumulation is termed *Ballana–Masmas aggradation* on the basis of its evident chronological correlation with the episode of dune formation and Nile aggradation at Ballana and the Masmas Formation at Kom Ombo.

Returning to some of the other Dibeira-Jer silts near Wadi Halfa, it is clear that this Ballana–Masmas aggradation is not the same event as that represented in the older fluvial deposits at Sites 443 and 1018 in Sudanese Nubia. The older deposits at these sites reach 153 m and are separated from the subsequent Nile deposits by a very pronounced, deep erosional surface (de Heinzelin 1968: Atlas Figure 12). These older Nile sediments should represent an undated aggradation certainly older than the Ballana–Masmas, as this term is here employed.

The only dated Nile sediments in this area that seem chronologically to precede the Ballana–Masmas aggradation occur at Site 1017 and are about 2000 years older than the earliest date for the Ballana. The similarity in elevation, with a maximum around 148 m at Site 1017 compared with 145 m for the younger silts (the vertisol, silts, and interfingering dunes) at Sites 443 and 1018, might indicate either that the maximal level of the Nile was stable for a period of about 4000 years or that the sediments at Site 1017 belong to an episode of aggradation 2000 years earlier. This question cannot be resolved with the data at hand, but our inclination is to view the sediments at Site 1017 as recording a preceding and separate aggradation for which the original term *Dibeira-Jer* should be reserved. (However, see revised date for Site 1017 discussed below.)

It should also be noted that there is no possibility of physically correlating the dated sediments at Site 1017 with the presumably older and higher Nile sediments at Sites 443 and 1018 or the beaches previously regarded as representing the maximum of the Dibeira-Jer aggradation. These Nile sediments may indeed date with the Dibeira-Jer aggradation at Site 1017; however, they could just as well refer to some older event or events.

An example of such an older event seems to be recorded at Sites 440 and 1440 (de Heinzelin 1968: 23, Atlas Fig. 15). Here a silt underlies an extensive complex of dune sands terminated by an incipient soil overlain, in turn, by silt and fluvial sand units up to around 153 m above sea level, a similar elevation to that of the older fluvial sediments at Site 1018. Two cultural layers were found within the dune at Site 440. The upper cultural layer was associated with the soil; the lower one lay within the dune about 1 m below. A radiocarbon date of 12,390 BC ±500 years (WSU-290) was obtained on charcoal from the upper layer. The date must be rejected as obviously much too young for both the indicated stratigraphic position and the associated archaeology.

While there are minor differences between the two assemblages, possibly due to the sample size, they are sufficiently similar to be regarded as within the same industry (Shiner 1968: 630–637). The lithic collections have high values for Levallois, and the dominant tools are denticulates. There was one example of a biface foliate resembling those from some Aterian sites. The general impression is that of the Mousterian complex, particularly the Denticulate Mousterian, possibly with an Aterian affiliation, and with only minor differences evident. It also closely resembles the two assemblages from the Nilotic Goshabi Formation in the Wadi El Melik area south of Dongola, Sudan. Although the Goshabi Formation was regarded as equivalent to the Sahaba at Wadi Halfa on the basis of similar areal extent (Marks, Shiner, and Hays, 1968: 319; de Heinzelin, 1971), the silts are not dated and could well be far older than the Sahaba, as the associated archaeology suggests.

Older silts that may precede the Dibeira-Jer as seen at Site 1017 are also reported from two localities along the west bank of the Nile at Wadi Halfa by the Colorado Expedition. One of these is at Site 6G30 (Irwin, et al. 1968: 5–9), which contained a Khormusan assemblage. It has a radiocarbon date of greater than 34,050 BC (ibid., p. 110), which until recently (see below) seemed too old for the archaeological material and other dates then available from the Khormusan industry. If the date is correct, as now seems likely, then the underlying Nile silts have to be older than 30,000 BC.

The other locality in this area is Site GB32 (Irwin, et al, 1968, p. 16) where a Halfan assemblage is controversially dated by radiocarbon at 23,750 BC ±2,500–3,700 (GXO-410) and occurs at the top of a sandy silt covered by another unit of fine dark gray silt. The site is at an elevation of 141 m above sea level, or about 20 m above the Nile floodplain. Elsewhere, there are several dates on Halfan assemblages that are several thousand years later (between 18,000 and 15,000 BC), but if the date is correct, the silt containing the industry may be equivalent to a Nile aggradation reported downstream, the Korosko Formation of Butzer and Hansen (1968).

The aggradation represented by the Korosko Formation is dated 25,250 BC ±1000–900 years (I-2061). Exposures of this unit occur at both Kom Ombo and in Egyptian Nubia, and are preserved to elevations of 34 m above the modern floodplain (Butzer and Hansen, 1968, p. 324). Although it is not possible to correlate with any of the undated older Nile sediments in Sudanese Nubia, most of which have been previously identified as the Dibeira-Jer Formation, it is now clear that the history of the Nile River is so complex that it cannot be reconstructed mainly on the basis of elevations. Only an extensive series of radiometric dates on these possibly numerous aggradations, preceding the first well-dated Ballana–Masmas aggradational episode, will permit the establishment of a firm sequence.

A further complication is suggested by a recent evaluation of the Middle Palaeolithic in Egypt (Wendorf and Schild, in press, b), in which three sequential stages are proposed. There are, from early to late: (1) Mousterian, found both along the Nile (Marks 1968a) and in several sites in the Sahara (Schild and Wendorf 1975); (2) Aterian and Aterian-related, also both along the Nile (as the Nubian Middle Stone Age, Chmielewski 1968; Guichard and Guichard 1965) and in the Sahara (Wendorf and Schild, in preparation); and (3) the Khormusan (Marks 1968b), known only along the Nile. Recent work at Bir Sahara and Bir Tarfawi in the Egyptian Sahara has shown that both the Mousterian and the Aterian settlements there occur with significant wet phases, and that these are separated from each other by an arid episode. A series of radiocarbon dates from

Bir Sahara and Bir Tarfawi indicate that both the Mousterian and Aterian occupations in the Sahara date before 44,000 years ago, although how much before is unknown. A pronounced, long interval of aridity follows the Aterian, and it now seems likely that the Sahara was not only extremely arid but also unoccupied from before 44,000 years ago to around 7000 BC, when a widespread Terminal Paleolithic occupation occurs. The Terminal Paleolithic sites also occur simultaneously with the onset of an interval of increased moisture, although not as moist as during the preceding Mousterian and Aterian wet phases.

This proposed three-stage structure for the Middle Paleolithic represents a significant change in our previous concept of these industries. For example, the Khormusan initially was assigned to the Late Paleolithic, primarily because of two lines of evidence. The first, and perhaps the most important factor, was the comparatively late age of the two radiocarbon dates then available (18,950 BC ±280 years, WSU-203, from Site 1017, and 15,850 BC ±500 years, WSU-215, from Site ANW-3); and the second feature which favored a Late Paleolithic assignment for the Khormusan was the high frequency of burins in the Khormusan assemblages. Except for the burins, however, the Khormusan is both typologically and technologically closer to the Middle Paleolithic. Furthermore, numerous burins are not necessarily a reliable index for the Late Paleolithic. There are several undoubted Middle Paleolithic assemblages known from Central Europe that contain very high proportions of burins (see, for example, Krukowski 1939; Kowalski 1969). More recently, three additional radiocarbon dates have been obtained from Khormusan sites, one greater than 36,000 years ago (GXO-409, Irwin *et al.* 1968), the second greater than 41,490 years ago (SMU-106), and the third a rerun on the remnant of WSU-203 from Site 1017, of 33,800 B.P. ±3350 years (SMU-245). It is not known if the younger date obtained by the Washington State University laboratory is due to inadequate pretreatment or to a malfunction in the electronics. In any event, the finite age obtained by Southern Methodist University laboratory may be due to minute humate contamination, since the remnant of the sample could not be completely pretreated. As a group, these three new dates cast doubt on the previously obtained younger dates from the Khormusan and suggest the possibility that the younger samples were contaminated. It is significant that the Khormusan assemblage from which the 41,490 date was obtained (Site 34, Industry D) is both stratigraphically and typologically one of the most recent in that industry. An age of more than 42,000 years for the Khormusan industry would also suggest a pre-Debeira-Jer assignment for the silts in which these sites occur.

While many of the questions posed by these re-evaluations cannot be clarified at this time because many of the key localities are deeply buried beneath the waters of Lake Nasser, it nevertheless seems highly likely that the older silts in the Wadi Halfa area were far more complex and have a far greater time range than we originally believed.

Nilotic sediments immediately preceding those of the Ballana Formation were not recognized in Upper Egypt, possibly because of the emphasis of the recent work on those deposits that yielded assemblages of Late Paleolithic age.

The sediments deposited during the Ballana–Masmas aggradation were recognized with certainty in only two areas: El-Kilh and Isna. The tops of the fossil floodplain silts range from 5 m to 6 m above the floodplain at El-Kilh in the south, and from 4 m to 5 m at Isna, some 50 km to the north, indicating a decline of the surface in reference to the modern floodplain. These silts are slightly higher than those of the succeeding aggradation at El-Kilh but slightly lower at Isna, a situation that may be attributed to the difference in the angle of the river slope in the two areas.

It is also interesting to note that, according to our observations, the gradient surface of the Ballana–Masmas silts is steeper than that of the succeeding Sahaba in relation to that of the modern floodplain, thus suggesting a lower base of erosion for this earlier silt. This may simply be due to a lower sea level during the interval of the Ballana–Masmas aggradation.

The striking lithological feature of the Ballana–Masmas aggradation is the interfingering of extensive dune fields with silts along the west bank of the river. A comparable situation occurred during historic times (Butzer 1959, 1961). The modern El-Khefoug landscape, which is particularly well developed between Mallawi and Beni Suef, seems to be a similar phenomenon (Said *et al.* 1970: 55). Except for the dune interfingers, the silts that were studied are massive, homogeneous, and very monotonous in their structure, representing a typical floodplain deposition; no signs of wadi activity were observed in the worked areas. This agrees with the observations by Butzer and Hansen in the Kom Ombo area for their Masmas Formation, which, according to radiocarbon dates, is equivalent to the Ballana aggradation. To quote these authors, "Local wadi activity was minimal during this Nilotic aggradation, and was certainly no greater than at the present time. [1968: 102]."

From these statements and our own observations, it would seem that the evidence throughout the Nile Valley from Nubia to central Egypt is in general agreement that the final phases of the Ballana–Masmas aggradation occurred during an interval when the climate of Egypt was similar to that which prevailed during historical times and has persisted until today. Local rainfall, if any, must have been sparse. There was little vegetation beyond the floodplain, and dunes, driven by prevailing westerly winds, were extremely active along the west margin of the valley.

The chronology of the Ballana–Masmas aggradation is one of the best established in the entire Nile sequence. From Nubia, there are five dates, all on charcoal:

14,440 BC ±500 years (WSU-201, believed to be minimum), Site 443
15,850 BC ±500 years (WSU-215), Site ANW-3
16,155 BC ±1200 years (I-863), Colorado Site 6B27
16,650 BC ±550 years (WSU-318), Site 8859
17,200 BC ±375 years (WSU-332), Site 2014

At Kom Ombo, there are two dates clearly associated with the Masmas Formation, both on carbonate:

15,150 BC ±400 years (I-2178)
16,350 BC ±310 years (I-2060)

From Upper Egypt at El-Kilh (Site E71P1), there are five dates, all on shell from the top of the Ballana–Masmas floodplain silt, apparently at the maximum level of the aggradation:

15,000 BC ±350 years (I-3238)
15,300 BC ±300 years (I-3249)
15,500 BC ±300 years (I-3418)
15,650 BC ±300 years (I-3419)
15,850 BC ±330 years (I-3417)

The Isna area has also yielded two dates from the top of the dune facies:

15,640 BC ±300 years (I-3415)
16,070 BC ±330 years (I-3416)

Another date in an apparently similar stratigraphic situation comes from Site E6102, near Dandara:

14,880 BC ±300 years (I-3427)

The stratigraphy where these dates were obtained indicates that the dunes in these particular localities had already been formed when the occupations occurred on their surfaces.

Another date evidently related to this event is from carbonate plant replacement at the base of a flat dune near the eastern fringe of the dune field at Site E71K9X near Isna—14,880 BC ±290 years (I-3420). This date may possibly relate to the very end of the dune deposition.

These 16 dates ranging from around 17,000 BC to 15,000 BC suggest that the events of Nile aggradation and dune formation may well have lasted 2000 years.

In addition to this consistent series of dates, however, there are four others that must be rejected. Two of these rejected dates are from Colorado Site 6B27. As noted previously, these are regarded as too recent because they strongly conflict with the associated archaeology:

4,200 BC ±400 years (I-864), Colorado Site 6B27
7,325 BC ±500 years (GXO-122), Colorado Site 6B27

The other two rejected dates cannot be stratigraphically evaluated, but on the basis of the related cultural materials they may fall within the Ballana–Masmas aggradation. Both dates, however, are too recent in view of the chronology discussed earlier. One of the dates is from a sample collected from the surface at an early site of the so-called Dabarosa industry (Colorado 6B29), and is dated 13,150 BC ±750 (GXO-122). The other was a compound sample from two Halfan sites, 6G29 and 6B34, and was dated 13,020 BC ±1420–730 years (GXO-576). In both instances the archaeological materials are closely related to assemblages from other sites that on stratigraphic and radiocarbon evidence are placed within the Ballana–Masmas event.

The chronology of the seemingly arid Ballana–Masmas period suggests a possible correlation with one or more warmer European oscillations. One likely candidate is the so-called Laugerie interstadial (or Bordes' Wurm III/IV interstadial), which has a series of conflicting radiocarbon dates. Two dates on burned bone from the transition from Middle to Upper Solutrean, believed to be at the confine between Wurm III and the beginning of the Laugerie interstadial at Laugerie-Haute, are 17,650 BC ±140 (GRN-4442) and 17,790 BC ±200 (GRN-4495). Above it, at the top of Upper Solutrean and, thus, near the end of the Laugerie interstadial, are two other dates, also on burned bone—17,920 BC ±190 years (GRN-4605) and 18,050 BC ±240 years (GRN-444, Vogel and Waterbolk 1967: 113). These two dates do not follow the sequence of radiocarbon dates developed for the earlier phases of the Solutrean in this rock shelter and, consequently, should be used with caution (Vogel and Waterbolk 1967: 116–117).

A possibly more reliable date from this interstadial comes from the Upper Solutrean layer at Abri Fritsch, where charcoal gave a date of 17,205 BC ±225 years (GRN-5499, Leroi-Gourhan 1969: 20). This would closely coincide with the earliest date associated with the Ballana–Masmas aggradation.

Another oscillation that may be correlated with the Ballana–Masmas is the Lascaux, which has two radiocarbon dates—14,050 BC ±500 years (Sa-102, Leroi-Gourhan 1969: 20) and 15,240 BC ±140 years (GRN-1632).

Except for the first two, none of the dates seem to define the upper or lower limits of these two oscillations. It might be appropriate to regard the arid interval of the maximum of the Ballana aggradation as possibly generally contemporaneous with both oscillations and the colder interval that separates them, particularly if the long chronology for the Ballana–Masmas of more than 2000 years is acceptable.

During this interval, in the restricted geographic area between Luxor and Idfu, two different archaeological complexes occur in the Nile Valley; and insofar as the available radiocarbon dates are concerned, they were contemporaneous. They have been named the Idfuan and the Fakhurian. This situation closely parallels that previously noted in Nubia, where three distinctly different industries seemingly simultaneously occupied the same geographic area during the Ballana–Masmas aggradation. These are the ending phases of the Khormusan industry (ANW-3, Marks 1968b), unless we accept the suggestion that the entire Khormusan is significantly older, the Halfan (443, 1014, 1018, 1020, 8859, 6B32, and 6G20-6B35, Marks 1968c; Wendorf 1968b; Irwin, Wheat, and Irwin 1968), and the Dabarosa (6B29 and 6B27, Irwin, Wheat, and Irwin 1968). This is a very unusual situation and strongly contrasts with observations for many parts of the Old World, where at this time strongly similar technocomplexes were developing over large areas where prehistoric societies were utilizing similar microenvironments. Here along the Nile, in spite of the closely similar microenvironments being exploited, the industries are entirely different, not only typologically and statistically but also technologically. This can mean only that at least some of these diverse groups came to the Nile with an already established typological and technological model for their tool kit and that the local Nilotic environment led toward little, if any, equalization of these tool kits. The cause of this suggested movement of diverse groups to the Nile Valley could well have been the arid conditions indicated by the climatic reconstruction for the maximum of the Ballana–Masmas period. Such arid conditions would have narrowed the livable areas of the desert to the Nile Valley.

The Idfuan industry, found concentrated in the El-Kilh area but also occurring at Isna, is dated between 15,850 and 15,000 BC. Some facies share technological resemblances with the Halfan farther south. The Idfuan sites are frequently large (i.e., E71P1), but they are probably composed of several clusters of cultural remains, possibly reflecting several occupations. In a few cases there were small, restricted concentrations (i.e., E71P6) suggesting small social units. The occurrence of dense cultural material through more than 30 cm of silt almost certainly implies several reoccupations of specific selected localities by similar groups. The occupation debris at one site (E71P1) is spread over a broad, flat surface, which must mean that this particular site was occupied mostly during the lower-water stage. Other sites (E71P6 and E71P7) have occupations on hill slopes at the very edge of the silt and were possibly settled during high water. A third site situation (E71K9 and E71K10) is at the river edge of an extensive dune field. Considerable depth and density occurs at all three site situations; however, the depth of the cultural horizons in the sites on slopes and at dunes could more likely have resulted from natural phenomena than those found within the flat silts.

The subsistence economy of the Idfuan was diverse, with no clear-cut emphasis. Three main sources are reflected in the remains: large mammal hunting, with *Bos* and hartebeest most common, though hippopotamus and gazelle are also represented; fishing, concentrated mainly on the large Nile catfish; and shellfish gathering, apparently restricted to *Unio*.

The technical characteristics of the Idfuan industry clearly suggest a clustering of the assemblages into two main groups, one containing a high frequency of the Levallois method of flaking and the other entirely lacking in Levallois.

There are three sites (E71P1, E71K8, and E71K10) known as representatives of the Levallois. Only one of these, Site E71P1, has been studied in detail. It is an unusually large site, but there was no apparent distribution cluster visible on the surface. A casual inspection of the tools, however, suggested that some forms tended to occur more commonly in different parts of the site. For this reason the site was arbitrarily divided into four areas (A–D), with Area A the farthest to the north and upslope and Area D at the south end of the site and downslope.

The four areas do not differ as far as the debitage and core typology are concerned, but they do have statistically significant differences within their tool kits. Among the cores, slightly less than half are Levallois, including the Halfan variety. Other cores include opposed-platform, both same side and opposite side blade cores with preceding core preparation; single-platform cores for both blades and flakes; and changed orientation cores with transversely crossing scars, as well as a few discarded and unpatterned changed orientation cores. Most of the cores are between 30 mm and 45 mm in length. More than 70% are made on local wadi chert; the remainder are made on Nile chert.

In the debitage the blades tend to be short—between 2 cm and 4 cm in length, with the longest around 7 cm long. Microblades and bladelets are the most numerous and represent more than 90% of the blade category. Most of the flakes are also small, the majority less than 3 cm in length. The Levallois Index is slightly below 10.

The variation in the tool kits is reflected in two distribution clusters. At the northern end of the site (Areas A and B), there is a very high Typologic Levallois Index; burins are low to absent; Ouchtata bladelets are also very rare or absent; and the most common tools are retouched blades and flakes, of which elongated pointed blades with basal blunting are significant. Notched and denticulated pieces are also numerous.

At the southern end of the site (Areas C and D), the tools are generally similar but differ in four main elements: (1) the presence of numerous pieces of the Ouchtata bladelet group, significant (2) burin and (3) scaled piece indices, combined with (4) values for retouched pieces nearly half as high as at Areas A and B (Figures 164–169).

The main typological indices at Site E71P1, Areas A and C are shown in Table 2.

There are four known sites that are characteristic of the non-Levallois group: E71P2, E71P6, E71P7, and E71K9. These sites all lack any trace of Levallois technology and share a generally common technological base. Opposed-

Table 2. Main Typological Indices at Site E71P1, Areas A and C

	A, surface	*A, T 2*	*C, surface*	*C, T 5*
ILty (mostly Halfan)	13.5	13.8	17.2	12.1
Burins	3.0	—	8.4	8.4
Ouchtata	<1.0	—	—	18.2
Notches and denticulates	15.8	26.7	19.6	19.7
Truncations	3.0	<1.0	4.0	2.3
Scaled pieces	1.5	—	8.1	6.1
Retouched pieces	18.0	24.1	9.2	11.0
Limited retouched pieces	23.3	25.0	17.2	15.9
Endscrapers	—	<1.0	6.8	2.3
Basal blunting	18.0	5.2	1.4	<1.0
Sidescrapers	1.5	<1.0	<1.0	<1.0
Backed elements	<1.0	2.6	3.6	3.3
Perforators	<1.0	<1.0	<1.0	<1.0

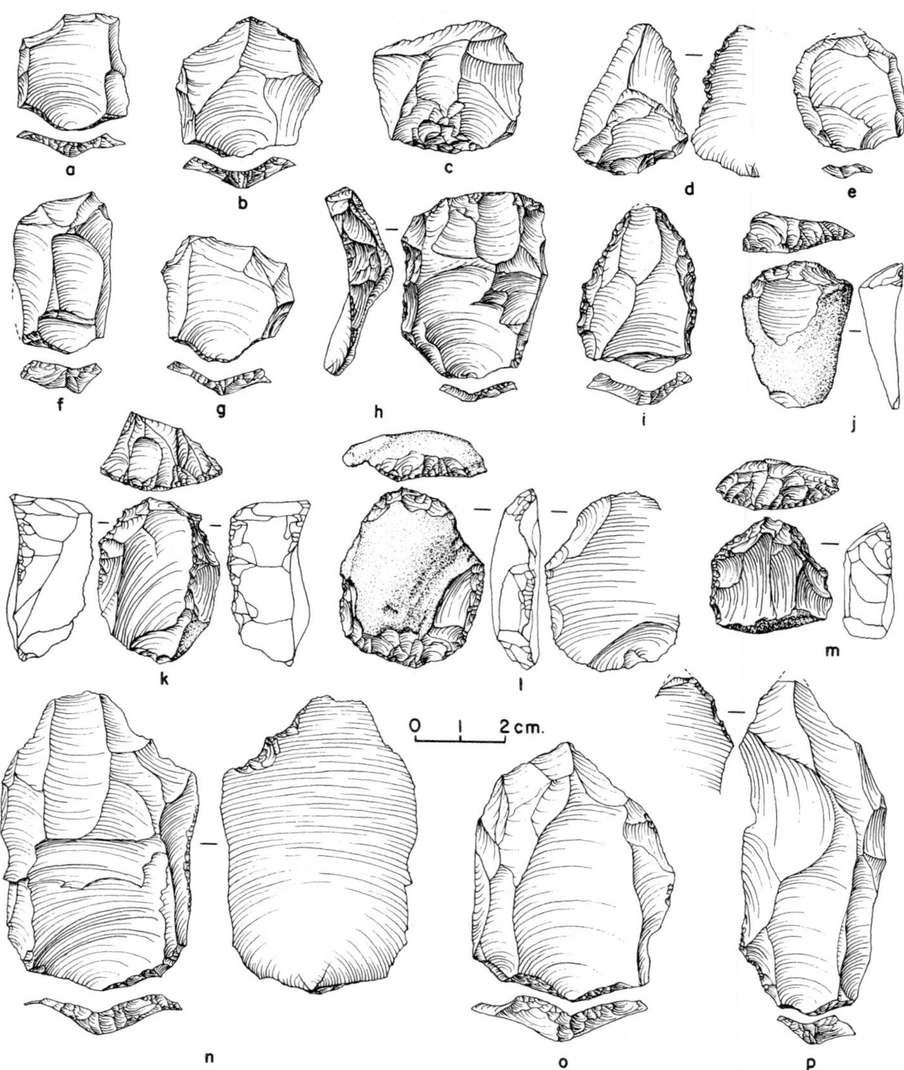

Figure 164. Tools from Site E71P1, Area C: (a–c) Levallois flakes; (d) Levallois flake, retouched; (e–g) Halfa flakes; (h–i, n–p) Halfa flake, retouched; (j) endscraper on flake; (k) keeled endscraper on flake, unilateral; (l) double endscraper on flake, retouched; (m) endscraper on flake, unilateral.

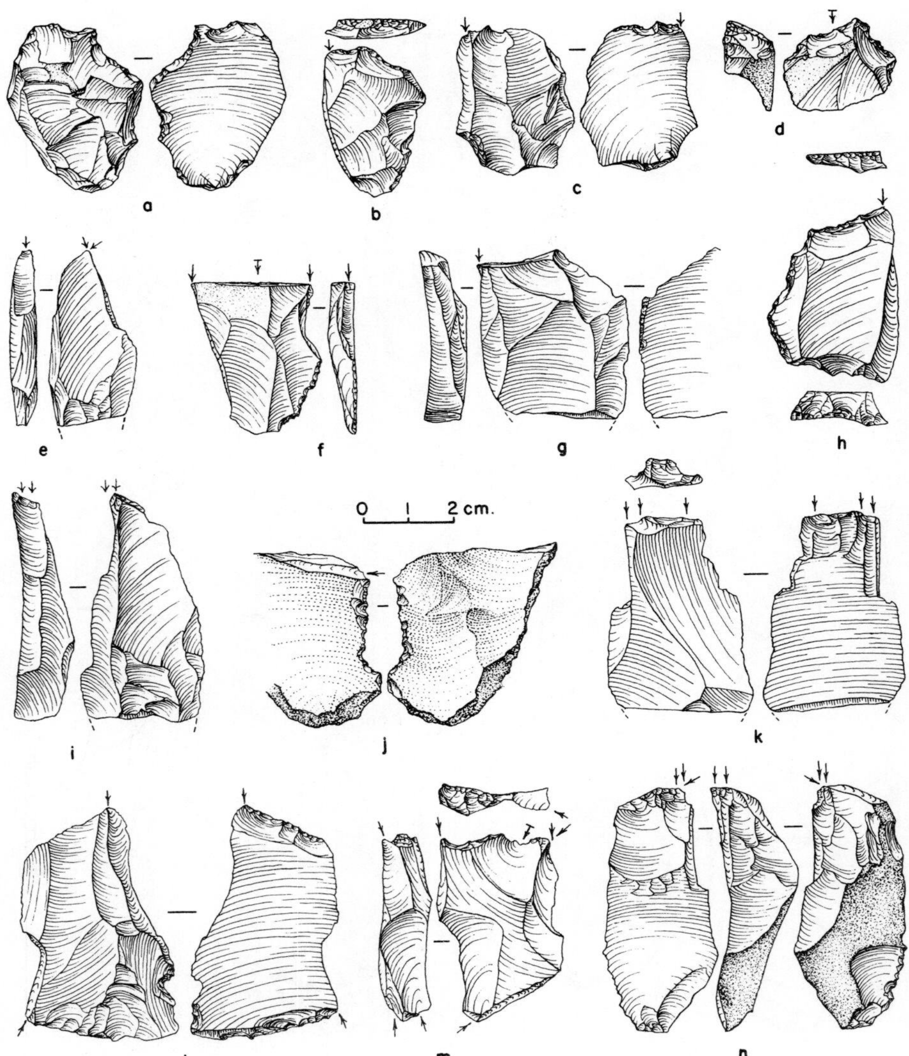

Figure 165. Tools from Site E71P1, Area C: (a) borer; (b–c, e–n) burins; (d) groover.

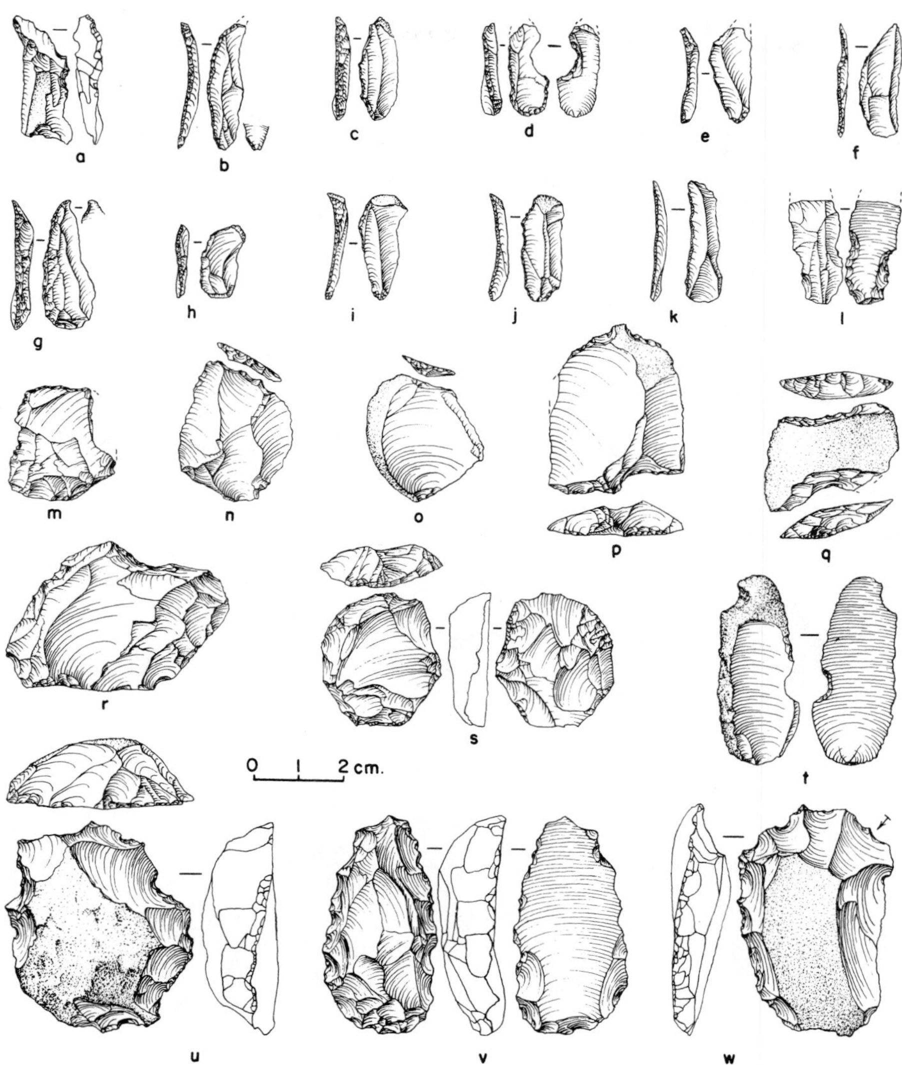

Figure 166. Tools from Site E71P1, Area C: (a, c) Arch-tipped bladelet; (b) convex-backed pointed microblade with inverse retouch; (d) convex-backed pointed microblade, notched; (e–g) pointed microblade with Ouchtata retouch; (h–j) Ouchtata retouched microblade; (k) straight-backed pointed microblade; (l) strangled bladelet; (m–o) distal truncated flakes; (p) basal truncated flake; (q) double-truncated flake; (r) notched flake; (s) combination tool; (t) notched blade; (u–w) denticulated pieces.

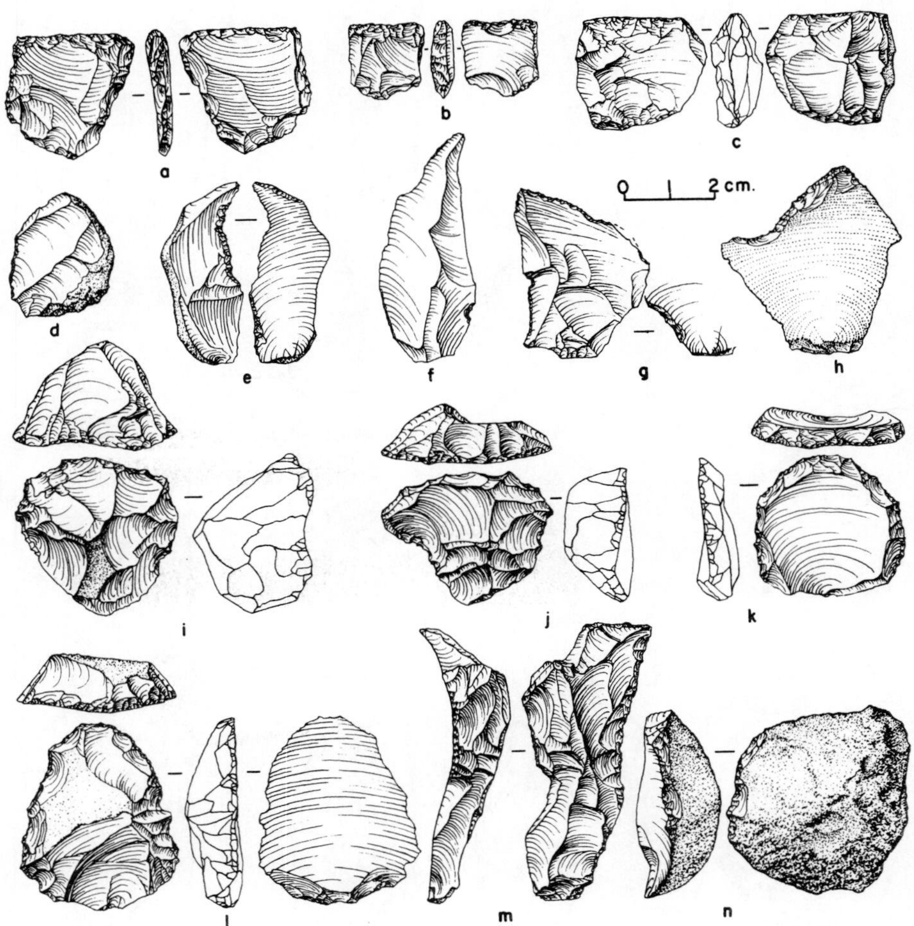

Figure 167. Tools from Site E71P1, Area C: (a–c) scaled piece; (d–h and m) retouched pieces; (i–l) core scrapers; (n) sidescraper.

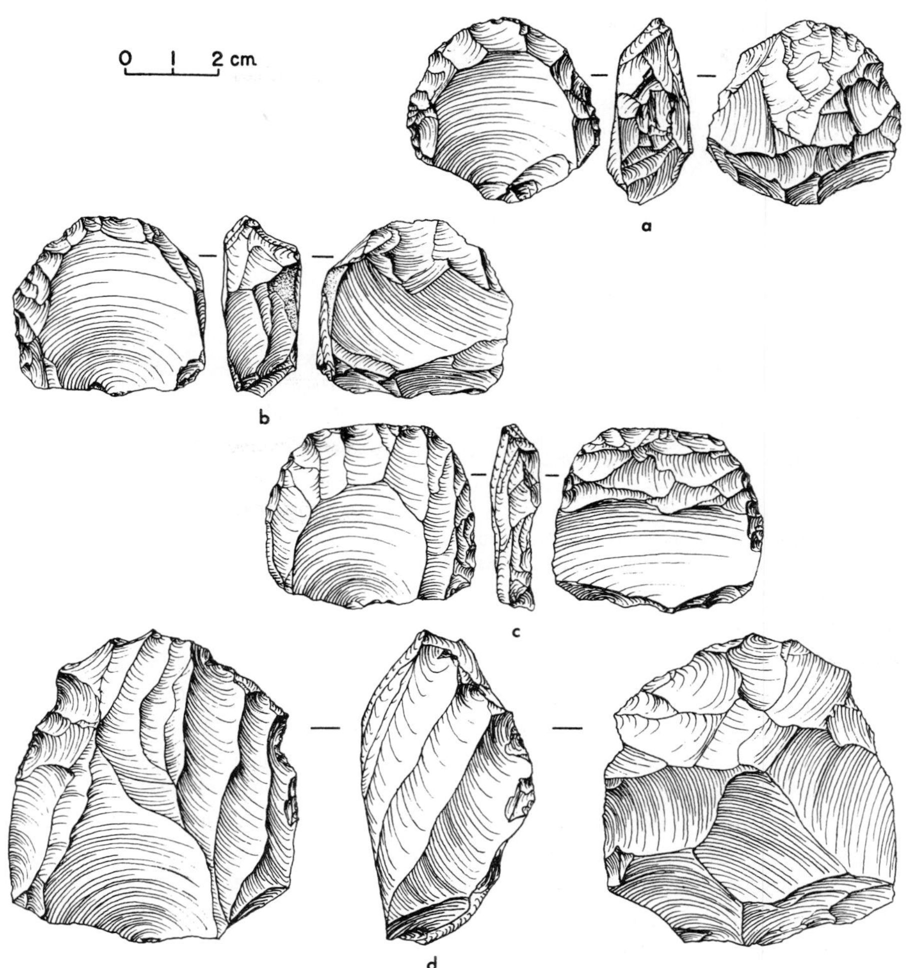

Figure 168. Cores from Site E71P1, Area C: (a–b) Levallois; (c–d) Halfan.

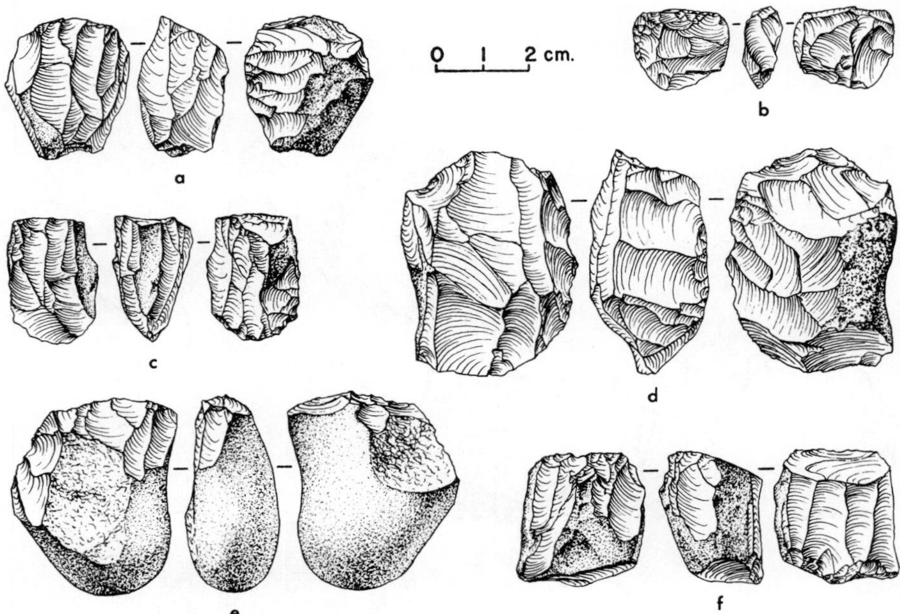

Figure 169. Cores from Site E71P1, Area C: (a) ninety degree; (b) bipolar; (c) multiple; (d) opposed platform; (e) single platform, faceted; (f) opposed platform, opposite sides.

platform blade and bladelet punch method cores form the most characteristic group. Most of them have traces of previous preparation of sides, backs, and preflaking surfaces. During the flaking some of them passed from blade through bladelet to flake stage near the end of the exploitation. Single-platform blade, bladelet, and flake cores also form an important category. The flaking surfaces on these cores range from flat to rounded, the latter resembling conical cores. One of the most numerous categories is the flake core with unpatterned changed orientation. Of these, the most common are the globular variety.

Within this broad, non-Levallois group there appear to be considerable variations in the frequencies of certain tools. Each site is sufficiently different to merit separate consideration. All of them share an emphasis on retouched flakes and blades, which represent half or more of the total tools, while end-scrapers and backed elements are rare to absent; all of the sites have considerable values for notches and denticulates, and the frequencies of truncations are generally low (Figures 170–172). The assemblages differ in two or three elements, which permit subdivision into four groups:

1. Relatively high Ouchtata values (around 15%), coupled with a low burin index (below 3%—Site E71P6).

2. With very low burin and Ouchtata values (below 4% and 1%, respectively), but with high basal blunting (*ca.* 18%)—Site E71P2.

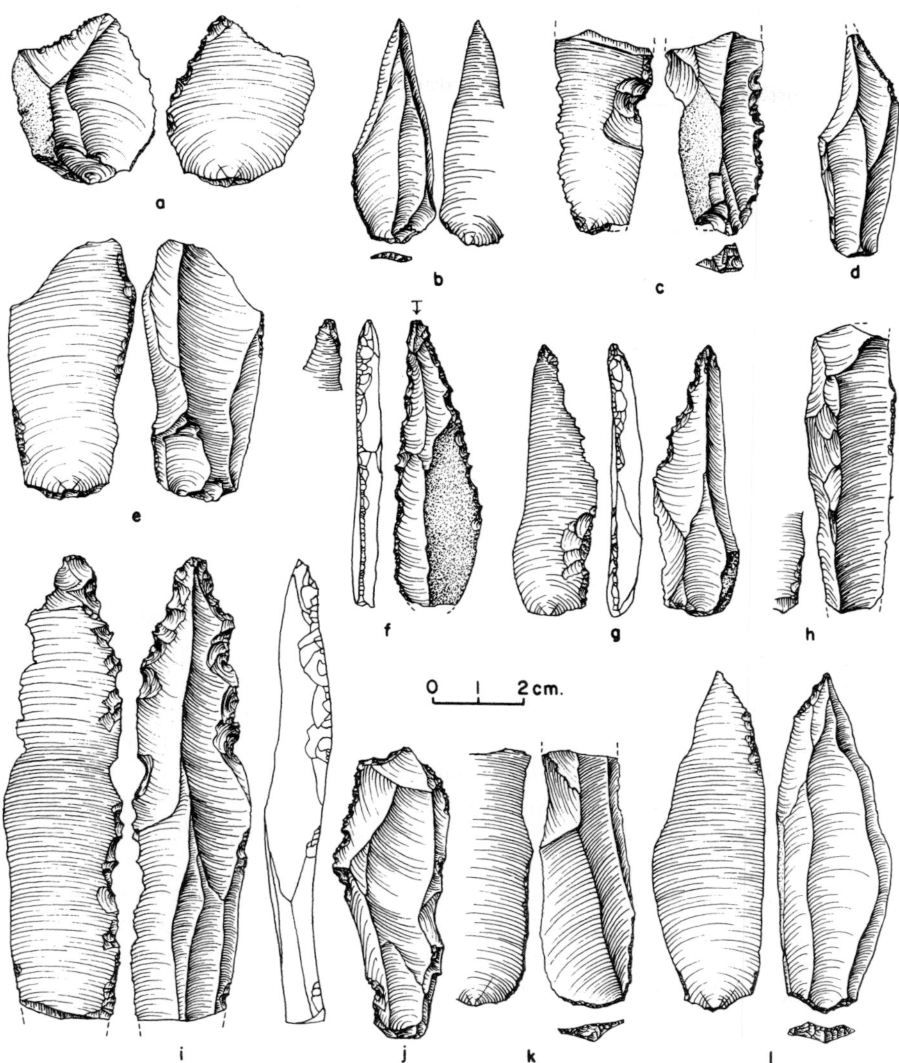

Figure 170. Tools from Site E71K9C: (a, c, j) denticulated pieces; (b) pointed blade with basal blunting; (d–e and h) retouched pieces; (f–g) borers on denticulates; (i) converging denticulate; (k) blade with basal blunting; (l) arch-tip blade with basal blunting.

3. High burin index (between 10% and 20%) and medium Ouchtata values (around 4%), together with low percentages for basal blunting—Site E71P7.
4. High burin index (around 20%), no Ouchtata, and considerable numbers of elongated, pointed blades with basal blunting (around 10%)—Site E7K9.

The main typological indices of the non-Levallois group are given in Table 3.

Table 3. Main Typological Indices for Sites E71P6, E71P2, E71P7, and E71K9 of th

	E71P6, surface	E71P6, T 1	E71P2, surface	E71P2, T 3	A, surfac
ILty			<1.0		
Burins	1.6	—	4.0	2.2	14.3
Ouchtata	11.4	16.7	2.7	—	3.4
Notches—denticulates	14.0	14.3	13.6	25.0	16.8
Truncations	—	1.4	1.4	—	5.9
Scaled pieces	<1.0	—	<1.0	—	—
Retouched pieces	25.4	17.1	31.3	22.8	20.2
Limited retouched pieces	35.7	39.8	31.9	37.0	31.1
Endscrapers	<1.0	1.2	1.0	—	<1.0
Basal blunting	5.9	4.6	12.7	9.8	1.7
Sidescrapers	—	1.1	<1.0	1.0	—
Backed elements (except Ouchtata)	4.9	2.3	—	1.1	4.2
Borers ± groovers	—	<1.0	<1.0	1.1	<1.0

The second complex associated with the maximum of the Ballana–Masmas aggradation, termed the Fakhurian industry, is known from only one cluster of sites located just north of Isna (E71K1–E71K5). There are two radiocarbon dates available that place this industry between 16,070 and 15,640 BC, making it slightly older than the mean for the Idfuan dates but overlapping with them. Three of these Fakhurian sites, all small, are situated on the crest of small, sandy knolls at the fringe of an extensive dune field, where the dune and silt interfinger. The other two, about the same size, are close together within the dune field.

Only the three sites at the margin of the dune field are known to have been occupied at the very end of the time when the sand and silts were in the process of overlapping. The other two are both undated but are supposedly of about the same age. There are minor differences between the two groups of sites, but the factors responsible are unknown.

In comparison with most of the Idfuan sites, the Fakhurian concentrations were small and yielded no evidence of internal clustering. The size of the concentrations and the distribution of the artifacts at the Fakhurian sites may indicate that these localities were not repeatedly reoccupied, as was suggested for several of the Idfuan settlements.

The lithic assemblages of the Fakhurian industry were studied by Lubell (1971, 1972), who noted that the cores in these assemblages are characterized by the absence of Levallois technique and by an emphasis on three major core forms: opposed platform (between 27% and 53%), single platform (24% to 35%), and changed orientation with transversely crossing scars (8% to 18%). The bipolar flaking technique is also present, but in low frequency.

on-Levallois Group

A, T 1 and 4	B, surface	B, T 2a (10–40 cm)	C, surface	C, T 1	Surface Area A	T 2
8.6	13.4	24.2	21.4	5.9	19.3	21.6
7.9	<1.0	4.2	—	—	—	—
12.2	22.4	13.7	15.5	21.6	27.2	23.4
4.3	9.6	4.2	3.6	—	3.6	1.7
—	1.0	1.1	—	—	<1.0	3.3
18.0	17.7	11.6	25.0	27.5	17.2	12.4
35.3	28.8	34.7	23.8	43.1	13.4	9.2
—	1.0	1.0	2.6	—	4.3	5.8
5.0	—	1.1	1.2	5.9	6.0	10.8
1.4	2.0	3.2	1.0	—	<1.0	—
4.2	3.8	2.1	3.6	2.0	1.3	1.7
<1.0	<1.0	—	1.2	—	2.8	6.7

The flake and blade debitage contains a high percentage of microlithic pieces. It is also high in blades, bladelets, and microblades (ranging from 26% to 32%), but these tend to be relatively short and wide.

The tool kit includes four major classes that characterize the industry (Figures 173–175). These are backed bladelets (ranging from 20% to 51%), straight and arch backed, as well as numerous Ouchtata group bladelets in some of the assemblages; retouched pieces (from 16% to 32%); perforators, mainly double backed with both ends pointed (9–15%); and notches and denticulates (7–15%). Other tools include endscrapers, which are present but variable (1–3%). Table 4 gives the main typological indices for several Fakhurian sites.

Table 4. Main Typological Indices at Fakhurian Sites.

	E71K1	*E71K3*	*E71K4*	*E71K5*
Endscrapers	10.5	3.3	8.0	6.1
Core scrapers	3.7	2.5	1.4	0.2
Perforators	9.2	15.5	9.8	9.7
Burins	3.1	2.5	2.8	1.7
Composite tools	0.5	—	—	—
Backed elements	20.0	24.2	25.1	51.4
Notches and denticulates	9.6	15.2	13.9	7.4
Truncations	6.0	6.5	6.0	6.1
Scaled pieces	2.9	0.2	1.1	0.2
Retouched flakes	17.5	10.6	12.1	4.3
Retouched bladelets	14.6	16.6	17.7	11.6
Sidescrapers	1.8	1.3	1.3	0.3
Varia	0.7	0.9	0.8	0.6

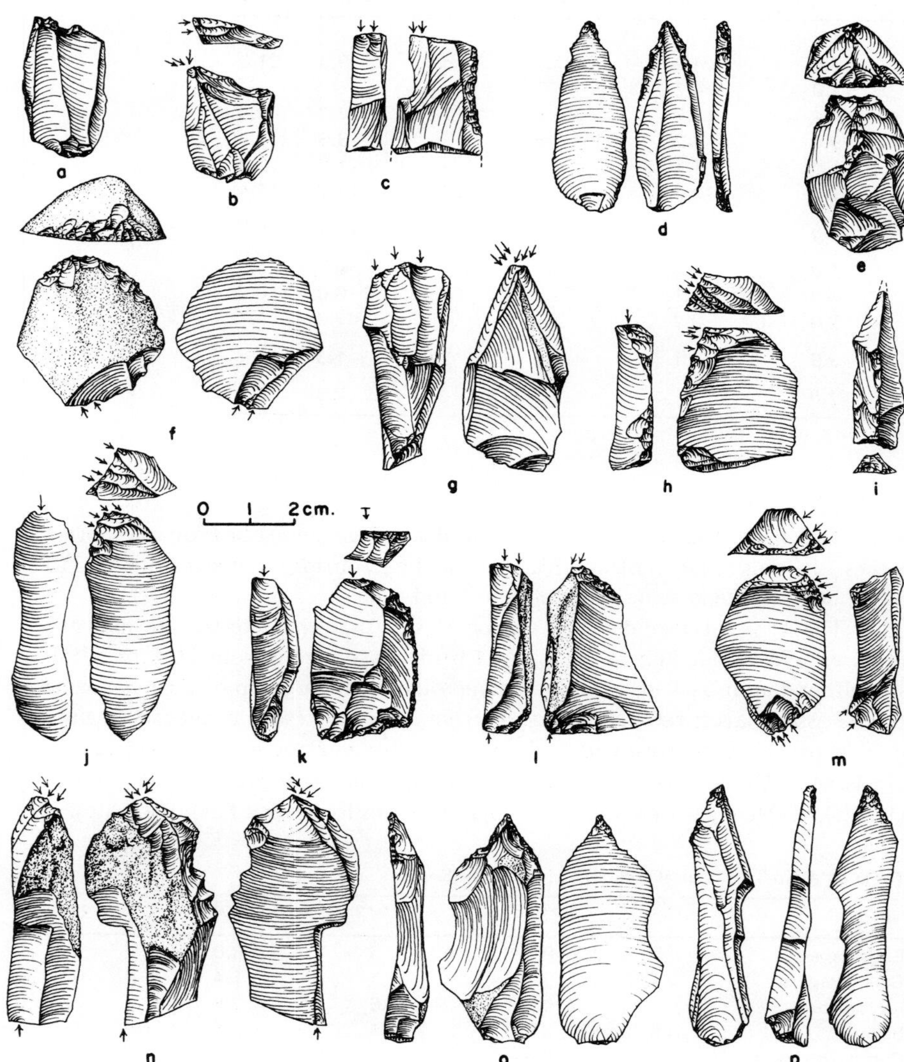

Figure 171. Tools from Site E71K9, Area C: (a) notched piece; (b–c, f–h, j–n) burins; (e) scraper; (i) basal truncated bladelet; (d, o–p) borers.

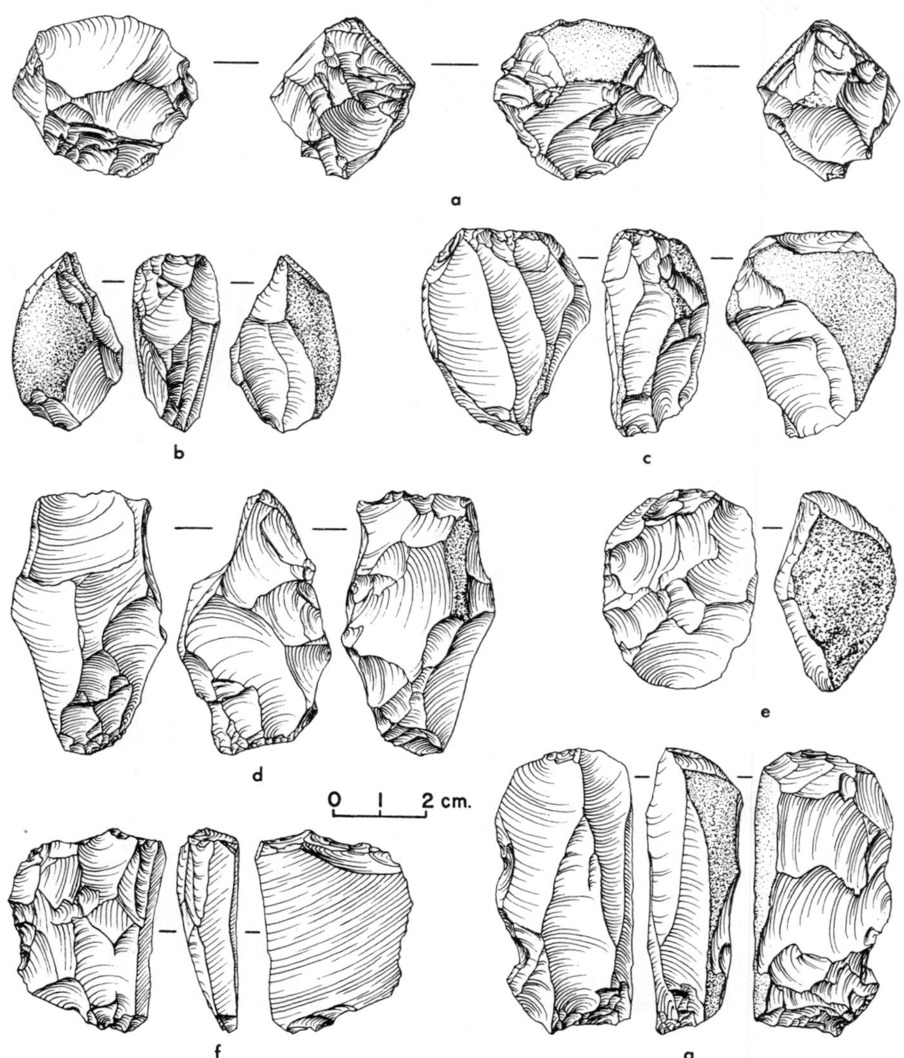

Figure 172. Cores from Site E71K9, Area B: (a) globular; (b) opposed platform, twisted, blade; (c) opposed platform, opposite sides, blade; (d) opposed platform, side preparation, twisted; (e) opposed platform, side preparation, flake; (f–g) opposed platform, side preparation, blade.

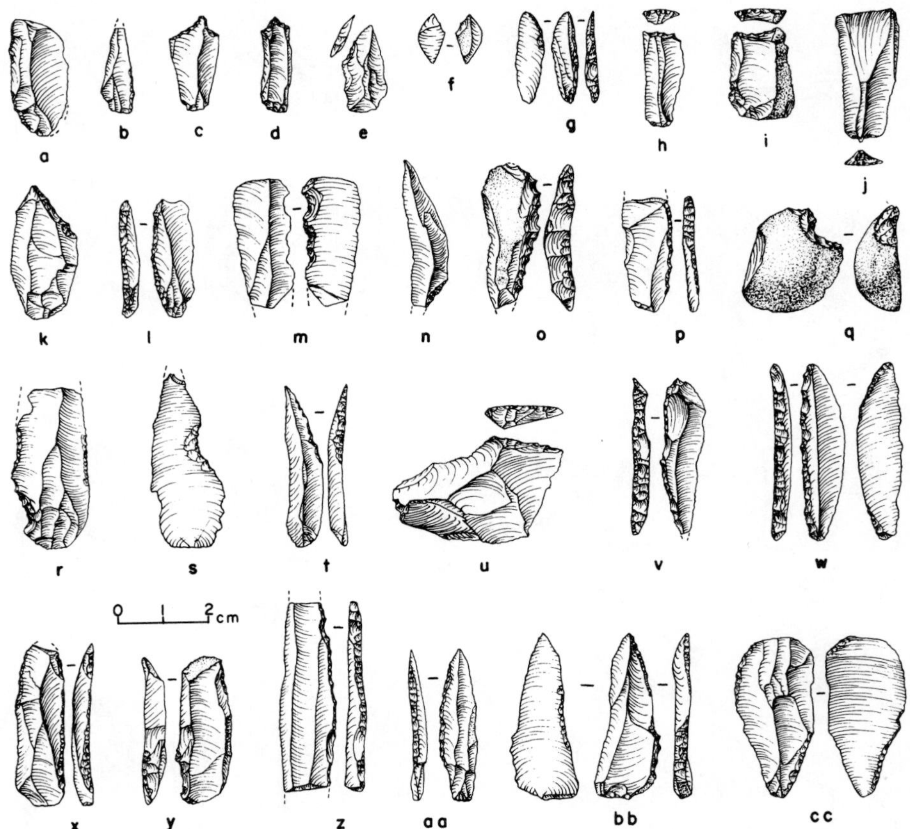

Figure 173. Tools from E71K3, Fakhurian industry: (a–b) Ouchtata microblade; (c) perforator; (d) graver; (e) piquant triedre; (f) microburin; (g) backed and retouched microblade; (h–i, k, u) distal truncated pieces; (j, n) basal truncated piece; (l, v) obtuse straight-backed bladelet; (m, o) microdenticulate; (p) partially backed microblade; (q–s) notched piece; (t) arch-tipped bladelet; (w, bb) backed and retouched bladelet; (x, y, aa) partially backed bladelets; (z) fragment backed bladelet; (cc) retouched bladelet.

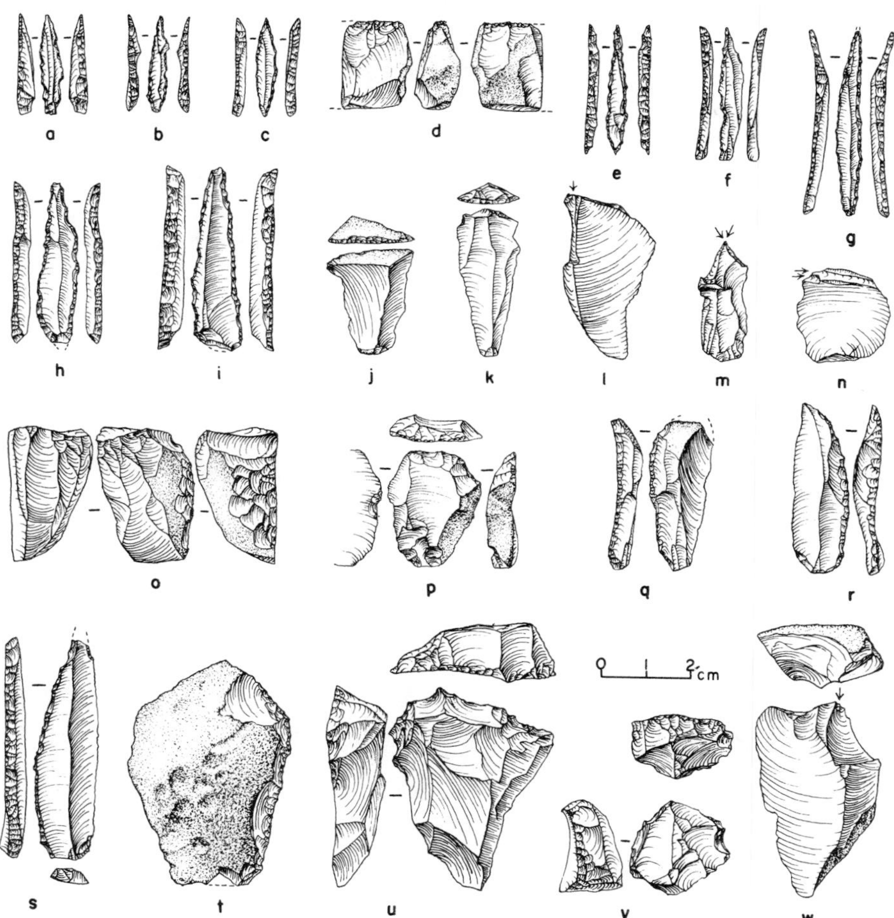

Figure 174. Tools from Site E71K3, Fakhurian industry: (a–c, e, g–i) double-backed perforators; (d) scaled piece; (f) perforator on backed bladelet; (j) end raclette; (k) endscraper on bladelet; (l–n, w) burins;(o) core scraper;(p) endscraper on retouched flake; (q–r) arch-backed bladelet; (s) arch-backed and retouched blade; (t) sidescraper; (u) denticulate endscraper on broken denticulated flake; (v) core scraper.

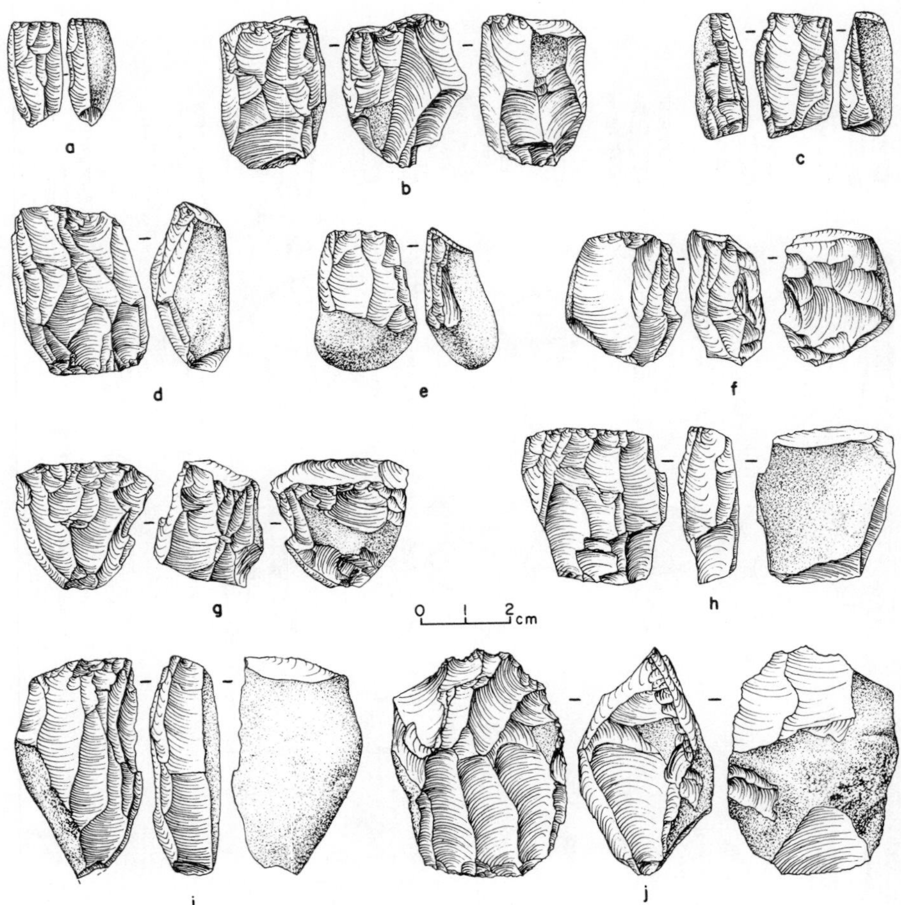

Figure 175. Cores from Site E71K3, Fakhurian industry: (a, e) single platform, blade; (b) opposed platform, opposite side, flake; (c–d, h–j) opposed platform, blade; (f) change of orientation blade; (g) pyramidal (atypical), blade.

Faunal remains were recovered from three of the Fakhurian sites: two along the dune margin and the third from within the dune field. These show marked differences, but it is not clear if these indicate economic variations or if the differences are because of the various conditions of preservation and collection. For example, at Site E71K1, where the bulk of the collection was taken from the dune surface, most of the remains are from large mammals, of which hartebeest and *Bos* are the most numerous (more than 100 bones of hartebeest), while only seven individuals of fish and a few *Unio* are represented. On the other hand, at Site E71K3, where a bone breccia occurred at the foot of the sand knoll, washed in and mixed with cultural material, fish dominate the faunal remains, with more than 110 individuals recovered from a very small trench. Among the large fauna found here, again hartebeest is predominant with 45 bones, followed by rabbit, *Bos*, gazelle, hippopotamus, and possibly lion (the only example found). At both these sites the fish remains consist almost entirely of large Nile catfish. Clearly they were specialized for the exploitation of these fish.

The few remains from the site within the dune (E71K4) are hartebeest and *Bos*; however, it should be stressed that the absence of fish in the instance of this site, and others in similar situations, is not necessarily an indication of a different pattern of economic exploitation.

The Deir El-Fakhuri Recession

The previous interpretation of the Nilotic Sequence by the present authors and others (Wendorf *et al.* 1970a, b, c; Said *et al.* 1970) proposed that a term, *The Deir El-Fakhuri Formation*, for a series of pond sediments that were believed to represent a recessional feature. However, because of additional data—including radiocarbon dates, the subsequent analysis of associated archaeological materials, and the results of diatom and pollen analyses—it seems more likely that the pond sediments of the so-called Deir El-Fakhuri Formation may not record a period of recession but, in fact, the early phase of the subsequent Sahaba–Darau aggradation as reflected within the special microenvironment of a closed dune field adjacent to the river. Our present understanding of these events now limits the Deir El-Fakhuri recessional interval to the period of Nile downcutting between the maximum of the Dibeira-Jer aggradation and the following Sahaba.

This recessional interval is not a local event. Butzer and Hansen (1968: 149) report a seemingly contemporaneous decline of at least 20 m at Kom Ombo, while de Heinzelin (1967: 322) supposes that the Nile fell no less than 4 m during the episode of downcutting that separates the Early and Late Sahaba formations.

No information is available to indicate the maximum depression of the level of the Nile during this recessional episode; however, at Isna it clearly fell to below 83 m above sea level (Site E71K18), or at least 2 m below the maximum of the Ballana–Masmas silts in that area, and almost certainly considerably lower. In the Isna area the next sediments preserved in the stratigraphic record are those already believed to be of an early Sahaba–Darau age, slightly before 12,000 BC. Thus it seems likely that around 3000 years may be represented in this interval of downcutting.

Among the tentative records assumed for this event is the series of so-called noncalcic soils at Sites E71K18, E71K12, E71K13, and E71K14D; however, no thin section or chemical examinations of these supposed soils were made, and the brownish horizon at Site E71K18 and the limonitic stains at Sites E71K12, E71K13, and E71K14D may all be due to oxidation caused by the subsequent ponds that developed in this area. Furthermore, the tops of the dunes at E71K12,

E71K13, E71K14, and E71K15 are cemented by heavy concentrations of calcium carbonate that may well have masked the upper horizons of a soil, if any were present.

Another presumed record of this recessional event is the net of vegetation casts observed at the top of the dune at most of the sites where the supposed noncalcic soil also occurred. This vegetation, however, most likely developed during the subsequent ponding episode. The tubular nature of the vegetation casts suggests an aquatic environment.

There remains only the possibility of wadi activity as a stratigraphic record of the recession. One such unit occurs in the Dishna area (Site E71M5B) prior to the Sahaba siltation, but the wadi deposit there is not dated beyond being pre-Sahaba. Other wadi activity that may partially correlate with this recessional event may be the fine-grained wadi alluvium of the so-called Malki member of the Ineiba Formation. According to Butzer and Hansen's observations (1968: 117), in the Kom Ombo area the Malki member unconformably overlies the Masmas Formation, now believed to be contemporaneous with the Ballana–Masmas aggradation. Freshwater marl from the base of this Malki member gave a radiocarbon date of 15,450 BC ±300 years (I-2179). The date may be regarded as slightly too old if most recent dates (*ca.* 15,000 BC) from the Ballana–Masmas sediments are correct, but when the standard errors of the dates are considered they overlap.

While the presence of sedimentary units formed during this recessional interval could not be clearly demonstrated, there are several different archaeological complexes presumably present along the Nile during the period between the maximum of the Ballana–Masmas and the succeeding Sahaba–Darau aggradation. One such complex may be represented at Site E6102, which occurred on an old surface deeply buried below the floodplain in the canal near Dandara and at an elevation only 3 m above the present Nile. The stratigraphic situation here is far from clear, but the site was undoubtedly occupied during an interval of low Nile levels, either the Deir El-Fakhuri or a slightly earlier event. The test excavations were not extensive enough to determine the size of the site, nor were there any associated fauna. The assemblage (Figures 176–178) has not been studied in detail, but the main typological indexes are given in Table 5.

Table 5. Main Typological Indices at Site E6102

ILty	16.6
Burins	1.4
Notches and denticulates	28.8
Endscrapers	1.0
Backed elements	1.0
Retouched pieces	44.4
Borers and groovers	2.0
Truncations	1.0

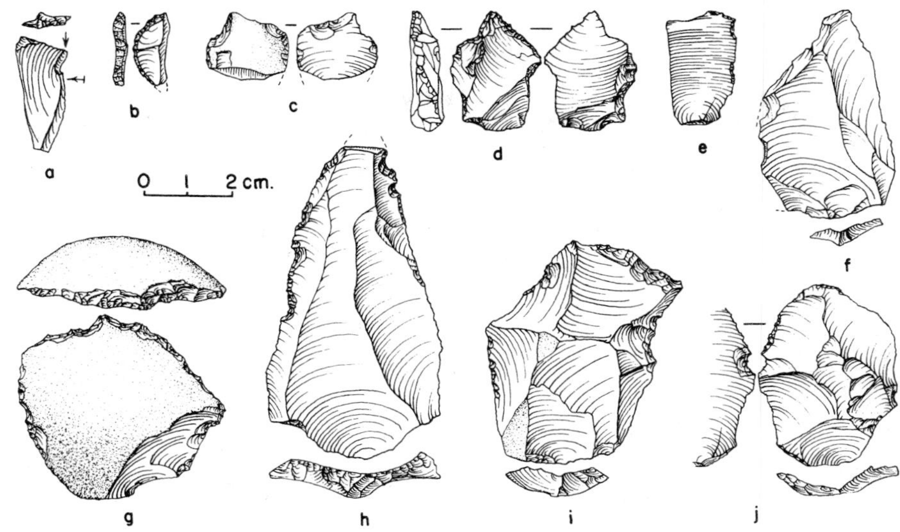

Figure 176. Tools from Site E6102: (a) burin on straight oblique truncation; (b) arch-backed pointed flake; (c) borer; (d) multiple groover; (e) groover; (f) Levallois flake; (g) denticulate on flake; (h) Levallois point, retouched; (i–j) Levallois flakes, retouched.

Two other archaeological complexes of the Deir El-Fakhuri interval are represented at Sites E71K12 and E71K13, each containing distinct lithic technological and typological entities. These two sites were studied by Phillips (1973).

The technological attributes of the assemblage from Site E71K13 may be summarized as follows: Wide and flat opposed-platform bladelet cores represent nearly three-fourths of all cores. Single-platform cores, mostly for blades, represent about 15% of the collection. A minor group, about 5% have opposed platforms with an additional platform perpendicular to the earlier ones. The flake and blade debitage contains a high frequency of well-made bladelets (around 30%), generally quite flat, parallel sided, and blunt at the distal end. More than 90% of the debitage is on local wadi chert; the remainder are made from Nile pebbles.

The most characteristic and highly dominant group is the Ouchtata retouched bladelets, accounting for nearly 80% of all tools. (Figures 179–180). Next in importance, around 8%, are backed bladelets, of which the most numerous are straight or arch backed with blunt ends. A few are straight or arch backed with pointed ends. There are also rare backed and obliquely truncated bladelets. Minor tool categories, between 4% and 5% each, are notches and denticulates and retouched pieces. Burins and truncations are rare, while end-scrapers and perforators account for less than 1%. The main typological indices for Site E71K13 are given in Table 6.

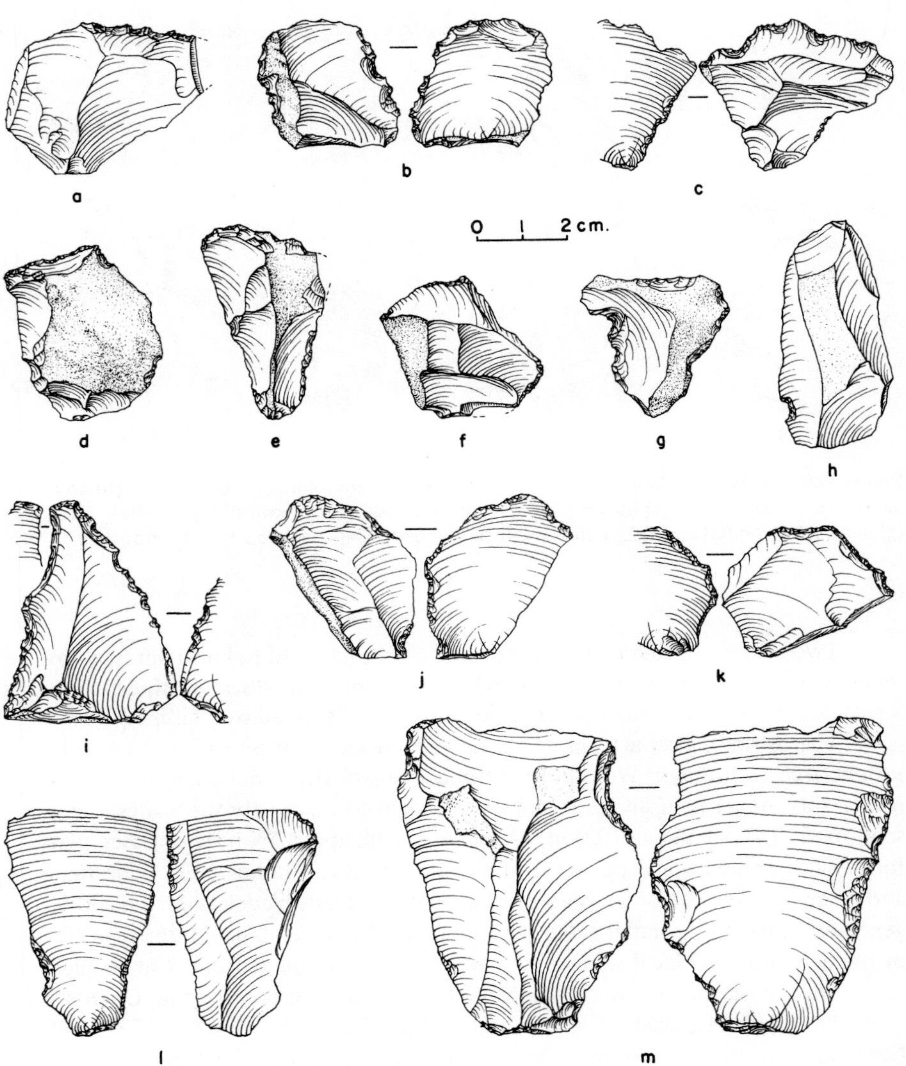

Figure 177. Tools from Site E6102: (a–c) denticulated flake; (d–f, j–l) retouched flakes; (g and m) notched flakes, retouched; (h) notched blade; (i) truncated flake.

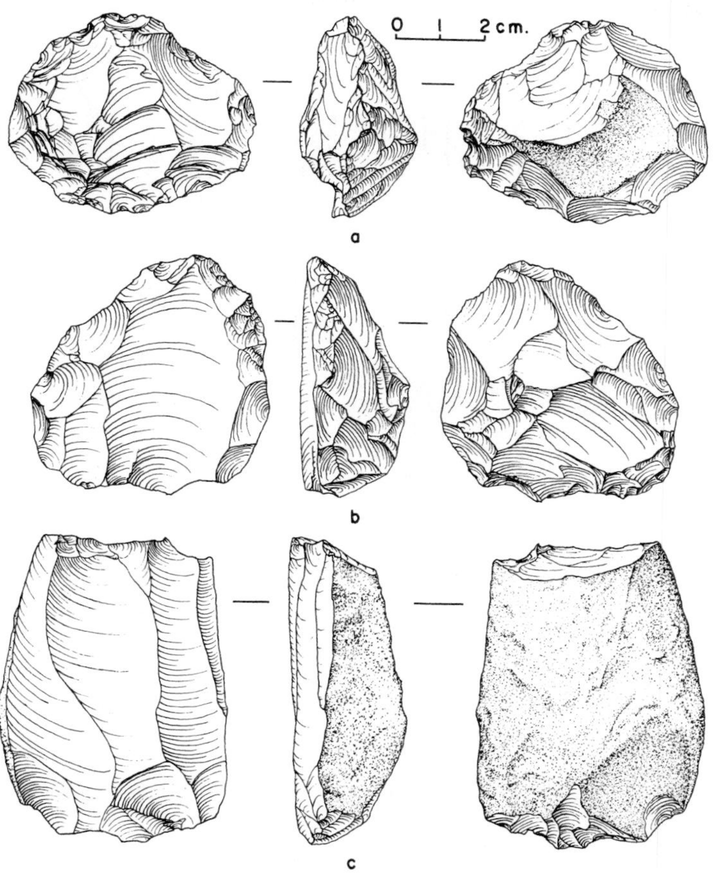

Figure 178. Cores from Site E6102: (a) discoidal; (b) Levallois; (c) opposed platform.

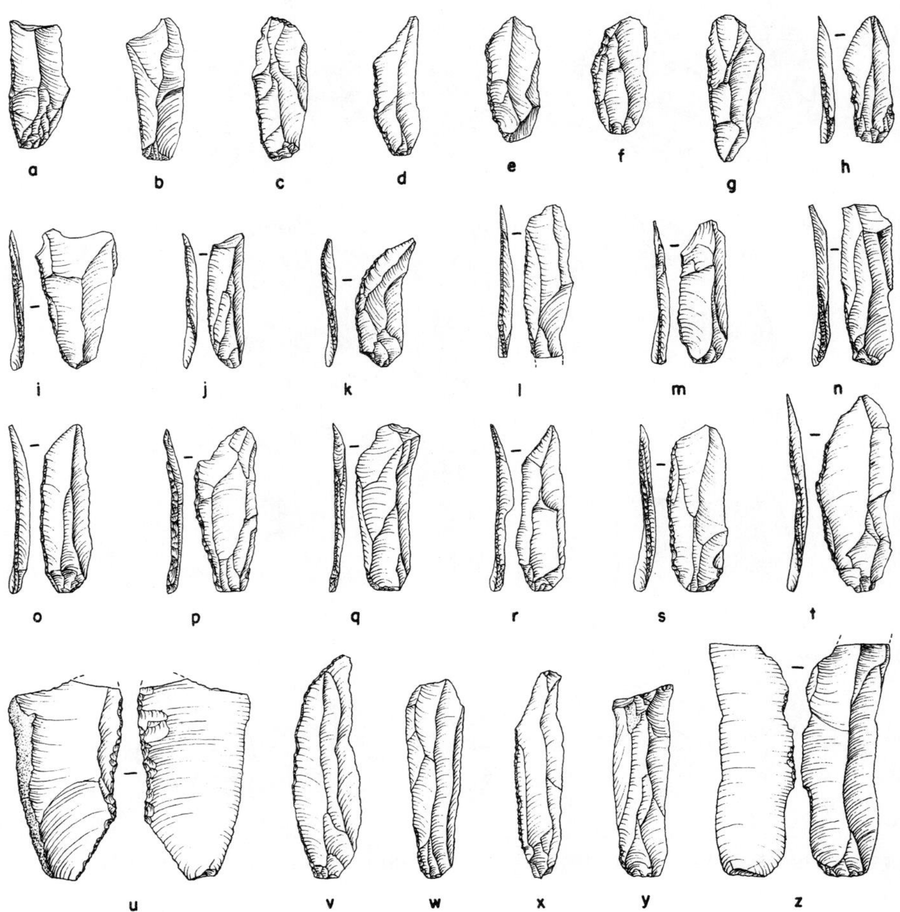

Figure 179. Tools from Site E71K13: (a–t, v–z) Ouchtata retouched baldelets; (u) retouched piece.

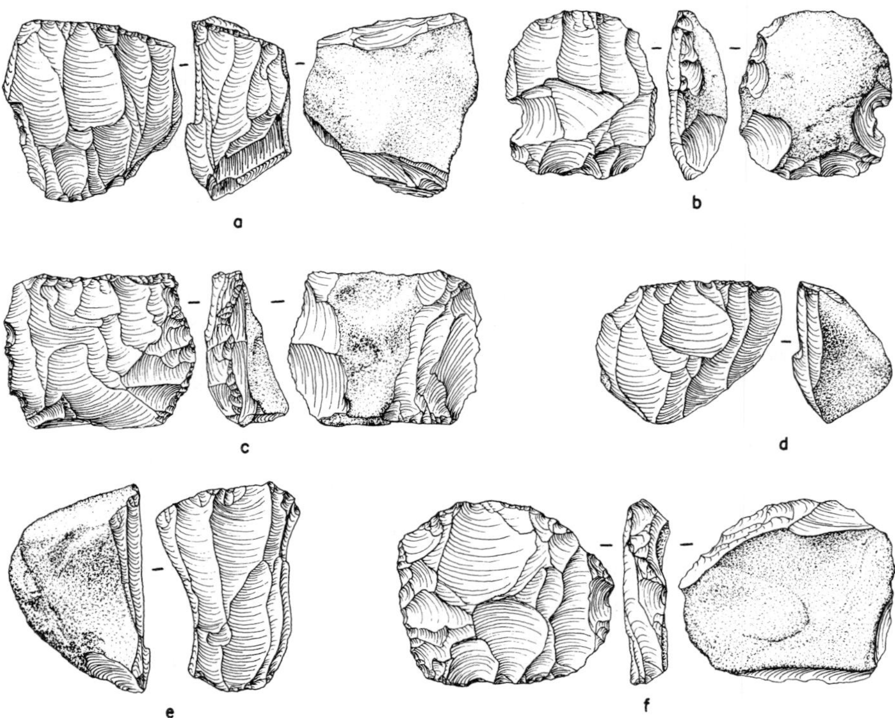

Figure 180. Cores from Site E71K13.

Table 6. Main Typological Indices for Site E71K13, all areas together (Phillips 1971)

Backed bladelets	8.5
Retouched pieces	4.9
Notches and denticulates	4.1
Perforators	0.01
Truncations	2.4
Ouchtata	78.4
Endscrapers	0.4
Burins	<1.1

A nearby site, E71K12, supposedly of the same age, has a quite different technology and typology, although it too is based primarily on bladelets. The cores here are predominantly elongated and rounded with opposed platforms and primarily for bladelets (around 45%). The next-highest frequency (around 4%) is single-platform cores, also mainly for bladelets. Minor core groups are the multiplatform and changed orientation varieties. Blades, bladelets, and microblades represent around 30% of the debitage, but in contrast with Site E71K13, more of the debitage (around 3%) is made on Nile pebbles; the remainder is of local wadi chert.

At this site the most important group of tools (Figures 181 and 182) are the backed bladelets (around 66%). They consist mainly of straight-backed and pointed pieces of various types (more than 50% of all tools). Many of these have retouched or truncated bases and retouched tips. Arch-backed bladelets are also important (around 4% of all tools). The remaining tools are retouched pieces (around 12%); notches and denticulates (10%); perforators (4%), of which the double-backed form is the most important; and Ouchtata retouched pieces (4%). Burins and endscrapers are of minor importance, around 2% or less. The main typological indices for Site E71K12 are given in Table 7.

Sites E71K12 and E71K13 both were certainly occupied before the ponds developed in the Isna area, because they occur within the top of the dune some 2 m lower than the pond sediments in the immediate vicinity. Our interpretation of subsequent events at these sites is that after the occupation a pond developed and the artifacts were spread vertically through the dune to a considerable depth by the action of vegetation on the soft, fluid sand at the bottom of the pond. There is a possibility, however, that these two sites were occupied prior to the Deir El-Fakhuri recession and just at the end of the Ballana–Masmas aggradation, but after the dune had been formed at this locality. As such, they may be closely similar in time and have similar settlement situations to the mid-dune field sites of E71K4 and E71K5 assigned to the Fakhurian industry.

Such an age is indeed suggested by the typological similarities, particularly in the Ouchtata group found in both Sites E71K13 and Site E71P6. The latter is classified as belonging to the Idfuan industry, and the occupation is tentatively placed at the very end of the Ballana–Masmas aggradation. There are, however, numerous typological differences that do not permit Site E71K13 to be regarded as a part of the Idfuan industry.

Another alternative, slightly conflicting with the preceding suggestion as to the age of Site E71K13, may be speculated on the basis of Site Gebel Silsila III in the Kom Ombo area, if the "Sebekian" from this site is indeed related to E71K13. The "Sebekian" layer at Gebel Silsila also seems to have a number of Ouchtata bladelets; however, a detailed comparison is not possible, since the assemblage at Gebel Silsila III has not yet been described except for a brief note

Table 7. Site E71K12, Main Typological Indices, All Areas Together (After Phillips 1971)

Backed bladelets	65.7
Retouched pieces	11.9
Notches and denticulates	9.4
Perforators	4.1
Truncations	4.1
Ouchtata	3.8
Endscrapers	1.1
Burins	2.2

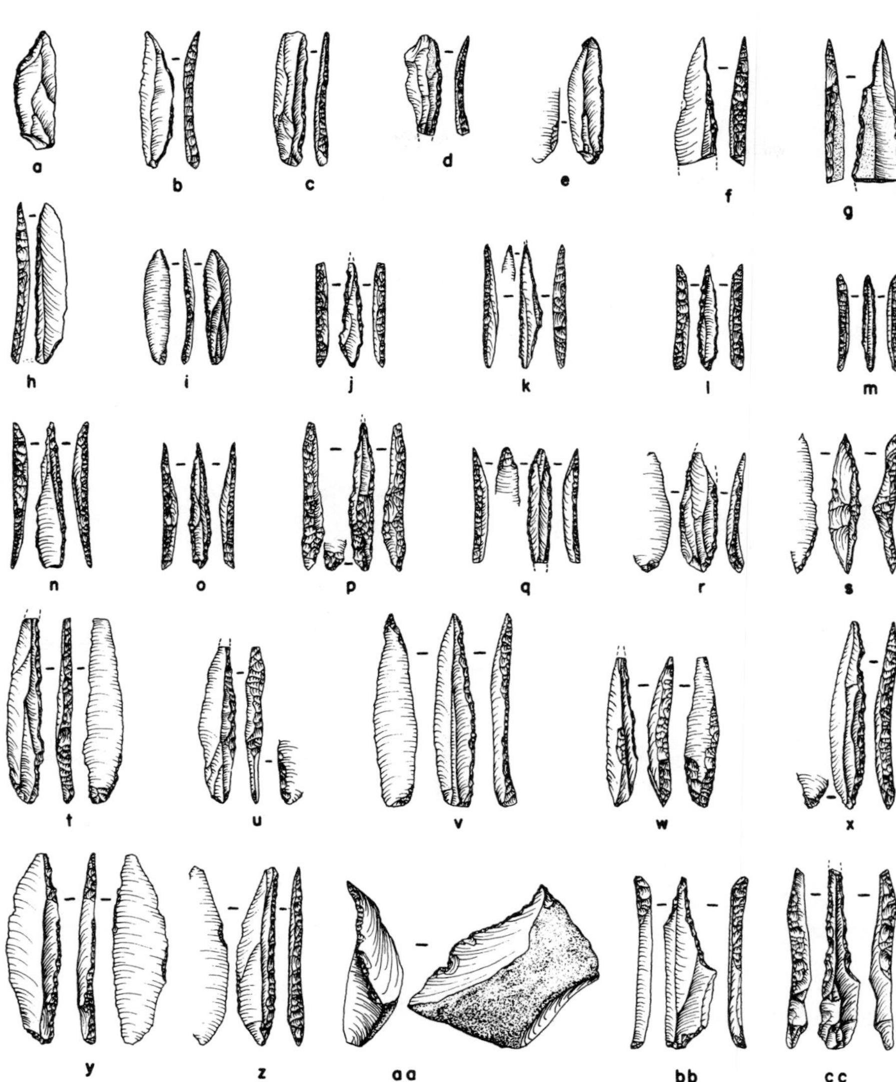

Figure 181. Tools from Site E71K12: (a–i, y–z) backed bladelets; (j–q) double-backed perforators; (r–x) backed bladelets with basal retouch or modification; (aa–cc) perforators.

(Smith 1968: 394–396), and there is no information available on the geological position. Five conflicting radiocarbon dates were obtained from the living floor at Gebel Silsila III: 14,050 BC ±800 years (M-1551); 13,250 BC ±700 years; 12,290 BC ±370 years (I-1201); 12,150 BC ±450 years (I-1292); and 11,611 BC ±600 years (Smith 1968: 396). Obviously the chronological position of Gebel Silsila III is by no means certain. It is further complicated by dates from

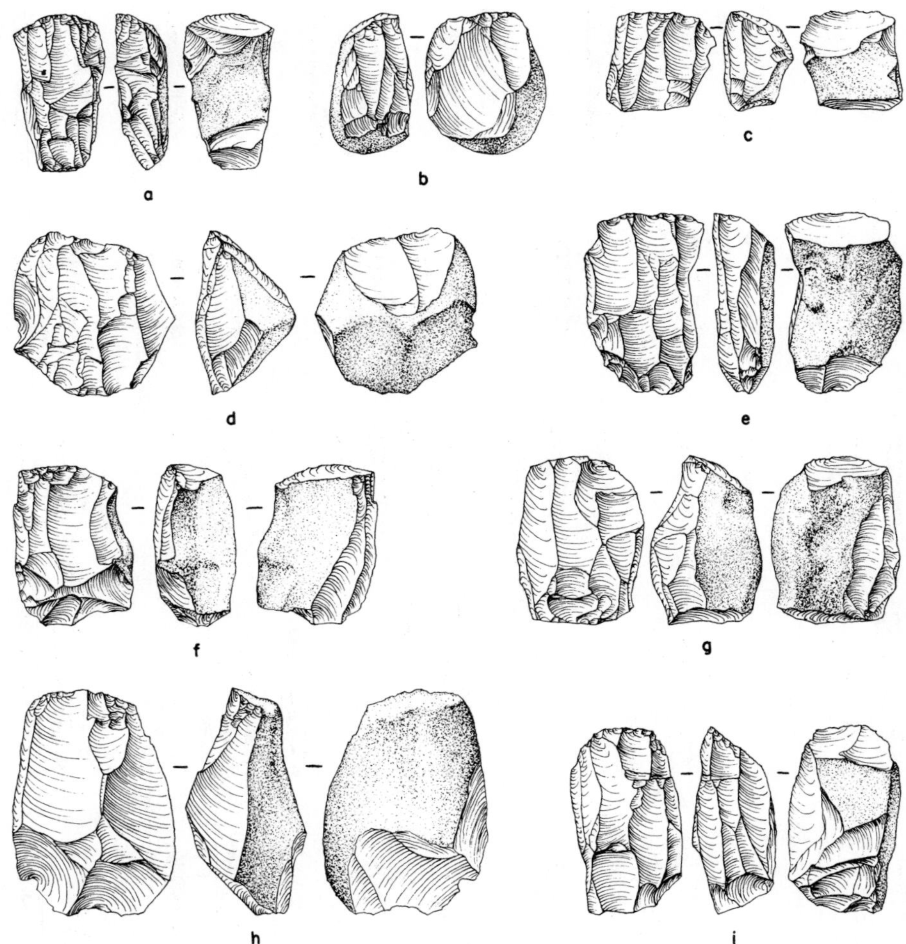

Figure 182. Cores from Site E71K12.

adjacent sites at Kom Ombo. The cultural layer at Gebel Silsila III is reported to overlie another assemblage assigned to the "Silsilian industry." At another nearby site an assemblage that seems to be closely similar to the Silsilian (Gebel Silsila 2B, Area II) has two radiocarbon dates—13,360 BC ±200 years (Y-1376) (Butzer and Hansen 1968: 114) and 12,440 BC ±200 years (I-5180) Phillips and Butzer, in press). Since the five dates from the living floor at Gebel Silsila III have a range of nearly 3000 years and many of them are older than dates associated with any Silsilian assemblage, it would be fruitless to speculate about the exact age of the "Sebekian" beyond observing that it probably postdates the Ballana–Masmas maximum and that it may be related either with the Deir

El-Fakhuri recessional interval or with the early part of the subsequent Sahaba–Darau aggradation. Because of the association of the Silsilian at GS-28-II with an early stage of the Sahaba–Darau aggradation (Phillips & Butler, in press), the latter is more likely.

The Silsilian is also seemingly very similar to the lithic assemblage at Site E71K20 near Isna, judging from the published illustrations (Smith 1968). Except for the similarity to the Silsilian, the assemblage from Site E71K20 appears to be unlike any other known material from Upper Egypt. The technology is expressed in the cores, where the most important form has opposed platforms. These include both short and elongated blade, bladelet, and flake cores. These usually show traces of side and back preparation. Two other important groups of cores are the single-platform and unpatterned changed orientation cores, the latter in most cases derived from other types.

The most important group of tools (Figures 183–185) is the truncations, which represent around 32% of all tools. Most of these are oblique distal on blades or bladelets, with clear traces of microburin scar left at the tip. An important group of these (3% of all tools) have ogival, rounded, or other retouched bases. A few have double truncations. The backed bladelet group, including Ouchtata, is next in importance, accounting for around 19% of all tools. Of these, arch-backed bladelets are the most common. Many of these arch-backed bladelets also have ogival bases. Notches and denticulates are also important (around 18%), mostly made on blades and bladelets. Bladelets with retouched ogival, blunt, or stemmed bases represent 10% of the tools. Microburins, both proximal and distal, also account for 10%. Burins, endscrapers, and retouched flakes and blades are unimportant in frequency, all accounting for less than 2%. The main typological indices for Site E71K20 are given in Table 8.

Table 8. Main Typological Indices at Sites E71K20 and GS-2BII, Trench B (Phillips, *in litt.*)

	E71K20	*GS-2B-II, T B*
Truncated bladelets, simple (including pieces with microburin scar)	28.1	37.1
Truncated bladelets with altered base (ogival, retouched, rounded, etc.)	3.2	10.2
Truncated bladelets, double	1.2	3.5
Truncated flakes	0.3	0.3
Backed bladelets	17.7	17.7
Ouchtata	1.8	1.4
Notches and denticulates	17.7	5.6
Retouched pieces	2.1	3.1
Blades and bladelets with altered base (ogival, retouched)	9.5	0(?)
Endscrapers	1.2	6.0
Burins	1.8	2.8
Microburins	10.3	8.8

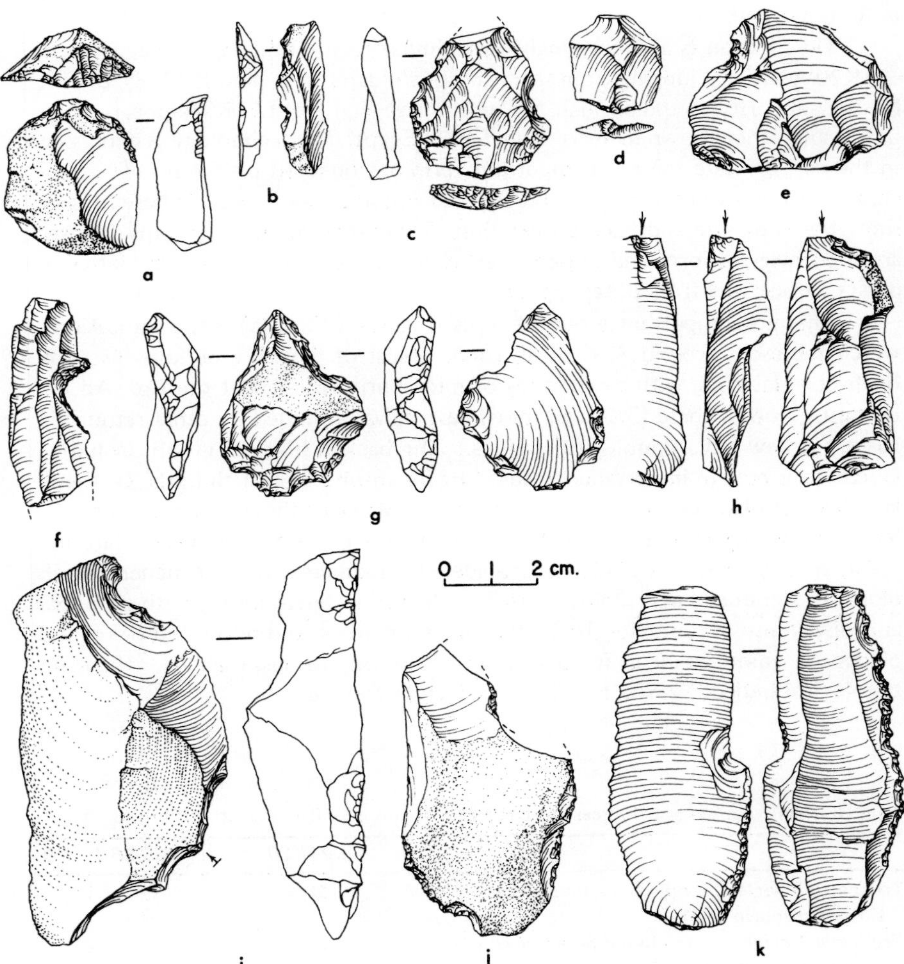

Figure 183. Tools from Site E71K20, Area B: (a) endscraper on flake; (b, i–k) denticulated pieces; (c) Levallois point, denticulated and broken; (d) Levallois flake; (e–f) notched pieces; (g) converging denticulate; (h) burin on truncation.

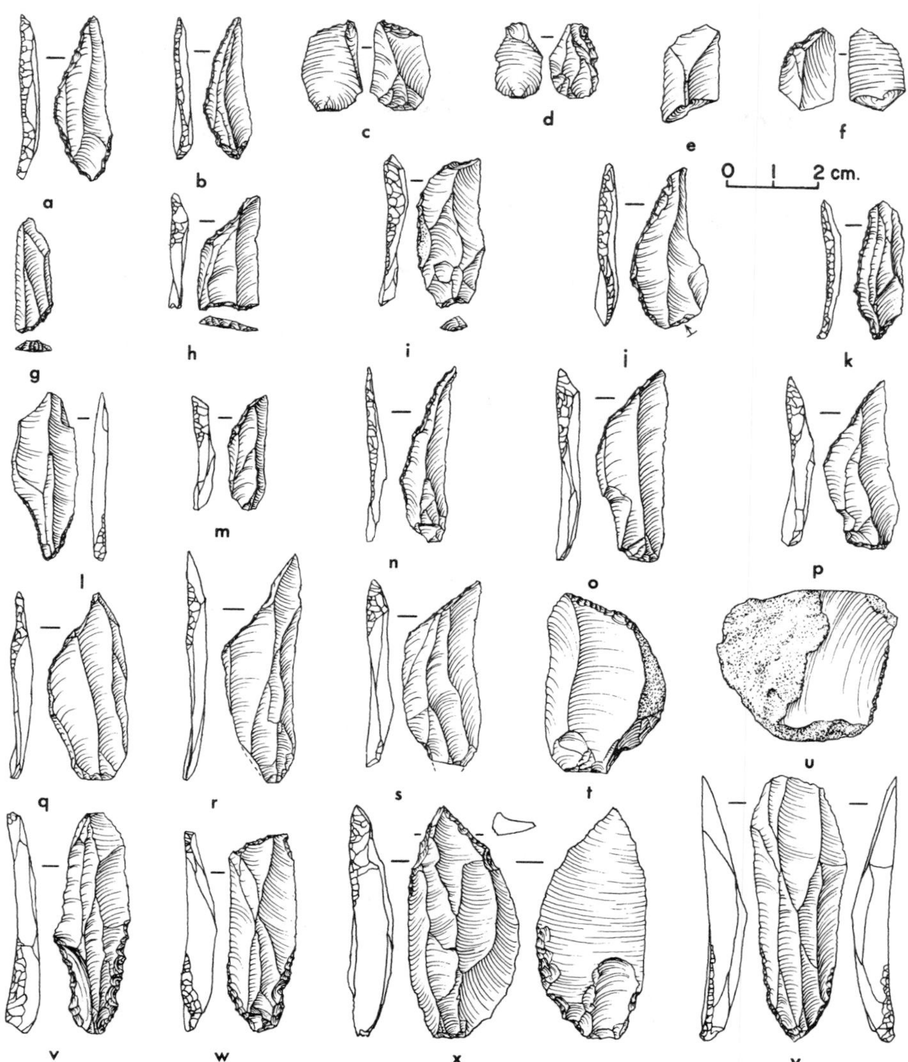

Figure 184. Tools from Site E71K20, Area B: (a–b) arch-backed bladelets with ogival base; (c–d) microburins; (e–f) central pressure microburin; (g) basal truncated bladelet with no trace of microburin scar; (h) double-truncated bladelet; (i) partially arch-backed and basal truncated bladelet; (j) arch-backed bladelet; (k) arch-backed bladelet with stemmed base; (l) bladelet with stemmed base; (m–o) left distal arch truncated bladelet with trace of microburin scar; (p–q) left distal concave truncated bladelet with no trace of microburin scar; (r) left distal concave truncated blade with trace of microburin scar; (s) left distal straight truncated bladelet with no trace of microburin scar; (t–u) retouched flakes; (v–w) blade with blunted base; (x) pointed flake with distal triming; (y) blade with ogival retouched base.

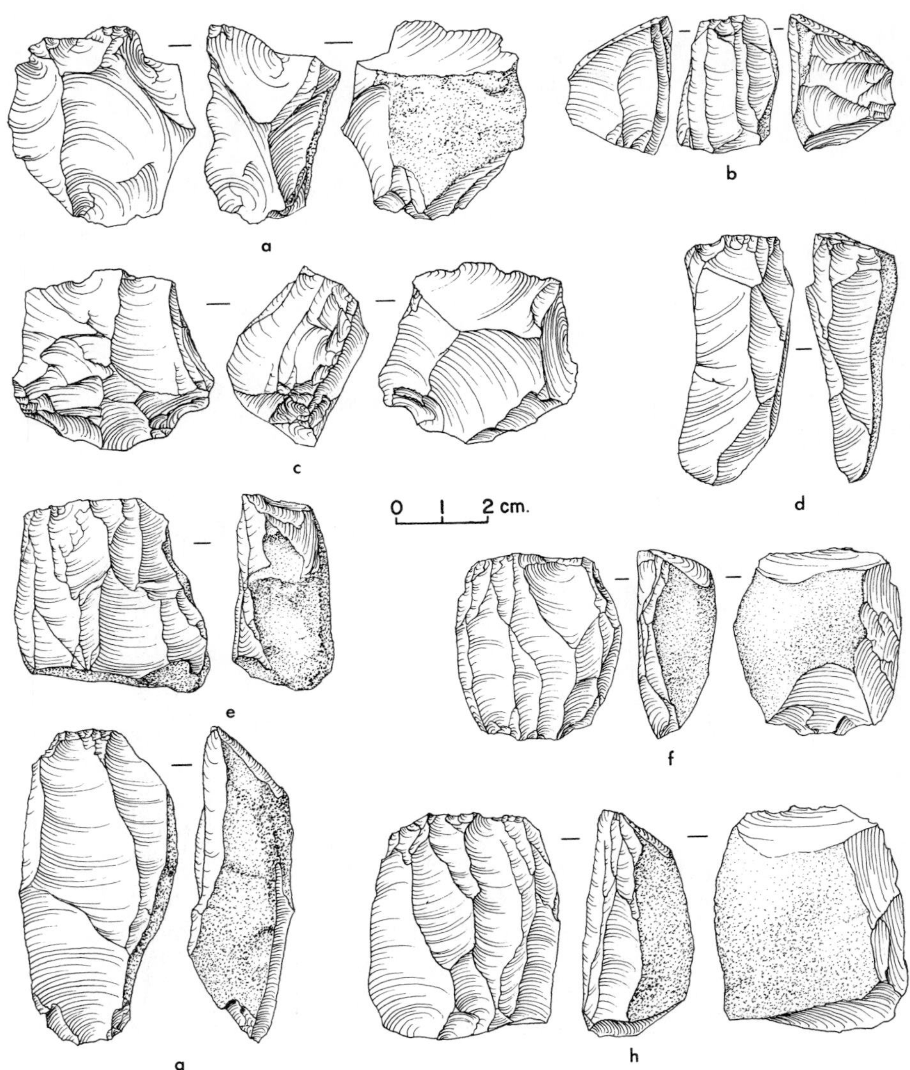

Figure 185. Cores from Site E71K20, Area B.

Site E71K20 is situated on the deflated surface of the Ballana dune with a few pieces apparently only recently exposed, at an elevation around 87 m above sea level. If this site is indeed contemporary with the Kom Ombo locality Gebel Silsila 2B, Area II, dated 13,360 and 12,440 BC, then silt sedimentation was not occurring at this elevation at Isna during the 12,000–13,000 BC period. At a later date, however, around 10,000 BC, silts did reach this elevation and covered the site area.

Rethinking the Sahaba Aggradation

As described by de Heinzelin (1967, 1968), the Sahaba Formation of Nubia represented the second large Nile aggradation associated with the modern Nile regimen. This large aggradation was originally subdivided into two segments separated by an episode of downcutting. It is now apparent, on the basis of numerous radiocarbon dates, that the early part of the Sahaba Formation of Nubia has to be considered as chronologically contemporaneous with the described episode of simultaneous siltation and dune sedimentation in Upper Egypt, as well as with an upper part of the Masmas Formation of the Kom Ombo area (Butzer and Hansen 1968). On the other hand, the late Sahaba Formation of Sudanese Nubia seems to be almost exactly correlative with the Darau Member of the Gebel Silsilla Formation of Kom Ombo and, as described in this study, the upper silts of Idfu, Isna, and Dishna. We therefore propose to name this episode of aggradation the Sahaba–Darau aggradation.

The series of pond sediments previously ascribed to the preceding Deir El-Fakhuri interval of downcutting and recession (Said *et al.* 1970; Wendorf *et al.* 1970) are now believed to represent an early phase of the rising Nile during the subsequent aggradation. The basic factor that led to this reassessment of the pond sediments is the absence of other evidence for a major climatic change that could produce permanent ponds in this area fed totally by local rainfall. Other factors have also influenced and supported this reassessment, although none of these are clearly decisive.

These ponds occur in two main dune areas: (1) at Tushka in Egyptian Nubia (Site 8905, Albritton, in Wendorf 1968: 856–864) and (2) near Isna in Upper Egypt. A close scrutiny of the sediments in the ponds at Isna discloses evidence of drying and surface erosion, as well as some Nile silt mixed with the pond sediments, in addition to one distinct layer of silt. The diatom analysis has shown a flora dominated by littoral and shallow water species. Furthermore, pollen analyses of the pond sediments have failed to yield evidence of abundant aquatic flora, and the total pollen spectra point to an arid grassland. Finally, the industry that occurs at the base of the oldest series of pond sediments (at Site E71K18) appears to be closely similar to the so-called Sebilian at Gebel Silsila 2B, Area I (Phillips, personal communication), from which two radiocarbon dates were obtained: 11,610 BC ±120 years (Y-1447) and 11,120 BC ±120 years (Y-1375) (Butzer and Hansen, 1968: 114, 136). These dates, if the correlation between the sites is correct, would suggest that the occupation at Site E71K18 occurred after the Sahaba–Darau aggradation had already begun.

It seems reasonable to suggest that the ponds were supported primarily by seepage from the Nile. This seepage presumably was able to penetrate the dune barrier, but only occasionally, during periods of exceptionally high floods, did actual Nile silts break through the barrier into the ponds. It seems likely, because of the thickness of the diatomites, that these ponds may have survived during most of the year or in some cases may even have been perennial. Two factors might contribute to this situation: reduced evaporation as a result of lower temperatures, and a more stable water table at the elevation of the dunes.

We have no evidence on the amplitude of the seasonal fluctuation of the Nile. It may have been less than today; thus the water table might have remained relatively more constant for a longer period. Butzer and Hansen (1968: 303) have suggested, however, that Nile floods during the Sahaba–Darau aggradation were at least as large as today and possibly larger. Their interpretation, however, is contingent on a correlation of their wadi deposits of the Malki Member of the Ineiba Formation with their Darau stage of the Nile (our Sahaba–Darau aggradation). The radiocarbon date of 15,450 BC at the base of the Malki Member strongly suggests, however, that it is at least partially contemporary with the preceding downcutting phase of the Deir El-Fakhuri interval. Furthermore, nowhere was there observed an interfingering of the Malki wadi deposits and Nile silts (Butzer and Hansen 1968: 117).

Regardless of whether the Nile floods during the Sahaba–Darau aggradation were of the magnitude of those today or less, there still remains the probability of reduced summer temperatures, which might have assisted in the survival of some ponds through a longer period than is possible today. This is indicated primarily by the diatom flora from the ponds. These diatoms are dominated by cosmopolitan forms and include very few with tropical affinities. This contrasts markedly with the Holocene assemblage from the Fayum, where tropical forms are a strong component (Abdel Alem 1958).

An important feature of the Sahaba–Darau siltation is the interfingering of Nile deposits with wadi sediments, as is well represented in the Dishna area. Here an earlier silt of unknown age, but possibly Ballana–Masmas, separates a lower series of wadi deposits from an upper one. The upper wadi series seems to show a gradient passage from a high-capacity stream that was moving gravels and pebbles to one with much less capacity depositing a more or less suspended alluvium with only occasional gravels that clearly interfinger with the silt. On the basis of analogy with the modern Nile cycle, the interfingering of two wadi and Nile alluvia would represent the winter alluviation of the wadi followed by summer Nile floods. The passage from a high-capacity stream to one of reduced capacity seems to indicate a rising local base of erosion due to the Nile aggradation. Near the end of the Sahaba–Darau siltation, no evidence of interfingering wadi deposits was observed. This may indicate a reduced local rainfall during this part of the aggradational episode.

Other wadi deposits possibly of Sahaba–Darau age are the previously mentioned Malki Member of the Ineiba Formation in the Kom Ombo area. Butzer and Hansen believe (1968: 116), in spite of the absence of evidence of interfingering, that they were contemporary.

Evidence of interfingering wadi deposits and Nile silts was also observed in Egyptian Nubia along the east bank of the river (Giegengack 1968: 116–124), where an equivalent Nile sedimentation, according to the radiocarbon dates and elevation, is interrupted by wadi gravels through most of the period of deposition, with the major intensity at the beginning of the sequence.

In Upper Egypt, except for these occasional wadi deposits interfingering with the silts in the earlier part of the aggradation, the Sahaba–Darau silts appear as massive and monotonous units with heavy mineral contents and granulometric measurements identical with those from the preceding Ballana–Masmas silts, a situation generally similar to that previously noted by Butzer and Hansen in the Kom Ombo area (1968: 470). It is obvious that the restricted number of samples analyzed is insufficient to demonstrate the small statistical differences between these silts shown by Butzer and Hansen (1969: 470), but all of them fall within the variability range of the Darau and Masmas silts of Kom Ombo.

There is, however, some evidence of dune forming, possibly near the end of this event. At Sites 8898 and 8899 at Ballana in Egyptian Nubia, there were three occupation floors that yielded unmistakable Sebilian artifacts within an aeolean dune (Wendorf 1968: 807–831). Two of the floors were superimposed and separated by more than a meter of sterile, stratified dune sand, an indication that the dune was still moving after the first Sebilian occupation and, indeed, continued to form after the second occupation (de Heinzelin, 1968: Atlas Fig. 71).

Elsewhere in Nubia (Sites 8886, 8888, 8863, 8883, 1042, 2013, 2005, and 8881), the Sebilian industry repeatedly occurs either within or on the eroded surface of the Sahaba sediments. In Upper Egypt, the same stratigraphic position is indicated (Sites E61M1 and E71P3). Unless we assume an unusually long sequence for this industry and virtually no change for more than 5000 years, which seems highly unlikely, then we must assign a Sahaba–Darau age for the three Sebilian occupation floors at Ballana and their enclosing dune sediments. If this dating of the dunes is correct, then the aeolean activity was of limited areal extent, because dunes of this age have not been recognized elsewhere.

The beginning of the Sahaba–Darau aggradation is believed to date slightly before 12,000 BC on the basis of the oldest dates from a series of radiocarbon measurements from this unit in both Nubia and Upper Egypt. The oldest date that may reflect the rising Nile during an early part of the Sahaba aggradation comes from the base of an interdune pond at Tushka in Egyptian Nubia. Unless there was a very considerable increase in local rainfall not otherwise indicated at this time, the pond is likely to have been a result of seepage from the adjacent river. The date, on charcoal, is 12,500 BC ±490 years (WSU-315).

There are other dates from the Tushka that have to be rejected. Another sample of charcoal from the same stratigraphic unit dated only 400 BC ±300 years (WSU-315a). The sample was evidently contaminated. Similarly, there are several dates on carbonate fractions from cemented material at the base of other nearby fossil ponds that yielded dates that seemingly do not reflect the initial development of the ponds but are probably contaminated by exchange of CO^2 (Wendorf 1968: 940). These dates are 7780 BC ±120 years (WSU-444), 8580 BC ±126 years (WSU-4156), and 9540 BC ±70 years (WSU-417 and WSU-442 combined).

Other old dates that can be definitely related to the Sahaba–Darau aggradation come from Channel B at Gebel Silsila 2B, Area II at Kom Ombo. These dates are 13,360 BC ±200 years (Y-1376) on charcoal and 12,440 BC ±200 years

(I-5180) on shell (Phillips and Butzer, in press). The dates are related to the Silsilan archaeological material "in an overflow tertiary channel [ibid.]" associated with Channel B of Butzer and Hansen (1968). Recently Phillips and Butzer (in press) have taken the position that the industry is rather contemporaneous with the date on shell; it is suggested that the charcoal was "floated" into the bed from an older sediment and therefore is derived.

At another site within Channel B, Gebel Silsila 2B, Area I, regarded by Butzer and Hansen (1968: 140) as younger than Area II, two radiocarbon dates were obtained—11,610 BC ±120 years (Y-1447) on *Unio* shell and 11,120 BC ±120 years (Y 1375) on charcoal flakes (Reed 1965).

Butzer and Hansen place the beginning of their Darau Formation, the equivalent of our Sahaba–Darau aggradation, around 15,000 BC (1968: 149), possibly basing this assumption on the radiocarbon date obtained at the Khor El-Sil archaeological site. That site, supposedly located within the terminal silts of the Manshiya channel, gave a date on shell of 15,050 BC ±600 years (I-1297) (Butzer and Hansen 1968: 142). The Manshiya Channel is regarded by these authors to be "broadly contemporary [ibid.]" with the basal deposits of Channel A at Gebel Silsila 2, the oldest of the channels placed within the Darau Member of the Gebel Silsila Formation. However, a radiocarbon date connected with Channel A, on *Etheria elliptica,* "in a position of growth at the south end of Site Gebel Silsila 2A [Butzer and Hansen 1968: 135]" indicated an age of 11,900 BC ±200 years (Y-1806).

The Manshiya Channel seems to have only a general geomophological association with the Fatira Channel, of which Channels A and B at Gèbel Silsila are the bifurcating part (Butzer and Hansen 1968: Fig. 31). If indeed the date from the Khor El-Sil site is correct and the Manshiya Channel is to be considered within the Darau Member, then it is necessary to assume a much older date for the beginning of this channel and, therefore, associate at least all dates between 16,000 and 15,000 BC with the beginning of the Darau Member, a position that could not be accepted with the data at hand.

Among the other dates possibly attributable to this event is one from Ballana in Egyptian Nubia of 12,050 BC ±240 years (WSU-329), obtained on charcoal from a hearth on the surface of a sand dune covered by a thin veneer of silt that is presumably of Sahaba–Darau age. The hearth was associated with an assemblage of the Ballanan industry. Unfortunately the elevation, at 22 m above the modern floodplain, is too high to date the beginning of this event. It merely indicates that the silt here, possibly representing the end phase of the Sahaba–Darau, was deposited after 12,000 BC.

At Akasha in the Second Cataract area, there are two dates on shell, presumably from within the Sahaba silts and covered by 20 m of uninterrupted silt that are believed to represent Sahaba–Darau aggradation (Fairbridge 1962, 1963). The two dates are 9,700 BC ±300 years (I-532, Trautman and Willis 1966: 179) and 10,770 BC ±350 years (I-929, Buckley *et al*. 1968: 270). Both dates are from the same layer at the same locality. The younger is unacceptable in view of the thick Sahaba silt overburden reported to overlie this horizon.

Further inference in regard to the age of the early phase of the Sahaba–Darau aggradation is provided by the archaeological assemblage from Site Gebel Silsila 2B, Area I, dated between 11,610 and 11,120 BC. The industry was tentatively identified as Sebilian, but according to J. Phillips (personal communication), who is now studying this collection, the material is closely similar to that recovered from Sites E71K18, Areas A–E and E71K6, Area B, all located near Isna. The several assemblages at Site E71K18 occurred at the base of pond sediments at an elevation of between 82 m and 83 m. In the reconstruction proposed here these ponds reflect the earliest sediments in the Isna area that can be associated within the Sahaba–Darau aggradation, and if the correlation is correct, a date in the vicinity of 11,500 BC would be indicated for both the beginning of the ponds and the initial phase of aggradation.

In the same area near Isna, a slightly higher and younger series of pond sediments at Site E71K14, Area A has yielded another radiocarbon date of 10,740 BC ±240 years (I-3421) on carbonates at an elevation of 87 m above sea level and below the upper diatomite at this locality.

There is still another date from silts presumably representing the Sahaba–Darau aggradation in Upper Egypt: 11,430 BC ±770 years (I-3440) on charcoal near the upper edge of a wedge of younger silt at Site E6104. Because of the particular stratigraphic situation where this sample was collected, however, its exact position within the Sahaba–Darau sequence cannot be determined. The date would suggest a placement fairly early in the sequence of deposition.

Near the top of the silts assigned to the Sahaba–Darau aggradation along both the east and west banks is a pronounced layer of baked silt recording an extensive fire that swept a long section of the Valley, at least from Isna in the south to Dishna in the north. This burned layer is, without exception, in the upper part of this episode of siltation. It serves as a distinct chronostratigraphic marker layer. Only one radiocarbon date—10,550 BC ±230 years (I-3424) on carbonaceous sand from Kimbelat, north of Luxor—is available for this event, but numerous samples of burned silt for paleomagnetic dating were submitted to R. Dubois. The results are not yet available.

Another similar date comes from wood found near the top of a fluviatile sand unit with lenses of silt at about 138 m above sea level, or 16 m above the floodplain, at Site 3400 between Wadi Halfa and the Sudan–Egyptian frontier (de Heinzelin 1968: Atlas Fig. 50). The date is 10,600 BC ±460 years (WSU-202).

In the same general area, at Site 330 on the east bank near Faras, *Corbicula* from a thick bed of shells near the top of a massive silt believed to represent the Sahaba–Darau aggradation yielded a date of 10,300 BC ±100 years (WSU-109, Chatters 1968: 482).

Farther south along the Nile, in the Murshid area near the head of the Second Cataracts, a high silt channel possibly of Sahaba–Darau age has yielded two radiocarbon dates: 11,700 BC ±300 years (on shell, GX-421) and 11,020 BC ±300 years (on shell, GX-422, Drueger and Weeks 1966: 157). The absence of published information on this locality and the associated archaeological materials, as well as the complications of elevation and deposition within the cataract area, prevents a definitive evaluation of these dates and their associated sediments.

Egyptian Nubia has also produced a series of five dates associated with Nile silts seemingly of the Sahaba–Darau aggradation (Giegengack 1968; Stuvier 1969: 599). These dates are: 10,690 BC ±400 years (on shell, Y-1644); 10,440 BC ±120 years (on shell, Y-1645); 10,150 BC ±160 years (on shell, Y-1810); 10,060 BC ±200 years (on shell, Y-1809); and 10,060 BC ±160 years (on shell, Y-1808). There is an additional date from this area of 11,410 BC ±120 years (on shell, Y-1643) from near Abu Simbel; however, it is from a cultural pit dug in Nile gravel of unknown age and therefore does not date any Nile sediments.

There are several series of dates associated with very high Nile levels, around 30 m in Nubia (Site 34) to 22 m at Kom Ombo, or between 7 m and 10 m higher than the main body of the Sahaba–Darau silts. These very high Nile levels may record the final maximum phase of the Sahaba–Darau aggradation or, alternatively, several series of exceptional floods during the latter part of the episode. Neither the radiocarbon dates nor the stratigraphy of the several localities permits a conclusive selection between these two alternatives.

The first explanation as a terminal series of Sahaba events was offered by de Heinzelin (in Wendorf 1968: 45) and Butzer and Hansen (1968: 115–116), and has been followed by subsequent authors (Wendorf *et al.* 1970: 68). The second alternative is suggested here by the discrepancies within the radiocarbon dates associated with these high levels. The dates are as follows:

Wadi Halfa area, below the Second Cataracts:

12,850 BC ±100 years (on shell, WSU-107, Chatters 1968: 482, reported as 12,650 BC by de Heinzelin, in Wendorf 1968: 40)

9,460 BC ±270 years (on shell, WSU-189, Chatters 1968: 483)

9,250 BC ±150 years (on shell, WSU-106, Chatters 1968: 482)

Kom Ombo area:

10,550 BC ±120 years (on shell, Y-1446, Stuvier 1969: 598, reported by Butzer and Hansen 1968: 115 as 10,050 BC)

10,070 BC ±205 years (on shell, NV-1265, Geyh 1967: 234)

9,770 BC ±195 years (on shell, NV-1264, Butzer and Hansen 1968: 115)

The date of 12,850 BC must be rejected. It seems much too old for any Sahaba–Darau flood, and according to this reconstruction, the level of the Nile was much too low just prior to the Sahaba–Darau aggradation to permit a flood of this magnitude. The remnant from which this sample was collected could also represent an earlier high Nile aggradation from which a too-recent date was obtained.

Farther downstream, in the Dishna area of Upper Egypt, these high floods could be represented in the several silt layers within the Dishna playa deposits. If so, this would provide our best available means of dating the Dishna sediments and indicate an age prior to 10,000 BC for the archaeological materials in the upper part of the underlying Nile silts.

The recession from the Sahaba–Darau maximum is convincingly dated at Site E71P5 at the El-Kilh area in Upper Egypt. Here *Unio* shells, associated with other cultural material in a recessional bar inset against Sahaba–Darau silts, yielded a radiocarbon date of 9610 BC ±180 years (I-3760, Buckley 1969). The earliest date from the succeeding Arkin aggradation is from Gebel Halfa in Sudanese Nubia, where Nile oyster shells believed to date with the early phase of this aggradation gave a date of 9250 BC ±285 years (I-531, Trautman 1964: 271).

If we accept these two dates as correct, then the two most recent dates—9250 BC and 9460 BC on shell associated with the highest floods of the Sahaba aggradation—have to be rejected as too young. A date slightly older than 9600 BC is suggested for the latest of these high floods and serves to mark the end of the Sahaba–Darau aggradation.

The preceding summary of the radiocarbon evidence places the beginning of the Sahaba–Darau siltation slightly before 12,000 BC and its end around 9,700 BC. A comparison with the European sequence would indicate that the beginning of the Sahaba–Darau aggradation is slightly older than the so-called Meiendorf–Raunis interval, which begins the Oldest Dryas, with beginning dates around 11,600 BC (Menke 1968; Serebryanny 1969).

The end of the Sahaba–Darau, and the last exceptionally high floods, if the chronology we have suggested is correct, would be contemporaneous with an early phase of the Allerod interstadial (Vogel and Zagwijn 1967: 79; Van der Hammen *et al.* 1967). The final phases of the Sahaba–Darau after the burned layer, therefore, should reflect both the Bolling interstadial (around 10,400 BC to 10,000 BC) and Older Dryas (approximately 10,000 BC to 9,800 BC). In Europe, this period is characterized by numerous rather short-lived cold and warmer oscillations, which cannot be detected along the Nile from the present evidence. There is a possibility, however, that the climatic changes that affected Europe also had some bearing on the precipitation regimen in Ethiopia and were somehow responsible for the exceptionally high floods near the end of the Sahaba–Darau.

The limited data available on the climate along the Nile in Upper Egypt during the period of Sahaba–Darau aggradation suggest that there may have been slightly more rainfall during some parts of this event. This is suggested by the wadi activity, indicated particularly along the east bank in Nubia and at Dishna. The Nubian data are perhaps a more sensitive climatic indicator in that the headwaters of the tributary wadis are located in the higher Red Sea Hills of the Eastern Desert. The slight increase in rainfall indicated by the wadis might have been accompanied by lower summer temperatures, as suggested by the evidence of ponds that seemingly survived during most of the year. This is also supported by pollen analyses of the sediments from these ponds. These analyses indicate a short grass prairie landscape. It is also significant that the diatom flora include fewer tropical forms than Holocene sediments.

It appears also that during this period dune development was greatly reduced and limited to a few areas, and that these were possibly of only a local significance not yet fully understood. This situation contrasts strikingly with the conditions prevailing during the Ballana–Masmas aggradation.

The final phase of the Sahaba–Darau siltation was characterized by unusually high Nile floods and local playa development at the blocked wadi mouths, again indicating greater moisture and reduced temperatures compared with conditions prevailing today. Nevertheless the climate was undoubtedly arid.

Indications of several fluctuations in the moisture and temperature parameters during the period of the Sahaba–Darau aggradation may be found in the fossil salt crusts within both the Nile silt deposits and the overlying playa sediments in the Dishna area. At least three such fluctuations are shown—one in the silt below the burned layer and two in the ovelrying playa deposits. Butzer and Hansen (1968: 182) noted similar phenomena in the Kom Ombo area.

During the period of the Sahaba aggradation, at least four distinct lithic industrial groups were present in Upper Egypt between Idfu and Dishna, a straight-line distance of about 140 km. These four lithic industries do not have identical chronological positions, although some of them are possibly contemporaneous. The earliest industry has been named the Afian, and it was found at six separate concentrations, all located near the eastern edge of a fossil pond at Thomas Afia Village near Isna. All of the concentrations, except one that was badly deflated, are small and may represent nuclear family units. Because of their density and richness in both tools and waste products, they seem to have been occupied for a protracted period. The stratigraphic evidence for the five *in situ* localities would indicate that all are roughly contemporaneous.

The Afian assemblages show a certain variability in both their tool kits and their methods of flaking. Two facies seem to be represented. In the first group are Sites E71K18A, E71K18C, and E71K6B. The second group is represented at Sites E71B18D and E71K18E. In both groups the cores are mostly of the wide and flat opposed-platform variety for elongated small flakes and bladelets (around 50%). Some of them show traces of preflaking preparation similar to Levallois. The flaking platforms are often faceted and were constantly refaceted during the flaking. The true Levallois cores in some instances (i.e., E716B) may represent 20% of the total, the majority being the "bent Levallois" variety for the production of sickle-shaped flakes (Schild 1971). It is interesting to note that almost all of those "bent" cores were designed so that the flake would bend toward the right. Some of the assemblages have little or no Levallois. A few of the opposed-platform cores also have a third or even a fourth platform prepared perpendicular to the primary platforms. Single-platform cores are rare, as are the discoidal and globular varieties.

The sites in the second group differ in the cores by having high frequencies of rounded opposed-platform and single-platform varieties for bladelets. This is reflected in considerably higher frequencies in the blade group of debitage, around 30% as against 15% in the first group. The blades are also slightly longer in the assemblages within the second group, but they remain mostly in the bladelet category.

The tools represent from 16% to 20% of the total lithic material at each site, and may be classified into nine major cateogires (Figures 186–190). In the first facies of this industry, the most important are microlithic simple basal truncations (from 14% to 18%). This is followed by microburins, the by-products of the manufacture of the simple basal truncations, and geometric and semigeometric tools. They show more variation, however, ranging from 13% to slightly more than 30%. The geometrics and semigeometrics, which vary between 14% and 21%, are composed mainly of trapezoidal double truncated microlithic flakes, triangles, triangle-like short, usually unpointed microlithic flakes and, rarely, elongated scalene triangles with the long edge convex. Backed elements are also important but variable, ranging between 4% and 22%. They are also typologically highly variable, convex and straight, pointed and unpointed, and with both flakes and bladelets represented. Endscrapers represent from 6% to 9%. Notches and denticulates are less important, accounting for from 2% to 6%, and retouched flakes and blades vary from 4% to 8%. Burins are well made but very rare and do not exceed 1%. The main typological indices for sites of the first group in the Afian industry are given in Table 9.

Table 9. Main Typological Indices at Sites of the First Group of the Afian Industry—E71K18A, E71K18C, E71K6B

	E71K18A, surface	*E71K18C, surface*	*E71K6B, surface*
Basal truncations, simple, on bladelets and microflakes	17.9	14.1	16.7
Distal truncations, simple	4.2	2.1	4.3
Geometrics and semigeometrics	13.5	21.1	16.6
Backed elements, various	22.6	8.5	3.7
Microburins, ordinary and central pressure	12.8	20.7	33.3
Endscrapers	9.0	8.3	6.6
Burins	0.7	1.0	0.4
Retouched pieces	5.6	8.5	3.6
Notches and denticulates	2.4	6.6	2.8

The two assemblages in the second group differ by clearly higher percentages of endscrapers (around 17%) and retouched flakes and blades (15%) and by lower values of basal truncations (6%) and geometrics and semigeometrics (between 5% and 9%) and, accordingly, by fewer microburins (less than 10%).

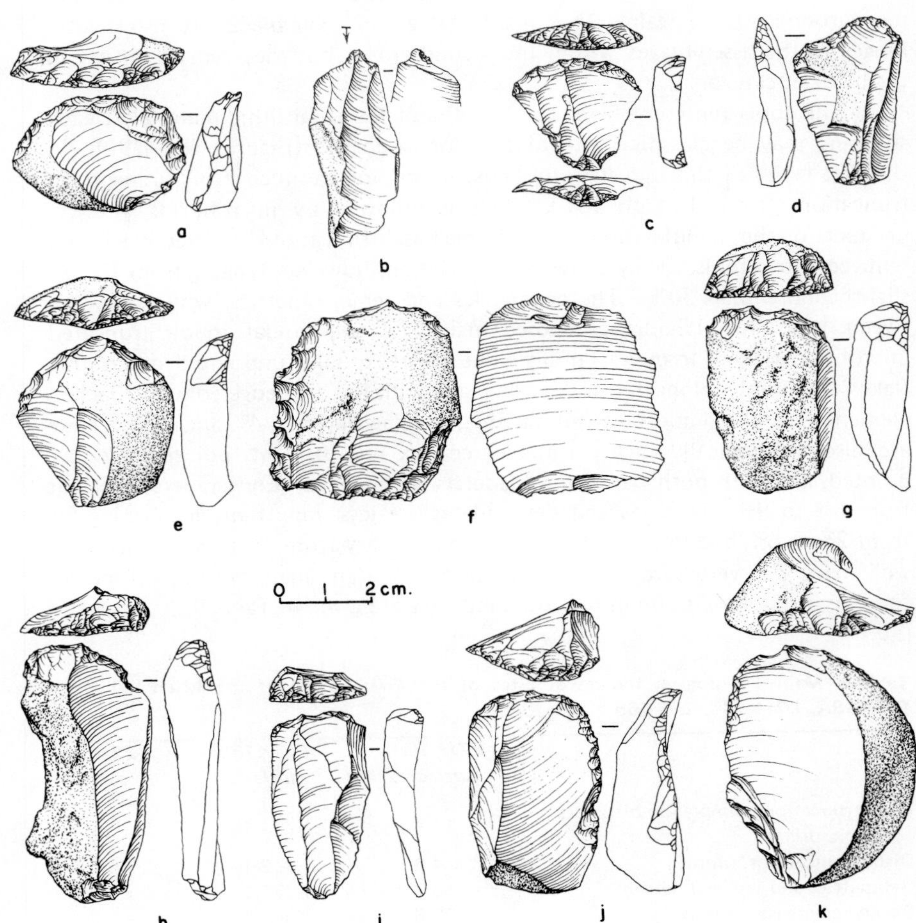

Figure 186. Tools from Site E71K18, Area C, Afian industry: (a) transverse sidescraper; (b) borer; (c) double endscraper on flake; (d) endscraper with nose or shoulder retouch; (e) ogival endscraper; (f) denticulated piece; (g) simple endscraper on flake; (h, i) simple endscraper on blade; (j) simple endscraper on flake; unilateral; (k) endscraper on retouched flake.

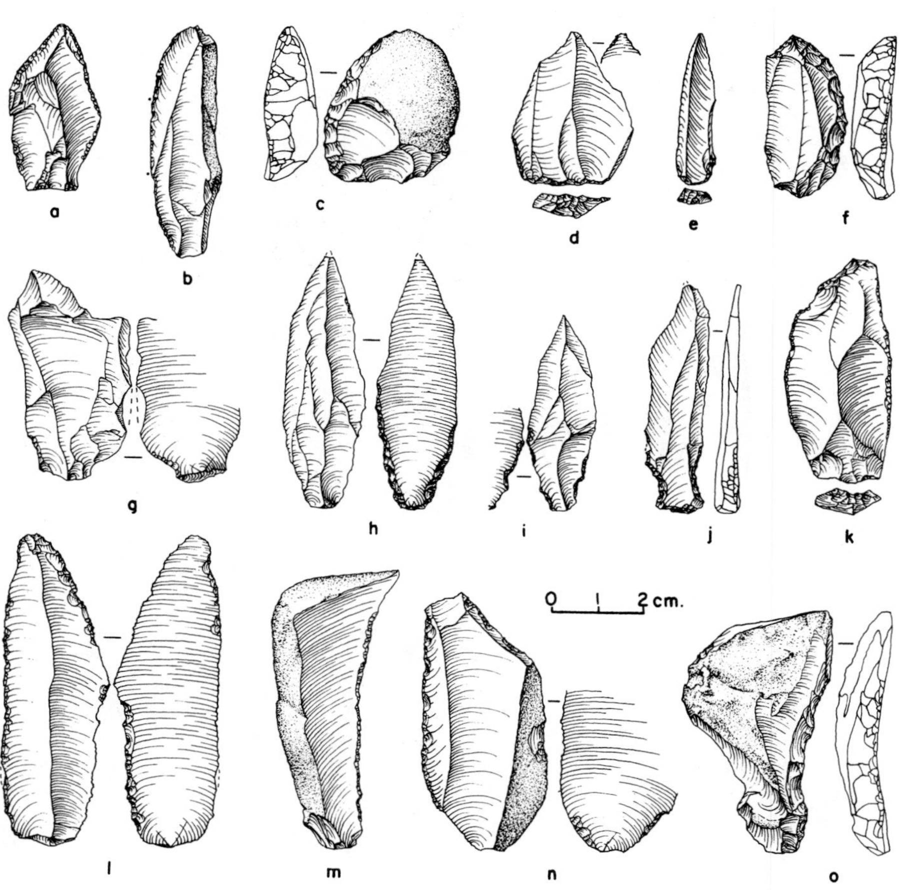

Figure 187. Tools from Site E71K18, Area C, Afian industry: (a, l) pointed bladelet with basal blunting, retouched; (b) retouched blade (edge ground); (c) sidescraper; (d, g) pointed flake with basal blunting; (e) pointed bladelet with rounded base; (f) varia; (h–j) pointed bladelets with basal blunting; (k) retouched blade, basal truncated; (m) retouched blade; (n, o) flakes with extensive retouch.

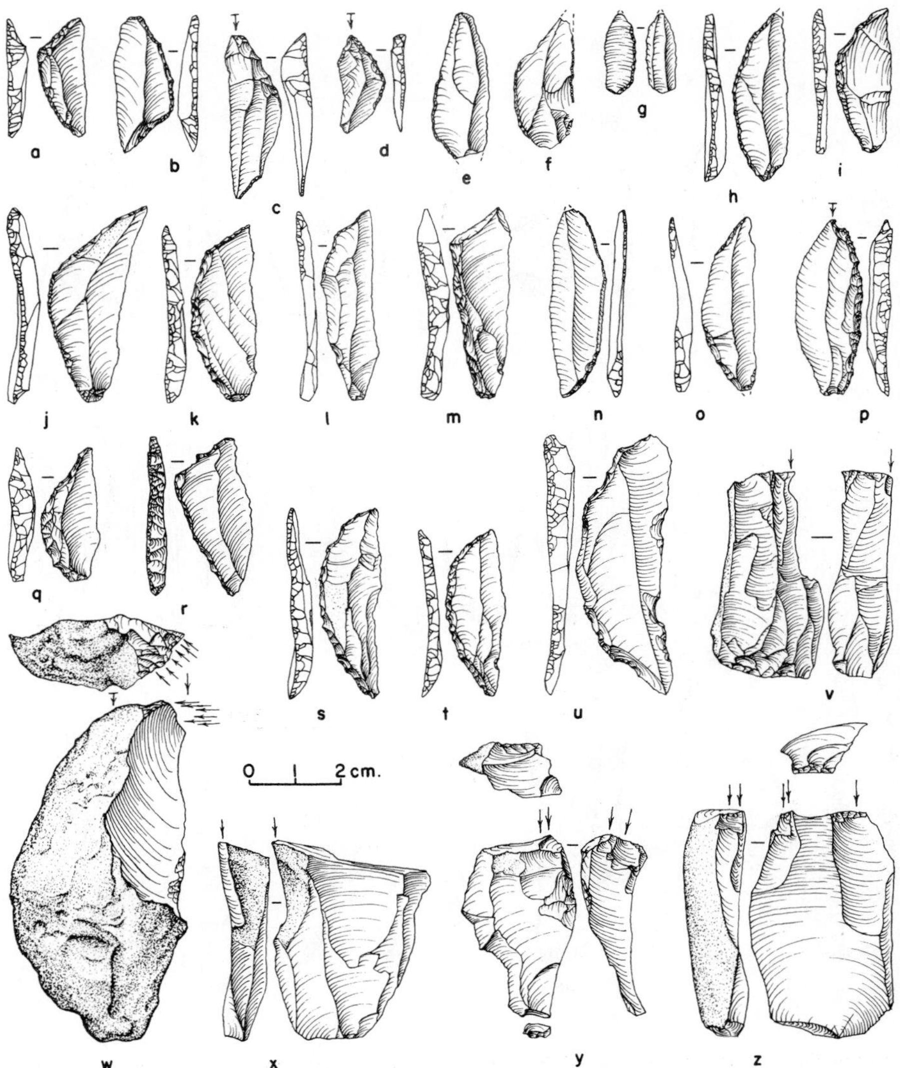

Figure 188. Tools from Site E71K18, Area C, Afian industry: (a) scalene triangle with convex backing and distal truncation; (b) scalene triangle with convex backing and basal truncation; (c) bladelet with arched tip, retouched; (d) flake with convex backing and ojival base; (e, f) Ouchtata retouched bladelets; (g) pointed bladelet with convex backing and rounded base; (h) pointed bladelet with convex backing and ogival base; (j–k) convex-backed and oblique distal truncated baldelet; (l) bladelet with arched tip; (m) LaMouillah point; (n, o) double-pointed bladelet with partial arch backing; (p, q, s, t) pointed bladelet with convex backing; (r) scalene triangle with straight backing; (u) convex-backed blade, partial; (v–z) burins.

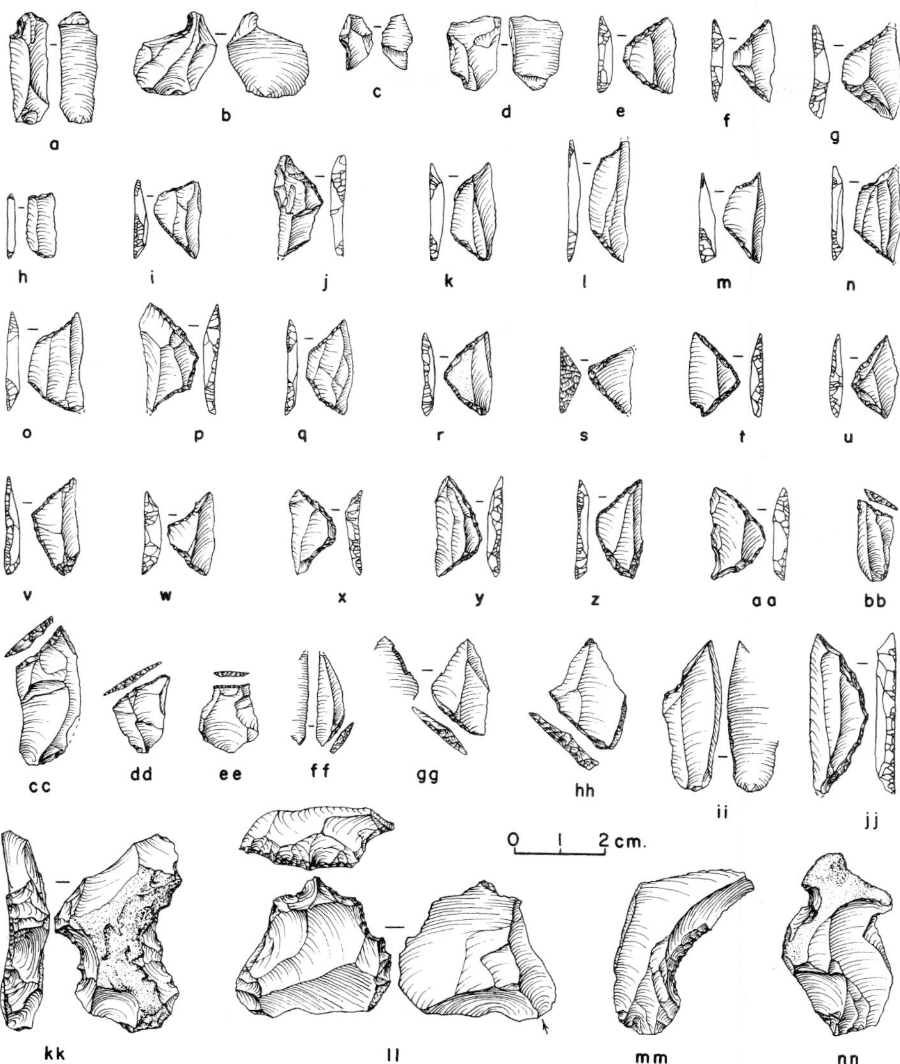

Figure 189. Tools from Site E71K18, Area C, Afian industry: (a, b) microburins, distal; (c, d) microburins, basal; (e–q) trapezes; (r–aa) triangle; (bb–ee) distal truncated piece; (ff–hh) basal truncated pieces; (ii) piquant triedre; (jj) lunate; (kk) strangled piece; (ll) combination tool; (mm, nn) notched flakes.

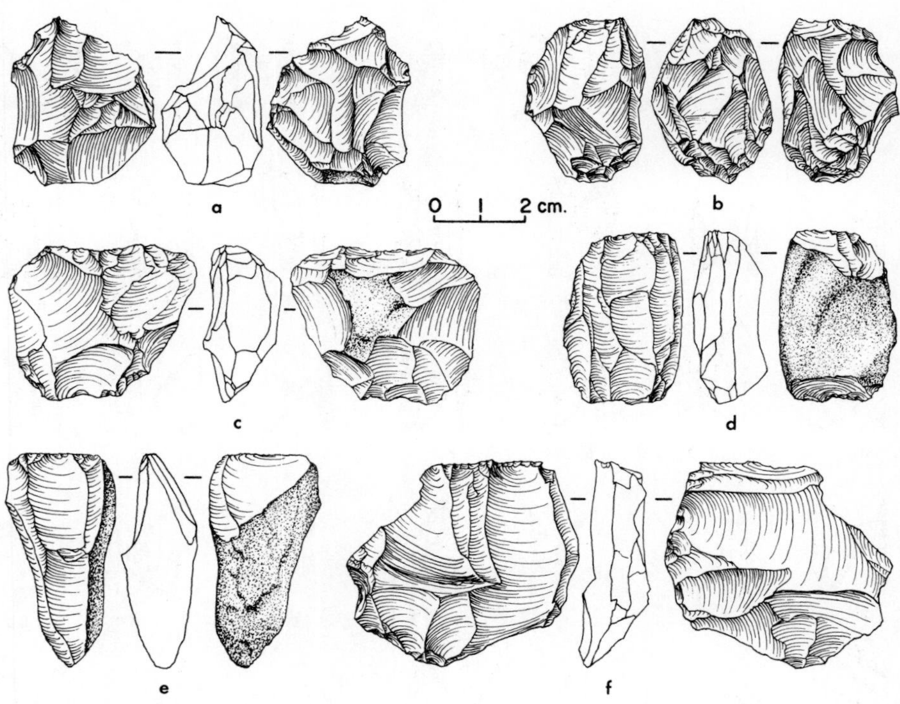

Figure 190. Cores from Site E71K18, Area D, Afian industry.

Table 10 gives the main typological indices for these sites assigned to the second group of the Afian industry.

Table 10. Main Typological Indices at Sites E71K18D and E71K18E, Second Group of the Afian Industry

	E71K18D, surface	*E71K18E, surface*
Basal truncations, simple, on bladelets and microflakes	5.3	6.2
Distal truncations, simple	—	0.4
Geometrics and semigeometrics	5.1	9.3
Backed elements, various	21.0	12.2
Microburins, ordinary	6.7	8.4
Endscrapers	16.5	18.4
Burins	0.7	2.2
Retouched pieces	16.6	13.4
Notches and denticulates	9.1	9.2

The arch-backed and truncated pieces as a group suggest a pseudo-geometric entity that may have represented an incipient stage in the development of compound tools. The interest in this observation is enhanced when it is realized that if the Afian industry is correctly dated to around 11,500–12,500 BC, then it is probably the earliest massive manifestation of the microburin technology in Northern Africa.

Another site that seemingly belongs to the Afian industry is reported from Kom Ombo (Gebel Silsila 2B, Area 1), where it was tentatively identified as Sebilian (Phillips, personal communication). The distinctive feature of the Kom Ombo site is the presence there of numerous grinding stones (Reed 1966; Butzer and Hansen 1968: 172). No traces of grinding stones were recovered from any of the Isna sites, which clearly indicates a different economic exploitation, possibly due to seasonal activities. There is also the possibility that the Isna sites date slightly earlier, around 12,000 BC (the Kom Ombo site has two radiocarbon dates—11,610 BC and 11,120 BC) and were occupied before the utilization of ground grain became widespread.

Judging from the faunal complex recovered at the Afian sites at Isna, both fishing and large mammal hunting were pursued. Most of the fish were large Nile catfish, and the most common mammal remains were *Bos* and hartebeest.

In the same stratigraphic position and microenvironment, on the shore of either the same or a closely adjacent pond along which the Afian settlements occur, is a small, limited concentration representing an entirely different tool complex (Site E71K6, Area A). There the most common cores are the opposed-platform, fully prepared, rounded variety for bladelets and flakes. All other core forms are rare, including single-platform and changed orientation types. Levallois is absent. The frequency of blades and bladelets in the debitage is relatively high, attaining 27%. The blades and bladelets tend to be long, and microlithic pieces are rare.

Among the tools in the assemblage, the overwhelming component is endscrapers, which represent slightly more than 40% of the total (Figure 191). These are followed by retouched pieces (around 14%), followed by borers, made mainly on blades and bladelets, which account for 10% of the tools. Burins and backed elements, of which the most common are arch-backed bladelets, account for around 7% each. Notches and denticulates show a similar frequency. Truncated blades and bladelets are less common (5%), while microburins are very rare. This assemblage has no known analogies elsewhere along the Nile. The main typological indices are given in Table 11.

Three concentrations of the distinctive Sebilian industry were found in Upper Egypt, one of them within the upper part of the Sahaba—Darau silt, possibly preceding the widespread fire, which would indicate a date slightly before 10,500 BC (Hassan, 1972). The other two Sebilian sites were on the eroded surface of the Sahaba but gave clear indications of having once been in the upper part of that unit (Hassan & Wendorf, 1974). This stratigraphic position would place the Sebilian slightly later than both the Afian industry and the lithic com-

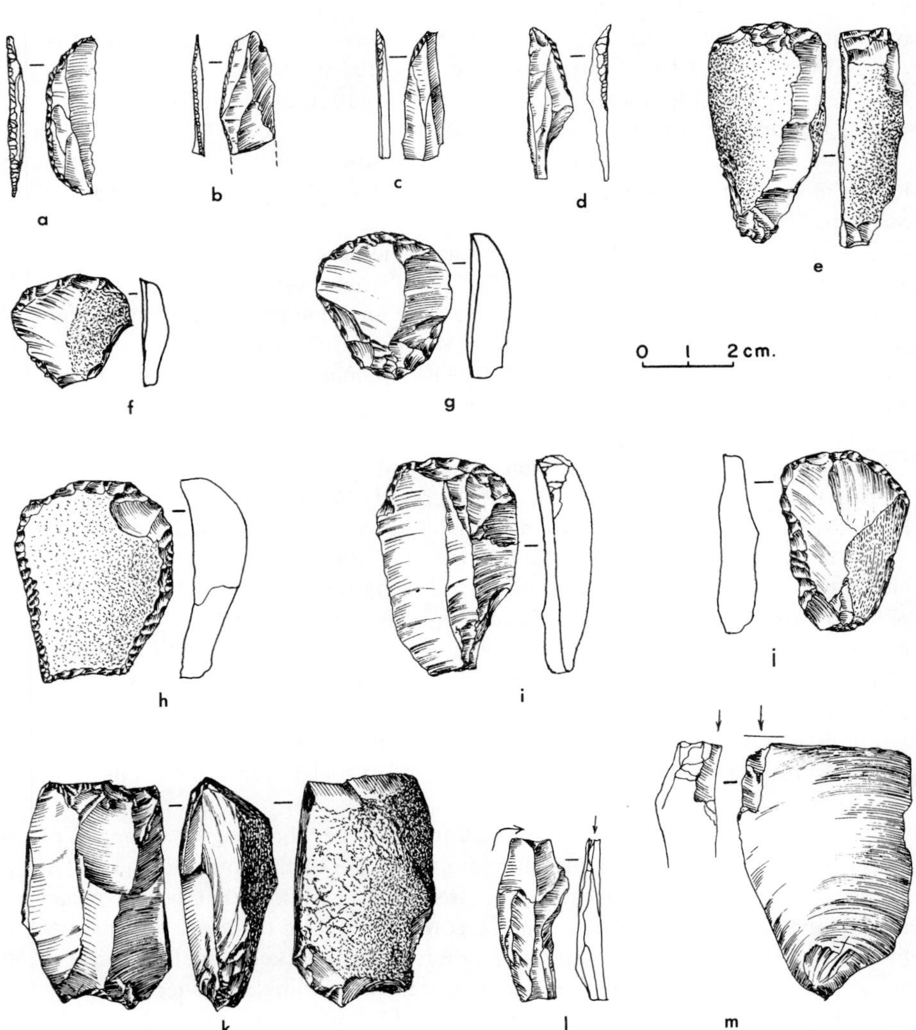

Figure 191. Tools and core from Site E71K6, Area A.

Table 11. Main Typological Indices for Site E71K6A, Surface

Endscrapers	41.2
Burins	8.1
Perforators	9.3
Backed bladelets	6.8
Ouchtata	1.2
Truncated bladelets and blades	5.6
Microburins, ordinary	1.8
Retouched pieces	14.3
Notches and denticulates	6.8

plex at Site E71K6, Area A. One of these assemblages does not significantly differ from the Sebilian, which is well described from farther south in Nubia, and consists primarily of truncated and backed and truncated flakes (Marks 1968: 461–531). The other two assemblages have higher frequencies of retouched pieces, as well as notches and denticulates (Figure 192). In all other respects they are similar (Hassan, in press). Table 12 gives the main typological indices for the Sebilian sites in Upper Egypt.

Table 12. Main Typological Indices of Sebilian Sites (Hassan 1972a, Hassan & Wendorf 1974)

	E71P3	*E61MIA*	*E61M1B*
ILty	20.0		
Endscrapers	2.3	—	2.0
Notches and denticulates	4.7	13.9	10.6
Burins	0.8	1.5	4.4
Truncations (basal, basal and lateral, lateral, distal, proximal–lateral, partial) on flakes	54.0	33.9	49.4
Backed flakes	8.5	—	—
Retouched pieces	9.2	20.9	16.4

In Upper Egypt the most numerous and richest sites associated with the Sahaba–Darau aggradation belong to the Isnan industry. Sites assigned to this industry occur in three widely separated areas: one large group near Isna and a second group near Nagada, both on the west bank, and a third series of sites in the Dishna area.

Some span of time is represented in these occupations. The earliest precede slightly the widespread fire, while the youngest date after the fire and just precede the final phase of the Sahaba–Darau aggradation. A range from around 10,600 BC to 10,000 BC is indicated.

In the Isna area the sites are surprisingly large, without any indication of internal clustering, as might be expected if they represented numerous repeated reoccupations. They seemingly represent a constant and long-lasting settlement of a large population. The fact that the sites are both numerous and large suggests a demographic explosion that may find its explanation in a new economic base.

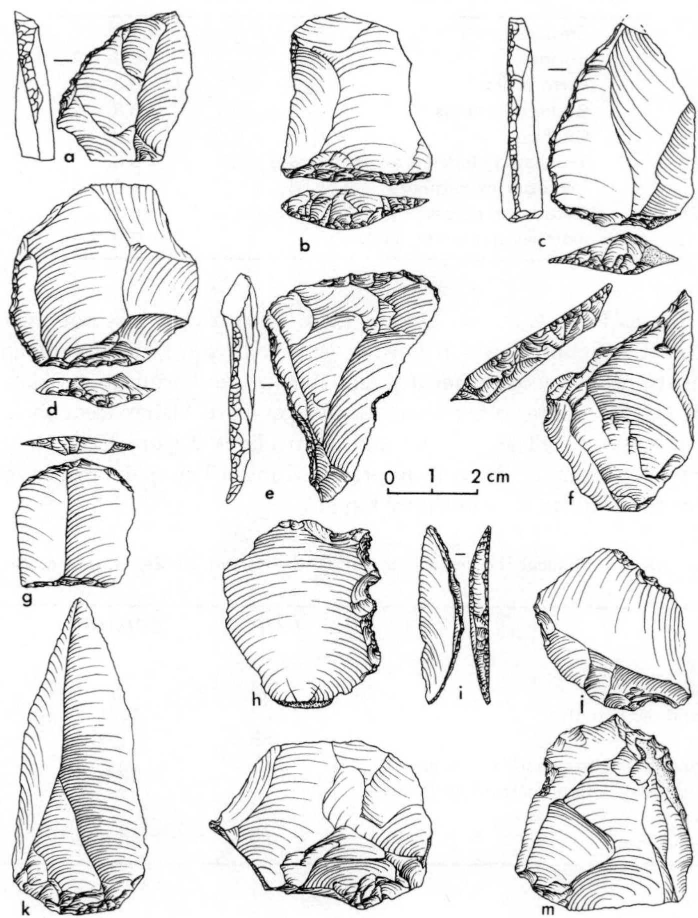

Figure 192. Tools from Site E61M1, Areas A and B, Sebilian industry: (a) oblique distal truncated flake; (b) basal truncated, partially backed flake; (c) backed, basal, and oblique distal truncated flake; (d) partially backed, basal truncated flake; (e) backed and distal truncated flake; (f) oblique distal truncated flake; (g) endscraper with basal truncation; (h) denticulated flake; (i) lunate; (j, l) retouched flake; (k) blade with basal truncation; (m) notched flake.

The same situation is not evident in all areas where the Isnan industry occurs. For example, the sites at Nagada seem to be slightly smaller than those at Isna, although they are still numerous. At Dishna, on the other hand, the sites are both numerous and large, but in most cases they clearly represent several reoccupations of the same locality. The Dishna sites are believed to reflect the specialized activity of workshops connected with quarrying.

One of the surprising features of the Isnan sites is the absence of fish remains. Unlike the previous occupants of this area, these hunted only large mammals. The decline in fishing as a source of food may be related to the appearance of the new food resource represented by ground grain. The associated pollen strongly suggests that this grain was possibly barley, and significantly, this large-grass pollen, which is tentatively identified as barley, makes a sudden appearance in the pollen profile just before the time when the first Isnan settlements were established in the area. This may indicate a change in local conditions favorable for this particular grain that permitted it suddenly to colonize the area, and this, in turn, attracted the new settlers.

The Isnan assemblages used primarily large nodules and slabs of Eocene flint, which was presumably quarried out of the cliffs of the Thebes Formation rather than collected from nearby wadis or gravel bars. The cores are large and often exceed 7 cm in length. The method of flaking is hard hammer throughout. The biggest group of cores, representing more than 50% of this category, is of the unpatterned, changed orientation, globular variety for the production of flakes. The next most important categories are the single- and opposed-platform cores for flakes. Blade cores are rare and mainly of the single-platform category, although there are a few of the opposed-platform type. Preparation is very restricted and is confined mainly to the striking platform.

In the debitage blades are rare, and the overwhelming group is flakes, most of which are large and thick, with big butts and large bulbs.

There is firm stratigraphic evidence to support a chronological subdivision of the Isnan industry; however, there appears to be very little change in the tool kit, and this is reflected primarily in minor changes in the frequencies of a few tool groups (Figures 193–196). The main feature is an extremely high percentage of endscrapers. In the oldest assemblage (E71K14D) they account for almost 64%, and in a stratigraphically younger assemblage (E71K14A) they represent 55%. Notches and denticulates represent around 19% in the older assemblage and only 11% in the younger. Burins, mostly made on snaps, account for only 3% in the older assemblage but increase to 13% in the younger. Backed elements, including arch-backed blades and bladelets and an occasional backed piece with two perpendicular truncations, are very rare or may be absent, while retouched pieces are more numerous, ranging from 5% to 7%. Of the tools from the *in situ* collection, up to 15% display lustrous edges from grass cutting (Figure 197). A few grinding stone fragments with deep concavity were also present (Figure 198).

One of the Isna sites belonging to this industry, E71K22, is more variable than the others (Figure 199). Its stratigraphic position above the burned layer indicates that it is at least as recent as E71K14A, and it may be slightly later. This may be suggested by the slightly lower frequency of endscrapers (45%) and the higher percentage of burins (17%). Here, also, backed bladelets with perpendicular truncations are more common than elsewhere (around 5%), and a few trapezoids occur. Table 13 gives the major typological indices. Three Isnan sites are also compared in a cumulative graph in Figure 200.

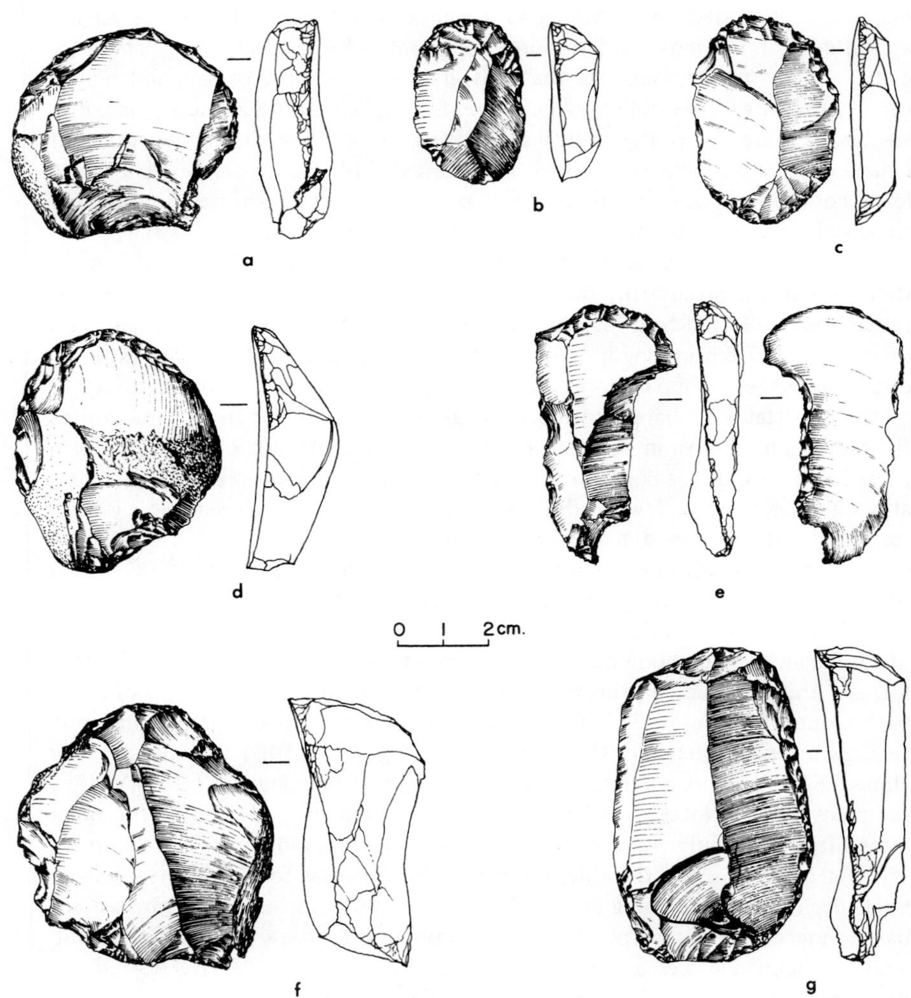

Figure 193. Tools from an early Isnan site—E71K14, Area D. All endscrapers.

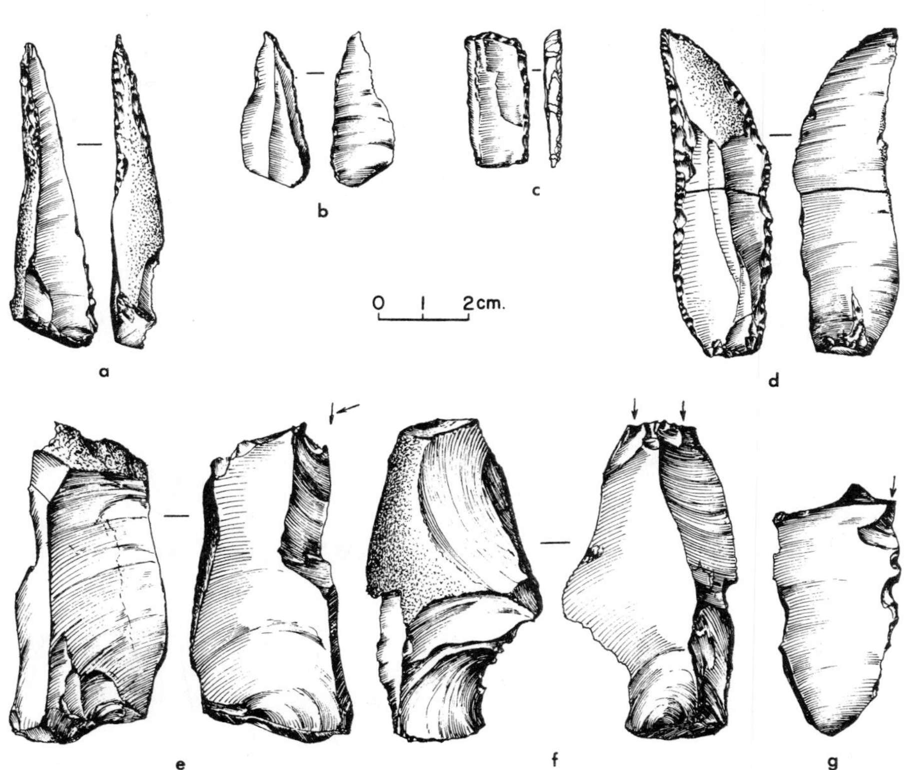

Figure 194. Tools from an early Isnan site—E71K14, Area D.

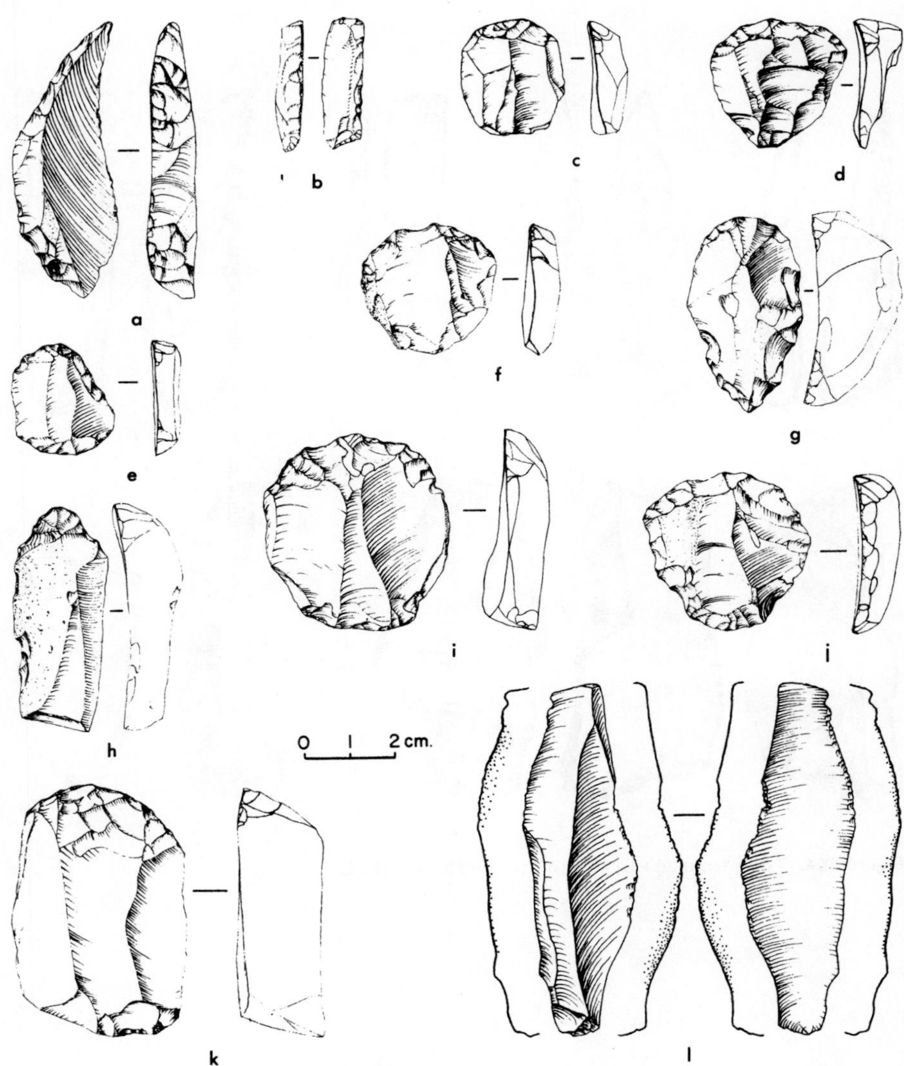

Figure 195. Tools from a later Isnan Site—E71K15.

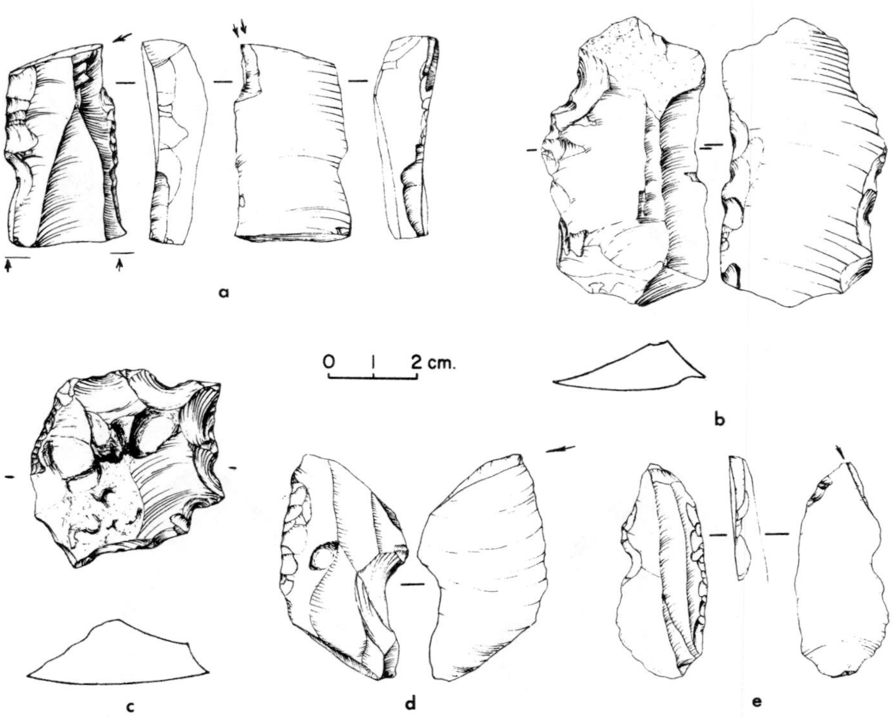

Figure 196. Tools from a later Isnan site—E71K15: (a, d, e) burins; (b, c) denticulated flakes.

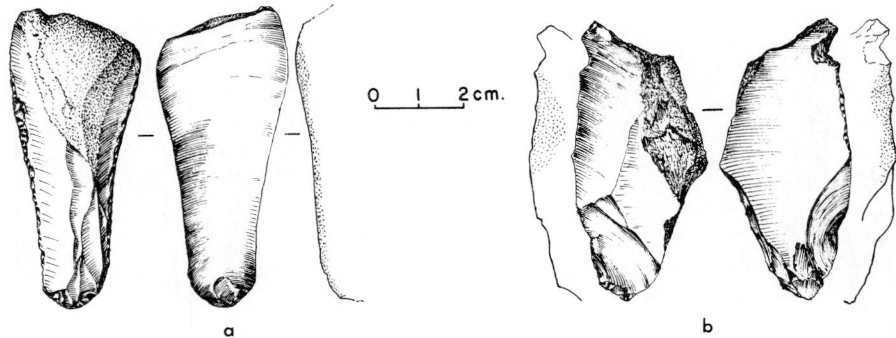

Figure 197. Pieces with lustrous edges from Site E71K14, Area A.

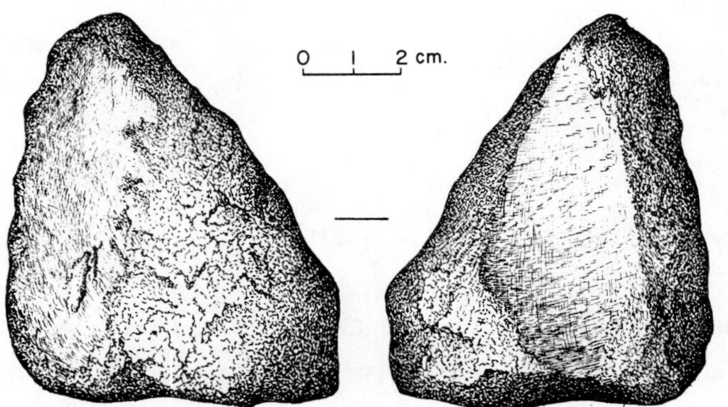

Figure 198. Fragment of grinding stone from an early Isnan site—E71K14, Area D.

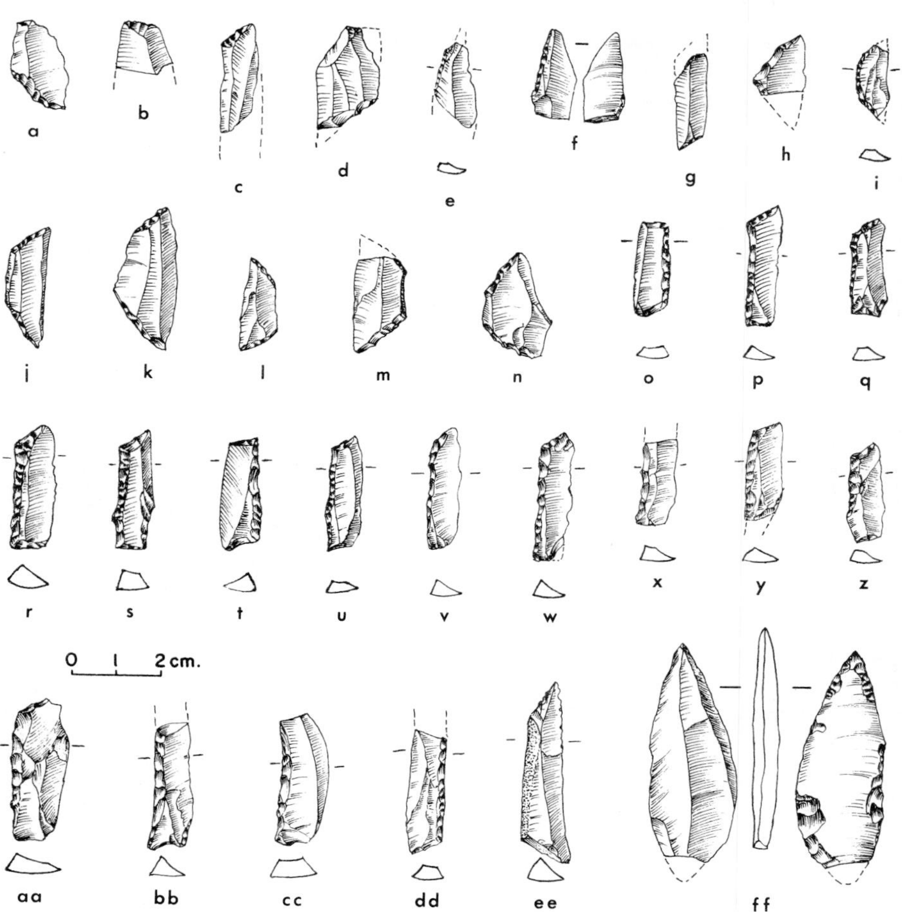

Figure 199. Tools from Site E71K22, Isnan industry.

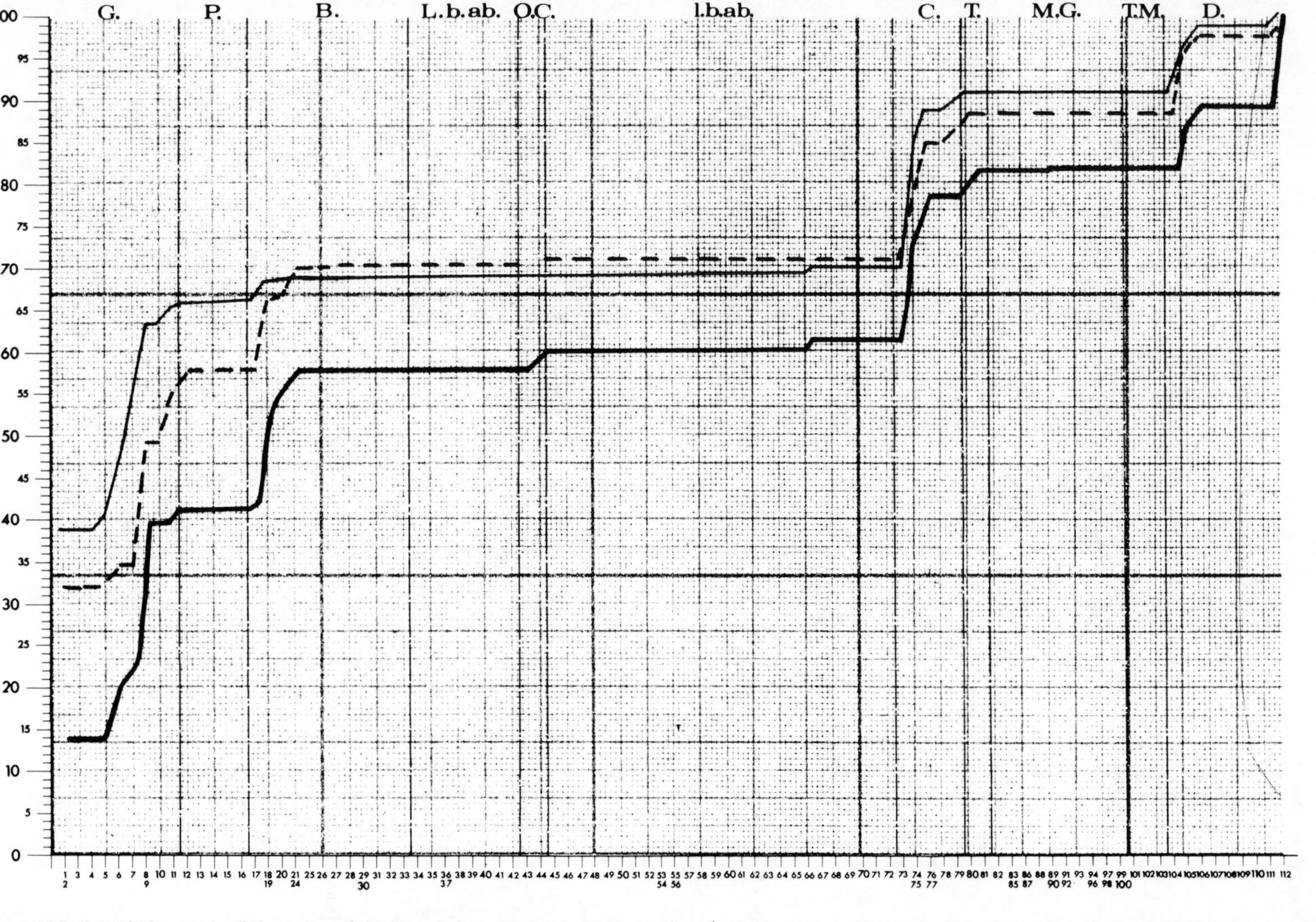

Figure 200. Cumulative graph of three sites of the Isnan industry based on Tixier typology (restricted counts, Categories 101–103 excluded): Site E71K14, Area D—thin continuous line; Site E71K14, Area A—broken line; Site E71K22, surface—thick continuous line. Sample from E71K14, Area D based on 1092 pieces of a total of 1181 pieces. Excluded were undetermined endscrapers (18), undetermined burins (2), undetermined tool fragments (68), rectangles (1), and transverse burins on truncation (1), included in Category 112. Sample from E71K14, Area A based on 966 pieces from a total of 1091. Excluded were atypical endscrapers (11), undetermined burin fragments (22), undetermined tool fragments (90), Corbiac burins (5), and burins combined with becs (2), transfered to Category 112. Sample from Site E71K22 based on 1189 pieces from a total of 1391 pieces, of which the following were excluded: undetermined fragments of endscrapers (144) and unidentified tool fragments (58). Also, Category 112 includes burins on straight truncation (5), single-blow transverse burins (19), single-blow transverse burins, double (1), atypical burins on truncation (4), unidentified fragments of burins (9), borers and/or flat-faced points (40), borers combined with truncations (1), endscrapers combined with truncations (1), pieces with thinned tips (4), and double-truncated backed bladelets and thin fragments.

Table 13. Main Typological Indices from Some Isnan Sites

	E71K14D, surface	*E71K14A, surface*	*E71K22, surface*
Endscrapers	63.5	54.8	45.0
Burins	2.7	12.5	16.9
Notches and denticulates	18.6	11.4	14.4
Retouched pieces	5.2	7.4	4.1
Backed blades	0.1	—	—
Backed bladelets (without Ouchtata and truncated)	0.6	0.1	0.5
Single- and double-truncated backed bladelets (including rectangles)	0.1	—	4.6
Ouchtata	0.1	—	—
Truncated blades and flakes	1.1	0.6	1.0
Truncated bladelets and microflakes	0.2	0.9	1.3
Double-truncated bladelets and microflakes (trapezoids)	—	—	0.4
Microburins, Krukowski	0.1	—	—
Microburins, ordinary	—	0.2	—
Sidescrapers	1.7	1.2	1.3
Perforators (borers, beaks)	0.8	1.00	0.1
Flat-faced points with borer or perforator tips	—	—	2.9(?)

At Dishna the several localities assigned to the Isnan industry differ from those in the Isna area by a much higher frequency of notched and denticulate tools as well as retouched flakes and blades. As a consequence the endscraper and burin indices are lower. In spite of these differences, however, it is felt that the Dishna sites are properly assigned to the Isnan industry and represent special quarry activities connected with the exploitation of the Eocene flint exposures at the nearby cliffs. The close similarities in the tool kits are expressed in the hard-hammer and large-core technology, the rarity of backed elements, and emphasis on endscrapers and burins for those tools outside the groups represented in the notches, denticulates, and retouched pieces.

The cores at the Dishna sites appear to be similar to those from the Isna area; however, in some localities blade debitage is more frequent (from 5% to slightly more than 20%) than at Isna. There is also considerable variability among the Dishna sites in tool frequency, ranging from slightly more than 1% to around 12% of the total assemblage.

As previously noted, in all these sites the tool kit is dominated by two main categories (Figure 201): notches and denticulates, which may vary between 11% and 43%, and retouched flakes and blades, which range between 30% and 70%. Endscrapers are more constant, with frequencies between 6% and 20%, but most around 15%. Burins range from 1% to 16% but usually account for around 6%. Sidescrapers are rare to absent, the highest frequency being around 5%. Truncations are always below 2%, and backed pieces (mostly blades and bladelets) are very rare or absent. Table 14 gives the main typological indices for several Dishna sites.

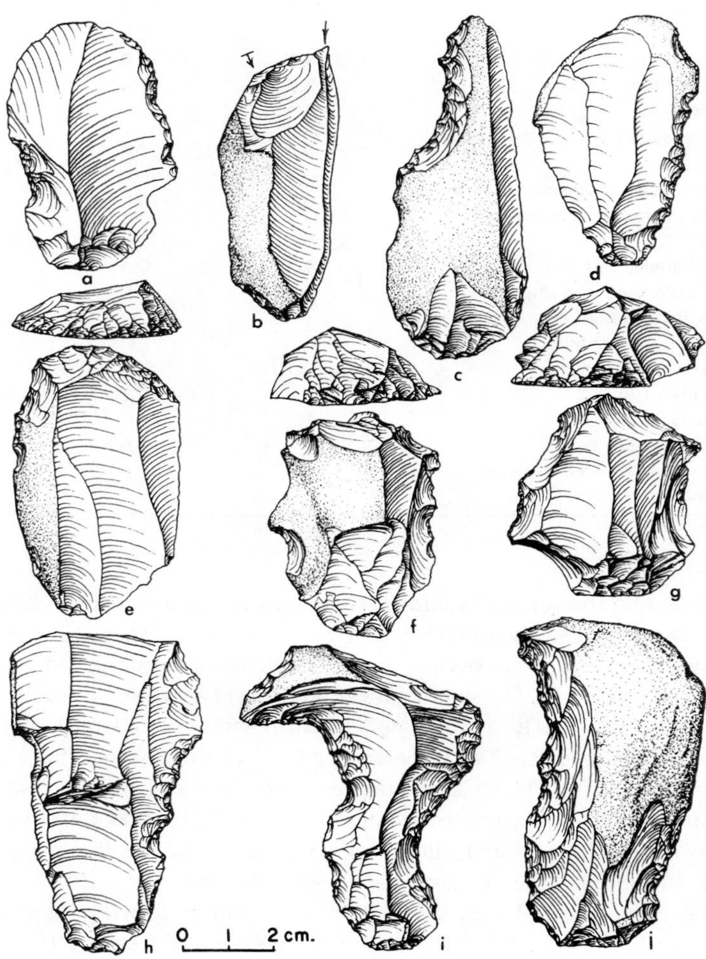

Figure 201. Typical tools from sites near Dishna assigned to Isnan industry (Sites E61M6, Area D; E61M10, Areas B and C): (a) notched flakes; (b) burin; (c) meganotched flake; (d) denticulated flake; (e) simple endscraper; (f) denticulated endscraper; (g) simple "thick" endscraper; (h) denticulated flake; (i) strangled flake; (j) concave sidescraper.

Table 14. Main Typological Indices from Some Dishnan Sites

	E61M2A, B	*E61M3B, C*	*E61M5A*	*E61M7A*	*E61M7C*	*E61M10B*	*E61M10C*	*E61M9A*	*E61M6C*
Endscrapers	10.4	17.3	15.7	14.8	21.8	5.6	16.8	14.0	14.7
Burins	6.7	1.1	6.3	6.9	16.5	1.3	5.1	2.6	1.5
Notches and denticulates	28.9	27.5	32.6	32.8	16.5	14.1	20.6	32.0	11.3
Retouched pieces	49.4	33.3	32.2	30.5	26.4	70.3	47.4	46.1	30.3
Backed elements	—	—	—	0.4	—	—	4.1	—	—
Truncated elements (mostly flakes and blades)	—	1.0	—	0.4	—	—	1.5	0.5	1.1
Sidescrapers	4.2	—	5.2	2.3	2.0	0.5	3.7	3.6	—
Perforators	—	—	1.0	—	—	—	<1	—	—

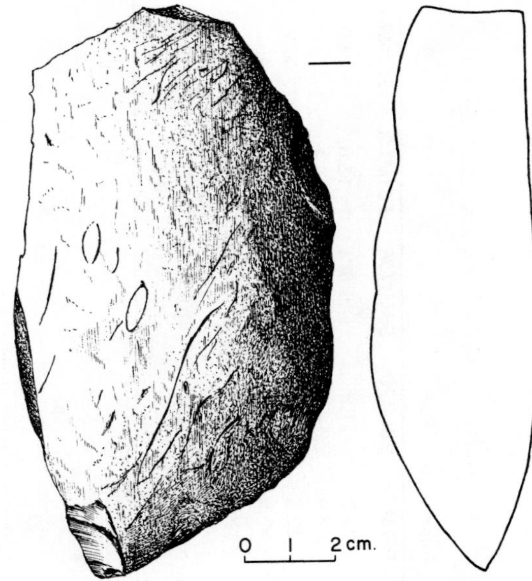

Figure 202. Chert slab with incised lines suggesting outline of elephant.

One locality (E61M9) yielded an interesting plate of Eocene chert on the cortex of which are evidently engraved numerous lines, two ovals around the center, and a possible elephant head with eye and trunk (Figure 202).

The Post-Sahaba–Darau Recession

In previous publications (Wendorf 1970a, b, c; Said *et al.* 1970), the downcutting that followed the Sahaba–Darau aggradation was referred to as the Dishna recessional interval. The tentative reassignment of the playa sediments in the Dishna area to the final phase of the Sahaba–Darau aggradation, however, would indicate that this name is not appropriate, since no deposits of this period were recorded in the Dishna area. This reassignment of the Dishna playa sediments to the terminal phase of the Sahaba leaves few deposits that can be associated with the beginning of the post-Sahaba–Darau recession. The only possible deposits of this period known in Upper Egypt were at Site E71P5 near El-Kilh. Here Nile sediments clearly inset against the eroded massive Sahaba silts contained an industry and *Unio* shells that dated 9610 BC.

In Nubia, de Heinzelin (1968: 47) recognized a similar phase of downcutting of the Sahaba sediments and called it the Birbet Formation. The type locality was at Dibeira West 6, where a poor collection of occupation debris was found on an eroded surface identified with this event and covered by a later silt.

The amount of decline could not be established either in Upper Egypt or in Nubia, although it possibly exceeded 20 m in Nubia if the interpretation of flood levels at Site 3400 is correct. In both areas the evidence of the lowest levels during this period is undoubtedly deeply buried under the modern floodplain.

The scarcity of exposures is responsible for the paucity of archaeological data that can be related to this period. The single known site (E71P5) yielded an assemblage (Figures 203–205) that contains a high frequency of retouched pieces (up to 46%), with medium values for endscrapers (around 16%) and notches and denticulates (about 14%). Burins are low (2%); truncations (of which some are basal truncated while others are basal truncated and backed flakes) are slightly higher, accounting for around 7%. Sidescrapers on flakes represent 4%. Backed flakes and blades are very rare, with a maximum index of around 3%. A few geometrics, including triangles and trapezes, represent about 3%. There are also very rare bifacially flaked stemmed projectile points. Grinding stones also occur, and some of the chipped tools have lustrous edges.

The assemblage seems to have close similarities with the Isnan industry, although the frequencies are different. This might be accounted for as changes that occurred in time within the industry, since the site is about 400 years later than the youngest site assigned to the Isnan industry.

A comparison and correlation of Late Pleistocene events along the Nile is shown in Table 15.

Later Nile Sediments

In Nubia abundant geological and archaeological data are available for the interval between the post-Sahaba–Darau recession and the development of the modern floodplain. In that area, following the Birbet recession, the level of the Nile rose to a maximum of 13 m above the modern floodplain during the Arkin aggradation (de Heinzelin 1968: 47–48). A radiocarbon date places the maximum of this event near 7410 BC ±180 years (WSU-175), while the base of this aggradation is probably dated by the Nile oyster shell from Gebel Halfa that yielded a radiocarbon age of 9250 BC ±285 years (I-531). Following the maximum, according to de Heinzelin (1968: Fig. 5), there was a gradual decline of the Nile until around 3350 BC, when there was a sudden drop that "exposed larger surfaces of the river bed, and incipient soils could develop."

There is some evidence, however, to suggest that this decline was not smooth but, rather, broken by several microaggradations and declines. These fluctuations seem to be represented by the group of levee remnants in the Arkin area at Sites DIW-51, DIW-53, and DIW-50. These sites are located on a sequence of levees that seem to record a series of declines followed by microaggradations at 9 m, 6 m, and 5 m, respectively, above the modern floodplain. Site DIW-51, at 9 m, is dated 5750 BC ±120 years (WSU-176), and Site DIW-50, at 5 m, has three dates—3650 BC ±200 years (WSU-174), 3460 BC ±150 years (SMU-1), and 3830 BC ±150 years (SMU-2).

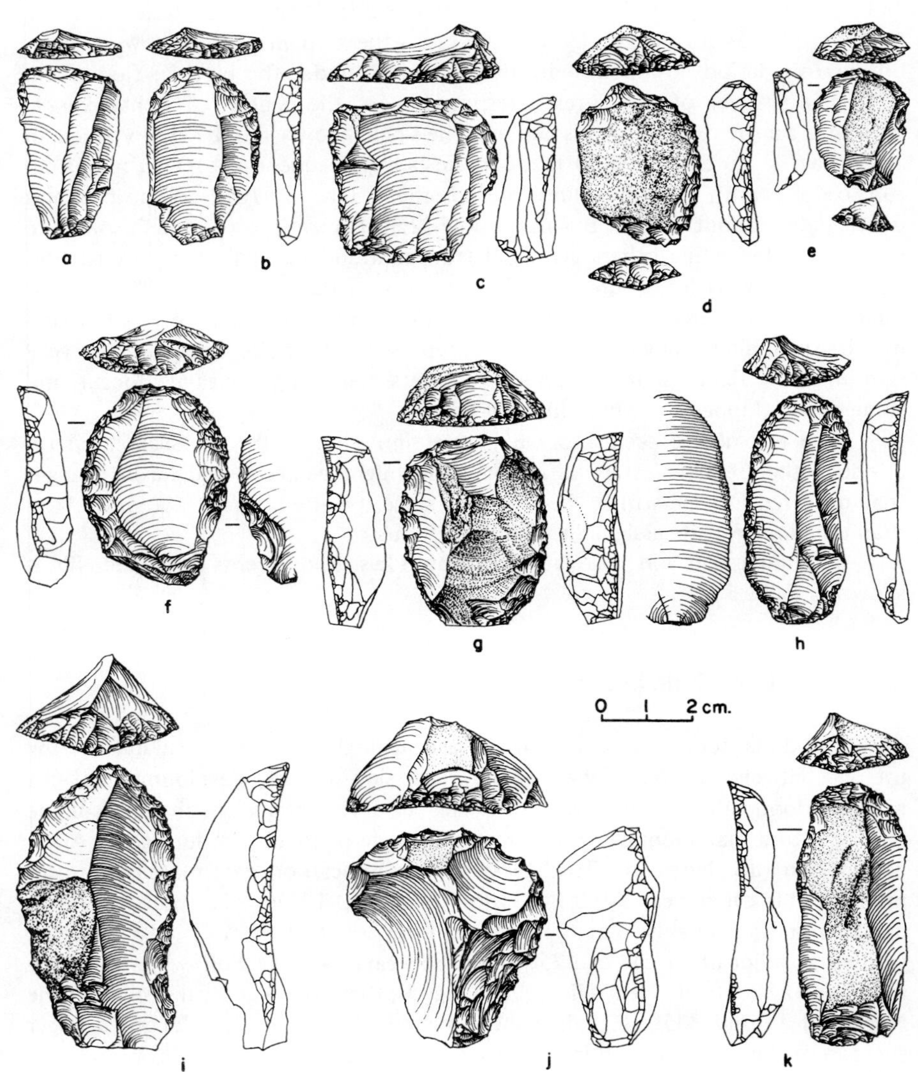

Figure 203. Tools from Site E71P5.

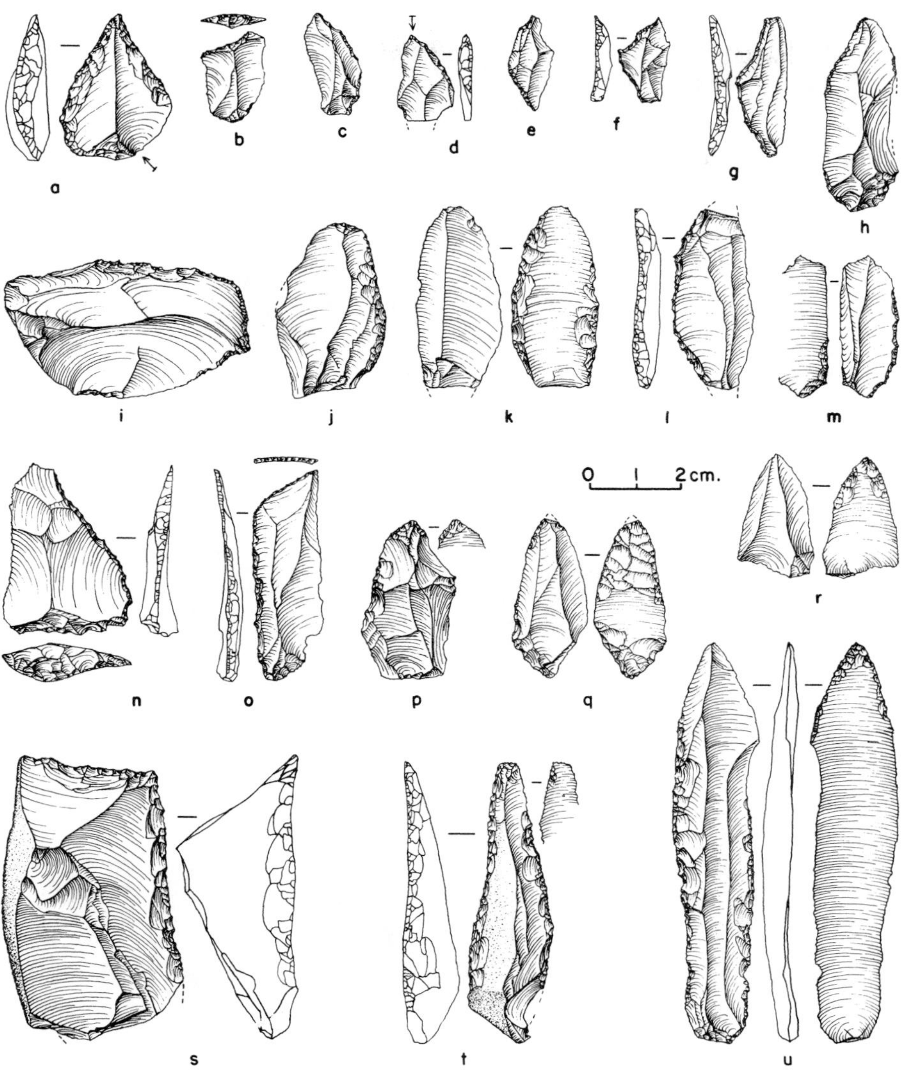

Figure 204. Tools from Site E71P5.

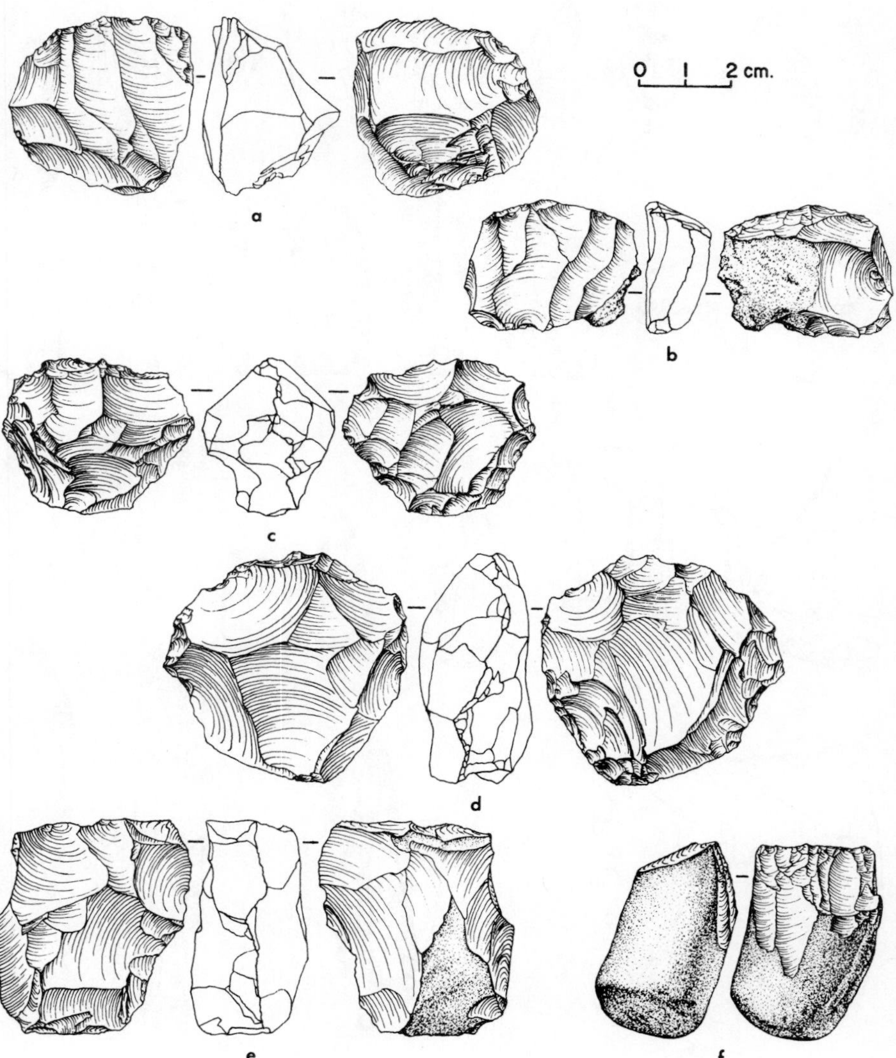

Figure 205. Cores from Site E71P5.

Table 15. Summary of Late Pleistocene Events Along the Nile from Nubia to Dishna

General Subdivision	*Nubia (names of formations & members according to de Heinzelin 1968)*			*Kom Ombo (names of formations and members according to Butzer and Hansen 1968; chronology after Phillips and Butzer)*		
Minipulsation of Arkin, El-Kab Catfish Cave & Dibeira West 50	*Arkin*	Aggrading floodplain silts at Dibeira West 50 High floods at Catfish Cave, floodplain at Dibeira West 53(?) Channel & levee at Dibeira West 51 Nile bar at Dibeira West 1 (*ca.* 13 m afl.) Oyster bed at Gebel Halfa (9,250 ±285) Birbet downcutting	Neolithic: 3,460 ±150, 3,640 ±200, 3,830 ±150 Occupation: 5,110 ±120 Shamarkian: 5,750 ±120 Arkinian: 7,410 ±180	*Arminna Member, Gebel Silsila Formation*	Suballuvial	
Sahaba-Darau Aggradation	*Late Sahaba*	High floods (up to 30 m afl.), Site 34 Silts & fluvial sands at *ca.* 16 m afl., Site 3400 (10,600 ±460) Hearth at Ballana on dune covered by silt seepage ponds at Tushka	Ballanan: 12,050 ±240 Occupation: 12,550 ±490	*Darau Member, Gebel Silsila Formation*	High floods (*ca.* 10,000) Channel C stage (*ca.* 10,500) Channel B stage (*ca.* 15,000–11,000) Channel A stage (*ca.* 15,000–12,500)	Occupation at KS-IV(?) Occupation at GS-2B, GS-1-XIII, GS-2B-11–Silsilian Occupation at GS-2A, complex KS-II/III
Deir El-Fakhuri Recession		Downcutting				
Ballana-Masmas Aggradation	*Ballana Early Sahaba*	Fossil soil covered by silts at GB27, Dune at 443, dune interfingering with silt at 8859 (*ca.* 16 m afl), and with vertisol at 1020 (*ca.* 22 m afl). Silts at GB32 (*ca.* 20 m afl).	Darbarosan: 16,155 ±1200 (in paleosol) Halfan: 14,550 ±500 (minimal) at 443; 16,650 at 8859; 17,200 ±375 at 1020 Late Paleolithic: 23,750 ±2,500/3,700	*Masmas Formation*	*ca.* 22,000–16,000	
	Dibeira-Jer	Fluvial sands & silts at 1017 (*ca.* 24 m afl) and channel sands at ANW-3 (*ca.* 19 m afl.) Dune, fluvial sand, and silt at 34 (*ca.* 28 m afl); paleosol at 6G30(?) Silt, dune, paleosol, and silt sequence at 40 and 1440 up to 31 m afl (?).	Late & Middle Khormusan: 15,850 ± 500 at ANW-3 15,850 ± 280 (1017) ? both too young Khormusan: older than 41,490 41,490 at 34D; older than 36,600 at 6G30			
Downcutting (?)		Downcutting ?				
Qena Sands		Silt, dune, paleosol, and silt sequence at 440 and 1440 up to 41 m afl (?)	Denticulate Mousterian ? below and in paleosol at 440; slightly older than 34,050 at 6G30.	*Korosko Formation*	Terminating *ca.* 24,000	
Dandara Silts						

Table 15. Summary of Late Pleistocene Events Along the Nile from Nubia to Dishna (cont).

General Subdivision	*El-Kilh Area*			*Esna Area*		
Minipulsation of Arkin, El-Kab Catfish Cave & Dibeira West 50		Silts & fluvial sands at El-Kab Recessional fluvial sands	Occupation at El-Kab—5980 ±160; 6040 ±150; 6400 ±160—Shamarkian Occupation at E71P5—9610 ±180		Silty sand & molluscan fauna at Village No. 4—8,450 ±470; 7,380 ±160.	
Sahaba-Darau Aggradation	*Fluvial sands & silts*	Truncation	Occupation at E71P3(?)—Sebilian	*Nile silts, seepage ponds*	Burned layer Upper diatomite or pond sediments 10,740 ±240 (E71K14A) "Middle silt" & pond sediments Lower pond sediments and diatomites Reworked dune sand & silt (E71K18)	Occupation at E71K14A, E71K15, E71K22(?)—Esna Occupation at E71K14D—Esnan Occupation at E71K6B, E71K18—Afian, E71K6A Possible at E71K20—Silsilian
Deir El-Fakhuri Recession		No sediments			Nile recession & possible soil formation(?)	Occupation at E71K12 & E71K13(?)
Ballana-Masmas Aggradation	*Massive silts*	Dune (?) at E71P7	Occupation at E71P1—15,850 ±330; 15,650 ±300; 15,500 ±300; 15,300 ±300; 15,000 ±300; E71P2; E71P6; E71P7—Idfuan	*Massive silts*	Dunes with occasional seepage ponds 14,880 ± 290 (E71K9X)	Fakhurian: Occupation on dunes at E71K1—16,070 ±330; E71K2; E71K3—15,640 ±300; E71K4(?); E71K5(?); E71K9—Idfuan

Dandara Area

Downcutting	Slope sediments	Sangoan-like assemblage in secondary position (E6103)
Qena Sands	Erosion responsible for rolling landscape Locally derived gravel & cobble cover Red soil possibly correlative with the one below Coarse sands & grit in massive, thick, homogeneous unit Thick red soil Two units of massive silts >37950 (E6103) Sandy silts & marls	
Dandara Silts		Late Acheulian (?) at E6101

Table 15. Summary of Late Pleistocene Events Along the Nile from Nubia to Dishna (cont).

General Subdivision	Makhadma Area			Kumbelat Area		Dishna Area		
Minipulsation of Arkin, El-Kab Catfish Cave & Dibeira West 50					Wadi gravel & pebbles			
Sahaba-Darau Aggradation	*Silt, fluvial sands*	Fluvial sand with mollusk Burned layer	Occupation at Area A (11,430 ±770) E6104	*silt* *Erosion*	Burned layer—10,550 ±230 Dune sands	*Playa behind levee*	Upper playa Intercalated layers of Nile silts & playa Lower playa	
						Upper silt levee	Burned layer Wadi gravel & sand (second series) becoming finer upward Thin silt layer	Occupation at E61M9, Occupation at E61M1, E61M2, E61M3, E61M5A, E61M6, E61M7—Esnan (quarry facies); E61M10—Sebilian
Deir El-Fakhuri Recession							Wadi gravels & pebbles pebbles—first series (?)	Occupation at E61M5B
Ballana-Masmas Aggradation								
Downcutting		Fine sandy slopewash, Late Paleolithic slope sediments with cobbles, boulders & gravels in coarse sand matrix.	Occupation at Area D C. Rolled middle Paleolithic. E6104		Wadi (?) pebbles & gravels (?)			
Qena Sands		Erosion responsible for rolling landscape Locally derived gravel & cobble cover Coarse, sands & grit in massive, thick homogeneous unit. Sandy silt (?)			Erosion Thick red soil			
Dandara Silts					Massive silt			

The 6 m aggradation recorded at DIW-53 is dated 5960 BC ±120 years (SMU-4, on charcoal). This date conflicts slightly with that obtained at DIW-51, although they overlap within their standard errors. The archaeology and stratigraphy would suggest an age around 5000 BC or even slightly later.

Another date that may somehow be related to this microaggradation is reported from Catfish Cave in Egyptian Nubia (Wendt 1966). Here, at 16 m above the modern floodplain, Nile silts are preserved in a cave and associated with an occupation floor. Charcoal from within these silts yielded a date of 5110 BC ±120 years (Y-1646). An episode of siltation at that elevation and at that date is extremely difficult to relate to the sequence known elsewhere. Perhaps the silts in the cave represent a series of unusual floods like those at the end of the Sahaba, rather than a major episode of siltation. There are no floodplain sediments of this age developed at this elevation, but they may possibly be high floods associated with the microaggradation at DIW-53.

In Upper Egypt only one site is known that records the history of the Nile for the interval between the post-Sahaba–Darau recession and the development of the modern floodplain. On the east bank, across the river from El-Kilh at the Old Kingdom fortress of El-Kab, Vermeersch (1970) has recorded a series of Nilotic sediments in an area now under cultivation. He has called these deposits the El-Kab Formation. The stratigraphic position of these silts is 4 m lower than another unit of silts probably assignable to the Sahaba–Darau aggradation.. The archaeological industry associated with the younger El-Kab silts yielded three radiocarbon dates on charcoal—6400 BC ±160 years (LV-393), 6040 BC ±150 years (LV-464), and 5980 BC ±160 years (LV-465).

The site consisted of two main occupation layers, but there appear to be no significant differences between them. The assemblages represent a microlithic blade complex composed primarily of backed bladelets (30% and 35%), of which straight backed are the most numerous, together with shouldered bladelets. There is also a very high frequency of microburins (about 35%). Minor elements include arch-backed bladelets (2%), bladelets with arched tip, double-backed perforators (3%), endscrapers (1%), and a few geometrics, including lunates, triangles, and trapezes (around 2%). The cores are mostly the single-platform type for bladelets and flakes.

In spite of the slightly different classifications employed, the assemblage recalls very much the oldest Shamarkian assemblage from Site DIW-51 in Nubia, dated at 5750 BC (Schild *et al.* 1968: 695–705). The two sites differ mainly by the seemingly higher frequency of arch-backed bladelets at DIW-51 and the extremely high percentage of microburins at El-Kab. The general structure and typology, however, are very similar. Placement within the Shamarkian industry is clearly indicated. The El-Kab Formation, judging from the radiocarbon dates, probably represents the same microaggradation as at Site DIW-51.

The history of the post-Sahaba–Darau Nile seems to be well recorded in the Fayum depression, where at least four succeeding Holocene lakes are noted. On the basis of a series of radiocarbon dates and associated archaeology, the oldest or Paleo-Moeris lake is likely to be contemporaneous with the Arkin aggradation. The next or Pre-Moeris lake, with its maximum around 6000 BC, most certainly records the microaggradation that was reported from the El-Kab area and from DIW-51. The following Proto-Moeris lake, whose maximum could be dated around 5000 BC, must have been filled by the same Nile floods that left sediments in Catfish Cave in Nubia and possibly covered the occupation at DIW-53. The Moeris lake, which started to rise around 4000 BC and reached its maximum around 2800 BC, is closely contemporaneous with the microaggradation at DIW-50. Finally, the decline in the level of the Nile, possibly the Qadrus event in Nubia, may have led Amenemhat I to initiate human control of the Fayum entrance and the Bahr Youssef Canal.

It would seem, therefore, that the Fayum Depression records the events of the Post-Sahaba–Darau Nile more sensitively than the Valley proper. This is primarily because these more recent deposits are, for the most part, buried under the modern floodplain downstream from Nubia. There is, however, the danger of the Fayum's being hypersensitive and having been filled by a series of very high floods that are not of major significance in the history of the Nile. Nevertheless even these unusually high floods must be related in some way to generally higher Nile levels. A correlation of events in the Fayum and along the Nile is given in Table 16.

The Terminal Paleolithic assemblages from the Fayum Depression share a number of technological and typological attributes and clearly cluster into a single industry, which has been named the Qarunian after Lake Birket Qarun. The preferred raw material utilized in these sites was small, rounded chert pebbles from the Oligocene conglomerate of the Gebel Qatrani Formation, which is extensively exposed on the plateau above Qasr El-Sagha.

The cores in these Qarunian assemblages are predominantly the single-platform variety for flakes and blades, with no preparation except for the platform. They are uniformly small (less than 5 cm long), and most are between 3.5 cm and 4.5 cm in length. Opposed platform cores are extremely rare, as are cores with changed orientation. The blade group of debitage represents around 13% of the total assemblage and is composed almost entirely of bladelets.

The tool kit is dominated by backed blades and bladelets, which account for more than 50% of the tools (Figures 206–208). Within these, backed blades are a small minority, around 3%. Pointed arch-backed bladelets, often with retouched or truncated bases, are the most important variety within this group (18%–30%), followed closely by pointed straight-backed bladelets, also often with retouched or truncated bases. These represent from 14% to 18% of all tools. Other minor backed-bladelet categories include shouldered and blunt tip varieties. Notches and denticulates account for 9% to 17%, while geometric elements, mostly triangles and trapezes, are very low, usually less than 5%. Basal and distral truncations, mainly on bladelets, may vary from 3% to 9%. Microburin technology is poorly represented, (always below 4%); of these, the

Table 16. Correlation of Events in the Fayum Depression and in the Nile Valley

Nile Valley	*Lakes in depression*	*E29G1*		*E29H1, Subbasin*	
		Sedimentary units	*Cultural events*	*Sedimentary units*	*Cultural events*
Aggrading floodplain silts at Dibeira West 50 (3460 ±150, 3650 ±200, 3830 ±150	Moeris	Sediments recently deflated Silty sand Erosion	Grinding stone at T. 7 (*ca*. 18.5 m)	Sediments recently deflated	
	Recession below 9 m				
High floods at Catfish Cave 5110 ±120	Protomoeris	Cemented sand Sandy silt Deltaic beach with swamp layer Deltaic beach sand	Occupation at Area E—5190 ±120 (19 m)	Beach sands with maximum water reach up to *ca*. 24 m Alternating layers of silty sand, sandy silt, and swamp sediments frequency burned Stratified sand Truncation	Occupation at Area C (17 m)
	Recession below 12 m				
Subaggradation at El-Kab (6400 ±160, 6040 ±150, 5980 ±160) and Dibeira West 51 (5750 ±120)	Premoeris	Clayey, sandy silt Deltaic beach with swamp layers Lacustrine sand	Occupation at Area B (*ca*. 17 m) Occupation at Area F Occupation at Area A—6150 ±130 (15 m)	Deltaic beach Lacustrine sand with swamp layers	Occupation at Area A—6120 ±115 (15 m)
	Recession below 10 m	Desiccation, burning			
Maximum of Arkin aggradation Dibeira West (7440 ±180)	Paleomoeris	Thick diatomite Lacustrine sand Diatomite Lacustrine sand			

Table 16. Correlation of Events in the Fayum Depression and in the Nile Valley

E29H1, bottom of Basin X	*E29G3, Area A*		*E29G3, Area B*		*E29G2–Kom W*		*Qasr El-Sagha (E29G6)*	
Sedimentary units	*Sedimentary units*	*Cultural events*	*Sedimentary units*	*Cultural events*	*Sedimentary units*	*Cultural events*	*Sedimentary units*	*Cultural events*
Diatomite	Deltaic beach Sandy silt with snails Erosion	Washed down charcoal Washed down charcoal—3210 ±110	Deltaic beach Sandy silt	Old Kingdom occupation at *ca.* 20 m Slabs on L-shaped mound Fayum A occupation—3910 ±115 at *ca.* 17 m	Sediments recently deflated Deltaic beach	Kom W top (Fayum A) at 20.6 m Kom W base 3860 ±115 at *ca.* 17 m	Deltaic beach	Stone pavement, (landing facilities) at 22.3 m Old Kingdom pottery buried in beach sand (*ca.* 22 m) Old Kingdom pottery reworked down shore (18.5 m)
Red soil (?) at *ca.* 9 m Recessive beach with root casts								
Loose sand with snails grading into diatomaceous snail breccia Truncation	Diatomite Fluvial sand							
Desiccation cracks	Wadi cutting Swamp sediment	Occupation at Area A—5550 ±125 (12 m)						
Sandy silt	Diatomite Fine, silty sand							

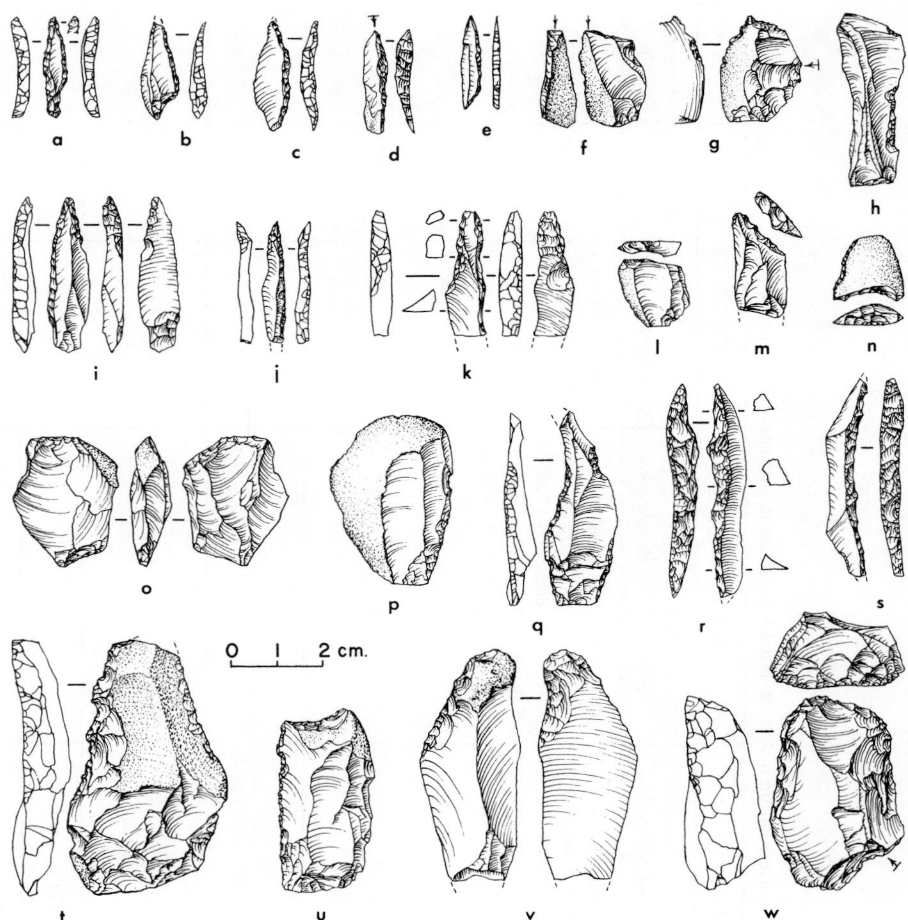

Figure 206. Tools from Site E29G1, Area E, Trench 4: (a) double-backed perforator; (b) *pointe a cran*; (c) arch-backed pointed bladelet; (d) straight-backed pointed bladelet; (e) scalene triangle; (f) burin; (g) groover; (h, p, v) retouched pieces; (i) perforator; (l, m) distal truncations; (n) basal truncation; (o) scaled piece; (q) partially backed and retouched blade; (r) hump-backed blade; (s) straight-backed blade; (t) denticulate; (u) distal truncation on retouched piece; (w) endscraper; (j, k) borers.

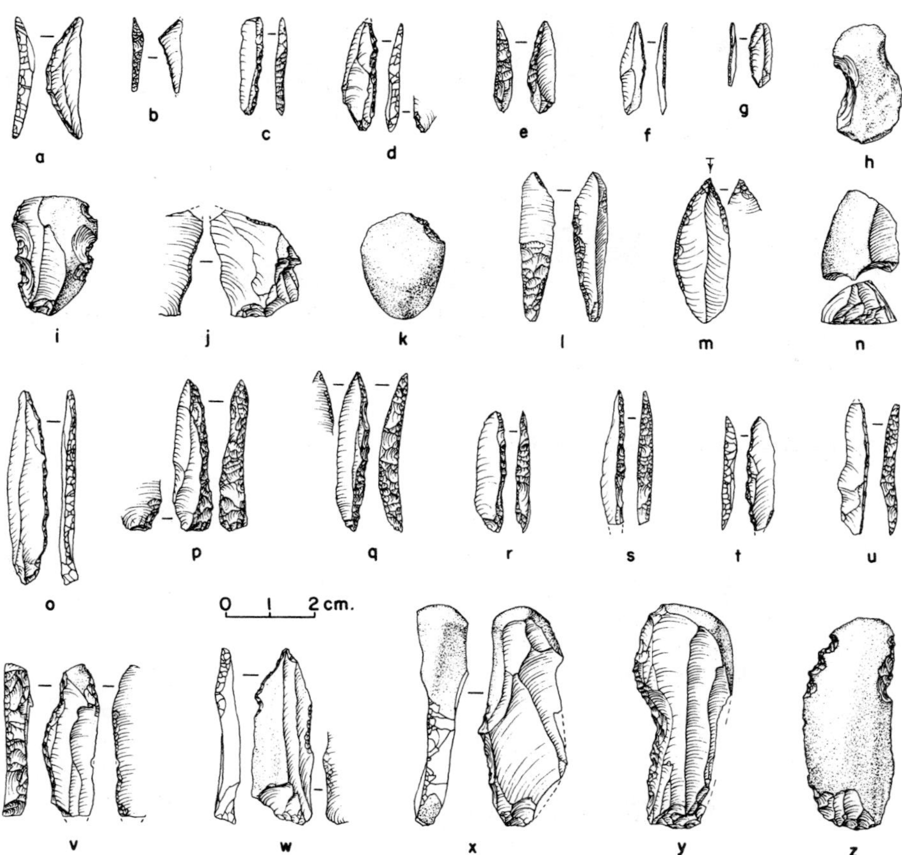

Figure 207. Tools from Site E29G3, Area A, Qarunian industry: (a) lunate; (b) scale triangle; (c) backed microblade fragment; (d) straight-backed partial microblade; (e) arch-backed partial microblade; (f, g) Ouchtata retouched microblade; (h) notched flake; (i) denticulated flake; (j, k) retouched flakes; (l, m) partial bladelets with normal and inverse retouch; (n) basal truncated flake; (o–q) arch-backed pointed bladelets; (r–u) straight-backed pointed bladelet; (v) arch-backed bladelet with inverse retouch; (w) groover, partially backed bladelet; (y) notched and retouched blade; (z) denticulated bladelet.

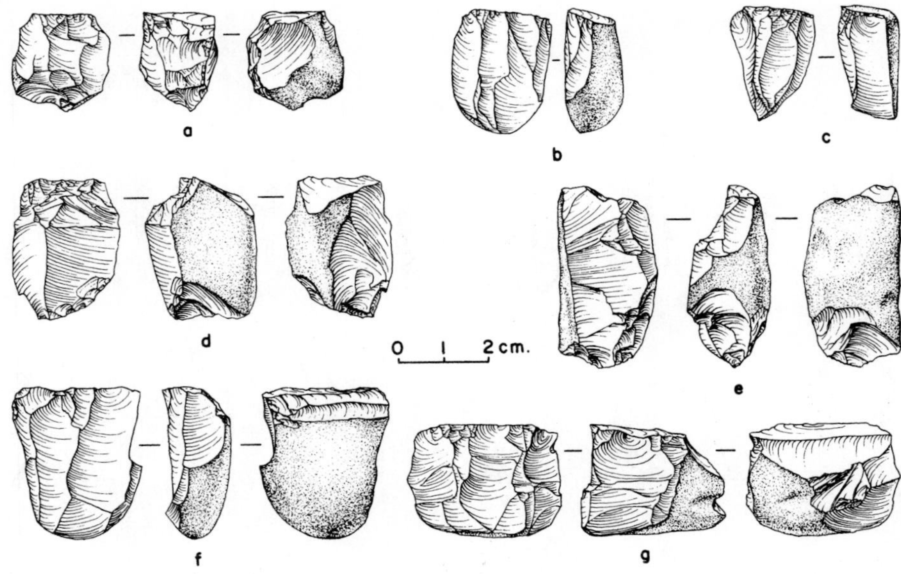

Figure 208. Cores from Site E29G3, Area A.

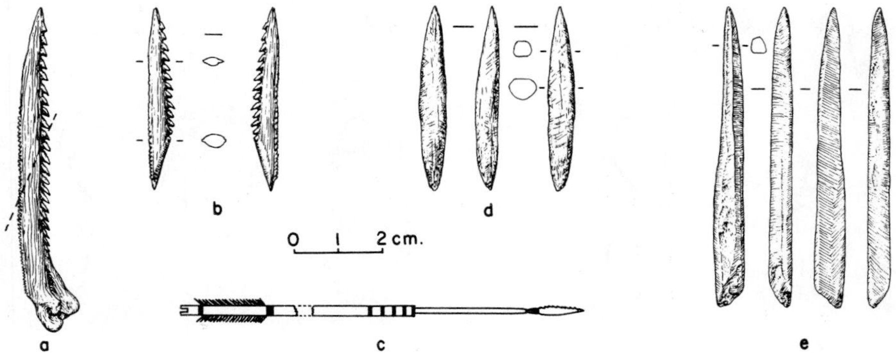

Figure 209. Bone tools from Site E29G1, Areas A and E: (a) unmodified pectoral spine from catfish; (b) point made from similar catfish pectoral spine; (c) Predynastic arrow from W. B. Emery, *Archaic Egypt*, 1961, p. 114, showing barbed point similar to (b); (d, e) bone points.

Krukowski variety forms the largest group. Endscrapers are usually present but very rare. There are no burins, and the few examples are atypical and may be cores. Double-backed perforators are present but extremely rare. Bone tools are also present but never common, and most of these are small "harpoons" made of modified catfish jaws (Figure 209). A series of Old Kingdom or Predynastic arrows from a tomb at Sakkara had several similar fish jaw points cemented to ivory foreshafts, which, in turn, were mounted on reed shafts

(Emery 1961: 113–114). There are also a few rather short, double-pointed, cylindrical bone points in the collections, like those reported from the Fayum by Caton-Thompson and Gardner (1934: Plate XLVII).

The Terminal Paleolithic Qarunian assemblages from the Fayum, characterized by extremely high percentages of backed bladelets and very low geometric components, seem to form a distinct industry, but one that falls within the general Nilotic and North African lithic complex. The close resemblance between the Qarunian and the Shamarkian is evident from an inspection of the cumulative graph comparing an assemblage from each industry (Figure 210). The main typological indices for two Qarunian assemblages are given in Table 17.

The Qarunian sites represent an economy that was clearly dependent on fishing as the major source of food. Large-mammal hunting and the grinding of grain were also practised, but these activities were not important at these localities. The Fayum Terminal Paleolithic sites, however, may reflect seasonal fish-harvesting occupations. It is quite likely that a very different economic emphasis might be indicated for the same group when they utilized a different microenvironmental situation, or in the base camps wherever they were located.

The first true Neolithic economy, with ceramics and food production, indicated by cultivated wheat and barley and domesticated animals, occurs in the Fayum around 4000 BC and presumably at the same time along the Nile proper. These Neolithic communities appear to have no connection, insofar as lithic components are concerned, with the preceding Terminal Paleolithic. The lithic technology in the Neolithic communities is based predominantly on flakes

Table 17. Main Typological Indices from Some Qarunian Sites

	E29H1A culture layer	*E29H1C culture layer*
Backed blades	2.3	2.8
Straight-backed bladelets (including pieces with altered bases)	14.1	12.7
Arch-backed bladelets (including pieces with altered bases)	18.9	29.3
Ouchtata	3.1	1.7
Other backed bladelets	12.6	21.0
Truncated bladelets and microflakes	3.1	8.8
Triangles	1.5	3.3
Trapezoids	—	1.1
Microburins, Krukowski	3.8	1.7
Microburins, ordinary	—	1.1
Endscrapers	—	1.1
Burins	0.7	1.1
Double-backed perforators	0.7	—
Other perforators	—	1.7
Retouched pieces (mostly bladelets)	9.4	—
Notches and denticulates	17.3	8.8

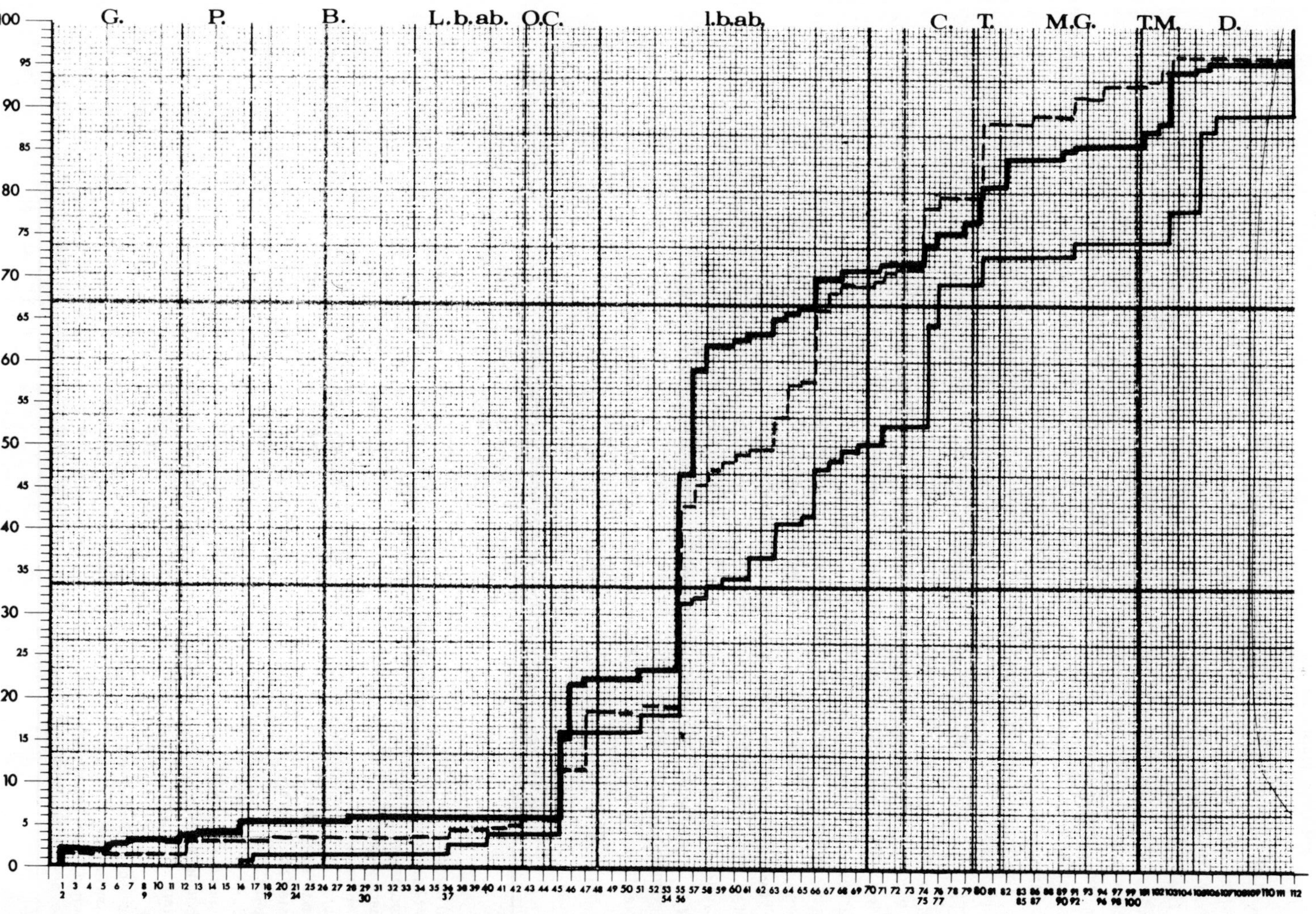

Figure 210. Cumulative graph of two sites of the Qarunian industry and one Shamarkian site, based on Tixier typology. Site E29H1, Area A—thin continuous line (128 pieces); Site E29H1, Area C—broken line (182 pieces); Site D1W-51, southern part—thick continuous line (622 pieces). Graph shows close similarity of two industries, an observation that is supported by the similarities in the main indices for the two groups.

produced by the hard-hammer technique. Bifacial tools made on thin tabular flint are common, as are stemmed and concave base projectile points, while the backed blades and bladelets, so common in the Terminal Paleolithic sites, are rare to absent in the Neolithic assemblages. A gap of about 1200 years separates the latest dated Terminal Paleolithic site from the earliest Neolithic community, but this seems to be far too little time for this basic transformation of lithic industries to occur. The appearance of a new population seems to be the best explanation. If so, the new population, and not its Paleolithic predecessors, was responsible for the development of the Egyptian civilization.

Appendix A

Diatoms from the Site E71K14, Area A, Trench 1, Upper Diatomaceous Silt (Unit 4, Figure 31)

WIESLAWA PRZYBYLOWSKA-LANGE

Diatoms from Site E71K14, Area A, Trench 1 Upper Diatomaceous Silt (Unit 4, Figure 31)

		Upper diatomite		
	Ecology	*1*	*2*	*4*
1. *Melosira ambigua (Grun.) O. Mull.*	(?)	+	r	r
2. *Melosira granulata (Ehr.) Ralfs.*[1]	alkaliphilous	+		
3. *Melosira varians Ag.*	(?)		+	+
4. *Cyclotella Meneghiniana Kutz*[2]	(?)	+		+
5. *Synedra capitata Ehr.*	alkaliphilous (–indifferent)	r	r	r
6. *Synedra ulna (Nitzch.) Ehr.*	alkaliphilous (–indifferent)	c	c	c
7. *Synedra ulna v. aequalis (Kutz.) Hust.*	alkaliphilous (–indifferent)	vc	vc	vc
8. *Synedra ulna v. biceps (Kutz.) Schonf.*	alkaliphilous (–indifferent)	vc	vc	vc
9. *Eunotia praerupta (Ehr.) Hust.*	acidophilous			+
10. *Coconeis placentula Ehr.*[3]	indifferent (–alkaliphilous)	c	c	r
11. *Coconeis placentula v. euglypta (Ehr.) Cl.*	indifferent (–alkaliphilous)	r	r	r
12. *Anemoeoneis sphaerophora (Kutz.) Pfitz.*	alkalibiontic	+	· r	
13. *Navicula criptocephala Kutz.*	alkaliphilous	+	+	
14. *Navicula cuspidata Kutz.*[4]	alkaliphilous			+
14a. *Navicula cuspidata Kutz. forma kratikularna*	alkaliphilous	r	r	r
15. *Navicula oblonga Kutz.*	indifferent (–alkaliphilous)	r	+	r
16. *Navicula radiosa Kutz*	indifferent	r	+	+
17. *Navicula sp.*	(?)	+	+	
18. *Pinnularia gibba v. linearis Hust.*	indifferent	r	r	
19. *Pinnularia viridys (Nitzch.) Ehr.*	indifferent	r	r	
20. *Caloneis silicula (Ehr.) Cl.*	alkaliphilous	+		
21. *Amphora ovalis Kutz.*	alkaliphilous	r	r	
22. *Amphora ovalis v. libyca (Ehr.) (Ehr.) Cl.*	alkaliphilous	r	r	r
23. *Amphora ovalis v. pediculus Kutz.*	alkaliphilous	r	r	r
24. *Amphora venete Kutz.*	indifferent		+	
25. *Cymbella affinis (Kutz.)*	alkaliphilous	+		r
26. *Cymbella cistula (Hemp.) Grun.*	alkaliphilous	r	+	+
27. *Cymbella cymbiformis (Ag. Kutz.) V. H.*	(?)	+	+	
28. *Cymbella lanceolata (Ehr.) V. H.*	alkaliphilous	+	+	

	Ecology	Upper diatomite 1	2	4
29. *Cymbella ventricosa Kutz.*	indifferent	+	+	
30. *Cymbella sp.*	(?)	+	+	+
31. *Gomphonema constrictum Ehr.*	indifferent		+	
32. *Gomphonema constrictum v. capitatum (Ehr.) Cl.*	indifferent			+
33. *Gomphonema lanceolatum Ehr.*[4]	alkaliphilous	r		
34. *Gomphonema parvulum v. micropus (Kutz.) Cl.*	indifferent	r	+	+
35. *Epithemia sorex Kutz.*[4]	alkaliphilous	r	r	
36. *Epithemia turgida (Ehr.) Kutz.*	alkalibiontic	vc	vc	vc
37. *Epithemia turgida v. capitata Fricke*	alkalibiontic	c	c	c
38. *Epithemia turgida v. granulata (Ehr.) Grun.*	alkalibiontic	r	r	r
39. *Epithemia zebra (Ehr.) Kutz.*	alkalibiontic	r	r	r
40. *Epithemia zebra vmporcellus (Kutz) Grun.*	alkalibiontic	c	c	r
41. *Rhopalodia gibba (Ehr.) O. Mull.*	alkalibiontic	r	r	r
42. *Rhopalodia gibba v. ventricosa (Ehr.) Grun.*	alkalibiontic	r	r	+
43. *Nitzschia amphibia Grun.*	alkaliphilous	vc	vc	c
44. *Nitzschia sigmoidea (Ehr.) W. Sm.*	(?)	+		
45. *Cymatopleura elliptica (Breb) W. Sm.*	alkaliphilous		r	x
46. *Surirella ovata Kutz.*	alkaliphilous	+		

[1]Deep water specimens.

[2]Having rather restricted distribution; cold temperature.

[3]Littoral forms.

[4]Cosmopolitan with topical affinities.

r = rare
c = common
vc = very common
+ = present

Appendix B

Mineral Analysis of Samples from Site E71K14, Areas A and D

ROMAN CHLEBOWSKI

Mineral Analysis of Samples from Sites E71K14, Areas A and D

	Lower silt 14A	*Loose dune 14A*	*Hard dune 14A*	*Lower diatomite 14A*	*Middle silt 14A*	*Upper diatomite 14A*	*Fine pond sediments 14D*	*Beach sediments 14A*	*Upper silt 14A*	*Upper silt 14D*
Heavy										
1. Anatase	trace	—	trace	—	0.5	0.5	—	—	—	trace
2. Andalusite	trace	0.5	trace	0.5	—	trace	—	—	trace	—
3. Apatite	trace	—	—	0.5	0.5	—	trace	—	trace	trace
4. Biotite	1.5	1.0	1.5	1.0	2.0	0.5	0.5	1.5	0.5	1.0
5. Zircon	5.0	8.0	9.0	11.0	8.5	8.0	10.0	9.0	5.0	9.0
6. Dysten	1.0	0.5	1.5	0.5	2.5	1.0	1.0	—	2.0	1.5
7. Epidote	6.0	7.0	3.5	6.0	6.0	9.5	5.0	6.0	6.0	6.0
8. Glauconite	1.0	trace	trace	0.5	0.7	0.5	0.5	0.5	1.0	1.0
9. Garnet	1.5	2.0	1.5	2.5	1.0	2.0	1.8	1.5	3.0	1.5
10. Hornblende	34.0	25.0	35.0	26.0	32.0	28.0	24.0	28.0	34.0	34.0
11. Monazite	0.5	trace	trace	—	0.3	0.5	0.2	—	trace	trace
12. Pyroxenes	11.0	18.0	10.0	10.0	10.0	12.0	9.0	16.0	10.0	6.0
13. Rutile	2.0	1.5	2.5	2.0	2.5	1.5	3.0	2.5	3.0	1.0
14. Staurolite	1.5	1.5	3.0	2.0	1.0	3.5	9.0	3.0	1.5	2.0
15. Sillimanite	—	0.2	trace	trace	—	trace	trace	trace	—	trace
16. Tourmaline	1.5	1.5	2.5	3.5	2.5	2.0	2.0	2.0	2.0	1.5
17. Opaque minerals	33.0	33.0	30.0	34.0	30.0	30.0	41.0	30.0	32.0	35.0
Light										
1. Quartz	87.0	91.0	95.0	81.0	88.0	82.0	82.0	92.0	93.0	86.0
2. Potash feldspars (mainly microclime)	5.5	2.5	3.5	5.5	6.0	4.5	6.0	2.5	4.5	7.5
3. Plugioclase	1.0	1.5	1.0	2.0	2.0	1.5	0.5	1.5	trace	1.5
4. Calcite	5.0	3.5	—	11.0	2.5	11.0	11.0	3.5	1.0	3.0
5. Muscovite	1.5	0.5	0.5	0.5	1.5	1.0	0.5	0.5	1.5	2.0

Appendix C

Analysis of Grain from Sites E71K14 and E71K15

JANINA KOSSAKOWSKA-SUCH

Analysis of Grain Size from Sites E71K14 and E71K15

	Loose dune K14		*Top of dune (cemented) K14A*		*Lower diatomite K14A*		*Middle silt K14A*		*Upper diatomite K14A*	
	g	*%*	*g*	*%*	*g*	*%*	*g*	*%*	*g*	*%*
Above 2.00 mm	—	—	—	—	0.15	0.40	0.02	0.02	0.51	0.95
2.00–1.0	0.15	0.08	0.45	0.02	0.69	1.98	0.29	0.32	1.36	2.61
1.00–0.75	25.05	12.90	14.07	6.50	1.90	5.44	1.21	1.32	1.80	3.36
0.75–0.50	1.40	0.73	2.37	1.10	0.30	0.85	0.14	0.15	0.10	0.18
0.50–0.25	85.00	43.80	49.20	22.80	0.25	0.70	1.81	1.98	1.42	2.65
0.25–0.125	56.00	28.90	59.45	27.60	4.59	13.20	6.66	7.15	6.75	12.60
0.125–0.09	12.66	6.72	26.15	12.10	3.32	9.53	13.15	14.34	9.00	16.85
0.09–0.06	3.53	1.55	18.75	8.70	2.57	7.40	8.89	9.72	4.50	8.40
below 0.06	10.21	5.32	45.35	21.00	20.91	60.50	59.43	65.00	28.06	52.40
	194.00	100.00	215.74	100.00	20.91	100.00	91.60	100.00	53.50	100.00

Upper silt K14A		*Pond sediment K14D*		*Upper silt K14D*		*Sand interfingering with upper diatomite K14A*		*Lower silt K14A*		*Pond sediment K15*	
g	*%*	*g*	*%*	*g*	*%*	*g*	*%*	*g*	*%*	*g*	*%*
0.28	0.39	1.70	1.09	0.65	0.46	—	—	1.78	1.75	—	—
0.52	0.72	1.70	1.09	1.44	1.02	0.14	0.11	0.33	0.34	0.02	0.01
0.75	1.03	1.88	1.21	3.14	2.25	3.47	2.86	0.42	0.43	0.72	0.49
0.10	0.14	0.25	0.16	0.43	0.30	1.27	1.05	0.14	0.15	0.01	0.01
1.54	2.12	22.10	14.30	7.40	5.22	47.80	39.40	4.32	4.23	5.45	3.71
5.29	7.30	54.80	35.35	8.10	5.72	53.50	44.10	8.22	8.10	43.17	29.40
7.01	9.70	35.10	22.60	7.25	5.12	8.42	6.96	8.29	8.15	67.62	45.95
3.25	4.50	9.78	6.30	4.75	3.36	1.87	1.55	6.85	6.75	13.10	8.90
53.71	74.10	27.86	17.90	108.76	76.55	4.80	3.97	72.15	70.10	16.96	11.53
72.45	100.00	155.17	100.00	141.92	100.00	121.27	100.00	102.50	100.00	147.05	100.00

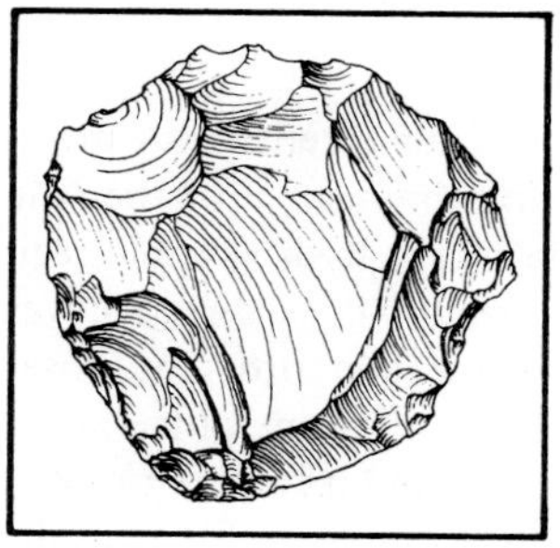

Appendix D

Heavy Mineral Analysis of Some Pleistocene Sediments in the Nile Valley

FEKRI A. HASSAN

Introduction

The mineralogy of Nilotic sediments has received the attention of many investigators because of its implications for deciphering the history of the Nile and determining the age of the establishment of the recent hydrographic regimen. Initially, the mineralogic composition of recent Nile sediments was revealed as a by-product of investigations for economic and other purposes (Judd 1886, 1897; Cayeux 1929; Bowman 1931). Later, an outstanding systematic study of the recent sediments of the Main Nile and its tributaries was undertaken by Shukri (1950, 1951). In addition, Shukri presented the results of heavy mineral analysis of older sediments, some of which were exposed in prehistoric sites. The results of a systematic study on the Quaternary sediments in the Fayum Depression soon followed (Shukri and Azer 1952). The authors utilized the stratigraphic classification formulated by Sandford and Arkell (1929) in locating their samples. Samples were obtained from "Plio–Pleistocene" gravels, "Lower Paleolithic" gravels. "Middle Paleolithic" sands, and "Upper Paleolithic" and "Post-Paleolithic" (historic) deposits. On the basis of their analyses and by analogy with the mineralogy of the sediments of the recent Nile tributaries, Shukri and Azer (1952) concluded that the Ethiopian tributaries were connected with the Nile in Lower Paleolithic times, but that the influx of material from these tributaries was not as great as in Middle Paleolithic and more recent times. Unfortunately, the dating of the terraces by Sanford and Arkell, which formed the basis for Shukri and Azer's conclusions, is unreliable. It was not until the 1960s that a more coherent stratigraphic framework became established (see, for example, Butzer & Hansen 1968, and Wendorf *et al.* 1970, and this volume).

Revision of the prehistory of Egypt and Nubia has also undermined some of Sandford and Arkell's conclusions. For example, the Sebilian industry, used to define the Upper Paleolithic in Sandford and Arkell's classification, has been bracketed recently between *ca.* 13,000 and 10,000 BC. (cf. Smith 1966; Marks 1968). It may be also noted that the so-called "Lower Paleolithic" sediments in the Fayum region did not contain any "Lower Paleolithic" artifacts and were identified as such solely by analogy with "Lower Paleolithic" terraces in the Nile Valley proper. Temporal variation in the mineralogy of Nilotic sediments, in the light of the recent work on the stratigraphy of the Quaternary sediments of the Nile, is the subject of this study. The results indicate that the modern Nile regimen was in existence during the Late Acheulian.

Samples

The samples investigated were obtained from geological sections exposed at archaeological sites and from formations of older age. The first group of samples were obtained from the geological sections at Site E6101 (Dandara and

Qena units), Site E71C2 (Nag El-Zamami area, Sahaba and Deir El-Fakhuri deposits), Site 68/2 (Mahgar Canal, Sahaba unit), Site 67/2B (El-Kilh area, Dibeira-Jer unit), and Site 67/8A (Isna area, Deir El-Fakhuri deposits), and Sites E61M1-10 (Dishna area, Dishna playa deposits). Samples from older formations, unassociated with archaeological material, were obtained from Kom El-Shellul Formation (Pliocene) and the "Lower Pleistocene" deposits at Abydos (Sohag, left Bank), Wadi El-Aball (Beni Suef), Wadi Talun (near Mena House, Giza), and El-Kola (Nag Hammadi, right bank).[1]

The Kom El-Shellul Formation consists of marine deposits of late Pliocene age. It consists of a section of cross-laminated sand overlying a section of fossiliferous limestone with *Ostrea cucullata*, marl, and shale. The sample analyzed was obtained from the top sand bed. The Abydos deposits are represented in a chain of hills which outskirt the Limestone Plateau in the neighborhood of El-Balyana (Sohag). A section of 12 m of cross-laminated sands is overlain by 10 m of shale. The section is capped by 3.5 m of conglomerate mixed with travertine followed by 2 m of Red Breccia (*Brocattelli*). The samples were obtained from the lower sandy beds. The deposits at Wadi Talun consist of a very thick section (about 80 m) of cross-laminated sands, topped with gravels and sands (10 m). Wadi El-Aball sediments consist of brownish sand with heavily patinated gravels, which crop out in low hills on the east bank of the Nile near Beni Suef. The El-Kola deposits consist of reddish to pinkish sands, which crop out near El-Kola (Nag Hammadi) beside an irrigation canal.

The Dandara unit is represented in a remnant knoll of silt and a few layers of very fine sand, near Hathor Temple (Dandara, Qena province). The sands of Qena Unit overlie unconformably the Dandara silt and appear in several localities in the same area. The Dibeira-Jer, Ballana and Sahaba Units consist of Nilotic silts, which are reported from many localities in Nubia and Upper Egypt. They belong to the Nile aggradational episodes. The Deir El-Fakhuri deposits, which are associated with the Sahaba aggradation, consist of pond sediments. The Dishna playa deposits belong to the terminal part of the Sahaba aggradation. The formation of the playas was interrupted by siltation as a result of an episode of exceptionally high floods (*ca.* 10,000 BC.). Detailed description of these upper Pleistocene formations may be found in this volume and in Said *et al.* (1970).

The samples were disaggregated by gentle crushing and treated at first by dilute hydrochloric acid to free them from their calcareous content. Ferruginous

[1]All samples were collected by the author, except those from Isna, El-Kilh, and Dishna, which were supplied by R. Said. I wish to express here my debt to Dr. Said for this material and for his encouragement. The samples from Dandara (Qena), Mahgar Canal (Qena), and Nag El-Zamami (Luxor) were collected in conjunction with the Joint Expedition of Southern Methodist University, the Polish Academy of Science, and the Egyptian Geological Survey (1968) under the direction of Fred Wendorf. It was a great privilege for me to have been a member of the expedition, and I am deeply grateful to Dr. Wendorf for that opportunity.

samples were boiled in a stannous chloride solution. The samples were then washed thoroughly, dried, and sieved. The fraction of 0.062–0.125 mm was then separated by wet sieving and dried.

The dry 0.062–0.125 mm fraction was separated into heavy and light crops using bromoform. Part of the heavy mineral crop was separated by micro-splitting and mounted in Canada balsam on slides. Two or three slides of each sample were usually prepared.

The slides were examined microscopically for identification and the minerals present were counted. Chlorite, muscovite, and biotite were not counted with the heavy minerals. The value of their specific gravity makes their separation by bromoform incomplete. A number of around 300 grains was counted, and the resulting counts were expressed in percentages.

Results and Discussion

The results of the heavy mineral analysis are listed in Table D–1. The major mineral constituents consist of: amphiboles represented mainly by greenish hornblende; pyroxenes, represented predominantly by augite; epidotes, represented mainly by pistachite; and opaque minerals, represented mostly by magnetite and ilmenite. Rare constituents include apatite, corundum, fluorite, garnet, kyanite, rutile, sillimanite, staurolite, topaz, tourmaline, and zircon. These minerals are described in detail by Shukri (1950, 1951) and Shukri and Azer (1952).

Marked variations exist in the frequency of these mineral constituents, but the variations in amphiboles, pyroxenes, and epidotes are especially significant, first because they are present in appreciable amounts that minimize random deviations and, second, because of the sensitivity of these minerals to the source of Nilotic material. The significance of these minerals in detecting changes in the source of the material delivered into the Nile has been noted by Shukri (1950, 1951). At present, the Nile has two systems of tributaries: the Ethiopian tributaries, represented by the Blue Nile and the Atbara, and a complex system that contributes to the White Nile. The material contributed by the Ethiopian tributaries which dominates the Nilotic sediments today is characterized by their richness in pyroxenes (Table D–2). In contrast, the White Nile sediments are extremely poor in these minerals. The frequency of epidotes in the sediments of the White Nile also is about twice their frequency in the Ethiopian tributaries.

The frequency of amphiboles, pyroxenes, and epidotes in the Main Nile and the White Nile is shown in Fig. D–1 to serve as a point of reference. It will be immediately clear from this figure that the frequency of the above mentioned minerals in the Dandara, Sahaba, and Dibeira-Jer units is very similar to that of the recent main Nile with its dual system of tributaries dominated by the Ethiopian system. A sample of marl obtained from the top layers in the Dandara unit (Site E6101, previously referred to as 68/8), dated "more than 39,900

Table D–1. Percentage of Heavy Minerals.

		Opaque minerals	*Hornblende*	*Augite*	*Epidote*	*Others*
Kom El-Shellul		95.0	+	—	+	4.5
Abydos						
	1	59.5	1.0	—	20.0	19.5
	2	60.0	+	—	22.5	17.0
	3	58.0	+	—	22.0	19.5
	5	84.5	—	—	12.0	4.0
Wadi el Aball		73.0	+	—	12.5	14.0
Wadi Talun						
	1	56.0	7.0	—	28.0	9.0
	2	49.0	10.0	—	31.5	9.5
	3	45.5	8.0	—	41.5	5.0
	8	46.5	14.5	—	22.5	16.5
El-Kola		47.0	7.0	—	20.0	26.0
Dandara Unit						
Dandara	4	29.0	31.5	15.0	13.5	11.0
	6	36.5	31.0	19.0	11.0	2.5
	7	27.0	13.0	30.0	14.5	15.5
Qena Unit						
Dandara	1	20.0	24.5	11.5	25.5	18.5
	2	14.0	40.0	13.0	20.0	13.0
	3	45.5	8.5	13.0	17.0	16.0
Dibiera-Jer Unit						
El-Kilh Site 67/2B		17.5	31.5	28.0	16.0	7.0
Deir El-Fakhuri deposits						
Isna Site 67/8A		25.0	49.0	2.5	11.0	12.5
Nag Zamami, Luxor		23.0	25.0	27.0	16.5	8.5
Sahaba Unit						
Isna		24.0	28.0	23.0	13.5	11.5
Nag Zamami 1		42.5	15.5	25.0	9.0	8.0
Nag Zamami 2		26.5	27.0	31.0	8.0	7.5
Mahgar Canal, Qena		48.0	6.0	21.0	9.0	16.0
Dishna Playa deposits						
Dishna		27.5	20.5	22.5	14.0	15.5

Table D–2. Frequency of Major Heavy Minerals in the Recent Sediments of the Nile Sediments[a]

	Opaque minerals	*Amphiboles*	*Pyroxenes*	*Epidotes*
White Nile	26.0	35.0	1.0	21.0
Blue Nile	15.0	56.0	15.0	11.0
Atbara	12.5	6.5	75.0	+[b]
Blue Nile and Atbara	14.0	31.0	45.0	6.0
Main Nile (north of Atbara)	28.0	32.0	30.0	6.0

[a] After Shukri (1951).

[b] (+) less than 1%.

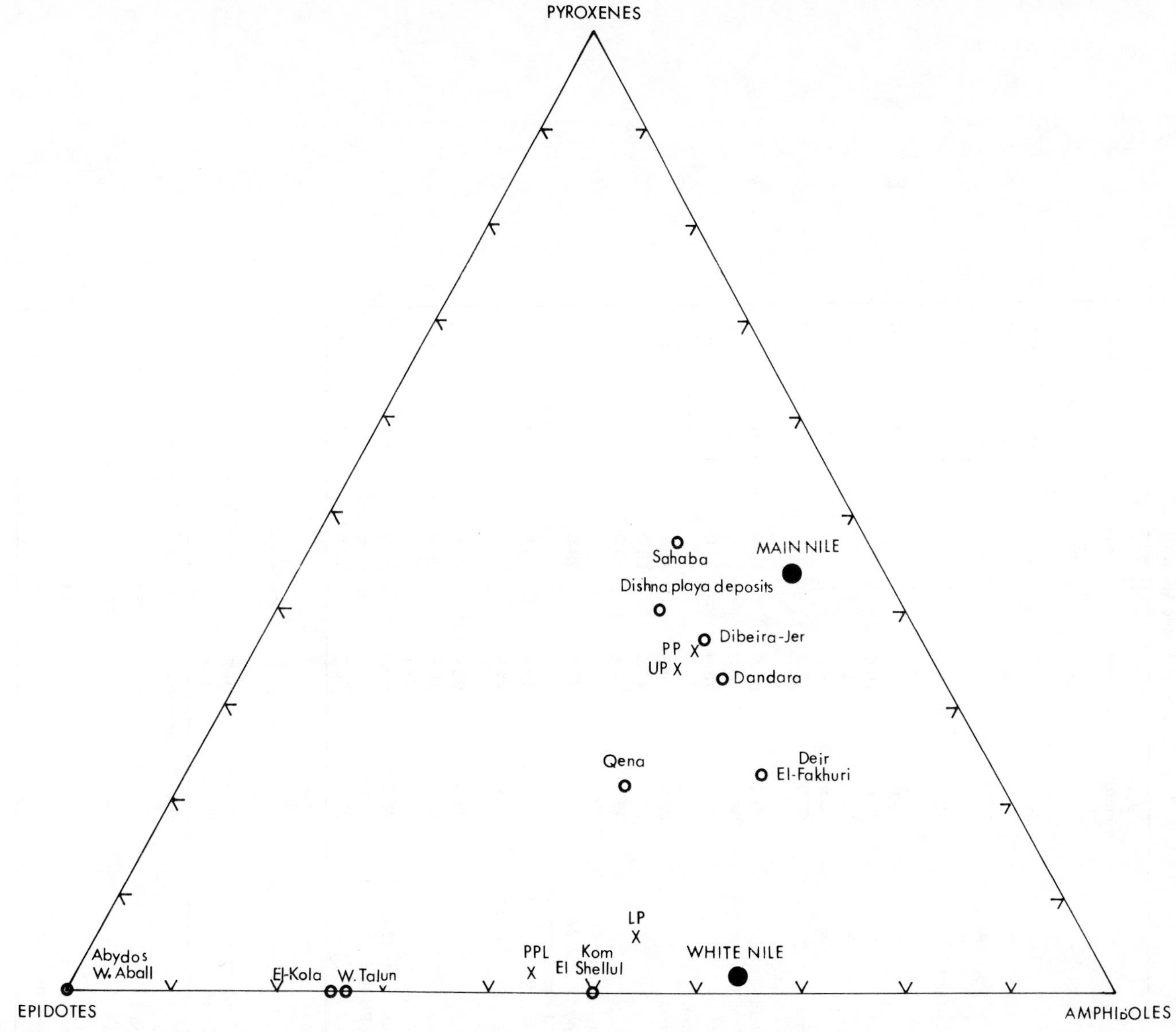

Figure D–1. Frequency of pyroxenes, epidotes, and amphiboles in some Quaternary and recent Nile sediments. PPL, LP, MP, UP, PP refer to Shukri's (1951) Plio–Pleistocene, Lower Paleolithic, Middle Paleolithic, Upper Paleolithic, and Post-Paleolithic, respectively.

years BP (I-3423) [Said *et al.* 1970: 44]." Late Acheulian artifacts were also found *in situ* in this formation at Site E6101 (ibid). There is, then, little doubt that the modern Nile system was fully established with as great an influx of material from Ethiopia as in more recent and present-day times by the later part of the Lower Paleolithic.

The implication of this result for the dating of the establishment of the recent Nile system and the history of the Nile are of great importance. These implications have been discussed by Wendorf *et al.* (1970: 1163) and Said *et al.* (1970: 47–48) when the preliminary results of mineral analysis were available. The Dibeira-Jer silts once viewed as representative of the first episode of silt deposition by the modern Nile regimen (de Heinzelin 1968: 47) no longer qualify as such (see Wendorf and Schild, this volume).

Older sediments from Abydos, W. El-Aball, El-Kola, and Wadi Talun lack the pyroxenes and show a relatively high content of epidotes (Table D–1). The deposits of the Pliocene sediments at Kom El-Shellul are also deficient in pyroxenes. In this respect, these sediments are similar to those of the White Nile in which the frequency of pyroxenes is very low (Fig. D–1).

It is interesting to note that the Deir El-Fakhuri deposits exhibit a lower content of pyroxenes than that of either the Dibeira-Jer or the Sahaba units (Table D–1 and Fig. D–1). These seem to represent ponding intervals with somewhat greater non-Ethiopian influx.

Qena sands exhibit a definite reduction in pyroxenes compared with Dandara silts. These sands were deposited under conditions of local rainfall in Egypt as evidenced by the presence of locally derived gravel. The gravels were derived from the basement, complex rocks of the Eastern Desert hills. The Nile course was thus located west of its present location, and the local influents were sufficiently competent to transport the gravel over a long distance. Local rainfall and perhaps an increasing influx from the non-Ethiopian tributaries might have diluted the Ethiopian element. A reduction in the Ethiopian contribution is also probable.

The Dishna playa deposits contain a mineralogic suite very similar to that of the Sahaba and thus do not seem to reflect a different hydrographic setting from that under which the Sahaba silts were deposited.

It may be instructive here to compare the present results with those obtained by Shukri and Azer (1952). It is obvious that the so-called "Upper Paleolithic" sediments, which would be regarded today as "Late Paleolithic," and the "Middle Paleolithic" sediments are very similar to those of the Dibeira-Jer, Sahaba, and Dandara units, as well as the recent Main Nile (Figure D–1). On the other hand, the so-called "Lower Paleolithic" and "Plio-Pleistocene" sediments are similar to the older Wadi Talun, El-Kola, and Kom El-Shellul deposits, all bearing greater resemblance to the White Nile than to the Main Nile. It would seem then that by comparison with the Dandara unit, Shukri's so called "Lower Paleolithic" sediments are pre-Late Acheulian. Our understanding of the early phases of the development of the River Nile will undoubtedly be vastly improved when reliable dates are obtained on the old Nilotic deposits not covered by the range of radiocarbon dating.

To recapitulate, during the Pliocene and Lower Pleistocene, the hydrographic system of the Nile was greatly different from that of today. Connection with the Ethiopian tributaries was not yet established, or if it did it was at such a scale that it did not leave a perceptible evidence in the mineralogic record. The Nile was fed primarily from its White Nile sources and from the local tributaries in Egypt and the Sudan. The modern Nile system, with a major discharge from the Ethiopian tributaries was in existence by the end of the Lower Paleolithic.

References

Bowman, T. S.
1931 Report on borings for oil in Egypt, Section 3, Eastern Desert and adjoining islands. *Geological Survey of Egypt.*

Butzer, K. W.
1959 Contribution to the Pleistocene geology of the Nile Valley. *Erdkunde* **13**:46–67.

Butzer, K. W. & C. L. Hansen
1968 Les roches sedimentaires de France: Roches siliceuses. *Mem. serv. Carte geol. France.*

Fairbridge, R. W.
1963 Nile sedimentation above Wadi Halfa during the last 20,00 years. *Kush* **11**:96–107.

DeHeinzelin, J.
1968 Geological history of the Nile Valley in Nubia. In *The prehistory of Nubia,* edited by F. Wendorf, Vol. I. Dallas: Fort Burgwin Research Center and Southern Methodist Univ. Press. Pp. 461–531.

Judd, J. W.
1886 Report on a series of specimens of the deposits of the Nile Delta, obtained by the recent boring operations undertaken by the Royal Society: *Proceedings Royal Society* **61**:32–40.

Marks, A. E.
1968 The Sebilian industry of the Second Cataract. In *The prehistory of Nubia,* edited by F. Wendorf, Vol. I. Dallas: Fort Burgwin Research Center and Southern Methodist Univ. Press. Pp. 461–531.

Philip, G. & Youssk
1965 Mineral composition of some Nile Delta sediments near Cairo. *Bulletin of the Faculty of Science (Cairo)* **39**:231–252.

Said, R., F. Wendorf, & R. Schild
1970 The geology and prehistory of the Nile Valley in Upper Egypt. *Archaeologia Polona* **12**:43–60.

Sandford, K. S. & W. J. Arkell
1929 *Paleolithic man and the Nile-Fayum Divide,* Publ. X. Univ. Chicago Oriental Inst.

Shukri, N. M.
1950 The mineralogy of some Nile sediments: *Quarterly Journal of the Geological Society, London* **105**:511–534; **106**:466–467.
1951 Mineral analysis tables of some Nile sediments. *Bulletin of the Institute Desert (Cairo)* **1**:10–67.

Shukri, N. M. & N. Azer
1952 The mineralogy of Pliocene and more recent sediments in the Fayum. *Bulletin of the Institute Desert (Cairo)* **1**:10–53.

Smith, P. E. L.
1966 The Late Paleolithic of Northeast Africa in the light of recent research. *American Anthropologist* **68**:326–355.

Wendorf, Fred, Rushdi Said, & R. Schild
1970 Egyptian prehistory: Some new concepts. *Science* **169**:1161–1171.

Appendix E

X-Ray Mineralogy of Some Quaternary Nile Sediments

FEKRI A. HASSAN
ABDEL-KADDER ATTIA

Samples were washed thoroughly with distilled water and treated with H_2O_2 to remove decayed organic matter, if present. The samples were them disaggregated using a mortar with a rubber pestle to prevent grinding. The clay fraction was separated from the sample by a 200-mesh screen. The samples were then immersed in a 4% solution of sodium hexametaphosphate for 24 hours in 1-liter glass cylinders. Three oriented slides were prepared for each sample: one was used as such (untreated); the second was glycolated; while the third was heated at 550° C for 1-½ hours. The X-ray diffractograms were obtained with nickel-filtered copper radiation (λ = 1.5418 Å) at 36 kv and 16 ma potential using a scanning speed of 1–2 θ/min.

Many of the samples, namely those from the Sahaba unit (Isna, Nag El-Zamami), Deir El-Fakhuri (Isna, Nag El-Zamami), and Qena unit (Dandara, Qena) did not give a conspicuous pattern. Such result is frequent, particularly in the case of montmorillonite-rich clays. Such poor diffraction patterns can result from (1) amorphous ferruginous oxides, (2) the presence of exchangeable cations which produce poor reflection, and (3) degraded structure resulting from diagenesis.

Clear patterns were obtained, however, for samples from the Dandara unit, the Dishna playa sediments (terminal Sahaba beds), Dishna lower "wadi" beds (basal Sahaba or pre-Sahaba), and older sediments (Plio–Pleistocene to Lower Pleistocene?). The peaks (basal reflection maxima) indicate that the clay mineral groups present in the samples examined consist of montmorillonite, illite, kaolinite, and chlorite (Figure E–1). Montmorillonite–illite structure is also observed. Montmorillonite was identified by a broad peak at about 14 Å, which shifted upon glycolation to 15–17 Å. Illite was identified by diffraction maxima at 10, 5, and 3.3 Å, which do not change upon glycolation. Chlorite is indicated by diffraction maxima at 4.7 Å and 14 Å, not affected by glycol treatment. Kaolinite is indicated by a diffraction maximum at 7, which disappears upon heating, and by another maximum at 3.5 (also characteristic of chlorite).

Montmorillonite is the predominant mineral group in all samples examined. Illite and kaolinte are less prominent, and chlorite even less so. The pattern of Pleistocene modern Nile sediments, including that of the Dandara unit, resembles strongly that of a recent sample from Qena (Figure E–1). El-Gabaly and Khadr (1962), Hamdi (1967), and Venkatarathnam and Ryan (1971) also report that recent Nile sediments are similarly rich in montmorillonite. In addition, a study by Butzer and Hansen (1968) revealed that the sediments of the Korosko, Masmas, and G. Silsila Formations consist predominantly of montmorillonite.

The strong resemblance between the diffraction pattern of the sample from the Dandara Formation with other sediments deposited under the modern Nile regimen is in agreement with the results of heavy mineral analysis (Hassan, in this volume). It must be noted, however, that a sample from older Nilotic sediments, which are attributed to a different Nile regimen without the Ethiopian tributaries, showed a great richness in montmorillonite (Figure E–1). Illite was also present, but kaolinite was underrepresented. Giegengack (1968), however, observed that the clay fraction in early Nile gravels consists mainly of kaolinite.

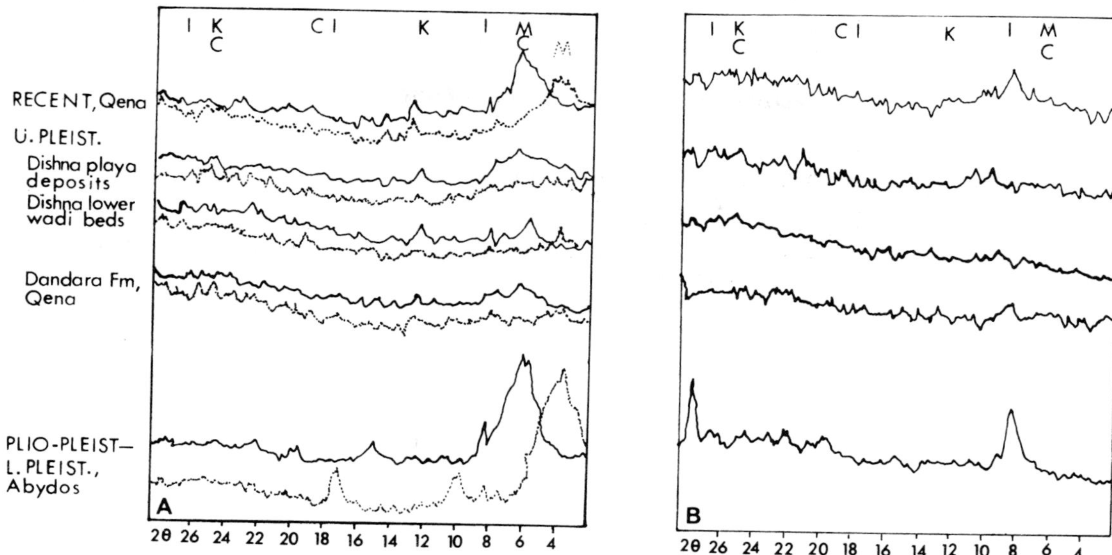

Figure E–1. X-ray diffractograms of the clay fraction of some Quaternary Nile sediments and a recent sample from Qena; (A) untreated (solid line) and glycolated (dotted line) samples; (B) heated samples; (M) montmorillonite; (K) kaolinite; (I) illite; (C) chlorite.

Further work is needed on the clay mineralogy of the sediments ante-dating the modern regimen before their identity can be clearly understood. A systematic study of the clay mineralogy of recent Nile sediments of the different tributaries of the Nile also would be useful in tracing mineral provenances. The abundance of montmorillonite in the sediments belonging to the modern Nile system, for example, seems to be in accordance with the high frequency of this mineral group in the late Pleistocene sediments in Ethiopia (Finck 1961). Generally, montmorillonite is a common weathering product of basalt in Africa (Grim 1968). Extensive exposures of basalt are widespread in Ethiopia and are major contributors to the material delivered into the Nile (Shukri 1950).

References

Butzer, K. W. & C. L. Hansen
1968 *Desert and river in Nubia.* Madison, Wisconsin: Univ. of Wisconsin Press.

Finck, A.
1961 Classification of Gizira clay soils. *Journal of Soil Science* 92:263–67.

El-Gabaly, M. M., and M. Khadr
1962 Clay mineral studies of some Egyptian Desert and alluvial soils. *Journal of Soil Science* 13:333–342.

Giegengack, Jr., R. F.
1968 *Late Pleistocene history of the Nile Valley in Egyptian Nubia.* Ph.D. dissertation, Yale University.

Grim, R. E.
1968 *Clay mineralogy.* McGraw-Hill: New York.

Hamdi, H.
1967 The mineralogy of the fine fraction of alluvial soils of Egypt. *U.A.R. Journal of Soil Science* 7:15–21.

Shukri, N. M.
1950 The mineralogy of some Nile sediments: *Quarterly Journal of the Geological Society (London)* **105**:511–534;**106**:466–467.

Venkatarathnam, K. & W. B. F. Ryan
1971 Dispersal patterns of clay minerals in sediments of the eastern Mediterranean Sea. *Marine Geology* 11:261–282.

Appendix F

Granulometric Analysis of the Sand Fraction of Some Quaternary Nile Sediments

FEKRI A. HASSAN

Samples for this study were obtained from the Dandara unit (Qena), Qena unit (Qena), Dibeira-Jer unit (Nag El-Zamami, near Luxor), Sahaba unit (Nag El-Zamami, near Luxor; Mahgar Canal, near Qena), Dishna playa deposits (terminal Sahaba, Dishna), Deir El-Fakhuri deposits (Isna), and Ballana sand (Ballana Formation, Isna; Nag El-Zamami). Samples from older sediments were obtained from Abydos (Sohag) and El-Kola (Nag Hammadi).

Samples were disaggregated, when necessary, by hand. The carbonate fraction was then removed with dilute hydrochloric acid. Fifty grams of the dried sand were screened through a set of sieves with openings of 2.0, 1.0, 0.5, 0.25, 0.125, and 0.062 mm. A mechanical shaker was used for a period of 30 min. The weights of the fractions of the different size grades were then estimated. From these results, the percentiles 1, 5, 10, 16, 84, 90, 95, 99, the first and third quartiles (Q_1, Q_3), the median (Md), the mean (M_z), the sorting coefficient(S), the skewedness (S_k), and the graphic Kurtosis (K_G) were calculated. The following formulae given by Folk (1966) were used:

$$S = \frac{\phi_{84}-\phi_{16}}{4} + \frac{\phi_{95}-\phi_5}{6.6}$$

$$S_k = \frac{\phi_{84}+\phi_{16}-2\phi_{50}}{2(\ 84-16\ )} + \frac{\phi_{95}+\phi_5-2\phi_{50}}{2(\ 95-5\ )}$$

$$K_G = \frac{\phi_{95}-\phi_5}{2.44(\phi_{75}-\phi_{25})}$$

$$M_z = \frac{\phi_{16}+\phi_{50}+\phi_{84}}{3}$$

The average values of these statistical parameters for each stratigraphic unit are shown in Table F–1. The results are also represented graphically in Figure F–1. The sands of the old Nile sediments which ante-date the modern Nile system are medium in size, whereas those of the Dandara unit, the Sahaba unit, and the Ballana sand are fine grained. The sands of the Dibeira-Jer unit, Dishna playa sediments, and Deir El-Fakhuri pond sediments are very fine grained. The only medium grained sands belonging to the modern Nile regimen are those of the Qena unit. In this respect they are similar to the older Nile sediments.

The sands of the Dandara, Sahaba, and Dibeira-Jer units are moderately well sorted. The Dishna playa sands are well sorted. The Deir El-Fakhuri pond sediments are very well sorted. In contrast, the sands of the older Nile system, the Qena deposits, and the Ballana dune sands are moderately sorted, with a wide range of size grades. The frequency curves of the sizes of all the sands, however, show a unimodal distribution of grain sizes (Figure F–1). All are also negatively skewed (Table F–1), indicating a predominance of the fine sand fraction over the coarser grades. The peaks of the frequency curves of the grain size distribution are strongly pointed (leptokurtic, $K_G > 1.0$) in all the sands of the modern Nile system. The sands of the older Nile regimen, on the other hand show less pointed, blunt peaks (platykurtic).

Table F–1. Granulometric Indices of the Sand Fraction of Some Quaternary Nile Sediments, in "phi" terms.

	P_1	P_5	P_{10}	P_{16}	Q_1	Md	Q_3	P_{84}	P_{90}	P_{95}	P_{99}	S	S_k	K_G	M_z
Old Nile sediments	–0.6	–0.1	0.2	0.5	1.0	1.6	2.2	2.4	2.6	2.9	3.4	0.99	–0.16	0.80	1.42
Dandara unit	–0.4	0.7	1.2	1.5	1.8	2.3	2.6	2.7	2.8	3.0	3.4	0.64	–0.33	2.83	2.15
Qena unit	–1.0	–0.3	0.1	0.7	1.0	1.5	2.0	2.1	2.3	2.7	3.2	0.83	–0.24	2.07	1.41
Dibeira-Jer unit	1.1	1.9	2.3	2.7	3.0	3.5	3.8	3.9	3.9	3.9	4.0	0.61	–0.51	1.17	3.33
Sahaba unit	0.2	0.8	1.3	1.7	1.9	2.2	2.6	2.8	3.0	3.1	3.6	0.63	–0.03	1.80	2.23
Dishna playa deposits	1.9	2.5	2.9	3.1	3.3	3.7	3.8	3.9	4.0	4.0	4.0	0.43	–0.34	1.60	4.57
Deir El-Fakhuri deposits	1.0	2.7	3.2	3.3	3.4	3.6	3.8	3.9	3.9	3.9	4.0	0.32	–0.29	1.27	3.58
Ballana dune sand	0.5	1.0	1.4	1.6	1.8	2.5	3.0	3.2	3.4	3.7	3.9	0.80	–0.24	2.19	2.44

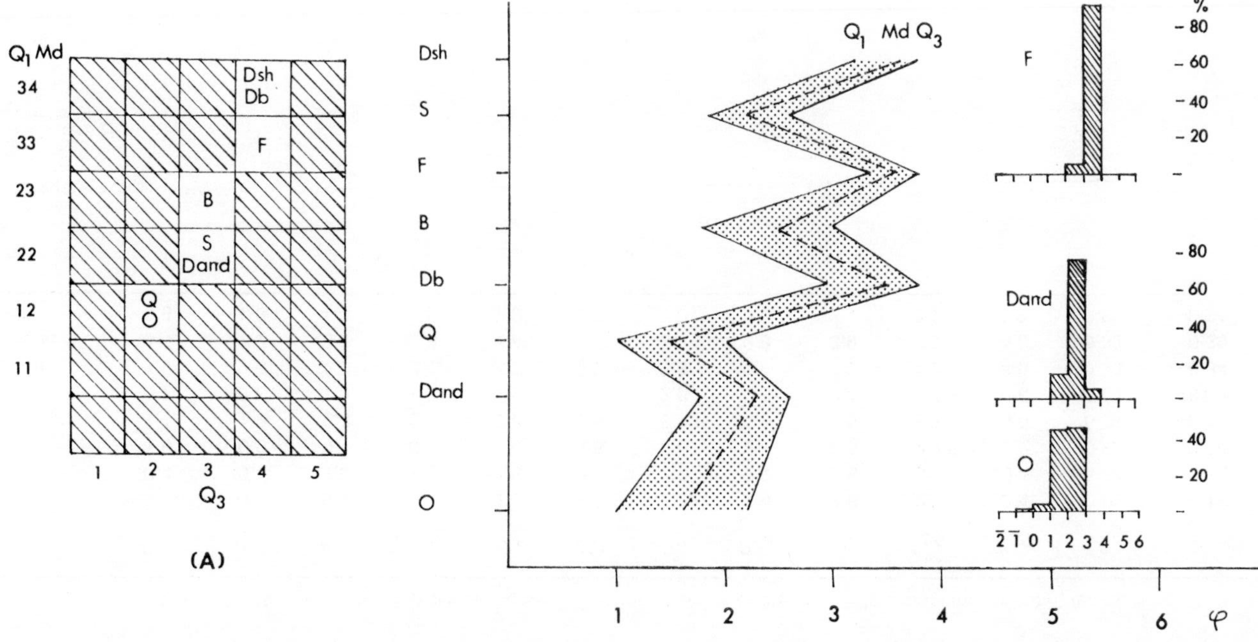

Figure F–1. Graphic presentation of the granulometric characteristics of some Quaternary Nile sediments. (A) is a presentation after the method of Doeglas (1968), which reveals the granulometric resemblance between the sediments of the Old Nile regimen (O) and the sands of the Qena Formation (Q), between the sands of the Dandara Formation (Dand), the Sahaba Formation (S), and the Ballana sand (B), and between the Deir El-Fakhuri sands (F), the Dibeira-Jer sands (Db), and the Dishna playa sediments (Dsh). (B) presents the granulometric results in a temporal order. The older Nile sediments (bottom) are coarser and less well sorted than the majority of the sediments of the modern Nile regimen (the degree of sorting is revealed by the distance between Q1 and Q3; the smaller the distance, the greater the degree of sorting). The histograpms reveal the degree of homogeneity in size sediments of the Nile regimen as opposed to the lesser homogeneity in older Nile sediments.

Generally, then, the sands of the modern Nile system are moderately well to very well sorted, fine to very fine grained, with a unimodal size frequency distribution, and characterized by a sharp peak (leptokurtic), whereas the sediments of the older Nile system are medium in size, moderately sorted, with a unimodal size frequency distribution, and with a blunt peak (platykurtic). There are, nonetheless, pronounced differences between the granulometry of the sediments of the modern Nile regimen, dependent on their depositional environments, and probably upon variations in the composition of the Nilotic material. The sands of the Qena unit, for example, are more akin to the sands of the older Nile system (Figure F–1A). The sands of the Dandara unit, the Sahaba unit, and the Ballana sand are very similar granulometrically (Figure F–1A), forming a group distinguishable from another, which includes the Deir El-Fakhuri unit, the Dibeira-Jer unit, and the Dishna playa sands. The Deir El-Fakhuri and the Dishna playa sands, however, are well to very well sorted, corroborating the field identification of these deposits as belonging to pond or playa depositional environments. The Dibeira-Jer sediments are moderately sorted and seem to have been deposited in a flood basin, some distance from the main river channel.

References

Doeglas, D. J.
1968 Grain-size indices, classification, and environment. *Sedimentology* **10**:73–100.
Folk, Fobert L.
1966 A review of grain-size parameters. *Sedimentology* **6**:73–93.

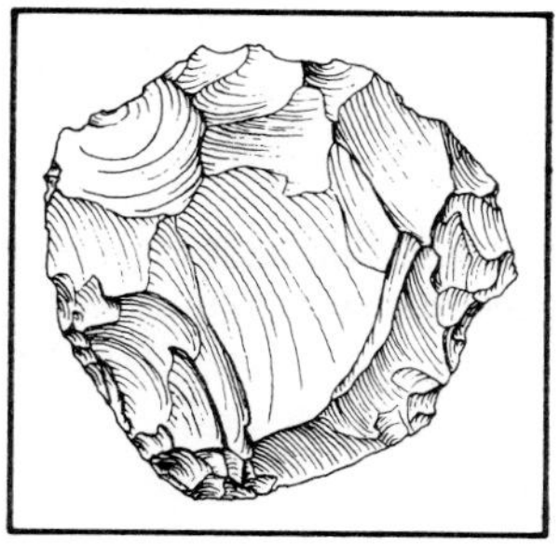

Appendix G

Freshwater Mollusks and Mammals from Upper Palaeolithic Sites Near Idfu and Isna

A. GAUTIER

The material described in this study was collected mainly in 1967 by F. Wendorf and his collaborators at a series of Upper Paleolithic sites in southern Egypt (Wendorf & Said 1967). Additional material was collected at some of these sites by the author during the 1968 field campaign.

The sites are now being dated by radiocarbon and paleomagnetism. For the purpose of this work, it suffices to say that the sites span approximately the period between ±22,000 BC and ±8000 BC, sites E71P1, E71P2, E71K1, E71K2, and E71K3 being the oldest, Site E71P5 the youngest (see Table G–7). In addition to freshwater mollusks and mammals, the sites also yielded many fish remains and a few bird remains. The fish remains are reported on by P. Greenwood. The bird remains will be studied by P. Ballmann, who kindly informed me that they pertain to water birds of different sizes (anseriforms and ralliforms).

Mollusks

At a few sites mollusks were collected in direct stratigraphic relation with the occupation or from adjacent strata. These sites (E71P5, E71K1, E71K18, E71K10, K71K9, E71P1) are listed in what follows in the same stratigraphic order as the mammalian remains listed in Table G–7. The identifications are based mainly on Mandahl-Barth (1954) and Martin (1968), in which full descriptions, bibliography, and other information concerning most of the collected species can be readily found.

Site E71P5, Area A: Corbicula sp. (*1 specimen*). Specific identification was impossible, as only a ventral margin fragment was found in coarse sand adhering to a large bone fragment. The site lies on a late recessional sandbar of the upper silt, which is probably correlative with the Nubian upper Sahaba Formation (de Heinzelin 1968). In this stratigraphic position one would expect *Corbicula vara* to occur. The specimen was probably transported by water currents into the sandbar.

Site E71K18, pond sediments: Lymnaea natalensis (one crushed limonitized cast); *Bulinus truncatus* (many); *Corbicula vara* Gardner s.l. (2).

Site E71K18, diatomite of upper pond: Valvata nilotica (many); *Cleopatra bulimoides* (1); *Bulinus truncatus* (many); *Gyraulus costulatus* (many, but less than *Valvata nilotica*).

Site E71K18, upper pond, below diatomite: Valvata nilotica (2); *Bulinus truncatus* (many); *Gyraulus costulatus* (2).

Site E71K18, lower pond: Bulinus truncatus (several); *Gyraulus costulatus* (2). The first sample is a mixture of several levels, from which the larger mollusks were collected in the field; hence, it does not contain the smaller species. The other collections were made in the diatomite and the lower part of the upper pond, and in the lower pond sediment. No countings were made, as the sampling error is considerable. First, the collections contain material sorted in the field (mostly *Bulinus truncatus*). Second, samples were treated in the laboratory; but as the hardened sediment could not be loosened very easily, many specimens (mainly larger ones) were broken in the process of preparation.

In Europe, samples of freshwater mollusks containing many specimens referrable to only a few species would be considered as indicating small bodies of water (cf. Sparks and Grove 1963: 194). This probably also applies to Egyptian samples, which were taken from sediments identified on stratigraphic evidence as pond deposits on a rather gently undulating topography.

Site E71K9, Area A: Lanistes carinatus (many); *Cleopatra bulimoides* (many). The shells were collected from dark, silty sand on the site and in its vicinity. *Lanistes carinatus* is an ampullarid preferring swampy conditions. The skulls are very well preserved and the species probably lived on the spot where the sediment was deposited. Many of the *Cleopatra* specimens are rolled and damaged. In Nubia, *Cleopatra bulimoides* predominated in the Sahaba Formation, where it was apparently accumulated in sand and gravel bars by current action (Martin 1968: 77). The dark, silty sand forms a thin veneer on the dunes containing the industry. This veneer seems to be a deposit with mixed character, for it has been described as a silty sand. It could be a lateral facies formed during a period of maximal aggradation over the higher dune topography, characterized by silt with an autochthonous *Lanistes carinatus* population mixed with fluviatile sand containing transported *Cleopatra bulimoides* It is probably related to the middle silt or the lower Sahaba Formation in Nubia.

Area around Site K9: Lanistes carinatus (many); *Cleopatra bulimoides* (many); *Bulinus truncatus* (1); *Corbicula vara* Gardner s.l. (2). This surface collection was made for radiocarbon dating. As the provenance of the material could not be established exactly, the sample was discarded. It is comparable to the sample from Site E71K9, Area A. *Bulinus truncatus* is a species occurring in the Sahaba Formation (Martin, 1968, 74). *Corbicula vara*, represented by rolled separate valves and one rolled bivalve specimen, was probably swept into the thin deposit of mixed character overlying the dunes in the same way as *Cleopatra bulimoides.*

Site E71K10: Cleopatra bulimoides. Many specimens of this species were collected from a loose, fluviatile surface sand at this site. The specimens are rolled and damaged, indicating transport by current action. This shore sand is probably comparable in age to the dark, silty sand at Site E71K9, situated in the same area.

Site E71K1: Lymnaea natalensis (1); *Bulinus truncatus* (1); *Lanistes carinatus* (some fragments); *Cleopatra bulimoides* (1); *Unio abyssinicus* (many). The unionids were found in clusters of broken and complete separate left and right valves. They are directly related to the occupational level and were probably eaten. The gastropods are derived from the silty veneers interbedded with the dune sand. They were collected in the deposits exposed in Trench 2 and on the surface. Preservation of this material is excellent, indicating that the specimens are autochthonous.

Site E71K3: Bulinus truncatus (1); *Unio abyssinicus* (1). The two specimens were found in the vertebrate collection. As at Site E71K1, *Unio abyssinicus* had been eaten. *Bulinus truncatus* was collected in coarse sand adhering to a bone fragment; it was probably swept into the deposit.

Site E71P1, Area 1: Cleopatra bulimoides (22); *Unio abyssinicus* (1).

Site E71P1, Area 3: Unio abyssinicus (many). As at Site E71K1, the broken and separate valves of *Unio abyssinicus* are from consumed mollusks. *Cleopatra bulimoides* is a fossil from the lower silt in which the industry was collected. The specimens are less damaged than those found at other sites and show no traces of rolling and transport.

All the identified mollusks are present in the Nile deposits in Nubia, except *Lymnaea natalensis* (cf. Martin 1968). Descriptions of this polymorphous species can be found in Mandahl-Barth (1954: 67–71; 1968: 39–40) and Leloup (1953: 9–16). It is common in many parts of tropical and southern Africa. According to the list compiled by Adam (1957: 74–75), it has been described from Pleistocene and Holocene deposits in the Fayum, Qasr-El-Sagha and Kharga Oasis, among others, by Gardner (1932, 1935). *Lymnaea cailliaudi* from the Fayum and Kharga Oasis, recorded by the same author, is not a different species but is synonymous with *Lymnaea natalensis.* The collections from Dungul Oasis at the Laboratory of Palaeontology (University of Ghent) contain several specimens of this species collected at a site whose age and significance I do not know (Site 8811).

The number of samples and species per sample are limited, and our knowledge of the ecology of most species is not detailed enough to allow for paleoecological analysis. *Unio abyssinicus* probably indicates colder waters than today (cf. Martin 1968). The same applies to *Corbicula vara,* which I would rather consider a subspecies of *C. consobrina* and not a distinct species, as accepted by Martin (ibid.). As in Nubia, the water seems to have been colder in Lower Egypt during the Upper Pleistocene. The few other inferences of ecological and general paleontological nature given in the text are not in contradiction with the depositional history of the sediments considered.

The stratigraphic value of the material is also very limited, as most species span very long periods. Moreover, our knowledge of the subfossil and fossil freshwater mollusks of Egypt is poor. At any rate, there exist no contradictions between the molluscan samples and the ages attributed to the deposits.

Mammals

Nesokia indica (Figure G–1).

About 40 fragments found at Site E71P1, Area 1, Site E71K1 Site E71K3 and Site E71K18, Areas C and E are referrable to this rodent. The material consists of lower jaws or lower-jaw fragments, a few upper-jaw fragments, and some postcranial remains. X. Misonne kindly checked the identification and supplied information concerning this widely distributed rodent.

Some measurements[1] are given in Table G–1 and compared with those

[1]Abbreviations used in the measurements are L. (length), H. (height), TR.D. (transverse diameter), A–P.D. (anterior-posterior diameter), W. (width), min. (minimum), max. (maximum).

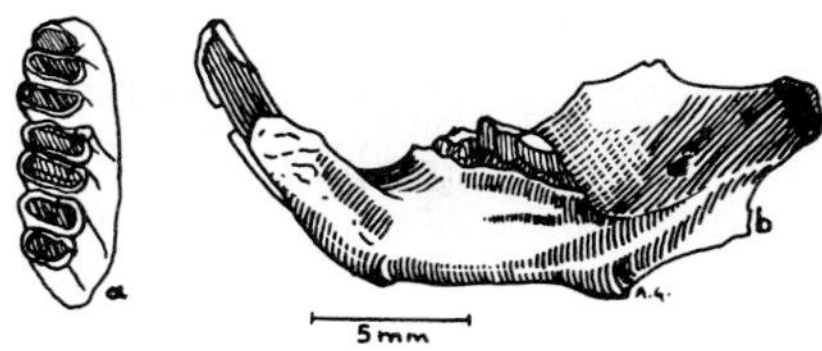

Figure G–1. *Nesokia indica*: (a) left lower teeth row; (b) left mandible. Both from Site E71K1.

taken on skulls at the Institut Royal des Sciences Naturelles de Belgique (IRSNB) and a few measurements found in the literature.

From Table G–1 one can deduce that the more reliable measurements are the alveolar lengths, as the masticatory length is to a certain extent a function of the degree of wear. The alveolar lengths indicate that the specimens from southern Egypt are larger than the samples from India, Syria, and northern Egypt. The Dead Sea specimen is somewhat larger. The Dabarosa specimen is smaller than the southern Egypt specimen and compares in size with Syrian specimens and probably with recent specimens from Suez. Although more data are required, one may probably accept that the southern Egypt fossil specimens belong to a population characterized by large size. This might indicate ecological conditions more favorable than those prevailing today in northern Egypt and those in Upper Pleistocene times in the northern Sudan.

The collected material does not belong to the group of consumed animals. Relatively many remains were found, representing quite a number of individuals, at Sites E71K1 and E71K18. Probably *Nesokia indica* established colonies on the location of these sites. At Site E71P1 only two specimens, pertaining to one individual, were found. This might be due to the hazards of collecting or to the fact that no colony existed on the site.

Table G–1. Measurements of *Nesokia indica* (in mm)

	Southern Egypt[3] *(Upper Paleolithic)*	*Dabarosa West*[2] *(Upper Paleolithic)*	*Suez*[3] *(recent)*	*Dead Sea*[3] *(recent)*	*IRSNB*[4] *(recent)*
L.M1–M3	10.0	–	7.5/9.3	8.0/10.5	6.5/8.0 (India)
(masticatory/	–	–	8 /9.3	–	7.0/8.1 (India)
alveolar)	–	–	–	–	7.2/9.0 (Syria)
L.M1–M3	8.2/10.2	–	–	–	6.7/9.4 (Syria)
(masticatory/	8.1/10.2	7.2/9.2	–	–	6.7/7.9 (India)
alveolar)	7.9/10.1	–	–	–	–/8.3 (India)
	7.9/10.0	–	–	–	7.0/9.2 (Syria)
	8.0/ 9.7	–	–	–	7.3/9.2 (Syria)
	–/ 9.6	–	–	–	–

[1]Sites E71K1, E71K5, E71K18, Areas C and E.

[2]Specimen shown in Robinson (1966: Fig. 1).

[3]Anderson (1902: 286–288).

[4]IRSNB, Reg. 10255, 10256 (India), 10235, 10236 (Syria).

Whether the colonies were established before or after human occupation is difficult to establish. Burrowing animals can cause notable disturbance of original stratigraphic relations and intrude into sediments geologically much older than the animals themselves. The sites at which *Nesokia* occurs are all surface and subsurface sites. Hence, Nesokia can have burrowed in the existing sediment at any time, as long as the ground was soft enough.

Nesokia indica does not occur today in southern Egypt. Anderson (1902: 286–188) records it from Suez, where specimens were captured near the banks of the Sweet Water Canal between Big and Little Shaluf. The numerous burrows and tortuous, well-padded runs, indicating an important population, were found concealed among sedgy grass and stunted, spiny shrubs. The local name for this rodent is *girdi*. A distribution map in Misonne (1959) also indicates the presence of *Nesokia indica* in the Nile delta. According to Robinson (1966), referring to Hoogstraal (1963: not seen), the species is also found in the Fayum marshes. Gautier (1968: 96) records some unidentified rodent fragments from Ballana in southern Egypt. They were found at Halfan Site 8859, which probably dates from the very beginning of the Sahaba Formation (±17,000 BC) (Wendorf 1968: 794–805). The molars in this small collection are indistinguishable from those of the fossils described earlier, and the Ballana rodent can now be put on record as *Nesokia indica*. Robinson (1966) describes fossil *Nesokia* from Dabarosa West in Northern Province in the Sudan. It was collected by the University of Colorado Museum Expedition at Sudanese Antiquities Service Site 6B28, situated 1 km west of the Nile River and 1.5 km west of Wadi Halfa. This site also yielded a human mandible, artiodactyls (now being studied by C. H. Reed) and *Lepus capensis.* Typologically it compares to Site 443, described in Wendorf (1968), from which a radiocarbon date of 14,500 BC has been determined. *Nesokia* is represented by a left mandible with complete teeth row (measured specimen, Table G–1) and a right mandible with M1 only.

Today *Nesokia indica* seems to be restricted to the area mentioned because there the ground is wet year round. Although irrigation is common in the narrow band of arable land on both sides of the Nile in Nubia and Egypt, it is seasonal, and there are periods when the soil is dry and hard, so that burrowing is difficult or impossible. According to Robinson (1966), the presence of *Nesokia* during the Upper Pleistocene in Nubia could indicate that the seasonal fluctuations of the Nile level had little effect on the area near the river and that a stable water table existed.

This higher water table could indicate a more humid climate than that prevailing today. More likely it was connected with the higher average Nile level and the greater discharge of the Nile during its floods. More water was stocked in the flooded sediments, which did not dry out completely in the periods between floods. The shallow fossil ponds found in southern Egypt (Site E71K18) might be another proof of such a situation. Whether they were connected with a more humid climate or with the greater flood height of the Nile, the fact that the soil probably did not dry out certainly affected the vegetation. It probably was much more luxurious and dense than today in Nubia as well as in southern Egypt. Hence, it could support more game than it would today without human interference.

Small Unidentified Rodent

At Site E71K3 a rodent smaller than *Nesokia indica* is represented by one molar tooth. It has not yet been identified.

Lepus capensis

Sites E71K1 and E71K3 yielded quite a lot of material pertaining to a lagomorph. At Sites E71K9, Area A and E71K18, Areas C and E, remains were collected that are too fragmentary for correct identification. They agree in general size and appearance with the material from Site E71K1 and E71K3 (Table G–2). In Table G–7 they are listed with a question mark.

In general size and pattern of the jugal teeth, the material agrees well with specimens of the Cape hare at the IRSNB and the figures in MacInnes (1953: Figures 17, 20, 25, 26). Several subspecies of *Lepus capensis* have been described from the Sudan and Egypt (Anderson 1902; Setzer 1956). I doubt if they can be separated on osteological differences. At any rate, the fossil material is too scanty for súbspecific identification, and osteological details on most described subspecies seem to be insufficient for statistical comparison. Hence, the material is put on record as *Lepus capensis.*

Lagomorph material was also collected in Sudanese Nubia at Sites 1017 and 1021 (Gautier 1968: 80). This material seems to be specifically identical with the material from Egypt. The identification *Lepus* sp. should be changed to *Lepus capensis.*

Hippopotamus amphibius

Hippopotamus is not well represented in the collection. Tooth fragments were found at Site E71P1, Areas 1 and 3, Site E71P2, and Site E71P7, Area B. Identifiable postcranial remains are also rare. At Site E71P1, Area 1 a first phalanx and a fragment of a vertebra were collected. Site E71K3 yielded a distal epiphysis of a metapodial (not fully grown) and some doubtful fragments of vertebrae. No measurements of this material can be given.

Table G–2. Measurements of *Lepus capensis* (in mm)

Scapulum, TR.D. articular process	±12.0
Mandible, L. P2–M3	±15.0
Humerus, TR.D. dist.	± 9.5
Radius, TR.D. dist.	± 6.9–7.6
Femur, TR.D. dist. epiphysis	±14.2
Calcaneum, total L.	±26.5–28.5

Table G–3. Measurements of Carnivores (in mm)

Hyaena sp.	
Scapulum, TR.D. articular process	41
Max.D. articular surface	32
Min.D. articular surface	22
Felis libyca (?)	
Radius, TR.D. dist.	±14
Tibia, TR.D. prox.	±24.9

Hyaena sp (?)

At Site E71K1 very poorly preserved remains of an occipital condylar skull region were found. They seem to pertain to a skull somewhat larger than a reference skull of domesticated dog, the condylobasal length of which is 183 mm. Site E71K9, Area A yielded an articular process of a scapulum that agrees in general morphology with the articular process of scapula in dogs. It is somewhat larger than the scapulum of a dog standing ±65 cm at the withers. Measurements are given in Table G–3. Tentatively this material can be put on record as *Hyaena* sp. If the generic identification is correct, the specimens should very likely be referred to *Hyaena hyaena*.

Felis libyca (?)

At Site E71K3, proximal moieties of carnivore tibia and metapodial were found. At Site E71P1, Area 1, the distal moiety of a radius probably representing the same species was collected.

Morphologically the material agrees with comparative material of European wild and domesticated cat at my disposal. Measurements are given in Table G–3. The material seems to pertain to an individual about 1.4 times larger than a domesticated cat, the condylobasal skull length of which is 74 mm. Probably the material can be referred to the wildcat *Felis libyca.*

Bos primigenius

The aurochs is well represented in the collection. The size and general morphology of the material compare very well with the size and general appearance of aurochs material collected in Nubia (Gautier 1968). Measurements are given in Table G–4. One upper molar (M3) seems to be exceptionally large; it may pertain to a very developed bull.

Alcelaphus buselaphus (Figure G–2)

This antelope is represented by many cranial and postcranial remains. They agree in general form and size with the material collected in the northern Sudan (Gautier 1968). Some measurements are given in Table G–5.

In the Sudanese collection no horn core fragments were present. Therefore it was not possible to specify exactly which hartebeest the remains represented. Fortunately the Egyptian collection contains horn cores (Figure G–2). They have been compared with figures of the several hartebeest in Wells (1959: 125,

Table G–4. Measurements of *Bos primigenius* (in mm)

Dentition, L/W P^3	21.8–17.0						
P^4	20.5–19.2						
M1–2 ±	28.5–33.8–±24.6–25.2						
M3	35.0–35.5–24.7–25.0 (40/27.4)						
M1–2	34.5–36.3–16.8–17.3						
Atlas, TR.D. prox. articular surface	±130						
TR.D. dist. articular surface	±125						
Scapulum, Max.D. articular process	75	±80					
Max.D. articular surface	–	58					
Min.D. articular surface	–	48					
Tibia, TR.D. dist.	± 74						
A–P.D. dist.	± 52						
Astragalus, L.	78	83	90	105			
TR.D.	50	55	–	–			
A–P.–D.	45	47	–	–			
Calcaneum, L.	192	–					
TR.D. prox.	± 47	47					
A–P.D. prox.	± 53	±53					
Max. TR.D.	70	–					
Max. A–P.D.	80	–					
Naviculo-cuboid, TR.D.	67	70					
A–P.D.	72	–					
Cannon bone, TR.D. prox. mt.	85	93					
TR.D. dist. mt./mc.	76	68	±90				
Phalanx II, L.	44	45	46	46	52	52	55
TR.D. prox.	32	37	34	35	44	44	48
TR.D. dist.	28	29	29	31	44	42	49
Phalanx III, H.	39						
TR.D.	27						
L.	70						

Figure 4). Comparable horn cores seem to be present in the *A. buselaphus* group and the *A. lelwel* group, but between these two groups marked differences still exist. In *A. buselaphus* the horn cores are U-shaped when viewed full face, and the tips are turned outward. In *A. lelwel* the horns are V-shaped when viewed full face, and the tips are not turned outward. The collected horn cores seem to belong to the type found in the *A. buselaphus* group. This group occurred in North Africa and Egypt and became extinct in historic times. Anderson (1902: 337) records that in 1895 *Alcelaphus buselaphus* had been found at a two-day journey west of Lake Qarun (Fayum).

Gazella rufifrons and Gazella dorcas (Figures G–3 and G–4)

Gazella is represented by approximately 50 identifiable fragments (Table G–6) The identification of this material is based on the collected horn cores, which belong to two quite different types. Seven horn cores or horn core fragments pertain to a species with relatively short nonlyrate horns (Figure G–3), the cross-section of which is somewhat flattened with a posterio-mesial blunt angle. This cross-section is quite comparable to that of a *Gazella dorcas* horncore shown by Gentry (1966: 63, Figure 7). One other horn core clearly belongs to a form with lyrate horns (Figure G–4). Its cross-section also compares to the *Gazella dorcas* cross-section shown by Gentry.

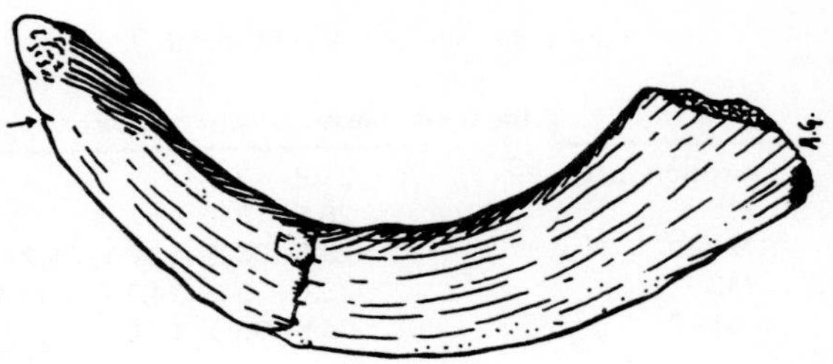

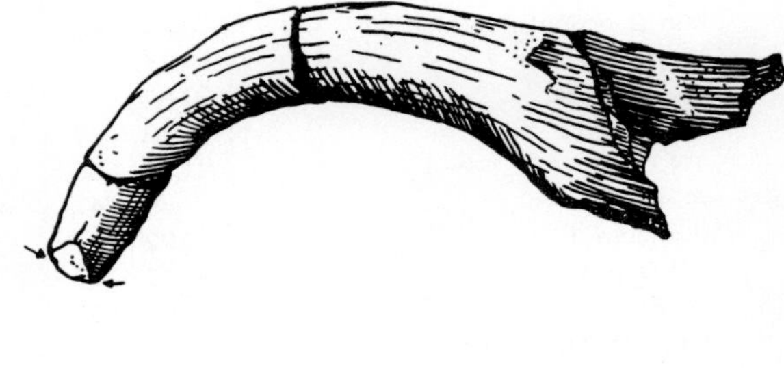

Figure G–2. *Alcelaphus buselaphus*, a pair of fragmentary horncores. The arrows indicate cutting traces (approximately × 0.25).

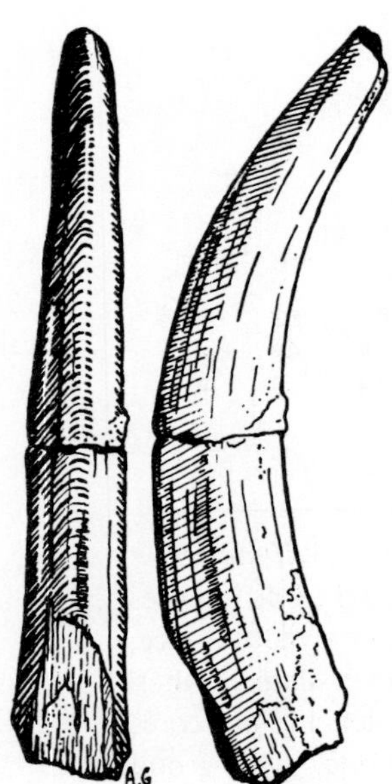

Figure G–3. *Gazella rufifrons*, horn core (approximately × 0.5).

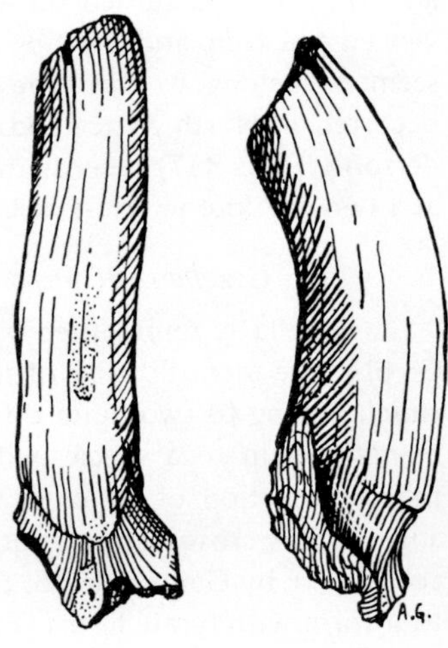

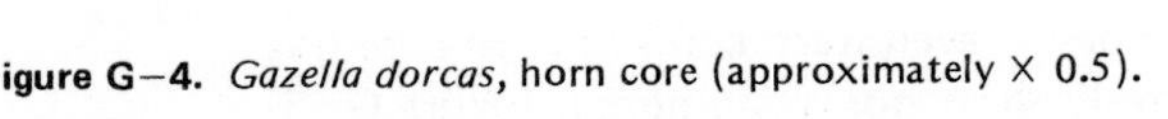

Figure G–4. *Gazella dorcas*, horn core (approximately × 0.5).

Table G–5. Measurements of *Alcelaphus buselaphus* (in mm)

Upper jaw, L.–W	M2–3	23.0–23.2–14.5–16.0				
M3		21.4–22.1–13.2–14.0				
M1		11.0–7.5				
M2		20.0–10.5				
M3		27.0–9.1				
Lower jaw, L.–W.	P2	9.9–10.0–5.1–7.2				
P3		±11.0–13.2–6.2–7.6				
P4		±14.0–16.3–8.5–9.7				
M1		±21.0				
M1–2		19.3–23.4–10.0–11.8				
M2		23.3–±11.0				
M3	28.1	28.1–32.0–9.4–10.5				
L.P2–P4		33.8–38.5				
Humerus, TR.D. dist.		51.0	51.0			
A–P.D. dist.		54.0	53.5			
Radius, TR.D. prox.		60.0	–			
A–P.D. prox.		32.0	–			
TR.D. dist.		–	48.0			
A–P.D. dist.		–	35.0			
Femur, TR.D. dist.		±65.0				
A–P.D. dist.		±91.0				
Tibia, TR.D. dist.		47.0	46.0			
A–P.D. dist.		37.0	38.0			
Calcaneum, L. max.		102.0	–	–		
TR.D. prox. tuberosity		23.0	24.0	–		
A–P.D. prox. tuberosity		30.0	31.0	–		
TR.D. max.		35.0	–	33.0		
A–P.D. max.		37.5	–	–		
Astragalus, L. max.		52.0	51.0	49.5	48.0	
TR.D. max.		±35.0	35.0	35.0	32.0	
Naviculo-cuboid, TR.D.		44.0	39.0			
A–P.D.		39.0	35.0			
Cannon bone, TR.D. prox.		43 (mc)				
TR.D. dist.		42.0–46.0 (mc)		35.0 (mt)		
Phalanx I, TR.D. prox.		21.0–23.0				
Phalanx II, L.		40.5	40.0	39.0	39.0	37.0
TR.D. prox.		–	±19.0	19.0	20.0	20.5
TR.D. dist.		–	16.5	17.0	16.5	–
Phalanx III, H.		29.0	28.0	28.0	26.0	
L.		±59.0	±56.0	±56.0	±54.0	

The nonlyrate horn cores are very comparable with those collected at the older sites in northern Sudan (Gautier 1968: 93–95). Remains of *Gazella* from these older sites were identified as *G. rufifrons*. This identification referred only to the large size of the remains and the fact that the horn cores seem to be somewhat more compressed than in *G. dorcas*. General considerations concerning the present-day distribution of *Gazella* in Sudan were thought to corroborate this identification. It was not mentioned that the Sudanese horn cores are nonlyrate and relatively short. These two characteristics exclude an identification of the

Table G–6. Measurements of *Gazella* spp. (in mm)

	Gazella rufifrons			*Gazella dorcas*
Horn cores, L. ant. base–apex	±175	—	—	—
A.P.D. near base	30	—	33	31
TR.D. near base	22	—	25	23
Horn core index	73	—	75	7.4
A–P.D. middle	27	27	—	26
TR.D. middle	19	18	—	20
Atlas, TR.D. ant. articular surface	±46			
TR.D. post. articular surface	±44			
Scapulum, max.D. acetabulum	21.5			
min.D. acetabulum	19.6			
max.D. autalulum and notch	26.9			
mc., TR.D. middle	13.3	—		
TR.D. dist.	±21	20.9		
Tibia, TR.D. prox.	±32 (not fully grown)			
TR.D. dist.	25.2			
A.–P.D. dist.	21.5			
Phalanx I, L.	37.9			
TR.D. prox.	10.5			
TR.D. dist.	9.2			
Phalanx III, L.	31.0			
H.	14.2			
TR.D.	8.2			

older Sudanese *Gazella* as *G. thomsoni*, which has long horns, or *G. dorcas*, which normally has lyrate horns. It now seems fairly certain that the older Sudanese *Gazella* remains and the nonlyrate *Gazella* horn cores of southern Egypt should be referred to the red-fronted *Gazella* or *Gazella rufifrons*.

The lyrate *Gazella* horn core from southern Egypt is referrable to *Gazella dorcas*. It probably has a somewhat greater size than horn cores of the present-day *Gazella dorcas* in Egypt. D. A. Hooijer (1961: 45–48) identified *Gazella dorcas* from Ksar'Akil that are larger than comparable material of recent *Gazella dorcas* measured by the same author. This would conform to the general rule that Pleistocene representatives of several extant mammals are often larger than their living descendants (cf. Kurten 1968).

The older remains of *Gazella* cannot be separated, as they are too few for statistical treatment. However, as *Gazella dorcas* is represented by only one horn core and *G. rufifrons* by seven specimens, very likely the greater part of the material has to be assigned to the redfronted *Gazella*. The *Gazella dorcas* horn core was collected on the surface at Site E71K1, together with some other *Gazella* remains. Hence, it is possible that this material is intrusive. As for preservation, the surface material is comparable with the other *Gazella* remains from this and other sites. This is a weak argument in favor of contemporaneity of the surface finds with those referred to *Gazella rufifrons*.

In the light of the foregoing, it seems necessary to review all the *Gazella* material from the Sudan. As already mentioned, the older sites yielded horn cores very comparable with most of those found in Upper Egypt. At the C-group sites *Gazella dorcas* was identified, mainly because the remains are smaller than at the older sites.

The few horn core remains of the C-group sites have been compared with the *Gazella* horn core from Site E71K1, surface. One of the more complete specimens seems to exhibit a slight torsion. The other more complete specimen is more rounded in the upper part than the *Gazella rufifrons* horn cores from the northern Sudan. According to Gentry (1964: 358), the horn cores in female *Gazella dorcas* diverge slightly from the base upward, while those of *G. thomsoni* and *G. rufifrons* are parallel. A female skull fragment from the C-sites seems to have diverging horn cores. Hence, the evidence suggests that the C-group *Gazella* is indeed *Gazella dorcas*, although the material is rather poor and does not exhibit clearly the diagnostic features of *Gazella dorcas* horn cores.

Gentry (1964: 354) suggested that *Gazella dorcas* would be the extension into North Africa of the Palearctic *G. dorcas* stock. Hence, it might be that *G. dorcas* arrived in northern Sudan when climatic conditions were deteriorating (cf. Gautier 1968: 93). Possibly it was present in southern Egypt at a much earlier date than in Sudanese Nubia.

Unidentified Ruminant

At Site E71K1, surface, two specimens were collected that seem to be referrable to a bovid smaller than hartebeest and larger than *Gazella rufifrons* or *G. dorcas.* Both specimens, a proximal fragment of a humerus and a shaft fragment of tibia, are too incomplete for measurement.

Discussion

In Table G−7, the sites have been arranged in a general stratigraphic order based on the combined evidence of stratigraphic relations, radiocarbon dating, and typology. For the sites in Nubia (Gautier 1968), not much information can be gained from this tabulation. Even by combining collections of comparable age or thought to belong to a definite period, no meaningful shift in the frequency of the main game animals becomes visible. This is due mainly to two factors. First, most of the samples are very small. As can be seen, the sites that yielded more remains contain more species. This indicates that our image of the hunting habits of Upper Paleolithic man from the site concerned is an impoverished one. Very extensive collecting at each site would probably yield more evidence of hunted fauna. Second, differential preservation of bone remains has probably occurred. Indeed the differences in size and robustness between the three main ruminants are marked.

The collected material of most game species (aurochs, hartebeest, *Gazella*, hare) contain very young as well as older individuals. Aurochs and hartebeest

Table G–7. Frequency of Mammalian Remains per Site

Site	*Bos primigenius*	*Alcelaphus buselaphus*	*Gazella*[1]	*Lepus capensis*	*Hippo-potamus amphibius*	*Nesokia indica*	*Other faunal elements; remarks*
E71P5, A	3	1	—	—	—	—	fish
E71K15	—	2	—	—	—	—	(only a pair of hartebeest horn cores)
E71K14, A	25	±15	4	—	—	—	
E71K14, D	1		—	—	—		
E71K9, X	—	3	—	—	—	—	
E71K18, A	—	3	—	—	—	—	fish, bird
E71K18, B	10	1	—	—	—	—	fish
E71K18, C	2	3	1	3(?)	—	12	fish, bird
E71K18, D	1	2	2	1(?)	—	—	fish
E71K18, E	2	3	?	—	—	1	fish
E71K13, C	3	11.	1	—	—	—	
E71K12, D	—	1	—	—	—	—	
E71K9	8	9	1	—	—	—	fish
E71K9, A	11	±50	—	5(?)	—	—	fish, *Hyaena hyaena* (?)
E71K9, C	3	2		—	—	—	fish
E71K10	1	2		—	—	—	
E71P7, B	5	—	—	—	1	—	fish, bird
E71P6	3	2	—	—	—	—	
E71P1, Area 1	15	19	3	—	3	2	*Unio abyssinicus*, fish, bird, *Felis libyca*(?)
E71P1, Area 2	2	2	—	—	—	—	fish
E71P1, Area 3	36	±50	6	—	2	—	fish
E71P2	9	4	1	—	1	—	fish
E71K1	71	±100	23	17	—	21	*Unio abyssinicus*, fish, bird, (one horn core *Gazella dorcas*), medium-sized ruminant
E71K3	8	±45	7	32	1 + 4(?)	6	*Unio abyssinicus*, fish, bird, small rodent, *Felis libyca*(?)
E71K2	—	—	—	—	—	—	
E71K4	15	±30	—	—	—	—	
E71K5	2	—	—	—	—	—	

[1] *Gazella rufifrons and Gazella dorcas*

are frequently represented by such compact bones as calcaneum, astragalus, phalanges, and distal cannon bone fragments. Teeth and tooth fragments of these species are also quite common, as they preserve well. Almost lacking are proximal fragments of humerus and femur. These are easily destroyed by weathering or by scavengers, which prefer these parts of long bones. Most of the material is rather fragmented. This is due to weathering in subdesertic conditions and the fact that the material has been broken and fractured during butchering. Many specimens show clear evidence of this activity.

On two specimens traces of cutting not due to butchering are visible. One is a small rib fragment (hartebeest?) with many transverse scars produced by a burin. The second, probably also a small rib (hartebeest?), shows traces of scraping parallel to the long axis of the bone and crossed by one deep burin scar. These two specimens, which indicate that bone was probably used for toolmaking, were collected at Site E71K1. Better evidence for such activity was found at Site E71K15. This site yielded only a pair of incomplete hartebeest horn cores (Figure G–2). On one horn core cutting traces are visible, the intention of which was removal of the tip; on the other horn core the tip has been removed by cutting at approximately the height at which the cutting traces occur on the other specimen.

As in Nubia (Gautier, 1968), aurochs, hartebeest, and *Gazella* form the most important game. Hippopotamus, hares, and at least one other ruminant were hunted only occasionally, if we can accept the evidence of Table G–7. The carnivores (*Hyaena*, wild cat) may have been killed by man for several reasons. The most interesting find is *Nesokia indica*, which probably indicates a more luxurious and denser vegetation along the stretch of the Nile Valley under consideration during some period(s) of the Upper Pleistocene. The presence of *Gazella dorcas* should also be mentioned.

Acknowledgments

I am indebted to the Belgian Ministerie voor Nationale Opvoeding en Cultuur and the Wenner Gren Foundation. Both provided grants that enabled me to join the 1968 field campaign in southern Egypt. This experience provided me with a better background for understanding the archaeological and geological problems involved in the investigations carried out along the Nile. I also want to thank X. Misonne for his help with rodent identification and P. Robinson, who provided information concerning fossil *Nesokia indica* from Sudanese Nubia and loaned specimens for comparison.

References

Adam, W.
1957 *Mollusques quaternaires de la region du lac Edouard. Institut Parcs Nat. Congo Belge, Exploration Parc National Albert, Mission J. de Heinzelin, (Brussels)* **3.**

Anderson, J.
1902 Zoology of Egypt. *Mammalia (London).*

De Heinzelin, J.
1968 Geological history of the Nile Valley in Nubia. In *The prehistory of Nubia*, edited by F. Wendorf, Vol. I. Dallas: Fort Burgwin Research Center and Southern Methodist Univ. Press. Pp. 19–55.
Gardner, E. W.
1932 Some lacustrine Mollusca from the Fayum depression. A study in variation. *Mem. Inst. Egypte* **xviii**.
1935 The Pleistocene fauna and flora of Kharga Oasis Egypt. *Quarterly Journal of the Geological Society (London)* **xci**. Pp. 479–515.
Gautier, A.
1968 Mammalian remains of the Northern Sudan and Southern Egypt. In *The prehistory of Nubia,* Vol. I, edited by F. Wendorf, Dallas: Fort Burgwin Research Center and Southern Methodist Univ. Press. Pp. 80–99.
Gentry, A. W.
1964 Skull Characters of African Gazelles. *Annals & Magazine Natural History (London)* **vii** (Ser. 33): 353–382.
1966 *Fossil Antilopini of East Africa.* In *Fossil mammals of Africa,* No. 20. London: British Museum of Natural History.
Hooijer, D. A.
1961 The fossil vertebrates of Ksar'Akil, a palaeolithic rock shelter in the Lebanon. *Zoolog. Verhandelingen Rijksmuseum Natuurlijke Historie Leiden* (No. 49).
Kurten, B.
1968 Pleistocene mammals of the old world. In *The World Naturalist.* London: Weidenfeld & Nicolson.
Leloup, E.
1953 Exploration hydrobiologique du lac Tanganika. Vol. III, fasc. 4. In *Gasteropodes.* Brussels: Instut Royal Sciences Naturelles Belgique.
MacInnes, D. G.
1953 The Miocene and Pleistocene Lagomorpha of East Africa. London: British Museum Natural History. In *Fossil mammals of Africa,* No. 6.
Mandahl-Barth, G.
1954 The freshwater mollusks of Uganda and adjacent territories. *Ann. Mus. Roy. Congo Belge, Ser. in 8°, Sciences Zoolog. (Turvuren).* **32**.
Martin, F.
1968 Pleistocene mollusks from Sudanese Nubia. In *The prehistory of Nubia,* Vol. I., edited by F. Wendorf, Dallas: Fort Burgwin Research Center and Southern Methodist Univ. Press. Pp. 56–79.
Misonne, X.
1959 Donnees sur les rongeurs d'un foyer de peste indien. *Bulletin Institut Royal Sciences Naturelles Belgique, T.* **xxxv**, (No. 17).
Robinson, P.
1966 Fossil occurence of Murine Rodent *(Nesokia indica)* in the Sudan. *Science* **154** (No. 3746): 264.
Setzer, H. W.
1956 Mammals of the Anglo-Egyptian Sudan. *Proceedings U.S. National Museum (Smithsonian Institute)* **106** (No. 3377): 447–587 (10 figs).
Sparks, B. W. & M. A. Grove
1963 Fossil non-marine Mollusca from Mongunn, North-East Nigeria. *Overseas Geology and Mineral Resources,* (London) **9** (2): 190–195. London.
Wells, L. H.
1969 The Quaternary giant hartebeests of South Africa. *South African Journal of Science* **55** (No. 5): 123–128.
Wendorf, F. (Ed.)
1968 *The prehistory of Nubia.* Dallas: Fort Burgwin Research Center & Southern Methodist University.
Wendorf, F. & R. Said
1967 Palaeolithic Remains in Upper Egypt. *Nature* **215** (No. 5098): 244–247.

Appendix H

Animal Remains from Localities Near Dishna

A. GAUTIER

The archaeological work near Dishna did not yield many palaeontological or bioarchaeological remains. The few samples collected are reported on mainly for the sake of completeness. They were taken from late Upper Pleistocene and Epi-Pleistocene deposits on sites between Nagada and Dishna. The identifications are based mainly on the authors listed in the references.

1. Near El es Zamami, in beach sand at ±6 m above and on slope to present-day human occupation level. Age probably comparable with end of Sahaba Formation in Nubia. Mollusks: *Corbicula vara* (monotypical accumulation).

2. Site E6104, Area A, trench 1 (near El-Makhadma), collection in burned layer and adjacent layers. Mollusks: *Valvata nilotica* (f)[1], *Gyraulus costulatus* (f), *Bulinus truncatus* (f), *Gabiella senaariensis* (l).

3. Site E6104, Area C, trench 1 in artefact zone. Vertebrates: several fragments of one molar, probably of hartebeest (*Alcelaphus buselaphus*).

4. Site E6104, in poorly sorted sand at same level as lower silt exposed in other profiles of the site. Relation to this silt unknown. The mollusks occur mainly in stratified bands. Mollusks: *Valvata nilotica* (ff), *Gyraulus costulatus* (ff), *Bulinus truncatus* (ff), *Corbicula vara* (r). The assemblage seems to be characteristic of a silt (see other collections), yet it occurs in ill-sorted fluviatile sand. This may indicate that the deposit represents part of a sandbar or a levee away from the main stream channel.

5. North of Site E6104, indurated silt at same general topographical level as lower silt at Site E6104 and probably of same age. Mollusks: *Valvata nilotica* (ff), *Gyraulus costulatus* (ff), *Lentorbis* sp. or *Segmentorbis* sp. (l), *Bulinus truncatus* (ff), *Ferrissia* sp. (f), *Corbicula vara* (r). The assemblage is richer than that at Site E6104, Area C, Trench 1, mainly because the sample was processed in the laboratory.

Ferrissia sp. has not been identified specifically because the specimens are not fully grown; moreover, the genus is badly in need of revision. *Ferrissia isseli* and *F. clessiana* have been recorded from Quaternary deposits in the Fayum and in Kharga Oasis, respectively, by Gardner (1932, 1935). Martin (1968) described *Ferrissia* from one site in Nubia.

Lentorbis or *Segmentorbis* sp. is badly preserved, but does not resemble any of the species of both genera I have seen until now. *Segmentorbis angustus* has been recorded from the Quaternary in the Fayum, the Kharga Oasis (Gardner 1932, 1935) and the Kurkur Oasis (Leigh 1968).

6. Site E61M10, Area B, artefact concentration. Mollusks: *Valvata nilotica* (3), *Gyraulus costulatus* (f), *Bulinus traulatus* (f), *Gabiella senaariensis* (ff), *Corbicula vara* (3). Vertebrates: One small fishbone; one bone fragment of a medium-sized mammal.

7. Site E1M10, Area D, artefact concentration. Mollusks: some fragments of a unionid (*Unio abyssinicus?*) maybe consumed. Vertebrates: two fragments of some molariform teeth (*Bos primigenius* or of comparable size).

[1] Letter in parentheses is an estimate of the frequency of occurrence (ff - very frequent; f=frequent; r=rare) or the exact number of specimens.)

8. Site E61M9, Area C, trench 1, in burned layer and down below to ±25 cm. Mollusks: *Lanistes carinatus* (fragment). Vertebrates: A few small bone fragments pertaining to small fish and medium-sized mammals; one complete phalanx and a proximal moiety of a phalanx of a small mammal.

References

Gardner, E. W.

1932 Some lacustrine mollusca from the Faiyum Depression. A study in variation. *Mem. Inst. Egypte* **xviii.**

1935 The Pleistocene fauna and flora of Kharga Oasis Egypt. *Quart. Journ. Geol. Soc. London,* **xci.** 479.

Gautier, A.

1968 Mammalian remains of the Northern Sudan and Southern Egypt (in The Prehistory of Nubia, ed. F. Wendorf, Vol. I, pp. 80–99).

in press *Freshwater mollusks and mammals from Upper Palaeolithic Sites in Southern Egypt.*

Leigh, E. G.

1968 Fossil mollusca from the Kurkur Oasis. In *Desert and river in Nubia,* edited by Butzer, K.W. & Hansen, C. L. Madison: Univ. of Wisconsin Press, Appendix. Pp. 513–515.

Mandahl-Barth, G.

1954 The freshwater mollusks of Uganda and adjacent territories. (Ann. Mus. Roy. Congo Belge, Serie in 8°, Sciences Zoolog., vol. 32, Tervuren).

Mandahl-Barth, G.

1968 Revision of the African Bithyniidae. *Revue Zool. Bot. Afriq.,* Bruxelles, **lxxviii**: 129–160.

Martin, F.

1968 Pleistocene mollusks from Sudanese Nubia. In *The prehistory of Nubia,* edited by F. Wendorf, Vol. I. Dallas: Fort Burgwin Research Center and Southern Methodist University. Pp. 56–79.

1968 *The prehistory of Nubia.* Dallas: Fort Burgwin Research Center & Southern Methodist University.

Wendorf, F. & Said, R.

1967 Palaeolithic remains in Upper Egypt. *Nature* 215 (No. 5098): 244–247.

Appendix I

Animal Remains from Archeological Sites of Terminal Paleolithic to Old Kingdom Age in the Fayum

A. GAUTIER

Introduction

Several archaeological sites in the Fayum excavated by F. Wendorf and his team during the field season early in 1969 have yielded animal remains. As usual, preservation of the material is poor because of weathering and diagenesis under desertic conditions following fragmentation during butchering. The sites are listed according to their age in Table J−7. They range from Terminal Paleolithic (Sites E29H1 and E29G1), with a radiocarbon date around 6000−5000 BC to Neolithic (Site E29H2), with radiocarbon dates around 3800 BC (Site E29G3), to Predynastic (E29G5), and Old Kingdom (E29G4), with estimated ages of 3500−3200 BC and 3000−2600 BC, respectively.

The most interesting sites are the Neolithic ones. Site E29H2 is the type site (Kom W) of the Neolithic Fayum A (Caton-Thompson & Gardner 1934). Unfortunately only a few bone specimens were collected at that site. Another Neolithic Fayum A site E29G3, however, yielded a sizable sample. When working in Egypt with F. Wendorf and his crew in 1968, the author visited this site and collected a few interesting specimens that supplement the 1969 collection. They have been included in this study (see sheep and goat).

The paleontological remains of archaeological sites in the Fayum were never studied extensively. Andrews (1903) and Caton-Thompson & Gardner (1934) give few details. They list pig, sheep and goat, hippopotamus, dog or jackal, turtle, crocodile, and fish (Nile perch?) for the Fayum Neolithic (Kom W). Bivalves used as tools were identified as *Spatha cailliaudi* and *Mutela dubia*; according to modern nomenclature, these shells should be called *Aspatharia cailliaudi* and *Mutela nilotica*. Other Neolithic specimens are elephant and hartebeest (*A. lelwel*, according to Andrews).

As pointed out by Higgs (1967) and Reed (1959, 1960), the presence of certain domestic animals in the Fayum Neolithic has not yet been substantiated by careful analysis. It is hoped that the present contribution, although limited, supplies some of the missing information.

Description of the material

Unionid (Caelatura sp.?)

At Site E29H2, Trench 2, Layer 8, some fragmentary remains of bivalve shells were collected. They are too small to allow a definite identification. Possibly they pertain to *Caelatura aegyptiaca*, a common unionid of the Nile Valley.

Turtle

The Predynastic site E29G4, yielded one incomplete humerus, which, as far as I have been able to ascertain, represents a turtle. It approaches in size and morphology the humerus of an animal labeled *Testudo graeca*, with a carapace measuring about 35 cm, found in the collection of the department of biology of University of Ghent. As only one specimen was collected and in the absence of well-identified comparative material, no definite identification of the material can be given.

Nile Crocodile (Crocodylus niloticus)

Many fragments of skull, mandibula, and vertebrae of crocodile were collected at the Old Kingdom Site E29G5. They pertain to two animals whose length can be roughly estimated at 250 cm. One fragment of the mandibular symphysis with part of the anterior ramus shows clearly that the animals belong to the group of crocodiles without elongate rostrum: The symphysis does not project behind the fifth dental alveole. Also, it appears from the various skull fragments that the animals had relatively slender snouts. Both observations indicate that the specimens can be asigned to *Crocodylus niloticus*, which was formerly very common in Egypt and many parts of Africa (cf. Arambourg 1947: 456–461; Wermuth & Mertens 1961; Villiers 1958).

Canids (Canis spp.)

At three sites, canid remains were collected, of which a short description follows, while measurements are given in Table I–1: Site E29G1, Area E, Trench 4—a proximal fragment of a humerus: Site E29H2, Trench 1, Layer 5—a fragmentary mandible with P2–M2 row and alveole for M3; Site E29H2, Trench 2, Layer 1—a thoracic vertebra of a young animal; Site E29G3, Area B, surface—a

Table I–1. Measurements of Canids (in mm)

E29G1, Area E, Trench 4	
Humerus, TR.D. prox.	±29.0
E29G3, Area B, surface.	
Tibia, TR.D. dist.	±24.0
E29H2, Trench 1, Layer 5	
Mandible, L. P2–M3	58.5
L.P3–M2	45.0
L.P2	7.3
L.P3	±7.8
L.P4	10.0
L.M1	±18.0
L.M2	7.0
E29G4, surface	
Mandible, L.P3–M2	±52.0
L.M1	±20.0
L.M2	±9.0
Pelvis, max. TR.D. acetabulum	±19.0

fragmentary distal moiety of a tibia; Site E29G4, surface—a jaw fragment with roots of P3–M2; a fragment of innominate bone.

The mandibles have been compared with European protohistoric dogs and wild canids, which still occur in the Near East and Egypt. Measurements for the former (*Canis aureus, C. lupaster, C. lupus*) can be found in Kurten (1965). As far as I have been able to ascertain, there are no reliable morphological differences between the smaller wild canids, domestic dogs, and the material from the Fayum, which, however, is poorly preserved.

The jaw from Site E29G4 has the size of small *C.* (*a.*) *lupaster*, or wolf jackal, but in view of the age of the site (predynastic) it could pertain to a rather large domestic dog. The more complete jaw from the Neolithic site, E29H2, is smaller than recent and fossil (Palestine caves) wolf jackals as measured by Kurten (1965) and falls within the range of recent *C. aureus*, or golden jackal.

Many authors consider *C. lupaster* as a subspecies of *C. aureus*, the difference between typical *C. aureus* and *C. a. lupaster* being mainly one of size. Generally the wolf jackal is considered as a typical North African animal (hence the alternative name Egyptian jackal), while the golden or common jackal is found from Dalmatia to India and Sumatra (cf. Zeuner 1963). The ranges of both animals, however, appear to overlap in North Africa and the Near East (cf. Kurten 1965; Ducos 1968), but generally speaking, one may accept that the jackal in Egypt is characterized by large size. Therefore the Neolithic Fayum mandible (Site E29H2), being smaller than typical *C.* (*a.*) *lupaster*, may be referrable to a domestic dog of the size of the common jackal. A definite identification, however, is impossible.

The two postcranial fragments that have been measured (Table J–1, Sites E29G1 and E29G3) are apparently both larger than their homologs in *C. aureus*, of which I measured one specimen in the Institut des Sciences Naturelles de Belgique (IRSNB). The E29G1 specimen probably pertains to a wolf jackal, as the site is Terminal Paleolithic; the Site E29G3 specimen represents either a dog or a wolf jackal. A definite identification is, however, impossible.

Small, Badger-like Carnivore

Site E29G3 yielded a fragmentary distal moiety of a humerus (distal transverse diameter: ±27 mm) that agrees in size and morphology with its homologue in *Meles Meles*, the palearctic badger. Comparision with other carnivores that are said to occur in northern Egypt (*Mellivora, Ichneumon,* etc.), as far as they are represented in the collection of the IRSNB, yields no good results (differences in size and/or morphology).

The badger does not occur in North Africa today, but its distribution includes Palestine, and I wonder if the species may not have lived in Lower Egypt in former times. As only one specimen was collected and in the absence of ample recent osteological material, no definite identification is attempted.

Hippopotamus (Hippopotamus amphibius)

Hippopotamus is represented at several sites by some bones, including easily identifiable specimens such as a mandibula fragment with broken P3 and

Table I–2. Measurements of *Hippopotamus amphibius* (in mm)

Mandible, L.P4	35
L.M1	49
L.M2	60
Scapula, max. TR.D. articular end	±150
Tibia, TR.D. dist.	105
Phalanx I, L.	69

P4–M2 row, a fragmentary upper molar, a distal moiety of a tibia, and a first phalanx. Less typical specimens include a poorly preserved scapulum, an incomplete second phalanx, a rib, and some tooth fragments. The measurements (Table I–2) fall in the range of the modern form (cf. Hooijer 1950).

Hartebeest (Alcelaphus buselaphus)

Several sites yielded postcranial remains that agree in size and morphology with *A. buselaphus* as described from other sites in Sudan and Egypt (Gautier 1968, App. G). A few fragmentary and some complete teeth are also referrable to hartebeest. Measurements for this material are given in Table I–3.

Unidentified Medium-sized Antelope

Such a game animal is represented by a distal moiety of a metacarpal at Site E29G3. The distal transverse diameter is 30 mm, which appears to be too small for hartebeest (cf. Table I–3). Until now I have been unable to identify the species represented. Although comparable in size, it certainly does not represent *Ammotragus lervia* (Barbary sheep).

Gazella (Gazella dorcas)

Gazella is represented by postcranial remains and a few teeth collected at four sites, the oldest of which (E29G1, Terminal Paleolithic) yielded the largest sample. The measurements fall in the range of *Gazella dorcas*, as identified from C-group sites in northern Sudan (Gautier 1968), and the material probably pertains to that species (Table I-4). From Upper Paleolithic sites in the Sudan, the somewhat larger *G. rufifrons* has been recorded (ibid.). Upper Paleolithic sites in Egypt have also yielded *G. rufifrons*, but it appears that *G. dorcas* is present too, although much less frequent (Gautier, App. G) . *G. dorcas* is considered a palearctic invader in Africa (cf. Gentry 1964). Apparently it moved southward

Table I–3. Measurements of *Alcelaphus buselaphus* (in mm)

Radius, TR.D. dist.	46.2
Astragalus, L.	±47.0
Calcaneum, L.	±98.0
Mt–mc, TR.D. dist.	±38.0–±45.0
Phalanx I, TR.D. dist.	16.0–±18.0

Table I–4. Measurements of *Gazella dorcas* (in mm)

M3, L.	±16.0
Scapula, min. TR.D. glenoid cavity	±18.0
Humerus, TR.D. dist.	23.0
Radius, TR.D. dist.	19.0
Tibia, TR.D. dist	21.0
Calcaneum, L.	52.1
Astragalus, L.	52.1
Phalanx I, L.	36.6–38.8
Phalanx II, L.	20.0

during the late Quaternary, replacing *Gazella* spp. in the African stock. Its presence in the Terminal Paleolithic of the Fayum does not contradict the preceding comments.

Aurochs and Domestic Cattle (Bos subspp.)

Remains of *Bos* were found at five sites dating from Terminal Paleolithic to Old Kingdom. Unfortunately the material is insufficient for statistical study. Also, osteometric data on primitive Egyptian breeds of cattle are lacking. Measurements for some specimens are given in Table I–5. Most of them indicate animals smaller than the large bovid, *B. primigenius*, from other Sudanese and Egyptian sites of the Upper Paleolithic (cf. Gautier 1968, in press).

Site E29H1, of Terminal Paleolithic age, yielded remains containing a large phalanx and other fragments apparently derived from heavy bones. In view of the site's age and the robustness of the material, the cattle present can be referred to *Bos primigenius.* Site E29G1, of comparable age, yielded only a few tooth fragments.

The sample from the Neolithic site, E29G3, contains several measurable specimens that are generally smaller than their analogs in wild cattle. This indicates that the material probably pertains to domestic cattle, although aurochs may

Table I–5. Measurements of *Bos* subspp.[1]

$\overline{P2}$–$\overline{P4}$, L.	±46(N)	
$M\overline{3}$, L.	±38(N)	
Radius, TR.D. dist.	90(OK)	
Calcaneum, TR.D. prox.	32(N)	–
Max. TR.D.	–	50(N)
Tibia, TR.D. dist.	63(N)	
Astragalus, L.	68(N)	
Mc, TR.D. prox.	±75(OK)	–
TR.D. dist.	–	59(N)
Phalanx II, L.	45(N)	
Phalanx III, L.	±89(TP)	±70(N)

[1] N=Neolithic; TP=Terminal Paleolithic; OK=Old Kingdom

still be present. The measurements have been compared with the quantitative data on the cattle of Manching (Iron Age, Bavaria, Schneider 1958: Durr 1961). The specimens tend to cluster in the upper size range of this small breed (mean height at the withers: ±113 cm).

The Predynastic site, E29G4, yielded only a few fragmentary specimens, the status of which is uncertain. Some complete sesamoids agree in size with those of large modern cattle.

The sample from the Old Kingdom site, E29G5, contains remains of a well-developed bovid, as indicated by the measurements of a distal radius and a proximal metacarpal. Both fall in the size range of small wild cattle. Aurochs was still hunted during Pharaonic times in Egypt, and possibly the measured remains pertain to a game animal. The remains may also be derived from a large domestic animal, possibly an ox.

Sheep (and Goat?) (Figure I–1)

Remains of *Ovicaprini* were collected at all sites younger than Terminal Paleolithic, but only Neolithic Site E29G3 yielded a large and interesting sample. Most of the E29G3 material cannot be identified as to species, but some specimens (fragmentary metapodials, radius, humerus, innominate bone) show morphological details that have been described by Boesneck *et al.* (1964) as more typical or frequent in sheep. The measurements and relative proportions of the complete metacarpal are also characteristic of sheep.

The small samples from Sites E29G4 and E29G5 contain some specimens ascribable to sheep (third phalanx, metapodial fragments, humerus). The remains from Neolithic Site E29H2 are indeterminable as to species.

Measurements for the postcranial material from Site E29G3 (Table I–6) have been compared with those for various archaeological and recent samples in Euproe as given by Herre *et al.* (1960), Polloth (1959), and Pfund (1961). As they tend to cluster in the upper range of the size variation found in the European samples, the sheep (and goat) of the Fayum Neolithic must have belonged to (a) breed(s) of fair stature. This is borne out clearly by the dimensions of the complete sheep metacarpal, which is equaled only by the largest archaeological and recent specimens recorded in the literature cited earlier. Possibly it belonged to a ram.

In 1968 the author collected at Site E29G3 several skulls and the remains of three animals. One separate fragment is part of a skull with a small, rather pointed horn core with slightly everted tips; in cross-section it is subcircular [Figure I–1(B)]. At first sight one is tempted to identify this fragment as goat, but in view of the subcircular cross-section, the fact that the horn core is directed outward, and the fact that the fronto-parietal suture probably forms an angle, it seems more likely that the specimen represents a young sheep with horns not yet well developed. A comparison with the goat remains of Es Shaheinab (Bate 1953) Toukh (Gaillard 1934), and modern small goats (cf. Epstein 1946, 1971) points in the same direction.

The larger fragments have been pieced together into two incomplete skull roofs [Figure I–1, (A) and (C)] that show several characteristic features of sheep

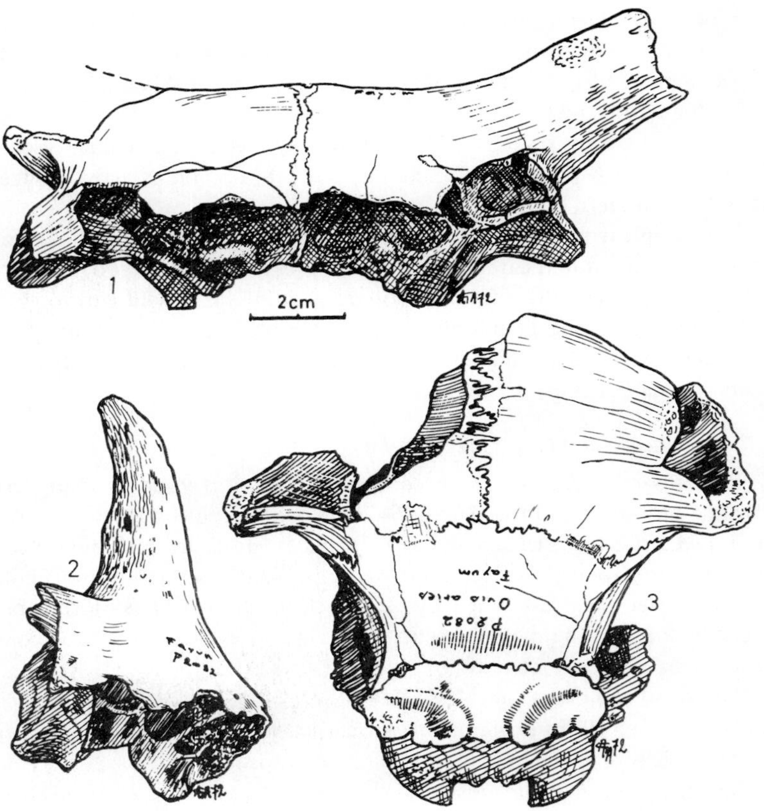

Figure I—1: (a) Anterior view of sheep skull, Fayum Neolithic A, Site E29G3, Area B; (b) approximate anterior view of sheep skull fragment with small horn core, Fayum Neolithic A, Site E29G3, Area B; (c) upper view of sheep skull, Fayum Neolithic A, Site E29G3, Area B.

as described by Boessneck *et al.* (1964) and Boessneck (1969). These features are also illustrated by the relative proportions of the smaller skull (Table J—6). In specimens the cores have an oval cross-section and form a very wide angle with the skull roof. In the larger skull part of the left horn core is sufficiently preserved to indicate that the left horn was probably slightly twisted clockwise when viewed from the front.

The oldest known sheep of ancient Egypt is *O. longipes palaeoaegypticus*, a long-legged breed with corkscrew horns (Duerst and Gaillard 1902). Lately the presence of well-developed horns in the ewes of this breed has been questioned by Ducos (1968), who bases his argument on an alternative interpretation of the Dehuti-hetep relief. However, there exist various representations of *O. a. palaeoaegypticus* in groups (cf. Zeuner 1963; Keller 1909), and it would be surprising if all of these depicted only male animals. Moreover, it appears that the breed

Table I–6. Measurements of Domestic Sheep (and Goat?) (in mm)

Skull, L. akrokranion-bregina	±51.0		
L. akrokranion-lambda	±18.0		
Min. TR.D. between temporal lines	±43.0 (84%; 250%)[1]		
Horn cores, TR.D.	±31.0	21.5	21.0
A–P.D.	±30.0	31.0	25.0
L.	–	–	54.0
L. $P\bar{2}-P\bar{4}$	23.0	–	
L. $M\bar{1}-M\bar{3}$	51.0	55.0	
L. $P\bar{2}-M\bar{3}$	74.0	–	
L. $M\bar{3}$	23.1	–	
Scapula: min. TR.D. glenoid cavity	24.0	–	
Humerus, TR.D. dist.	34.1–37.0		
Radius, TR.D. prox.	34.2		
Tibia, TR.D. dist.	±26.0–31.0		
Astragalus, L.	33.1–35.2		
Calcaneum, L.	64.3		
Phalanx III, L.	28.0[2]		
Mc, L.	±153.0		
TR.D. prox.	±27.0		
TR.D. diaph.	16.2		
TR.D. dist.	28.6		
Index TR.D. diaph./L.	10.5		
Mc–mt, TR.D. dist.	24.8–±28		

[1] Measurement expressed in percentage of L. akrokranion-bregina and akrokranion-lambda.

[2] Site E29G5, Predynastic; all other measurements from Site E29G3.

changed in the course of time and that hornless ewes are figured in younger representations (Epstein 1971: 69).

Sheep comparable with the Egyptian breed mentioned are known from various archaeological sites in Asia (Catal Huyuk, Mesopotamia, Palestine, Mohenjo-Daro). Discussions as to whether these sheep are all derived from one basal stock or a result of parallel variation are purely academic, as no good criteria exist on which theories of descent can be based (cf. Zeuner 1963; Boetger 1958; Epstein 1971; etc.). Nevertheless it appears likely that these screw-horned sheep are closely related and that such a form was introduced in Africa during the Gerzean or during an earlier period. Indeed the oldest reliable record is at Toukh (Gerzean); older records are not well substantiated by osteological evidence.

The Fayum skulls with the larger horn cores are comparable in general morphology with the more complete type specimen of *O. l. palaeoaegypticus* from Toukh. The cross section of the horn cores of this form is oval, with a depression on the posterior half of the median side, followed by a blunt posterio-internal angle or keel (cf. Duerst & Gaillard; Gaillard; Ducos 1968: 63, Fig. 15,

n. 16). As already mentioned, the cross-section of the Fayum horn cores is oval and without indication of a posterio-median depression and a posterio-internal keel. However, the specimens are very incomplete and somewhat eolized, so that poorly expressed morphological details may have been obliterated. Moreover, the more complete specimen pertains to an animal with poorly developed horns (Figure I–1).

In conclusion, we may say that although the evidence is incomplete, the Fayum sheep seem to belong to a large breed with outward-directed horns twisted in a corkscrew fashion. In all probability it is related to the breed called *O. l. palaeoaegypticus* (Duerst & Gaillard 1902), also known as the corkscrew-hair sheep (Zeuner) or the hairy thin-tailed sheep (Epstein).

Discussion and Conclusions

In Table I–7 the absolute frequencies of the several animals encountered are listed per site. The number of identified specimens per site is limited, and statistical treatment has not been attempted. It is clear, however, that the Terminal Paleolithic sites are dominated by the game animals already encountered at comparable sites along the Nile Valley toward the south. These animals are hartebeest, *Gazella*, and wild cattle.

Younger sites are dominated by domestic animals, but game was still on the menu. Moreover, it is very likely that *Ovicaprini* were the dominant domestic animals. Indeed bones of smaller animals such as goat or sheep are less resistant to destructive processes during fossilization than the larger and heavier bones of cattle. Hence, their chances of being conserved in an identifiable state are less than those of cattle. Nevertheless the *Ovicaprini* appear to be much better represented than cattle. It should also be noted that within the group of the *Ovicaprini* no specimens typical of gaot were recognized, but some specimens can be definitely asigned to sheep. Sheep, hence, may have been much more important than goats. The specimens pertain in all probability to the breed described as *O. longipes palaeoaegypticus.*

The presence of domestic sheep in the Fayum is not surprising. According to Higgs (1967), domestic sheep or goat was already established in Cyrenaica (Hauah Fteah) as early as ±4800 BC. Unfortunately the evidence is scanty, and nothing is known about the breed(s) present.

The presence of domestic cattle in the Neolithic A is not well substantiated by osteological evidence, but the size of the material is indicative of rather large domestic cattle, probably related to the long-horned breed of early historic times in Egypt. The question as to whether dogs were present in the Fayum Neolithic A cannot be solved either. To me it appears very likely that they already formed part of the technological outfit of the Fayum Neolithic A people, who kept sheep and possibly other gregarious domesticates. The osteological evidence, however, is inconclusive.

Table I–7. Frequencies of Fragments of Different animals.

Site	*Hippopotamus*	*Hartebeest*	*Gazella*	*Cattle*	*Sheep/goat*	*Other faunal remains; remarks*[1]
G5, surface	3	2 (?)	2	11	5	fish (4), crocodile (3)
Trench 1, cultural layer	—	—	—	—	—	bird (4), crocodile (3)
G4, surface	1	1 (?)	—	4	18	fish (3), bird (12), wolf jackal or dog (2), crocodile (31), turtle
Trench 1, cultural layer	—	—	(?)	—	(?)	bird (4)
G3, Area B, surface	—	—	—	20	99	badger (?) (1), wolf jackal or dog (1), medium-sized antelope (1)
Area B2, surface	—	—	—	1	13	
Area B3, surface	1 (?)	—	5	4	30	
H2, Trench 1, Layer 3	—	—	—	—	3	
Layer 4	—	—	1	—	6	fish (1)
Layer 5	—	—	—	—	4	wolf jackal or dog (1)
Trench 2, surface	—	—	—	—	1	
Layer 1	—	—	—	—	1	wolf jackal or dog (1)
Layer 2	—	—	1	—	—	
Layer 4	—	—	—	—	1	
Layer 8	3	—	—	—	—	bivalve (2)
Layer 9	1	—	—	—	—	
G1, Surface	2	5	1	—	—	fish (1), hippopotamus mandible
Area A, surface	—	6	—	—	—	
Trench 1, surface	—	—	3	—	—	
Trench 1, cultural layer	—	4	—	—	—	bird (2), fish (1)
Area B, surface	—	—	—	4	—	
Area C, surface	2	2	—	—	—	bird (2)
Area E, Trench 4	—	9	18	—	—	fish (3), wolf jackal (1)
H1, Surface	—	6	—	—	—	
Area B	2	10	—	7	—	
Trench 18	—	9	—	—	—	

[1]The number in parentheses is the number of specimens.

Andrews (1903) and Caton-Thompson (1934) list pig and elephant among the animals from the Neolithic in the Fayum. Apparently pig is quite frequent at Kom W (frequency: pig, 5; goat–sheep, 8; ox, 9) while elephant was found only once. The absence of pig from the present collection is difficult to explain. Possibly it indicates that small samples such as those studied here and, apparently, those referred to by Caton-Thompson and Gardner (1934) are not wholly reliable.

References

Andrews, C. W.
1903 Notes on an expedition to the Fayum with description of some new mammals. Geological Magazine (*London*). x(Dec. IV): 337–343.
Arambourg, C.
1947 Contribution à l'étude géologique et paléontologique du Bassin du Lac Rodolphe et de la Basse Vallée de l'Omo. Part 2: Paleontologie. *Mission Géologique de l'Omo* 1932–33 **I** (Fasc. III); *Museum Naturelle Histoire (Paris).*
Bate, D. M. A.
1953 The vertebrate fauna. In *Shaheinab*, edited by A.J. Arkell. New York & London Oxford Univ. Press. Pp. 11–19.
Boessneck, J.
1969 Osteological differences between sheep *(Ovis aries Linné)* and goats *(Capra hircus Linné)*. In *Science in archaeology*, edited by D. Brothwell & E. Higgs. London: Thames & Hudson. Pp. 331–358.
Boessneck, J., M. H. Muller, & H. Teichert
1964 Osteologische Unterscheidungsmerkmale zwischen Schaf *(Ovis* aries Linné) und Ziege (*Capra hircus* Linné). *Kühn-Archiv.* **78** (H.1-2): 1–129.
Boettger, C. R.
1958 *Die Haustiere Afrikas*. Jena: G. Fischer Verlag.
Brentjes, B.
1965 Die Haustierwerdung in Orient. *(Neue Brehmbücherei Wittemberg Lutherstadt)* **334.**
Caton-Thompson, G. & E. W. Gardner
1934 *The Desert Fayum.* London: Royal Anthropological Institute of Great Britain and Ireland.
Ducos, P.
1968 L'origine des animaux domestiques en Palestine. *Publ. Instit. Prehist. Univ. Bordeaux,* Mém. (No. 6).
Duerst, J. & C. Gaillard
1902 Studien über die Geschichte des ägyptischen Hausschafes *Recueil Trav. Philol. archéol. Egypt (Paris)* **24**:44–76.
Durr, G.
1961 Neue Funde des Rindes aus dem keltischem Oppidum von Manching. In *Stud. vor-und fruhgeschichtlichen Tierresten Bayerns,* **2**: *Tieranat.* Instit. Universität München.)
Epstein, H.
1946 The Hejas dwarf goat. *Journal of Heredity* **37**(11):345–352.
1971 *The origin of the domestic animals of Africa.* New York, London, Munich: Africana Publ.
Gaillard, C.
1934 Contribution á l'ètude de la faune prèhistorique de l'Egypte. *Arch. Mus. Historie Naturelle* (Lyon) **14**(3):1–25; 1–12.

Gautier, A.
1968 Mammalian remains of the Northern Sudan and Southern Egypt. In *The prehistory of Nubia*, Vol. I, edited by F. Wendorf. Dallas: Fort Burgwin Research Center & Southern Methodist Univ. Press. Pp. 80–99.
Gentry, A. W.
1964 Skull characters of African gazelles. *Ann. & Magazine Natural History* (London) **VIII** (Ser. 13): 353–382.
Herre, W., G. Nobis, H. Requate, & Siewing, G.
1960 *Die Haustiere von Haithabu.* Neumünster: K. Wachholtz Verlag.
Higgs, E. S.
1967 *Domestic animals.* In *The Haua Fteah (Cyrenaica)*, edited by C.B.M. McBurney. London: Cambridge Univ. Press. Pp. 313–323.
Hooijer, D. A.
1950 The fossil hippopotamidae of Asia, with notes on the recent species. *Zoolog. Verhand. Rijksmus. Natuurk. Hist. Leiden* (No. 8).
Kurten, B.
1965 The carnivora of the Palestine caves. *Acta Zoolog. Fennice* (Helsinki) **107.**
Lortet & Gaillard
1907 La Faune mommifiée de l'ancienne Egypte. *Arch. Mus. Lyon, t.* **IX**(2): 1–130 (184 figs.).
Pfund, D.
1961 Neue Funde von Schaf und Ziege aus dem keltischen Oppidum von Manching. In *Stud. vor-u. frühgeschichtlichen Tierresten Bayerns,* **11**: *Tieranat.* Instit. Univ. Munchen.
Polloth, K.
1959 Die Schafe und Ziegen des Latène-Oppidum Manchings In *Stud. vor-u. frühgeschichtl. Tierresten Bayerns.* Tieranat. Instit. Univ. München.
Reed, Ch-A.
1959 Animal domestication in the prehistoric Near East. *Science* **130** (No. 3389): 1629–1639.
1960 A review of the archaeological evidence on animal domestication in the prehistoric Near East. In *Prehistoric investigations in Iraqi Kurdistan; Studies in ancient oriental civilization,* No. 31, edited by Braidwood R.J. & Howe. Chicago: Oriental Institute, Univ. Chicago Press.
1961 Osteological evidence for prehistoric domestication in southwestern Asia. *Zeitschr. Tierzüchtung u. Züchtungs biologie, Bd.* **76** (Hft. 1): 31–38.
Schneider, F.
1958 Die Rinder des Latène-Oppidums Manching. In *Stud. vor-und frühgeschichtlichen Tierresten Bayerns,* **5.** Tieranat. Instit. Univ. München.
Villers, A.
1958 Initiations Africaines. XV. In *Tortues et Crocodiles de l'Afrique Noùe Francaise.* I.F.A.N. Dakar.
Wermuth, H. & Mertens, R.
1961 Schildkroten. Krokodile. In *Brückenechsen,* **9.** Jena: Fisher.
Zeuner, A.
1963 *A history of domesticated animals.* New York: Harper & Row.

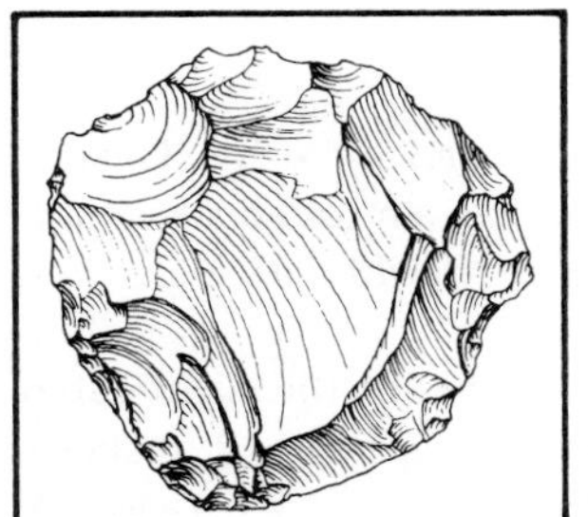

Appendix J

Fish Remains from Upper Paleolithic Sites Near Idfu and Isna

P.H. GREENWOOD
ELIZABETH J. TODD

Introduction

Without exception, the fish remains consist of isolated and often damaged bones. Some 2500 bones can be identified, and there is an almost equal number of small fragments from neurocranial roofing bones of clariid catfishes; these cannot be identified further.

The fragmentary nature of the material, combined with the slight osteological differences between extant species of the families represented, makes it impossible to identify the species of fish from which the bones are derived. At best a generic identification is possible, but more often only a familial identification can be made with certainty. For example, the clariid catfishes *Clarias* and *Heterobranchus* are osteologically very similar. However, two bones (the palatine and the articular) show fairly marked intergeneric differences, which are usually detectable in the fossils. Thus at some sites we are able to identify both genera from these bones, but since the bulk of the clariid material does not exhibit any generic characteristics, it can be identified only to the familial level.

For each site we give an estimate of the minimum number of fish represented in the material and an estimate of their size range. The number of fishes is based principally on paired bones, the higher number of a left or right element being taken as the minimum number of fishes present. The possible size range is calculated by direct comparison of the fossil bone with its counterpart in an extant species. The figure in parentheses after the bones listed is the total number of specimens from that particular site.

Site Reports

Site E71P1, Area 1

Family *Clariidae*: Supraorbital (1); numerous fragments of neurocranial roofing bones. Judging from the size differences in the tubercles ornamenting these bones, several different individuals are represented; no estimate of their size range is possible.

Site E71P1, Area 2

Family *Clariidae, Clarias* sp.: numerous fragments of neurocranial roofing bones; lateral ethmoid (2); frontal (1); supraoccipital (3); articular (1); ceratohyal (2); fragment of epi- and ceratohyal (1). At least three fishes present (based on the number of supraoccipitals); size range 45–90 cm standard length.

Site E71P1, Area 3

Family *Clariidae, Clarias* sp.: numerous neurocranial fragments; ethmoid (20); lateral ethmoid (37); infraorbital (2); frontals (52); fragments of parasphenoid (21); supraorbital (16); supraoccipital (9); pterotic (?) (1); palatine (1 and 2 fragments); operculum (3); vomer (2); dentary (32); fragments of hyoid arch elements (73); urohyal (4); articular (69); quadrate (22); pectoral girdle elements (mostly cleithra) (13); pectoral fin spines (24); branchiostegal ray fragments (?) (4); centra (11 and several fragments). At least 50 fishes are represented (based on the number of articulars); size range 14–100 cm standard length. Since the articular is generically identifiable (see "Introduction"), it seems reasonable to assume that the clariid remains can all be referred to the genus *Clarias*.

Family *Cyprinidae, Barbus* sp.: a fragment of pharyngeal bone with some teeth attached; the articular heads of two dorsal fin pterygiophores. Probably two fishes are represented; size range 35–45 cm standard length. The size range of these fish, and the morphology of the pharyngeal teeth preserved, indicates a similarity with the extant *Barbus bynni.*

Site E71P1, Area 6

Family *Clariidae, Clarias* sp.: numerous fragments of neurocranial roofing bones; frontal (4 fragments); supraorbital (4); parasphenoid (4 fragments); palatine (2 and 2 fragments); dentary (3); articular (20); epihyal (16); ceratohyal (11); cleithrum (2 fragments); pectoral fin spines (3). At least 11 individuals are represented (based on the number of articulars); size range 20–95 cm standard length.

Family *Cyprinidae, Barbus* sp.: one left lower pharyngeal bone and teeth; the morphology of the teeth is very like that of the extant *Barbus bynni*. This bone is estimated to be from a fish *ca*. 60 cm standard length.

Labeo sp.: one right lower pharyngeal bone and teeth from a fish of indeterminable size. Unfortunately none of the characters preserved permits identification of the species.

Site E71P2, Trench 2

Family *Clariidae,* probably *Clarias* sp.: some neurocranial fragments (roofing bones) and one ethmoid. The various sizes of the neurocranial bones suggest that at least two fish are represented.

Site E71K4, Trench 2 (0–20 cm)

Family *Clariidae, Clarias* sp.: several fragments of neurocranial roofing bones; ethmoid (1); dentary (3); articular (2); operculum (1); ceratohyal (1); head of a hyomandibular (1). The number of dentaries preserved indicates the presence of at least two fishes, but the sizes of the other bones suggest as many as four individuals in the size range 40–90 cm standard length.

Site E71K1

Family *Clariidae, Clarias* sp.: many fragments of neurocranial roofing bones; frontals (7); lateral ethmoids (8 and some fragments); ethmoid (4); ethmoid and vomer (1); supraoccipital (fragments); pterotic (1); sphenotic (2); supraoperculum (2); supraorbital (5); operculum (1); palatine (2); hyomandibular head (1); epihyal (24); hypohyal (3); ceratohyal (3); urophyal (1); articular (9); quadrate (2); dentary (5); pectoral girdle (fragments); cleithrum (1); centra (28).

At least six fishes are present (based on the number of articular bones); size range 20–110 cm standard length.

Family *Cyprinidae, Barbus* sp.: centrum of a fourth vertebra; an anterior caudal vertebra; the haemal arch and the proximal part of the spine from the second preural vertebra. Probably only one fish is represented by these bones, which are from an individual 50–60 cm standard length.

Family *Cichlidae*: a damaged centrum (from a fish *ca*. 15 cm standard length) is tentatively referred to this family.

Site E71K3

Family *Clariidae*: Both *Clarias* (51 palatine bones and 213 articulars) and *Heterobranchus* (3 palatine bones) are represented (see "Introduction"). Thus the remaining clariid bones can be identified only to family. But considering the predominance of *Clarias* species over *Heterobranchus* (108 individuals compared with 2), it seems probable that most of the bones should be referred to *Clarias*. This material from Site E71K3 comprises ethmoid (79 and several fragments); lateral ethmoid (106 and several fragments); vomer (22 large and several small fragments); frontals (8 and several fragments); parasphenoid (several fragments); basioccipital (5) and basioccipital attached to the fused anterior vertebrae (2); dentary (112); articular (213); palatine fragments (23); quadrate (117); hyomandibular (2); hypohyal (75 and several fragments); epi- and ceratohyal (6); ceratohyal (56 and 60 fragments); epihyal (70 and some fragments); branchiostegal rays (many fragments); operculum (12); interoperculum (16); supraorbital (106 and a few fragments tentatively identified); preorbital (46); infraorbitals (31); cleithrum (many fragments); pectoral fin spines (180 from the proximal end and numerous fragments from the distal end); centra (920 and numerous fragments); tripus (5 and some fragments thought to be tripodes).

Family *Cyprinidae, Barbus* sp.: articular head of the first dorsal pterygiophore; an almost entire first dorsal pterygiophore; three damaged lower pharyngeal bones (two left, one of indeterminable side); two isolated lower pharyngeal teeth. A piece of ossified fin ray and a fragment of operculum are tentatively referred to this family and genus. At least two individuals are represented; both are in the size range 40–45 cm standard length. The size of these fishes and the form of the lower pharyngeal bones and teeth suggest comparison with *Barbus bynni*.

Family *Cichlidae*: three centra and a first anal pterygiophore are referred to this family; all could be from a species of *Tilapia*.

Indeterminable percoid fishes: a fragment of branchiostegal ray and four fragments of fin rays (spinous) are from percoid fishes but cannot be identified further. The branchiostegal ray resembles one from *Lates niloticus* (family *Centropomidae*).

Site E71K9, Area A

Family *Clariidae, Clarias* sp.: two articulars (both left side) from fishes 40–50 cm standard length.

Site E71K9, Area C

Family *Clariidae*: fragments of neurocranial roofing bones and part of a pectoral spine (including the articular head). At least one fish (*ca.* 25 cm standard length) is represented.

Site E71P7, Area A

Family *Clariidae*: neurocranial fragments, particularly roofing bones, a fragment of frontal, and (tentatively) part of a branchiostegal ray. It is impossible to give an estimate of the number of individuals represented in this sample, or of their sizes.

Family *Bagridae*: A dorsal fin spine is referred to this catfish family because of its resemblance to the dorsal spine of *Chrysichthys auratus.*

Site E71P7, Area B

Family *Clariidae*: represented by some fragmentary neurocranial roofing bones and part of a dentary.

Site E71K18, Area A

Family *Clariidae, Clarias* sp.: numerous fragments of neurocranial roofing bones; supraoccipital (1); fragments of parasphenoid; vomer (1); suborbital (1); supraorbital (5); quadrate (4); articular (7); dentary (6); palatine (2); interoperculum (1); ceratohyal (1); epihyal (1); urohyal (1); cleithrum (2 and some fragments); coracoid (1); pectoral fin spine (11); centra (10 and some fragments). Part of a basioccipital is tentatively referred to this family. At least seven fishes are represented in this sample (based on the number of pectoral fin spines); they are in the size range 15–80 cm standard length.

Site E71K18, Area B

Family *Clariidae*: One palatine may be from a *Heterobranchus* species; 27 articulars, however, are from *Clarias.* Thus it seems likely that the rest of the clariid bones present could be referred to that genus—many fragments of neurocranial roofing bones; lateral ethmoid (3 and a fragment), frontal (2and some fragments); supraoccipital (2); supraorbital (11); part of a suprapreoperculum; preorbital (4); operculum (fragments); sphenotic (?) (fragments); palatine (1); quadrate (2); articular (27); dentary (12); epihyal (3); ceratohyal (12); urohyal (1); fragments of branchiostegal rays; posttemporal (fragment); cleithrum (10 and many fragments); coracoid (1); pectoral spine (19 and some fragments); centra (5). At least 15 individuals (based on the number of articulars) are represented; their size range is 25–40 cm standard length.

Site E71K18, Area D

Family *Clariidae*, probably *Clarias* sp.: neurocranial roofing bones (fragments); articular (1); pectoral fin spine (1). At least one individual is represented the bones are estimated to be from a fish (or fishes) 35–50 cm standard length.

Site E71K18, Area E

Family *Clariidae*: part of a right epihyal from a fish about 50 cm standard length.

Site E71K5, Area A

Family *Clariidae*, probably *Clarias* sp.: fragments of neurocranial roofing bones, part of a dentary, and a pectoral fin spine. At least one fish is represented, but the sizes of the different bones indicate that more were present and that they were in the size range 40–65 cm standard length.

Discussion

The fish fauna represented by these fossils are, taxonomically speaking, very depauperate when compared with the ichthyofauna of the present-day Nile or with contemporary fossil fauna from Nubia (see Greenwood 1962). The predominance at all sites of one family (the Clariidae), and probably one genus (*Clarias*), is noteworthy.

If, as seems likely, human selectivity is involved, then the material is probably more a reflection of fishing techniques than of the ecological conditions obtaining at the time of deposition. Nevertheless the comparison with the Nubian sites is of interest because human activity can be assumed to have influenced the species composition of those deposits.

Of course the fish fauna might be a reflection of ecological conditions, which would then influence the species available to the fisherman. If this assumption is made, then throughout the period covered by the deposits the habitat represented would be a shallow swamp or swampy lake perhaps connected with or near open, better oxygenated water from which the species of *Barbus, Labeo,* and presumed *Lates* could be obtained.

From the evidence available to us, we cannot reach any definite conclusions as to which interpretation is more likely.

References

Greenwood, P. H.
1968 Fish remains. In *The prehistory of Nubia,* edited by F. Wendorf. Dallas: Fort Burgwin Research Center and Southern Methodist Univ. Press.

Appendix K

Wear Patterns on Some Lithic Artifacts from Isnan Sites

ROMUALD SCHILD

FRED WENDORF

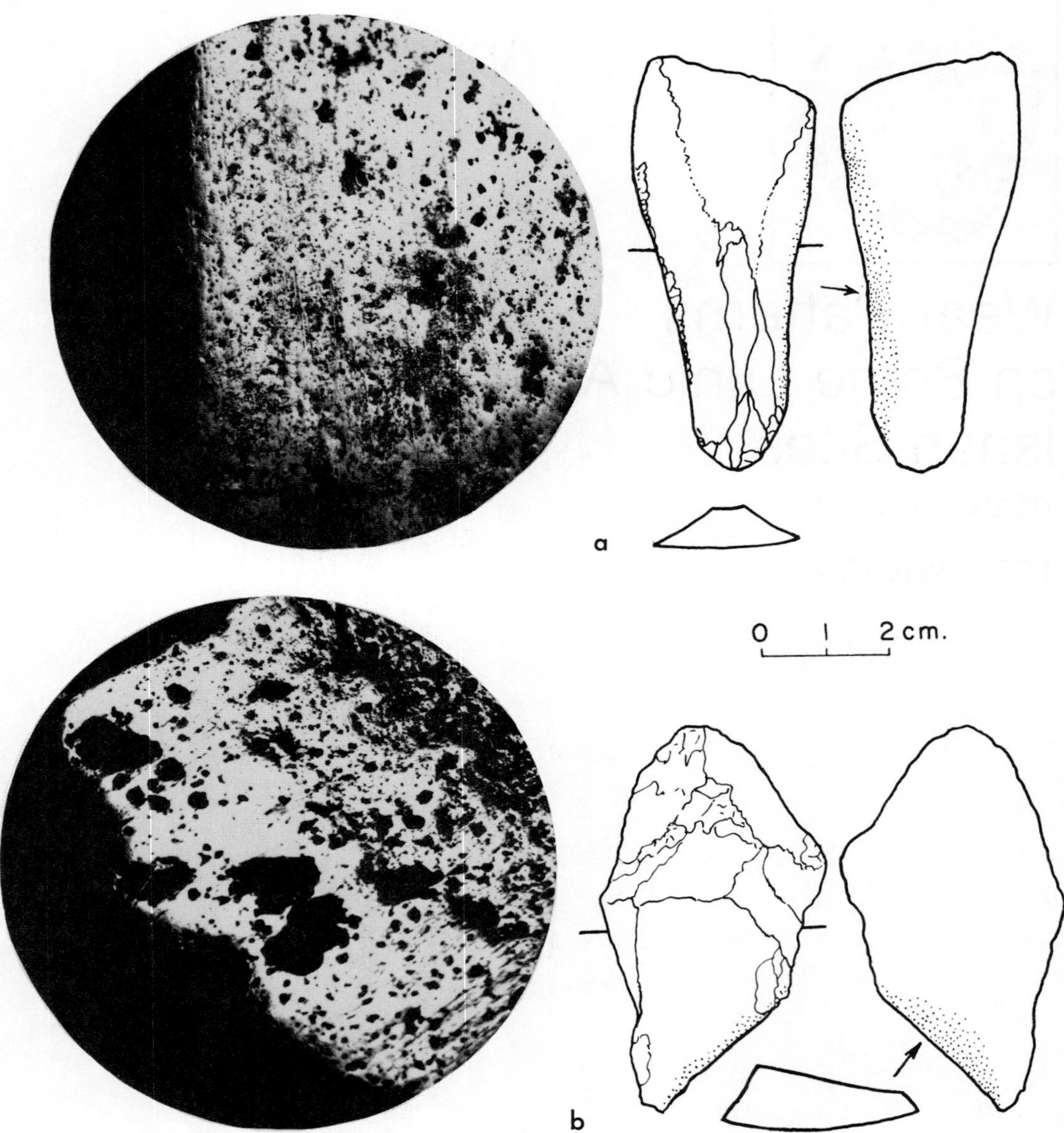

Figure K–1: Microphotographs showing traces of use on two sickles from Sites E71K14, Area A and E71K15. Arrows point to photographed spot. Magnification × 260. Photography by K. K. Pollesch.

A series of artifacts, mostly naturally backed flakes and a few retouched pieces, from Sites E71K14, Areas A and C, and E71K15 show extensive traces of lustrous edges of the type known as sickle sheen. All the pieces showing sickle sheen were examined under an MT-3, Epitype 2 (Karl Zeiss, Jena) metallographic microscope under magnifications ranging from 100 "times" to 300 "times". The pieces were not coated, but were placed at 90° toward the lens. This position permits detailed observation of worked edges and adjacent surfaces and shows the maximum relief.

The naturally backed flakes show damage that resembles a lunar landscape, with larger and smaller craters located close to the working edge and never extending beyond the range of the sheen [Figure K–1 (b)]. This is typical for Neolithic sickles in Europe (Semenov 1964). The working edge is blunted, and there is a delicate striation developed approximately 90° toward the edge or slightly inclined. The retouched pieces have this sheen developed along one entire edge, as seen on the retouched blade in Figure K–1 (a). The striation on these pieces is parallel with the edge, and the lunar-like landscape is less developed, although evident.

From these observations it is obvious that the naturally backed pieces were used in the hand without hafting and with a forceful cutting motion at a right angle and without a sawing motion. The pieces with parallel striation and the sheen developed along the entire edge were possibly mounted in a handle that permitted their use in a saw-like manner and with less force. In all instances the sheen is well developed and indicates extensive use of the sickle.

References

Semenov, S. A.
1964 *Prehistoric Technology*. London.

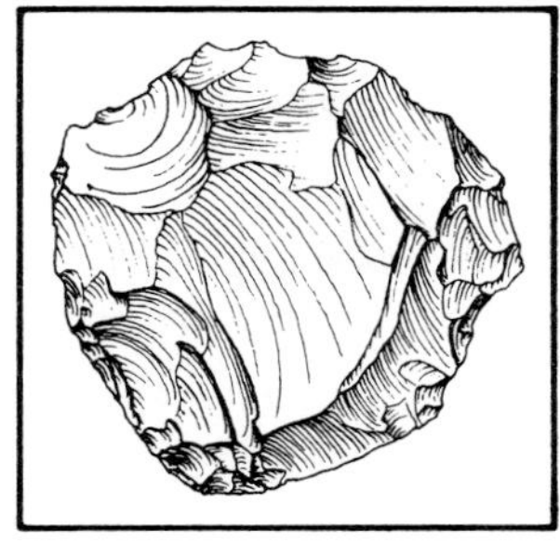

References

Aleem, Anwar Abdel

1958 Taxonomic paleoecological investigation of the Diatom-Flora of the extinct Fayorem Lake (Upper Egypt). *University of Alexandria Bulletin* **2**:217–44.

Attia, M. I.

1954 *Deposits in the Nile Valley and the Delta.* Cairo, Egypt: Papers of the Geological Survey of Egypt, 356 pp.

Baedeker, Karl

1929 *Egypt and the Sudan; Handbook for Travellers* 8th Revised Edition, New York: Scribner.

Ball, John

1907 *A Description of the first Aswan cataract of the Nile.* Cairo, Egypt: Egypt Survey Department, 121 pp.

1939 *Contributions to the geography of Egypt.* Cairo, Egypt: Government Press.

Beadnell, H. J. L.

1905 *The topography and geology of the Fayum Province of Egypt.* Cairo, Egypt: Papers of the Geological Survey of Egypt, 101 pp.

Brown, R. H.

1892 *The Fayum and Lake Moeris.* London: Edward Stanford.

Buckley, James D., Milton A. Trautman, & Eric H. Willis

1968 Isotopes radiocarbon measurements vi. *Radiocarbon* **10.** (No. 2) 246–294.

Butler, Barbara

1974 Analysis of skeleton from site E71K1. In *The Fakhurian: A late paleolithic industry from Upper Egypt and its place in Nilotic prehistory,* edited by D. Lubell. Cairo, Egypt: Papers of The Geological Survey of Egypt (58).

Butzer, Karl W.

1959 Die Naturlandschaft Aegyptens Wahrend der Vorgeschichte und dem Dynastischen Zeitalter. *Abh., Akad. Wiss. Lit. (Mainz), Math.-Nature, Kl.* (No. 2) 81 pp.

1960 Archaeology and geology in ancient Egypt. *Science* **132**:1617–1624.

1961 Archaeologische Fundstellen Ober-und Mittelaegyptens in ihrer geologischen Landschaft. In *Mitteilungen des Deutschen Archaologischen Instituts Abteilung Kairo,* Vol. 17. Pp. 54–68.

Butzer, Karl W. & Carl L. Hansen

1968 *Desert and river in Nubia.* Madison: Univ. of Wisconsin Press.

Caton-Thompson, G.

1946 The Levalloisian industries of Egypt. *Proceedings of the Prehistoric Society* **12***(4): 57–120.*

1952 *Kharga Oasis in prehistory.* London: Athlone Press.

Caton-Thompson, G. & E. W. Gardner

1929 Recent work on the problem of Lake Moeris. *Geograph. J.* **73**:20–60.

1934 *The Desert Fayum.* London: Royal Anthropological Institute.

Caton.Thompson, G., E. W. Gardner, and S. A. Huzayyin

1937 Lake Moeris; Reinvestigations and Some Comments. *Journal of the Royal Anthropological Institute,* **61**:301–308.

Chatters, Ray M.

1968 Washington State University natural radiocarbon measurements I. *Radiocarbon* **10** (No. 2); 479–498.

Chavaillon, Jean & Jean Maléy Chavaillon

1966 Une Industrie sur Galet de la Vallee du Nil (Soudan). *Bulletin de la Societe Prehistorique Francaise* **63**(2):65–70.

Chmielewski, W.

1965 Archaeological research on Pleistocene and Lower Holocene sites in Northern Sudan: Preliminary results. In *Contributions to the prehistory of Nubia,* edited by Fred Wendorf. Dallas: Fort Burgwin Research Center and Southern Methodist Univ. Press.

1968 Early and Middle Paleolithic sites near Arkin, Sudan. In *The Prehistory of Nubia,* Vol. 1, edited by Fred Wendorf. Dallas: Fort Burgwin Research Center and Southern Methodist University Press. Pp. 110–147.

Churcher, C. S.

1972 *Late Pleistocene vertebrates from archaeological sites in the Plain of Kom Ombo, Upper Egypt.* Toronto: Royal Ontario Museum Life Science Contribution 82.

Currelly, C. T.

1913 *Catalogue General des Antiquites Egyptiennes du Musee du Caire, Nos. 63001-64906: Stone Implements.* Le Caire.

diCesnola, Arturo Palma

1960 L'Industria Litica della Stazione de Abka. *Kush* **8**:182–236.

deHeinzelin, Jean

1968 Geological history of the Nile Valley in Nubia. In *The prehistory of Nubia,* edited by Fred Wendorf, Vol. 1. Dallas: Fort Burgwin Research Center and Southern Methodist Univ. Press. Pp. 19–55.

1971 Geology: Ed Debba to Korti. In *The prehistory and geology of Northern Sudan,* assembled by Joel L. Shiner. Mimeographed report to the National Science Foundation.

El-Akkad, S. & A. A. Dardir

1966 *Geology and phosphate deposits of Wasif, Safaga Area,* No. 36. Cairo, Egypt: Geological Survey of Egypt, Pp. 1–35.

El-Hinnawi, M. & T. El-Deftar

1970 Geological map of the Limestone Plateau, Western Desert (Scale 1:50,000). Cairo, Egypt: Geological Survey of Egypt, Cairo.

El-Naggar, Z.

1966 Stratigraphy and classification of type Esna group of Egypt: *American Association Petroleum Geologists Bulletin* **50**: 1455–1477.

Emory, W. B.

1961 *Archaic Egypt.* New York: Penguin

Fairbridge, Rhodes W.

1962 New radiocarbon dates of Nile sediments. *Nature* Vol. **196**:108–110.

Faris, M. I.

1947 The contact of the Cretaceous and Eocene rocks in the Taramsa–Tukh Area

Bull. Inst. Egypte **28**:73–85.
Gardner, E. W.
1934 Some lacustrine mollusca from the Fayum Depression: A study in variation *Memoirs of the Institute of Egypt* **18.**
Gardner, E. W. & G. Caton-Thompson
1926 The recent geology and neolithic industry of the Northern Fayum Desert. *Journal of the Royal Anthropological Institute* **lxi**:301–308.
Geyh, M. A.
1967 Hanover radiocarbon measurements. *Radiocarbon* 9:218–236.
Giegengack, R. F. Jr.
1968 *Late Pleistocene history of the Nile Valley in Egyptian Nubia.* Ph.D. dissertation, Yale University.
Green, David L., George H. Ewing, & George J. Armelagos
1967 Dentition of a Mesolithic population from Wadi Halfa, Sudan. *American Journal of Physical Anthropology* **27**(1):41–56.
Guichard, Jean & Genevieve Guichard
1965 The Early and Middle Paleolithic of Nubia; A preliminary report. In *Contributions to the prehistory of Nubia,* edited by Fred Wendorf. Dallas: Fort Burgwin Research Center and Southern Methodist Univ. Press. Pp. 57–116.
Guichard, Jean & G. Guichard
1968 Contribution to the study of the Early and Middle Paleolithic of Nubia. In *The prehistory of Nubia,* Vol. 1., edited by Fred Wendorf. Dallas: Fort Burgwin Research Center and Southern Methodist University Press. Pp. 148–93.
Hamdan, G.
1964 Egypt—The land and people. In *Guidebook to the geology and archaeology of Egypt,* edited by Frank A. Reilly. Amsterdam and New York: Petroleum Exploration Society of Libya, 6th Annual Field Conference, El-Sevier.
Hassan, Fekri A.
1972 Note on Sebilian sites from Dishna Plain. *Chronique d'Egypte* **47**:11–16.
1974 *The archaeology of the Dishna Plain.* Papers of The Geological Survey of Egypt (59)
in press *The Sebilian of the Nile Valley: Some new concepts.* In Paleoanthropology, edited by L. G. Freeman. The Hague: Mouton.
Hassan, Fekri A. & Fred Wendorf
1974 A Sebilian assemblage from El Eilh "Upper Egypt" *Chronique d'Egypte* **49**:211–221.
Hester, James and P. Hoebler
1970 *Prehistoric settlement patterns in the Libyan Desert.* University of Utah Papers in Anthropology 92, Nubia Series 4. Salt Lake City: Univ. of Utah Press.
Hume, W. F.
1911 The effects of secular oscillations in Egypt during the Cretaceous and Eocene periods. *Quarterly Journal Geological Society* (London) **67**:118–148.
1965 *Geology of Egypt: The stratigraphical history of Egypt from the close of the Cretaceous period to the end of the Oligocene.* Cairo: Geological Survey of Egypt. 743 pp.
Irwin, Henry T., Joe Ben Wheat, & Lee F. Irwin
1968 *University of Colorado investigations of Paleolithic and Epipaleolithic sites in the Sudan, Africa.* University of Utah Papers in Anthropology 90. Salt Lake City: University of Utah Press.
Issawi, B.
A review of the Upper Cretaceous–Lower tertiary stratigraphy in Central and Southern Egypt. (Manuscript in preparation).
Jomard, E. F.
1918 Memoire sur le Lac de Moeris. *Description de l'Egypte: Antiquites, Memoires,* Vol. 1. Paris, Pp. 79–114.
Kleindienst, M. R.
1967 Brief observations on some Stone Age sites recorded by the Yale University Prehistoric Expedition to Nubia, 1964–1965. *Congres Panafricain de Prehistoire, Dakar, 1967.* 111–112 pp.

Kowalski, S.
1969 Zagadnienie Przejscia od Paleolitu Srodkoweg do Gornego w Polsce Poludniowej w aspekcie postepu technicznego. *Swiatowit* **30**:5–21.

Krukowski, S.
1939 Paleolit. *Prehistoria ziem polskich.* Krakow: PAU.

Krueger, Harold W. & C. Francis Weeks
1966 Geochron Laboratories, Inc., radiocarbon measurement ii. *Radiocarbon* **8**:142–160.

Leroi-Gourhan, A.
1969 La Chronologie de L'Abri Fritsch d'apres l'analyse pollinique et le Carbone 14, in *Livret-Guide de l'excursion A4 Berry-Poitou Charentes.* VIIIth Inqua Congress, Paris, 1969.

Linant, de Bellefonds
1843 *Memoire sur le Lac Moeris.* Alexandria.

Little, O. H.
1936 Recent geological work in the Fayum and in the adjoining portion of the Nile Valley. *Bull. de L'Institut d'Egypte* **18.**

Lucas, A.
1926 *Ancient Egyptian materials.* London: Edward Arnold.

Lubell, David
1971 The Fakhurian: A Late Paleolithic industry from Upper Egypt and its place in Nilotic prehistory. Ph.D. dissertation, Columbia Univ.
1974 *The Fakhurian: A Late Paleolithic industry from Upper Egypt and its place in Nilotic Prehistory.* Cairo: Papers of The Geological Survey of Egypt (58).

Marks, Anthony E.
1968a The Mousterian industries of Nubia. In *The prehistory of Nubia,* Vol. 1, edited by F. Wendorf. Dallas: Fort Burgwin Research Center and Southern Methodist Univ. Press. Pp. 194–B14.
1968b The Khormusan: An Upper Pleistocene industry in Sudanese Nubia. In *The prehistory of Nubia,* Vol. 1, edited by F. Wendorf. Dallas: Fort Burgwin Research Center and Southern Methodist Univ. Press. Pp. 315–391.
1968c The Halfan industry. In *The prehistory of Nubia,* Vol. 1, edited by F. Wendorf. Dallas: Fort Burgwin Research Center and Southern Methodist Univ. Press. Pp. 393–460.
1968d The Sebilian industry of the Second Cataract. In *The prehistory of Nubia,* Vol. 1, edited by F. Wendorf. Dallas: Fort Burgwin Research Center and Southern Methodist Univ. Press. Pp. 461–531.

Marks, Anthony E., Joel L. Shiner, & T. R. Hays
1968 Survey and excavations in the Dongola Reach, Sudan. *Current Anthropology* **9**(4):319–23.

Marks, Anthony E., Joel L. Shiner, Frank Servello & Frederick Munday
1971 Flake assemblages with levallois techniques from the Dongola Reach. In *The prehistory and Geology of Northern Sudan,* assembled by Joel L. Shiner. Mimeographed report to the National Science Foundation.
1970 *Preceramic Sites.* The Scandinavian Joint Expedition to Sudanese Nubia Publications, Vol. 2, edited by Torgny Save-Soderbergh. Helsinki: Scandinavian Univ. Books.

Menke, B.
1968 Das Spatglazial von Glusing. *Eiszeitalter and Gegenwart* **19**:73–84.

Myers, O. H.
1958 Abka Re-Excavated. *Kush* **6**:131–41.
1960 Abka Again. *Kush* **8**

Nakkady, S. E.
1951 Stratigraphical study of Mohamid District. *Bull. Fac. Sci. Alexandria Univ.* **i**:17–43.

Petrie, Sir. Wm. M. Flinders
1889 *Hawara, Biahmu, and Arsinoe.* London.

Phillips, James L.
1970 Oeuvre recente sur L'Epipaleolithique de la Vallee du Nil: Rapport preliminaire. *L'Anthropologie* **74**(7–8):573–81.

1972 North Africa, the Nile Valley, and the problem of the Late Paleolithic. *Current Anthropology* **13**(5):587–90.

1973 *Two final Paleolithic sites in the Nile Valley and their external relations.* Cairo: Papers of the Geological Survey of Egypt (57).

Phillips; James L. & Karl W. Butzer

in press A Silsilian occupation site (GS2B-11) of the Kom Ombo Plain, Upper Egypt: Geology, archaeology, and paleoecology: *Quaternaria* **16**.

Reed, Charles A.

1966 The Yale University prehistoric expedition to Nubia, 1952–1965. *Discovery 1* (2):16–23.

Said, Rushdi

1960 Planktonic Foraminifera from the Thebes Formation, Luxor, Egypt. *Micropaleontology* **6**:277–286.

1962 *The geology of Egypt.* New York: Elsevier. 337 pp.

Said, Rushdi, Claude C. Albritton, Fred Wendorf, Romauld Schild, & Michael Kobusiewicz

1972a Remarks on the Holocene geology and archaeology of Northern Fayum Desert. *Archaeologia Polona* **13**:7–22.

Said, Rushdi, C. Albritton, F. Wendorf, R. Schild, & M. Kobusiewicz

1972b A preliminary report on the Holocene geology and archaeology of the Northern Fayum Desert. In *Playa Lake symposium*, edited by C. C. Reeves, Jr. Lubbock: Icasals Publication No. 4. Pp. 41–61.

Said, Rushdi & B. Issawi

1965 Preliminary results of a geological expedition to Lower Nubia and to Kurkur and Dungul Oases, Egypt. In *Contributions to the prehistory of Nubia,* edited by F. Wendorf. Dallas: Southern Methodist Univ. Press. Pp. 1–28.

Said, Rushdi & H. Sabry

1964 Planktonic foraminifera from the type locality of the Esna Shale in Egypt. *Micropaleontology* **10**:375–395.

Said, Rushdi, Fred Wendorf & Romauld Schild

1970 The geology and prehistory of the Nile Valley in Upper Egypt. *Archaeologia Polona* **12**:43–60.

Sanford, K. S.

1934 *Paleolithic man and the Nile Valley in Upper and Middle Egypt.* Chicago: Univ. of Chicago Oriental Institute Publication (18).

Sanford, K. S. & W. J. Arkell

1929 *Paleolithic man and the Nile–Fayum Divide.* Chicago: Univ. of Chicago Oriental Institute Publication (10).

1933 *Paleolithic man and the Nile Valley in Nubia and Upper Egypt.* Chicago: Univ. of Chicago Oriental Institute Publication (17).

1939 *Paleolithic man and the Nile Valley in Lower Egypt.* Chicago: Univ. of Chicago Oriental Institute Publication (46).

Schild, Romauld

1971 Nowa, Nieznana Odmiana Lewaluaskiej Metody Rdzeniowania z Poznego Paleolitu w Gornym Egipcie (A new variety of the levallois method of flaking from the Late Paleolithic of Upper Egypt). *Archaeologia Polski* **16**:75–84.

Schild, Romauld, Maria Chmielewska & Hanna Wieckowska

1968 The Arkinian and Shamarkian industries. In *The prehistory of Nubia,* Vol. 2, edited by F. Wendorf. Dallas: Fort Burgwin Research Center and Southern Methodist Univ. Press. Pp. 651–767.

Schild, Romauld & Fred Wendorf

1975 New explorations in the Egyptian Sahara. In *Problems in prehistory: North Africa and the Levant*, edited by Fred Wendorf and Anthony E. Marks. Dallas: Southern Methodist Univ. Press.

Schweinfurth, G.

1886 Reise in das Depressionsgebiet im Umkreise des Fajym. *Zeitschrift der Gesellschaft fur Erdkunde zu Berlin* **xxi**.

Schweinfurth, G.
1903 Steinzeitliche Forschungen in OberAegypten. *Zeitschrift fur Ethnologie e.* 798.
1904 Steinzeitliche Forschungen in OberAegypten. *Zeitschrift fur Ethnologie* **5**:766.
1905 Recherches sur l'age de la pierre dans la Haute-Egypte. *Annales du Service des Antiquites de l'Egypte. Le Caire.*
1909 Uber Altpalaeolithische Manufakte aus dem Sandsteingebiet von Oberagypten. *Zeitschrift fur Ethnologie s.* 735.
Serebryanny, L. R.
1969 L'aspect de la Radio-chronometrie a l'etude de l'Histoire Tardi-glaciaire des regions de glaciation ancienne de la Plaine Russe. *Revue de Geographie Physique et de Geologie Dynamique* **xi** (No. 3); 293–302.
Shafei, A.
1940 Fayum irrigation as described by Nabulsi in AD 1245 with a description of the present system of irrigation and a note on Lake Moeris, *Bulletin de L'Institut d'Egypte* **20**:283 –327.
Shiner, Joel L.
1968a The cataract tradition. In *The prehistory of Nubia,* Vol. 2, edited by F. Wendorf. Dallas: Fort Burgwin Research Center and Southern Methodist Univ. Press. Pp. 535–629.
1968b Miscellaneous sites. In *The prehistory of Nubia,* Vol. 2, edited by F. Wendorf. Dallas: Fort Burgwin Research Center and Southern Methodist Univ. Press. Pp. 630–650.
1968c The Khartoum variant industry. In *The prehistory of Nubia,* Vol. 2, edited by F. Wendorf. Dallas: Fort Burgwin Research Center and Southern Methodist Univ. Press. Pp. 768–790.
Siirianen, Ari
1965 The Wadi Halfa region (Northern Sudan) in the Stone Age. *Studia Orientalia* **30**(4):3–34.
Smith, Philip E. L.
1966 The Late Paleolithic of Northeast Africa in the light of recent research. *American Anthropologist* **68**(2):326–55.
1967 New investigations in the Late Pleistocene archaeology of the Kom Ombo Plain (Upper Egypt). *Quaternaria* **9**:141–52.
1968 *A revised view of the later paleolithic of Egypt. La Prehistoire: Problemes et Tendances.* Paris: Editions du Centre National de la Recherche Scientifique.
Sterns, F. H.
1917 The paleolithic of the Eastern Desert *Harvard African Studies* **1**.
Stuvier, Minze
1969 Yale natural radiocarbon measurements **ix**. *Radiocarbon* **11** (No. 2):545–658.
Trautman, Milton A.
1964 Isotopes, Inc., radiocarbon measurements iv *Radiocarbon* **11** (No. 2): 545–658.
Van Der Hammen, Th., G. Maarleveld, I. C. Vogel, & W. H. Zagqijn
1967 Stratigraphy: Climate succession and radiocarbon dating of the last glacial in the Netherlands. *Geol. en Mijnbouq* **46** (No. 3): 79 – 95.
Vermeersch, P.
1970 Une Nouvelle Industrie Epipaleolithique a Elkab en Haute-Egypte. *Chronique d'Egypte* **45**(89):45–67.
Vignard, Edmond
1921a Une Station Aurignacienne a Nag Hammadi (Haute-Egypte), Station du Champ de Bagasse. *Bulletin de L'Institut Francais d'Archaeologie Orientale* **18**:1–20.
1921b Les Stations Paleolithiques d'Abou del Nour a Nag Hammadi. *Bulletin de L'Institut Francais d'Archaeologie Orientale* **20***:89.*
1923 Une Nouvelle Industrie Lithique, le Sebilien. *Bulletin de L'Institut Francais d'Archaeologie Orientale* **22**:1–76, and *Bull. Soc. Prehist. Fr.* **25**:200–220.
1928 Une Nouvelle Industrie Lithique, le Sebilien. *Bulletin de la Societe Prehistorique Francaise* 25:200–220.
1934a Les Microburins Tardenoisiens du Sebilien: Fabrication, Enpolis, Origine de

Microburin. *Congres prehistorique de France 10^{e} Session*, pp. 66–106.
1934b Le Paleolithique en Egypt. *Memoires de L'Institut Francais d'Archaeologie Orientale* **66**:165–75.
1935a Le Microburin est-il Sebilien? *Bulletin de la Societe Prehistorique Francaise* **32**.
1935b Le Paleolithique en Egypte: Melanges Maspere. *Mem. Inst. Fr. Archaeol. Orient* **66**(Fasc. 1): 165–175.
1947 Une Station de Sebilien III, a Reggan Taourirt, dans le Tanezrouft, Sahara Central. *Bulletin de la Societe Prehistorique Francaise* **44**:293–313.
1955a Menchia, Une Station Aurignacienne dans le Nord de la Plaine de Kom Ombo (Haute-Egypte). *Congres Prehistorique de France 14^{e} Session, Strasbourg*, pp. 634–53.
1955b Un Kjoekkenmodding sur la rive droite du Wadi-Shait dans el Nord de la Plaine de Kom-Ombo (Haute-Egypte). *Bulletin de la Societe Prehistorique Francaise* **52**:703–8.
1955c Les Stations et Industries Sebiliennes du Burg el Makkazin, Region de Kom-Ombo (Haute-Egypte). *Bulletin de la Societe Prehistorique Francaise* 52:436–52.
1957 Pointe de vue nouveau sur L'Industrie du Champ de Bagasse pres de Nag Hammadi (Haute-Egypte). *Bulletin de la Societe Prehistorique Francaise* **54**:298–313.

A. V. Vinogradov
1964 Sebilskaya Kultura Urajone Dakki. (In Russian).

Vogel, J. C. & H. T. Waterbolk
1967 Gronigen radiocarbon dates vii. *Radiocarbon* **9**:107–155.

Vogel, J. C. & W. H. Zagwijn
1967 Gronigen radiocarbon dates vi. *Radiocarbon* **9**:63–106.

Wendorf, Fred (Ed)
1965 *Contributions to the Prehistory of Nubia.* Dallas: Fort Burgwin Research Center and Southern Methodist Univ. Press.
1968 *The prehistory of Nubia,* 2 volumes and atlas. Dallas: Fort Burgwin Research Center and Southern Methodist Univ. Press.

Wendorf, Fred & Rushdi Said
1967 Paleolithic remains in Upper Egypt. *Nature* **215**:244–47.

Wendorf, Fred, Rushdi Said, Romauld Schild
1970a Egyptian prehistory: Some new concepts. *Science* **169**:1161–1171.
1970b Late Paleolithic sites in Upper Egypt. *Archaeologia Polona* **12**:19–42.

Wendorf, Fred, R. Schild, & R. Said
1970 Problems of dating the Late Paleolithic age in Egypt. In *Radiocarbon variations and absolute chronology*, edited by I. U. Olsson. Nobel Symposium 12, Uppsala; Stockholm Almquist and Wiksell.

Wendorf, Fred & R. Schild
in press (a) The use of ground grain during the Late Paleolithic of the Lower Nile Valley, Egypt. In *Papers of the Burg-Wartenstein Symposium No. 56* (held August *19–27, 1972, on the Origin of African plant Domesticates*), edited by J. R. Harlan. The Hague: Mouton.

Wendorf, Fred & Romauld Schild
in press (b) The Middle Paleolithic of the Lower Nile Valley and the adjacent Desert. In *Papers of the IX Congres International des Sciences Prehistoriques et Protohistoriques. Nice*, edited by H. de Lumley.

Wendt, E.
1966 Two prehistoric archaeological sites in Egyptian Nubia. *Postilla* **102**:1–46.

Whitehouse, Frederic Cope
1882 Recent explorations in the desert near the Fayum. The Lake of Moeris. *Proceedings of the Society of Biblical Archaeology* (London).

Youssef, M. I.
1968 Structural pattern of Egypt and its interpretation. *Am. Assoc. Petroleum Geologists Bull.* **52** 601–614.

Za'Atout, M. A. & A. Gad
1961 *Geology of the High Dam Area, Aswan, Egypt.* (Internal Report), Cairo, Egypt: Geological Survey Egypt.

Subject Index

A 6
B 7
C 8
D 9
E 0
F 1
G 2
H 3
I 4
J 5